THE PROFESSOR

THE PROFESSOR

Arsène Wenger at Arsenal

Myles Palmer

Dedication

For Johnny Brooks, Keith McCormack, Vic Brooks, Chick Gilks, Steve Shaw, Dave 'Fido' Findlay, Mal Chadwick, John Turner, Dick Labrom, Kevin Taylor, Keith Bell, Dave Murby, Sean Hobson, Joe Matthews, Bob Crow and John Storey – the Manchester University footballers who gave me so many of my happiest Wednesdays and Saturdays.

This edition published in Great Britain in 2003 by
Virgin Books Ltd
Thames Wharf Studios
Rainville Road
London W6 9HA

Published in paperback in 2002 by Virgin Books Ltd

First published in hardback in 2001 by Virgin Books Ltd

A catalogue record for the book is available from the British Library.

ISBN 0 7535 0876 1

Typeset by TW Typesetting, Plymouth, Devon
Printed and bound in Great Britain by
Mackays of Chatham PLC

CONTENTS

ACKNOWLEDGEMENTS

I have many people to thank for their assistance and cooperation in the writing of this book, first among those my journalist friends, especially Nigel Bidmead, Philippe Auclair, Gary Jacob, Kaz Mochlinksi and, in particular, the prolific and inspirational Rob Hughes, the man Sepp Blatter and I regard as the conscience of football. The first draft was twice as long as this version and much of the material which survived the edit was included because of what Rob wrote in his foreword. Sincere thanks are also due to Ian Grant for creating *www.anr.uk.com*, our website, where I kick ideas around. We have been heartened by most of the e-mails we have received. Conversations with Mitch Lawrence, Alexis Grower, Doug D'Arcy, Stewart Joseph, Kelvin Lewis and Mark Jacob have been entertaining and illuminating. I am also indebted to Alex Fynn, who persuaded me to write a preface saying what was in the book, who it was for, and why it was written.

FOREWORD BY ROB HUGHES

Early in his Arsenal reign, Arsène Wenger was asked what kind of people most irked him. 'Superficial people,' he replied. 'People who don't really commit themselves in what they do or what they say.' Monsieur Wenger need have no concerns on that score over this book. The author, Myles Palmer, must have been in front of him at ninety per cent of the press conferences Wenger has given in London – always in the front row, always with the most direct questions, always committing himself in the front line of journalism.

The fascination of this biography is that the more Palmer researched and probed, the more it became apparent that Wenger in particular, and perhaps football managers in general, is better judged on what he does rather than on what he says. It is my own observation that Arsène Wenger, wonderfully expressive in French, German, Italian, Spanish and English and capable of making himself understood in Japanese, has fifty-fifty vision: he sees every sin of his opponents and next to none in an Arsenal shirt. But he likes people who commit themselves, and he got accustomed at post-match press conferences to the inevitable Myles Palmer interjection, 'What was your view on Patrick Vieira's red card, Arsène?' It was ever thus, with Wenger since 1996 and with George Graham in the decade that preceded him. Both managers, I'm quite sure, came to accept Palmer for what he is: a fresh, persistent, inquisitive mind; a loaded gun firing the questions most match reporters hope somebody else will risk.

Wenger and Palmer make, on the face of it, an odd couple. Behind those rimless spectacles, and with that intense and studious air, the manager from France looks like a Strasbourg University economics graduate – which he is. In his black leather jacket, tousled hair often hidden beneath a cloth cap, Palmer could pass for the sociology student he once was at university in Manchester in the Rolling Stones era. And while Wenger has been besotted since childhood with the game of football, especially the German game just over the border from Alsace where he was raised, the young Myles became beguiled by overseas soccer because of the exploits abroad of Burnley Football Club. Today, though, Palmer's children are committed Highbury fans, his own proclivity more towards Deportivo La Coruña than Derby County, more Lazio than Luton, more FC Porto than Pompey. So long as Wenger is here, bringing foreign knowledge to the Premiership, Palmer's antennae will be reaching outwards.

There are other dichotomies. Wenger has a remote side to his nature that not even those who grew up in the same village have fathomed. He was a solemn child, they say, always *très, très privé.* But football was always at his core, German football, because it was teams from across the border that most often beat his home side, Duttlenheim. Palmer, by contrast, is an eclectic person. He was never a footballer or a musician, but writes on both. He possibly matches Wenger's intensity when he is scratching out a book, but needs the physical outlet of swimming in a London pool or Tai Chi to free the mind; and he takes holidays where Wenger goes on scouting missions, in Europe or South America.

'I am anxious,' Wenger admitted on the eve of his first Arsenal match. 'I want the players to continue the wheel of success.' Whether they have or they haven't, I leave to Myles Palmer to discuss. But although Wenger has now become an Arsenal man, the feeling persists that he has left a little of himself in Japan, where the locals were astonished by his attention to detail when the Frenchman studied the correct way to take sake before he arrived in Nagoya. Will he go back there, or will he be seduced one day by the lure of Germany – Bayern Munich, the national side perhaps?

His period in Japan, Wenger has said, taught him to control his emotions. Or at least not to reveal them. We know he has a girlfriend and a four-year-old daughter, Leah, who live with him in Totteridge within easy driving distance of Arsenal. We know he is happier bringing overseas players to Highbury rather than placing his trust in English runners because of the thirty players he has brought to Arsenal all but Matthew Upson are foreign. On Wenger's first day in charge, two typically instinctive goals from Ian Wright, an atypical Englishman, gave the Frenchman a win at Blackburn Rovers. Wenger waxed lyrical on his inheritance, on the rock-solid defence and the unorthodox striker. He kept the defence, and over time discarded the goalscorer. 'Ian Wright,' he once penetratingly observed, 'is a celebration specialist. It looks spontaneous, but I think he thinks about it.' Gradually, from midfield onwards, Arsenal became a French force: Vieira, Petit (then Pires), Henry, Wiltord. They spoke the common language, they were London's 'Les Rouges', but the manager who brought them to Highbury insists it is not a matter of prejudice, more of price and availability.

You must read between the lines. Wenger is an alchemist, blending his migrant brew at the most traditional of English clubs. It possibly helps to observe such things through maverick eyes, and Myles Palmer has those (the subjects of his biographies to date are Woody Allen and Mark Knopfler). To expect a conventional football book about this manager from this writer would be to miss the point, and the fun. After all, it is not so much a matter of quoting Wenger as interpreting him.

PREFACE

Arsenal's training centre at Shenley, shining like a glass spaceship among the green fields of Hertfordshire, is a haven of privilege, a sporting campus where footballers prepare for their weekly exams in the Premiership and the Champions League. After a few visits to this luxurious high-tech building you start to realise that the world looks different from inside Shenley. When you are there only two things matter: the next match and preparation for the next match. That is the life of a footballer and that is the life of a manager: matches and preparation for matches. Everything else is remote, secondary, peripheral, barely relevant.

It is from here that the civilised French technocrat Arsène Wenger views the challenges of the coming days and weeks. He operates within the narrow grid of a 58-match fixture list, so his main concern on any given day is the mood and fitness of his players. In the first half of any season he is especially concerned that his new players are adjusting, improving, fitting in, getting ready to contribute significantly. Managing a football club which tries to win every match is a very, very testing job – physically, mentally, emotionally.

This book has been written for Arsenal fans and for anybody who is interested in understanding the pressures and frustrations of being a Premiership manager. Where I have gone into detail about a controversial incident, a big match or a press conference it is because I consider it to be either a turning point in an Arsenal season, or especially illuminating about Wenger and the way he works with his players. Football, the only sport that matters, is a series of big moments, or rather moments that seem to be big at the time but not quite as big later. They always seem more cut and dried in hindsight, mainly because memory and media always compress, package and simplify.

By using a lot of my own notes, scribbled down in the heat of the moment, I have tried to do three things. Firstly, to give a taste of what nearly happened, what could have happened and what did happen in the days since Wenger's arrival at Highbury. Secondly, I wanted to show that there is a very fine line between success and failure in football – a whole season can come down to one game or one goal. You have to go through bad luck and injuries and heartbreak to achieve success, and it is those disappointments which test your character (I had forgotten, for instance, just how precariously balanced Arsenal's campaign was in November and December 1997). Thirdly, I wanted to try to capture how Wenger relates to newspaper reporters and how they relate to him.

This book has themes and arguments, but it basically says that Arsène Wenger is an excellent manager but not perfect, and that Arsenal is a very well-run club but not perfect. *The Professor* quotes Wenger so extensively that readers can make up their own minds about the French maestro, although it must be remembered that he does not define himself by what he says. He defines himself by the players he buys and sells, by the squads he has built and by the way his team plays. He has no time for hobbies because he lives his life through his team and through the matches they play. When he was asked what he does to relax, he said, 'I watch football.' He once told my French journalist pal Philippe Auclair that he is so interested in football that he would manage a team without a crowd. As Michel Platini said, in his inimitable Gallic way, 'Arsène want always his team to play well. Technically, a beautiful style, and I think that's why, perhaps, he is a success.'

PROLOGUE: MISSION STATEMENT

The twenty-second of September 1996. A Sunday morning in a hospitality suite in the Clock End at Highbury. Arsenal chairman Peter Hill-Wood stands on a small stage covered in red cloth, welcoming the assembled television crews, journalists, radio reporters and photographers. He is about to introduce the new Arsenal manager, who has flown in overnight from Japan. This press conference is a big moment, one the fans and the media have been wondering about for weeks. Everyone wants to know: who is this Arsène Wenger?

Is he a hard case like George Graham?

A blarney merchant like Terry Neill?

A tactician like Don Howe?

A chequebook cowboy like Ron Atkinson?

A brilliant bully like Brian Clough?

An inarticulate genius judge of horseflesh like Bob Paisley?

A combative workaholic like Alex Ferguson?

The main problem at Arsenal is an ageing team. The team will have to change and at the same time continue to be successful. We do not know how long the period of transition will prove to last, nor how expensive or painful it will be. The challenge is a fundamental one which all modern businesses have to face: the management of change.

A tall, slim Frenchman walks in and steps up on to the dais. Arsène Wenger is, we quickly realise, a completely different animal. He is not like George Graham, not like Bruce Rioch, not like anybody we have seen before. He has an ambassadorial presence. He is firm, calm, diplomatic and very articulate, handling a variety of testing questions with great fluency. He is authoritative, but in a friendly, accessible way. He seems to be a man of great analytical intelligence. Everything he says makes sense and he does not waste many words. It is a flawless performance, and while it is a valuable press conference in the sense that he answers each question honestly and clearly, without the usual evasions, it is something else too, something like a political or military briefing, almost a lecture. A mission statement.

Clearly, Arsène Wenger is a gentleman rather than a well-groomed bully on his best behaviour. A gentleman is someone who can be trusted. A gentleman's word is his bond. A gentleman has good manners and is public-spirited. A gentleman has firm principles and unimpeachable integrity. A gentleman has an aura of charm and intelligence. A gentleman, above all, is someone who can demonstrate grace under pressure, and Arsène Wenger will need that quality above all in his new job.

Today's football managers are powerful figures, household names, superstars of the biggest sport in the world, ringmasters who try to control forty players and fifty reporters, but they are also lion-tamers who put their heads in the lion's mouth twice a week. That is pressure. They live and die by decisions made in front of 40,000 people and twelve television cameras. It is a highly nerve-racking job, but it is well paid. And somebody has to do it.

They have also become, in this Sky-hyped age of the Premiership, vital news providers. The managers want to be liked by the viewers and listeners and readers and they need the approval of the reporters who transmit their predictions, reactions and excuses. Arsène Wenger knows he has to walk a fine line, knows he has to be very careful about what he says while appearing to be friendly, reasonable and candid. If reporters like him they will tend to ignore his mistakes and forget to highlight the occasions when he contradicts himself. However, his words must have substance, especially topical substance, because he is feeding a machine which services a huge appetite for news about football clubs and star players. And if that tightrope is not tricky enough to walk, he has to talk informatively about his players knowing that they will see and hear and read what he has said. Every manager uses the media to wind up a player at times, to challenge him, to punish him, to remind him of his responsibilities.

So what did Wenger say at that inaugural press conference that so impressed everyone? First of all he said that he had been frustrated by the delay in securing his release from Nagoya

Grampus Eight, who had now hired Portuguese coach Carlos Queiroz. 'I had the feeling that I put Arsenal in an awkward situation. It was a very difficult situation for the board, which was severely attacked. Fortunately, the team has done very well and is in a good position. That makes me quite confident for the future.'

He had been offered the job over a month before, in the second week of August, and had not taken long to make up his mind. 'I love English football because the roots of football are here. I like the spirit of the games, and at Arsenal I like the appearance of the club and the potential of the club. It's another step in my personal development. I've worked and been successful in France for ten years, and I've been successful in Japan for two years, where I had to create something from nothing and had to adapt personally. To go to another country with a football club at a high level and be successful is a very big challenge for me.'

He admitted that he had also been approached by the FA. 'Before I had contact with Arsenal Glenn Hoddle had contacted me. When he took over the international team he asked me if I would take over as technical director of the FA. I asked him for time to think it over, and we agreed that I would call him back in August. But then I had contact from Arsenal. I told Glenn I would take over at Arsenal because I love to work on the field. I am not at an age where I would like to work in administration. So I chose Arsenal because I think it's better for me. I think I know all the best players in England. I know all the international players, I know all the clubs, I know how the teams play, the organisation. Some of the grounds I don't know, but generally I think I know what's going on here. I was always interested when I started my career. I went every year to other countries to see how they were working and I think I have a good knowledge of international football.'

Press reports had already been linking him with South American stars like Leonardo and Ortega, and with German midfielder Matthias Sammer, but he denied an interest in any of them. 'The people who write those stories have good imagination – and expensive imagination. There's no truth in them at all. I have some ideas about players I might sign, but nothing concrete.When you speak about players you want you always end up paying double what they're worth, and many times you don't make the agreement.' When asked about new acquisition Patrick Vieira, he said, 'I think he's a great midfielder because he's a fighter. He's able to win the ball. And he's a very good passer.' He emphasised that Vieira, at the time an under-21 international, would be a great asset to the French national team in the future.

He was asked if he had a message for the Arsenal fans. 'My aspiration is that when Arsenal fans come here they are happy. It's up to the players and me to present the game that they love. Also, I want the fans to help us in difficult periods of the season when they are inside the gates. Because no team can be attractive and fantastic for the whole season.' He added that the absence of a manager in recent weeks had not caused a crisis in morale at the club – quite the opposite. 'I was very surprised. I read all the press but every time I had contact with the board they were very strong and very determined.

'I have the feeling today that the team also reacted very well. So the crisis was around the club but never inside the club. I feel only one pressure, my inside pressure to win and to do well. When you are in a job as long as I've been now, you get used to the outside pressure. The only important pressure is what you feel from yourself, to be strong, to work hard, to make an attractive game, and to go on and win the game. All the rest, I'm used to it now. Of course at the beginning of my career it was not easy, but these kind of pressures are much easier now.'

He said he hoped to marry continental sophistication with the red-blooded fighting spirit of English football, giving Arsenal the best of both worlds. 'That's my challenge. But I think English football has changed in the last four or five years. Everything is internationalised today. Could you imagine four years ago that Ravanelli and Juninho would play in Middlesbrough? The way of playing has changed very quickly, and I don't see a big difference now between English football and the game in other countries. In Euro 96, England played more technically than some other countries, more of a passing game. I think the difference is very small now.'

The new boss continued to preach evolution rather than revolution. 'I want the team to develop what they are doing now.

Football made of movement, a collective game of quick passing and quick movement. I think we will have to improve, and that will be the main target of every player, individually and collectively. I would like to bring in my collective touch, the way I see things. You can never say in advance how long it will take, but for the players to get used to my way of working will take two months. I like real, modern football. That means compact lines, of zones, of quick, coordinated movements with a good technique. I play 4–4–2 if I can. It is very adaptable because you can change easily to 4–3–3 or 4–5–1. It is really strange because in Europe people are going to the English system of 4–4–2 and England is going the other way. But with three at the back you have to come a little deeper, and I like offensive football and winning the ball early. It is much more difficult to pressurise up the field with three at the back.

'There are two challenges. The first is for me to adapt to the team and the qualities of English players. The second is for them to adapt to my ideas. I want to improve the squad with my ideas, and if we really need somebody, I'll try to bring somebody in. I don't want to destroy the strengths of the team, the spirit, the mental strength they showed in a difficult period before I arrived. There are many talented players here. But after I assess them maybe we'll bring one or two young players in.'

Football is much bigger in England than in France, a point he acknowledged. 'The game is important here. You have the feeling that you're working with something that is part of the life of the people. That's very exciting. People carry on supporting, from father to son, and you really live with your club, and that gives you the feeling that you always have somebody behind you. Arsenal did well in the recent past, and also in the distant past. I think I can help this club be successful and take a further step forward. And after me somebody else will come in and help the club even more. The life of a club never stops. Also, the spirit of the players. They are always able to fight to reverse games. You can see a game where one team is leading 2–0, but anything can happen here because the players have a generosity that you don't find in Latin countries.'

Wenger is a personal friend of the vice-chairman, David Dein, so he was asked whether he thought, if things did not work out,

Dein would get rid of him. 'If you are a friend or not, when things don't work well you will always have problems. I don't think that will affect our friendship. The work is one thing and the friendship is another. What is important on one side has nothing to do with the friendship. The work is the work, and it has to be effective. If I'm here it's not because I'm a friend of the vice-chairman of Arsenal. It's because the board of Arsenal think I have the right qualities to work here, and it's up to me to prove they made the right choice.' He denied, however, that he was under pressure to be an instant success. 'I want to win every game. That's the only important pressure for me. Instant success is demanded everywhere, it's the same all over the world. I believe you have to work with your ideas, do quality work, and after that hope for the best.'

For Arsenal to introduce a new manager in this way on such a day was unprecedented. Peter Hill-Wood, a gracious old-Etonian banker, apologised for interrupting our Sunday, thanked us for coming, and invited us to stay for lunch. I chatted briefly with David Dein and his friend Danny Fiszman, and then joined assistant manager Pat Rice for lunch. We talked about Spurs and Gerry Francis.

Overall, Arsène Wenger came over as a serious technocrat who knew he was accepting a serious responsibility. He was everything we wanted him to be and more than we expected. His opening address was memorable because he somehow hit on exactly the right mixture of realism, optimism and humility. When it was all over we could safely point to a number of qualities in the new manager. We could say that Wenger was straightforward ('I love English football'), very ambitious ('I want to win every game'), a traditionalist ('the life of a club never stops'), idealistic ('my aspiration is that when Arsenal fans come here they are happy') and wholly comfortable when it came to accepting full responsibility ('it's up to the players and me to present the game that they love'). He was also pragmatic ('I don't want to destroy the strengths of the team, the spirit, the mental strength they showed in a difficult period before I arrived'), an experienced manager confident about his qualifications for the job ('I want to improve the squad with my ideas').

Luckily for Wenger, midfielder Patrick Vieira, whom Arsenal had signed on his recommendation, had already played twice by mid-September and shown his class. The twenty-year-old, who was signed from AC Milan for £3.5 million, had come on as a substitute for Ray Parlour in a 4–1 demolition of Sheffield Wednesday, then made a superb first start in a 2–0 victory at Middlesbrough which hoisted Arsenal up to third place in the table. Arsenal fans had long craved somebody who could pass the ball in midfield, so they welcomed Vieira. The powerful, skilful, exciting number four was exactly what Arsenal needed. Had any of those fans been able to ask the new manager one question that day, it would probably have been, 'Please sir, can you sign six more like Vieira?' David Dein had sent videos of each game by courier to Japan and Wenger had addressed the team's biggest and most long-standing problem even before he had arrived.

Although his arrival seemed to have been messy, there was a feeling that it might turn out to be remarkably well timed. He did not have to follow George Graham directly, and since Chelsea now had Ruud Gullit at the helm, it seemed less risky, less radical, for Arsenal to hire an overseas coach. In terms of British football, and in terms of Arsenal's history, that September gathering proved to be a milestone, a signpost pointing to a promising future.

Listening to Arsène Wenger that day, you could not help thinking: this guy is different class. If this guy is half as good at talking to footballers as he is at talking to us then Alex Ferguson will have a serious rival again. George Graham built a winning team, but this guy might go one step beyond that. This guy might build a great team, a magnificent team, a thrilling team that can win everything in sight: the Premier League, the FA Cup, the European Champions Cup, the Grand National, the Olympic Games, everything!

In the days following that Sunday press conference I called friends with global connections in football to ask about Wenger. One said, 'He's a runner-up, not a winner. He finishes second too often.' Another said, 'A cautious man who likes weak people round him. He's aristocratic, rich, doesn't need football. Why did he spend seven years in a tax haven in Monaco? And why go to Japan?

A backwater, a graveyard. The stadiums are full because it is hyped so much, but the Japs don't know what they're watching.'

All of which made the next few years an interesting prospect.

1. FRANCE

I think you'll find that managers do go in phases. There are certain facets of the game that they concentrate on, and then they move on. They're always changing, they're always learning, they're always maturing, aren't they?

Mark Hateley, ex-Monaco striker

Arsène Wenger was born in Strasbourg on 22 October 1949 and grew up in Duttlenheim, a village of 2,500 people ten miles south-west of the city. His father, Alphonse, was a businessman and restaurateur, but also a football enthusiast who managed the village team in which his sons played. The Alsace region, of which Strasbourg is the capital, had been the subject of a territorial struggle between France and Germany for hundreds of years, but the area had been very much under French control since the end of the Second World War. Still, in the footballing world Racing Club de Strasbourg were always beaten by German teams, so the teenage Wenger, football already his passion, became fascinated by German clubs.

His father took him to see games in Germany, where Borussia Mönchengladbach became his favourite team. This was where his love of exciting, penetrating football first took hold. 'I was attracted by a game of movement, of counter-attack, based on speed and dynamism. That was what mattered to me,' he later recalled. The bright schoolboy knew that a goal was the most exciting moment in a football match, but he could also see that the moment when one team lost the ball and the other team gained possession was a moment alive with many thrilling possibilities.

Despite this passion already coursing through his veins, Gilbert Guntzburger, an older team-mate of the teenage Wenger in the 1968/69 FC Duttlenheim amateur side, remembered Arsène as a boy who had a more solemn disposition than his brother. 'He was so very serious. He was exactly the opposite of his older brother Guy. Guy liked a drink and a laugh. Not Arsène.' Serious, but in love with football. Alsace at that time was an area steeped in religion and the boys had to receive permission from their priest to go and play football because that meant missing vespers, the evening prayers. The young footballers, cycling past the church on their way to the pitch, used to cross themselves.

The community was so small that it was hard to find eleven boys of similar age, so Arsène did not play team football until he was twelve. But he was a regular from then on, and a decent player. A picture of Alphonse and a fourteen-year-old Arsène with the 1963/64 Duttlenheim team is still kept in the club office. Claude Wenger (no relation), now in charge of publicity at FC Duttlenheim, remembered his former team-mate as a good dribbler, a two-footed midfielder who could score goals. 'He was the club's top scorer with thirteen in 1968/69. But he had such intelligence, such vision. Those were his greatest assets.'

At that time Raymond 'Max' Hild, the coach at Mutzig, an amateur team in the Third Division, discovered the eighteen-year-old Wenger playing for Duttlenheim, signed him and made him his captain. Together they won the Alsace Cup. When Hild moved to Vauban, another amateur club, he took Wenger with him, and in 1978, when Hild became coach of Strasbourg, he once again persuaded Wenger to go with him, to join his first professional club. So the lanky amateur followed his coaching guru from club to club, but he continued his studies in economics, sociology, German and English and graduated from Strasbourg University.

Hild recalled, 'As a player he was an attacking midfielder who would score around eight goals a season from distance. He was not so good with his head around the opposing goal, but he could certainly use it to read the game. Mental speed was his great strength. He played eleven championship games and a UEFA Cup tie, but building clubs from the foundation is where his future always belonged.' Strasbourg reporter Michael Kapfer, who used to watch Wenger play from the press box, said, 'He had two or three games for the first team when they won the French Championship in 1979. But the match I'll always remember is the away leg of a UEFA Cup tie in the German town of Duisburg. It was the only European tie he ever played – he wasn't in the home leg when we drew 0–0. He played as a central defender in the away leg. It was an absolute disaster as Strasbourg lost 4–0. Arsène stayed an amateur because he chose to remain at university.'

Educated people are usually more aware of what they do not know, and Wenger realised that speaking English would be useful to him, as well as helping him with his studies, so he came to England during the close season. He later said, 'When you are a professional footballer, you spend your holidays at Club Med. Me, I bought an air ticket to London. A friend advised me to go to Cambridge where I hired a bike and enrolled on a three-week English course. My team-mates thought I was mad.'

Not only mad – too high-brow as well. Robert Felix, a back-room man at Strasbourg, remembered how Wenger never quite fitted in with the other players, who liked him but found him too sophisticated, and added that the Frenchman 'could play anywhere and he could be relied upon. But the truth is he was not really good enough to be a professional. I think that was the reason he did not turn pro, more than wanting to stay at university. He knew he was not good enough.'

Max Hild says that Wenger was about thirty when he finally asked him if he could help to coach the kids at Strasbourg, even though coaching 'wasn't a career he had ever thought about. His goal was to succeed his father at the Comptoir de l'Est, the family car-parts business.' Nevertheless, Wenger earned his manager's diploma in Paris in 1981 and he became Strasbourg's youth coach the same year. Robert Felix recalled him being 'brilliant with the youngsters. A perfect example for all young players. Even then he was a big man with an aura. You knew he was going to become a great coach.'

In 1983 Wenger moved to the French Riviera to take charge of the Cannes youth scheme, and a year later he was offered, and accepted, his first job as a manager. Aldo Platini, father of Michel, said, 'Arsène stood out at coaching meetings. I recommended him for his first job as a senior coach with my club Nancy.' In Wenger's first season in charge there, 1984/85, Nancy finished twelfth in the league and at the end of his second season they were eighteenth and had to win a play-off match to avoid relegation. The tiny club stayed up but continued to struggle, unable to afford the kind of players Wenger wanted, and the following year they were relegated. Aldo Platini said, 'It wasn't Arsène's fault. He had no money to spend. Monaco wanted him halfway through his spell with us. He wasn't sacked. He simply left us to join them.'

Mark Hateley joined Monaco from Milan in 1987 just as Wenger was arriving from Nancy. A tall, ebullient striker, the son of Tony Hateley, a big centre-forward who scored 200 goals for Notts County, Aston Villa, Chelsea, Liverpool, Coventry and Birmingham, Mark Hateley was greatly encouraged to learn that another English player, Glenn Hoddle, would be playing with him. 'At that particular time Glenn was supposed to be signing for Paris Saint Germain but hadn't signed on the dotted line,' he said. 'His agent was my agent. He had a chat with Wenger and we got him down to Monaco with us. We had an Ivory Coast player, Fofana, a very, very quick winger, but apart from myself and Glenn it was mostly French players.'

Hateley had left Portsmouth when he was 21, when English football training was still archaic. He immediately began to profit from the more professional training routines used in Italy, where even the smaller clubs prepared in a more technical, intelligent and detailed manner. He was pleased to see that Monaco under Arsène Wenger was no different. 'The training abroad was way in front of the British scene and it's only recently that we've got on to the same wavelength. Training camps, *retiros*, had been in existence for twenty years when I arrived. Milanello had been there long before that. At Milan you did your running, you did your weights, your diet was monitored. You were educated, and when you're a young lad you're easily educated anyway. We had a lot of doctors – the medical side was very, very good. It was the same at Monaco.'

But he found it hard, after playing in front of 80,000 people in Milan, to play in front of much smaller crowds in the principality. 'That was the most difficult thing about it. Summer season was good in Monaco because you had a lot of tourists there who would come and watch the games, so you could be getting between nine and thirteen thousand. But the winter periods you were as low as three thousand. That was the hardest thing we had to battle with. That's where self-motivation comes in.'

Hateley won most of his England caps when he was at Milan, partly because he suffered a serious injury at Monaco which stopped him playing for nineteen months. Most French fans, he reckoned, judged strikers purely by their goal tallies, 'but I don't think Wenger saw it like that. It was very much a team game and I was a team player. I worked very, very hard for the team and I used to create more goals than I would score. The first year we won the league and the cup and I finished second top goalscorer behind Papin. All in all it was a great experience and a great year for myself and Glenn. That first season was fantastic for me, for all the players, for the club, everybody. Monaco hadn't won anything for a long, long time, so to win the league and get into the European Cup was a feat beyond anybody's imagination.'

George Weah, a naive teenager from Liberia, was also brought in to Monaco during Wenger's first season. Wenger later recalled having to be very patient when he worked one-on-one with Weah. 'He came and he was nobody and he was on his own. He worked a lot because he had the desire. When you are a manager and you feel the appetite of somebody you'd be guilty if you didn't try to help. What makes you sad is when you meet talent and he hasn't the desire to achieve something. It's a bit like being a father, where you help a child achieve something. If you give them a good education and if they make their way, you're happy.' Hateley was impressed by Wenger's new signing, despite the fact that Weah came into the team in his position. 'It wasn't till I got the injury in the October of the second season that George came into the team. That's where he came through. He had unbelievable ability. He would do some unbelievable things with the ball. And, as you would expect from a nineteen-year-old, some unbelievably poor things, like tripping over the ball, or something silly.'

In Mark Hateley, George Weah and, later, Jurgen Klinsmann, Wenger had three genuine centre-forwards, all of whom could head the ball, yet when he went to Arsenal he never signed that type of player. 'Perhaps he went through a phase,' said Hateley. 'I think you'll find that managers do go in phases. There are certain facets of the game that they concentrate on, and then they move on. They're always changing, they're always learning, they're always maturing, aren't they? I liked to head the ball, and Klinsmann could head the ball, but we had more to our games than just heading the ball. George Weah was the same.'

Jean-Pierre Hopp, a friend of Wenger's from Nancy, went to visit him a year after he had taken over at Monaco and was amazed by his selfless commitment to the cause. 'The car park at the training ground was full of Mercedes, BMWs and Porsches – and parked alongside was Arsène's Renault 17. I've never seen a coach as determined and committed as him. He had a girlfriend back in Strasbourg but hardly ever had the time to see her.' Mark Hateley had a similar impression of the young workaholic coach. 'When I was at Monaco, Arsène was very, very intense. Every spare minute was football. It was football, football, football.' It was something of a shock for the England striker because his previous coach had been much older and more philosophical. 'Nils Liedholm, when I was at Milan, was sixty years old and had played in World Cup Finals and was well respected. He'd got all the knowledge of a footballing man. When I was 21 he was ideal for me because he had bags of time for me. I went from that to Arsène, who taught me something else, a lot about discipline and self-belief. He added that to my game.'

It was Wenger who first saw that Glenn Hoddle had coaching potential, although that development seemed improbable when Hoddle and Hateley were playing together, as the latter recalled. 'We sat down and talked about the game, I think all players do that. But when players are playing the one thing they've got on their mind is playing the game and nothing else. You don't think about not playing, and then going into coaching. You always think you're gonna keep playing. But that time does come. It was unfortunate for Glenn that he didn't come abroad at an earlier age. Michel Platini once said that had Glenn been born a Frenchman he'd have played over a hundred games for France.'

Hateley laughed when asked what system Monaco used to play under Wenger. 'We played the system where you have to win! With good players you can play any formation. Whether it's 4–4–2, you're interchanging all the time, 3–5–2, whatever you wanna play. We played with wide men sometimes and we played with three at the back at other times. We had Patrick Battiston playing at the back for us, and Amoros at full-back. We had a lot of good players who could play in different positions at different times in the game.

'Another young lad coming through was Emmanuel Petit. He was just coming into the set-up. He was a centre-half originally, then a left-back, and midfield on and off. Honestly, when he was a young sixteen-year-old he was ever so strong. Physically very strong, running very strong. Absolutely non-stop. Very few of us can do that. He had all the attributes and he was always gonna be a good player.'

Hateley later played for Glasgow Rangers, does radio work in Scotland now, and also has a Champions League show on Thursday nights on Scottish television, but he recalled that phase of his career, working with Wenger in a warm climate on the Riviera, with great affection and gratitude. 'Living down on the south coast, you have the heat and the Mediterranean diet: fish, salads, pasta – it's all conducive to a healthy lifestyle and weight loss.'

In 1989 Monaco got to the French Cup Final but lost 4–3 to Marseilles. They also reached the quarter-final of the European Cup, losing 1–0 to Galatasaray at home and drawing the second leg in Cologne, where UEFA had decreed they must play after crowd trouble in Istanbul. Two years later they took their revenge on Marseilles by beating them 1–0 to win the French Cup. The following year they won through to the final again but the match was cancelled after a major stadium accident during the other semi-final in Bastia, as a result of which 3,000 people were injured and twenty killed. That tragedy happened the night before Monaco were due to meet Werder Bremen in Lisbon in the Cup Winners Cup Final. The team, traumatised by the accident which involved friends of the players, lost the final 2–0.

In 1994, Wenger's Monaco were European Cup semi-finalists, and their line-up included Klinsmann, Youri Djorkaeff and the brilliant Belgian Enzo Scifo. They beat AEK Athens and Steaua Bucharest to reach the last eight, which was in two mini-leagues of four clubs. There they defeated Spartak Moscow and Galatasaray but lost twice to the mighty Barcelona, then managed by Johan Cruyff. But they qualified for a semi-final place, only to come up against an awesome AC Milan team which included the likes of Paolo Maldini, Marcel Desailly and Dejan Savicevic. They were soundly beaten 3–0, and Milan went on to thrash Barcelona 4–0 in the final.

After seven seasons of consistently good results, and having proved that he could discover talent as well as work with stars, Wenger had become much more successful as a coach than he ever was as a player, and his reputation grew apace. Bayern Munich wanted him, but Monaco refused to let him leave. A man of integrity, Wenger did not walk out on them. Ironically, a few months into the following season, 1994/95, after some indifferent results, he was sacked. It was time for Wenger to move on, to move away.

Years later, in January 2001, Wenger stated that bribery and corruption had influenced his decision to leave his native country. 'One of the reasons I moved away from France was that I suffered from that when I was manager of Monaco.' He was referring to the match-fixing scandal involving Marseilles president Bernard Tapie, who was eventually jailed for a year for bribing three Valenciennes players in a 1–0 win in 1993, en route to the club's fifth consecutive French title. Marseilles were stripped of their 1993 European Cup and relegated. 'Everybody knew they did it many times, bribing three players on one team. We were runners-up to them every year. I don't think it is a problem in English football. Our credibility depends on honest football. We knew it was happening in France although I was never approached to throw a game. It is down to officials and regulations in football to protect the game. I'm in football because I love football. I am happy that the players are earning a lot of money because I have always fought for that. But it has brought a lot of people to the game who don't care about football, only money.'

Having turned away from French football, Wenger decided to take his expertise to the other side of the world.

2. JAPAN

He's a god there. He did a good job at Grampus Eight, took over a struggling team, lifted it all up. Stojkovic, the big star there, was under-performing and he got him playing again, to everyone's delight.

Steve Perryman

Tokyo had staged the Olympic Games in 1964 and Japan had continued to boom right through the sixties, seventies and eighties, enjoying unprecedented economic growth. During that time the Japanese built up powerful, world-famous corporations which did business on every continent, companies like Sony, Toyota and Nissan. Japanese society is corporate in flavour, with hierarchies that everyone understands and a general assumption that people work towards shared objectives under highly qualified leaders. In mainstream Japanese life company workers live together, work together, achieve together and even play together.

The most popular sports in Japan in 1995 were sumo wrestling, baseball and golf, but Japan wanted to bid for the 2002 World Cup so they had launched their first professional football league in May 1993. The J-League comprised ten clubs – Kashima Antlers, Jef United, (Mitsubishi) Urawa Red Diamonds, Yomiuri Verdy, Yokohama Marinos, AS Flugels, Shimizu S-Pulse, Nagoya Grampus Eight, Gamba Osaka and Sanfrecce Hiroshima – each backed by a major company and each allowed three foreign players. It was agreed that no game should finish in a draw, so golden-goal extra time was played followed by penalties if necessary.

A few of these J-League clubs were formed from already existing amateur teams such as Nissan, but since the football clubs themselves had only just been created there was no history of rivalry or acrimony between them. The Japanese saw sport as entertainment rather than as tribal warfare, so the atmosphere at games was fresher, more innocent; there was a lot of female support and no need for heavy policing or strict segregation. Visiting team buses were never bombarded with abuse or rude gestures, fans were not hypercritical when a player made a mistake

17

and it was safe for the teams to travel to other cities by *shinkansen* (bullet trains) without fear of being harassed.

Nagoya is the Detroit of Japan, an industrial city of two million people situated 150 miles west of Tokyo. The city had spent £12 million on a new stadium with a 30,000 capacity and in 1993 imported Gary Lineker and two Brazilians as their three overseas players. The following year they signed the former Yugoslavia captain Dragan Stojkovic. Other teams followed suit. Zico, the Brazilian star of the 1982 World Cup, came out of retirement to play for Kashima Antlers, although he had already reached the age of forty.

The trade was not just in players, although French coaches were not exactly fashionable in 1995. But Wenger had done well at Monaco and earned a reputation as a cultured technician of the game. He was respected as a team-mechanic, someone who could create a harmonious squad, refine individual players and combine them to create a balanced, efficient unit. He was also known for his diplomacy, for his knack of tailoring what he had to say to fit the person or group he was addressing, so his personality was as important as his knowledge. When people talked to him they found a multilingual man with an impressive command of detail, but one who could also see the bigger picture, the landscape beyond his next match. He also had the patience to work with young, inexperienced players, which some top coaches lack.

So the question was not: why did the Japanese want him? It was: why did Wenger go there? Why would a football coach in his prime, who had won the French Championship and led his side to the semi-final of the European Cup, move to a league in Asia which was barely two years old? It was a bold leap into the unknown for Wenger, who had left tiny Monaco, a playground which has a beach, harbour and casino to go to work in the most industrialised country on earth, a nation of 126 million on three big islands, a land of vast factories full of robots, of spa towns built around sulphurous hot springs, of white-faced geisha girls and sushi delivered by scooter boys, of mist-filled valleys which only occasionally revealed the magnificent scenery?

The stink of corruption, of course, in part drove him away from his homeland, but fundamentally Wenger is a teacher who always wants to learn more, a man with a curiosity about other cultures, an interest in disciplines outside football and an ability to look outwards and forwards. Clearly, he is a singular personality, a man marching to the beat of his own drum, and at that time he had a postgraduate mentality about his career. He realised that this was an opportunity to learn, to broaden his horizons, which might never come again, so he took it.

Wenger joined Grampus Eight in January 1995. Two weeks after he arrived he was contacted by Werder Bremen president Fritz Bohme, who wanted him to replace their Bayern-bound coach Otto Rehhagel. Once again the timing of a possible move into the Bundesliga was wrong. Wenger said later, 'I had to tell them, sorry, but how can I leave Grampus Eight when I have only just arrived?' Bremen's general manager Willi Lemke, who flew to Nagoya with Bohme to talk to Wenger, paid him some extraordinary compliments. 'Arsène is almost too good to be true,' he said. 'You would not expect somebody like him in a business like football. He is such a respectable, decent person.'

One of Wenger's players during his first season in Japan was Masaru Hirayama, a college defender who had joined Grampus Eight in the summer of 1994. A knee injury soon ended his pro career and he went to work at Keishin High School in Fukui, where he now teaches social studies and coaches the school team. Hirayama said that he learned a lot in the short time he was with his French mentor. 'Wenger pulled the club from the bottom to second place in one year,' he said. 'I watched the team keep winning as Wenger coached. He is an able manager, very charismatic. He was amazingly considerate too, and would give personal advice to each individual player.'

Another who recognised the quality of Wenger's impact on Grampus Eight was Dr Christopher Hood, a British academic living near Nagoya when the J-League started in 1993 and who had begun to follow the club when Gary Lineker was signed. 'If there's ever been a case proving how important a manager is,' he asserted, 'then Arsène Wenger's time at Nagoya Grampus Eight is it, because he went in there and he didn't really change the playing squad a great deal but turned their fortunes round overnight almost. And once he left, again without great changes in playing personnel, the team slumped. It was so obvious that their success was down to him personally. So I think his attitude must have fitted in with the Japanese people and players and he must have also been able to control the non-Japanese players in the team, because sometimes they can be the harder players to control. They tend to be well-established players and sometimes get a little bit arrogant and need to be put in their place now and again. I dare say Wenger was quite good at doing that. If you can control Stojkovic you can control anyone. He certainly managed to get the best out of him.' Hood claimed Grampus Eight were a highly entertaining side. 'They were regarded as a very attacking team and a very effective force.'

As someone who has lived in the country and studied it, Hood believed that foreigners who are work-obsessed, like Wenger, can function very well there and enjoy themselves. 'I think Japan is a country that suits people like that. If you look at the people who study in Japan they tend to be, on the whole, quite loner-type figures, people who like to be able to mix with their own friends when they want to be with friends, and completely shut themselves away when they want to be shut away. Japan very much suits that mentality. There's not so much pressure on people always to be mixing and doing things. It's the sort of country where you can be yourself and do what you want to do. In some ways that's surprising because it's always thought of as a conformist society, but I think in Western countries, although we always talk about individualism over here, there's a lot more pressure to conform and go along with what other people are doing. Whereas in Japan you can step back and do what you want to do.'

Steve Perryman hugely enjoyed his experience there after a difficult first six months. Perryman had originally gone to Japan in 1996, to Shimizu S-Pulse as assistant manager to Ossie Ardiles, after managing Brentford between 1986 and 1990, saving Watford from relegation, and a brief spell in Norway managing Start. In 1999, when Ardiles resigned to join Croatia Zagreb, Perryman took over as manager. 'You've got thinking time in Japan,' he said. 'I read somewhere that Wenger said that Japan gave him back his faith in soccer, and I know what he means by that. You work abroad, I suppose it could be anywhere, but for me in Japan, I felt such a surge of energy. You get rid of all the things that are dragging you down. Trips up the motorway and back for six hours. You just concentrate on soccer and that's the beauty of living there.'

For Perryman, as for Wenger, there was the realisation that working in other countries brings out parts of the self that are obscured or suppressed by one's native culture. His twenty-month stay in Japan forced Wenger to explore qualities in himself that were not needed in France, or not available to him then. He later said that his time at Nagoya had made him more calm and composed, and he regarded that as crucial to his development as a manager. He was an immigrant who did not know the language and that made it easier to ignore distractions and focus his energy on what was important: working with his team and winning matches. Japan was also the perfect place for experimentation with tactics and set-up. 'In Japan it was easier to bring in something because professionalism was young,' he recalled. 'Everything was new – they accepted that – and it was more easy to change things. Here in England you have more than a hundred years of history. Any time you want to change something, you must convince everybody, because of the history.

'In Japan I learnt a lot about myself and how I could be,' Wenger added. 'I was very fortunate to have an experience whereby I was still working in football but outside the European mainstream. I had a lot of letters, but I could hand them over for someone else to deal with. I could not understand what people were saying to me or what they were writing in the newspapers, so I did not have that to worry me. I realised that football was what I enjoyed, the rest was just people's opinions. So since I came back into European football with Arsenal I take the same approach. I concentrate on the football, on training the team. I can be happy doing that. The rest is not important so I don't let it affect me.'

Wenger made it clear that at that time his own private agenda was more important to him than a high-profile job in Europe. 'Certainly that decision and my work over there created less of an impression than if I had been coaching Bayern. But as far as my personal and professional plans are concerned, I brought back a lot of satisfaction and a lot of pleasure.' He remains convinced that quitting Europe was a sound decision, and a very educational one for him, although his life in Japan was somewhat monastic. 'I learnt there how to take hold of something by letting go. That's beneficial at any level. When I got back I was much more lucid, more detached, more serene. I had the impression of having passed a couple of years in a convent where I devoted everything I had to my work.'

Perryman concurred with Wenger's views on the Japanese experience. His main source of job satisfaction came from his players listening carefully to him, wanting to learn the game, whereas footballers in Britain are more stale and cynical. 'I don't think the English professional puts in too much overtime or too much of his own thought. I think it has become a bit too humdrum and normal for them.' Where Britain has dumbed down, and behaviour has deteriorated, Japan has a culture where teachers and leaders are respected for their knowledge. 'The players give you their eyes and ears because they're happy to play for you. When I take the kids to school, they walk up to the teachers and formally bow and greet them.'

Perryman talked about Japan and about Wenger on Sky's *Soccer Extra* in January 2001. During that programme he made it clear that, despite the presence of Brazilians such as Dunga and Jorginho, the general standard of football in Japan was well below that of Europe. Most of the Japanese players, he said, are young and naive; 'Overall, the top in Japan is mid-Division One.' When asked if Arsène Wenger was still held in high esteem there, he said, 'Yeah, he's a god there. He did a good job at Grampus Eight, took over a struggling team, lifted it all up. Stojkovic, the big star there, was under-performing and he got him playing again, to everyone's delight. Just reorganising it. Being Wenger, he's got a comment about everything: the way the league should be structured, when you should play, when you should rest. He led them down every street, really. Which they needed, to be fair.'

Perryman also pointed out that the English style of man-management, with aggressive shouting in training and in the dressing room, is utterly alien to the Japanese, where the pride of the individual player cannot withstand a bawling out in front of his team-mates. That scenario, so common in the world in which Alex Ferguson and George Graham grew up and worked, is a non-starter in the J-League. If the coach screamed abuse at a footballer he would be so humiliated that he might go AWOL for three weeks. 'There is a vast difference in culture. You cannot pin a player one to one in a team meeting. Get them in the office one to one, absolutely no problem, say what you want and they take it that you're trying to help them. In an English team meeting, you would need to do it, because if you didn't do it the other players would think: you're soft; he's missed the point, he's left him alone. You have to do it, everyone expects it. In Japan you don't do that. It's in private. Of course, in team meetings you're making your general points all the time.' The phlegmatic Wenger was made for the part. Japan's culture suited his supportive, conciliatory style of man-management. He is able to control his temper in almost every situation, and since he hates shouting at his players anyway, working in a country where calmness is regarded as a strength rather than a weakness was ideal for him.

I have an e-mail pal, Katsumi, a 36-year-old football fan who travels to Europe occasionally on business. He was in France during the World Cup in 1998, and on the day after the England–Argentina quarter-final in St Etienne he bumped into Arsène Wenger on a train and was amazed when Wenger asked him, in Japanese, 'Where do you live?' Katsumi said, 'He changed Grampus quickly and totally. While he was in Nagoya he picked up several talented young players, including Hirano, Mochizuki and Oiwa. The three contributed a lot to the team and were selected for the national side. But once he left Nagoya in 1996, the team started breaking up. The club called in Portuguese coach Carlos Queiroz, but soon he was replaced by Japanese coach Tanaka, an assistant of Wenger. Nagoya supporters still dream of the Arsène days. He is a legendary person here in Japan.'

3. BOOZE AND IGNORANCE

There is no doubt in my mind we are blinkered and backward as a sporting nation.

Peter Hill-Wood, Arsenal chairman

At some English clubs in the early nineties players did not even bother to warm up before a game. They were allowed to sit around in the dressing room, reading newspapers and watching the horse racing on television, until ten to three. Heavy drinking was also widespread among footballers, who always claimed they could 'sweat it out' at training the next day. Jimmy Greaves and George Best drank like fish, after all, and still played like gods. It was just bonding, fraternity, solidarity, footballers socialising together for the sake of team spirit. Boys will be boys.

Striker Mick Quinn, a bright Scouser who played for Newcastle, Coventry and Portsmouth, used to love a night out with the boys. When Quinn was at Coventry he was on the plump side of stocky and the fans nicknamed him Sumo, but he scored the first hat-trick of the Premiership at Highbury and Ian Wright, no less, told him it was some of the finest finishing he had ever seen. Quinn, now a racehorse trainer, loved pop music, playing cards, gambling on horses and getting blotto. 'If Tony Adams is an alcoholic, I should be dead,' he told me in 1996. 'It's a load of bollocks. He's a heavy drinker, but what footballer isn't? And Tony is blaming a semi-final defeat by Germany in Euro 96 for driving him back to the bottle? While Gareth Southgate, the guy who missed the penalty, is sleeping at night? I think Tony's got to sort his head out.'

Arsenal players seemed to make more than their share of news headlines, as opposed to sports headlines. In 1989 Paul Merson had been fined £350 for drink-driving and failing to stop at an accident, and he was banned from driving for eighteen months. Merson and Steve Bould were later disciplined by the club after drunken, rowdy behaviour at a sponsor's dinner-dance at the Swiss Cottage Holiday Inn. Tony Adams, the captain, used to lead the hard drinkers in a regular session at Ra Ra's, a private club in Islington, and those booze-ups, like everything else in football, were based round the fixture list. If Arsenal did not have a midweek game they usually had Wednesdays off, so Tuesday night was the best opportunity to go out and get bladdered. These gatherings, as Adams later admitted, became known as the Tuesday Club.

Trouble was almost inevitable from time to time, especially in the close season. In May 1990, Paul Merson, Nigel Winterburn and two other players were sent home from a club tour of Singapore following a late-night drinking session. Late that year Adams was jailed for drink-driving even though the incident had happened in May, just after the season finished. His trial was postponed three times, the authorities obviously deciding to use his conviction as a high-profile example to frighten drinkers over the Christmas/New Year holiday. The implied message was: if we can put Tony Adams in Chelmsford prison, we can put you in as well.

The shenanigans did not stop there. In October 1993 Adams and Ray Parlour were accused of yobbish behaviour when a fire extinguisher was set off, drenching diners at a Pizza Hut restaurant in Hornchurch, Essex. Scotland Yard confirmed that police had received five complaints of assault. Adams and Parlour were among a party dining in the restaurant on the Thursday evening after England's 2–0 World Cup qualifier defeat by Holland in Rotterdam. Police said that some of the diners alleged that one of the players used a table knife to remove the pin from one of the restaurant's extinguishers, and that a second player then picked up the extinguisher and began spraying water round the room.

In August 1994 Paul Merson was under police investigation when he left the scene of a car crash in Mill Hill. His Land Rover Discovery had collided with a Nissan Micra, a wall and finally a tree. Both cars were badly damaged and witnesses said that Merson vanished before police arrived, leaving a friend to face questions.

Three months later Merson sold his 'my gambling/cocaine/booze hell' confessions to the *Mirror*. It was predictable that Tory MPs in particular would demand his prosecution for drug abuse. Sir Nicholas Fairbairn, the former Solicitor-General for Scotland, said it was 'appalling' that Merson should be paid by a newspaper for admitting to substance abuse. Merson's revelations caused the usual uproar: big club, young footballer, played fourteen times for England, tragically gone off the rails, set a bad example to the thousands of impressionable young people who idolise him. Police said they wanted to interview Merson, who at the time lived in a mock-Tudor house near St Albans, but he had gone abroad with his wife Lorraine and their two young sons, Charlie (three) and Ben (eighteen months). The Football Association, meanwhile, insisted that disciplinary action should be secondary to Merson's rehabilitation.

Merson had first snorted cocaine in a Hertfordshire pub toilet after drinking nine pints of lager. He claimed that the buzz helped him to overcome his shyness. Like Tony Adams, he was a binge-drinker; furthermore, and unlike Adams, he gambled every day. When an ankle injury stopped him playing football he became bored and gambled even more heavily. His debts began to mount, so he started snorting more coke to cheer himself up. It was a classic vicious circle.

That same month, November 1994, Ray Parlour was involved in a serious fracas at the south-coast World Holiday Centre in Bognor Regis, Sussex. Arsenal had no game on the Saturday because England were playing Nigeria at Wembley the following Wednesday, so he and some mates had driven down to Bognor for a night out. Someone smashed him in the face with a glass during a brawl and he needed four stitches in a large gash above his left eye. It was a typical footballer-in-punch-up incident, and the *Mirror* gave it the usual tabloid treatment: RAY PARLOUR ALMOST BLINDED IN NIGHTCLUB BRAWL sang the headline. A witness said, 'He was in the Manhattan revue bar and the row started when someone bumped into him. People started squaring up to each other and then all hell broke loose. It really all went off when Parlour came out with the line "Don't you know who I am?"' Friends whisked Parlour away from the club before security men could question those involved, but he was forced to withdraw from the England under-21 squad as a result. When a fan bumped into Parlour outside the ground on his way to the Arsenal box office and saw that he had a big stitched-up gash on his eyebrow, the fan said, 'Jesus, Ray, what happened to your eye? Did you do that playing football?' Parlour replied, 'I wish.'

The following summer, in May 1995, Arsenal went on an end-of-season tour to Asia where they played three games. After their final match in Hong Kong several players went out for an all-night drinking session in the Wanchai girlie bar district, where Parlour was said to have drunk twelve pints. A taxi driver was preparing his car for the Sunday-morning shift when Parlour made his way towards the vehicle, threw prawn crackers on to its bonnet and punched the driver. The man's nose needed five stitches. Parlour pleaded guilty to assault at the Eastern Magistrates Court. His lawyer, Adrian Huggins, told the court that Parlour could remember nothing about the incident, but that he nevertheless wanted to apologise to the 65-year-old driver and to the people of Hong Kong. He was fined 2,000 Hong Kong dollars (about £170), but was later fined more than £5,000 by the club. Inevitably there was talk that his future as a player at Arsenal was in jeopardy.

As this story was hitting the headlines, the *Sunday Mirror* dredged up witnesses who had taken speed and Ecstasy with John Hartson in Ibiza, even though the alleged incident had taken place just before he was transferred to Arsenal from Luton Town for £2.5 million, a deal which made him the most expensive teenager in British football history. 'He hadn't been to sleep from the night before,' said the witness, 'and he was still buzzing off his head. He was asking about "Es". He knew what was what. I can spot an amateur a mile off. He had money falling out of his pockets and had loads of women around him purely because of the football thing.'

Despite the headlines, it was not just Arsenal players behaving badly. Hundreds of pro footballers reckoned that a good booze-up was a reward for winning a game, and the best way to drown their sorrows if they lost. All clubs had drinkers, many had heavy drinkers, but most managers tended to turn a blind eye until the law was broken, which it often was.

Mick Quinn served three weeks in Winchester prison for driving while disqualified. He told me, 'Footballers think they can go by the grace of God and enjoy birds, booze, betting and everything else. Half the time they seem to be able to do whatever they want, to be above the law. I was shell-shocked. All of a sudden, from living in a four-bedroom detached house I was cooped up in a twelve foot by twelve foot cell with criminals. It was not a modern, open prison. I was banged up in a Victorian regime for 23 hours a day. I was let out for three twenty-minute walks every day.'

There were, however, dissenting, sensible, practical voices in the wilderness, minds open to the healthier regimes operating on the continent. Back in 1993 I did an interview with Roger Spry, the conditioning coach Ron Atkinson had taken with him from Sheffield Wednesday to Aston Villa, and he happened to mention a scientifically-minded manager at Monaco who treated footballers like finely tuned athletes. At first I thought the man's name was Arthur Venga.

At that time Ron Atkinson was the king of 'personality' bosses, famous for his flash suits and gold jewellery but shrewd enough to employ Spry and Dave Sexton, the most invisible major figure in English football, as first-team coach, showing Dalian Atkinson and Dean Saunders how to make clever runs for each other. Spry is a former kick-boxing champion who has worked with boxers and golfers as well as footballers. He says it is difficult to describe his job to people. 'They say, "What d'you do?" And I say I'm a conditioning coach. They don't realise that you're like a mechanic: you've got to get your player in tip-top condition. You have to oil him, you have to feed him and prepare him. It's a holistic thing.'

This lack of knowledge about conditioning depressed Spry, and he worried about the long-term prospects for English football while it was dominated by the FA and by club managers whose minds were closed to continental training methods. He had worked outside England and could see the difference in approach. 'I worked with two of Norway's players when I was with Start in Tromsö, right up in the Arctic Circle. A friend of mine, an English guy, Stuart Baxter, had invited me over. I was there for almost six months. Then I was offered a job in Portugal, so I went there.' The J-League had just started in Japan, and Baxter, who was also disillusioned with English football, went out there to coach Sanfrecce Hiroshima.

One conversation I had with Spry was in June 1993, just after the fiasco in Oslo when Graham Taylor's England team blundered to a 2–0 defeat at the hands of Norway in a World Cup qualifier. Spry, a neighbour of Taylor's in Sutton Coldfield, was angered by that shambles. 'In England everything's based on effort and commitment. That's fine against fools, but when you play against people who have superior technique and are willing to match your courage and commitment, they're gonna wipe the floor with you. It's often an embarrassment to be an Englishman abroad. We're so far behind, we're ridiculed. But we're so insular that we don't even realise what other football nations think of us.'

Spry said that lucrative television deals had begun to generate more money than ever in English football, but that the game here was still built on a shallow foundation of limited players whose technical development had been woefully neglected. 'Every other country in the world, bar none, has had an influx of foreign coaches. But people still say "That wouldn't work over here." But what is the most traditional English game, apart from football? It's rugby league. Ten years ago rugby league was dull, dire, full of fat guys running around like headless chickens, lots of effort but no technique. Then the Australians started to come over and all of a sudden the game started producing exciting stars like Ellery Hanley and Martin Offiah. And people say, "This is a totally different game!" But *why* is it a different game? Because of an influx of foreign ideas.'

Spry mentioned a Czech manager who had failed in England, Josef Venglos, who was in charge at Aston Villa in 1990/91. 'We need special people to come into English football, with special personalities. No disrespect to Josef Venglos, because he's a very good coach, but he's had the same problem in every country he's gone to. He's too nice a guy to ruffle feathers. The one thing you don't need in England is a shrinking violet. You need someone to come in with all guns blazing and say, "What you've been doing is crap! We're doing it this way from now on!" '

At that time Spry was preparing to address a symposium in Helsinki on the development of youth players. He said that England had exported coaches for decades, but never imported them for fear of losing a club's precious 'Englishness'. In the early to mid-nineties, with the game in something of a crisis, it was time to wake up or join Austria and Iceland in the European Third Division. 'It's time for a revolution in English football. It's totally lacking in imagination, innovation and creativity. It's got to be done. When you see Norway, a small country, streets ahead of us in technique, fitness, commitment, everything, it's tragic, really. But the time for talking, for feeling sorry for ourselves, has gone. We've got to say, "Right, let's do it! There are the knowledgeable people available, let's get them together and do it!"'

In his own area of expertise, Spry said that English football was decades behind. Many people in English football still did not realise that conditioning enhances skills and prevents injuries. If the body is not flexible enough to make certain shapes, the ball cannot be controlled properly, and many injuries are caused during a game when the body tries to make shapes it should have been making a hundred times a week in training. 'I used to find it sad. Then I found it frustrating. Now I just get angry, because all these claims that we have the fittest footballers in the world are rubbish. That is the biggest fallacy in world football. By continental standards we are unfit. Players assume in this country that you can mess around in training, abuse yourself all week, and it will be all right on Saturday. It's the it'll-be-all-right-on-the-night syndrome. It's totally ridiculous. It doesn't work. The best foreign players do all their talking during training, on the pitch, not to the press.

'I've worked with Brazilians, Frenchmen, Spaniards, Portuguese, Kuwaitis and Australians, and every single one of them has been surprised at how quickly skills can be learnt. Some of the Villa players are doing things they didn't believe they could do a year ago. Not because they're incapable of doing it, but because no one had ever shown them. From a very early age players should be encouraged to be bilateral. Everything should be developed equally, both left and right. The South Americans learn to use every part of the body that's legal. If we see a British player backheel the ball we say, "Ooh, look at that!" Over there they say, "If it's legal, learn how to use it." How many players have you ever seen in Britain pass a ball with their knees? I've seen our players control it with their chest, and then with their foot, which takes a helluva lot of time. You can, as the ball comes to you, just swivel and play the ball with your knee. Many South Americans can play the ball thirty metres with their knees, accurately, in one flowing movement. And it's not because they're more technically gifted, it's because they've got more parts of their body in the right condition to give them that range of movement.

'Our whole game is based on linear running. A lot of their conditioning is based on short, sharp, explosive movements, repeated over and over again, with or without the ball. That's the very big difference. A lot of my friends, particularly the Brazilian coaches, have said that the thing that they've got as a nation is teachable, and the thing that we have is not. That never-say-die attitude is one of our greatest strengths. They are very, very frightened that one day the British will train continental-style, because they say that with our attitude plus that potential ability, we'll be unbeatable.'

Spry admitted that real progress towards modern methods at an English club would be impossible without a very brave, forward-thinking chairman. The trouble is, he added, most chairmen want success yesterday. He had not been surprised to see Arsenal soundly beaten 3–1 in a November 1991 European Cup tie at Highbury by Benfica, whose coach was Sven-Goran Eriksson. 'I've talked to Arsène Wenger and Sven-Goran Eriksson about having an international exchange of some of their good young players. Can you imagine the benefits if three of AC Milan's players came and spent a month at Villa and three of our players went over there? What an incredible learning experience! Or even better, what if AC Milan said to me, "Roger, come and help with our training for a month and we'll send our coach over to Villa for a month." Or I could go to Monaco or Marseilles or River Plate. For the good of the game those ideas should be explored.

'I know that Wenger goes from Monaco to the AC Milan training ground regularly and he's welcomed with open arms. There is so much fear in this game. If someone who really knows what they're doing comes in and you don't know what you're doing, and you've been bullshitting and bluffing for fifteen years and getting away with it, when somebody with real knowledge walks in everybody thinks, "Jesus Christ!" '

I conducted several interviews with Roger Spry over a three-year period between 1993 and 1996, but neither of us could have guessed then that a fitness revolution would indeed come to England in 1996 and that it would be launched by his pal from Monaco. If Arsène Wenger had read every detail on the Highbury crime-sheet, the full list of misdemeanours by his players, he would not have believed it. He would have asked, 'Can a team that has won six trophies in eight years really be such a gang of boozers, gamblers and outlaws?'

4. 1996/97: THE SEASON OF ANALYSIS

The Arsenal AGM is a small piece of theatre which takes place every year at Highbury at noon on the first Thursday of September. The club had been so stable over many decades that nothing much usually happened at this meeting, apart from the approval of the accounts, the re-election of the directors and a few tame questions – sometimes, veterans claimed, from 'plants', people primed to say certain things to provoke certain responses.

But the 1996 AGM was the most stormy in living memory, notable for Peter Hill-Wood's explanation of Bruce Rioch's sudden departure and Jarvis Astaire's revelations about David Dein's frustrating summer. One shareholder caused an uproar by asking why Dennis Bergkamp had been signed for £7.5 million when his friend, a solicitor and agent, had been offered the Dutchman for £5.5 million. The ensuing debate made it clear just how difficult it is to sign talented footballers in a highly competitive European transfer market.

Directors are always nervous when they change managers since managers vary a lot in ability, and hiring a new one is the most important decision they make. A competent manager can keep a team ticking over, a good manager can improve a team, and a very good manager can win trophies. But all managers can lose their way, all can suffer bad luck, and all take big risks when they buy players.

The meeting began with Hill-Wood making an opening address, as he does every year, and the disposal of formal business. Hill-Wood is a City gentleman who worked for Hambros bank, has an American wife and spends a lot of time in New York. The AGM can be the most nerve-racking day of his year.

'In view of events of the past fortnight,' he began, 'I will explain more about our decisions and their timing. When Bruce Rioch joined us we agreed on a different role for the manager. As time went on he seemed to become less than happy with his role. He didn't sign his contract until very recently, although it had not been altered since last February. We felt that Bruce didn't share our vision for the future of the club, and after a series of discussions over some months the board reached the decision that he was not the right man for our job. You know that he took us into Europe, for which we thank him very much. I would have to agree that the timing of Bruce's departure was both inconvenient and undesirable, but there is no ideal time to release a manager. Much has to do with finding a replacement, and of course activities in the transfer market to strengthen our squad.

'We have acted in the best long-term interests of the club. We have identified a replacement of considerable international reputation who has agreed to join us. We cannot announce his appointment officially as we have given an undertaking not to do so. All being well, a statement will be made very shortly and we expect to have him with us by the end of September.

'The two major changes in the manager's area of responsibility are, first, the transfer negotiations, and second, youth development, which we felt needed a radical overhaul. We have recently appointed Liam Brady as head of youth development. He's very experienced in all football matters both in Europe and in the UK. And we hope we will soon get back to the old days when more of our star players were homegrown.

'The first change I mentioned regards our operation in the transfer market. The way it works is that the manager identifies the players he wishes to buy or sell, and the responsibility is given to David Dein and Ken Friar to do the deals in conjunction with the manager, in what are often very complex financial arrangements. Much has been made of the so-called failure of this system in the past year. It cannot work if the players identified by the manager are, for one reason or another, unavailable to us. And I think it is fair to say that although every player Bruce proposed to the board was pursued, overall his list proved to be impractical. In a very short time we have acquired two new players, Patrick Vieira and Remi Garde, both of whom were signed in time to qualify for this year's UEFA Cup. No doubt there will be more to follow during the coming season. The club has significant funds at its disposal to purchase quality players, but we will not break the bank on one superstar. We all know that there are three or four more pieces of the jigsaw to be put in place.

'The board has taken these steps in the best long-term interests of the club. We are confident that we are planning for a bright future ahead. In the meantime, Stewart Houston has shown that he has the full support of the players, and the performance in our first two games was, I thought, excellent, with everyone showing total commitment. That's all I have to say. I'll now be happy to take questions.'

A shareholder said, 'I'd like to ask Mr Fiszman, who is now the main shareholder, to give his view of the future of this club, and whether there are funds coming into the club.'

Nobody had expected Danny Fiszman to speak on any such matter. Hill-Wood quickly replied, 'I did say that we have substantial funds available, so that, I think, answers that question. Mr Fiszman doesn't have anything to add to that.' There was some ironic laughter. Fiszman, a diamond dealer brought up knowing the value of security and anonymity, is one of London's most invisible millionaires. Sightings of him are rare, comments even rarer.

The board was then asked to spell out their short-term objectives for the club, over the next two years. 'The short-term ambitions are to get the right squad together and win another trophy,' Hill-Wood replied. 'I don't think we had a particularly bad season last year. We finished fifth – fourth equal in fact. We got into Europe. But I don't think anybody in this room would think that the squad we have is actually going to challenge Manchester United just at the moment, so it needs to be strengthened and we hope that it will be. This club needs success. We all want it, none more so than the board of directors. If you look around the stadium, it's a magnificent stadium. We've spent about £40 million over the past ten years on it, we've got the best pitch in the land. Things aren't all bad. We want them better. The board are accountable and we take our responsibilities very seriously, we try our best. Sometimes it doesn't prove good enough but I promise you we will continue to try.'

Another shareholder changed the subject. 'The club has been subject to a campaign of vilification from the tabloid press which I find, as a supporter of over thirty years, extremely upsetting. The club seem unable to counter the fact, fiction or innuendo which is reported almost daily in the newspapers. A company that has a turnover of over £20 million should be much more adept at handling the media and I would suggest that you employ somebody who is capable of giving the correct information, so that the supporters and shareholders know the facts.

'There are other points which require unequivocal answers. One is the Bergkamp transfer. I know for a fact that Bergkamp was offered to this club for £5.5 million. The person that offered him to the club was told, a day before the transfer, that Arsenal were not going to sign him because he was going to break the wage structure. I would also like to know if a former employee of the club, who works now as an agent, was paid commission by the selling club on overseas transfers. I'd also like to know – and I wrote to you about this, I don't know if it's correct or not – about a rumour that he got £35,000. Why was he only sacked last week? Can we have direct answers to the questions and no fudging because I am extremely hurt by what's going on in the media. We love this club. People are not here today to hear the club accounts, we are here out of love for this club.' This emotive speech was greeted by loud applause. The shareholder was encouraged to continue. 'It's a big part of my life and I know that everyone who has made the effort to be here feels the same way. We want straight answers. We want to hear decent things about the club. We want to pick up a newspaper, like we used to do, and be proud to be an Arsenal fan.' There were cries of 'Hear, hear!'

Hill-Wood said, 'So far as the handling of the press is concerned, we do give them facts as we are able to give them, and they interpret them in different ways, often in not very helpful ways. We are considering the appointment of a PR man, a press officer, and I think your suggestion is one we take very seriously. So far as Bergkamp is concerned, I was not aware of what you said. I'm not doubting you, but I personally was not aware that he was offered to us at £5.5 million. When he was finally offered to us he was a lot more than that.'

David Dein seized the microphone and stood up. 'I know who you're talking about. Your very good friend Mel Goldberg did not do the deal. The deal was directly completed with Inter Milan. I played a part in it, Ken Friar played a part in it, and I have to tell you this: we could not have bought Dennis Bergkamp for one single penny cheaper than £7.5 million. That is a statement of fact. He could easily have gone to Barcelona, never mind what your colleague thinks he could have achieved, because in the end he did not do the deal and could not do the deal, because Inter Milan – and we have letters to prove the fact – were not selling for £5.5 million. That's all I've got to say. If anybody here would like us not to have bought Dennis Bergkamp for £7.5 million they should say so now. We could sell him for twice as much.'

This prompted some shouting and heckling. Dein spoke again. 'I take it as an offence that you are questioning our integrity. Every last cent went to Inter Milan and we were delighted to have pen put to paper on his contract because we thought it was an excellent buy. He could have gone elsewhere for more money, but he chose to come to Arsenal. That is the bottom line.'

The shareholder who'd asked the Bergkamp question then said, 'He is the only good buy we have made since Ian Wright, but the point remains that he was offered for £5.5 million –'

'By an agent who could not consummate that deal,' the vice-chairman cut in. 'How do I know? Because I did the deal personally, with Ken Friar, with Inter Milan. That's the bottom line. Not somebody who says I could have got him cheaper because he couldn't do the deal.'

Dein was applauded warmly for that. People were enjoying the aggro, which went far beyond anything veterans had ever seen at an AGM.

Hill-Wood got proceedings back on track by picking up the thread about Arsenal's relations with the press. 'They are very good at their job. They're very good at making you say things you probably shouldn't say. They collar the players at the most unlikely moments when they're probably not on guard and we can't, I'm afraid, gag them totally. We try and advise them to be cautious about what they say, but they don't always manage to do that. These press reporters are very clever. They trip me up periodically and they trip the players up. There's not a lot we can do about it. It's often the same players because some of the players are sensible enough not to say anything while others are a bit talkative. When we have a press officer hopefully that will take some of the sting out of it. I get called, and I know Mr Dein does and Mr Friar does. We get calls at all times of the day or night. If we could divert those to one central point, which is exactly what the Football Association have done and I think the PR that they've got has improved greatly, I think it would improve with us as well. So it's a very sound suggestion.'

Jarvis Astaire, the Wembley director and boxing promoter, his mind obviously still on the Bergkamp outburst and transfer issues generally, stood up to say that although he was not an Arsenal supporter, he was a shareholder and close friend of David Dein. Astaire said he was 'nobody's poodle' and had not been set up to defend Mr Dein or anybody else, that he had remained a shareholder for thirty years because he had always respected the club. Like many of the older people present he had grown up regarding Arsenal as the MCC of football, an institution where stability, probity and sportsmanship were highly valued. 'I am therefore in a position to tell you first hand that during the course of Euro 96 this summer I spent most days in the company of Mr Dein attending matches. And because we were close together, and he had his phone with him, or he was in my car while I was driving, he took me into his confidence to a large extent.

'He did try desperately to obtain the very few players who were available. He was frustrated on a number of occasions when the names of some of the most prominent foreign players came up, including those who have signed for other clubs, because Bruce Rioch didn't feel happy or confident enough to have those players join this club under his management. There is not the slightest doubt about that. I am making a statement of fact. I have no axe to grind. I can tell you that there was one player that the manager was happy about, and that's Seedorf. I was present when Mr Dein had a number of conversations, very difficult conversations, with Sampdoria about trying to sign Seedorf, but by that time, by the time the manager agreed that he wanted him, Real Madrid had already done a deal verbally, and the deal went through and that was the end of it. But I can assure you that there was tremendous frustration felt by Mr Dein about the lack of confidence and imagination on the part of Mr Rioch.'

Since there had been stories in the papers speculating about the imminent arrival of a certain French manager from Japan, people wanted to know why the chairman was still keeping everyone in the dark about his identity.

'I don't think anybody's in the dark,' Hill-Wood said. 'It's been one of the worst-kept secrets of the year. It's just that we did give an undertaking. It may sound odd to you when everybody and his uncle knows who is coming, but I can't say formally.'

A shareholder countered, 'Speaking as a lawyer, an undertaking to whom, Mr Chairman?'

'An undertaking to Mr Wenger and to his –'

This slip of the tongue meant that the rest of the chairman's response was drowned out by the sort of laughter often heard in the House of Commons during Prime Minister's Questions.

'It's a technicality,' said Hill-Wood.

The meeting ended soon after that.

So this was the state of London's number one sporting institution in September 1996. Arsenal was a football club which had enjoyed eight years of stability and success followed by eighteen months of trauma and turbulence. Their most educated fans were still furious with the cowardly way in which George Graham's sacking had been handled. They were also very disappointed that Bruce Rioch had signed no new players and deeply embarrassed by the avalanche of bad press.

WELCOME TO ARSENAL, MR WENGER!

Sooner or later a continental manager is going to break through and have success in England.

Don Howe

The Frenchman from Japan arrived in England to find that the champions were Manchester United and the biggest star in the country was Eric Cantona. His former Monaco player Glenn Hoddle had just started as England coach with a 3–0 World Cup qualifier win in Moldova, Ray Wilkins had resigned at QPR, John Major was Prime Minister but the director of the club he supported, Matthew Harding, had just given a £1 million donation to Tony Blair's New Labour. George Graham had been in the wilderness for nineteen months, but when Howard Wilkinson was sacked by Leeds Graham was appointed manager the following day, 10 September – the day on which Arsenal lost 3–2 at home to the young Wenger's favourite team, Borussia Mönchengladbach, in the UEFA Cup. Nine days after Ray Wilkins left QPR, Arsenal caretaker boss Stewart Houston quit Highbury to go to Loftus Road. On the very same day Tony Adams admitted he was an alcoholic.

Arsenal's Peter Hill-Wood was probably the first chairman to own up publicly about England's old-fashioned football culture. On the subject of Wenger's appointment, he said, 'This signals a new era for us. I believe Arsène Wenger is going to be a great success and drag football in this country into the twentieth century. There is no doubt in my mind we are blinkered and backward as a sporting nation. Look at the British results in Europe, they were not good, including ours. We keep telling ourselves we have the best league in Europe, but it is not true. We need to catch up with the continentals and we think Arsène is the man to help us.' Wenger said, 'It is my dream to take over a club in a top European league and if I didn't take the opportunity now it may never happen.'

Arsène Wenger was the first Frenchman to manage an English football club. His first official day at Highbury would be 30 September, and he would be in charge for the Blackburn Rovers game twelve days later. He was believed to be on a salary of £2 million spread over a three-year contract. He met the players for the first time at the training ground on Monday, 23 September, the day after his press conference, and watched them work with Pat Rice. 'I know how I want them to play,' he said. 'Now I just have to wait and see if they can adapt to that. I am not in a hurry to buy players. It is not the best time to buy at this stage of the season anyway. The teams with good players don't want to sell and they are overpriced. And first I want to give the players here a chance. I want to watch them more. We are third in the league and the results are not too bad. We have a good team. But the squad is quite small if we have to play in everything – Europe, Premiership and cup competitions. If we stay in the UEFA Cup maybe we will have to bring in someone new.

'I spoke to all the players for about five minutes and told them I would be speaking to them individually after the Sunderland game on Saturday, so I can get to know them. I won't take over until next week so I just observed what was going on in training. I want to give confidence to the players first. I am someone who needs challenges. I like to win and I try every day to be better than the day before. I have a lot of failings but if I have one quality it is that I like to give.'

First impressions can be deceptive, but Wenger seemed to be a formidably intelligent man who talked about facts. He took the time to digest the important facts and built his views on those facts – a healthy sign. Opinion is cheap, but professional football is a game of goals and assists and clean sheets. It is, above all, about results. Results are everything. Results win trophies, results make and break careers. Results create big games, big seasons, big money, big opportunities. Wenger also had a cool head. One tabloid had quoted the 1995 World Footballer of the Year George Weah as saying, 'Arsène is the best coach I have ever played for and I would love to play for one of his teams again in the future. He brought the best out of me as a footballer. I owe all my success to him.' Wenger simply said that signing his former protégé from AC Milan was 'impossible'.

He spent that first afternoon studying videos of the Borussia Mönchengladbach game with Pat Rice. 'My first impression is that the players here are aware of what they must do in Germany,' he said. 'The experienced players know it will be difficult but they are used to battles. I believe we can get a result. We were unlucky in the home game with Dennis Bergkamp's injury, but we created a lot of chances. Borussia are also a strange team. One week they win 4–0, the next they lose 4–0. If Pat asks me about something I will try to help him. He will be in charge of the team and make the decisions, but I feel it is important to be here this week. I will be an observer. I will be in the dressing room and on the bench, nothing more. I'll only give my advice if he asks for it. He knows the club, he knows English football, he knows the players very well and he is a pure Arsenal man. I will not become the manager until next Monday.'

It was a bizarre twist of fate that the Frenchman from Alsace was joining Arsenal just as they were about to visit Borussia Mönchengladbach, the German team whose thrilling counter-attacks had first fired his imagination. History was against Arsenal, who had never come from behind to win in Europe after losing a first leg at Highbury. Tony Adams, a substitute for hamstring victim Lee Dixon at Middlesbrough the Saturday before, was starting his first competitive game for eight months after two knee operations. He had not been named in Glenn Hoddle's squad for the World Cup qualifying tie against Poland on 9 October.

The starting eleven for the Borussia game, in 3–5–2 formation, was the side that finished the game at Middlesbrough, which Arsenal had won 2–0: Seaman; Bould, Adams, Linighan; Keown, Vieira, Merson, Platt, Winterburn; Hartson and Wright. This makeshift team was deeply unbalanced, with four centre-backs and only one good midfield player, Vieira. Despite that handicap Ian Wright scored the first goal just before half-time after Hartson had headed on Merson's free-kick. It was his fifteenth goal in seventeen European games, but then Stefan Effenberg slid a pass behind Linighan for Juskowiak to make it 4–3 on aggregate. Early in the second half Merson made it 4–4 with a twenty-yarder into the top corner, but Effenberg restored Borussia's lead after 75 minutes, then Juskowiak scored again to seal Arsenal's fate.

Wenger had watched the first half from the stand and spent the second half on the bench. Pat Rice, ebullient as ever, tried to put a positive spin on the defeat and said that Wenger had suggested a couple of changes. 'One of them was to go to a back four and add extra width to the attack, and of course I took his advice. We've come out of this with a lot of credit and will bounce back in typical Arsenal style.'

It was clear to all that Arsenal's famous rearguard, which had conceded twelve goals in the last six games, was crumbling. Chris

Davies, in the *Daily Telegraph*, reported that Arsenal's 'success in recent seasons has been based on the most solid of defences. Age is catching up with most of the back players and Wenger, who is said to prefer a back four, will no doubt make a commanding stopper a priority. Andy Linighan's weaknesses were again cruelly exposed by Borussia's speedy forwards while Arsenal had nobody with the touch and vision of Stefan Effenberg, the game's outstanding performer.'

Wenger obviously had some work to do. Former Arsenal manager Don Howe, among others, realised that 'Players judge a manager on whether he knows football. The players will want to hear him talk about football. If he comes across as having good football intelligence there will be no problem. Sooner or later a continental manager is going to break through and have success in England, and if Wenger gets success the Arsenal supporters will accept him like anyone else. Supporters want to see their team win.' Glenn Hoddle reminded Arsenal fans that Wenger 'has an English mind but also a German mind, which is very disciplined'. He said that the Arsenal players would find the new manager honest, straightforward and approachable, but ruthless too if a player stepped out of line. 'That's when the German side comes out.'

Wenger himself seemed buoyant after the defeat in Cologne. 'My challenge is to mix the English style to a more continental way. Also I am conscious that I have to win over the supporters because they don't really know me and I am foreign. But if they reject me it will not be because I am foreign. They will reject me if I don't do a good job.'

OLD GUARD TRY NEW IDEAS

Other teams noticed that we were still flying after eighty minutes, and when Tony, Martin, Wrighty and I were on England duty the other players started asking what we were taking.

David Seaman

According to David Seaman, Arsène Wenger arrived and did exactly what Roger Spry said Josef Venglos should have done at

Villa. He said: 'Right, we are doing it my way from now on!' In *Safe Hands*, his autobiography, Seaman wrote: 'Arsène made it clear that there would be total change straight away. There was no messing about. He told us, "This is how I run training and this is how I expect you to eat and look after yourselves." He said we could not carry on eating what we had been used to stuffing down ourselves, as it was no good for us as professional athletes.'

This was, in fact, an over-simplification of what happened. At first the new manager asked the players to train in the afternoons as well, but they refused to do that. So Wenger, whose credibility was low after he had made them switch to 4–4–2 at half-time in Cologne when they were winning 2–1, decided to compromise with a longer session in the morning. A masseur, Mark James, was employed for the first time and the players now had lengthy warm-downs after training and matches. Wenger said, 'I like players to relax with massages and hot baths. I believe they are helpful, physically and psychologically.' He had studied physiology and was an expert on flexibility, nutrition and the best ways to protect a player's body against fatigue. He knew how muscles worked and had also studied plyometric training, an advanced technique which involves jumping, bounding, one-legged hopping, skipping and other exercises which are specific to a particular muscle. Jumpers, sprinters and hurdlers train by doing multiple jumps over a series of obstacles such as low hurdles. These exercises, aimed at strengthening the lower body, can only be done by athletes who are already strong and well conditioned. They add power to existing strength. Arsenal's training ground at London Colney, which they shared with University College London, had antique facilities such as big white baths and a canteen worthy of a Second Division club, so Wenger immediately moved their training base to Sopwell House, a nearby hotel which had a gym, a pool, a jacuzzi and a good restaurant. The players now changed at Sopwell, took a coach down to the training pitch, then came back to the hotel. Sopwell had been used by Croatia, Portugal and many other visiting football teams before matches at Wembley.

The players found that their diet had been revolutionised. Steak, chips, scrambled eggs, baked beans, sugar and junk food were forbidden. Wenger brought in dieticians to explain the benefits of pasta, boiled chicken, steamed fish, broccoli, raw vegetables and lots of water. He also flew in Philippe Boixel, the French national team osteopath, every month to work on the realignment of the players' bodies, and the biochemist Dr Yann Rogier talked to them about the value of dietary supplements such as vitamins and minerals. The players began to receive vitamin injections and to take tablets, including creatine, an amino acid produced naturally in the liver and kidneys which is mass-produced artificially and widely sold in tablet or powder form at health-food stores. Creatine replenishes energy in the muscles and reduces fatigue, so it is most beneficial to sprinters and footballers, who do brief but intense bursts of running. It had been used by British Olympic athletes in Barcelona in 1992. Wenger, however, made it clear that the supplements were optional.

David Seaman noticed that the innovations had an immediate impact on the whole Arsenal squad, whose levels of energy and concentration were now much higher. 'Other teams noticed that we were still flying after eighty minutes, and when Tony, Martin, Wrighty and I were on England duty the other players started asking what we were taking. They copied what we were doing and carried on with it when they went back to their clubs, and most of them said they felt better for it. When this got back to Arsène, he made a point of warning us not to tell the other players exactly what we were doing and taking. At that stage this was all new to the English league and he wanted to keep our edge for as long as possible.' Wenger's training techniques were the distillation of two decades of research, practice, observation and careful thinking, so he must have been annoyed that his methods had been revealed to his rivals in such a careless manner.

Work on the training pitch became more scientific, with fewer long runs and cross-country runs but much more timed running in the form of bleep-tests, where players run back and forth while an electronic device emits a timed signal. Wenger believes that players can over-train, so he made it clear that from now on sleep, rest and relaxation would be very important.

George Graham had never allowed journalists or broadcasters to watch Arsenal's training sessions, and Wenger kept up this tradition. In *Addicted*, his best-selling autobiography, Tony Adams stated that Wenger liked to keep his training methods to himself, but he did reveal that sessions sometimes lasted only 45 minutes: 'stretching and a warm-up, then a ten-minutes-each-way small-sided game and finish with a run round the pitch'. Seaman confirmed that Wenger was out on the training pitch with them every day and always knew exactly what he wanted his players to do. He always had his stopwatch with him and was a martinet about the timing of their work (the word 'martinet' originates in France: Jean Martinet was a seventeenth-century army drill-master notorious for his brutal methods). 'Everything is geared to his watch,' Seaman wrote. 'He knows how long any training or tactical discipline should last and will stop it right on the button. Sometimes he drives us mad. We could be playing an eight-a-side game on a smaller pitch with a bigger goal. The score is 2–2 and it has been a really good, tight game but, when the time he has allowed for it is up, he will always step in and stop it. We all say, "Let's go on until the next goal wins it," but he never changes his mind. We have to stop and move on to the next exercise. There is no arguing with him.' Wenger had a fitness coach working with him, but Adams believed that the manager knew professional footballers inside out and could tell whether a player was fully fit just by watching him run. 'He is a thinker, a listener, and he cares a great deal about the welfare of players,' said Adams.

Wenger's first game in charge of Arsenal was on 12 October 1996 at Blackburn, and that was when he first introduced his players to the stretching exercises which were to become an important part of their lives. 'He called us all down to the hotel ballroom,' Adams recalled, 'and put us through the routine for half an hour. There was some joking among the boys, who were all pretending still to be sleepy and putting on the tiredness, because we probably feared change. But just because it was different didn't make it wrong. It helped that we went on to win the game that day and now it is second nature to us.'

The way Wenger treated his players as people was related to the way he treated them as footballers. He saw football as a game for adults and young adults, so instead of telling them exactly what to do on the field he gave each player the responsibility for his own game, which allowed a more exciting and more varied style of play to evolve, with defenders like Bould and Adams encouraged to bring the ball forward far more than they ever did under Graham, who only wheeled the big men up for set-pieces. Dennis Bergkamp was another who responded positively to these new ideas. He had been sulking since Bruce Rioch, the manager who signed him, had been sacked, and had stopped going into the players' lounge. Bergkamp hated boozers, so Wenger's approach was a breath of fresh air for him. Whenever the Dutchman had smelt drink on the breath of team-mates in the morning he made a point of hounding those players in training matches, giving them a hard time to make them wish they had not indulged the night before.

Wenger was unbeaten after his first four Premiership games against Blackburn, Coventry, Leeds and Wimbledon, but everything was still new to him. He learned something every week: what each player could do in training, whether he could reproduce it in matches, how often he could do it, and whether he did it more often home or away. He watched his players carefully to see how brave, how skilful and how determined they were, and he surveyed them with a fresh, unprejudiced eye, making an inventory all the while, gathering a definitive dossier of information on the basis of which next summer's big decisions would be made. He was making small, specific judgements but also an overall judgement about Arsenal's style of play. Would a different style be more effective with this group of players? If so, how quickly could that new style be created? Will new players be needed? If so, how many? Can the club afford them?

In terms of media relations, Wenger worked with Clare Tomlinson, who had joined Arsenal from the FA after Euro 96, and they decided that he would do press conferences but not give one-on-one interviews to English journalists. Wenger came with no baggage and he decided to travel without baggage, without favourites. He was still trying to figure out the English game and assess the challenge posed by other Premiership clubs anyway, and he had not known any British reporters when he was a player. That sensible approach protected him in the early days when his English was not as good as it is now, buying him time to figure out what the media needed and wanted. That decision has never been reversed, even though most other Premiership managers do interviews as well as press conferences.

MANCHESTER UNITED 1 ARSENAL 0

They are so disappointed, so frustrated. I also learnt that they have solidarity when they lose. Maybe David Seaman felt he made a mistake but everybody was all right.

Arsène Wenger

After a couple of months at the helm Wenger realised that his main rivals were going to be Alex Ferguson at Manchester United, Kevin Keegan at Newcastle, Brian Little at Aston Villa and George Graham at Leeds.

Ferguson had arrived at Old Trafford in 1986, the same year in which Graham arrived at Arsenal. Graham had soon built the powerhouse midfield of Marwood, Davis, Thomas and Rocastle, which showed Ferguson what was needed to win the league. Once, at Highbury after a game, Ferguson had marvelled at the tackling and running power of David Rocastle. 'What an effort the boy Rocastle puts into his game,' he said, pointing out that such hard work by the tenacious Rocky was of great benefit to Lee Dixon, who played behind him.

When Wenger first came to Old Trafford Ferguson was just embarking on his second decade in charge, but United had suffered a disturbing sequence of results. They had lost 5–0 at Newcastle, then 6–3 at Southampton before coming back to Old Trafford to play Chelsea, who beat them 2–1. So, coming into the game with Arsenal on 16 November, the champions had conceded thirteen goals in their previous three games, and Roy Keane was suspended. The young David Beckham had taken his place in central midfield. The game was played in front of

55,210 people, the biggest crowd in the history of the Premiership.

The real action opened with Cantona playing a superb pass across the penalty area, picking out Beckham, whose instant shot hit the post with Seaman well beaten. Bergkamp then put Wright in on the left, but his touch was poor and he had to chase the ball as it ran into the box. Schmeichel raced out, feet first, grabbed it and then jumped up, enraged, suggesting Wright had kicked him. Fierce words were exchanged. Referee Graham Poll cautioned Wright but replays suggested that the striker's outstretched right foot had not connected with the Danish goalkeeper. It looked like Schmeichel's histrionics had got the fiery striker a booking. Seaman had earlier been injured when Solskjær's boot caught him in the chest – he was found to have a cracked rib.

The only goal, when it came in the middle of the second half, was the most untidy, self-inflicted goal Arsenal would concede all season. Giggs closed down on Dixon, who half-volleyed a wonky backpass, and Seaman made a pig's breakfast of his clearance. He should have kicked the ball into Row Z or let it go out for a corner, but he chose to stop the ball with his foot and kicked it straight to Nicky Butt, who jabbed it across the open goal towards Poborsky. As Winterburn intervened the ball hit his arm and dribbled over the line. A farcical goal to concede.

'We lost the game on details, offensively and defensively,' the manager said afterwards. 'In the big games you make one or two small mistakes and you pay for it. That's why we are unhappy today. Because we have the feeling that we could have done more and come back with at least a draw.' He was, however, impressed by Arsenal's team spirit, even in defeat. 'They are so disappointed, so frustrated. I also learnt that they have solidarity when they lose. Maybe David Seaman felt he made a mistake but everybody was all right.' The Frenchman placed huge emphasis on this *esprit de corps* and would continue to do so for the next five years. 'With the internationalisation of the game today, you have many foreign players in the team, and you do not always have the right spirit. You have to find a real balance. If you bring players in, you have to make sure they have the right spirit.'

ARSENAL 3 SPURS 1

The real revelation of a player's character is not in his social life but in how he plays. In my social life I can hide my real personality . . .

Arsène Wenger

After six weeks and seven games the manager did a press conference before his first North London derby and his thoughts represented a half-term report on the players he had inherited. When one reporter mentioned Patrick Vieira's creative touches, the manager said something interesting. 'What is creative?' he asked. 'For me, being creative is scoring goals. That is why, for me, beauty is efficiency. It is not about making nice movements. The crowd love him because he does the right thing at the right moment, not because he's beautiful to watch. I see players who do wonderful things outside a match but once in a match they are disasters because they cannot do them when they are needed.'

Wenger was at his most professorial during a discussion of the alcoholism and behaviour in general. 'The real revelation of a player's character is not in his social life but in how he plays. In my social life I can hide my real personality, but when I'm playing I show really how I am. It's important for me to win while respecting the rules. Sometimes if a player is really dirty on the field but outside in life he is so nice, at important times in his life he will become like he is on the field. When you argue with the referee you are not concentrating on the game and you lose two or three seconds. I know that sometimes a player needs to release his frustration. It depends on the personality. Maybe Ian Wright sometimes needs to say something in order to be better in the next move. But it's better to have a high level of concentration. Look at how we lost at Manchester United – a small thing.'

He pointed out, however, that he had been very impressed by the professionalism of his players. 'I have a deep respect for my squad. We have an experienced team. Some people say that we have an old team but the mental side must still be young because these players are ready to take on anybody to win games. For me, being a professional is not just playing once a week, and playing well from time to time, it's trying to be at your best every time. For this you need a strong mentality. For a professional player, it's not normal every day to get up in the morning and say, "OK, let's go on with the fight." You need a special attitude. Winners are those who are able to do it. When you have players like I have who have been doing it for ten years, that means there is something special inside them which makes them want to win.

'I am surprised by the technical quality of the defenders. English defenders had a reputation for just kicking the ball. You should come to training and see that our five defenders are technically good. Tony Adams and the other ones are able to play. They last so long because they have the quality. If they had only physique they couldn't last.'

Arsenal needed to be at their best on 24 November because they had not beaten Spurs at Highbury for five years. There had been some scuffling stalemates when the sides were managed by those old cronies George Graham and Terry Venables, who used to come in to face reporters together, thereby making sure that the press conference was also a goalless draw. This time Wenger was pleased to see Dennis Bergkamp, his star player, inspiring the Gunners to victory.

The Dutchman won a penalty early on when Clive Wilson fouled him in the box, and Ian Wright converted. It was 1–0 at half-time. Wright missed several chances in the second half before Andy Sinton hit a shot which rebounded from the base of the post, hit the head of the diving John Lukic, and crossed the line for an unusual own-goal. The rest of the game was tense, but some good football was played. Arsenal scored twice in the last three minutes to win the match. Bergkamp flicked on a Paul Merson throw and Adams, charging forward, hit a shot which went in off right-back Steve Carr. Then Merson found Wright on the right side and he hit a long cross beyond the far post. As the cross came down on the wet, slippery grass, Bergkamp killed the ball with one devastating touch, knocked it five yards past Carr, burst across the startled defender and smashed his shot past Ian Walker. Carr tried to grab him round the waist but he was a scarecrow, a man of straw, against the explosive force of the Dutchman, who had decided where he was going before the ball had even bounced. Dennis Bergkamp had administered an outrageous *coup de grâce* by passing the ball to himself. It was a classic goal which decided the game and lifted the ecstatic North Bank fans from their seats in salute. The handsome 3–1 win was the highlight of the season so far.

Beating Leeds 3–0 in October had put Arsenal top of the table, but after losing at Old Trafford they had dropped to third. Next up, on the last day of November, were league leaders Newcastle at St James's Park.

Injuries to key players are a big part of every manager's life and Wenger now found that he was without Seaman, who was to miss nine Premiership games with that cracked rib, and Bergkamp, who had strained a thigh muscle while warming up at Anfield for a midweek Coca-Cola Cup tie which Liverpool had won 4–2. So Arsenal had lost their last two away games and now had to face a trip to Newcastle with John Lukic in goal and John Hartson partnering Wright. On the day, Arsenal were rescued by a fine performance from Paul Merson, who often carries the ball more than Bergkamp does.

A very unusual incident occurred early in the game which could have put Arsenal off their stride. A ball was played down the field towards the Arsenal penalty area. Tino Asprilla was ten yards offside, strolling back in his nonchalant way, and when the long ball came towards him he allowed it to bounce between his legs, leaving it for an onrushing Alan Shearer, and obliging Tony Adams to run round him. When Adams and Shearer barged each other, Adams was sent off by Graham Barber for a professional foul.

But it was Arsenal who took the lead when Hartson made a pass down the left side and Wright craftily allowed big centre-back Darren Peacock to reach the ball first, then knocked him off balance with a neat nudge. He crossed to the far post where flying wing-back Lee Dixon scored with a diving header. Dixon had always liked steaming into the box and what made this one fun was that David Ginola, his old adversary from the Paris Saint Germain ties in the Cup Winners Cup, had failed to track his run. Ginola, however, soon replied with a good cross and Shearer rose above Hartson to head the equaliser. Wenger was entitled to wonder about the marking. Since Bould and Keown were on the field, why was neither of them marking the England striker as he went for the kind of header ten million English football fans had seen him score fifty times? The organisational intelligence of Adams was missed.

The winning goal was a jammy one, but Wenger probably felt his team deserved some luck after having had Adams so harshly dismissed. Merson dribbled straight down the middle of the field and tried a 25-yard shot which hit Ian Wright on the ankle and broke into his stride. Wright deftly slipped the ball past the advancing Srnicek. So Arsenal had played for over an hour with ten men and beaten the league leaders to go top of the table. Overall, Wenger was delighted with his team's form. Unfortunately, this victory at St James's Park was as good as it got because a 3–1 win over Southampton on 4 December was their only victory in five Premiership matches that month.

As 1996 drew to a close, Arsenal were still very much an English side with eight Englishmen plus Bergkamp, Vieira and Garde. Of those three, the first two were key players, as was illustrated on 28 December during the game against Aston Villa at Highbury, where the first goal in a 2–2 draw illustrated their attacking potential. Vieira, back in the side after missing three games, took the ball off Savo Milosevic and poked it towards Bergkamp, whose through-ball put Wright in. Mark Bosnich did not come out, so Wright had time to get his head up, check the bottom corner and fire past the keeper's right hand. Wenger admitted that his side could not sustain their game in the second half of that match because Garde, Bergkamp and Parlour had not had enough competitive football recently. He talked about maintaining a high tempo and finding a balance between getting balls forward quickly and keeping possession. Clearly, his favourite style of football was not as patient as that favoured by Bruce Rioch. He did not like too much pretty possession play, preferring quick penetration – slicing through the heart of the opposition's defence as soon as possible. This conception of the game was Milan-influenced, which is hardly surprising given all those trips he made to their training ground while at Monaco. Wenger favoured powerful, skilful athletes who could press ferociously, win the ball and pass it quickly into dangerous areas.

HARTSON GLIMPSES TRANSFER THROUGH RED MIST

I think we outplayed them tonight. Tactically, I think we got it right. I thought they ran out of ideas in the last twenty minutes.

George Graham

When Arsenal played Middlesbrough on New Year's Day 1997 they won 2–0 with goals by Bergkamp and Wright, a victory which kept them in second place. Both goals came from mistakes and John Hartson was sent off in an incident which seemed to sum up his self-indulgent life.

Hartson had already served a three-match ban earlier in the season and had come on as a 64th-minute substitute for Bergkamp. Within two minutes he had thrown the ball away after a tackle on Bryan Robson, Boro's player-manager. Referee Mike Reed gave Hartson a yellow card for that, but a minute later he swore at Reed despite not being involved in the play at that time and was shown the red card.

Wenger had just gone four straight games without a win, his worst sequence since taking over, and he badly needed three points. Arsenal were 2–0 up and his irresponsible centre-forward had been sent off only three minutes after coming on, leaving his team-mates to play twenty minutes with ten men. A better side than Middlesbrough might have saved the game, especially when a penalty was awarded not long afterwards. Fabrizio Ravanelli, who had been felled by Steve Bould, sent his spot-kick into the North Stand via the crossbar.

Inevitably, Wenger was asked after the match about his team's deteriorating discipline. Was four red cards in the last eight games a worry?

'It's fifty per cent,' the manager joked.

But that's not the kind of consistency you want, is it?

'That's right. I think maybe some red cards I can understand. But it's less understandable when you speak with the referee.

Because we had a red card with Steve Bould at Liverpool, Tony Adams at Newcastle and even Ian Wright. It's a game, it happens; it's a reaction, they played the ball. It's always understandable. This one, I first must check what happened with the referee and with John Hartson. It was not in the game.'

Ian Wright's second goal was his 166th for Arsenal and the 200th of his career. Wenger said this was a great achievement. 'It's a symbol of a big career. I think 200 league goals is fantastic. It's really incredible.'

A steward then came in and handed Wenger a pale blue sheet of paper – a copy of the referee's report.

The *Sun*'s Brian Woolnough asked, 'Does it say there what he called him?'

The reporters giggled, but Wenger said only that Hartson's first yellow card was for a foul and the second for foul and abusive language. 'Too many red cards,' he conceded, 'but I cannot condemn the behaviour of my team because, as I explained to you before, the three red cards we got before we didn't deserve.'

Middlesbrough was a valuable win, but Hartson would now miss another three games. Wenger continued to give nothing away regarding his own feelings about the Hartson dismissal, but it looked as if this particular red card could have long-term significance for the Welshman.

The next three games were all against Sunderland. Hartson played and scored in a 1–1 draw in the FA Cup on 4 January; the tie was replayed at Roker Park on the 15th and the Gunners won 2–0. In between those two games Arsenal faced them in the league and lost 1–0. They beat Everton and West Ham after that, and then, on the first day of February, George Graham showed his old team how to keep clean sheets.

This goalless draw at Elland Road was a prequel to the FA Cup fourth-round clash at Highbury three days later. On that day Graham made sure he did not lose at his old club by employing defensive methods which had won both domestic cups for Arsenal in 1993. Rod Wallace scored the early goal, then roamed around in the Arsenal half with Brian Deane, holding the ball up well as various players broke in support at great speed. Graham had put the quick, tenacious Gary Kelly on to Merson and Gunnar Halle on to Wright, with Carlton Palmer trying to shackle the more skilful Vieira in midfield. Merson worked his socks off, but was hard pushed just to keep possession of the ball let alone make a good dribble or pass. Parlour and Dixon, two players with great drive, made no impact on the right because every Leeds player was as quick and determined as they were. Hartson came on at half-time, hit the post with a header and missed another two chances in injury time. So in two games against Leeds Arsenal had failed to score. Without Bergkamp the goals had simply dried up. Wright, who was having a bad spell anyway, missed his classy passes.

The match, although a disappointing stalemate, provided observers with a chance to compare Graham's personality with Wenger's. Graham, self-regarding as ever, used the first person singular rather than the plural. The Leeds team seemed to be a vehicle for his ego just as much as the Arsenal team was for Wenger's, but the Frenchman seemed more modest and democratic about it. Graham is one of the best tacticians in British football but a lot of his tactics are about nullification, about stopping football being played rather than playing football. He is the sultan of stopping, the nabob of negation. Wenger prefers to believe that the pursuit of excellence will produce the right results as well as enjoyment for players and supporters.

'I thought first half we played very well,' said Graham. 'I thought Arsenal looked a bit jittery at the back, a few set-pieces, a few moves. I thought we'd maybe pinch a few more goals in the second half. They played into our hands really, bringing on John Hartson. I think they started going long ball. The last half hour I think it was very easy for us. Although it was very tiring physically, I thought we handled it well.' He explained his team selection and tactics with no hint of an apology.

'Radebe phoned in this morning, he had the flu. He was really ill. I really needed him to either pick up Merson or Wright. So that was a big problem. So I had to push in Kelly from the right wing, bring in young Harte at full-back. It messed me up a little bit. But I actually thought they coped very well. I thought Kelly on Merson was absolutely outstanding and Halle was probably the man of the match. We had to adapt to a very physical side. I think we outplayed them tonight. Tactically, I think we got it right. I thought they ran out of ideas in the last twenty minutes.'

Wenger thought Leeds had defended well but Arsenal had missed chances. 'I think we had a bad start, an unlucky goal against us, and after that we tried to play to keep the ball on the ground. We tried to play quite well, maybe with not enough mobility in the first half. In the second half when John Hartson came on we could not keep the patience to keep the ball on the ground, and tried very hard to play long balls to put the Leeds defence under pressure. We couldn't find the right balance between playing long balls and keeping the balls on the ground and having patience. But the team gave everything. They fought like crazy until the last minute so we can say, once again, that Arsenal was Arsenal, with the fighting spirit.' He admitted that his team had hit far too many long balls. 'But we had many chances, when John Hartson hit the bar and the post, and if he had scored we'd have said the opposite. So if you don't score you are wrong.'

Nine days later Wenger sold Hartson to West Ham for £3.2 million. The transfer divided the fans. Some said it was Arsenal's best result since beating Parma 1–0 in the 1994 Cup Winners Cup Final, others that the club would have got the same money for him come the summer. Clearly, a coach who admires fast, slim footballers could never have enjoyed the sight of Hartson, a lumbering carthorse of a player, on the training pitch every day. He was also a boozing bachelor who was fond of junk food, and a gambler who allegedly put Paul Merson's bets on for him after Merson told everyone he had given up gambling. Hartson symbolised the bad old days of English football. What was the point of teaching what Wenger had begun to teach and then keeping a walking, talking contradiction on the payroll?

A few months later Sky commentator Martin Tyler made an extraordinary comment to me about the goalless Premiership game at Elland Road. He reckoned he had pinpointed the moment which had convinced Wenger to sell Hartson. 'There was a pass on for Ian Wright, who had come on; there was a break on, and it needed a cool first-time ball on a very dodgy pitch. But John took an extra touch, and when he played it Wright was offside. John was playing safe rather than stab it and have it go off his sock.'

When Arsenal went to White Hart Lane on 15 February it was probably the first time both teams had ever played with three centre-backs. A dull 0–0 draw was no surprise. The surprise was that Rosenthal and Iversen contributed more to the game than Wright and Bergkamp, who were tentative because they had not played together for nearly a month. Spurs' keeper Ian Walker only had to make two saves, one from a volley by Bergkamp, the other when he tipped round a Keown header. Wenger admitted it was a fair result and said both defences played very well, especially John Lukic. When asked about Wright and Bergkamp, he said, 'I think both showed a little bit of lack of competition. For different reasons. One because he was suspended for three weeks, and the second one because he was injured and came back and had just one game. Ian Wright had just one game in five weeks. And of course that is very important for the strikers. A midfielder can play, but a striker – you need to be sharp to make a difference.'

Wenger was proving to be a pragmatic character, a positive thinker, someone who had a firm grasp of the arithmetical possibilities from his remaining fixtures. Football, like politics, is the art of the possible. Wenger was disappointed that his team had wasted a chance to go top of the table, but he remained bullish about their prospects. 'Mathematically, we are in a good position,' he said. 'We are there with twelve games to go. We play seven at home, five away. Everybody comes to Arsenal and it's not so bad. We played at West Ham and Leeds and Tottenham, three difficult games. We won at West Ham and played two draws at Leeds and Tottenham and made five points out of three away games, so it's not so bad.' He talked about 'decompression' following the midweek FA Cup defeat against Leeds, which was a very tense night for everyone.

Arsenal had recently been linked with a seventeen-year-old French striker who wanted to leave Paris Saint Germain, so I asked Wenger, 'Are you trying to get Anelka before the transfer deadline?'

Wenger smiled wearily and said, 'It's impossible. We will try to bring somebody in before the transfer deadline, that's for sure. But if you ask me if we are close I'd say no. But we cannot be far away because the deadline is not far away.'

Arsenal's next match was at Highbury against Manchester United, for which Eric Cantona was suspended. Wenger said, 'I feel every time, every game, it's a game we must win. But this one maybe even more. We have to think that if we play well, if we give everything, if we have the support that we will have, I'm sure, at Highbury, we have a chance to beat Manchester.'

WRIGHT JUMPS ON SCHMEICHEL'S LEG

There are things that happen in every game of football.

Arsène Wenger

One of the talking points before the game on 19 February was that Ian Wright, who was in sight of the club's all-time scoring record, had never scored against Manchester United in a league match, and he had publicly accused Peter Schmeichel of making a racial remark after their flare-up three months earlier. The referee for the game was Martin Bodenham, who was notorious for letting a lot of fouls go unpunished, which usually meant an open, exciting, free-flowing game.

Wright missed two chances in the first eight minutes. The first was a one-on-one with Schmeichel, the second a diving header where he missed the ball by two inches. Roy Keane was captain of United for the first time and his partner, wearing the number ten shirt, was David Beckham. When Gary Neville played a ball down the right Tony Adams was deceived by the bounce and Andy Cole fired a low shot neatly past Lukic. Then a Giggs–Poborsky–Cole move ended with Solskjær making it 2–0.

Adams went off at half-time, Stephen Hughes came on, Arsenal switched to 4–4–2 and Hughes soon smashed a shot against the post. The rebound went to Bergkamp, who touched the ball instantly to Wright, and he rammed it into the net. It was a sublime demonstration of lightning reflexes by both players, but the flag was up for offside. Then Hughes started another move, Merson played the ball in behind Irwin, Parlour crossed low and Bergkamp hit an unstoppable shot between Schmeichel and his near post.

By this stage, with the score at 2–1 and having missed those two early chances, with a third shot unluckily deflected off Ronny Johnsen's leg, not to mention the disallowed goal, Ian Wright was an incident waiting to happen. So when he sprinted after a through-pass and Schmeichel came out of his penalty area feet first and the whistle went for offside, Wright kept on running and jumped two-footed on to the United goalkeeper's outstretched leg. It was spectacularly dangerous play, easily the most outrageous Premiership foul of the season, and it had Alex Ferguson catapulting off the bench in fury. Amazingly, Bodenham did not even give Wright a yellow card, so he must have had a very poor view of the incident.

Schmeichel played on after treatment, and then Bergkamp hit a beautiful early cross to create a wonderful chance for Wright. It was a ball he could, and probably should, have chested down, but he chose to go for a stooping header which he mistimed, the ball bouncing tamely into the ground. He clearly did not want to chest down the ball in case Schmeichel came at him feet first again. So Manchester United beat them for the second time that season. Scottish managers were beginning to be a problem for the Frenchman. George Graham's Leeds had shut down and beaten Arsenal that month, and now Alex Ferguson had handed Monsieur Wenger his first Premiership defeat at Highbury and moved clear at the top of the table, five points ahead with a game in hand.

One of the unwritten rules in football is that a manager does not attack his own players in public. Every manager expects loyalty from his players and in return for that he defends them, so after the Schmeichel assault Wenger naturally tried to pour oil on troubled waters. 'There are things that happen in every game of football,' he said. It was a ridiculous comment, but Wright had put him in the embarrassing position of having to defend the indefensible.

Wright's wretched period continued with a story about his affair with Tina Hodgson, a waitress at TGI Fridays in Mill Hill, North London. The News of the World headline had read SOCCER STAR WRIGHT CHEATS WITH BURGER BAR BEAUTY. Wenger did not, of course, involve himself in the private lives of his players, but Wright's embarrassing publicity was harming the team. He had not been the same player since the story came out and he had not scored in his last four games. He still needed eleven goals to beat Cliff Bastin's record, but it was now obvious that he would not do it before the close of the 1996/97 season. Wright was a huge star, a crowd favourite, but he was becoming less reliable. His private life was splashed all over the tabloids and he was more undisciplined than ever. He would soon be starting his tenth domestic suspension at Arsenal in five and a half years.

On the day of the Arsenal–Wimbledon game, Sunday, 23 February, Wright's problems worsened when the *People* produced another scoop: IAN WRIGHT SCORES WITH BBC GIRL. It seemed that Wright, who had always been bubbly, quotable and amusing, had been seduced by showbusiness. He had become a luvvie, more of an actor than an athlete. Venetia Williamson-Noble was a 26-year-old Radio One researcher he had met at the previous year's Brit Awards ceremony at Earls Court in London. The couple had begun to see each other secretly, but were later seen together at nightclubs. In December 1996, Wright went to the *Top of the Pops* Christmas party at the BBC studios in Elstree, Hertfordshire, and she had been his after-match guest in the players' lounge. Wright's wife Debbie admitted that she and Ian had not been living togther as man and wife for a year, but that they still loved each other and were trying to work it out.

On a more promising note, it was announced that Arsenal had completed the signing of Nicolas Anelka, the young striker from Paris Saint Germain, only days after Wenger had pronounced it 'impossible'. Another boost for the club was the selection of Patrick Vieira for the France squad, an honour which was well overdue.

There were just eleven league games left when Wimbledon came to Highbury, where Arsenal were always going to struggle without Adams and Keown. Their three centre-backs that day were Scott Marshall, Remi Garde and Steve Bould, and there was a misunderstanding as soon as the first long ball came over. Lukic came out, Garde let the ball bounce then headed it back, but the ball went for a corner. Arsenal cleared the corner weakly to Neil Ardley, whose cross was volleyed in by Vinnie Jones for the only goal of the game.

In February *Match of the Day* screened their Goal of the Month competition as usual, but for Wenger's men February was the Month of the Goal. They had recorded no league victories and scored only one goal, by Bergkamp in the defeat at Old Trafford. Wenger betrayed a hint of grouchiness. After the Wimbledon game he complained that it was 'not a regular championship' if some teams had more time to recover from their previous games than their opponents. This was a valid point, but one that was never mentioned by British managers. Our domestic league is a rough-and-tumble competition where everyone always says: be first, never say die, never complain, take each match as it comes and do not worry about whether things should be organised more fairly.

On 6 March referee and ClubCall man Kenny Goldman told me that his friend had just refereed the Arsenal–Norwich Combination Cup game. Anelka's registration had come through during the first half so he was allowed to go on, and he looked very good, even though Arsenal lost the tie 3–1. The gossip that week was all about Ian Wright's head being messed up by his marital misdemeanours. Could this talented French kid replace the fading goalscorer? If so, how soon?

In March Arsenal beat Everton, Nottingham Forest and South-ampton by the same scoreline, 2–0, then on the 24th they lost 2–1 at home to Liverpool in a match notable for Robbie Fowler's sportsmanship in attempting to persuade the referee not to give a penalty when he had tumbled over David Seaman. Fowler missed the penalty, but Jason McAteer scored from the rebound. In April they disposed of Chelsea and Leicester, but then stuttered with 1–1 draws against Blackburn and Coventry, while Kevin Keegan's Newcastle, the attacking team which leaked too many goals, finished in fine style with two wins, two draws and four clean sheets. The highlight of Newcastle's run-in was their 1–0 win at Highbury on 3 May. Arsenal picked up a final win against Derby on the 11th but ended the season in third place, level on points with Newcastle (second) and Liverpool (fourth) but losing out on a place in the new Champions League to the former on goal difference. Brian Little's Aston Villa and Ruud Gullit's Chelsea finished fifth and sixth, seven and nine points behind respectively.

Arsenal had matched the champions, Manchester United, on the road, both clubs winning nine away games, but they had lost crucial home games to United in November, Wimbledon in February, Liverpool in March and Newcastle in May. They had also lost twice to United and to Liverpool, and neither had they managed to beat Aston Villa. Wenger knew that in the 1997/98 season he would need to win those games against his closest rivals. He would need to beat Manchester United, Liverpool and New- castle at Highbury. And such victories would of course have a value beyond the arithmetic, since it is vital, in all sports, to beat your biggest rivals. It would be an easier job if Wenger could just figure out how to improve his team, so he asked himself a few fundamental questions. How can we score more goals? How can we win those awkward home games against Aston Villa, Liverpool, Leeds and Manchester United? How can I get more out of Bergkamp?

The most difficult question was: Who should I let go? David Platt had started 27 Premiership games in midfield but had not been tackling. He functioned quite well within the team unit but played as if he had a glass knee. In a team playing power football, trying to win the ball early, this was a major flaw. One recalled a rather ominous remark by Sven-Goran Eriksson, Sampdoria's coach when Platt was there, which was hardly reported outside Italy. He had said that Platt's knee injury did not necessarily have to be career-threatening. Discerning fans rated Platt a bad signing at £4.75 million, an ageing crock.

Aside from Platt, Arsenal's style of play, with Bergkamp and Merson doing the creative stuff, passing to each other when they were not feeding Wright, had been working fairly well – as long as Wright was scoring. In 1996/97 he scored 23 goals in thirty starts and five sub appearances. Unfortunately, Bergkamp had scored just nine from open play, Merson only six. The manager had seen all the matches and had watched all the videos, so he knew that Merson usually passed to Wright, his mate. He decided that Merson and Bergkamp were too similar, and that Merson's presence in the side reduced the impact of his most creative attacker. Arsenal's style of play was still based on the 3–4–2–1 formation Wenger had inherited from Rioch, which Tony Adams had persuaded him to retain for the rest of the season. But that system meant that too much time was spent feeding the flanks, not enough feeding Ian Wright.

Wenger realised that this was a turning point in his Arsenal career, a time when he had to build carefully and re-motivate his key players, especially his most gifted player, Dennis Bergkamp. He said, 'He's 27, and I told him at his age you become a huge player or you go backwards.' Wenger had challenged his star in a very clever way. He was saying: the next five years can be your best, you can be a genuinely great player if you want to be. The following season promised to be very interesting. As Manchester City manager Malcolm Allison once said, 'Coaching is not about what players you've got. It's about what you get out of the players you've got.'

5. 1997/98: THE SEASON OF THE DOUBLE

At 2 p.m. on Tuesday, 17 June, Arsenal called a press conference which told us a lot about the ambitions of the new manager and the quality and type of footballer he wanted on board from now on.

Wenger was wearing a beige suit and had a new, very short hair cut. He was especially genial and charming when I had a word with him before the reporters came in and settled down. He said that Luis Boa Morte, the young left-winger he had just signed, had missed the final of that summer's under-21 Toulon Tournament through suspension, not injury.

The manager was joined on the stage by David Dein and two of the new players. Dein, briskly businesslike and brimming with bonhomie, said simply, 'I'm delighted to welcome Emmanuel Petit, who has interrupted his holiday to come over, and Marc Overmars, who signed for us yesterday.'

Emmanuel Petit was blond with a pony-tail. He was wearing a sky-blue suit made of soft towelling-type material like that used for an infant's baby-gro, a see-through shirt and a medallion. He looked like a Californian soap star – the body of an athlete, the face of an actor. Was he hard enough for the Premiership, or was he another Frank Leboeuf? Overmars wore charcoal pinstripe trousers, matching waistcoat and a white T-shirt. This was a formal meeting, a big turning point in his life, but his manner was relaxed and cocky. The most frequently quoted transfer fee for Overmars was £7 million, but the true figure was just over £5 million.

Wenger said that the club's basic challenge was to improve the structure of the squad by bringing in some new players and younger players. 'We also wanted players who are used to winning, used to the pressure in the big clubs, and who are winner-types. I think Emmanuel Petit and Marc Overmars have proved before that they are used to being in clubs where you have to win, and that's very important to us. They play in positions where we wanted to sign some players. On the other side we also signed some younger players like Boa Morte from Portugal and a young German player called Alberto Mendez, and of course Gilles Grimandi, who is a defender who played also in Monaco. That's the five purchases we have made in recent times. It's not all over yet. We might still bring in one, maximum two, players.'

Dein echoed the manager's enthusiasm. 'Marc Overmars is a big signing for us, as indeed is Emmanuel and his colleague Gilles Grimandi, who is still on holiday. All five players will be reporting for training at the beginning of July. So it is exciting times at Arsenal Football Club.' He also pointed out that since Wenger had taken over nine months ago ten players had left the club and as many had joined, emphasising that all the new players were on four- and five-year contracts without any escape clauses.

Wenger then waxed lyrical over his new Dutchman. 'Marc Overmars is a player of class. He has qualities that are very difficult to find now. He's a winger-type who can go in the space, is a good dribbler, and we needed this type of player. We had a problem this season [1996/97], especially at home. Don't forget that we were maybe the best away team but we lost the championship at home. I think we needed more power and more speed at home, and more penetration. I think Marc has won everything until now. He's won the European Cup, the World Club Cup, and championships, but he's still very young and ambitious – 24 years old is the best age for a football player. The four or five years he has in front of him are the best ones, and that's why I went for him.

'They're adaptable players. For example, Petit can play in every position on the left side, in midfield, central or on the outside, or in defence. When I started him in competition he was a central defender on the left side, but he's a technical player and he went into midfield. I think both Marc and Emmanuel are very adaptable in a 3–5–2 or a 4–4–2 system. We will take the best option. But in my choices it was very important that they would be adaptable in different systems because in modern football you need some-times to change the system for one or two games. Basically, we would like to go to a 4–4–2 but it's not decided.'

Overmars confirmed that he had talked to Bergkamp before making his decision. 'I spoke with him a few times, of course, about the club. He said many good things.' He was then asked whether Arsenal had tried to sign him a few years ago. 'It started with a meeting with Mr Dein two years ago. At the time I was playing with Ajax and winning all the prizes. I think I'm now a good age and I feel very good about this transfer. I think the time is right. As Mr Wenger said, we'll play a little bit different. I like it because of the space; with my speed and quality I can use it very good here. At Ajax you've got your own position and you have to keep in your position, so this will be a little more space and freedom, and I like it.' Overmars confirmed that he was fully recovered from a serious knee injury and Dein said that he had just played thirty games for Ajax.

One key issue that summer was whether Wenger would sign any British players. There had been talk that England's left-back Graeme Le Saux was leaving Blackburn, whose board said he could go when a club paid £7.5 million for him. Wenger said he would not pay that sort of money and the *Mirror* reported that a swap, David Platt plus £5 million, was a possibility, although it seemed unlikely that Blackburn boss Roy Hodgson would fancy that deal. Platt was absent from Arsenal's pre-season friendly in Strasbourg on 25 July, said to be watching his horse run in another part of France. Le Saux eventually went to Chelsea – for £5 million.

Wenger continued on the squad strength theme. 'If you want to have an interesting role in the championship you need a bigger squad than we had last season. We were lucky because we had many players over thirty, and not many injuries. But we had Tony Adams out from January to June, only on seventy per cent of his possibilities, and David Seaman out for nineteen games. And we were out of the UEFA Cup and quickly out of the FA Cup. I think that's why we need a bigger squad than we had last season if we want to be more ambitious. It's very difficult to admit, but sometimes I was glad we weren't involved in more competitions because we just didn't have the players to play every three days.

'We have two departments at Arsenal now who work very hard to improve the quality inside the club, the youth department and the professional department. In the professional department I think Arsenal had the best players between 28 and 35 years old. But between 20 and 28 the best players are at Manchester United and at Liverpool. We had no choice, in this age category, but to go abroad. What was crucial was the spirit. That's why we wanted to get in winner-types because of the specific Arsenal spirit, which is a winner-type who will never give up. Emmanuel and Marc are these type of players. The spirit is more important than the nationality. I think they will fit in and integrate well because of their qualities.'

Wenger was asked to justify his 'no choice but to go abroad' view. 'It just says that the best players between 20 and 28 are at Manchester United, Newcastle and Liverpool. We are ambitious. When you are ambitious you always want the best quality. If we had equal quality in England we wouldn't go abroad. But the quality is important for us because we have a big ambition. When you go abroad you look for the spirit of the players. If the spirit of the players is right and the ambition is right, then you don't say, "I won't take these players because they're not English." The good quality players between 20 and 28 are already at the big clubs in England. McManaman, Fowler, Campbell – look who plays in the national team. All the younger players who play in the national team are not at Arsenal. It's very difficult to get these kind of players. So when you have the ambition we have, and you want the quality of players we want, you have to go abroad.

'For me, when you change more than three players in a team, you always take a technical risk because you change the deep structure of the team and the deep balance of the team, mentally and technically. So we have taken a risk, but we would have taken the same risk – maybe a little bit smaller because you don't have the adaptation problem – by buying just English players. When you take more than three new players you always have a problem of unbalancing the team, or creating a new balance in the team. But we had no choice. We couldn't just go on and on until the team dies.'

These were sweeping generalisations coming from a manager who had worked in England for just nine months, particularly the comment about having no choice but to go abroad, which was utterly dismissive of all the players in the lesser Premiership teams, not to mention any hidden potential within the Nationwide leagues. Wenger was, in effect, saying that there were no decent left-wingers in the Premiership (except Ryan Giggs), no good young stoppers (except Sol Campbell) and no skilful forwards (except Steve McManaman and Robbie Fowler). Still, he was being realistic when he implied that he could not hope to sign those players as their prices would be prohibitive and their clubs would not sell them anyway, let alone sell them to Arsenal. Even if those players were for sale, they might not want to play for a French manager.

Emmanuel Petit was obviously looking forward to a new experience. 'The football in England, for me, is the best in Europe. When I was young I saw the football in England. I think it's better than in Italy, France and Spain because it's spectacular, it's funny and it's a game. That's why it's very good for me to play here.'

Overall, the day was a hugely promising moment in Arsenal's history. David Dein was like a dog with two tails, which was hardly surprising since signing these five players had been a lot more fun than last summer's manic phone calls from Jarvis Astaire's car.

Meanwhile, young Nicolas Anelka was headed for the Far East to take part in the under-20 World Cup being held in Malaysia in July that year. The French side was coached by Gerard Houllier, who had said before the tournament that his team could win it. Thierry Henry was the captain of a gifted side which included Stéphane Dalmat, David Trezeguet, Peter Luccin and Mikael Silvestre, but the French players found it very difficult to adapt to the heat, especially in their first game against Brazil, which they lost 3–0. Anelka did not respect Houllier's tactics, so the manager was furious and dropped him for the next match. France beat Mexico in that match to reach the quarter-finals, but Henry was injured and did not play against Uruguay, against whom Anelka missed a penalty. France went out, Argentina beat Uruguay 2–1 in the final, and the Republic of Ireland finished third. Anelka hated being blamed for the failure of the team, so he was in a really negative frame of mind when he returned to England. Arsenal programme editor Kevin Connolly reckoned Wenger only gave Anelka the number nine shirt to cheer him up before the new season started.

When the 1997/98 season got under way on 9 August, Wenger had by then managed Arsenal in thirty Premiership games, had met all the opposing managers and sized them up, and seen their teams play on television and video many times. This new season was his first complete campaign and the first in which he had detailed knowledge of his opponents and an intimate understanding of the resources at his disposal. He had already worked with Petit and Grimandi at Monaco, and he knew that Overmars was intelligent.

BERGKAMP'S PURPLE PATCH

It was the best hat-trick I've ever seen.

Martin O'Neill

By the end of July the whisper from the Arsenal training ground was that the atmosphere was very good and the squad was vibrant. My friend Alexis Grower's accountant pal Lionel Martin, who handled Emmanuel Petit's house purchase and mortgage, said all the players were buzzing. Lambros Lambrou, the young solicitor who interviews the players for the club programme, said that Dennis Bergkamp was fired up and talking about winning everything in sight. One wondered, though, how Ray Parlour felt now that his manager had signed Overmars, Boa Morte and Mendez, three wingers. Paul Merson had been sold to Middlesbrough for £5 million, so would Parlour be next on the transfer list?

There was no such doubt hanging over Tony Adams, who was still a very important part of Wenger's plans. He now felt he had a very understanding manager who was helping him to get his private life back in order. When Adams was young he was a warrior-leader, constantly winning fifty-fiftys and high balls and scoring vital goals in semi-finals and derbies, playing like a man with a rage to win. He was a footballer's footballer. Defenders admired him and forwards respected him as a formidable opponent. Unfortunately, Adams would miss the first month of the new season through injury.

As promised, Wenger changed his system to 4–4–2 and things went well in August. Arsenal started with a 1–1 draw at Leeds, where Ian Wright scored, and then Wright scored both goals in a 2–0 defeat of Coventry at Highbury, both tap-ins, one from a misjudged Richard Shaw back pass. He now needed only two more goals to beat Cliff Bastin's club record of 178, which had stood since 1946.

Two points were immediately obvious about Wenger's dynamic new style of play. The first was that it was designed to make the best use of his three most talented players, Vieira, Bergkamp and Wright, allowing for maximum penetration by the two strikers. Secondly, however, it looked as if Bergkamp and Wright would have to score all the goals because Parlour and Overmars rarely got into shooting positions. Neither of them had track records as goalscorers anyway.

Arsenal's third game, on 23 August, was at Southampton, where both Bergkamp and Wright were tightly marked by Francis Benali and Ken Monkou. Thankfully, Overmars scored the first goal. The winger's strike was a big relief to Wenger, who did not want to be over-dependent on his front two for goals, especially as Wright was injury-prone and often suspended. David Seaman was at fault for the equaliser, failing to come for the cross which Neil Maddison headed in. Remi Garde also had a shaky match at right-back – the return of Lee Dixon was needed. And in Adams' absence Ostenstad gave Grimandi a lot of trouble. Wenger was forced to bring on reserve Scott Marshall to handle him. If there was a turning point in the match, it was when Benali stood on Bergkamp's foot off the ball, then stood on his foot again. On the second occasion the Dutchman grabbed Benali's head and threw him to one side like a rag doll, then started playing like a man possessed. Arsenal won 3–1, Bergkamp scoring twice.

The mistake by Seaman was worrying. Had his bottle gone? Seaman had already enjoyed one great season at QPR and five great seasons at Arsenal, so he had made his mark, won a championship and three cups. What he had done against Millwall in the League

Cup in 1993, against Sampdoria in the Cup Winners semi in 1995, and against many other teams, was magnificent and stayed in the fans' memories. In one game at White Hart Lane he saved four shots from Gary Lineker that would have been goals against any other keeper. In countless big games he made a difference because he had more presence than any of his rivals. One-on-one he was superb, standing up and making strikers work very hard for their goals. He made catching cannonball shots look effortless, and he also had very long arms. The QPR players had admitted that in shooting practice he used to sicken them by saving shots nobody else could have reached. Seaman was England's number one goalkeeper, but recently he had gone through a divorce, had suffered some injuries, and Euro 96 had made him a national hero. He capitalised on that, started to live the celebrity lifestyle, guided by his new wife, who became his agent, and at the same time he began to look vulnerable on the field. He had had a poor season 1996/97 and there was a feeling that he might never be the same player again.

Arsenal's next game was at Leicester on 27 August, with Ian Wright still needing those two goals. Leicester had just won at Liverpool and drawn 0–0 with Manchester United, and they shared an extraordinary, pulsating match in which three of the six goals scored came during injury time. The scorers were Bergkamp (9 minutes), Bergkamp (61), Emile Heskey (84), Matt Elliott (91), Bergkamp (94) and Steve Walsh (96).

In the sixties and seventies fans always talked about George Best, Bobby Charlton and Peter Osgood 'turning it on', but by the nineties football was such a tight team game and there was far less scope for one player to dominate a match. But Dennis Bergkamp certainly turned it on at Filbert Street. He was, in this mood, untouchable and unplayable. His first goal came when Overmars shaped to cross into the box, instead pushing a pass back for Bergkamp, who hit a right-foot floater into the far corner. Vieira put him through for his second, a stabbed shot which spun up off advancing keeper Kasey Keller and dropped in under the bar. After that Arsenal let Leicester back into the game. Platt had failed to reach a clearing header for Leicester's first goal, but he redeemed himself deep into injury time by picking out Bergkamp with a long pass for the Dutchman's hat-trick. Bergkamp juggled the ball with hypnotic skill before scoring what everyone thought was the winner. And then Leicester came back to make it 3-3.

It was apparent to all that Wenger had made Bergkamp a better player, a hungrier, more aggressive competitor. He had played for his country in Euro 92, USA 94 and Euro 96, but there was no tournament in 1997 and the summer break had obviously sharpened his appetite for the game. Martin O'Neill was gracious enough to admit that Bergkamp's 'was the best hat-trick I've ever seen'. Another hat-trick awaited the Dutchman: incredibly, the top three in the August Goal of the Month competition on *Match of the Day* were all Bergkamp goals.

Ian Wright had not been himself at the Dell, and during the Leicester match he had four chances, two of which he would normally have scored. Anelka replaced him for the last thirteen minutes. After the final whistle a frustrated Wright did something very stupid: he ran forty yards from the bench in order to confront referee Graham Barber about the amount of injury time he had allowed. Barber pointed to six goals, six substitutions and an injury to Lee Dixon to explain the six-minute extra minutes. Wenger may have thought, 'If Ian gets a ten-match ban and fails to score in the next couple of games, this Cliff Bastin distraction could go on until Christmas!'

Adams was still missing and everyone knew that if he had played rather than Grimandi, Leicester would not have scored three goals. But it was too soon to write Grimandi off, since all foreigners take time to acclimatise. Petit was improving already.

The 1997 AGM was a very quiet meeting, with David Dein absent on UEFA business, and everyone wanted to know whether the club was staying at Highbury. Peter Hill-Wood said, 'We are not moving, we want to stay here, we are looking at sites we might go to in five years' time, but it is far too soon to talk about that.'

Arsène Wenger charmed everyone again. He said he could not sign a top, top striker to play when Ian Wright was suspended because top, top strikers cost £15 million, but we think Anelka will be a top striker. He said he thought the team was playing some good football, but the new players would take time to settle in. Someone asked: 'Are you going to go off and coach France?' He said: 'No, I've already turned that down.' One shareholder proposed a motion that negotiations to extend Wenger's contract be started not next week, not tomorrow, but now, in this meeting. Someone else said, 'Ian Wright's always in trouble, why don't we sell him?' That suggestion was loudly booed by the majority of shareholders. So, overall, the AGM was gentle, routine stuff, nothing like last year's ructions. Stability had returned to Arsenal FC and that was vital. In football, the club is very important, although nobody ever talks much about the club because they always talk about the team. A good club will often produce a good team, and a very good club will sometimes produce a very good team. But if a club is badly organised, and divided off the field, that will show in the team's performances. What happens behind the scenes at a football club always shows on the field. The next game was at home to Spurs and it was a fierce, fast noisy 0–0 draw in which Arsenal played some excellent football and hit the frame of the goal three times. Spurs skipper Sol Campbell stood up, never went to ground, never allowed Wright to turn him in the box. He was a colossus, especially after being booked early on. After that he was on a knife-edge, one slightly late tackle away from sending the Highbury crowd ballistic, demanding his expulsion, but he continued to make brilliantly timed tackles against two sharp strikers. Wright missed two good chances and Bergkamp was booked for a bad tackle on Campbell. He had also been booked at Southampton and Leicester.

Even though Arsenal had not beaten Spurs, Wenger must have been pleased. For a side with three new players – Overmars, Petit and Grimandi – they were performing well. But a few questions still nagged: How would they handle being a goal down? And how could they raise the tempo if they were already playing at 100 mph?

WRIGHT FINALLY BEATS BASTIN'S RECORD

*What motivates me is an ideal of thinking how football should be. And to try
to get near this way of playing. And to try to improve all aspects of my
personality that can help me get near this ideal way of playing football.*

Arsène Wenger

In the second week of September Ian Wright went off to Wembley
with Seaman to play for Glenn Hoddle's England against Moldova.
He scored twice in a 4–0 victory. Three days later, on 13
September, he played against newly promoted Bolton, who could
not handle Arsenal's whirlwind tempo. Wright scored a hat-trick
in a 4–1 victory. After scoring his first goal he raced away to
celebrate, pulling up his shirt to reveal a specially printed Nike
T-shirt which read 179 JUST DONE IT. He had got over-excited,
though, flaunting the T-shirt after the strike which *equalled* the
record of 178 goals. The record-breaker, however, was not long in
coming.

Bolton's manager Colin Todd admitted that Arsenal's high-
tempo style had overwhelmed them. 'We tried to slow the game
down,' he said, 'but when we regained the ball we gave it back to
them in our own half, which caused us problems.' When Wenger
came in after the game I asked him if he thought Ian Wright more
relaxed after the Moldova game. 'Yes. It helped him a lot. He was
calm in front of the goal. It brought his confidence back, maybe
eased the pressure off him a little bit because he had not to wait a
week for the game with everybody thinking "When do you break
the record?" It's like when sometimes you see a tennis player when
they have only one point to finish a game.

'We had a bad start, we were 1–0 down, it could have made the
team nervous but we were lucky to come quickly back and go into
the lead very quickly. The image I would like to keep is the joy of
the whole team when he broke the record, along the line where
everybody came to congratulate him. It just shows that everybody
in the team was concerned by it and that shows how well he's
accepted by the whole team and how happy everybody was. It's a
historical moment for the club because maybe we will have to wait

a hundred years for somebody to beat the record. He's a quick thinker, a quick brain in the box, and he has the physical power to react. His second quality is that he's an explosive player, but he's very quiet and calm in front of goal at the right moment. And that's very rare. Usually the explosive players are very nervous in the finishing. And that is one of his qualities. And his third quality is mental: he wants it. He has the appetite. He has a huge one.'

Why did you take him off?

'It was one way to give him a celebration. The game was won and he deserved it. The second thing was he has played on Wednesday and he has to play on Tuesday, so I wanted to spare him some minutes and also to give a little bit of a chance to Anelka.

'I think international level has made him aware that he has not only to score goals but to play for the team. Ian Wright scored two goals against Moldova but he also made one for Gascoigne and he's shown at international level he's not only a goalscorer but a complete player now. He'll feel he has achieved something but it won't make him quiet or release his appetite. He will stay like this his whole life. He wants to be successful. Now I think in his mind he wants to make two hundred, then more. That's the way champions are. They always want more. They want to go further. They're hungry.

'When you want to be successful in life you have that for ever. I believe that some people with a weak motivation can have a strong one for certain periods of their life, but if you are strongly motivated for something you keep that for your whole life. What motivates me is an ideal of thinking how football should be. And to try to get near this way of playing. And to try to improve all aspects of my personality that can help me get near this ideal way of playing football.'

What was your first impression of Ian Wright?

'That he was funny. That he was alive. Frankly, that was the impression of the whole team. The team, together, were all happy.'

Has working with Ian Wright changed you?

'It's difficult to say. I think I'm today better than ten years ago in my job, but I'm not sure. Because I tried for ten years to improve every year. I really think that having an experience in Japan helped me to adapt to different people, totally different to how I think you should behave. Maybe ten years ago I would have thought, "This guy's really crazy", or I'd have been a little bit harder with him, or been less tolerant.'

How long can he go on?

'Nobody knows. But at his age you have to think short-term because your body can let you down a little bit, or you get an injury. Today you could say two years, maybe. But nobody knows. I explained that to the older players, that they cannot think three or four years ahead, just go from year to year. Always the most difficult part of the job is to take decisions like that. You might have thought that two years ago it was the right moment for him to stop already. Now he plays well.'

Wenger said that he had never let a player go who had done well later, admitting that he had not been ruthless enough at times when it came to decisions like that. He said it was hard, when a player had fought for you for seven or eight years, to suddenly tell them they had to leave. 'It's not easy, especially when they still play well. And sometimes you have to anticipate that because you feel, if you're in a big club, you can't take the risk of the team going down if two or three players cannot perform any more like you want. It depends on the characteristics of the player. Take Patrick Vieira now. When he's 33 he might have problems getting the ball back. But while he may not win the ball back as he does today, he will play much better with the ball, so that's why the decision is difficult. He could still be efficient for the team, but not as a ball-winner. So you have the problem of balancing the whole team when you take the decision.'

Arsenal's next game, on 16 September, was a UEFA Cup tie in Greece against PAOK Salonika. The Gunners were now unbeaten in six games, but would be without Bergkamp for this match because Greece was just too far to drive. Before the match *The Times*' Brian Glanville asked Wenger if he would be using Anelka and the manager replied, 'There's a chance, yes.' It was an important remark. At that stage the eighteen-year-old Frenchman had not yet started a game for Arsenal, and Wenger had to choose between sticking with a 4–4–2 playing Anelka alongside Wright, or playing safe with David Platt in a five-man midfield. George Graham would have packed the midfield and ground out a draw, but Wenger gambled on Anelka.

Just three months earlier Wenger had talked about flexibility, about changing the system for one or two games, but before this match he probably thought: 'Why change it for one match? I have just changed from 3–4–2–1 and brought in new players, so is it worth changing the system again just for one match? If I dump my new 4–4–2 framework I will be throwing away eight weeks' hard work. I fancy us to score one goal against anybody. So I'll keep the system and bring in Anelka for Bergkamp. I have to show faith in Anelka and I have to be seen to pick him, otherwise people will say I have not replaced Hartson and I only have two strikers.'

On the night Arsenal played carefully and fairly well for an hour, then Salonika scored and the Greeks started to play well themselves. Seaman made an awesome save, clawing away a free-kick which was going into the top corner, but Ian Wright lost the ball too much, missed Bergkamp's passes and could not combine with Anelka. There was no rapport there, no understanding at all. Ultimately, Wenger's 4–4–2 looked too rigid because it lacked Bergkamp's creative vision and skill. Vieira and Petit looked too similar in the middle of the park and Wright did nothing except get booked for dissent, miss a half-chance that fell slightly behind him, and shoot just wide with his left foot when Overmars set him up. Overmars produced Arsenal's best effort, clipping the outside of the post. Salonika's best player, Frantzeskos, ran inside Winterburn, just onside, and scored after 61 minutes to give PAOK a 1–0 win. Winterburn had stepped up perfectly, but Bould was blocked from doing the same thing. The Spanish referee had been excellent and very few refs could have spotted that minor obstruction.

It was this game, perhaps more than any other, which illustrated what a mixed blessing Ian Wright was in 1997. That night might have crystallised Wenger's thinking about his star striker. Wright, a finisher of genius rather than a footballer of genius, was now dividing the fans and the critics. He could be electrifying but also clueless, sometimes both in the same game. Wenger the tolerant man-manager could forgive his man's aberrations, but Wenger the analyst would have looked at the immediate needs of his team and seen that although Wright was still scoring goals, he was giving the ball away more than ever. The team had been geared to him for too long and had become unbalanced. If another player played badly Arsenal could still win, but they now found it virtually impossible to win if Wright played badly because he gave the ball away so much. Wenger might have summed up the Ian Wright conundrum as follows: he sometimes plays well and scores. But, more often, he plays badly and scores, or he plays badly and does not score. He never plays well, does not score, and Arsenal win anyway. And he never plays badly, does not score, and Arsenal win anyway. So, if Wenger was the analytical thinker we believed him to be, he could only draw one conclusion from the available facts: Ian Wright was a menace, a Liam Gallagher to Bergkamp's Noel, a lout who grabbed the headlines while the quiet man wrote the songs.

The game in Salonika showed, once again, that Arsenal did not pass the ball well without Bergkamp. Like any great team player, Bergkamp improved the play of those around him. A good team is always balanced, and Bergkamp balanced Arsenal. He made the team swing. When he was absent the attack was like a door hanging off one hinge. Another obvious conclusion to draw: the squad was still too thin. One striker would not fly, the other would not keep his mouth shut, the third was a moody novice. With Bergkamp removed from the frame, Wenger needed another half-striker who could carry the ball and play Wright in a few times. Merson used to do that job, but Wenger had sold him to Middlesbrough.

The next match, on 21 September, was at Chelsea, which gave supporters a chance to compare Wenger with another foreign manager, Ruud Gullit, who had joined the club as a free-transfer player from Sampdoria in May 1995. He was just 33 when he took over as player-manager, and he had quickly signed Gianluca Vialli, Frank Leboeuf and Roberto di Matteo. But if we judge managers by what they do rather than by what they say, Arsenal was a much healthier club than Chelsea. Gullit, in his first job, was an impatient chequebook manager who bought current internationals on top wages, a policy which started when he and Mark Hughes joined the club. Wenger, the experienced manager in his fourth job, was more patient, signing unknown youngsters, a couple of solid pros, and Overmars.

His approach was that of a perceptive Chief Scout, someone who makes development deals which address current needs while also investing in the future.

The actions of both coaches in the transfer market had made clear and interesting statements. Ruud Gullit's signings sent this message: I will probably not be here long, so I want to win trophies now with stars who know how to win trophies. Arsène Wenger's signings sent a different message: we need a younger, more athletic, more skilful team that can take us into the next century. Compared to Wenger, Gullit was really just Ron Atkinson with dreadlocks.

The game at Stamford Bridge was the first time that season Arsenal had had a chance on the Sunday to make ground on Manchester United, Liverpool and Blackburn, all of whom had drawn the day before. In fact, it was a winner-goes-second match, but the Gunners were lethargic early on and Gustavo Poyet scored from a corner. They raised the tempo immediately. Vieira passed to Wright, who headed to Bergkamp, who produced an ice-cool finish past Ed de Goey, and when Wright later flicked the ball up, a Michael Duberry header fell to Bergkamp and his left-foot shot bounced in for 2–1. Chelsea came back with a Zola equaliser from a Mark Hughes cross that Seaman would have caught three years earlier, and then Nigel Winterburn scored a sensational winner with a 25-yard shot. Ian Wright was hardly in the game. When he did get the ball he usually lost it.

Apart from the continuing brilliance of Bergkamp (on the Sky Sports *Super Sunday* programme he won man of the match with 91% of the viewers' votes), Wenger was delighted to see Petit having his best game so far, making some good passes and becoming stronger as the game went on. When Arsenal went 1–0 down Petit almost immediately made a burst forward into the box. The pass never came but the idea was right, evidence that Petit was a winner type, as Wenger had claimed. Arsenal were now second in the Premier League, Chelsea three points behind but with a game in hand. Wenger had now been at Arsenal for a year. He must have been pleased that his side had shown a very competitive attitude and had reacted well to their first defeat of the season in Greece. They had also reacted well to going a goal down at Chelsea, raising the tempo and equalising quickly before going 2–1 up. Wenger must have believed that the PAOK tie was retrievable in the second leg.

The main feature of the season so far, of course, was that Dennis Bergkamp had improved so much. He was getting more of the ball now and had better players round him. And why was he getting more of the ball? Because Merson had mostly passed to Wright, his mate. Then Overmars arrived, became Bergkamp's room-mate, and passed to him much more than Merson had done. Remarkably, Bergkamp now had seven goals in seven Premiership games – and four yellow cards. He was fired up all right, maybe too fired up. Continuing at this rate he would get twenty yellow cards by the end of the season – and 38 goals!

BERGKAMP'S PURPLE PATCH CONTINUES

I'm a long time in the job. In two or three days you can quickly destroy what you've built up for a long time. We just have to keep humility and try to go to the next game, and start again.

Arsène Wenger

The West Ham game at Highbury on 24 September was the night when Ian Wright was honoured with an elaborately choreographed ceremony which showed that football had now officially become showbusiness. Four white boards were placed in a square in the centre circle with the words IAN WRIGHT WRIGHT WRIGHT, and four lines of kids stretched diagonally to the corners of the ground wearing the shirts of every club Wright had scored against, including the European sides like Paris Saint Germain and Auxerre. The two teams came out without him, then the hero came out on his own to deafening applause. It was like Sky Sports hype for a

Naseem Hamed world title fight. All that was missing was the announcer's voice saying, 'And now, ladies and gentlemen, would you please welcome, from Croydon in Surrey, in the blue corner, wearing the white shorts, the lightweight champion of Egoland . . . Ian Wright, Wright, Wright!' Chairman Peter Hill-Wood gave the cuddly superstar a silver cannon in a red velvet box, and they posed for pictures with Junior Gunners as the fans cheered his greatest goals playing out on the Jumbotron screens. When nets containing 179 red balloons were opened it began to look as if the kick-off would be delayed, but the razzmatazz suddenly stopped and stewards ran on to dismantle the boards.

Then the match started, and the Dutch master was razor-sharp, slicing through the Hammers like cheesewire through Cheddar. Bergkamp was electrifying in Arsenal's 4–0 win, reminding us that the most exciting thing in football is a big man with skill and pace. Inevitably, Wenger was asked if he thought this was Bergkamp's best-ever display for Arsenal. 'You like to say yes every time,' he replied, 'but I think the whole team played well and we had good speed in our game, it was more fluent. The fluency of the game was good. It was not all easy because West Ham gave us some problems in the air in the first fifteen to twenty minutes where we were a little bit too stretched, but after that every time we came out we looked dangerous. We could score goals with our chances and we had some very good moments in the game today.

'Dennis is a playmaker and a striker. He's a mixture. He's a player who is in a perfect position as a second striker. If you put him in midfield he'll lose too much strength to work and will not be efficient. But when he is in a free role as a striker, he likes it, or a free role in midfield – you feel he always knows which position is the biggest threat to his opponent. Sometimes it's up front, sometimes he's in between the lines, sometimes he's in midfield. He has the experience now to know where he is always dangerous for the opponent. He's a playmaker and an important link between midfield and attack.'

Can Bergkamp get any better?

'Yes, I would say yes. There's no limit for improvement for every player. He lost his concentration a little bit in the second half.'

'Did you tell him that?' I said. Some reporters giggled quietly and Wenger did not answer the question – which answered the question.

Did you consider resting him the second half?

Wenger smiled and said, 'We cannot rest him. But it's good to see that when we had to change some players, the players who came on played well in the collective pattern we want to play.'

Brian Glanville of *The Times* then asked whether Wenger thought the team depended on Bergkamp too much.

'It is a worry, of course. I don't want to deny the importance of Dennis Bergkamp in our team, but I think in Greece we did not see the real Arsenal team. Not only was Bergkamp missed, but we missed the whole team.'

Was this the best performance since you've taken over, or the best first half anyway?

'Maybe, maybe the most fluent one. And where we had the most speed in our ball circulation. That's what we try to improve; we don't manage always to do it. But the team was close to what we would like. But I still think we can improve. In every sector we can win the ball quicker, we can be better off the ball, we can have more accuracy in our passes in the last 25 yards, we can be stronger in the set-pieces. We have a lot of work to do.'

And we thought George Graham was a demanding coach. His team had just played with superb flair and efficiency, sliced a decent West Ham side to ribbons and won 4–0, but the manager was still saying there was a lot of work to do. But, Wenger continued, 'for us every game is difficult. When you win the games you have the feeling that you've done well, you have the confidence. Without the confidence you cannot play. Against us, against Arsenal, every team will try to fight and try to give its best. What is concerning me is not the other team but my team. That my team goes into the game trying its best and trying to play the best football we can.'

Brian Woolnough of the *Sun* asked him to elaborate on a comment Wenger had made about the players enjoying themselves.

'When you love the game, that's what first brings players to football. When you're a professional player sometimes the fact that you play professionally, it becomes too much like work, you lose a little bit of this appetite. When you lose that you're a little bit less good. Everybody always says "You have to win, you have to win." Of course, we know it. But it's not because you know that you have to win that you win. It's best, first of all, to love what you do. And if you want to love what you do it must not be compulsory, it must be something you want to achieve and that you enjoy.'

These comments pointed up the difference between Graham and Wenger. Both are serious coaches, but the importance of player enjoyment never seemed to loom large in Graham's thinking at Arsenal. He wanted to keep his job, and the best way to do that was by winning trophies, so he always told the players that they were in the results business rather than the entertainment business or the pursuit-of-excellence business. The priority was winning because a winning team needs no apologists. For Graham, winning meant never having to say you are sorry. Wenger's aims are more ambitious, more risky, perhaps more fragile, because his Arsenal team reaches for the stars. His players, re-humanised by the holistic training techniques and made to feel more valued by big pay rises, would always take more of the credit for any trophy they won under Wenger than they ever did under Graham, who was always the biggest star at Highbury. He made sure he earned more than the players and he made sure that nobody threatened his power. He could be a master of disinformation when he wanted to be – naming, for instance, suspended players in his squad on a Friday night – but Wenger is a master of transparency who seems to tell you almost everything.

When Wenger was asked whether he thought his team was now doing better than he had anticipated at this stage of its development, he replied carefully by emphasising the fragility of a team, a mood, a winning sequence. 'I'm a long time in the job. In two or three days you can quickly destroy what you've built up for a long time. We just have to keep humility and try to go to the next game, and start again what we did tonight, and try to improve what we did tonight. Sometimes you try and it doesn't work. We could be disastrous at Everton in the next game. What is important for me is that we have a consistency since the beginning of the season.

That shows that we have a quality, and even if we play badly in one game, what we've done until now won't fall away. We've shown in seven, eight games that we had the quality in every game – not always in ninety minutes, but you could see, you could feel the desire to play together.' As he said this last sentence, Wenger rubbed his fingers together, as if feeling the quality of cloth.

I said, 'The players put a lot into the Chelsea game and a lot again tonight. Can you keep that up physically twice a week for eight months?'

'No, I would say no. That's why a strong team is there in March and April. We have our weak moments physically throughout the season, that's why the collective game, the organisation, is important. You cannot play the whole season at the speed we played in the first 45 minutes. It's good to have a collective base for when you are physically a little less strong so you don't lose too many points.'

Anyone new to a Wenger press conference would have put the Frenchman down as a straight shooter who gives genuine answers to questions. Clearly, he would not over-praise his team in September – no coach would. But he was happy enough. His team had already done enough to make the period up to Christmas interesting for themselves and for the fans. The big question was: how long could Bergkamp maintain his dazzling form? Lambros Lambrou had reported in July that he was fired up, and he was still flying at the end of September. His performances were absolutely phenomenal. Lambros said after the West Ham match, 'What impressed me most was in the second half when he cut in from the left, outpaced everyone in a sprint across the field and hit a dipping shot just past the post. That showed how strong he is and how motivated he is.'

Lee Dixon was injured for the game at Everton on the 27th and Grimandi again struggled at right-back, but Wright and Overmars put Arsenal 2–0 up. Then Everton came back with two goals early in the second half. It was not the best preparation for the return with PAOK at Highbury the following Tuesday, Arsenal's fourth game in ten days. Overmars was not fully fit for that match and Wright again kept losing the ball, but victory looked possible after

Bergkamp swerved inside his marker and scored with a wonderful shot, side-footed low across the keeper. Unfortunately, they never really looked like scoring again and the tie was drifting towards extra time when Seaman booted a goal kick straight to a Greek player on the halfway line. Two passes later Vrizas beat Adams and produced a classy finish to equalise. It was not even October and Arsenal were out of Europe already.

They began to concentrate on the title race with a vengeance. Barnsley were thrashed 5–0 on 4 October, but afterwards Wenger spoke about how traumatic being knocked out by Salonika had been, and that in his opinion it showed at the start of the game. 'I had problems to recognise my team in the first fifteen minutes because nothing was going well. For fifteen minutes I thought maybe the shock had been bigger than I thought it was. And after that of course Dennis brought us back into the game, and then it was a little bit easier.'

Wenger had taken Wright off after he had scored and put Anelka on, but the teenager had a frustrating time. So I asked: Is Anelka trying too hard to impress? Does he just need to be calmed down?

'I try, I try. He just needs one day to come on and to touch his first ball and to score a goal. It's strange because he's not a goalscorer type, he's a team player, much more than a usual striker. But you have the feeling when he comes on now his only obsession is to take the ball and run at everybody and score his goal. And that's where he's wrong. But he's young. You had a bad impression of him today. He has not shown ten per cent of what he's capable of doing.'

Bergkamp, yet again, had put in a stunning performance, running the show and scoring two goals. Was there anything left to say about the Dutchman?

'He's among the best players in the world. It looks so easy for him to score goals. And his goals are so spectacular because most of his goals are from outside the box. He scores goals like a midfielder. And he doesn't need three touches. All his goals are two touches or one touch.'

Brian Woolnough asked whether or not Bergkamp's dislike of the spotlight off the pitch was more apparent this season.

'Yes, but he's much more under the spotlight this season than last season or the year before because everybody would like him to explain why he scores so many goals and why he plays so well. But I enjoy it when a player keeps a constant focus on what is important, which is his game and his life. Sometimes when you are like Dennis now you can go somewhere different every night, but he doesn't do that. So I enjoy him very much. Because he knows what is really important in his life, and he does it well.'

Is there anything he can't do as a footballer that you'd like him to do?

'I think he could improve his heading, and he could sometimes get more in the box. Sometimes when we have a break he makes his run towards the ball instead of going up into the box. Because when he makes his runs behind defenders he's very strong physically and I would like him to score five or six goals a season with his head. Because, if he wants to, really, he's a good header. But he doesn't like it. So when you look at the percentage of goals he scores, it's amazing, for a striker, how many goals he scores outside the box. He has been educated in Holland, and in Holland people play always on the ground and combine always on the ground. You look at Ajax, where they score most of the goals on the ground, so they are not educated to score in the air. But he's not bad in the air.'

Does he tend to take it easy when Arsenal are winning 4–0?

'That's a problem of all the talented players – they have to fight against that themselves. But it's not obvious concerning Dennis because he likes perfection. The problem for Dennis at that stage of a game is that he wants to do things that are too difficult sometimes. He likes to be so perfect that he sometimes misses goals because he tries some difficult things. But you must understand that it's rare in games and in the season that the players can do the things they enjoy in the game, so when you're 4–0 up and 5–0 up there are moments when you get a little bit more freedom.'

Which players are in his bracket?

'Among players today, Zola. He is the same type of player but Dennis is stronger physically. But Zola at 28 was a Dennis type. A little bit more activity in midfield, but a little bit less a goalscorer than Dennis. In his early career, Roberto Baggio was the same type of player: efficient, not really a striker, not really a midfielder, but efficient in scoring goals, difficult to mark, not good in the air, but very skilful. And Cantona, but Dennis scores more goals than Cantona, and maybe runs a little bit more.'

Why was Bergkamp not more successful when he was playing in Italy?

'You cannot play well when you're unhappy, that's for sure. But why was he unhappy? It was two things: he couldn't settle down and he was in a team which didn't play the football he likes. He went from a very offensive team to a very defensive team at Inter. He came from Ajax, where they play with two wingers and two strikers, and went to Inter, where they play with man-to-man marking, with a sweeper, and him on his own up front – so that wasn't the best team for him. Because Dennis, when he has something in his mind, he's very difficult to change. He's intelligent. He knows what he wants. He wants to win the games.

'To have a balanced life makes it always easier for the managers. It may be harder to gain his confidence when you come at the start, but a player who comes every morning and has had a good sleep and has good family relations, it's easier than someone who is never at home and is not happy at home. But for me the most important thing is not the private lives of the players, it's not my concern. For me it's how much they love their job, and he loves his game. That's why he's a great player. It's always the same. You can speak about a player, but at the end of the day, does he really love to play? Does he really love the game? Could you call him tomorrow to come and play a game with friends? If he has that, for me, that's a characteristic of the big player: he loves to play.'

Although he never used the term, Wenger had just summarised the modern era of the half-striker, an animal which evolved because creative players were kicked out of midfield. When Milan's Arrigo Sacchi and copycat coaches turned midfield into a war zone with fierce pressing, playmakers in that part of the field became virtually obsolete. The invention had to come from the last third of the field rather than the middle third. And on the evidence of the last two months, Dennis Bergkamp was the supreme exponent.

STRUGGLING WITHOUT OVERMARS

Arsène is a wonderful example of an open-minded approach. I think he's done a fantastic job for the cause of other foreign coaches.

Martin Tyler, Sky Sports commentator

The 5–0 thrashing of Barnsley had seemed like a perfect night for Wenger, but something important had gone almost unnoticed: Overmars had been injured and he would miss the next three Premiership games. Significantly, Arsenal would not score in any of those games.

First of all, though, the nation turned its attention towards Rome where England needed only to draw with Italy to qualify for the World Cup in France. It was in the Italian capital that Glenn Hoddle made a conceptual leap by playing Ian Wright as a defender, showing the kind of realism and tactical imagination Wenger had lacked in Salonika. Hoddle realised that England would not have the ball very much during the match, so he played just one up, Wright, and told him to chase defenders for ninety minutes. He knew a goalless draw would do, so he adopted a George Graham approach.

Rome was a night of immense tension – but it turned out to be a huge tactical success for Hoddle. Paul Gascoigne, returning to the city where he had played for Lazio, had lost his pace but retained his skill and strength, and he shuffled, turned, teased, played short passes and slowed the game down all night. He gave a masterful demonstration of keep-ball and this, added to Wright's fiery, aggressive closing down of the Italian backs, held England together.

Three nights later, on Tuesday, 14 October, Wenger picked a reserve team to play Birmingham City in the Worthington Cup. Only Lee Dixon of the regular starting eleven played (as captain), the team was Manninger; Dixon, Marshall, Grimandi, Upson; Mendez, Vernazza, Platt, Hughes; Wreh and Boa Morte. It was 1–1 after ninety minutes, but through the drizzle the 28,000 crowd watched Arsenal cruise home in extra time with goals by Boa Morte (his second of the night), Platt and Mendez.

91

Bergkamp played at Crystal Palace on 18 October but Hermann Hreidarsson, a strong Icelander, blotted him out in a 0–0 draw. The Dutchman picked up his fifth yellow card of the season and was now suspended for three games. Nineteen-year-old Luis Boa Morte, who had looked sharp against Birmingham midweek, was Overmars' replacement, but he did not look a Premiership player. He was quick, brave and skilful, but immature, a headless chicken.

Before the Aston Villa game on the Sunday of the following week, featured on Sky, I had a conversation with commentator Martin Tyler, whose apparently laid-back style disguises a tightly focused footballing intelligence and a wealth of detailed knowledge. Tyler's last match at Highbury had been the annihilation of Barnsley. He had interviewed Bergkamp and the manager on camera. After the Barnsley game, I said both to Dennis and to Arsène Wenger that I felt that Dennis, at this moment in time, was the best player in the world. Which is not a statement that I would make lightly. Arsène said, "Maybe there's somebody in Africa that we don't know about, but I know what you're saying. Yes, I can't think of anybody who's playing better. I know some Dutch commentators who follow Dennis very closely, and they believe we've added to his game." Tyler said that Bergkamp was now a better player because he had become more aggressive, but that it had cost him his place in three forthcoming games against Derby, Manchester United and Sheffield Wednesday. 'He's been sent off since he's been here, he's got this suspension. Clearly, this fantastic purple patch can't go on for ever, but there's no reason why it can't go on for another ninety minutes. If I was Brian Little that is what would be concerning me.

'There was a piece in *France Football* with Wenger. My French isn't that wonderful, but I think he was saying, "I want to improve the attacking side of our play. We are gonna let in more goals because of it, but we're already scoring more. That's the way I believe in."

'Petit's been an excellent signing. He played for France against South Africa for the first time in a couple of years, so it's been good for Petit as well as good for Arsenal. Overmars has been slower into his stride. Much has been said about him having to learn the role in left midfield, rather than play as a wide attacker. He's still a very exciting addition. He's had a very serious injury and you always worry about players coming back from that, but he's done enough in patches to suggest that he can play at a wonderful level.

'Arsène is a wonderful example of an open-minded approach. I think he's done a fantastic job for the cause of other foreign coaches. There's the difficulty of coping with the football lifestyle in England, with so many games, and the dressing-room mentality. Mickey-taking is a very important part of the culture. You've got to be cute enough in the language, and radiate the right respect. The impact that he's made is really incredible. And Arsenal is now the place to go to. It's now the fashionable boutique. Before it was a good functional product which would never let you down.

'I do subscribe to the view that had they bought short-term in January/February they were genuine candidates to win it last year. And they had a very good chance of finishing second for the Champions League. But on their recent European form they might not have got past the qualifying round if they'd finished second. That's the only negative I can think of in Arsène's year.'

The Aston Villa game ended goalless; Bergkamp, Wright and Parlour were all off form. The Dutchman had been suffering with flu during the week, Wenger told us later, and Parlour's wife had had their second baby on the Friday night. In the goalless draw against Spurs on 30 August Arsenal had hit the bar three times, but in this game they only hit the frame of the goal once, with a Vieira volley off a Bergkamp free-kick. Wenger was still using Anelka judiciously as a substitute. As long as he brought him on as a sub, and gave him 25 minutes, Anelka was a new player. Wenger was desperate to give him every chance to succeed while at the same time protecting him. The Villa match was notable only for the dismissal of the luckless Petit for laying hands on the referee. The official actually ran into him, so the resulting contact should not really have been deemed a push. Wenger said the club would appeal against this red card.

At the post-match conference a journalist asked, 'Are people starting to rumble how you play?'

'Guess what we want to do? Yes, maybe. But we have to find a way where we can put them under pressure more, and maybe work more on our movement off the ball. And when you see a player like Boa Morte today you see that he has some potential, but you also see that he misses experience, he misses movement off the ball, coming at the right moment – that's where you can sometimes win the game.'

When will Overmars be back?

'Next Saturday. We could have played him today but we were scared of a setback. Next Saturday at Derby, or maybe, at the latest, Manchester United.'

I asked, 'If you get a couple more nil-nils would you consider changing the formation from 4–4–2 to another system?'

'I would rather change the organisation of the team if we conceded goals. Because we were maybe a little bit too offensive. But I don't think it's because of the organisation that we don't score goals. We still have a very good attack, we've scored 27 goals even if we haven't scored in the last two games. It's due to the fact that some players are tired, don't look fresh enough. And we miss Overmars. It happens. You always have periods in the season when you don't score as I would like to score.'

Are you worried by the discipline?

'The best discipline is to score goals. We didn't score in the last two games. There's different kinds of discipline. There's a tactical discipline. If we hadn't been disciplined today we would have lost the game. There is a discipline with the referee, but I don't think we complained more to the referee than Aston Villa did.'

Did you talk to the referee?

'I have never talked to an English referee since I am here.'

'Why not?' one reporter came back.

'He'd get booked!' said another. Everyone laughed, including Wenger.

'I'd get the red cards as well. After the game – what can you change after the game?'

Wenger's overall approach had now become a slight worry because he seemed to see the game mostly in terms of speed, fitness and pressure. Would the fittest, fastest team win the championship? August, September and October had now gone and only time would tell whether the French professor was right.

But there were still question marks over Ian Wright. He was now a third of the way through his seventh season at Arsenal and Wenger could see that his team was very much limited by what Wright could and could not do. When Bergkamp scored against Salonika, Wright ran away to the crowd himself when he should have gone to congratulate the man who gave him the passes for most of his goals. He had done the same thing before: in Paris in 1995, when John Hartson scored against Real Zaragoza,Wright sprinted away towards the Arsenal fans as if he had scored himself. Perhaps, in his own mind, he had. Wenger could now tell in the first ten minutes what kind of game Wright was going to have. Early in the Villa game he must have groaned inwardly when Wright miscontrolled a pass from Boa Morte, letting it bounce behind him – Wright was going to have a stinker. Of course he could still nick a goal when he was playing badly, but Wenger needed more than that. Glenn Hoddle had done him no favours by picking Wright for the England match in Rome because that had taken his mind off Arsenal.

Wenger switched his team at Derby on 1 November, dropping Boa Morte after his two bad games against Palace and Villa, bringing back David Platt and putting Petit wide on the left. He picked Anelka with Wright again, as in Salonika, but it did not work. Arsenal controlled the first half happily enough without making a chance, Wright hit the bar with a penalty in the second half, and they ended up losing 3–0. On days like this, Nicolas Anelka, Christopher Wreh and Luis Boa Morte did not look as if they deserved to be on the same pitch as Dennis Bergkamp, Tony Adams and Patrick Vieira; many fans doubted whether they would ever prove good enough.

However, there was hope that patience would pay off with Anelka, who was still only eighteen. Michael Owen was well into a fine first season at Liverpool and he was nine months younger than Anelka. But Owen lived at home, had no worries, played most games and was only sometimes on the bench, whereas the Frenchman was still adapting to a new city and a new club. Still, if Wenger was right and Nicolas Anelka was a major talent, another George Weah, the patient, developmental approach was the right one. He might get five years and a hundred goals out of Anelka before selling him on to a club like AC Milan for £20 million.

So Arsenal had failed to score in their last three games without Overmars. When he returned to the side at Highbury against Manchester United on 9 November the Premiership champions were beaten 3–2, on a day notable for Anelka's first league goal, just eight minutes into the game. Overmars cut in and shot, as he did so often. The ball rebounded off Gary Neville towards the corner of the penalty area where Anelka retrieved it and, from the edge of the box, sent a high-velocity shot inside Schmeichel's near post. It was a thunderbolt which would have been a great goal against any opposition. Against Manchester United, it was sensational. Ian Wright, who was his ineffective partner that day, had been trying to beat Schmeichel for years and this kid had done it first time out. After this goal we began to glimpse the real Anelka. Much more relaxed now, he seemed to cruise around the pitch, elegant, skilful, able to change gear effortlessly, almost like a young Ruud Gullit. That afternoon, for this eighteen-year-old, the sky seemed to be the limit.

Vieira also got a goal, one made in Essex: a Parlour corner headed on by Adams, then a power-drive from the edge of the box which flashed past Gary Pallister's back and into the goal off the underside of the bar. When Ian Wright fouled Henning Berg a short while later some Muppets in the crowd began to chant, 'Ian Wright, Wright, Wright!' (With fans like that, it was no wonder he lost the plot so often.) But United did not roll over. Teddy Sheringham scored two brilliant goals before half-time, losing Grimandi to score with a typical header for the first, and then, after a flick-through by Giggs, beating Seaman with a superb low shot into the corner.

The match stayed at 2–2 from the 40th minute to the 82nd, when Wright set up Wreh for a shot which deflected off Gary Neville; Schmeichel, on the deck, clawed the ball off the line and Neville cleared for a corner. Parlour took it, and Platt, out-jumping Beckham, sent a stunning header into the top corner. It was by far his best goal for Arsenal.

ARSENAL 1 BLACKBURN 3

The last half hour was the worst since I came here.

Arsène Wenger

When Arsenal played Blackburn on 13 December at Highbury it was business as usual when Marc Overmars scored the first goal. The roof started to fall in when Jeff Kenna hit a cross and Tim Sherwood nudged Dixon away, leaving Jason Wilcox to equalise. Then Chris Sutton climbed above Keown in midfield and headed on Tim Flowers' kick down the middle, Kevin Gallagher raced towards the penalty area, Adams came across but did not tackle, and the Scot hit a stupendous dipping left-foot shot over Seaman to make it 2–1. Another simple pass down the middle released Sherwood one-on-one with Seaman, who came late and feebly failed to claim the ball in front of Sherwood's boot. The ball went loose, and with no defender anywhere in sight Sherwood had time to make it 3–1 and complete the rout. The absence of Vieira, who was on the bench, proved highly significant. The last time Petit had been partnered by Platt, a fortnight before against Liverpool, Arsenal lost 1–0.

Wenger must have been as shocked as everyone else to see Tony Adams dominated by Chris Sutton. Adams was the strong man who had seen off every centre-forward in the league – John Fashanu, Les Ferdinand, Alan Shearer, Graeme Sharp, Mark Hughes, all the strikers who could jump, back in, hold you off, nudge you before the ball arrived. Nobody could outpower Adams, although a tough striker might occasionally battle out a draw with him. He had been the rock on which the team was built. They had won six trophies with him in the side and few fans seriously believed that Arsenal would have won any of them without him. But now he seemed a hollow shell, unrecognisable from the indomitable warrior the fans knew and loved.

It looked as if Arsenal were a team with just two gears: top and overdrive. They attacked at high speed, scored first, and then needed to score a second goal. The style Wenger had created played to his strengths, but on this occasion they were Blackburn's strengths as well. The irresistible force met an even more irresistible force. Arsenal were simply overwhelmed by a team playing power football with more power than them. In the past twelve years they had sometimes been beaten by defensive teams and skilful teams, but they had never been out-bombarded before.

Roy Hodgson was understating the case when he said his men had done a good afternoon's work. 'At half-time I thought we'd played reasonably well in the first half, but we went a goal down from our free-kick, a ball headed back into midfield and kicked over our back four who were maybe a little bit high there. And Overmars this time got his run perfectly right and Tim, unfortunately, having got it right the time before, got it wrong and we're 1–0 down. But I didn't really think we were out of the game. I thought if we kept playing the type of football we'd played in the first half maybe the chances would come. They did, and luckily we took them.'

Arsenal had now lost four of their last six Premiership games. Apart from the Derby and Liverpool defeats, they had also lost 2–0 away at Sheffield Wednesday on 22 November. The victory over Manchester United and a 1–0 win at Newcastle, whose minds were on their forthcoming Champions League tie against Dynamo Kiev, were crumbs of comfort. Wenger had been seething after losing to Liverpool, although it was not too apparent unless you watched his face very carefully. Two weeks later, after the Blackburn débâcle, he was even angrier – and this time it was much more obvious. He still spoke rationally after the match, but his fury went far beyond anything he actually said, even though what he said was strong and true enough. 'It was a fight,' he said. 'They lasted longer in the fight than we did. The last half hour was the worst since I came here.'

So one naturally wondered, would Wenger now sign some younger players who could play ninety minutes rather than an hour? Or would he slow Arsenal's game down and give his side a couple of extra gears? Did this team have the craft to slow the game down? The next game, on 22 December, was against Wimbledon, another physical team. Would he bring back three centre-backs? With results going the wrong way Wenger seemed a slave to 4–4–2, to formation, shape and pace. He seemed too scientific, not intuitive enough, not enough of a gambler, not flexible enough, someone who stuck stubbornly to his own rules come what may.

Later on the day of the Blackburn match it was announced that there had been another Ian Wright incident after the game. A few weeks earlier, when Wright had broken the club's goal record, some fans had chanted for their hero below the window of the dressing room, which overlooks the street, and Wright had conducted their cheers and thrown out his shirt, or some such souvenir. Now they were jeering him and Wright, incredibly, insulted the fans from the same window.

Wenger had now been the manager for fifteen months, but he had bottled the Ian Wright situation, had not yet unloaded David Platt and had not started to rebuild the defence for the future. Wright had become less productive with every game that passed and the back four was falling apart in front of his eyes. Overmars had under-achieved, and while Petit had a great engine he still did not look like a world-class midfield player. Parlour was a good competitor who had improved a lot, but could he improve much more? Wenger had uncovered one unquestionably great player, Patrick Vieira, while Remi Garde and Gilles Grimandi had been competent at best.

However, the Blackburn defeat, and the team meeting which followed, was the catalyst which turned Arsenal's season round. The senior players said that the foreigners were not giving the back four enough protection, so Wenger asked Petit and Vieira to play more as anchormen, with Petit, the more experienced of the two in that role, playing deeper while Vieira pushed forward to add his forceful presence in attack. Sometimes, though, Petit went forward and Vieira stayed back more – it depended on the opposition and the state of the game, and Petit was to prove himself very good at reading those situations.

The game against Wimbledon, a Monday night Sky game, had to be abandoned halfway through at 0-0 owing to a floodlight failure, the third Premiership blackout that season. Sabotage by a Malaysian gambling syndicate was later blamed. The game was rescheduled for later in the season, so Arsenal's first chance to bounce back after being bombed into submission by Blackburn came on Boxing Day against Leicester, the team that had stubborn-ly refused to succumb to that Dennis Bergkamp hat-trick back in August, which now seemed a very long time ago. But Wright, Overmars and Bergkamp did not seem to be on the same wavelength. Bergkamp's form had faded since he had returned from suspension, although he did place a free-kick on Platt's head for the first goal. Then Bould lobbed forward and Steve Walsh, Ian Wright and Matt Elliott raced for it, Keller came out of his goal, and Walsh volleyed the own-goal of the season high over his goalkeeper's head. Then Seaman idiotically dribbled past Heskey and lost the ball to Cottee, who passed to Izzet, who set up Lennon to knock in past Dixon on the line, but Arsenal just managed to hang on to the 2–1 win.

Wenger had said that he needed goals from midfield, but anyone who watched Arsenal carefully could see that the front three usually shot on the run and only passed to each other. They almost never passed to Parlour, Vieira or Petit. There was very little play round the ball, no passes laid back for 25-yard shots, not much passing in the box and no real variety, just rapier-quick thrusts and many passes forward, not sideways. It was an entertaining style of play which created a lot of chances, but it was one-dimensional and it meant that the midfielders only scored from set-pieces.

Wenger, however, asserted that this win against Leicester would help Arsenal get back to their normal way of playing. He then sent Adams to Cannes in southern France for intensive rehabilitation work. There was a rumour that the captain had been back on the booze the night before the Wimbledon game, which he did not play in, so he might have been sent away to dry out although the official story was that his ankle was not right, an injury which had upset his body's balance and caused a nagging back strain. There was even a suggestion that he might retire at the end of the season, or after the 1998 World Cup.

Ray Parlour was the best player on the field two days later at White Hart Lane in a 1–1 draw, and Grimandi had his most solid game so far. Keown managed to snuff out Jurgen Klinsmann, who had returned to play under Christian Gross and save Spurs from relegation, and at the other end Anelka was unlucky with a shot which hit the post. Arsenal dominated the second half without creating much. Alan Nielsen scored for Spurs, then Ramon Vega equalised for the Gunners, Parlour's shot deflecting off him past Ian Walker, his third own-goal of the season. One was still wondering whether Wenger would change his two-gear approach, but Wenger, interestingly, reckoned his players had recovered their confidence. Maybe, but could they dominate their last fifteen games as they had dominated their first fifteen? The players would naturally be more tired from January 1998 onwards and teams knew what to expect now. So when Arsenal played them again would they not just defend deeper, make the game last longer, wait for the storm to blow out after seventy minutes then score goals when Wenger's elderly defenders were wobbling?

By the end of 1997 Arsenal had played twenty, won nine, drawn seven and lost four. The same results again would mean a third- or fourth-place finish, so a pronouncement by Wenger at this time was worrying. He said that he hoped Ian Wright would stay for the next two years and see out his contract – a comment which must have have been just a polite soundbite. If Ian Wright was still at Arsenal in 2000, Arsène Wenger would not be. In January 1998 Wright was due to start hosting his new television chat-show on LWT. Did the manager approve of this new distraction?

Arsenal's FA Cup third-round tie was against Port Vale on a wet and windy day. Vale played 3–5–2, soaked up pressure and used the ball cleverly in their occasional counter-attacks, while Arsenal hit far too many long balls at Bergkamp, who most of the time was either offside or unable to reach the ball because it was overhit or windblown. They rarely looked like scoring in a 0–0 draw, but the Coca-Cola Cup fifth-round tie at West Ham on 6 January worked out neatly for them. Seaman made a silly, clumsy challenge on Kitson to concede a penalty, but Hartson hit the post from the spot. After that, Wright and Overmars scored. Arsenal scoring first meant that Petit did not have to do anything except chase and tackle. At that stage in his first season Petit was still mostly a presser, better when the other team had the ball, so the situation suited Arsenal's midfield.

Then tabloid reports said that Benfica were very keen to sign Ian Wright, but the timing seemed bizarre – except, perhaps, from

Wright's point of view. That is, if his point of view was: Got my record, got my place in the history books, got my silver cannon, cheerio!

GRAHAM'S BACK-HANDED COMPLIMENTS

I thought they would have really been up there with United. I don't know why, it's not for me to say. I thought they'd be challenging United a lot closer.

George Graham

On 10 January Arsenal played Leeds at Highbury. Marc Overmars, who was beginning to show signs of being a better player than he had been so far, scored the first goal, Jimmy Floyd Hasselbaink equalised, then Overmars grabbed the winner.

After the game George Graham was at his most mischievous, tossing out back-handed compliments and wind-ups. 'When you get a team like Arsenal who have got outstanding individuals,' he said, 'and you can keep them quiet for three-quarters of the game, and all of a sudden one of them comes to life, that can win the game for them. I think that's what happened.'

Did you try to sign Overmars?

'Yes.'

At Leeds or Arsenal?

'At Arsenal. We couldn't afford him at Leeds.' Graham laughed at his own joke. 'He's not taken off yet, has he? I don't think so. When you've got that talent, you can be quiet for long periods. They've got him, they've got Wright, they've got Bergkamp. They were a lot more physical today, Arsenal – I thought they did well in that department. I thought it was a difficult game, first half. Arsenal were up for it physically and I think we matched them quite well. The ball was in the air too much. I thought Seaman was putting us under pressure with long kicks all the time – it reminded me of my days here. Not all of them, some of them. For me, we only saw the real Arsenal in the last twenty minutes after they scored. I thought they looked a bit nervous. But we didn't capitalise on it. We showed them too much respect.'

Bill Pierce of PA Sport asked, 'You said at the start of the season they had the players, didn't you?'

'I thought they would have really been up there with United. I don't know why, it's not for me to say. I thought they'd be challenging United a lot closer. With the quality they have, a lot of quality.'

I put the first two questions to Arsène Wenger.

George Graham said he thought Arsenal were up for the physical battle today – do you agree?

'Yes, it was of course a very physical battle, we expected that. I think they came here to frustrate us. The players were up for the battle, every ball was a fight. First, I think we could cope with that. Secondly, we did master our nerves and didn't speak too much with the referee, and didn't forget to play football. Sometimes it's difficult to have a fight because you forget to play.'

Were you worried that all the Benfica publicity would affect Ian Wright's performance?

'No. I think he played very well. I was not really worried. The answer is always on the field, not in the newspapers. And I think he has shown how great his spirit was, and for me he played a great game today.'

Has Ian told you he wishes to stay at this club?

'He cannot say to me every day when I see him that he wants to stay at the club. But he didn't say to me that he wants to leave.'

Is Overmars coming good now, at last?

'For me, he's a great player. Like many great players you expect always more than they produce. But you look at the players in the winger position in the midfield and you look at how many goals he's scored since the beginning of the season, and how important the goals were – who is the player in his position in the English championship who's scored more goals than Marc Overmars? And he works very hard for the team. Of course he takes many risks, and sometimes he loses the ball when you think he shouldn't have lost it, but when he manages to go through he's always a threat. I think he had some great games at the beginning of the season, then he was injured and he was out for three or four weeks, and it took him some time to come back. He didn't play well for a while because he had a kick on his laces on his right foot.'

His instep?

'His instep. And he couldn't kick the ball with his right foot. Since two weeks only he can do it again. And since those two weeks he's played much better. Because I had always the feeling that he does not put his foot in at the right moment, or doesn't go in the box. And you cannot understand why he didn't do it, and suddenly he discovers he can do it again.'

I asked, 'Is that why he stopped taking corners?'

'Yes. We took him out of the corners because he couldn't kick the ball.'

Has he got over his big injury?

'I think so. It is one you never can forget about, because I had the same kind of injury. In the specific position where you were injured, you always try to avoid this position. Because it is in your mind. But in every other aspect he's recovered. Listen, it's difficult to find, all over the world, players who play on the sides and are young. He's young, he's 24. He has won everything – the European Cup, the World Club Cup – and can run without the ball. He has great movement, he understands the game, he can run with the ball, he can work for the team. He has the speed.'

Bill Pierce asked: 'Petit's perfomance?'

'I was pleased with the performance of Petit today, and I must say, as well, at West Ham. It was a continuity of what he did at West Ham.'

Is today's win special because it's George Graham?

'He's welcomed by the fans because he's done very well for the club. That is normal. For me there's no special animosity. I just would like to do as well. And of course it's important to win our games at home in front of our fans. No, I cannot say that it's anything special on that side. I just had the feeling before the game that it was a very, very important game for our Premier League position because we had a win against Leicester, we went away to Tottenham, we had the two cup games and then we came back here against Leeds who are threatening our position at the top of the table, among the first four or five. I thought that for us to win at West Ham was important and to build on that with another win was crucial for the team. I think we have shown today that we can do it.

'It takes some time for players who come from foreign countries to adapt. They are surprised at the beginning. They come and say, "That's not football!" And I think when you go abroad you have to adapt and show that you can cope with it. They are at the stage where they are showing that they are doing it. You see players like Petit who at the beginning of the season would have lost his nerve much more than today. Now he knows what is expected of him. Because some players who were considered to be physical in foreign countries, and come here, they still have to go up a step to be at the English level. I'm surprised sometimes now when I watch continental games, that I get bored. Even if technically it's better. You just miss the intensity, you get used to it here. And when you look at a game on TV or if you go abroad, you think, "What's going on here? It's not alive." The passion is so big here, the commitment so high. You adapt, or you have to go. And the referees permit more than abroad. If you watch games in Italy, for example when players in the box go down, it's a penalty. Or every tackle, especially in the air – they allow much more here in the air. And here in the air the fights are much more important. It takes some time for the players to adapt.'

You seemed very calm during the game.

'When I was younger I was much more excited on the bench. But now I have some problems to get quickly up.'

Naturally, everyone laughed at this.

Were you surprised when the referee did not book anybody in the first fifteen minutes?

'No, it was a relief for me because we have some players who have three or four bookings. We had all the bookings early in the season, and so we have already had our suspensions, and the teams who have better behaviour have them now. We had our suspended players in November and they will have them in January and February.'

Brian Woolnough asked, 'Do you get the impression that Dennis is suffering because he's not scoring? His body language suggests he's very frustrated with himself.'

'I think he's improving in the last two games. He needs a goal now. If you score ten goals and suddenly you don't score any more, you get frustrated. But now in nearly every game he's man-marked, and really man-marked, with defenders holding him. Referees here are not used to man-marking.'

I said, 'Can you work on a style of play which gives him the ball facing the goal?'

'Yes. If the whole team is technically very good, it's easier to give him the right ball in the right space. But it's not always easy. Here at Highbury the pitch is narrow, so there's less space to play to him. Dennis is a winner and he's much more influenced by the results of the team. In our first twenty goals, eighteen were scored by Ian and Dennis. Other managers are not stupid. They say, "We'll stop them, then who will score?" I was always worried about that. If you have a third player, and a fourth player, who can score it gives always more room to Bergkamp, of course.'

Again the question about Ian Wright's future was put to Wenger – has he asked to leave?

'No.'

If he asks you on Monday, will he be allowed to go?

'No.'

He seemed to give a farewell wave to the fans. It looked a bit like goodbye.

'That's your interpretation.'

Mike Walters of the *Mirror* joined in. 'He often waves to the fans, we accept that. But this looked like a deliberate thank you and goodnight.'

'Goodnight maybe, but goodnight is not goodbye.'

Woolnough again: 'Is he in your long-term plans?'

'Listen, he has a two-year contract. You cannot be in the position we are in the middle of the season and let your strikers go away and not have people to replace them.'

Would you be prepared to let him go at the end of the season?

'I can't answer this question, I can only answer short-term questions. But short-term for me, it's difficult to say. I still think one day he will go, but he should not go to Benfica now. Because for me Ian Wright has to play in the World Cup, and to play in the World Cup he must stay in England. I have to defend the interests of our club. It would be irresponsible. If you think like that, you could take any player anywhere, even if he's under contract. That's not feasible. Football is so different when you go to a foreign country, you need some time to adapt. That's just too dangerous.'

But will Wrighty play in the World Cup?

'If he battles like today, and at West Ham, he will go, I'm sure.'

Woolnough persisted: 'Have you discussed this whole thing with him?'

'No. What was really important for me was the game today. When we have some time off, maybe we can talk about his future. For the moment we need the concentration of everybody.'

Do you have a good relationship with Ian?

'Yes, but he's a player. When he doesn't play well, the relationship is less good. When he plays well, it's good. That's normal. But overall, I'd say I'm very happy with the relations I have had with him since I've arrived.'

Then Martin Thorpe of the *Guardian* picked up the line of questioning. 'Have you told him leaving now will harm his chances of playing in the World Cup?'

'No. I will have a chat with him about this story because it came out in the press. But it's like that with Ian Wright. Tomorrow maybe Manchester United wants to buy him. I don't know what his priorities are, I don't know what is his desire. It depends what is your priority in life. I think the biggest priority is always to play at the highest level. And money should always be the consequence of the quality of your performances. Listen, I'm not a businessman, I'm a football manager, so what interests me is sport, and much less money. I haven't seen great players who do not make money today. It existed twenty or thirty years ago.'

I said, 'Does he have to get permission from the club to host a television show?'

'The television show?'

'You're the first guest!' Woolnough quipped.

'It depends, if it doesn't interfere with his training.'

'Can somebody be a regular television star and a Premiership goalscorer at the same time?'I asked.

'Not a regular one, no, but he can have one TV show if it doesn't take up too much time.'

Attention then turned to the club captain. Is Tony Adams fit now?

'He's come back from France. He was at the game today and he looks great. All the tests he had were positive. He came back in a very positive mind. He will train normally on Monday.'

That night, the Arsenal–Leeds game was featured on *Match of the Day*. When the highlights were over, viewers were treated to final proof that Ian Wright had completely lost the plot.

Jon Champion: 'Clarify your position. That's hard work and goals at Arsenal? Not Benfica?'

Wright (looking ridiculous in a big floppy black hat with a Nike swoosh): 'Well, wherever I'm playing, that's how I'm gonna do it. I've always tried to do that.'

Champion: 'Wherever you're playing? Does that indicate a doubt in your mind?'

Wright: 'I wouldn't say it's a doubt in my mind. I couldn't lie and say it's something that doesn't interest me. It's a fantastic opportunity at this stage. It's something that I would have definitely looked at. But the door was closed on it early doors and I couldn't really do anything about it.'

Wright, who usually grinned and flashed his gold tooth, seemed depressed, sounding like a defendant in the dock. He shrugged and said he would have liked to go but 'Everybody knows how much I love Arsenal.'

For Wright to try to walk out in January while the team was still in the hunt for three trophies was evidence that he did not love Arsenal. It was amazing to hear him say on BBC television that he wanted to go to Benfica but the club had told him he could not go. His words made him seem greedy, ungrateful, petulant, submerged in self-pity. Ian Wright Wright Wright had got it wrong wrong wrong by turning into everything a professional footballer should not be. And he had obviously not yet given up on his hope that Arsenal would let him walk away. His sullen grumbling was perhaps the most disgraceful interview ever aired on *Match of the Day* and Wenger must have watched it and wept. He must have thought, 'Excuse me, Ian, there is nothing to discuss. You are under contract for the next two years. And I'm going to put your

I-wanna-go-to-Benfica interview on a tape loop in the Arsenal Museum and label it HOW NOT TO CONDUCT YOURSELF AS AN ARSENAL PLAYER.

Wenger never said what he really thought of his striker's selfishness, but he rarely picked him after that. In fact, Ian Wright never scored another goal for Arsenal after that interview.

In the FA Cup third-round replay at Port Vale on 14 January, Bergkamp took a pass from Grimandi 25 yards out and, with almost no backlift, sent a sublime shot floating into the top corner. Wright tweaked a hamstring, Vale equalised and the tie went to extra time and penalties. Arsenal won the shoot-out 4–3 after Islington-born Allen Tankard sent his spot-kick over the bar.

Noel Whelan scored the first goal for Coventry at Highbury three days later, but it was the pacy Darren Huckerby who posed the biggest problem. Seaman hurt his hand when he tipped over one blistering shot from Huckerby (he chipped a knuckle and missed the next thirteen games) and then Keown pulled a hamstring chasing him. When Paul Williams unwisely headed back to goalkeeper Magnus Hedman, Bergkamp intercepted to score his first Premiership goal since early October. And the Dutchman was instrumental in his side taking the lead, touching the ball back to Lee Dixon whose shot deflected to Anelka, who buried it. Vieira had been booked early on for clattering into Huckerby, and when Coventry took a free-kick on the left Vieira inexplicably jumped like Michael Jordan as the ball sailed towards him and slapped it with his left wrist. Referee David Lodge awarded a penalty and gave Vieira his second yellow card for swearing at him. Dion Dublin converted, and the game finished 2–2.

In the FA Cup fourth-round tie at Middlesbrough on the 24th Arsenal moved on comfortably enough with a 2–1 win, both moves for the goals started by long passes from Adams to Anelka. Taking the first of them, Anelka found Bergkamp who flicked the ball through for Overmars, whose shot beat Schwarzer all ends up. The goal was so good that even Anelka smiled and congratulated him. The second came from a textbook counter-attack after a Middlesbrough corner: Adams hit a long, high clearance to Anelka on the left and his crossfield pass picked out Parlour, who took one touch and buried his shot. This was the geometry of demolition and Wenger must have wondered why on earth it had been such a struggle against Port Vale. Bergkamp, once again, had shown himself a master at releasing other players at pace. And in this team of speed merchants, Parlour was beginning to show that he too could accelerate from box to box in less time than it takes to pull the pin from a fire extinguisher.

Keeper Alex Manninger made the game closer than it needed to be with a rush of blood to the head at the other end. When Mustoe hit a long ball down the middle, Manninger raced ten yards beyond his penalty area, and Merson cruised round him and hit a shot which sweetly bisected Bould and Adams before rolling into the net. Merson had scored 98 goals for Arsenal in 427 appearances and now he had scored one against them. Adams teased Manninger about this aberration for years afterwards: 'You're not gonna give me a heart attack today, Alex? You're not gonna come flying out past me, are you?'

TEN WINS IN A ROW

I deeply feel that the team was never as low as people said, but we were at a dangerous moment when the team could have gone both ways, and where we needed small but important victories.

Arsène Wenger

Tony Adams looked strong, fast and determined against Chelsea in the Coca-Cola Cup semi-final first leg at Highbury on 28 January, nothing like the hollow man we had seen in the 3–1 tanking by Blackburn. This was the real Adams again. Arsenal won the match 2–1 with goals by Overmars and Hughes.

'Big match, big performance?' I asked Wenger. After a year and a half I had started to talk like him.

'I thought so, yes. It was a big performance, but a big performance where the right score should be 4–1, I would say. I had nearly the same feeling at Middlesbrough where we created many chances. We did it again tonight and couldn't take our chances. But collectively the performance was good. I had really the feeling that at 2–0 we could kill it. Not by one, but by two or three more. I still think if we had scored the third goal we could have scored more, because they were struggling at the time. And after it was 2–1 they had hope again, it was more difficult. We were a little bit selfish in the last twenty minutes around the box – we had some people in better positions. But overall I'm pleased with the quality of our game.'

Wenger would soon regret those missed chances. In the second leg at Stamford Bridge on 18 February Petit was momentarily distracted, fiddling with his ponytail, when Chelsea scored two of their goals in a 3–1 win. Had the Frenchman's golden locks been securely tied, as they were later, Arsenal might well have ended up landing the domestic treble. The 2–0 win over the same opposition in the Premiership on 8 February was at least some consolation.

In the meantime, Manchester United, who had been on top of the table since October, had faltered slightly. On the last day of January they were beaten by Leicester when Tony Cottee scored at Old Trafford. Arsenal were at home to Southampton that day. The first half was scrappy, but then Manninger made a fantastic save from a Matthew Oakley shot and three goals in seven minutes gave the Gunners a 3–0 win.

United's slip-up was what everyone at Arsenal had been waiting for, as Wenger was quick to acknowledge. 'First our victory is important. But the fact that Manchester United lost at home gives more chances to everybody. Before the game nobody could believe that they would lose at home, because they looked invincible until now. But they have their bad time now. They've lost now a few games in the last four, I think they've lost three. I always said it's maybe over to win it but not over for second place. But now it looks open for everything.'

Going on to talk about Arsenal's improved form, he said, 'I think the unit is stronger, and tactically they understand each other better. I think as well some players needed a bit of time to settle down and adapt to English football. Gilles Grimandi sometimes looks lost, but in the last two games has played well. With so many new players it takes time.'

Will Ray Parlour play for England in the forthcoming friendly with Brazil?

'It would really be the surprise of the season, the biggest improvement of the season. Nobody would have said before the season started that he would have been an international in February, but on the other hand it would be one game more for him. He deserves it. He had another great game today. And he looks like improving on his final ball. His work rate is fantastic. But of course international is another step. But, if he doesn't make it in the short term, in the long term it must be his ambition. In the World Cup, or after. He's only 24 years old, Ray Parlour, so he can be in now. But in the next World Cup, for sure, he must be one of the players.'

Wenger was also delighted that Adams' spell in rehab seemed to have worked so well. 'I think that's the best I've seen Tony since I'm here. He looks really sharp again. Not only today, but on Wednesday at Chelsea, in his movement. He is not handicapped any more, he really looks like a player, all his movements are back. He still has problems in his back. He must always do his rehabilitation work and be very careful in his postures. He's an organiser, and I think he lost that a little bit when he wasn't physically ready. And now he has it again. He speaks to everybody, and reads the tactical problems on the field. That's why he's very important. When you are not right yourself you cannot care about other players on the field. When you get up every morning and you cannot walk, you cannot feel like jumping around and kicking the ball.'

Is Manchester United's monopoly of the Premier League now getting a bit boring?

'Yes, but it's important that the best team wins the championship, and if they're the best team we shouldn't want them not to win it just because it's Manchester United. It's open. The team that has so far gone through the season without any bad times is Blackburn. If you look at the tables they are the team that's lost less games than anybody else. They are the most consistent team since the beginning of the season in the championship. Because until now they have had no bad time. I expect them to have one. But mainly I expect us not to have another one. If you'd asked my players a week ago, they'd have said, "No, we've got no chance to win it." But if you win your games and Manchester United doesn't, after a while everybody thinks, "Why shouldn't we do it?"

'United went to Chelsea and won 5–3. And three weeks later they've lost three games, nobody knows why. That's how unpredictable football is. I'm not excited because I still think some teams are in a better position. We are still eight points away from Manchester United with a game in hand. We have to win this game, but we'd still be five points behind. That means they must lose two more, and we must win these two. But you never know. If they have a real bad time and we have a real good time, it's not impossible.'

In early February ClubCall man Dickon Geddes spoke about a Swedish striker Arsenal had wanted. 'Right at the end of my piece I said to him, "Arsène, there's a rumour that Andreas Andersson was here on Friday. He passed a medical, then Arsenal pulled out and he signed for Newcastle." Arsène just smiled and said, "Yes, he did sign for Newcastle." Which is as near to an admission as you'll ever get.'

Between 15 and 25 February Arsenal played Crystal Palace three times, needing a replay at Selhurst Park to get through to the FA Cup quarter-final. On 8 March they met West Ham at Highbury in that quarter-final and drew 1–1. Wenger hated the extra burden of these replays. 'For me the most important thing is the championship. So every time we play one more game it reduces our chances to be fresh in the championship games. So I cannot be happy. But on the other hand, in the quarter-final of the FA Cup you cannot calculate – you have to give everything to go through.'

In the Premiership Arsenal were going along steadily enough. Chris Wreh scored a fine goal to give them a 1–0 win at Wimbledon on 11 March, and then came the big game at Old Trafford, where Overmars delivered yet again, scoring the only goal from a flick-on by Anelka on 79 minutes. Those six points, and especially the win at Old Trafford, proved to be the turning point in the title race, psychologically as well as arithmetically.

In the West Ham replay at Upton Park on 17 March Wenger started Anelka and dropped Wreh, who had started in Manchester. Bergkamp had a night of frustration where everything he tried to do for 35 minutes did not work, and then as soon as something did work he was fouled. He played a one-two with Anelka and was going for the return pass when Steve Lomas held his shirt, so he lashed out fiercely with his left arm, smashing Lomas across the mouth, and was sent off. Anelka scored with a flashing shot just on half-time, but Hartson got a late equaliser. When the game went to penalties, Hartson and Abou hit the same post, and Manninger saved from Berkovic, leaving Adams to score the winner. Arsenal would now play Wolves in the semi-final on 5 April.

On 28 March Sheffield Wednesday arrived at Highbury. It was the first warm Saturday of the year and by this stage of the season all the remaining matches were vitally important, the margin for error almost nil. After a wretchedly nervous first five minutes, when Arsenal could not string two passes together, they annihilated Wednesday, creating several good chances before Overmars floated a perfect ball forward to give Bergkamp a side-foot past Pressman from seven yards. Wednesday improved in the second half but Seaman, back after his knuckle injury, did not have a shot to save. Ron Atkinson commented, 'First half, they outpowered us completely and gave us a right good tanking. We were very lucky to be only 1–0 down. Second half, we made a better fist of it, carried the game to them a little bit more. At one stage I thought they had fifteen on the park.'

Wenger's thoughts were now almost exclusively on the title race. 'If you look at the championship, we lost only four games and in January we were the only team with Manchester United and Blackburn. Since then they have lost, but we couldn't win away. The difference between Manchester United and Arsenal in January is they won more games away than we did. So we have reduced the difference by winning at Wimbledon and Old Trafford. So what has become important now is to win the home games and try to get more points away.'

Overmars had another great game against Wednesday. So why was he looking so frightening?

'He's a world-class player. He was a typical winger at Ajax. In Holland they use the wingers to create space for the midfielders, and that means they are in and out of the game. When he came here I gave him a different role where he was much more involved in the midfield, and I think that psychologically it took him some time to adjust to that. Physically it's much more demanding. He's very disciplined, he works very hard for the team, and every time we have the ball he makes his runs forward. So he has a very demanding physical role. So it took him some time to get used to that. In Holland, when you play at Ajax you know that in eighty per cent of the games, if you play at sixty or seventy per cent of your potential you win it. In England that doesn't exist. At Ajax, when they played PSV and Rotterdam, they had to be up for it. But when they played Nijmegen or Roda it was good enough to be at seventy per cent. To get used to fighting every game took him some time.'

Unlike George Graham, Wenger invariably owns up when experiments have not worked out, as he did when he was asked if Overmars could play on the right.

'No, that's really terrible. That's why I bought Boa Morte. One of my ideas, to give an option to the team, was that at home we could play with Boa Morte left and Overmars right. But he doesn't like at all to play on the right side.'

When he talked again about Tony Adams and his problems, Wenger managed to avoid mentioning the words 'booze', 'drink' and 'alcoholism'.

'Tony is thirty years old and he's always pushed his body too far. Since he has changed his way of life he has learnt to cope with his body and know himself much better. And now I'd say he knows when to push on, and when you go out of the game. He's improved a lot by knowing himself much better. He's a strong character and I think he's a very intelligent man. And tactically he's a great reader of the game, so he always knows what's going on on the field and what's wrong. So for a manager he's a very big support. He's a better player with the ball than I thought he was. All the defenders are better players on the ball than I thought they were, Bould as well, Keown as well. Of course Dixon and Winterburn, you know, they had to be able to play. But on the ball the central defenders are better than I thought. When you're a manager you're lucky if you have good players. If you have good players and leaders, it's a privilege. Because most of the time you have to fight to convince them, and that's why you like experienced players. They know what to do, they know how to react, so if your link with the manager is good, you're stronger.'

Wenger went on to say that he had a lot of respect for what Tony Adams had achieved in his private life, predicted that he would have a successful World Cup, and reiterated his faith in his players generally. 'I deeply feel that the team was never as low as people said, but we were at a dangerous moment when the team could have gone both ways, and where we needed small but important victories. In this kind of period, when you see that your confidence has gone, and you have to fight to win your confidence back, to have experienced players is good. Especially at Arsenal, a club with such a big pressure, where you always have to win. And if you don't win, everybody asks why. You need strong characters like Adams, Bould, Keown, Winterburn, Dixon, Seaman. That's very important in the bad periods of the season.'

This was very much a year in which Wenger's first team picked itself. Everyone knew what his best eleven was, so when key players were missing it was obvious. In any team there are four or five core players and the absence of any of them can be damaging, but Arsenal had the mental resilience and organisation to survive those absences, and that was something Wenger was very pleased about.

'We had many games without Seaman, we had many games without Adams, we had many games without Keown – he didn't play for three months – we had many games without Dixon, and we went through all that. Petit was out for a while, Vieira was out for a while, Parlour was out for a while; Overmars was out, Bergkamp was out, Ian Wright is out. But every time we found the spirit and the strength to get over that. That is what we have to do. We have done it before, gone through it. And that should give us the strength, especially as we are in a not too bad period now.'

Was Wright's hamstring a worry?

'I'm more concerned about Ian Wright than about his injury. When Ian Wright is going well you must put him in jail to keep him out of the game. His impatience, his love of the game, is a big asset when he's fit. But his enthusiasm when he's injured is terrible for him. He thinks he can come back and play when there's no pain. We need to be over-patient because he's impatient. He's pushing you every day. When he wakes up the next morning and doesn't feel any pain, he thinks he can play the next day.'

What about Bergkamp's suspension?

'We can keep him sharp. Last time he had a three-game suspension it lasted five weeks. This time it is only two weeks. I'd say he can keep himself physically fit and keep his concentration although that's hard when you're not playing.'

A Chris Wreh goal at Bolton on 31 March made it four Premiership 1–0s in a row, and there were some decidedly manageable fixtures coming up. Before that, though, there was the small matter of an FA Cup semi-final. Tony Adams did a typically candid press conference before the match against Wolves at Villa Park, during which he explained how Wenger had helped him to rebuild his career. The *Mirror*'s John Dillon wrote that the skipper's transformation was like the Frankenstein story in reverse: Wenger had inherited a monster and turned him back into a man. 'He has great knowledge and insight into people,' Adams said. 'It has helped to extend my career when it could have been over. He's pointed out things that have improved my self-awareness and made me think a lot more about how I play. It makes me wonder how I did things before. It was probably just on instinct. He gets his point over very well. He is a very, very intelligent man, although it may appear that he's aloof because he is detached. But he's a nice guy. It's just that he's standing back and watching all the time. People who are filled with fear and insecurity may take that the wrong way. They panic because he is scrutinising things and weighing them up. But he has no fear. He's not insecure, so he can be honest about things.'

Adams could also be honest since he had already confessed everything – about how his Sundays used to be all-day booze-ups during which he might down twenty pints of Guinness, how he kept a crate of cheap champagne in the boot of his car, how he was embarrassed by his blackouts and bed-wetting, how he smashed glasses on his head to amuse his mates, how he could not remember knocking his bedroom door completely off its hinges one night at the England hotel. After Wednesday night games at Wembley he sometimes stayed up all night, on one occasion stumbling into Arsenal's training ground early the next morning and telling physio Gary Lewin, 'For God's sake, don't let the gaffer see me like this!' But now the dark days of the eighties and early nineties were behind him. 'The way I was going, I was dead. As far as I was concerned, there was no football left in me. But together we have given Tony Adams the chance to play on. Me and Arsène – the pair of us have done it.'

Adams could not remember big chunks of his past life, but oblivion was no longer an option for him. He said that if Arsenal lost to Wolves it would hurt, but he would not be trying to escape the reality of it by going down the pub. On the contrary, 'I'll feel the joy more sharply if we win. I have different ways of enjoying things nowadays when in the past I knew only one way. When you abuse alcohol, you suppress everything – good feelings as well as bad. My recollections of our past successes are patchy. I don't regret anything, but for me it's pretty simple now. I can sense the pain and the pleasure. And it's real.'

In an interview with *L'Equipe*, translated on to a website by Liz Ireland and headlined MY STRENGTH IS IN MY SERENITY, Wenger made it clear how he felt about Adams and his fellow defenders. Money could not buy the kind of commitment shown by players such as Adams, Bould, Dixon, Winterburn and Keown, and he valued the loyalty they showed to the club, to him and to each other. They knew they were part of something special, and they wanted to play together for as long as possible for a club and a manager who had treated them very well. 'In England,' Wenger reminded his fellow countrymen, 'there is a deep morality on the part of players. There simply aren't any mercenaries there yet! The jersey means more than anything. It's simple: at Arsenal, I work with five players who have spent more than ten years at the club. And when we discuss their contracts, the first thing each of them says is, "I'd like to stay, if I can."'

Against Wolves at Villa Park it was Chris Wreh, the erratic Liberian, who again scored the only goal of the game to put Arsenal into the FA Cup Final. Their opponents in that final, Newcastle, visited Highbury on 11 April and found Nicolas Anelka in awesome form. He took a pass from Wreh, dummied Stuart Pearce and rifled his shot into the far corner for the opening goal. Then he stabbed in at the far post after Parlour had burst between Batty and Pearce and crossed from the right. Then Vieira cruised forward from the centre circle and hit a thirty-yard thunderbolt into the top corner to make it 3–0. This was an intimidating preview of the final for Newcastle and their fans. When Warren Barton latched on to a ball over Bould's head and finished superbly, it was the first goal Arsenal had conceded in nine Premiership games.

At Ewood Park two days later, Dennis Bergkamp returned from suspension and destroyed Blackburn, who were 3–0 down after fourteen minutes. A Remi Garde throw went off the head of Henchoz to Bergkamp, who took one touch and rammed his shot across keeper Alan Fettis. That was after 75 seconds, his fiftieth goal for Arsenal. Soon after that Bergkamp released Parlour in a similar position and he fired through Fettis for 2–0, then Parlour scored again.

Since the teams had last met just before Christmas, when Ian Wright was fading, Arsenal had become defensively sounder, and they were now able to attack from deep positions with devastating directness. Blackburn found this out when they took a free-kick and the ball was headed out by Petit to Winterburn, who launched a seventy-yard pass down the middle of the field. Anelka left everyone trailing in his wake, headed the ball on and dummied the keeper before scoring from close range. It was 4–0 at half-time. Amazingly, it started to snow and an orange ball was brought out. Kevin Gallagher went on to volley a very sweet goal, but it was little consolation. 'Before the game we were very focused, very concentrated, very professional,' said Wenger, revealing what everyone could have guessed.

It was clear that the Anelka of April 1998 was a totally different player to the Anelka of October 1997. He looked powerful, confident, fast and was a great turner, able to stop on a sixpence inside the box and unbalance his marker. It was just a shame, in hindsight, that his excellent first goal for the club against

Manchester United back in November had come when Arsenal were struggling. When the team improved in the new year, Anelka took off and never looked back.

This demolition of Blackburn was repeated against Wimbledon, Arsenal playing the football of champions to win 5–0. Adams sent a booming header into the net from Petit's inswinging corner in the eleventh minute, Chris Wreh scored the fifth in the 89th. In between Overmars had released Anelka on the left, spurted forward to support and surprised Neil Sullivan with a low shot across him. Anelka exploded forward again to set up Bergkamp to make it 3–0 in nineteen minutes. In the second half Seaman came out of his box and hammered a long pass to Bergkamp, and from that Anelka and Overmars set up the long-awaited first goal by Petit. On the same day Manchester United were held 1–1 at Old Trafford by Kenny Dalglish's Newcastle, so the bookmakers now had Arsenal odds-on for the title.

After the Wimbledon victory, Wenger said, 'The joy and the excitement of the players to play together was what came out of that game. The pace we had in the game, our quick passing, always looked dangerous. The Blackburn game gave us more confidence offensively, because we had many games when we won only 1–0, 1–0, 1–0 and always had the feeling that one day we could concede a goal and we would not win it. Then we scored three against Newcastle, then four against Blackburn, and that maybe released the feeling that we only rely on defensive efficiency.

'We still have a difficult programme: five games to play, three away and many players away this week with the national sides. That's always very disturbing. We play at Barnsley and this game is very, very important for us. It's the only important game for us because it's the next one. We are focused and we know how difficult it will be. But I think they are just concentrated on enjoying what they do together. That's what comes out of the game when you watch it.

'Anelka was not happy after the game because he didn't score. But I was very happy with him because he's showing us, from game to game, that he's improving. His power, the holding-up of balls, bringing other players in is better. He was tremendous in the first half. With Bergkamp, him and Overmars we have such pace it's always very difficult for defenders.'

Wenger again spoke of how proud he was of the spirit and perseverance his squad had shown through the bad times a few months before. 'We never gave up. In our worst period in the championship we kept the desire to do well and to improve. We came back very slowly into this championship with some small results, some draws, and slowly back into it by winning 2–1 or 1–0. And we had many cup games. But if you look at our run since Blackburn, we had some good results in the Coca-Cola Cup and some good results in the FA Cup, and in the championship since then we have done very well. The miracle is that everybody who came in did well. And that what we've done so far is more the result of a squad than of individual players. Matthew Upson is nineteen years old. It's the first time he's played in the back four in such an important game and he does well.'

Brian Woolnough asked him to elaborate on the sense of 'joy' he had mentioned.

'It comes from confidence and it comes from early goals. Also from an acceptance of a common way to see the game and how to play it. When the players meet anybody during the week, they get told, "You have to win, you have to win." Since I've been in the job people say to me, "You have to win on Saturday." We know it. We know we have to win, but to win you have to enjoy what you do first, and to have the same approach and the same way to do things. The game is not only work. It's work because you have to do it every day, and if you don't enjoy it you cannot bring out in the game what you could feel today.'

Are you surprised it's all going so well?

'I'm never surprised to do well. My ambition is to do it. What we can say today, five games before the end, is that it is still possible. The way to do it is to try to do well at Barnsley and keep the way we played today. I think the championship in England is more difficult than anywhere else, maybe. The commitment is higher than anywhere else in the world. Listen, last night I had the choice between Cannes against Nantes on French TV and Middlesbrough against Manchester City in Division One. And after half an hour I switched to Middlesbrough–Manchester City. Because there was more passion around the field.'

I asked, 'When you won the league with Monaco, was it a home game or an away game?'

'We won the league without playing. It was the night before and our competitors lost, so we won the league without playing, with six games left to play.'

When asked if he had studied Arsenal's history, Wenger said he knew something about it but had resolved to do things his own way.

'When you're a manager you can only be efficient if you respect your own view of football. Could I go on like Arsenal played before? I just wanted to do things my way, but keep the strong points, and try to keep my own feeling of football. You must be a little bit lucky when you change things because you need to be successful. In a big club like this you must be successful because there's always a big force to push you backwards to do things like they did before. If you do things differently and you start to lose, people say to you, "Listen, my friend, let's do it like before and let's be efficient first." So the change must be very slow.'

Is Anelka enjoying it now?

'He's an introvert type. It took him some time to feel relaxed. I always was concerned. I always kept believing in him because there was a tremendous difference between what he did in training and what he did in the games. For me, it was more of a nervous problem. And he's slowly getting rid of it. He had the feeling that he doesn't play enough, and that if he plays and is not successful immediately he'll be out of the team again.'

Woolnough then asked the really important question, and this time Wenger, unusually, did a Geoff Boycott. He just played a straight bat and knocked the question firmly back down the wicket. It was a small but significant exchange.

Will it be hard to leave Anelka out now if Wright's fit?

'I'm here to solve the problems we have now. For the moment we don't have that problem.'

But Wright has to play for Arsenal to go to the World Cup?

'I think so. Usually a striker and goalkeeper are special positions. They rely a lot on confidence. If every time a striker plays and thinks he has to score or he's out of the team, I don't think you're helping him. I think Anelka will play in Sweden on Wednesday, and if he does well he has a good chance of playing in the World Cup. My interest is the club. I have only to consider Arsenal, not England. If I can combine their interests I'll do it. If Ian Wright is the best striker available at that moment he will play.'

Arsenal were now top of the table for the first time since October and needed to win just three of their last five games. Petit was interviewed on *Match of the Day* and said, 'I think against Blackburn we played our best first half. But for the moment we play good football, we are very confident, we don't lose, and we enjoy to play together. You can see it on the pitch and it's really fantastic.'

Wenger also spoke, saying that the mental attitude and focus was right but, as usual, he took nothing for granted. 'At the moment things work well. I think the integration of foreign players and the mixture between English and foreign is right at the moment. Basically, the individual attitude of every player is right inside the club, and that's why maybe they are doing so well. Because they are good players, and they respect the collective way we want to play. And that's why we are efficient.'

Dennis Bergkamp had scored twice against Barnsley at Highbury the previous October, and he produced his trademark goal at Oakwell: just outside the area, left side, minimum backlift, a right-foot shot curling round the keeper's dive and going just inside the post. It was his 22nd goal of the season. Then Overmars cut in from the left side, took Platt's pass on his body and went through to make it 2–0.

Arsenal now needed only two more wins, which made the Derby game at Highbury on 29 April a very nervous occasion. When Christian Dailly tugged Anelka's shirt in the box, he fell, the referee pointed to the spot, Bergkamp took the kick and Poom saved it. Then Bergkamp went off with a hamstring injury. The decisive moment came when Overmars tackled a defender outside the box, perhaps illegally, and the ball went loose to Petit, who smashed it low into the net for the only goal of the game.

That priceless strike set up the climactic day at Highbury the following Sunday against Everton, who were in relegation trouble and in no state to compete with Arsenal's pace, pressing and movement. The force was with Arsenal that day. Their momentum was irrepressible, elemental, tidal, unstoppable.

Wreh started the game with Anelka and the first goal arrived after just five minutes when Petit curved in another inswinging corner. Adams jumped above Bilic, who headed into his own net. Later, Petit was flattened by a two-footed tackle from Don Hutchison, and while he was down Overmars raced away to make it 2–0. The Dutch winger then scored a phenomenal and electrifying third goal, picking up the ball in the centre circle, zooming past Dave Watson and shooting low across Thomas Myhre to clinch the game and the title. Thousands of ecstatic fans jumped out of their seats and Arsène Wenger held the grinning Pat Rice in a fierce embrace. The Frenchman had finally lost his cool and grabbed his assistant in a bear hug that said: We've done it!

Then Tony Adams went galloping through on to a Bould pass and thumped the ball into the net with his left foot. For Adams the title-winning night at Anfield in 1989 had been an epic once-in-a-lifetime drama, but scoring this goal in this stadium in this game at this moment was sheer bliss – and from a pass by big, bald Bouldie. He will never forget that moment.

Wenger, calm again amid the hysteria after the match, said, 'Maybe it's the biggest satisfaction in my career until now. I'm very happy because we had a combination of exciting, entertaining football and efficiency.'

George Graham had always said that the BBC's Alan Hansen was the only pundit who ever gave Arsenal any credit. He had won titles with Liverpool and knew what it took to become champions. This time Hansen said, 'It's been a combination of English grit and determination and foreign talent. And it's bedded in together perfectly.' He then summed up Arsenal's season by saying, 'You get on a roll and you think: "Hey, we're invincible here." And I think that's what happened in the last ten league games.' Sir Alex Ferguson later admitted in his best-selling autobiography that this Arsenal charge had made them worthy champions. 'In the home stretch, they had put together a sequence of ten straight victories and only a truly special team could have done that in a league as tough as ours,' he wrote. 'They had notable quality in every department and Arsène Wenger deserves immense credit for integrating his English and foreign players into such a cohesive, powerful and highly motivated unit.'

In George Graham's 1989 and 1991 teams, some of the running power was at full-back, Winterburn and Dixon up and down the touchlines like yo-yos, putting in crosses. Now, in 1998, the running power was all in midfield and attack, and the full-backs stayed back a lot more. Now, Wenger had Patrick Vieira, a giant gladiator, partnered by Manu Petit, two technical masters of skirmishing and interception, two players who did the work of three, aided by the powerhouse breaks of the indefatigable Ray Parlour, all of them able to release a left winger who was, in effect, a striker. The first time a Petit through-ball put Overmars in for a goal we should have twigged it: Overmars was the new Ian Wright. He scored more goals than he made – sixteen in his first season in a new team – but he started his runs from different positions so we all thought he was a left winger. Or maybe, just maybe, he was a left winger the first time Premiership teams played against him, and when they played Arsenal again he had become a striker. By the time they had figured out that puzzle Overmars had added a Premiership medal to his extensive collection.

One could only wonder about Wenger's real attitude to Ian Wright now. He had not grasped the nettle straight away because Wright was still the big star, still a good goalscorer, and a comparable younger striker would have cost far more than the club could afford. But at the close of the 1997/98 season, Wenger had watched the games and studied the videos and he could see that Arsenal had become a much healthier and more efficient team without Wright. With him they were more vulnerable because games revolved around his form: Did he score? Did he miss? Did he lose the ball 29 times? His style of play was the same as ever – sometimes electrifying, often erratic.

One of the reasons Wenger had sold John Hartson was his dislike of target men. He had talked about hitting too many long balls against Leeds and he decided to remove that option and concentrate on what his team was obviously practising during the week. In football, the three principles of play are possession of the ball, supporting the ball, and penetration. The style of play Wenger created in 1997/98 emphasised the first and third principles at the expense of the second. There were not too many support runs into midfield, or into the last third, and not too many passing options, so there were few square passes. His brand of attacking football was more like fencing – full of sudden, fierce thrusts which were very well-aimed and very well-rehearsed. So it had proved hard to contain Arsenal, except by outpassing them (as Liverpool did) or outpowering them (as Blackburn did). The Blackburn trauma had been the turning point, and the return of a fit Tony Adams in mid-January was an immense stabilising influence on the rest of the season.

Petit was, we came to realise, a tremendous strategic player and it was his footballing intelligence, combined with that of Adams in defence and Bergkamp in attack, that allowed Arsenal to play the game so fast and so penetratingly. It was mostly narrow football suited to the narrow Highbury pitch, with players being supported by high-powered runs infield from Parlour and Overmars. Bergkamp already had a rapport with Overmars, and he developed a rapport with Parlour, who started to read where Bergkamp wanted the ball and where he wanted him to run. Both the 'wide' players were, in fact, narrow players, avoiding the touchlines a lot of the time, and both of them found it easy to link with Bergkamp, who was very astute in seeing where they were and where they were going. Overmars liked coming inside partly because he had smashed up his knee on a rock-hard December pitch when going outside a defender near the touchline, and Parlour liked it because he had never been a flank player anyway. In the Arsenal youth and reserve teams Parlour had always been in the middle, tackling, scrapping, winning the ball and running with it. He wanted to be in the middle of the action now, not watching it. Waiting around for a pass was not his game and never would be.

Basically, Wenger had put a new engine into an old machine. But it was the mixture of French horsepower and Dutch science that was so unique: Overmars and Bergkamp could suddenly drift into good positions to receive the ball and a lot of match-winning goals had flowed from that. Bergkamp was, with his countless assists and his sixteen league goals, better than ever, but the man who had unquestionably made the difference was Overmars.

Close study of the stats reveals this clearly. Arsenal did very badly when Marc Overmars was not playing. They missed him more than they missed Bergkamp, Adams or Vieira. No other winger in Europe could have joined Arsenal, settled into English football and scored twelve league goals to decide so many games. Dennis Bergkamp was PFA Player of the Year, and that was fully deserved, but reporters who voted for Footballer of the Year should have given that award to Overmars, not Bergkamp. His goals made the Double possible.

THE DOUBLE

When he leaves Arsenal, his legacy will be felt for many years. I am proud to see him so popular in England.

Max Hild

The FA Cup Final on 16 May looked like being more an extended lap of honour for winning the title than a normal final. With or without hamstring-victim Dennis Bergkamp, Arsenal were always going to beat Newcastle, who had finished the season thirteenth and 34 points behind them.

Within a few days of the title being won chairman Peter Hill-Wood had said the club wanted to offer Wenger a five-year deal at £1 million per season, which would make him the highest-paid manager in English football. 'Arsène has done a fantastic job and we'll sit down with him after the FA Cup Final and discuss whether he wants to extend his contract. I think we would be talking about a long-term deal and I would be delighted if he signed for five years. The way I feel right now he can stay here as long as he wants. I'm sure this is just the first of many championships for him.' Petit, however, said he was convinced Wenger would accept the French national team job eventually, but hoped he would first want to win more trophies at Arsenal. 'Knowing the kind of man he is,' Petit said, 'I believe he will see this as just the start.'

Meanwhile, Wenger had ordered the team to stay focused. 'The important thing coming up to a Cup Final is to keep up the momentum, so we must keep trying,' he said. He admitted, however, that he was already planning next season's Champions League campaign. 'Even when we were walking round the pitch in front of all those happy people, my first thought was about the European Champions League,' he said. 'I know I must keep those people happy. That means taking things on another step, winning the championship again and the Champions League – an even higher challenge. You must switch that quickly. It's why this job drives you slowly crazy. You never have time to enjoy the present.'

Before the final, Wenger said he would only play one style of football and nothing else. He admitted being very dogmatic about that and even recommended that other managers should be as stubborn as he was. 'Every manager can only be successful if he gets his team to play the way that he holds deeply within himself. When I came to the club I didn't consider too much what had been the style before, although I was aware of the tradition and heritage. I knew that the only chance we had of being successful was by playing how I felt we should. That's why we played the way we played. I respect what happened before because the club was successful. But we played the kind of football we did because it was the way we could be successful. I would not change my philosophy.'

It was at times like this, with so many celebrations going on, so much publicity, so much hype around the FA Cup Final, that Wenger's focus and detachment were invaluable. He was still able to concentrate fully, and he compared himself to a racing driver. 'When you watch somebody driving a Formula One car round a Grand Prix track you ask yourself why he's not scared, how he can do it. But when you ask him, he'll tell you it's because he just concentrates on what he has to do, thinks about the next curve. When you are a football manager, it's the same. It's hard to get away from the environment around you, but you learn that you have to do it. I've got to get with the business of winning it, that's my job.

'You're a manager because you love to win. That's the only thing that lets you survive. I believe that every career is made of winning and losing. But the people who learn from losing win more than those who don't. The quality of the players and their spirit is the most important. Even if you're a winner as a manager, you won't be unless the players are winners too. As soon as it is over, I will be looking ahead. Maybe that's why my job drives me on all the time too much – I don't remember what I did five years ago. No matter what happens at Wembley, I will be looking in front for the next one.'

On the big day itself, Ray Parlour took the bull by the horns and carried the game to Newcastle with a series of powerful runs. Arsenal's pace and defensive determination were phenomenal, even if their passing, without Bergkamp, was patchy. The match as a whole demonstrated, perhaps better than any other, that Wenger's particular trip was not so much finding players with greyhound pace but building a team's entire style around pace. The Petit–Overmars connection was always vital when Bergkamp was not playing since Arsenal needed to use the pace of Overmars in runs off the ball.

Teams are accustomed to defending against dribblers, but when a dribbler makes a good run off the ball and a team-mate finds him with a forty-yard pass, the opposition defence is usually split or seriously stretched and the keeper is often exposed to a one-on-one. When a Petit pass from the halfway line found the speeding Overmars, he stabbed the ball through the legs of keeper Shay Given before tumbling over him. His pace was important, but so was the timing of his run.

Few teams have ever been less nervous, less threatened, than Arsenal were that day while holding a 1–0 lead. But Newcastle did have a good spell: a Dabizas header clipped the top of the bar and Shearer went past Adams and hit a shot against the post. One wondered, just for a moment, whether Arsenal were a one-hour team. But then Parlour found Anelka somewhere on the hairy-scary border zone between onside and offside, there was no flag and Anelka flew towards the goal like a red and white arrow, scoring with a scorching shot. At nineteen years and 63 days he was the third youngest goalscorer in an FA Cup Final.

After a long, long season Arsenal were still showing huge hunger, fierce desire and the ability to score devastating goals.

Parlour still made a burst past Pistone and slammed a shot against the outside of the post; the game was already over, but not for him. This FA Cup Final performance showed that Wenger had evolved a very, very strong concept: a ball-winning machine that feeds supercharged strikers. Power football played relentlessly with huge authority at a very high tempo.

For Wenger there had been far more satisfaction in winning the league, of course, but the FA Cup Final is one of the world's biggest matches, watched by hundreds of millions of football fans all round the world. There was one unknown and unnoticed Frenchman at Wembley who enjoyed the victory too, and that was Wenger's special guest on the big day, the 69-year-old Max Hild, who had now retired after twenty years as Strasbourg's coach and general manager. Hild had been Wenger's guru, the biggest influence on his career. A few days later the Arsenal manager said, 'He stimulated my interest in the coaching side of football. He made me think about the game and I'm delighted he was able to be at Wembley on Saturday.'

A month earlier Hild had done an interview saying that Wenger's part-German heritage had proved invaluable to him. 'Alsace used to be part of Germany and Arsène has the rigour, discipline and sense of order for which Germans are known. He has an intellectual side and has never lost his spirit of inquiry. It doesn't always serve him well though. I told a director of AC Milan that Arsène would make a first-class coach for them, and he told me, "No, he looks too much like a schoolmaster to us." It is true that Arsène is an educator by nature. His greatest joy, like mine, is to discover young talent and make sure it flowers. It was an enormous risk to take kids like Anelka and Wreh from French football so young and transplant them into the English game. But Arsène had the patience and confidence to make it work for Arsenal. Vieira, another youngster, was barely known in England, yet Arsène had the nerve to make him one of the most important elements in his team.

'There is another important factor with Arsène. I first taught him how taking care of the body meant so much. He has deepened what I taught him by widespread reading and consulting experts in sports medicine. Now he is a master of his subjects. What and when we eat and drink is vital, so is rest. How else can you explain the remarkable transformation of Ray Parlour this season? He is now a fantastic athlete and Arsène has shown him the way. You might laugh when I tell you that muscle injuries can come from not eating the right food, even from not having the proper dental care. But Arsène knows it is no joke. He brings science to the job of preparing his players. He remains what he was when I met him, a student with a passion for football.

'When he leaves Arsenal, his legacy will be felt for many years. I am proud to see him so popular in England. He has no time for hobbies. When he returns home from an Arsenal match, he replays it on video to make a more objective analysis. I used to take him fishing. It's not really his thing, but he still wanted to know every tiny detail of how it was done and how all the equipment worked.'

Just for a few days, though, Wenger had earned the right to take it easy and bask in the glory of a well-deserved Premiership and FA Cup double.

6. 1998/99: THE SEASON OF ANELKA

Football clubs are driven by ambition, tradition and rivalry, so for each club there is deep meaning in beating certain other clubs. At the start of the 1998/99 season Arsenal were Double-winning champions, they had thumped Manchester United 3–0 in the Charity Shield with goals from Overmars, Wreh and Anelka, and the players felt that they could now win the Champions League before United won it. That motivated them more than anything else. It was a huge incentive.

During the close season Wenger had sold Ian Wright to West Ham for £750,000, thereby placing a huge amount of faith and trust in a relative novice with greyhound pace and great potential. David Platt had retired. New signings included Argentina's World Cup right-back Nelson Vivas from Lugano in Switzerland for £1.6 million and teenage left-back David Grondin from St Etienne for £500,000. Wenger had also made a bid for midfielder Ronald de Boer, who said, 'Arsenal have made a low bid but of course they are going to make a low bid. They are not going to show all their cards at the start. I am going to leave Ajax, that's for sure, and I know Arsenal are very interested and I would like to play there. It's a nice club, nice management, and it is very well organised.'

Although the new season offered the stimulating challenge of the enlarged Champions League, it was business as usual first in the Premiership. Arsenal beat newly promoted Nottingham Forest at Highbury in their first game on 17 August, then drew their next three games 0–0, against Liverpool, Charlton and Chelsea. Liverpool were being co-managed by Roy Evans and Wenger's friend Gerard Houllier, whom he had advised to go to Liverpool. Clearly there was a lack of executive bottle at Liverpool, where Evans did not command the respect of a group of scallywags who were under-achieving every season. The 1996 FA Cup Final had made it clear that the culture at the club was decadent. Both finalists had hosted press days at their training grounds before Wembley. At the

Liverpool press day the players had larked around, while the Manchester United players had taken their media duties seriously and given sensible interviews. Journalists who went to both events did not give Liverpool a prayer, especially when they saw the cream Armani suits that Ruddock, McManaman and company were wearing on the big day. United had won 1–0 with a goal by Eric Cantona, and half an hour later some of the so-called Spice Boys had been seen laughing in the banqueting hall. Roy Evans had kept his job for the next two years, and now, incredibly, Houllier, a former manager of the French national team, was being asked to share the reins.

After the Liverpool game on 22 August, Wenger said, 'Those who played in the World Cup Finals are not yet sharp, so this was a point gained. We could have scored early on and late on, but we didn't and that is why we lost two points.' He was referring to missed chances by Parlour and Bergkamp.

THE 1998 AGM

It's always a bit of a struggle between tradition and innovation. Tradition is what I would like to keep here. The very strong spirit of the English players.
Arsène Wenger

The 1998 AGM turned out to be a love-in starring Arsène Wenger and a spectacular collection of glittering silverware. On display from around 11a.m as shareholders gathered for the usual noon kick-off, set against a wall of scarlet baize, were seven trophies: the Premiership, the FA Cup, the Charity Shield, the FA Premiership Youth League, the Southern Junior Floodlit Cup, the Women's FA Challenge Cup and the Women's League Cup. Grinning shareholders posed in front of the cups while friends took photographs.

The event inside the North Bank Stand was slickly stage-managed. Hundreds of gold-painted chairs were arranged in rows with a central aisle leading to the altar, to make it feel like a place of worship, a cathedral. There were TV monitors every ten yards down the hall, and audio monitors so that everyone could see and hear clearly. David Dein, one of football's most energetic yuppies, was obviously determined to send out all the right signals: success, prosperity, enjoyment, technology. Yet, alongside that, Arsenal still seemed like an old gentlemen's club because it was fronted by chairman Peter Hill-Wood.

At noon the directors walked in to loud applause and cheers – what a buzz for the hero-executives! It was astonishing stuff for a formal shareholders meeting. AGM veterans said it had never happened before. The eight men, mostly wearing black or navy suits, sat down: Danny Fiszman on the left, then Arsène Wenger, Ken Friar (as usual at the chairman's right hand), Peter Hill-Wood, Dein, the Carr brothers and David Miles.

Back in 1995, when the directors came out after George Graham had been sacked just five months before, they looked as if they were about to face a firing squad. Hill-Wood, fidgeting nervously, said the club's lawyers had instructed him not to talk about Graham because it was sub judice, which caused great disgust and unrest in the room because no one believed that the Graham sacking, which did not go to court, could be sub judice at that stage. At the 1996 AGM, just a few weeks after Rioch had been dumped four days before the first league game against West Ham, the flak had started flying immediately. Now, backed by so many glittering trophies, the directors knew that 1998 was as good as it would ever get. Still, they could not have expected to be cheered on to the platform.

Hill-Wood, standing while the others were seated, whizzed through the formal business in about five minutes: acceptance of the accounts, the reappointment of auditors Kidsons Impey, the welcome to new company secretary David Miles and the re-election of directors. It was a case of 'Carried unanimously, thank you!' every time. Hill-Wood is likeable because he does not come over like a high-powered executive. He is old money, a banker who loves a gin and tonic, a trustworthy custodian of a deeply loved sporting institution. He never pretends to have all the answers at his fingertips, which is part of his charm. When closely quizzed by shareholders on a particular point, he will often get the answer from Ken Friar.

'It's a pleasure to be standing in front of the silver vaults,' said Hill-Wood. 'I think it's unlikely that any of us will see this again, so you'd better feast your eyes on it!'

The shareholders who spoke were mostly educated middle-class men, and they spoke well. But none gave his name.

One said, 'When will the stadium issue be resolved?'

'I wish I knew,' replied the chairman. 'The preferred route, as I think you all know, is to stay here.'

Another shareholder said, 'I may be old-fashioned, but I'd like to say that the manager is the most important employee of any football club, and it does concern me when I read in the press that at a number of clubs players are actually paid more than the manager. I'm absolutely appalled by this. I wonder whether you can assure me that Mr Wenger is the highest-paid employee of this football club? I certainly feel he ought to be. If he's not, why?'

Before Hill-Wood could reply to this, Wenger made a gracious, open-handed gesture towards the speaker and said, 'My agent!' People laughed loudly. Indeed, they laughed so loudly that the seriousness of the question, and the answer, became almost irrelevant.

'From the board's point of view,' Hill-Wood began, 'we believe that Mr Wenger is reasonably well paid, and he has committed himself to us for a further period of time. And I think he is satisfied with the salary. I agree with you. The most important task for the board of directors, in my view, is to appoint the best manager. I think we can genuinely say that we got something right.'

There was then a question about the Ticket Registration Scheme from a man who was registered, had got a ticket for the FA Cup Final but had not got one for the Manchester United game. Ken Friar explained the arithmetic: Highbury holds 38,000, there are over 20,000 season tickets, and 6,000 tickets had to be given to Manchester United fans. That left only 12,000 seats, but there are 15,000 fans on the registration scheme. The ground is simply not big enough.

One shareholder picked up on this and asked, 'Mr Chairman, there were reports that you made a bid for Wembley Stadium. Were they true? If it was made, can you give shareholders an indication of how it would have been financed?'

Hill-Wood replied, 'Yes, we did make a very genuine offer for Wembley. This was made up of a number of ingredients. There was a substantial cash payment that would have come from the bank, and through a method of securitisation, if you understand that term. Securitisation is where you sell up front a known stream of future income. So that was one method. We would have had to issue some more shares, which we would have done. And the balance was made up of delayed payments which were guaranteed but which were paid over a period of three or four years.'

Someone else then said, 'I'd like to ask Mr Wenger a question if I may. One of the biggest financial gains in the last year was the way he acquired Nicolas Anelka from Paris Saint Germain for a minimal fee. He's obviously worth a lot more money now. We are now spending a lot of money on our youth team and our youth development system. How are we going to stop people doing to us what Mr Wenger did to Paris Saint Germain? Secondly, I've read in the press over the summer that we have tried to buy various strikers. Could he tell me which ones he tried to buy and which stories were rubbish? And are there any plans to buy a striker before Christmas, in time for the second half of the Champions League?'

Hill-Wood turned to Wenger. 'Would you like to answer that now or later?' Wenger said, 'I can answer now.' There was loud applause. 'You know that, concerning Nicolas Anelka, there is a European rule that stipulates that football is a job like anything else, and if you are at the end of a contract, whether you are 18 or 20 or 24, you can move to a different country. That's why Nicolas Anelka was free. It's exactly the same for players who are eighteen and at the end of a contract. That means they could move to France. So you just try to compete financially. At the time I was told Nicolas was unhappy. He wanted to leave Paris; he would have gone to Madrid or Barcelona. That means they had lost their player. And maybe because I was French he came and became one of our players. We have no protection for our players going abroad if they are not under contract.

'Concerning the transfer market in the summer. When I arrived here two years ago we had a fairly good team, but we needed some younger players to rebuild the team. After four or five months of observation I came to the conclusion that it was not possible to improve the team by buying English players, just because the best young players were at Manchester United or Liverpool, so we had to go abroad to buy the players. I think we did reasonably well getting the players at what I believe was a reasonable price last season. We won trophies and we went into the market again. My first idea was to buy English because I still think it's very important for a club like Arsenal to have a British spirit, and to keep the basis of the English players and the spirit of the English players. And that's what we spoke about.

'It's always a bit of a struggle between tradition and innovation. Tradition is what I would like to keep here. The very strong spirit of the English players. I would say that innovation is to bring in some players who can bring different qualities and that's why, maybe, we were successful last season – because the mixture was right. My first target was stability. That means my first target, in the middle of the season, was to keep the players we had. Because, like you said, Anelka, Overmars, Petit, Vieira, Christopher Wreh, they're all young, they're all between 20 and 25. And the only way to protect yourself from the Bosman rule is to get them on long contracts. And today I'm very happy because we have a good team, and we have all our young players on long-term contracts, at least five to six years. That means we have good protection concerning the value of our team.

'Of course when I say stability I didn't imagine that Ian Wright would want to leave. But I knew he was close, one or two years away from his end, and that we had to buy a striker. And that it would be difficult for him to sit on the bench and not play. The second thing was that David Platt stopped, and that was very late. It happened on 7 July. So when he stopped his career we were in a situation on 8 July where we had to find some new players. Ian Wright, it happened just before the end of the World Cup. He signed for West Ham on 12 or 13 July, so it was late too. We went for strikers, most of them were foreign strikers. None of them was for me at the right value. The second problem we had was that I couldn't imagine bringing in a player who has achieved nothing, and he's better paid than the players who have achieved the Double.'

Wenger was interrupted by loud applause at this point.

'Unfortunately, we didn't make some deals because of that. When you phone up and you're Arsenal, the price of course is very high. But mainly we didn't want to go over the wages we have at the moment. I didn't want to destroy the spirit. So at the moment we are still in the market. I still think we are short and that we need to buy two players. We need to buy one striker, but it has to be the right one. And maybe one midfielder, a creative midfielder because we have so many games to play, and so many targets this season. We want to be the best. The competition is very hard but as long as we keep our quality we can do it.'

Wenger was then asked why he had sold Isaiah Rankin, a reserve striker who had gone to Bradford City for £1.3 million.

'Because he had in front of him too many players who were in a position to play in the top team. He was impatient. I thought that he wouldn't naturally make it this season, and he needed some first-team games. He was one of the players where if you keep him, he drops; if he drops, his value goes down and he isn't happy and he hasn't improved. If you are sure that he won't play for you this season, you give him a chance to make a career somewhere. If he makes a good career somewhere else, I'm very happy for him.'

This was applauded too.

One shareholder then mentioned his new contract: 'Mr Hill-Wood said ten minutes ago that you have committed yourself to the club.'

Hill-Wood replied for his manager. 'Mr Wenger has committed himself to a further four years.'

This bit of news brought deafening applause.

'Mr Chairman,' said another shareholder, 'to administer even the mildest of rebukes to a man who is responsible for the monumental achievement of winning a Double in his first full year as a manager would be churlish in the extreme. However, that said, might I respectfully remind those responsible for running the club that the almost equally great achievements under George Graham, of winning the championship in 1989 and 1991, were both followed by a year of under-achievement, due in large part to a failure to strengthen the squad.'

Hill-Wood said simply, 'I hear what you're saying.'

The next shareholder said, 'Mr Chairman, coming along today, with my wife, she said, "What's it gonna be like today?" I said, "It's gonna be wonderful, it's gonna be a party, we'll be rolling around in the aisles." I first supported Arsenal in 1941, I've supported them ever since and I've never seen an array of silver like that. So why don't we have a dance in the aisles and celebrate?'

This unexpected suggestion brought cheers and more loud applause. There were a couple more questions, and then the feel-good festival was over. The tribe had convened, had heard words of wisdom from the big chiefs, and now they just wanted Mr Wenger's autograph. The 1998 AGM had been a small triumph of magic theatre, a conjuring trick by directors who had come out to parade in front of a dazzling, blinding collection of trophies. Most proud winners stand behind their silverware, but the Arsenal board sat in front of them and simply disappeared. It was quite clever. None of us would ever see eight men hiding in front of seven trophies again.

LENS, KIEV AND PANATHINAIKOS

Panathinaikos played much better at Wembley than they did in Athens. In fact every team that has come to Wembley to face us has lifted their game because every team loves to play there.

Arsène Wenger

Arsenal recorded their fourth draw in a row at Leicester on 12 September, then turned their focus on the club's first ever Champions League game, to be played in the Stade Felix Bollaert in Lens where, less than three months earlier, England had beaten Colombia 2–0 in a World Cup group match. The Gunners played excellent football on the night but were let down by their lack of punch in front of goal. Bergkamp and Anelka missed five or six good chances and an Overmars strike in the 51st minute was not enough to win the game. Wenger took Bergkamp off near the end and put on Garde, an extra defender, but Smicer's corner was flicked on at the near post and Vareilles equalised in the 90th minute. The body language of Tony Adams suggested that he thought the goal was a mistake by Seaman. It was a disappointing start to the European campaign.

Arsenal showed their true ability in the next game that Sunday, turning on the style against Manchester United at Highbury and staging a rerun of the Charity Shield. When Beckham hit the target with a fierce free-kick which any other keeper would have tipped over, Seaman just held the ball nonchalantly above his head. Then Hughes flighted a free-kick perfectly and Adams got there ahead of Schmeichel to head into the net. And when Overmars released Anelka just before half-time Schmeichel saved his first shot, but he buried the rebound for 2–0.

Referee Graham Barber then sent off Nicky Butt for fouling Vieira on the edge of the box, even though he was not the last man, and when Beckham bottled a fifty-fifty with Winterburn, vanishing in a puff of smoke, the Clock End began to sing, 'Can we play you every week?' Designer Dennis was shaping the game freely now, slowing it down, speeding it up, slipping Anelka in, making moves that were triangular, rectangular, spherical, cylindrical, any shape you wanted, while Overmars toyed with Neville and Berg. At one point the crowd gave Vieira a standing ovation when he chased back into defence, mopped up and cruised away with the ball. New signing Freddie Ljungberg, who had recently impressed playing for Sweden against England, then made his home debut. He came on for Anelka after 79 minutes and scored his first goal from a pass by Bergkamp, lobbing the ball neatly over Schmeichel. Small, energetic, brave, resourceful and versatile, Ljungberg looked a steal at £3 million.

Alex Ferguson admitted afterwards, 'Arsenal were far better than us. Wanted to win it far more than we did. And I don't like saying that as manager of Manchester United. They were prepared to give fouls away to win the match. We were tiptoeing into tackles.' Wenger said, 'It reminded me a little bit of the Everton day when we won the title.'

The following Saturday Sheffield Wednesday beat Arsenal 1–0 at Hillsborough in a game notorious for Paolo Di Canio's push on referee Paul Alcock and a Martin Keown red card, which was later rescinded. There was also a tunnel incident involving Patrick Vieira, who was later fined £20,000 by the FA .

Wenger was trying to sign Nwankwo Kanu, on loan from Inter Milan until the end of the season. Kanu was 22 but had already had an astonishingly dramatic career, having been discovered at an under-17 World Youth tournament in Japan in 1993, when he scored six goals and was voted player of the tournament. Nigeria's plane had to overnight in Amsterdam after the competition and Ajax officials met Kanu at the airport and signed him. He played with Marc Overmars, who became his friend and gave him lifts, since he was too young to drive. Kanu won three Dutch titles with Ajax and played in the 1995 Champions League Final, coming on as a substitute against Milan in Vienna on a night when the other sub, Patrick Kluivert, scored the only goal of the game. A year later he captained Nigeria in the Olympics in Atlanta, when Nigeria beat Brazil and Argentina to win the gold medal.

He was signed by Inter for £1.3 million that summer, but a heart valve defect was detected and Inter president Massimo Moratti paid for him to be flown to a Cleveland clinic where he had pioneering surgery. He recuperated in California, but when he returned to Inter the club had changed its style, coach Gigi Simoni preferring to play defensive football with Ronaldo and Zamorano up front. Kanu hated defensive football, and although Moratti pleaded his case with Simoni, he had played only one game in the 1997/98 season and wanted a move. It seemed a huge gamble by Wenger.

Remi Garde deputised for Parlour for the Panathinaikos game at Wembley on 30 September, but looked apprehensive. It was the biggest game of his career. The game featured about twenty minutes of sparring – a couple of punches were landed, but there were no knockdowns – and after an hour one wondered whether Arsenal would be the first ever Champions League club to draw all six games. Then the keeper spilt a corner and Adams rammed it in for 1–0. Soon after, Keown headed in a Petit corner for 2–0. Anelka starred in some breathtakingly fast counter-attacks after that, but the Greeks got a goal back when Asanovic hit a free-kick which deflected to Maud, who headed in from five yards.

The next European game was Dynamo Kiev at Wembley on 21 October. For Wenger, it was exciting to pit wits with a legendary coach like Valeri Lobanovsky, who had created Kiev's wonderfully cerebral teamwork by using the same system for thirty years. He regarded it as one of the most interesting matches of his entire career, and if Arsenal could beat Kiev at Wembley it would be something of a quantum leap forward for the club. It would change the way Europe saw Arsenal. It would change the way Arsenal saw themselves. And it might even change the way Wenger saw Arsenal. But he knew that Kiev were one of the best eight teams in Europe, and he knew he would be facing them without Vieira and Petit, who were suspended.

On the night, Kiev were temperamentally as well as tactically disciplined. They defended deep and cleverly, and rarely fouled except in the last third to prevent a shot or killer pass. Their defenders were very cute at pushing up to narrow angles to pinch the ball or catch a striker offside, and their shape was so good that you did not notice how much running they did. They broke using two or three passes, often one-touch passes, and the whole team just rolled along with automatic movement into the right spaces.

Shevchenko, a slim powerhouse, took only four minutes to rob Overmars, zoom infield and attempt a shot. Early in the second half he smashed a dipper just past the base of the post. Then he took off on a preposterous run from the halfway line, nutmegged Adams, and forced Seaman to come out to him. Later on he chased Keown and shoulder-charged him off the ball, something you never see.

As Arsenal huffed and puffed against a mass of white shirts, who often nicked the ball and broke at awesome pace, Wenger could see that Kiev were the better side. But the better side does not always win. Shevchenko played a one-two with Bialkevich, went through and buried his shot, but the goal was disallowed – wrongly, as replays showed. Within sixty seconds of that, something remarkable happened: Lee Dixon outpaced Rebrov on the right, hit a superb cross to the near post and Bergkamp scored with a diving header from eight yards. One-nil to the Arsenal!

Anelka was still too immature to be a match-winner in the Champions League. He had been shooting from thirty yards, standing around in offside positions and overhitting passes, so

Wenger took him off, brought on Nelson Vivas and moved Overmars forward. When Overmars rounded keeper Shovkovsky, Luzhny managed to kick the ball off the line.

Arsenal's front six had been poor, apart from Parlour, but it looked as if their defence and a bit of luck had won the game – until the last minute of normal time when Bialkevich put the ball across the box and Rebrov equalised. There was no flag and the goal stood. In Lens, Wenger had taken a striker off when Arsenal were winning 1–0 and they had conceded a late goal. The same thing had happened again.

At an unusually chaotic press conference, Wenger said, 'I've heard their first goal was onside but the second was not regular.' On the Bergkamp goal, right after the disallowed goal, he said, 'You can never say when you score a great goal that it's unfair.'

Kiev were clearly the superior team. They had more skill, more possession, more shots, more corners and fewer fouls. They had smothered Overmars and outnumbered Arsenal in every part of the field; it was always four against three, three against two, two against one. And their two strikers, Andrei Shevchenko and Sergei Rebrov, were world class. The brave, dynamic little Rebrov, an ethnic Russian who had chosen to play for the land of his birth, Ukraine, was the scorer of so many late goals that the fans called him 'the Rescuer', while Shevchenko, a phenomenal footballer with a big engine, had proved to be bold, fast, creative, direct and as greedy as great goalscorers usually are.

Arsenal travelled to Kiev on 4 November for the return match without Bergkamp, Overmars and Adams. They were never going to win the tie, especially since Kiev, amazingly, had to win to stay in the competition. Anelka had also dropped out with a septic toe, but this made little difference, given his form in the first game. The side was: Seaman; Dixon, Keown, Bould, Winterburn; Parlour, Vieira, Petit, Vivas; Boa Morte, Wreh. Hughes and Grimandi were on the bench. Wenger was bluffing three positions, the two strikers and Vivas, but he watched a brave eight-man performance in which Petit, Vieira, Parlour, Dixon and Winterburn strove commendably.

The turning point came when Keown was outpaced and mugged by Rebrov. He should have put both hands in the air and let him go, but he allowed his shin to clip Rebrov's heel. Rebrov, of course, went down, then got up to score the penalty. Vivas had passed to Kiev players with uncanny regularity throughout the first half and was the man beaten when Golovko made it 2–0, and then he tripped Bialkevich when he was going nowhere and gave away a free-kick. Shevchenko was always going to hit a right-footed shot round the wall, so Seaman should have had a four-man wall with a big, brave man on the end, like Vieira. Instead he had a three-man wall with little Vivas, who ducked, and the ball flashed into the net for 3–0. Hughes, as sub, got a goal back late on.

Arsène Wenger was two strikers short. It was that simple. He went into the Champions League with only one proven striker, Bergkamp, who did not fly, and one exceptional novice, Anelka, so he was always going to be one injury away from trouble. With this strike force supplemented only by Overmars, Arsenal were struggling. It looked as if Wenger, a risk-taker when it comes to the development of players, was determined to turn Anelka into another George Weah. He was gambling that Anelka could learn enough in the first 25 games of the season to become a star in the second 25 games. The best way for him to learn quickly was to play every game. If he was in and out of the team he would learn slowly because he would be taking one step forward and one step backwards all the time. In 1997/98 Overmars had taken the pressure off Bergkamp, and so had Wright, but now, with Wright gone and Overmars more of a known quantity, the pressure was on Bergkamp again. He had to nurse Anelka, score more goals himself, and in a post-World Cup season that was asking too much. Wenger knew his strike force was threadbare, and he must have dreaded the situation that arose in Kiev. He should have signed two strikers to replace Wright and Hartson, but maybe he did not have enough money or could not get the players he wanted.

The Lens game at Wembley on 25 November turned out to be his biggest disappointment of 1998. Arsenal lost the game 1–0 because Petit was suspended and Bergkamp and Vieira had been injured the previous Saturday against Wimbledon. As a consequence, Arsenal lacked power and confidence. Adams was also a casualty: he had been playing with pain-killing injections but he was in agony and did not come out for the second half.

The team had overcome the absence of key players before and become champions, but this game, against a resourceful young French team, was a bridge too far. They missed four good chances and were outplayed overall. The 8,000 fans from Lens lit up the night in their orange and yellow colours, standing throughout the game, pogoing in unison, clapping rhythmically, singing lustily and having a high old time behind the goal. They were rewarded after 72 minutes when Smicer cleverly beat Dixon on the right and crossed low to the far post, where Debeve scored from three yards. The Arsenal defence had done their job but the linesman had not – Debeve was offside. England's champions were on their way out of the so-called Champions League with only one win in their first five games.

Two players were sent off in injury time by Swedish referee Anders Fisk. Parlour tried a one-two with Vivas, Rool obstructed him and Parlour lashed out, kicking the Frenchman in the chest. Then Dixon tangled with Vareilles, fell over and got Vareilles sent off. UEFA reviewed footage and suspended Dixon, which meant he would miss Arsenal's first European game the following season. It was very, very unusual for Ray Parlour to kick a player off the ball, even when provoked, and virtually unprecedented to see Lee Dixon feign injury. Those two incidents showed the pressure, the rage, the frustration, the intense disappointment which all the players felt, and which Wenger also felt. The Gunners had been outplayed by a lively, spirited small-town club from France. The second half, in particular, was abysmal. Had we ever seen an Arsenal team play with less belief?

Still, Wenger knew that the Champions League, like everything else in football, is a learning curve. No club wins it without being in the quarter-final or semi-final the year before. The competition is a very awkward, testing series of games against variously talented opponents in various cities in various weather conditions. You hope to start in phase one in your first year, progress to phase two a year later, then try to get into the quarters and semis. That process takes three or four years.

Managers suffer when the goals dry up and Wenger was suffering now. By the end of the Lens game, his attack had kept four clean sheets in a row. He had fielded a reserve team against Chelsea at Highbury in the Worthington Cup on 11 November and been hammered 5–0. Then came a goalless draw with Tottenham at Highbury and a 1–0 defeat away to Wimbledon. Overmars had now gone eleven games without a goal.

On the Friday after the Lens game Wenger told the Sunday reporters, 'My job is not to show anger or frustration, but to arrive at a logical analysis of what happened and try to work out why. There is no normal reaction any more in football. When you lose, it is always too negative. When you win, too positive. I try to give small problems small importance and the right importance to the right problems.' He insisted he had known all along that November could be a difficult month because Petit, Vieira, Bergkamp and Overmars had all been involved late into the World Cup. For those players, the problem was partly psychological. 'If you are winning games, you don't think you are tired. You feel well. But if you lose, you're tired – even if you do everything right physically.' He then admitted he felt guilty about the Champions League failure. 'I try to think, "What did I do wrong?"'

Wenger stepped up his efforts to sign Kanu, who was said to be demanding a £900,000 loyalty payment from Inter, who in turn wanted a 'buy back' clause in his Arsenal contract. Wenger naturally refused to give Inter that option. He was taking a calculated risk, but if it paid off and Kanu proved to be a match-winner in the Premiership, he did not want anybody else to benefit.

The bitter disappointment after crashing out of the Champions League so early proved hard to shake off, and performances dipped after the Lens defeat. So far in the Premiership Arsenal had played fourteen, won six, drawn six and lost two. At home to Middlesbrough on Sunday, 29 November, they conceded a goal to Brian Deane inside six minutes, and when Boa Morte came on for Wreh he was booed on to the field. Rarely, if ever, had an Arsenal substitute been booed on to the field. The crowd, unlike the Spurs crowd, was well known for being patient and forgiving with young players, but the team had so obviously run out of ideas and performances that ninety minutes was beginning to seem like three hours. When Lee Dixon hit a shot over the bar from thirty yards, the fans booed again. Somebody said, 'Hill-Wood's just walked out in disgust!' – presumably disgusted with the supporters' reaction, not with Dixon's shot. Middlesbrough brought eleven players back to defend, the crowd lapsed into nostalgia by chanting 'Ian Wright, Wright, Wright!', then, in the final minute, Anelka equalised, slamming in a shot off the underside of the bar. An agonising day for Wenger, but the late goal had at least earned a point.

December started with a 0–0 at Derby, followed by a surprise 3–1 win in Athens in the dead Champions League game against Panathinaikos, for which Wenger fielded a very young team which included teenagers Paolo Vernazza, David Grondin and Matthew Upson. The Greeks had four chances in the first half, but the four goals were scored in the last half hour, three of them by Mendez, Anelka and Boa Morte. Wenger said that Wembley had motivated their three opponents and that this was a factor the club had underestimated. 'Panathinaikos played much better at Wembley than they did in Athens. In fact every team that has come to Wembley to face us has lifted their game because every team loves to play there. What is disappointing to me is that we know now we could easily have won this group and gone through to the quarter-finals. But we dropped four points by conceding a last-minute equaliser in Lens right at the start of the competition, and another against Dynamo Kiev at Wembley. We were also beaten by an offside goal by Lens.' His biggest regret was that Arsenal had failed to win that first game in Lens. 'We learnt that in these games you get very few chances, and if you don't take them, you don't win.'

Since the directors had felt some guilt about inconveniencing their most loyal supporters by asking them to travel to another stadium in another part of London to watch their team, they had sold thousands of tickets at only £10 each. The *Daily Telegraph*'s John Ley did a piece pointing out that crowds of 73,000 had brought receipts in the region of £800,000 per game; failing to qualify for the next phase of the Champions League, however, had cost the club at least £5 million.

FERGUSON CALLS ARSENAL 'BELLIGERENT'

*Gerard is an open-minded and passionate man. I am the opposite: stubborn
and stupid. But sometimes stupid behaviour makes you win.*

Arsène Wenger

When Dennis Bergkamp scored twice at Aston Villa on 13
December and Arsenal went in at half-time 2–0 up, Wenger must
have thought his team had turned the corner at last. But then Dion
Dublin turned the game upside down and Arsenal walked off 3–2
losers. Wenger had always maintained that you needed experienced players, especially when results were not going well, and it
was two of those, Bergkamp and Overmars, who did a lot to help
Arsenal get their season back on track over the next few weeks.

Reports now stated that Real Madrid wanted Wenger to replace
their Dutch coach Guus Hiddink. The papers made much of the fact
that Wenger had so far failed to sign a four-year extension to his
contract which would keep him at Arsenal until 2002, but he insisted
that this was a minor matter. 'I've told everyone many times that my
word is my signature, and it's been that way for the twenty years I've
worked in football.' He said the contract discussions were about
'small, small details' which would be agreed within a week or so.

Early in the Leeds game at Highbury, five days before Christmas,
Wenger might well have begun to fancy the Real Madrid job when
Anelka crossed from the right wing. The cross went past everyone
in the goalmouth to Bergkamp at the far post, but the ball went
right under his left foot. Wenger had seen balls go past Bergkamp,
go beyond him, go behind him, go over his head, but he only saw
the ball go under his foot once every two years, if that. Was this
going to be another one of those days? Wenger had suffered far too
many of those days lately – Wimbledon, Lens, Middlesbrough and
Derby were the kind of days he wanted to forget. He sat there
watching his team play without rhythm and fluidity for 28
minutes. Then Anelka flicked on, Bergkamp was one-on-one, and
he poked the ball in for 1–0.

Leeds had certainly been the better team until the goal, but now
Arsenal hit a groove. Overmars skipped easily past Halle and

crossed for Anelka, who shot wide; Bergkamp put Petit through but his flick went over the bar. Early in the second half a slick move ended with a terrific left-foot shot by Vieira for 2–0, Hasselbaink replied with a cannonball, perhaps the hardest shot to go past David Seaman since Juan Esnaider's thunderbolt in the 1995 Cup Winners Cup Final, and finally Petit made it 3–1. Wenger had at last seen his team play as he thought they should play.

When West Ham came to Highbury on Boxing Day they made Ian Wright captain against his old club – and this seemed to inspire Anelka. We had never seen him in this mood. He was hyper-aggressive and super-confident, playing with real venom and tremendous two-footed skill. For once, everything about him was right. His body language screamed a simple message: Give me the ball and I'll score! Overmars made it 1–0 after eight minutes and Anelka was so compelling he seemed certain to make it 2–0. Why was he suddenly playing like this? To show Ian Wright who was the main man? But then Anelka picked up an injury, which was rare for him. Physio Gary Lewin went on to treat the ankle, but it was serious enough for him to have to leave the field after half an hour.

There was no further score, and afterwards Wenger was full of praise for Petit. 'He brings a balance. He knows when to drop back and he's the one who can find Nicolas and Marc. He sees openings very well. He can run for hours, he's a winner, he's an ambitious guy – and he's very consistent. The World Cup gave him more confidence.'

It was true that Petit had been phenomenally consistent for a long time. He had had a great year in 1998, and then he sustained it. He had taken his Arsenal form into the World Cup squad, earned a regular place in the team, scored in the final against Brazil, come back to London as a world champion, and, unlike others in France's team, taken his World Cup form into the new season and carried on playing brilliantly for Arsenal. At his old club, Monaco, Thierry Henry and David Trezeguet had barely bothered to raise a leg.

Two days later Patrick Vieira was sent off at Charlton and the newspapers had another field day about Arsenal's disciplinary record – which, admittedly, was unique. This was their eighteenth red card since Wenger's arrival 27 months earlier. More disturbingly, it was their fifth red card of the 1998/99 season, and it was only just after Christmas. On average, Arsenal were having a player sent off once a month.

Referee Uriah Rennie had made himself the star of the game by issuing seven yellows, Charlton's five cautions including one for Eddie Youds, who should have been sent off for a violent tackle from behind on Bergkamp which ended the Dutchman's participation in the match before half-time. Six minutes into the second half Vieira was looking to run away from Neil Redfearn when he impeded him, so he swung his arm back and caught Redfearn on the shoulder. Rennie sent him off. Three minutes later Mark Kinsella felled Parlour in the box and Overmars scored from the spot. Arsenal held on for a 1–0 win.

In the FA Cup third round on 4 January 1999, Arsenal were drawn away at Preston and Manchester United played Middlesbrough. Alex Ferguson met four Sunday reporters for an interview on the day after his 57th birthday and took the opportunity to make some very rude remarks about his nearest championship rivals. He talked about Arsenal's 'belligerent' style of play, saying that some Arsenal players liked 'a scrap'. He added, 'When they're not doing well in a game, they turn it into a battle to try to make the opposition lose concentration. The number of fights involving Arsenal is more than Wimbledon had in their heyday.'

Arsenal went 2–0 down at Preston, but then came back to win 4–2 with goals from Boa Morte, Petit (two) and Overmars. After the game Wenger described Ferguson's attack as 'clumsy' and said that every Premiership team should respect the others. 'We always try to play football,' he said. 'You do not win championships and cups by fighting. We respect every team and let the referees do their job on the field. I think we have to give a good image to the game, and it starts by respecting every other team. What he said does not bother me at all and I do not want to make a fuss about it. I think it was just a little bit clumsy on his part.'

Wenger admitted that Preston had dominated the early stages and said that the match had been close. 'Preston played like world champions for the first twenty minutes. They were quicker and more aggressive than us. It was like a poker game for them. They gave it everything early on and gambled on getting a lead they might be able to maintain. If they had got three they might have done it because I could not see us scoring. We came very close to making our exit tonight. We were two goals down by the time we woke up. And then I thought it might be one of those nights when their goalkeeper was the hero.'

Meanwhile, Alex Ferguson was telling reporters that he had sent a letter of apology to Wenger. 'Arsène Wenger has a right to be annoyed over this matter. I have already dropped him a note explaining the situation and I offered him the apology he deserved. It is not my policy to criticise teams and the way they play. People go on about it all being psychological warfare, but that is far from the truth on this occasion. I was stitched up and feel I have been betrayed.'

The matter did not rest there. Joe Lovejoy followed up his original piece in *The Sunday Times* a week later by strongly denying that Ferguson had been 'stitched up'. He said that the Manchester-based reporters were frightened of Ferguson and treated his quotes like tablets of stone. He noted that Ferguson had named biased referees, grasping agents and one player who was 'the biggest cheat in football'. Many Premiership managers talk off the record in this way, but Wenger never does so he never creates the opportunity for such misunderstandings to arise. Lovejoy made the point that, had he chosen to report Ferguson's remarks in full, the United boss 'would have been in serious trouble with m'learned friends'.

Wenger had always talked in a measured manner on every subject that came up in football, but the one topic that infuriated him (and still does) was systematic fouling against his players. When Vieira used an arm to free himself from the attentions of Charlton's Neil Redfearn, he had been sent off. The manager, as usual, defended his man vigorously, but this time he did it in a more emphatic way than ever before. He called Redfearn 'a cheat'. 'Do you know which player has committed more fouls than anybody else in the Premiership this season? I'll tell you who – Neil Redfearn. The people who sponsor the Premiership compile statistics on these things and his record is the worst. Just imagine what people would be saying now if that was an Arsenal player. And Dennis Bergkamp has spent ten days on the treatment table because of a dreadful tackle by another Charlton player. But again we never hear anything about that.'

Charlton boss Alan Curbishley joined the verbal war, and then the FA became involved through their new 'compliance officer' Graham Bean who said that the 'undignified squabble' must stop or misconduct charges could follow. Wenger said, 'I had a phone call from Graham Bean. I was surprised. I am surprised by the kind of job he is supposed to do. After the incident involving Patrick I was asked a question and I just said Redfearn was a cheat on that occasion. I just gave my opinion. He can call me fifty times and I don't know why I should change that view. We live in a democracy and Alan Curbishley has every right to have a different opinion. It doesn't change my respect for him. I didn't feel that, at any time, I attacked him or Charlton. At first you are surprised at all the attention. After that you wonder if you are right or not, then you get fed up with it and after that you ignore it. That is the stage we are at now.' Wenger said there was a danger that managers could lose freedom of speech. 'I can accept that sometimes some managers are fed up with Arsenal. You don't expect to say we are the greatest and the best all the time. I don't ignore critics. I think criticism is right sometimes, but I should be able to say what I believe is right. I don't know how Mr Bean can stop me saying what I believe is right unless he puts me in jail.' And on the subject of Alex Ferguson's apology, he said, 'If he has written the letter it must have been sent by horse because I haven't received it. But the comments didn't upset me and I accept what he said. We don't expect presents. If you are good enough you win, and if you are not you lose. That is why the game against Liverpool is so important. We need to beat Liverpool and we need to win our home games to stay at the top.'

Arsenal were at home to Liverpool on 9 January and desperately wanted to improve their poor record against them. In nine Premiership meetings between the teams Liverpool had lost just once, with seven wins. Roy Evans had bowed out in November and

Gerard Houllier was now in sole command. 'Arsène is a good football man and a good friend,' Houllier was reported as saying, 'and whatever happens we will stay friends.' Wenger, in turn, made one of his most enigmatic comments when he said, 'Gerard is an open-minded and passionate man. I am the opposite: stubborn and stupid. But sometimes stupid behaviour makes you win.'

Wenger had always wanted to sign Robbie Fowler, who would have benefited from a fresh start and would have enjoyed playing with Petit, Bergkamp and Overmars, but Houllier regarded Robbie almost as a son. Whether Fowler and Michael Owen were compatible was always in doubt, so Houllier might have been tempted to break up the Spice Boys and rebuild his team around Owen. He could have begun to finance that by selling Fowler to Wenger for £15 million, but it did not happen.

The match itself was wholly forgettable. With Bergkamp still injured as a result of the Youds assault, the erratic Boa Morte played up front with Anelka, so it was no surprise that, after a good tussle between Keown and Fowler, it finished goalless.

Arsenal's appeal failed to overturn Vieira's sending-off on Boxing Day, so he would miss the FA Cup fourth-round tie against Wolves on 24 January and two Premiership matches against Nottingham Forest and Chelsea before and after that. Wenger immediately called for an overhaul of football's disciplinary procedures, saying that a panel of experts should adjudicate on red-card incidents. 'After examining the evidence, they would have the power to let the ban stay, decrease or increase it. It would be, I think, more fair, and that's all we want at Arsenal, to be treated the same as everyone else. To call us a dirty side is unbelievable. It seems to us that it is always Arsenal players who are being watched and their every move examined. I would like to see other teams scrutinised in the same way. It might be worth watching a recording of our FA Cup match against Preston and the fouls on our goalkeeper, Alex Manninger. Their players just jumped into him and made no attempt to play the ball. We are not guilty of that kind of foul. Nobody mentioned that, though, which is frustrating for me.'

January was only eleven days old and 1999 had already been a controversial year for the Frenchman, but at least his team was showing signs of being able to score goals again. He had sent Tony Adams to Florida for some sunshine, rest and recuperation, and Adams now came back to first-team action on 16 January at the City Ground, where Arsenal beat Forest 1–0. He had missed ten games since coming off at half-time against Lens. Results improved steadily after his return to the team, prompting his manager to label his captain's injuries as 'a small problem'. 'The only problem for him,' Wenger went on, 'is how long he will want to go on. If he is motivated I think he can go on until he is 37 or 38. At the moment he looks very focused.'

KANU ARRIVES

It's the same type of gamble I took with Overmars and I will be happy if we can get the same kind of result. I try to calculate my risks, and with a talent like his, it is not a huge one.

Arsène Wenger

The day before Adams' return to the first team, Wenger finally landed Nwankwo Kanu, who passed a rigorous medical examination and signed a six-year contract. Arsenal had paid Inter £4.5 million for him. 'He will be a big asset for us,' the manager said. 'He can play as the main striker or off the main striker and has already proved himself at top club and international level. But his problem is that he has had very few chances at Inter because he is behind strikers there like Roberto Baggio, Youri Djorkaeff and, of course, Ronaldo.' There were parallels with Bergkamp's departure from Inter in 1995. He, like Kanu, hated defensive football, and now they were both playing for Wenger, an attacking coach.

But did happy times lie ahead? Anelka gave an interview to a French reporter at Sopwell House on Tuesday, 2 February 1999. The interview came out in *L'Equipe* three days later and was translated, predictably, into a *News of the World* back-page sensation on 7 February. For Anelka had said that Marc Overmars played for himself and never gave him a pass to score a goal. The pair had detested each other ever since Anelka had slagged off Overmars in a previous interview in *L'Equipe*.

At Upton Park on 6 February, after Arsenal had stuffed West Ham 4–0, the players walked off the field. Bergkamp and Overmars applauded the fans, but Anelka did not bother, and for the next game, the following Saturday against Sheffield United in the FA Cup, it looked as if Wenger might rest Anelka and play Kaba Diawara, his boisterous new loan striker who had understudied Sylvain Wiltord at Bordeaux. If Wenger did play Anelka against Sheffield United and he got injured, he would miss the game at Old Trafford on the Wednesday night, and he was already without Bergkamp and Petit for that game.

Kanu was on the bench and fans were intrigued to see him warm up. He was six foot five inches tall, a beguiling beanpole whose feet seemed to have the same degree of ball-control as a basketball player's hands. In an enjoyably competitive game Vieira scored with a header and Marcelo equalised with another header. Then, after 75 minutes, Grimandi got the wrong side of Lee Morris, stretched in the box, fouled him, missing the ball by inches, and referee Peter Jones waved play on when he might have given a penalty. Morris stayed down, injured. When the ball went down the other end, keeper Alan Kelly kicked it out of play near the halfway line. Morris had treatment, then limped off for more treatment. So Ray Parlour threw the ball down towards the corner flag for Sheffield United to collect, as you do, to give back posesssion to the team whose player has been injured, even when it is 1–1 in an FA Cup 5th Round tie with fifteen minutes to go. But Kanu, in his first sub appearance, intercepted Parlour's throw and crossed the ball to Overmars, who raced forward and tapped it into the net.

All hell broke loose. The visiting players protested and the game was held up for eight minutes. Sheffield United manager Steve Bruce called his players off, but Graeme Stuart persuaded them to stay on the field. Peter Jones did not have the power to disallow the goal, so it stood. It was 2–1, and for the rest of the match the 6,000 Blades fans sang, 'Shame on Arsenal, shame on Arsenal!' Those last eighteen minutes were all fear and loathing and dangerous nonsense: wild tackles by Sheffield players, anger from the visiting fans, stewards in fear of a riot. Peter Jones gave every fifty-fifty decision to Sheffield, which made things even more ridiculous.

On some days there is only one question to ask, and when Wenger came in I asked it. 'Did Kanu understand what he was doing?'

'No. He hadn't seen the injured player at the other end. He didn't realise the keeper had kicked it out deliberately.'

Wenger said that Arsenal had offered to replay the game. The FA approved that suggestion very quickly and the story was on PA Sports News by a quarter to six that evening – probably the fastest FA decision of the twentieth century. FA spokesman Steve Double confirmed, 'We have agreed for this game to be replayed. David Davies and Terry Annabel, the chairman of the Cup committee, discussed this situation within half an hour of the end of the game. It is an unprecedented situation. Everybody welcomes the sporting gesture by Arsène Wenger. He is to be congratulated.' The decision seemed to be a victory for common sense, but there was no discussion about what should happen were this kind of 'goal' ever to be scored again. Maybe the referee could consult the linesman, who could give a foul throw, even if it was not a foul throw, which would give possession back to the team which had the ball originally.

Kanu, naturally, was distraught. The man who had won the European Champions Cup in 1995 and Olympic gold in 1996, faced death on the operating table and survived to spend a year in limbo at Inter Milan before joining his little pal Marc at Arsenal, a new club where the manager believed in him so much that he had spent many months negotiating to buy him, had finally made his first appearance but had only been on the field for ten minutes before unwittingly creating a huge controversy.

Four days later Kanu made his first Premiership start at Old Trafford in the pouring rain. Arsenal were outplayed in the first half, and when Parlour fouled Ronny Johnsen just inside the box a penalty was given, but Dwight Yorke fired it wide. Then Kanu bamboozled Stam, Phil Neville tackled him and the ball broke to Anelka, who scored. Just after the goal Vieira was involved in another of his trademark incidents. This time he was beating Roy

Keane when the Irishman grabbed him, Vieira raised his arm in retaliation, and both players were shown yellow cards.

Arsenal's passing became much shorter after Anelka's goal as they tried to keep possession, but United equalised within ten minutes when Andy Cole headed his one hundredth Premiership goal. After that Arsenal had to defend stubbornly to earn a 1–1 draw; they had been outplayed for seventy of the ninety minutes. Vieira, however, had performed magnificently. 'He has everything you want from a midfielder,' his manager said. 'I don't think there is a limit to what he can achieve. It is hard to believe sometimes that he is still only 22.' Wenger also emphasised that Kanu, although he looked individualistic, was, above all, a team player. 'What I like most is his intelligence, the way he is aware of team-mates and always wants to bring them into the game. He does not want to do things individually. To me, he is a great player and he showed his strengths against Manchester United.' One suspected that Wenger saw himself as a Svengali of rehabilitation, that he enjoyed restoring stalled, problematic careers just as much as he liked turning raw young talents into international stars. He continued, 'It's the same type of gamble I took with Overmars and I will be happy if we can get the same kind of result. I try to calculate my risks, and with a talent like his, it is not a huge one.'

Ten days after the big controversy, on a Tuesday night, the Sheffield United game was replayed. The announcement of Marc Overmars' name was vigorously booed by visiting fans, as expected. It was a vivid, compelling match because it had that extra edge. As Overmars dribbled towards the Sheffield punters at the Clock End, they sang, 'One cheating bastard, there's only one cheating bastard!' But the Dutchman was fired up, ready to show them just how good he was, and he began to slice the Blades apart with deadly accurate shooting and passing. Early on Bergkamp played the ball forward, Hughes touched it on and Overmars hit a low left-foot shot under Alan Kelly, a super-clinical finish by the player Wenger had once called 'an efficient guy'.

Bergkamp, who had had four assists the previous Saturday in Arsenal's 5–0 demolition of Leicester City, also looked scalpel-sharp. Overmars hit a Beckham-style diagonal fifty-yarder from the halfway line, picking out Parlour's run, and Parlour cut it back into the box first time. The pass was not quite into Bergkamp's stride, but it gave him space to adjust his body shape and execute an exquisite chip which sent the ball sharply up, across Kelly's dive, and into the far side of the goal. At such moments it is Bergkamp's crowd, Bergkamp's stadium and Bergkamp's pitch. Why else did groundsman Steve Braddock create the finest playing surface in England? So that the ball will run true and such moments of skill will be possible. Braddock's immaculate pitch was Arsène Wenger's invisible player, his twelfth man, rolled and cut and manicured to suit his pace-based style of play.

There was another plus to the evening. Winterburn had come back, Nelson Vivas switching to the right. Playing full-back is a game of angles and good habits, so it is not easy to play left-back on a Saturday afternoon and right-back on a Tuesday night, but Vivas was now concentrating, tackling well, winning headers, passing accurately and looking skilful. A small man, he is very good at back-pedalling quickly to prevent passes being played over his head. When he mistimed a tiny backpass to Tony Adams at one stage during the Sheffield game, the skipper cleared the ball and gave him a little pat on the bum, as if to say, 'Don't worry about it – we got away with that.'

Against Leicester Anelka had scored a hat-trick, but after the game he had revealed something which made fans wonder just how unusual a character he really was. 'I was a little tired before the game,' he said. 'For a week I had been waking up in the middle of the night running with sweat. I don't know why. I had the impression of playing against ghosts. I don't know whether they are dreams or nightmares.'

After the Leicester game Bergkamp said that Anelka was similar to Michael Owen in his speed and finishing. 'I don't see a great deal of difference between them. Nicolas now needs fewer chances to score from. This season he is deadly. We are getting to understand each other more and more. Look at the statistics. He has opened the scoring in perhaps nine or ten games. He has hit crucial goals. You can see his speed and power, and the team is playing to his strengths. He beats goalkeepers with raw power. It is not just his speed, it is what he does when he gets in front of goal.'

Against Sheffield United, however, Anelka struggled all night against sharp, tight marking. On the Thursday we learned that Juventus executive Roberto Bettega had been at the game and that Juve were thinking of offering £20 million for Anelka. What might they have offered had they seen him play well? Would Wenger let him go?

The manager had been causing outrage on the continent by signing promising teenagers like Jeremie Aladière and German youngster Moritz Volz from underneath the noses of local clubs. He defended himself against accusations of poaching and vowed to continue scouting abroad for the finest young players. His view, as before, was that as the wages of established stars spiralled upwards clubs would be forced to concentrate on youth development. 'In my native France and in Germany, a lot has been said about Arsenal's player policy. In my own country the signing of Jeremie Aliadière created a sensation because the French don't want to lose their best talents. The sixteen-year-old players we signed were free agents and several other top teams in Europe wanted to sign them too.'

Anelka scored again in a 1–1 draw with Newcastle on 28 February, and then on 6 March Arsenal ended Derby's FA Cup run with a very late goal. The game had changed completely when Kanu came on in the last 25 minutes, grabbing the winner after a corner in the last minute. Keown's shot hit the Nigerian on the chest and he swivelled and lashed it into the net.

At this point in the season Wenger must have felt that he had assembled perhaps the strongest and most skilful squad of players in Arsenal's history: an English defence that was more durable than Stonehenge, a French engine room, a double Dutch threat in attack, an improving goalscorer who lived on Planet Anelka, and an all-star bench with a sparky Swede, a Nigerian ball-wizard and an Argentinian who was as versatile as a Swiss army knife.

When league leaders Manchester United and second-placed Chelsea drew their FA Cup quarter-final, Ferguson and Vialli said they really did not need another game and Fergie produced one of his classic wind-up remarks, a comment calculated to annoy Arsène Wenger. 'Arsenal are probably in the best position to win the championship after this,' he said. At that stage Arsenal were seven points behind United and three points behind Chelsea! Wenger dismissed the comment, saying, 'Is that his latest joke? Would he like to swap positions with us? I would certainly offer him that if I could.' It had become a point of honour for Wenger not to allow anyone to say that Arsenal were favourites to win anything. They had six of their remaining eleven league fixtures at home, but he insisted, 'It is much tougher for us to win the championship this year than at the same stage last year. Mathematically, we had it in our own hands then, but that is not the case now. The small chance we have is to keep winning our games and hope the other two will drop points.' The season had in fact turned out to be remarkably similar to 1997/98. With eleven games left Arsenal were seven points behind United with a game in hand; a year earlier they had been nine points behind with three games in hand.

Against Sheffield Wednesday on 9 March, Bergkamp was a Rolls-Royce marooned in London traffic, longing for a motorway, and the game was so dull that Wenger made a substitution at half-time, bringing on Diawara for Ljungberg. Diawara hit the post with a shot and then obliged Srnicek to make two brilliant saves. Petit and Kanu came on, and there were only seven minutes left when Petit found Bergkamp with a smart free-kick and he hit a shot which bounced past Srnicek at last. Overmars then picked out Kanu, who banged his shot high into the net, and went on to run sixty yards with the ball to set up Bergkamp for 3–0. Wenger was buzzing – three goals in five minutes, another three points, another clean sheet and another masterclass in demolition. He told reporters that the success culture within the club had inspired his new players, Kanu and Diawara. 'It's infectious,' he said. 'There is a pressure from the group to do well. For us it is important to do what we enjoy well, and when you come from outside and feel that, it's easier because there is a positive feeling about the game. They never know when they're beaten and refuse to give up. There's a lot of great characters in the team. You are a winner or not a winner, and if you are a winner, it's important for you to win throughout your whole life. They try to give everything to win and as long as they have a chance, they fight for it.'

Arsenal were now second in the Premiership. They won at Everton on 13 March, and a week later met Coventry at Highbury, where Kanu came on for Anelka after 76 minutes and made a priceless goal ten minutes from the end. He nutmegged Bosnian centre-back Konjic, then stumbled as Barry Quinn stretched into a tackle, just touching the ball away from Kanu. The Nigerian fell but still managed to shovel the ball square to Overmars, who fired a shot low into the corner of the net.

Once again Kanu had arrived and changed the game. Against Derby he had scored the winner in injury time and against Wednesday it was goalless when he came on for Anelka and Arsenal had ended up 3–0 winners. There was nobody like Kanu in the whole country, maybe the whole world. He divided seconds into nanoseconds, yards into inches. He reinvented geometry, seeing angles that did not exist for other players. Bergkamp was an elegant power player but not a great dribbler in the box, and when Anelka dribbled in the box he saw nothing but the goal. Kanu, however, seemed to create the game from moment to moment, could see team-mates and pass to them while dribbling in the box. He was the complete opposite of Anelka and therefore a perfect substitute for him. When he came on it really was a case of 'And now for something completely different'. Kanu was good at what Anelka was bad at.

At the press conference I asked, 'What is it about Kanu that allows him to come on and pick up the pace of the game and do something every time?'

Wenger smiled and said, 'Intelligence and class.'

Are you tempted to give him more than a fifteen-minute runaround when he's fitter?

–'Yes. We work hard on his fitness because he was out of the game for a long time. And he knows that as well. He works very hard at the moment in training, and we work on specific things. But you can see that this player, fit, can play in any team.'

Wenger was also delighted by Ray Parlour's goal in the win over Coventry. Tony Adams had lashed a long clearance up to Bergkamp; he had passed it square to Parlour, who had accelerated, swerved inside David Burrows and hit his shot with the outside of his right foot across Hedman into the far corner. He said that new England coach Kevin Keegan should feel very positive about Parlour. 'I think he's ready to play. He has shown again today that he can adapt to different positions. He's strong technically now. I'm very pleased with the goal he scored today because of the way he finished, he wouldn't have done that a year ago. He's calmer in the box, composed in the box, and less nervous in his finishing. I believe as well that he's the kind of player who lasts in a season. Because he has such tremendous stamina. When other players start to be tired he still keeps up with his same performances, or even improves. The more he plays, the better he is.'

Wenger's assessment of Coventry was generous. 'They cannot go down. What I've seen today, they cannot go down. Because they can frustrate everybody, they run like crazies. All eleven are very resilient. I was quite impressed by their passing ability. They missed maybe a second striker, like Whelan, and Boateng. I don't think they will go down.'

Bergkamp and Overmars missed the game at Southampton on 3 April after playing for Holland, which infuriated Wenger. 'Overmars has blisters after playing on hard ground and Dennis has returned with flu after being away. We had fifteen players away on international duty this week, so you cannot expect to come through without some casualties. But we have lost two significant players and you can see now why I do not like international matches being played at this time of year. They could have a different arrangement for international games. I do not think they should be played in March or April. It is everybody's concern, not just Arsenal's, because all over Europe championships are coming to a climax so every match is hugely important.'

At The Dell Kanu started his first game as Bergkamp's replacement, but the game finished 0–0 and he missed a second-half sitter when Anelka set him up with a square pass. He side-footed his shot and Benali blocked it on the line. Then Mark Hughes almost won the game with a diving header, but Seaman made a world-class save. 'We are very disappointed,' said Wenger afterwards. 'This is two points dropped.'

There was more bad news at the training ground, where Alex Manninger had been injured saving a shot from David Seaman. Wenger said, 'At first we feared Alex had a fractured wrist and that could have threatened his career. It is not as bad as that, but he will be out for the rest of the season.' John Lukic, who was 38, would now be on the bench.

The narrow win over Blackburn on 6 April brought Arsenal to within a point of Manchester United on a day when Bergkamp scored and Martin Keown was sent off for lashing out at Chris Sutton. The *Guardian*'s David Lacey picked up on this latest infringement. 'This could be the moment when Arsenal's perennially poor disciplinary record catches up with them. Emmanuel Petit, arguably their most influential player, will miss the semi-final through suspension following his third dismissal of the season. Arsène Wenger's two-and-a-half years in charge at Highbury have consistently offered the paradox of cerebral football let down by the hole-in-the-head school of indiscipline, even if Keown's flailing arm on Tuesday night was prompted by worries about his sick son . . . Red cards continue to sprout among Arsenal's performances like poppies in disturbed ground. When Wenger philosophises about his players and lists their qualities he comes across as the head of a science faculty enthusing over the examination results while down the corridor the students are about to blow up the lab for the umpteenth time.'

The point about Petit was important, since Arsenal would miss him at Villa Park on Sunday, 11 April, just as they had missed him in the decisive European game against Lens at Wembley back in November.

BERGKAMP'S PENALTY

The two teams are very close to each other, it was a smashing game, and in the end the luckiest won.

Arsène Wenger

For the manager who loved competition, the FA Cup semi-final was the defining moment of the 1998/99 season. His team still had a chance of winning a back-to-back Premiership and FA Cup Double, and no English club had ever achieved that. Back in 1991 Arsenal had become the major force in English football by overtaking Liverpool, then Arsenal were themselves overtaken by Manchester United, the biggest club in the country. Alex Ferguson made them the best team and their consistency in the nineties set the standard to which several clubs aspired. The Arsenal–Manchester United rivalry was therefore intense, and had been given an extra edge by a few well-publicised spats between Wenger and Ferguson.

This FA Cup semi-final was the biggest game of the English season and a contest of many dimensions and many duels: North versus South, Scotsman versus Frenchman, Stam versus Bergkamp, Keane versus Vieira, Giggs versus Overmars, Schmeichel versus Seaman. League leaders against defending champions for a place at Wembley. United had not beaten Arsenal for two years, but they were unbeaten in 21 games.

The game kicked off with Vivas in midfield for the suspended Petit, and Nicky Butt playing instead of Paul Scholes, who was on the bench. Gary Neville fouled Overmars twice in the first two minutes to earn the first yellow card. Vieira won a foul off Keane and then won a tackle with him. Nicolas Anelka hovered on the halfway line like a bullet waiting to be fired. He had scored twice for France against England at Wembley in February and had also scored six goals for Arsenal that month. He had also started four games against Manchester United and scored a goal in each; his presence, his potential, seemed to dominate the early minutes. Could he score the first goal? Could Arsenal launch him on one of those turbo-charged sprints?

When a Bergkamp pass finally released Anelka, Roy Keane chased him and made a crucial pass back. Then Cole fed Giggs and his shot flashed inches past the angle of post and crossbar. The game soon developed into a pulsating contest, with Jaap Stam outstanding as he made a great tackle on Parlour and blocked an Anelka shot. Schmeichel made two fine saves, tipping over an Adams header from a corner and stopping a Bergkamp rocket after Stam had cleared a corner.

Then Roy Keane had a 'goal' disallowed. Giggs beat Dixon and made a fine cross, Yorke headed on and Keane rifled his shot into the net off Keown. The linesman gave offside against Yorke earlier in the move, a deeply misguided decision which was very lucky for Arsenal.

Vivas, already on a yellow card, tripped Keane early in the second half and was lucky to stay on the pitch. United were dominating now and Anelka was peripheral, drifting around, dawdling, walking back from offside positions so that some Arsenal attacks had to slow down. Anelka had not yet scored in the FA Cup campaign and did not look as if he cared. He had decided to sulk, and Wenger must have been amazed and disgusted to see him outsprinted by Ronny Johnsen a couple of times. Pace has to be driven by desire. If you really want to win, really want to score, really want to get past defenders, you find another gear, but Mr Moody did not fancy it today.

In extra time Vivas stuck his elbow into Butt's face after the ball had gone and referee David Elleray sent him off. Ten Arsenal players were capable of beating many teams, but Manchester United was a slightly different proposition. Still, they held United comfortably and Bergkamp almost won the game twice in the last five minutes of extra time. His clever short pass released substitute Freddie Ljungberg into the box but he did not shoot first time and the chance slipped away; then he jinked past Keane and Ronny Johnsen, only for Gary Neville to make a covering tackle near the penalty spot. The defending by both teams had been exceptional.

The replay was at the same ground the following Wednesday night and Wenger restored Petit after his suspension. Alex Ferguson switched his attack, bringing in Sheringham, Solskjær and left-winger Jesper Blomqvist, all of whom played well in the first half. After seventeen minutes Beckham played a cute one-two with his mate Sheringham and then curled a 25-yard shot past Seaman. As passions spilt over Elleray dished out four yellow cards in seven minutes: Stam, Keown, Keane and Beckham went into his book. Then Bergkamp equalised after 69 minutes with a shot that took a big deflection off Stam, and four minutes later Keane was sent off for a rash tackle on Overmars, who had come on for Ljungberg.

Arsenal now had their strongest team on the field, the eleven who had won the Double, facing ten men with the score balanced at 1–1. It was a huge opportunity for victory and they almost took it. Ray Parlour had played with more bottle than craft, but in injury time he dribbled straight at Phil Neville in the box, swerved to the right, and Neville tripped him. Elleray gave the penalty. It was clear-cut and nobody protested.

Dennis Bergkamp had missed three of his last five penalties. One of those had been saved only the week before by Blackburn's John Filan, and now he had a penalty to take him back to Wembley for a repeat of the FA Cup Final he had missed through injury a year ago. He stood well back, looking composed, an erect, blond gladiator faced by a dead ball and a great Dane. The game was in stoppage time. If he scored, United could not come back. He ran up, struck the ball firmly to his right – and Schmeichel saved it. What drama!

The Dutchman had played superbly up to that point, and he continued to play well in extra time. He hit a fierce shot which Schmeichel saved. The unmarked Keown muffed a header from Parlour's cross, and when a Petit corner bounced and hit Johnsen the rebound flew towards Schmeichel, who parried it; Butt hooked away. Then a Bergkamp pass just eluded Petit in the box.

In the second half of extra time Patrick Vieira made the most catastrophic pass of his career. His tired crossfield ball was intercepted by substitute Ryan Giggs, who cruised past a desperate Vieira, swerved between Dixon and Keown, accelerated towards the corner of the six-yard box and hit a thunderous shot past Seaman at his near post. This strike, after a sensational slalom through the best defence in Europe, was the finest goal of Ryan Giggs's career because it was spectacular, because it was the most important and because it catapulted United into a position where the mythical treble was now a possibility. The title, the FA Cup and the Champions League were now within their grasp.

When Sky's George Gavin spoke to Wenger after the final whistle he looked and sounded very flat but spoke in a dignified way. 'It is not easy to take a defeat, but what you can demand of your team is that they give everything. They are very sad today of course because it was not our night at all and we were really, I think, unlucky. The two teams are very close to each other, it was a smashing game, and in the end the luckiest won. We had the chances to win. Especially, we had the penalty with a minute to go. So you expect, of course, to win the game. But that's football. We were a little bit unlucky, lost the ball in the middle of the park and Giggs did the rest. There were one or two rebounds for him, but Giggs is a great player. It was a fantastic goal. They have so many qualities in the middle of the park and up front that every ball you lose is dangerous. But there's no reproach. I would just like to congratulate my team. They were fantastic. They are very sad tonight. They have shown again they are a great team. Sometimes you can say that when you lose.'

Can you pick them up for the remaining league games?

'That's part of our job. We want to win, and if you want to win you have, of course, to survive disappointments. And we have to show that in the next game, that we can react. When you lose, of course you're very sad. But, at the moment, it's history. We just have to look forward.'

Alex Ferguson praised the courage and commitment of his team and defended the resting of Cole, Yorke and Giggs for the following week's Champions League semi-final against Juventus, as he had every right to do. He had been a manager since he took over at East Stirlingshire in 1974, and he knew that winning the game always justifies your team selection. 'I think we deserved the win,' he said. 'Over the two legs I think we were the better team. The players have played in agony to get the victory. Ryan Giggs has injured himself near the end also. There's a lot of pain in there. The two strikers and Blomqvist were magnificent. If I don't play them when they're playing well, when do I play them? Do you wait till you lose a game? No, you play them now.' Rotation had worked well for Ferguson that night, and the subject, already much discussed at Stamford Bridge, would become a big theme in English football over the coming three years as Liverpool, Leeds and Arsenal all became able to afford four good strikers.

Two years later I talked to Sky Sports commentator Martin Tyler about the Arsenal–Manchester United rivalry, particularly the crucial Old Trafford game in March 1998 and the 1999 FA Cup semi-final replay. Television is more important than the newspapers, so managers do the Sky and BBC interviews before they talk to the press. The broadcasters therefore see them immediately after matches when the adrenalin is still flowing, not twenty or thirty minutes later, so Tyler's impressions were illuminating.

'The win at Old Trafford in 1998 was really the key game because Arsenal had never scored a Premiership goal at Old Trafford up to that point. And Overmars was exceptional, which wasn't always the case away from home. But it didn't look as if it was gonna produce a goal. Then it did, and that shot of the Arsenal fans that Sky have used over and over again in the titles, of that demented guy behind the goal where Overmars scored, sums up what it meant to everybody. Then they believed they could win the league. Manninger played brilliantly in that game as well. Not with a great deal to do, but he came out at Andy Cole's feet when he broke away in the first half.

'Arsenal had the Indian sign on United until Dennis Bergkamp's penalty was saved by Schmeichel. I've never seen Wenger more angry after a game than that night. Not just losing the Cup, but losing that edge that they had over Manchester United. They'd had a very good recent record and they beat them again in the Charity Shield. The general feeling around that time was that the best Arsenal would beat the best Manchester United. That seems an extraordinary thing to say now. But through 1998 and 1999 that was what many people believed – if Arsenal got their best team out, which they didn't always do.'

There was a slightly strange, subdued atmosphere at Highbury on Monday, 19 April, everyone still digesting the disappointment of losing the semi-final. Wenger rested Anelka and Wimbledon played more defensively than they had ever done at Highbury, so Arsenal had to play a much slower, more patient passing game based around Kanu, who allowed everybody to link in and have a shot. Arsenal notched up 34 goal attempts, eighteen on target, and won 5–1. They followed that by going to Middlesbrough and winning 6–1, Kanu scoring memorably by flicking Parlour's cross between his own legs and into the far side of the goal. Anelka's reaction to being dropped against Wimbledon was to play out of his skin at Middlesbrough and score twice.

On Saturday, 1 May, Ian Wright surpassed all his misdemeanours at Arsenal after being sent off the pitch just twelve minutes into West Ham's game with Leeds by referee Rob Harris. Wright went straight to the referee's changing room and damaged his clothes. Harris was in his first season as a Premiership official and had showed Wright a second yellow card for 'acting in an aggressive manner towards an opponent'. Two other West Ham players were also sent off. Leeds won 5–1.

The following day, a warm, sleepy Sunday afternoon, Arsenal played Derby, Kanu starting the game with Bergkamp on the bench. Anelka put them ahead from a Parlour cross in fifteen minutes, and after that they emphasised accuracy and possession more than usual, spurting forward as spaces allowed, but mostly playing save-your-legs football, leaving Overmars to jog in the shade of the West Stand. Wenger said his team had suffered a lot from the heat and needed that special strength they had at the back. On Derby, he said, 'They know how to lose 1–0 here. They don't let us score the second goal.'

Wenger had crossed swords with Alex Ferguson and Alan Curbishley earlier in the season, and now, in the last month, he found he had upset Chelsea chairman Ken Bates by making some comments over the weekend about escalating wage bills in the Premiership. Bates was furious at headlines like WENGER AC-CUSES CHELSEA OF CHEATING, and he told the *Mirror*, 'He is an idiot for calling us cheats and he's also out of order because, as I recall, when he was coach at Monaco they survived on gates of 3,500 – because they were funded by Prince Rainier.' In his defence, Wenger said, 'I didn't mention Chelsea at all in what I said, or maybe once when I was asked about them and I answered that I did not know if they had an extra income. I also said that if clubs spent more than they can afford then that is nearly cheating, but I didn't mention any particular club. If Ken Bates is thinking of suing me then he must be a very sensitive boy, but I am not worried about what he says.'

SPURS 1 ARSENAL 3

A very good game. I thought Arsenal, in the first half, outstanding. On the break they were real, real quality tonight . . .

George Graham

Arsenal had been holding back during the heatwave against Derby because Wenger had always planned to play high-tempo football at Spurs on 5 May, a night game which would be much faster and fiercer. They put on a superb exhibition of collective commitment, pace and one-touch passing.

After sixteen minutes Petit took off on a powerhouse sprint, controlled Bergkamp's devastating pass with one touch and lifted it over Walker for 1–0. When Bergkamp's pass split Spurs again, Anelka powered through and finished with a flourish, an imperious flicked shot that looked so casual, as if he had done it a hundred times. Spurs were pressing, pressing, pressing, desperately chasing the ball, trying to close the gap in class through sheer energy. Then Vieira put an arm on the dribbling Ginola, who immediately crumpled, and a harsh free-kick was awarded. Darren Anderton's shot from 25 yards was very well placed, bouncing and skidding past Seaman into the bottom corner. Just before half-time Tim Sherwood elbowed Dixon and threw the ball in his face. From the kick-off, Anderton tangled with Vieira, who fell, Sherwood steamed in and, with the ball about six feet away, kicked Vieira in the groin area while he was on the ground. Petit was outraged and got a yellow card in a scuffle. Vieira had treatment for two minutes.

Dennis Bergkamp was also fiery, focused and explosive, playing as he had in the replay against Manchester United. Remarkably, he had already, in an hour, headed the ball more often than he had in all his 26 Premiership games that season. After 75 minutes Kanu came on for the Dutchman, but he only got one kick in eleven minutes until, suddenly, he produced a moment of genius. He controlled the ball on his chest, let it bounce, flicked it up over Luke Young's head and rammed his shot past Ian Walker for 3–1.

The 4,000 Gooners in the corner were celebrating happily enough, singing, 'We beat the scum three one!' and then suddenly pandemonium reigned there, the area transformed into a pulsating mass of jumping bodies and laughing faces. This could mean only one thing: Liverpool must have drawn! The final score from Anfield was indeed Liverpool 2 Manchester United 2, and the over-excited Gooners began to chant, 'Champions! Champions!'

The Arsenal players had given a performance of tremendous steel and nerve. George Graham, the master tactician who had so craftily squeezed the channels at Highbury to dig out a 0–0 in November, had got it all wrong in May because you should never defend that high up against pace. It was suicidal. Arsène Wenger, in contrast, was as satisfied as he ever will be in N17, talking about how thrilled he was with the first-half performance. 'Our passing was excellent, our runs were great, and every time we got through the first defending of Tottenham we were dangerous. So to go back at half-time with 2–1 was very difficult. We needed to be very strong mentally. We came back to the dressing room thinking it should have been 4–0, and it was 2–1. Of course we expected a reaction of Tottenham in the second half. They fought very hard and we had to be strong and well organised in the second half, and wait for our chance. Again we missed chances in the first twenty minutes, but after Kanu came on we scored the third goal. That killed it.'

Do you think you have a psychological advantage over Manchester United going into the last week?

'I don't know. We are consistent for a long, long time now, and we have to keep that consistency till the end. But we are not the only ones who are consistent because Manchester United has lost only three games, Chelsea as well lost only three games. It's difficult to predict now who will win it, and how they will win it.'

But surely it's in your own hands again? If you keep winning, and win by enough goals, you will win the championship.

'That's what we have to try. But don't forget that they have one more game to play, so if they win their games they have more chances to score goals. So that's why I think it's still in their hands.'

Brian Woolnough then asked him if there was a key to the victory over Spurs.

'The key was that maybe they played very high, and we found the space behind them with Dennis dropping off and finding Marc

Overmars, Ray Parlour and Nicolas Anelka with their runs. Because they played in a very high position. So as long as we could find Dennis when we won the ball, and he could feed our strikers, we were very dangerous.'

Graham was generous in defeat but showed flashes of anger when he talked about the first and third goals conceded by his side. 'A very good game. I thought Arsenal, in the first half, outstanding. On the break they were real, real quality tonight, especially in the first half. We got into the game just before half-time with a good free-kick, gave us a lift. I told the boys, second half, to be more positive. Second half, for half an hour, 35 minutes, I thought we did well. I thought we did very well. And then they broke again with real quality players.

'I thought some of the defending tonight was schoolboy. I really did. I thought it was disgraceful. I thought the first goal – on the training pitch I would sort it out in no time. And the last goal, terrible defending. There were too many chances. Arsenal had lots of chances tonight. I thought the back four were not good enough. But I'd give Arsenal credit for assembling a very strong squad there. Not only talented, but physically very strong, so they can take you on. Whatever way you wanna play it, they've got the answer to you.'

TITLE RACE GOES TO THE LAST DAY

Our contest with Arsenal is almost over. We've played Juventus, Inter Milan, Barcelona and Bayern Munich this season, but if I had to nominate the toughest side we have faced it would be Arsenal.

Jaap Stam

There was a rumour flying around that George Graham had said privately that Wenger would quit Arsenal when the legendary back four packed up, but Graham was too shrewd to say something like that in public. Remarkably, David O'Leary had no such inhibitions. Before the Leeds–Arsenal clash on 11 May, the penultimate game of the season, he said, 'Arsène has done a fantastic job but he has a lot of old defenders and there is a risk that they will all go at the same time. People say it's half the team, but for me it's more than that. In terms of resilience and discipline and all those things I learned at Highbury, it is *the* team. Replacing them is going to be a big job and a long job, and it may be that Arsène won't want the challenge of it. That's why I feel that Manchester United, with many more younger players, are better positioned in the long term.'

On the night, Leeds pressed so ferociously that Arsenal had Parlour, Petit and Vieira booked in the first 36 minutes. That was inhibiting, but it was an exciting match, despite the abysmal refereeing of Gary Willard, who took the names of nine players. Keown flattened Harry Kewell with a wild tackle in the box on 45 minutes, but Ian Harte blasted his penalty against the bar, and when Hasselbaink followed up Seaman made a superb save. Two minutes before that Seaman had made another miraculous save from a Kewell thirty-yarder which was flashing into the top corner.

The game changed after Kanu came on for Overmars and made some fabulous passes. Diawara also came on, for Parlour, and went close with a header which shaved the bar. Nigel Martyn saved at Kanu's feet and Jonathan Woodgate headed a Diawara shot off the line. But the turning point came on 75 minutes. Winterburn was lying on his back after a tackle and Alfie Haaland ran over him, smashing his knee into Winterburn's face and demolishing his nose. Doctors were called and play was held up for five minutes before the bloodstained left-back was taken off, to be replaced by Vivas. The delay interrupted Arsenal's rhythm at a crucial time, and after 86 minutes Harry Kewell crossed from the left and Vivas got on the wrong side of Hasselbaink, whose diving header killed Arsenal's title hopes.

Would Hasselbaink have scored that winner had Nigel Winterburn still been on the field? Wenger thought not. 'We made a huge tactical mistake at the far post,' he said. 'Vivas was not well positioned for the cross, but it's unbelievable that we made so many chances and did not score. We are guilty of not taking our chances.'

The Frenchman knew that his team now needed a miracle to retain the championship after their first defeat in the league since Aston Villa on 13 December. He said, 'We have given Manchester United the chance to win it now. I don't expect them to lose against Blackburn tonight and a point will be good enough for them. If they win, then the title will be over because I cannot see Spurs doing us a favour at Old Trafford on Sunday.' But he added, 'Everything is possible, and you have to be optimistic. If I was not optimistic I would not have survived sixteen years in management. But I would have to say that it's seventy per cent certain that Manchester United will get something out of the game at Ewood Park and only thirty per cent for Blackburn having a chance to win it. I would not bet all my money on Blackburn tomorrow night, but you never know. I will watch the game on television and hope. If Manchester United win, we will have to rely on Spurs, and I don't think they will go there and win. I just hope they fight like Leeds fought against us.'

Blackburn had been champions in 1995, but now they were at the foot of the table, having sacked Roy Hodgson and hired Brian Kidd, Ferguson's number two, in December. They needed to win to stay in the Premiership, but in the event they could only hold United to a 0–0 draw.

So the closest title race of the nineties went to the final day of the season, Arsenal trailing Manchester United by one point. Jaap Stam wrote a column in the *Telegraph*, saying 'Our contest with Arsenal is almost over. We've played Juventus, Inter Milan, Barcelona and Bayern Munich this season, but if I had to nominate the toughest side we have faced it would be Arsenal. They have quality running through the side and enormous self-belief which shows itself in their determination to win every game.' Arsenal were at home to Aston Villa, United at home to Tottenham. Would Spurs shock everyone by beating United to win the title for Arsenal? Strange things happen in football, but that would have been the strangest of all time.

Vivas continued at left-back against Villa, but when he suffered an injury Arsenal were totally disrupted. Petit went to left-back, Parlour moved inside and Ljungberg went wide right. As usual they struggled to create openings against Villa's three centre-backs.

In Manchester, George Graham had taken David Ginola off after four minutes because he was injured following (wait for it) a little push in the back from Gary Neville. Did Graham think Ginola might slam in one of his 25-yard thunderbolts to grab the headlines with a goal that would live for ever in the annals of infamy? With Ginola, you never knew. Could he be trusted to shoot over the bar as usual when a chance came? Graham apparently thought not, but of course nothing much, if anything, was ever said about that deeply mysterious substitution.

Back at Highbury, the highlight of the first half came after nineteen minutes when the stadium erupted at the news from Old Trafford: Les Ferdinand had scored! Four words that must never, never be spoken inside Highbury were now being muttered by thousands of people: Come on you Spurs!

Patrick Vieira miscontrolled a couple of early balls and then recovered to become the game's best player. He had a rocket shot saved by keeper Michael Oakes, a header kicked off the line, and later on he powered past Ugo Ehiogu and won a corner off Southgate. After the corner he had two more shots blocked. He had reinvented his partnership with Petit in this game, moving to left midfield to keep in close contact after the Golden Ponytail had been re-deployed at left-back.

David Beckham made it 1–1 at Old Trafford late in the first half, then the Arsenal crowd heard that Andy Cole had made it 2–1. Arsenal, meanwhile, continued to dominate Villa without scoring. Then Kanu came on to conjure a goal yet again, flicking in from three yards after a Petit corner.

So the last day of the season produced what Arsène Wenger had expected: Arsenal had won and Manchester United had won. Suddenly the tension and struggle and drama was all over. After a long, exciting season and some thrilling team performances, the final day turned out to be a victorious anti-climax.

In 1997/98 Arsenal had lost six games and become champions. Now they had lost four and finished runners-up with 78 points, the same number that had won the title a year before. They were unbeaten at home and had the best defence in Europe. In 38 games they had conceded only seventeen goals and diehard Gooners reckoned that phenomenal record the swansong of the greatest defence the world had ever seen.

Wenger was left feeling deeply dismayed that Arsenal had been unable to beat Kiev or Lens, but he was proud that his players had pushed Manchester United all the way in the Premiership. He had continued to play attractive power football, Anelka had developed rapidly, and the style was very exciting and penetrating. Other managers had begun to read his tactics and learned how to nullify Arsenal, so when the team stuttered they looked one-dimensional, lacking creativity, and collective confidence drained away. Then Wenger signed Kanu, who made a goal against Manchester United in his first game in February and became the team's supersub and talisman. If Arsenal needed a goal, Wenger put Kanu on and he usually scored or made one. So Wenger had kept faith with power football with an ace up his sleeve, an alternative, a Plan B – the Nigerian had scored six Premiership goals in five starts and seven sub appearances.

Most serious managers do an audit of their results when the last ball has been kicked, and Wenger must have wished he could have signed Kanu sooner. He had scored his first Premiership goal on 9 March when there were only eleven games left. Had Kanu arrived earlier and started playing in, say, November he would surely have made a difference in at least one of the 0–0 draws against Tottenham, Derby and Liverpool. If not, a single goal in the 1–1 draw with Middlesbrough might have been enough, in the final audit, to make the difference between winning the Premiership and losing it by one point.

Wenger also recalled the defeat at Aston Villa in December after Arsenal held a 2–0 lead and the 1–0 defeat at Wimbledon in November just before the Lens game. 'You are bound to think about these things,' he said, 'but, all in all, the team has performed magnificently. We had a slow start and the World Cup unquestionably affected some of our most important players. But losing the championship so narrowly is like losing a race by a yard.'

THE ANELKA TRANSFER SAGA

Real Madrid have not been in touch with Arsenal so there is nothing legal in what they are doing. The player has a four-year contract and any direct approach to the player is illegal.

Arsène Wenger

Back in April, Wenger had defended Anelka staunchly and shown huge tolerance. 'He is not an arrogant guy,' the manager insisted.

'He is reliable and shy, much more sensitive than people think. I sometimes put myself in his position and he is amazing for a twenty-year-old. He doesn't drink, he doesn't smoke, he is at training every day, he has played nearly every game this season. That deserves a lot of respect.'

But now the young striker said he was very unhappy. In mid-May, when Arsenal were on tour in Malaysia, Anelka said, 'The English press causes me enormous problems on a personal level. As they aren't going to stop, that marks out my road for me. The English journalists are all rubbish. They are frustrated players who never made it as professionals. It is pure jealousy.' Wenger immediately told Anelka to grow up and stop moaning. 'Anelka has no right to complain. The press has treated him relatively well. He has not been harassed or blamed. Invoking the press to justify leaving the club is a bad reason. They will be worse anywhere else. Leaving Arsenal would be an enormous strategic error. Here he is guaranteed the Champions League and is part of a strong team. He still has progress to make. I'm sure that if I chat to him, he will say he wants to stay. I think he's ninety per cent certain to stay.'

In the meantime, Wenger re-signed Bould, Winterburn and Dixon, all of whom were over the age of 35, on one-year contracts. 'I want at least three new signings for next season,' Wenger added, 'because the fixture list is crazy and we will need some experienced players, especially in the Champions League.' He was weighing up a possible £1.8 million bid for Dynamo Kiev right-back and captain Oleg Luzhny, even though that contradicted his policy of not signing players over thirty. The Ukrainian, at the age of thirty, was signed on 28 May. Wenger warned again that next season's expanded Champions League would be very demanding physically because clubs would be playing matches every week rather than once a fortnight. He reckoned that clubs would now need eighteen players of comparable quality. 'No one can really evaluate the influence of a weekly European game on the Premiership. Rotation of the squad will be a necessity. It will be very physically demanding and there will be more competition for places. Oleg is an important addition to our squad. He is a quality defender with vast experience at both international and club levels. He's a top-quality player and the price was right.'

The day after Luzhny was signed, Juventus refused to dismiss reports that representatives of the club were planning to visit London the following week to discuss a deal for Anelka. Their director-general, Luciano Moggi, said, 'I will not deny it but I will not confirm it either. I don't want to say anything as it might cause confusion.' Real Madrid had apparently agreed a £3 million-a-season deal with Anelka and his agents. This seemed a strange call by Madrid, since they already had two young strikers, Raúl and Morientes, friends who passed to each other. How would Anelka fit into that? Madrid were ready to make a £14 million bid, but this outrageous policy of negotiating with Anelka before agreeing a transfer fee with Arsenal left Wenger furious and meant that David Dein was more likely to do business with the elegant Italian Roberto Bettega, who had played with Liam Brady at Juventus in the 70s.

Wenger was, of course, still looking for new players himself. He was said to admire left-back Gianluca Pessotto, midfielder Edgar Davids and winger Thierry Henry, and the Arsenal manager was in Turin to watch Juventus play Udinese in a play-off to decide which club would be in next season's UEFA Cup. Juventus lost out, a dire situation for a club which had been Champions League winners in 1996 and finalists in 1997 and 1998. Wenger had agreed terms for Pessotto the previous summer, only for Juventus to pull out at the last moment.

On Thursday, 3 June, Anelka was with his national team in Clairefontaine, south-west of Paris, and was quoted as saying, 'I'd be surprised if I stayed at Arsenal. Coming here, I said to myself it could be the last time I left London. I think things are going to be settled in the coming days.' Arsenal supporters were told that Real Madrid had begun to talk wages with Anelka's agents three weeks ago, and Real claimed to have spoken to Arsenal. Real president Lorenzo Sanz said, 'It's true that we've started negotiations with directors of Arsenal. We still haven't made an offer so reports of Arsenal rejecting a bid are false. We continue working to bring him here.' But Wenger, who was now understood to want £20 million for Anelka, was talking to Juventus, who valued him at £15 million. Meanwhile, Anelka was saying, 'I want to go to Spain and nowhere else. Italy doesn't interest me. I don't like the game they play there. Spain corresponds more to my style of play. Strikers score more often, there are more spaces in defence, a bit like England.'

On Friday, 4 June, Wenger called for a FIFA investigation into 'illegal' approaches by Real Madrid, even though the results of such an investigation would probably not be available for weeks as FIFA usually handled more than a hundred disputes between players, clubs and agents at any one time. 'Real Madrid have not been in touch with Arsenal,' Wenger said, 'so there is nothing legal in what they are doing. The player has a four-year contract and any direct approach to the player is illegal. We will ask FIFA to look into this. What I should say to Real Madrid is that they should concentrate on solving their own financial situation, which is not very good. Nicolas is an Arsenal player. What is real is that the player knows what he is doing when he signs a contract. The basic thing is to respect the rules. You have to do what is legal. That is what we try to do. We don't expect any presents from clubs. As we speak, Nicolas is at Arsenal. If he is unfortunate enough to pick up a serious injury playing for France today, will Real Madrid pay his money? Of course not, it will be Arsenal.'

Meanwhile, talks took place in London between David Dein, Lazio director Massimo Cragnotti (the son of club president Sergio Cragnotti) and Vicenzo Morabito, the agent acting for Lazio, who had recently received £31 million from Inter for Christian Vieri, although Diego Simeone, rated at £7 million, went the other way as part of that world record deal. Dein and Wenger had decided to use the Vieri fee as a benchmark. By mid-June we were being told that Wenger rated Anelka at £28 million and that Dein had considered Lazio's £21 million cash offer for 24 hours before turning it down.

These hikes in prices were made not just to keep pace with market value, but also, in all probability, because of reflection on the Arsenal manager's part. He had, after all, hugely improved the young French striker through his coaching and advice, and Anelka's form during March, April and May had been awesome at times. Wenger had groomed him into the ideal centre-forward for a stylish power team which played the football Wenger had always dreamt about, football with speed, skill, energy, unstoppable attacks, unplayable strikers – the geometry of devastation, a high-powered football machine with enough momentum to blow the opposition away. Anelka's international career had taken off and he had played for France in a Euro 2000 qualifier in Moscow in October 1998, scoring the first goal in a 3–2 victory, and now he was playing against Russia in Paris. Petit and Wiltord scored but Anelka did not, which was hardly surprising with everything that was going on.

Also in June, midfielder Dietmar Hamann, who had joined Newcastle the previous summer for £4.5 million from Bayern Munich on a five-year contract, took the liberty of telling a German magazine that Arsenal were interested in him. Hamann, 25, said, 'Newcastle know what I want, and that is to leave. I can play Champions League football for Arsenal and that would be better for me and my career.'

Claude and Didier Anelka, Nicolas's brothers and agents, were proving to be utterly intransigent in the continuing negotiations with the Italian clubs and had sent a fax to Highbury saying, 'Nicolas does not want to play in Italy, he will never go to Italy. He wants to go to Real Madrid. That is the choice of his heart.' Claude, 31, was the elder brother, a former aspiring professional whose career was ended by injury. He was a part-time DJ at The Spot, a Covent Garden nightclub, and played Sunday football in North London with club owner David Blackwood. Didier, 29, had business qualifications and had negotiated with Madrid.

When this fax was delivered, Wenger was still trying to sign Roberto Muzzi for £7 million. With Lazio now threatening to withdraw their £21 million offer for Anelka, Wenger and Dein invited the young Frenchman to a crunch meeting in Paris which would decide his future, the Arsenal manager again expressing his shock at the underhand way in which Real's Sanz had courted Anelka. 'They are a big club run by little men. What they are doing is out of order.' Sergio Cragnotti had understandably refused to meet Real's demands for a £6 million payment to 'buy out' their option on Anelka.

Incredibly, agent Marc Roger now suggested that the striker could take Arsenal to the FIFA court for demanding that he observe the four-year contract he had signed only six months ago. Wenger must have wondered what planet all these people lived on. What a way to spend a summer! Still, there was better news when Cagliari agreed to accept £10 million for Roberto Muzzi.

On Tuesday, 22 June, Arsenal issued a statement saying that Anelka would be staying at Highbury. 'In the light of recent media reports, Arsenal FC would like to stress that it is our wish to retain the services of Nicolas Anelka. On Nicolas's impending return from holiday the situation regarding his future at Arsenal FC will be discussed and resolved.' This threat was enough to persuade the Anelka brothers to make a U-turn and agree to sign for Lazio. It looked as if Dein and Wenger had at last won the most squalid transfer battle in British football history.

In the last six weeks Wenger's frustrations had mounted as Anelka refused to speak directly to him or to David Dein while insisting that he would only move to Real Madrid, but now a resolution was in sight. As Nicolas and Didier prepared for their flight to Rome to meet Lazio officials, Anelka was all of a sudden singing a new song. 'Lazio are a prestigious club,' he said, 'and their squad is full of star players. I like their coach, Sven-Goran Eriksson, who has been successful wherever he has worked. I know what a fantastic city Rome is but above all it would be wonderful for me to play alongside Marcelo Salas. I still need to clarify my situation at Arsenal, then I will make up my mind.'

Wenger was by now desperate to complete the transfer so that he could concentrate on finding a replacement. Roberto Muzzi was still a strong possibility, and he still believed that Robbie Fowler could be available if the price was right. But Anelka was still proving elusive. By now it was obvious that Claude and Didier, knowing how persuasive Wenger could be when talking to footballers, wanted to make sure that their younger brother did not talk to the man who had trusted in his talent and made him France's top striker. The player Wenger had described as reliable and shy only ten weeks before was now hidden away in Martinique. In the *Mail on Sunday* on 27 June reporters David

Walker and Bob Cass discovered this and wrote a story under the headline ANELKA ON CHEAP TRIP THAT LEADS TO A FORTUNE, which made the whole story seem like a bizarre soap opera in which three scheming French brothers had made sure they were incommunicado. The Anelkas were staying at Buccaneers' Creek, 'a £56-a-night economy-class hotel' where there were no telephones in the bedrooms, so negotiations had to be conducted solely by mobile phone. This scenario made them seem subversive, as if it was a kidnapping. The brothers continued to talk to Lazio officials, who said a deal was imminent.

Wenger was on holiday in the Riviera, recovering from a knee operation, and he said that Anelka was risking his international career by leaving Arsenal. 'Two weeks ago, I was sure Anelka was going to stay, but today I'm a little more pessimistic because he is showing a real determination to leave us. By leaving us, Nicolas is taking a real risk, knowing that at the end of the season there is the Euro 2000 tournament.'

It was then reported that Real Madrid had pulled out of the chase, and that Lazio could now pay less than the £23.5 million they had offered the week before. A fee of around £20 million was now expected to clinch the deal. On 29 June Anelka was insisting that Arsenal could not complain about illegal approaches made to him since that was how Wenger acquired him in the first place. 'All the clubs do that,' he said. 'Arsenal did the same thing with me to get me to leave Paris Saint Germain. My priority is to join Real Madrid, but if that does not work out, why not Lazio? I prefer that than to return to Arsenal. I would have no problem going to Italy. I always planned to play there one day.'

These shabby events left Wenger in an extremely vulnerable position. July had begun, and the shrewd team-builder who had reconstructed his side so brilliantly two summers before found himself in a situation where he did not have Anelka or a replacement or the money to buy a replacement. He was now said to be keen on Brazilian striker Christian, 23, of Internacional of Porto Alegre.

On Sunday, 4 July, Anelka told the *Corriere dello Sport* that talks over his move to Lazio had stalled, partly because of new interest shown by Juventus and Parma. He admitted, however, that he thought Arsène Wenger a reasonable man. 'He's got the ability to listen to others. He's very fair. He's understood the reasons for my decision. I think that by Tuesday the transfer will all be sorted out. I'm an Arsenal player, but their club officials have to listen to my desires and to respect my wishes.' Of Dein, he said, 'He wants all the money he can possibly get out of the transfer.'

The next day Anelka went further, accusing Dein of thinking of 'money, money and only money'. 'David Dein is keeping this deal from going through because he wants to make as much out of it as possible. We were supposed to complete the transfer on Friday, but Arsenal got late inquiries from Juventus and Parma, so they asked for more time. It does not matter, however, because I want to play for Lazio. Arsenal are a big club, but Lazio have a virtual dream-team, filled with world-class players. It will be an honour to play alongside them.'

By Tuesday there was a new twist: Lazio had offered Arsenal a player plus £20 million. Wenger wanted Marcelo Salas, who was not available; Cragnotti offered one out of Alen Boksic, Fernando Couto, Pavel Nedved and Kennet Andersson.

Former Arsenal striker Alan Smith, who had played with Adams and Dixon in the 1989 championship-winning team, then entered the fray via his *Telegraph* column, lamenting the anti-social personality of Anelka, who always gave one-word answers when team-mates tried to make casual conversation, and the fact that he had no pals at the club apart from David Grondin, the young left-back who had recently been loaned back to St Etienne. He said that Anelka had never understood English dressing-room humour and thought that everyone was taking the mickey out of him. Smith wrote, 'On one occasion last year, as the team bus prepared to depart for an away game, somebody noticed that Anelka was missing. He was refusing to travel. Wenger had to get off and try to coax the player, via his brother, on to the coach. He did eventually succeed but only after listening to Nicolas's gripes about how the entire team disliked him. The times the loner did make it on to the bus, his first move was always to quickly slip on some headphones and watch a film intensely on his laptop. For the next four hours or so his eyes would never leave the screen.'

Early that July, Wenger sold Steve Bould to Sunderland for £400,000. The big defender had another twelve months of his contract to run, but Peter Reid had offered him regular first-team football. 'Arsène has been top class,' said Bould, who was 36. 'He said that if someone came in for me he would let me go if that's what I wanted. It's a chance of regular first-team football. But it was Arsène's fitness regime which has probably extended my career by two years, maybe more.' Bould, when asked, said he was convinced Anelka would be better off remaining at Highbury for the time being. 'I wish he was staying at Arsenal because he is a great player. I believe another two years under Wenger would have done him big favours. It's all about money, though. Football is big business, and who can knock him for what he is going to earn?' The solidarity expressed in that last line might have shocked some fans, but the game had been all about money for a long time.

Anelka's next move was to threaten a legal case that would allow him to join Lazio for no transfer fee, a development that was more extraordinary than anything that had happened so far. His lawyer, Marguerite Fauconette, said that she had discovered an obscure European employment law which would allow Anelka to walk out on Arsenal simply by paying them three months' wages in compensation (around £200,000). However, it turned out that any legal battle would be a test case because that particular European agreement did not yet apply in the United Kingdom.

Arsenal had by now suggested a swap deal involving a fee of £15 million plus striker Alen Boksic as one way to end the stalemate, but Boksic did not want to leave Rome. By this time Roberto Muzzi had said that he would rather join Udinese; Wenger had been interested in Inter Milan's young hot-shot Andrea Pirlo and Greek striker Nikos Maklas, a prolific goal poacher for Vitesse Arnhem who had just been signed by Ajax for £5 million. David Dein, however, was still holding out for £22 million from Lazio, with Didier Anelka saying, 'Nicolas wants to go to Italy and has definitely chosen Lazio for the seriousness and importance of the club. And also for the players who will be around him there. Nicolas wants the best, and today the best is Lazio.'

By Monday, 12 July, Dein was apparently ready to call Lazio's bluff and keep Anelka at Arsenal if the Italians did not increase their bid, although Cragnotti was saying, 'I will be making a new offer to Arsenal for Anelka tonight. We will make a small improvement to the offer but it will be our final offer and if that is not accepted by tomorrow night we will leave the negotiating table.' Dein was confident that Juventus would still top Lazio's highest bid, and since Wenger wanted Thierry Henry, that would be a better deal for Arsenal. Time, however, was running out and all the available strikers were being signed up.

Cragnotti then faxed Dein to inform him that unless Arsenal lowered their asking price of £22 million there was no possibility of a deal being done. The agents, Marc Roger and the Anelka brothers, were insisting on a huge cut for themselves, so Cragnotti was understood to have told Dein that 'the offer of £18 million cannot be modified due to budgetary restrictions and on account of the heavy commission that Lazio would have to pay to the agents of Nicolas Anelka'. The size of this commission was variously reported as £5 million and £6.5 million.

On Thursday, 15 July, lawyer Alisdair Bell, an adviser to UEFA, warned Anelka that he would not be able to walk out of his contract. 'George Michael tried to walk out on his contract with Sony and he wasn't able to,' said Bell. 'That incident is a good comparison to this. Michael demanded the same thing as Anelka is demanding now, and that result was subject to English law, as will this one. Being tied to a record company is like being tied to a football club – you can't just walk out.' Bell believed that if Anelka's move to Lazio did not happen the best he could hope to do was buy himself out of his Arsenal contract.

Anelka versus Arsenal had turned into an extraordinary battle of wills, a game played for very high stakes, but the saga had by now become extremely tiresome for everyone and the club had started to take some flak. In June it had been said that the Anelkas were greedy, but by mid-July people had started to say that Arsenal were greedy as well.

Over the weekend Lazio made their 'final final' offer, which still fell £4 million short of Arsenal's asking price. But this time

Cragnotti cleverly guaranteed to pay Arsenal the difference, in cash, if Lazio sold Anelka before 2003, which reflected Lazio's sensitivity to Arsenal's suspicion that their aim was to make a quick profit in an inflationary transfer market. Cragnotti's personal spokesman said, 'David Dein has been going round all over Europe saying we just want to make money out of Anelka, so we are offering to pay the difference if he leaves.'

Meanwhile, Wenger signed 25-year-old Brazilian left-back Silvinho from Corinthians for £4 million and established a training camp in Lyon to prepare for friendly matches against newly promoted St Etienne on 24 July and Monaco on 26 July. He now had to figure out which of his new players would be in the team and how they would manage without their main goalscorer. Life with Anelka had been difficult at times, but he would be hard to replace. Bergkamp and Overmars were injured for the St Etienne game, so he picked Kanu and Ljungberg up front with Silvinho on the left wing. The full team was: Seaman; Luzhny, Keown, Grimandi, Winterburn; Parlour, Vieira, Petit, Silvinho; Kanu, Ljungberg.

Wenger knew that the threat of Anelka's pace had dictated the shape of many Arsenal games, making them less compressed so that Vieira and the others had more space in midfield. The loss of their speedy striker therefore had a big impact all over the field. If Arsenal stopped attacking at lightning speed and played more passes, they were more likely to lose the ball in dangerous areas and be subjected to counter-attacks at times when they had too few players behind the ball. Indeed, both St Etienne goals in a 2–2 draw came that way. The keeper hoofed a big ball downfield, Luzhny headed forward, Vieira tried a risky short touch to Petit, the ball was intercepted and Aloisio scored. Then Vieira chested a ball and was fouled, Aloisio flicked the ball behind Grimandi and Revelles spun into space and hit a volley past Seaman from sixteen yards. Arsenal were 2–0 down after nine minutes and playing like strangers. Then Petit intercepted and Kanu produced a classy left-foot shot. Kanu then had another shot saved, but Ljungberg volleyed in the rebound. It was a very untidy game in which Parlour, who usually worked well with Bergkamp and Anelka, looked lost. After the goals the contest fizzled out in a parade of substitutes.

For the game against Monaco in Clermont Ferrand Boa Morte was up front alongside Kanu. Unfortunately, half of Boa Morte's passes went to his opponents and the other half were fifty-fifty balls. The game was dozy compared to the St Etienne match, played at sixty per cent of the tempo, but even with a slower game it was difficult for Arsenal to change their style of play. They did not make enough runs to support the main striker – they had lost that habit because neither Wright nor Anelka had passed very much. The team, struggling to adapt to life without Anelka, looked very frustrated. Vieira hacked someone down to earn a yellow card, and there was an incident between keeper Fabien Barthez and Winterburn. Petit made a comment about it and the referee walked across to the bench to speak to Wenger. 'I want you to take Petit off or I will send him off,' the official said. So Wenger put Stefan Malz, his new German midfielder, on for Petit.

At half-time Wenger experimented by putting Grimandi on for Upson and Luzhny on for Parlour, so that the Ukrainian was playing in front of Dixon in a 4–4–2. But now Vieira was having to carry the ball thirty yards when he would have preferred to push it down the channels. The Charity Shield against Manchester United was just days away, and Wenger must have thought, 'Alex Ferguson will love an Arsenal attack without pace. We terrified them in last year's Charity Shield when Anelka turned Stam inside out. But now they won't be scared of us!'

After the Monaco game Wenger issued an ultimatum, telling Anelka to find a new club within two days or return to Arsenal. 'If in 48 hours Anelka has not found another club we will consider him an Arsenal player, that he's coming back home to us.'

By this time the Lazio deal had broken down completely because they refused to increase their 'final final' offer of £20 million. Cragnotti had said, 'Lazio have decided to withdraw definitively from the negotiations to buy Anelka from Arsenal.' Wenger summed up the impasse by saying, 'The situation is very bad for Anelka's career. He doesn't gain anything with this and the club also loses. Arsenal and Lazio are in agreement so the fault lies with the player. What's happening this summer is abnormal because the contracts between players and clubs are no longer controlled by the directors.'

By Monday, 26 July, Ivan Speck was telling *Mail* readers that Anelka would become a Lazio player if he agreed to take a £4 million pay cut over four years so that Lazio could agree to meet Dein's £22 million asking price. The negotiations seemed endless, but nobody had yet asked the $64,000 question: Was Anelka mature enough to make it in Serie A, the tightest, most tactical league in the world? Without the help of Petit and Vieira? Without the passes of Bergkamp? Without the guiding hand of an ultra-sympathetic coach? The whole thing seemed ridiculous, and Arsenal were still, of course, paying Anelka £12,500 a week to behave in this ungrateful and devious manner.

Meanwhile, back at the saga, Marc Roger told *Soccernet*, 'We have yet to reach an agreement on Nicolas's personal terms because Lazio decided they wanted to pay him £4 million less to make up for what they are giving Arsenal. He is thinking things over at the moment. But I am hopeful I can persuade Nicolas to accept the new package Lazio have offered and that a deal can be concluded on Monday night.' The 'new package' was a five-year contract worth around £15.5 million. If Anelka refused Lazio's terms, Wenger would insist on his return to Arsenal, so it seemed certain the player would now back down, even though Roger and the Anelka brothers would have £1.5 million sliced off their commission as a result.

Then, amazingly, Real Madrid came back into the picture with a £23 million bid. Lorenzo Sanz claimed that Arsenal had been persuaded to abandon their complaint to FIFA and meetings had already taken place on David Dein's yacht in the south of France.

7. 1999/2000: THE SEASON OF HENRY

The 1998 Charity Shield had been a tremendous triumph, Arsenal thrashing United 3–0, but the 1999 rematch was approached with some trepidation. Wenger found himself playing his fiercest rivals at Wembley with half his team missing. In sweltering heat – the temperature hit 93 degrees inside the stadium – Arsenal struggled to adapt to playing without Anelka, Bergkamp, Overmars, Seaman and Adams. The plan was to feed Kanu and make narrow runs to support him, so Parlour had to cut inside looking for through-balls and Vieira had to use his power to run beyond the Nigerian.

Wenger must have been dismayed by the first hour. Most Arsenal–Manchester United games had been close, but United had been well on top in this one, Dwight Yorke making all the play and giving Grimandi the run-around, teasing, creating, making space, making angles. United had more rhythm, more understanding, more good habits. Then Beckham's dipping free-kick from thirty yards went in off the underside of the bar. Referee Graham Barber did not award a goal, but Yorke followed up to head home anyway.

Wenger could see that his experiment, playing Silvinho as a left-winger in front of Winterburn in a 4–4–2, was not working. The Brazilian could not find the right spaces to receive the ball because United pushed up, crowding the midfield. So he brought Boa Morte on for Silvinho and switched Ljungberg to the left.

The game changed immediately. Ljungberg fed Kanu, who fed Parlour, whose cross-shot hit the inside of the post. Then Irwin grabbed Vieira's shirt in the box, a penalty was given, and Kanu sent Mark Bosnich the wrong way to make it 1–1. Not long after that Kanu played Parlour in and his shot flew in off the far post for 2–1, and Nigel Winterburn, skipper for the day, led the Gunners up the 39 steps to collect the Charity Shield for the second time. It was a big day for Kanu, who had celebrated his 23rd birthday by scoring an immaculate penalty and creating the winner for Parlour. Remarkably, this was Manchester United's first defeat of 1999.

Wenger's post-match press conference began with confirmation that Nicolas Anelka had been sold to Real Madrid, although the contract was yet to be signed. He said, 'I am sure Arsenal will survive without Anelka, but I am not sure what would have happened had we not agreed the deal with Real. We have talked to Real and we are satisfied with their explanation of what went on before. Now I hope it is all over.' So Anelka had officially left Arsenal only fifteen months after becoming the third youngest goalscorer in an FA Cup Final. Conveniently, Davor Suker left Real Madrid to join Arsenal at the same time, for £1 million, and Thierry Henry arrived from Juventus for £8.5 million. Wenger commented, 'It would not be right for me to give you the figures, but I can tell you Suker has taken a substantial cut in wages. This is very unusual.'

The acquisition of this ageing goal poacher seemed like a shotgun wedding: Arsenal needed a striker quickly and Suker needed a club quickly. Suker was a patient predator who worked hard at being invisible and waited for an opening. Could the most passive poacher in Spain adjust to the rough-and-tumble of English football? Wenger had certainly transformed Petit and Overmars, given them new roles, made them look like world beaters, but they were younger. Could he rejuvenate Suker, who had been a problem for all four coaches he had played under at Madrid? Jupp Heynkes had fallen out with him, Fabio Capello had kept pushing him to deliver more, and Guus Hiddink had not picked him much. John Toshack had tagged him 'one of the Ferrari brigade' and then sold him.

Suker had previously played for Dynamo Zagreb and Seville. In 1996/97 he played the first of his 38 league games for Madrid under Capello, who had coached the club only for that season. He scored 24 goals and they won the title, but when Capello left and Heynkes took over, Suker had gone into decline. His stats over the last three years were those of a star who was going through the motions. He continued to play well for Croatia long after he stopped doing it for Real Madrid. He was the top scorer in France in 1998 with six goals, but it is never wise for a club manager to judge players in terms of performance at international level. Most millionaires can raise their game for a World Cup, but what are they like at Sunderland in February?

However, at the highest levels in all sports there is no substitute for experience. Anelka, for instance, had failed for Arsenal in the Champions League because he was far too raw. After his PAOK, Lens and Kiev experiences it was always likely that Wenger would sign experienced players such as Luzhny and Suker, whose arrival at Arsenal showed the way European football was going: the clubs in the Champions League were selling players to each other. Wenger had been severely disappointed by his European results; he had probably looked closely at those failures and privately vowed that such defeats must never be allowed to happen again.

Kanu partnered Bergkamp up front virtually throughout August for the first five Premiership games. Luis Boa Morte, so disappointing in his few appearances, was sold to Southampton for an undisclosed fee. Arsenal beat Leicester and Derby and drew with Sunderland, and then, on 22 August, played Manchester United at Highbury with a back five which contained, for the first time, three players Wenger had signed: Manninger, Upson and Silvinho (alongside Dixon and Keown). Ljungberg was in central midfield, and he put Arsenal ahead just before half-time, but without Adams and Petit one goal was never going to be enough. When Vieira lobbed the ball over Keane's head it went to Scholes, then Cole, then Keane, who equalised. Wenger brought on Overmars for Kanu, and then Suker for Henry, still trying to decide on his best team. Then Parlour lost the ball to Giggs and his shot deflected to Keane who made it 2–1. Both goals had come as a result of losing the ball in midfield and allowing Keane to run beyond the defence – the same problem they had had pre-season against Monaco.

When Arsenal played Bradford three days later, Vieira powered in a header from a corner, Parlour was chopped down in the box, and Kanu made it 2–0 from the spot. It was another short match at Highbury – just seventeen minutes long. The only question for the next 73 minutes was: Would Henry score? He missed one attempt from two yards, but Bergkamp was clearly determined that the Frenchman should break his duck. He had been down this road himself, and he had seen Anelka go down this road as well. Bergkamp knew how vital a striker's first goal was psychologically, so he fed Henry pass after pass after pass. Henry soon had a one-on-one but hit keeper Gary Walsh with his shot, then he cut in and had a shot saved. Wenger was using the second half like a pre-season game, looking at different combinations, checking things he would have preferred to see in July, bringing on Overmars for Henry, Suker for Bergkamp. The score stayed at 2–0, and when Bradford's cheeky Scouse boss Paul Jewell was asked whether Walsh had ever played better, he said, 'I thought he could have saved the penalty and come for the corner.'

Liverpool–Arsenal was Wenger's 150th game in charge. He had won 81 of those games but none against Liverpool, and that did not change on 28 August. Kanu was injured so Wenger gave Henry his first start at centre-forward, but Houllier knew all about Henry, having coached him in France's under-20 team, and he had by now changed Liverpool's culture. They played well and beat Arsenal 2–0.

THE 1999 AGM

It's always the same: if you lose a player late, you buy late. If you buy late, you can have problems at the start of the season.

Arsène Wenger

Thursday, 2 September saw Wenger again sitting at a long desk with the Arsenal directors, this time for a rather dull AGM. The best moment came when a shareholder brought up the subject of the protracted departure of Nicolas Anelka. 'If newspapers are to be believed,' he said, 'Real Madrid are £100 million in debt. How can we be sure we will get all of the five staged payments?'

Chairman Peter Hill-Wood replied. 'I did mention that we have a bank guarantee, or we will have it.'

'You have it, or you will have it?' said the shareholder.

'We will have it.'

'When will that be in place?'

'Tomorrow,' said Hill-Wood. There was loud laughter and considerable applause. Hill-Wood, embarrassed, quickly added, 'That is absolutely true.'

The first hour of the 75-minute meeting was routine stuff: the re-election of Hill-Wood and Clive Carr, predictable questions about relocation, media companies buying stakes in clubs, the state of the executive ladies' loos and the inaudibility of the public address system in the West Stand. Other perennials included, 'Can you stop bombarding us with pop music?' and 'Why don't you show the whole game on the big screens like Spurs and Aston Villa?'

Hill-Wood had to apologise for not being able to give news of progress regarding the relocation of the stadium, although two sites were under investigation. He said it would take four years to build a new stadium and move in.

A shareholder said, 'We went to Wembley last year for the Champions League games, and you've withdrawn the planning application to redevelop Highbury, so it's very clear to all and sundry that the board have made the decision to relocate away from Highbury. I really think they should come out and say this, so that the fans and shareholders are properly prepared for this.'

'It is our preferred option to relocate,' Hill-Wood confirmed. 'We've never really hidden that fact. Saying that we are definitely going to relocate, however, would be rather irresponsible. We don't know that we definitely are.' This was a change from the 1998 AGM, where the chairman had stated that the board preferred to stay at Highbury.

Another shareholder wanted to know if the purchase of Suker and Henry was dependent on the money from the sale of Anelka. Hill-Wood denied this was the case.

'With Anelka going, it was important to get a player in, or two players. One was not dependent on the other. We assumed Anelka was going. You basically buy a player when you can buy them. I think Mr Wenger is looking to strengthen the squad at any moment he can.'

One speaker said that he felt the lunatics were taking over the asylum, for he had read that on no account would Anelka be sold to Real Madrid. 'We don't get the money up front,' he added, 'as a colleague has mentioned earlier. The problem I have with that is that the two forwards were signed three days before the season started, which is not ideal preparation for the coming season. One the manager says is not fit, the other is obviously taking his time to get into the team. I would put it to the vice-chairman, if it wasn't linked to the Anelka transfer, would it not have been better to give said forwards a full pre-season, playing in the pre-season friendlies? Can the vice-chairman answer, please?

David Dein, always combative when criticised, said, 'We did not want to sell him. We did everything we possibly could to get him to remain with the club. He eventually returned to England, he was desperate to leave the club, and we managed to get an auction going between three clubs. We did not want to deal with Real Madrid. However, prior to doing so we made certain stipulations to get them to explain their conduct, which they did to our satisfaction. We had originally made a complaint to UEFA and to FIFA, which is now being dealt with by their officials. I can say no more on that. All I can tell you is that the deal we concluded was in the very, very best interests of Arsenal Football Club. On what we achieved, I would like to think you are satisfied.

'Turning to the new players, the timing of that was really very, very difficult. Trying to make sure a club is willing to sell a player. Very often they are not. We managed to get Thierry Henry and Davor Suker, albeit it was late. But it was important we got those two players.'

The shareholder interrupted. 'With respect, Mr Vice-Chairman, if I can have the right of reply to that. Davor Suker, I'm led to believe, bought his own contract out. He was a free agent who touted himself about for a number of months. It seemed to me and my associates that he was bought very, very quickly, as soon as Anelka was sold. My point to you is, surely it would have been a lot better if these players had been in place pre-season, achieving fitness and getting to know the other players before having to play for the first team in what has been an inauspicious start for the club this season.'

David Dein clearly did not relish being reminded of those months of Anelka aggravation. Speaking with controlled aggression, he said, 'I'd willingly swap jobs with you for one day, so you can see the problems we have to deal with. For us to get world-class players in, very often the timing is not ours.'

Another shareholder noted that while players' wage costs had gone up 60–70% over two years, directors' costs had increased by 300%. 'Is there any particular reason for this?' he asked.

The question again brought loud laughter.

'Well, the principal one,' Hill-Wood replied, 'is Mr Dein. He had a fairly substantial bonus which the Remuneration Committee felt he had earned fully. I supported that, and I don't think it's excessive.'

As usual, Hill-Wood was now impatient for the meeting to end. He does not enjoy being asked questions he cannot answer, and he knows that many of the shareholders are educated adults who have more experience of public speaking than the Arsenal directors. At any moment an accountant, solicitor or barrister might stand up and ask a really penetrating question. Amazingly, nobody asked why Arsenal were going back to Wembley for Champions League games again, when last season's experiment had failed.

The mood of the meeting changed after an hour when one shareholder went to a microphone and said, 'I would like to congratulate Mr Wenger on an outstanding season last year.' This sentiment was applauded immediately by some 400 people, about half of those present.

Hill-Wood then said, 'That's probably an appropriate moment to ask Mr Wenger to say a few words to you.'

This was what everyone had been waiting for. Arsène Wenger stood up and spoke for ten minutes. He was 49 but still had a youthful quality about him, and he came over as a decent, purposeful head boy giving a report to an assembly of grammar-school parents. He proved, once again, to be a master of these set-piece events, someone who knows how to press the right buttons. With a group of players he is persuasive, with a group of journalists he is plausible and informative, and once a year with the shareholders he is warmly intelligent and likeable. He seems to have a lot in common with the shareholders who are, like him, mostly middle-class. His words somehow manage to contain exactly the right blend of honesty, humility and ambition.

'Once again Arsenal has a huge attendance and I must say I enjoy that,' he said. 'That's why I would like to thank you for the huge support you brought to the team last year. Everyone takes it for granted that we get 38,000. I don't because I've worked somewhere before that didn't get that. I personally enjoy it very much.

'We are deeply disappointed that we didn't win the championship last year. We failed by one point, but we made 78 points like we did the year before and lost only four games. The basic target we have reached is to establish Arsenal Football Club at the top of domestic football for three years, as well as we can. It becomes always more difficult because many clubs have big potential in England, and almost everybody buys and tries to improve his team. I personally believe that my responsibility is to work on the short term – that means to make this club very successful every year – and as well in the medium term and the longer term. In the short term, I think we can look back over the last three years and say we've improved our stock, and we've heard a lot about transfers today.

'As the manager I feel responsible to the shareholders to look at the balance, the financial balance. We spoke about Anelka, about Suker. We lost Anelka this season but the financial benefit was great. We could have said, "You have to stay in the reserves for four years, to learn a lesson." But at some stage we had to respect the financial interest of the club today. The pressure to survive at top level is so big that we had to compromise a little.'

Interestingly, Wenger contradicted the chairman.

'To get the other players in, like you said, I'm not scared to say yes, it was linked to Anelka, of course. Why? Because the wages of top-class strikers are very, very big. In my opinion, for a long, long time, Anelka stays with Arsenal.' This was exactly what one had suspected during the Anelka soap opera that summer, that Wenger always hoped to take charge in July after convoluted negotiations had stalled and persuade his protégé to stay another year. 'It's always the same: if you lose a player late, you buy late. If you buy late, you can have problems at the start of the season. Suker was not our target early in the summer, for two reasons. One, he had a contract where he could buy himself out for £1 million. Two, his financial requests were too high. He came down to fit into our wage structure very late. That's why he came to our club very late.

'As well I've heard some questions about the midfield, why we don't have better cover. But there as well I want to be responsible for the longer term. I want to bring young players in. I've done that my whole career. I've put Petit in at eighteen and Thuram at eighteen, and of course they were not like today. But if you want to give a chance to the younger players, you have to have an opening there. That's one reason. Second reason, to find replacements on the international market for Petit and Vieira, for example, is very, very difficult.'

Wenger went on to say that if you have a very good player like Stephen Hughes who has a player like Manu Petit in front of him, and you buy another player, then another, the youngsters will never get a chance. He said that was why Arsenal worked very hard with the youth team, who should provide the basis of the side in the future with the addition of four or five players from outside the UK. In the long term Wenger said he would like a team that is 60% home grown, 40% continental imports.

He then touched on the stadium question and the long-term future of the club.

'This club worked very hard to build a new training ground. It is one of the most advanced in Europe and will help guarantee the future success of the club. We spoke about the ground. When I go out there, I love this stadium, but we are now 17,000 or 18,000 less people than some of our rivals, and tomorrow it will be 20,000 or 25,000 less than them. That means, at the end of the season, a huge difference. And if we want to compete with the top clubs, in the longer term, how can we keep up the pace? 'You talk about Anelka. But if you sit down with Anelka, and tell him: Listen, how much can you get at Real Madrid? If we can pay the same, he might still be here. But at the moment we cannot do it. And that is what we have to find. But maybe at some stage in the future we will be able, if we want, to keep the player.'

He finished by referring to the two recent defeats by Liverpool and Manchester United. 'We had a deep disappointment last week because we lost two games and that's not happened for a long, long time in the same week. And we have to redress the situation very quickly, because last year we lost four games only, and we didn't win the championship. This year we have lost two already.' He also said he would be very proud if Arsenal did well in the Champions League. 'I'd like to thank you once again for your support, and I hope we'll see each other again next year. And we'll be very happy because we've had a successful season. Thank you.'

The French maestro sat down to a storm of applause, and Hill-Wood wrapped up proceedings by saying, 'I think we've exhausted ourselves, and maybe you have too. Thank you very much for your attendance. I hope you've had an enjoyable season. We'll see you all again next year with a lot of silver, I hope. Thank you.'

At the 1998 AGM, after winning the Double, Wenger had answered questions, but that was obviously not on the agenda this time. It may never be on the agenda again.

FIORENTINA AND AIK SOLNA

If you keep scoring late, you believe you can score late.

Arsène Wenger

In September a manager is usually concerned about how his new players are fitting in and which ones can make a contribution to the team sooner rather than later. Wenger had signed a 31-year-old Croatian, a 30-year-old Ukrainian, a 22-year-old Frenchman and a 25-year-old Brazilian. Now that Overmars was fit again it looked as if the Croatian would be the first to claim a regular place.

Arsenal had often struggled against Aston Villa's 3–5–2 system, which stifled the pace of Wright and Anelka, so it was interesting when Wenger gave Davor Suker his debut in a home game against them on 11 September. In a crowded penalty area, where defenders outnumber opponents, they often create a comfort zone for themselves and switch off mentally. Suker had proved himself cute at moving away from a defender at the last moment to create a yard of space for a precise shot or header. In a low-scoring game, which Arsenal–Aston Villa usually was, he might do well.

On the day Suker was tightly marked by Gareth Southgate, the Villa captain, and just as the crowd was beginning to accept that it was a typical Arsenal–Villa game, where the Gunners had eighty per cent of the play but could not score, Julian Joachim got a goal from a Merson pass. But within a minute Bergkamp flicked Suker through to equalise. Early in the second half referee David Elleray penalised keeper David James for time-wasting when he held on to the ball, even though James was carrying a knee injury which prevented him kicking. Arsenal were awarded a free-kick eight yards from goal and Suker rifled it high into the Villa net. James was then substituted. Towards the end Kanu dribbled, fell, poked the ball to Overmars, took the return pass and made it 3–1.

Afterwards, Wenger said, 'We have link players but we needed a goalscorer, and Suker is obsessed by goals. We were dominating games in midfield but couldn't finish off teams. When Davor is inside the box he hits the target, and you can see how he loves to score. He reminds me of Wright both in his play and his attitude.' This was one of Wenger's stranger remarks, since Wright was fast, aggressive and kept losing the ball, while Suker was one-paced, passive and kept possession very well.

Three days later Arsenal's 1999/2000 Champions League campaign began. It looked like a challenging programme, kicking off with Fiorentina in Florence, AIK Solna at Wembley and Barcelona at the Nou Camp. Solna at Wembley was obviously the easiest game of the three, Barcelona away the hardest.

Fiorentina had led Serie A the season before, but then Gabriel Batistuta sustained an injury, morale had collapsed and they finished third. Italians maintain that Florence is a schizophrenic city with unforgiving supporters, a mercurial team and an interventionist president, the film mogul Vittorio Cecche Gori. Coach Giovanni Trapattoni now had a side unbalanced by new strikers Enrico Chiesa, noted for his explosive shot, and Predrag Mijatovic, a tricky, provocative Yugoslav. Their arrival meant that playmaker Rui Costa, the main provider for Batistuta, was being wasted in a deeper role. But then in Serie A many presidents collect stars who upset the balance and harmony of a developing team, a scenario Wenger would have found intolerable. On the night the diving of Mijatovic infuriated Arsenal, but they dominated the game. Overmars gave Ljungberg an early chance which Toldo saved. When the Dutchman put the Swede in with another cross, Toldo brought him down, then got up to save Kanu's penalty and clinch a 0–0 draw.

The next Premiership game was on 18 September at Southampton where Thierry Henry came on as a sub and scored with a terrific shot from just outside the penalty area. It was his first goal for Arsenal and it was a valuable one, since it was the only goal of the game.

Four days later a huge crowd of 71,227 turned up at Wembley expecting to see an easy victory over AIK Solna, who were managed by Stuart Baxter, the man Wenger had wanted as his number two when he joined Arsenal. The team was as expected, with Ljungberg wide on the right and Grimandi in midfield; Kanu, Henry, Silvinho and Luzhny were on the bench with Upson, Vivas and Lukic. In the second minute Overmars hit the best left-foot cross of his Arsenal career but Suker muffed the near-post header. Solna defended cleverly with a solid, compact 4–4–2 system, pushing up to the 45-yard line whenever possible. Nevertheless, Arsenal kept coming. After nine minutes Bergkamp played a pass to Suker, got the ball back in the box and hit the keeper. Then Vieira broke upfield, beat two men and slipped the ball square to Bergkamp as Suker made a run across the centre-back, creating a momentary gap. Bergkamp's pass found Ljungberg, who put Arsenal 1–0 up. After that it was one-way traffic.

Until the second half. Eight minutes after the restart, Winterburn, for only the second or third time in twelve years, was a fraction late coming out, playing Nordin onside, and suddenly it was 1–1. Time was running out when Wenger brought Kanu and Henry on for Overmars and Ljungberg. There were desperate moments towards the end. Two Swedes went clear of the Arsenal defence, looking offside, although the replay showed them onside. The striker delayed far too long, however, and allowed Winterburn to block. Suker produced an ambitious dipper from 25 yards, just over, then his exquisite backheel gave Henry an open goal, but he shot wide of the far post.

Frustration mounted. With two minutes left, Bergkamp began to foul defenders. But then Winterburn hoisted a good ball downfield and Suker headed on to Kanu. The Nigerian was wrestled to the ground by Brundin, but he still managed to hook the ball square to the unmarked Henry, who scored. Solna poured forward after that, and when Manninger punched out a cross, substitute Silvinho won the loose ball and flicked it to Bergkamp, who released Henry. The Frenchman raced away from inside his own half, took the ball right up to the keeper and gave Suker a tap-in. The score looked comfortable, but this was Arsenal's most uncomfortable 3–1 victory for decades. It might also have been the longest 91 minutes of Arsène Wenger's life.

He made five changes for Saturday's game against Watford, another hard-working team of journeymen who battled bravely. Wenger expected his side to score, of course, as the first half, then the second half went on, but when? Ljungberg crossed and Thierry Henry sailed in at the far post and missed the ball completely; then Ljungberg hit a low cross from the byline and Kanu failed to connect at the far post. Two sitters in two minutes. Would Arsenal convert a cross before Christmas? Ljungberg crossed again, and this time Kanu's header hit the post. Then Luzhny hoisted a huge throw to the near post and Kanu netted from four yards. The goal came three minutes from time, but as Wenger said afterwards, 'If you keep scoring late, you believe you can score late.'

KANU OUTSHINES RIVALDO

If you realise your ambitions so quickly, you start dreaming about new challenges.

Marc Overmars

Wenger must have felt he had a chance of winning in the Nou Camp on 29 September, mainly because his defence was so strong. He had said Arsenal must defend collectively, a sensible approach because Barcelona had more brilliant players than any team Arsenal had ever faced in their entire history.

Rivaldo was more dangerous than Shevchenko, Zidane or Batistuta because he could win matches with dribbles, long passes, short passes, long shots, headers, crosses and free-kicks. The Brazilian is tall, strong, durable, awkward and very good in the air, but he is only flesh and blood, and he had looked jaded against Betis the Saturday before, a game Wenger, with his usual thoroughness, would have watched on Sky Sports. Rivaldo could be stopped by tight marking and tough, fair tackling.

In the larger scheme of things, Wenger knew that Arsenal needed time to get the hang of playing against the big boys in Europe. The Champions League is a steep learning curve, and the big question was not so much whether Arsenal could get a point. It was: Can the team handle it? The biggest club ground Arsenal normally visit is Old Trafford and the Nou Camp is twice the size. Would they get stage-fright in Europe's biggest football theatre?

Surprisingly, Kanu, the supersub, started the game and gave an astonishing 93-minute performance. The Nigerian was hungry, brave and immensely resourceful. He foraged, feinted, dummied, turned, jogged and generally made himself available everywhere. He was better than Rivaldo. Sadly, Bergkamp played like a zombie. When Wenger put on two subs, Ljungberg and Suker, he left Kanu on and took off Bergkamp and Overmars. Louis van Gaal also made an unexpected striker switch when he selected the nimble Dani rather than Kluivert, the tall target man. But Dani was anonymous and Barcelona missed Kluivert's power in the second half when Arsenal raised the tempo. Wenger was delighted to see Overmars play his best game of the season so far. He had missed chance after chance all through September and had not scored a goal in his seven games. But he showed, once again, that he has the big-match temperament.

The match had been billed by Wenger as a let's-find-out-how-good-we-are exercise. On the evidence of the first 35 minutes the answer was: not good enough. Grimandi gave away two 25-yard free-kicks and Dixon had to kick a Luis Enrique header off the line. After 35 minutes Barcelona had enjoyed a mind-boggling 71 per cent of the possession. Manninger was flapping and punching, and when he spilt a tame Cocu shot the ball bounced up on to Vieira's thigh inside the six-yard box. Amazingly, Vieira took a second touch and wanted a third, so Luis Enrique came up behind him and poked it into the net from four yards. What a gift! What was Vieira thinking about? He should have whacked that loose ball into Row Z!

Bergkamp, having just witnessed the most idiotic goal Arsenal had conceded since he joined the club in 1995, reacted by kicking Rivaldo. It was an angry, dangerous kick on the ankle and he deserved his yellow card. Vieira also fouled Rivaldo, another yellow card. The Barcelona crowd jeered Davor Suker when he warmed up, howled when he took his white top off and screamed when he replaced Bergkamp after 73 minutes. He had only been on the field twenty seconds when he lunged in late on local hero Guardiola and kicked his foot. Not content with that, Suker chased across the field, allowed Winston Bogarde to clear the ball, then dived in fractionally late so that Bogarde's follow-through connected with his studs. It was a very bad foul and the crowd went ballistic. If Suker was a hate figure before that tackle, he was a demon now. His name went into the book, and Barcelona's concentration went out of the window.

The second half had been a different match, nothing like the first half, but now, suddenly, a third match started. Arsenal were still 1–0 down, but at last they looked capable of winning the game. Then Grimandi elbowed Guardiola when they were on the ground, right in front of the referee, and was sent off. The pendulum had swung dramatically towards Arsenal, but now it swung back.

Then, incredibly, within a minute of Grimandi's red card, Kanu equalised. When Guardiola jumped and missed the ball, Suker nodded it forward and Kanu nudged Guardiola off balance. While this was happening the Croatian readjusted his body position, just in case the ball rolled back towards his left foot. When the ball did exactly that, Suker hit a shot through Guardiola's and Bogarde's legs, wrongfooting Hesp, who managed to parry the ball with his right hand. It popped out to Kanu, who half-volleyed into the corner of the net from eight yards. The game finished 1–1.

Wenger must have been disappointed that half his team seemed to be overawed by the occasion. Manninger did not cope in the first twenty minutes and Bergkamp, Parlour, Vieira and Grimandi did not handle it either. So five of his eleven players did not really cope with the pressure of the event. But he must have been encouraged that they were, eventually, well worth a draw. The next game was Barcelona at Wembley and if Arsenal had an inferiority complex before the Nou Camp they should certainly not have one now. Barcelona versus Arsenal had been fascinating but Arsenal versus Barcelona promised to be pivotal. Not decisive, but pivotal. Because if they could beat Barca at Wembley they could also beat Fiorentina.

Vieira then proceeded to let his team down again at West Ham on 3 October, where Arsenal lost 2–1. He allowed himself to be wound up by Neil Ruddock, was sent off and came back to spit at the defender, which earned him an eight-match ban. He later apologised for his actions and said he was ashamed of himself. Maybe he was still upset about his blunder before the Luis Enrique goal.

The build-up to the second Barcelona game on 19 October highlighted how difficult it can be for coaches to handle superstar egos. A small mystery surrounded an Overmars feature in the *Mail on Sunday* by David Walker, a north-of-England-based reporter who does not normally cover London clubs. Overmars was quoted as saying, 'I went to England to win the league title and FA Cup with Arsenal. That happened quicker than I thought possible. If you realise your ambitions so quickly, you start dreaming about new challenges. My next aims are to win a major trophy with Holland and to win a league championship trophy with a club in another country.' He admitted that his current contract did not expire until 2004, but added, 'When I first joined Arsenal three years ago I asked for a clause so that I could leave for a set fee of £10 million. Arsenal wouldn't allow that. At the time it seemed like a bizarre amount. Now such a fee would be negotiated by most clubs. If I'd had that clause in my contract last summer I probably would have gone. It doesn't matter that the clause isn't there. We'll just see what the future brings.'

What did Wenger make of these extraordinary comments? We may never know, but Arsenal fans were furious. If those quotes were true, Marc Overmars believed that Arsenal could not win the Champions League. Could Wenger accept this? Could he accept that mercenaries rule? Could he accept that Marc Overmars might already want to leave?

Arsenal met Everton on Saturday October 16 and played their best football of the season in the second half and won 4–1. Then they moved to Wembley three days later and played Barcelona. Why were they hammered 4–2? Three reasons: Tony Adams had a bad night, cynical strategic fouls by Barcelona, and exceptional counter-attacks by the visitors. Adams was very unlucky to concede an early penalty when Cocu dived. He slipped on the second goal, then scuffed a left-foot shot into the ground from five yards. He might have done better with two headers.

Tactically, the game was the most interesting contest Wenger has ever lost in England. It looked as if Louis van Gaal had learned more from the Nou Camp encounter than Wenger had, so Barca had a superior game plan and would probably have won without the penalty gift. The way Barcelona played was cool, shrewd and relaxed. They did not support their attacks, did not use overlappers, did not flood the box, and only won one corner against Arsenal's thirteen. Their style was mathematical, geometrical and economical. Very little energy was wasted, very few passes were wasted, and they seemed to have thirteen players to smother every Arsenal move. There was an element of Muhammad Ali rope-a-dope about the night – Arsenal wore themselves out and never saw the punches coming. The pitch seemed to be full of spaces that the Barcelona players decided not to run into because they wanted to save them for later. The game would make for a superb instructional video because the near-misses were as good as the goals: Figo's left-foot rocket, which Seaman tipped on to the post, Figo's header just over the bar from Kluivert's cross on 49 minutes.

Wenger must have been grateful for the enthusiastic support of the Arsenal fans, who were passionate, optimistic and marvellous. No recent Arsenal crowd has been so supportive. When the penalty was awarded they sang 'Seaman! Seaman!' because the keeper had been a penalty-saving hero notably in big games against Millwall, Sampdoria and Scotland. When Luis Enrique made it 2–1 they sang 'We love you Arsenal, we do!' and at 3–1 down they roared 'Stand up for the Arsenal, stand up for the Arsenal!' And they still had enough left to get right behind the team when Overmars made it 4–2 after 84 minutes.

Wenger had had fair warning from Frank de Boer that Barcelona were cynical masters of the strategic foul forty yards from goal. Sure enough, after nine seconds, Guardiola grabbed Kanu, who had dispossessed him, and threw him on the ground. Then Cocu cheated with his dive. Swiss referee Urs Meier was deceived because it was a subtle, understated, elegant dive. He gave a penalty and Rivaldo scored superbly with a shot into the corner. Keown was off the field having treatment behind the goal when Arsenal, shell-shocked and furious, conceded a second goal just ninety seconds later, Figo making a terrific stretch to beat Winterburn and flick on for Luis Enrique, whose finish was perfection. Figo was carded for a foul on Vieira, and when Bergkamp juggled the ball past Abelardo the defender handled and also got a yellow. Reiziger then obstructed an Overmars run, but escaped a booking. Arsenal's four midfield players committed just three fouls in the game, while Barcelona's four notched up ten. Not a huge total, but it highlighted their strategic ruthlessness.

As Wenger stood up from the bench at the final whistle and we saw his face on TV, he looked humbled. Of course, this very testing competition is an education for the club, the players and the manager, so the fans sympathised with Wenger, doubting whether he had ever wanted to play at Wembley. The Champions League is home and away against the best in Europe and Arsenal's choice to play 'home' games away from its own stadium two years running will rank as one of the biggest own-goals in the history of English football.

The Chelsea game at Stamford Bridge on 23 October, the day after Wenger's fiftieth birthday, started badly. Dan Petrescu made the first goal and scored the second, and Arsenal were 2–0 down with about forty minutes to go against a team who were coming off a sensational 5–0 win over Galatasaray in Istanbul in the Champions League.

Most of the match was played in a monsoon, so the pitch was covered with surface water. The first Kanu goal came when Dixon crossed and the ball rebounded from Babayaro to Overmars, who hit a feeble shot from 25 yards that was going wide until Kanu stretched to control the ball with his left foot and toe-poked the ball hard enough for it to skim through the water and beat de Goey's right hand. With this goal, Kanu became the first player to score against Chelsea at Stamford Bridge in the Premiership that season. Then he scored again. Overmars, on the right, crossed left-footed, craftily, to the rear of a crowded penalty area, picking out Kanu, who cushioned the ball at an angle away from the goal, avoiding the nearest defenders, so that the ball rolled towards the corner of the six-yard box. He got to it just before Desailly and buried a right-foot shot at the near post for 2–2. It was reminiscent of Bergkamp's audacious pass to himself to score the third goal against Spurs back in November 1996.

The winner was the best goal ever scored from a bad pass by a striker who wanted to score the goal himself. When Wise made a poor pass Overmars chested the ball to Suker, who was wide right on the halfway line. Suker cruised infield on his left foot, beating Wise; Overmars scooted forward looking for a return pass from Suker, but the Croatian passed wide to Kanu, who was standing near him on his left. It was the wrong pass under the circumstances. It was a pass that had 'You get wide and cross for *me* to score the winner' written all over it. Kanu chased the ball to the touchline, but Albert Ferrer got there first and attempted to clear down the line. Kanu somehow blocked, regained the ball and continued to amble down the left touchline. Incredibly, keeper Ed de Goey charged out of his area and tried to tackle Kanu somewhere near the corner flag. As de Goey came at him left foot first, Kanu jabbed the ball with his right foot against his own left ankle so that it bounced up and hit his right knee. Desailly was by now running back to cover the near post. The Nigerian then took a very delicate touch with his right foot as Leboeuf also ran back to cover the goal. This set-up touch was perfect, but he was a yard inside the penalty area and a yard from the goal-line. It was a hugely unfavourable angle, but Kanu hit a tremendous curving shot which flashed past the two French defenders.

What a moment! What a goal! What a player! What an electrifying hat-trick! Chelsea 2 Kanu 3! Was this the finest late strike among Kanu's many late strikes? Was it the greatest hat-trick in Arsenal's history? Ian Wright had scored some sensational hat-tricks, Anelka got one in the 5–0 demolition of Leicester in February, and Martin O'Neill had said that Bergkamp's hat-trick against Leicester in August 1997 was the best he had ever seen, but Kanu had done more than that. The player Wenger had rescued from oblivion at Inter, the player he had waited a year for, the player he had gambled £4.5 million on had followed up his stupendous performance in the Nou Camp by putting on a one-man show which turned the game upside down. When all seemed lost Kanu had scored three goals in the last sixteen minutes to put Arsenal second in the table, one point behind Leeds.

BATISTUTA'S WONDER-GOAL

It's a real regret to me that Arsenal have not yet played to their full potential in the Champions League. We need to establish the club as one of the top teams in that league.

Arsène Wenger

Arsenal–Fiorentina was the crunch game of the club's 1999/2000 European campaign, and it looked like being a tight, low-scoring chess match. 'They play quite deep and wait for the right moment to strike,' said Wenger. 'I expect to be under pressure, but only for short spells, and then it is intense. They are like snakes, they have spurts and in five minutes they can kill you.' He admitted that his team had yet to earn recognition among the European elite. 'It's a real regret to me that Arsenal have not yet played to their full potential in the Champions League. We need to establish the club as one of the top teams in that league. Historically, that's what the club is missing. You are not a great team until you have done that.'

Wenger might have been expecting to be under pressure, but his players had won most of the important duels in Florence: Overmars had baffled Angelo di Livio, Keown had dominated Batistuta, and Luzhny had overpowered the fiery Jorg Heinrich.

Moreover, Barcelona's pace had been in midfield, Fiorentina's pace was in attack, so the Italians were more conventional – with the exception of Gabriel Batistuta, a shoot-from-anywhere centre-forward, a spectacular player who always goes for power, not placement. He gambles, fires cannonballs, so it is always going to be a sensational goal or a misfired rocket into Row Z – rarely anything in between. His Italian record was an amazing 134 goals in 219 league games.

On the night, Batistuta scored an exceptional goal with what seemed to be his third kick of the match. His first, a nasty late tackle after two minutes, almost broke Lee Dixon's ankle. His second, after 48 minutes, was a ridiculous overhead kick which sailed six yards over the bar. Then, in the 75th minute, the Argentinian scored the goal that knocked Arsenal out of the Champions League and proved, once again, that he is the greatest centre-forward since Marco van Basten.

The move that brought the goal justified Fiorentina's defensive strategy in the match. Vieira broke forward powerfully and promisingly but was tackled by Firicano. Adani hit a crossfield pass, Rui Costa laid it back to Chiesa, who found Heinrich just inside his own half, and Heinrich broke past Vivas and ran straight down the middle of the field as Rui Costa's run took Keown wide on the right. As Heinrich swerved past Adams, Batistuta was hovering onside and wide of Winterburn, on the corner of the penalty area. He stopped the pass with his right foot, and touched it forward instantly with his left, so that the ball went seven yards forward and he had to race Winterburn for it.

When Batistuta spurted forward past Winterburn, he was flying, like Colin Jackson going over the last hurdle in an Olympic final, and he knew he was going to shoot if he got there first. He was stretching but he lashed a volcanic shot through Seaman and high into the far side of the net. It was an awesome example of centre forward play, one of those special moments where an athlete suddenly has access to all his talent, all his power, all his training, all his experience, all his ambition, and makes a mark in the memory.

The whole move was superb – the dribble by Heinrich, the pass to Batistuta, the audacity and precision of the set-up touch, the electric movement – but the goal was astounding because of the velocity of the shot, the narrow angle and the fact that at the time the game was balanced on a knife-edge. It was the greatest goal I have ever seen in a one-goal game.

Afterwards, the articulate Wenger for once struggled to explain Arsenal's failure. He seemed dazed, like a boxer doing an interview ten minutes after being knocked out. 'We lost,' he said. 'We don't know why, but we lost. That's the reality now. We can't change it and we have to cope with that.' So Wenger was still the manager of the biggest medium-sized club in Europe, still frustrated, still just one elusive goal away from joining the big boys.

There were still eight weeks to go until Christmas, and the big story from now on would be the success or failure of his record signing Thierry Henry, who was only a sub in Arsenal's first four Champions League games and an unused sub in the fifth.

Quite simply, Wenger now needed to concentrate on making sure he got a return on Henry, his £8.5 million investment. If Thierry Henry did not score goals, Arsenal might not be in next season's Champions League.

SEEING RED – AGAIN

Freddie did not butt me. I don't know how he has been sent off for that. I have no problem telling the FA this.

David Ginola

Referees have a very difficult job now that television proves them wrong so often. Wenger very rarely adds to the barrage of abuse, but in the game at White Hart Lane on 17 November David Elleray made two big mistakes, and Wenger must privately have despaired when the Harrow teacher sent off two of his players.

He had picked Kanu with Bergkamp again, prompting fans to wonder why he had signed Suker and given him the number nine shirt if he was not going to play him. Suker was the only centre-forward at the club. Did Wenger now think the Croatian was only a twenty-minute player?

Spurs took an early lead when Iversen scored after seven minutes, and Arsenal were losing the key duels. Overmars was well contained by Carr, while Bergkamp was pushing up on Campbell, asking for the ball to feet, backing in, turning, beating him occasionally, but never getting near enough to the goal to do any real damage. Petit made a stupid late tackle on Chris Armstrong and Ginola teed up the short free-kick for Sherwood, whose right-foot shot went round the wall for 2–0. Vieira got on the end of a Petit free-kick after 38 minutes and powered a header in off the post to make it 2–1, and soon after that a mêlée started on the far side of the pitch and Ljungberg was sent off. Then substitute Dominguez teased Keown, the defender lunged in viciously, and Keown was sent off as well. Arsenal lost the match and finished with nine men.

When Wenger looked at the videotape of the Ljungberg red card he could see that the circumstances were quite bizarre. Bergkamp had a a tussle with Campbell, who pushed him over, so Elleray blew for a free-kick to Arsenal. Edinburgh came in for the loose ball after the whistle had gone and kicked it out with his left foot. Ljungberg, standing close, did not contest the fifty-fifty ball because he had heard the whistle go, but Edinburgh, following through, kicked Ljungberg with his right leg and ended up in a sitting position on the ground. The Swede was annoyed by this and pushed Edinburgh in the chest – a mild reaction in the circumstances. Clemence then pushed Ljungberg backwards, Ginola arrived but did not raise his hands, Iversen got between Ginola and Ljungberg but did not raise his hands either, Armstrong came up behind Ljungberg and pushed him in the back, Clemence pushed his right hand in Ljungberg's face and the Swede then put his left hand on Armstrong's throat. Dixon shoved his team-mate away as Armstrong continued with verbals. At the same time as Iversen pushed Armstrong away, a coin was thrown from the crowd and it hit Ginola on the head.

Elleray then sent Ljungberg off for a headbutt on Ginola. A yellow card for a tame push on Edinburgh would have been harsh, but a red card for a headbutt that did not happen was ridiculous. Ljungberg walked away across the field, turning briefly to give the ref a V-sign, and when the bionic eye of the camera followed him into the tunnel he could be seen angrily kicking a door. He had been the victim of gamesmanship by Armstrong, Clemence and

Edinburgh. 'Freddie did not butt me,' Ginola said afterwards. 'I don't know how he has been sent off for that. I have no problem telling the FA this. I was just looking at what was going on and I was then hit in the face by something.' Wenger said, 'Frederik is destroyed. He said he didn't do anything wrong.'

The referee got it wrong again when he gave Keown his first yellow card. Sherwood had played a bad pass to Ginola and the Frenchman was not going for it as Keown made his challenge. Keown did not tackle Ginola from behind because Ginola was never between him and the ball. He was adjacent to the ball, which Keown played. There was probably slight contact, so Ginola dived, trying to con the crowd and the referee. When Elleray, standing only six yards away, called this a foul, Tony Adams and Bergkamp both went ballistic. Elleray had made the game a farce.

Next day, of course, there were big headlines: Arsenal's 26 red cards under Wenger. David Miller suggested in the *Daily Telegraph* that chairman Peter Hill-Wood should be hauled up before the FA to provide an explanation, but Pat Rice did not seem too worried. When Pat was on television on the Monday morning he was shown a photo of Ljungberg making the two-fingered gesture. He was asked, 'What does he mean by that?' and Pat said, 'He was ordering two tickets for the Scotland–England game.'

Like most managers, Wenger lives each game, and the preparations for each game, but for him every match is part of a sequence, a bigger picture. He thinks about the British game, the European game, the global game, and how football reflects the way society is going. However, like any manager, his mood becomes more expansive after a big win. So after Arsenal hammered Middlesbrough 5-1 at Highbury the ideas flowed out of him just as the passes and shots flowed out of his team. He hit some bullseyes when he talked about the stylistic evolution of the Arsenal attack in the post-Anelka period, and how performances depend a lot on fitness. He admitted that the two Dutchmen often perform below their maximum because they are carrying minor injuries which restrict their running and undermine their self-confidence.

Since late 1997 it had been apparent that Wenger loved a certain style of football, a dynamic way of playing which depended on early passes and explosive acceleration. So, day by day, week by week, he had built and tested an Arsenal machine that could win the ball and score two seconds later. He prepared his team to play technical power football, always hoping for the days when they would produce a ninety-minute goalfest like the performance against Middlesbrough, where he saw Overmars score three goals and Bergkamp two. He had often talked about killing the game, and this was one of those days when Arsenal were overwhelming. It was an exhibition of fast, skilful, precise, penetrating football. They certainly killed the game. It was a case of Bang! Bang! Bang! You're dead!

Dennis Bergkamp played his best football since the FA Cup semi-final against Manchester United seven months earlier, making the first goal, scoring the next two and winning the penalty for the fourth. So I kicked off the press conference by asking Wenger about the Dutchmen. Had they found another mood, another level, today?

'Yes, they played very well, but I think overall it was a very good team performance. And I'm very happy for them that they scored because they missed that a little bit. We had a good creative game today – good passing, the right concentration for nearly ninety minutes. We lost it a little bit at the beginning of the second half when we were under a little bit of pressure and lost our game, but I'm quite happy that we had a good, creative game for eighty minutes. The challenge is to repeat it.'

Best performance so far this season?

'Over ninety minutes, defensively and offensively, yes. I think we had some quite good games this season, but we could never put together defensive concentration and offensive efficiency. For example, against Barcelona, at home, I personally believe that going forward we were outstanding, but defensively we were very poor.'

You looked like a hungry team today.

'We looked a hungry team. We looked like a team who had time to think about what happens to them. And who have the intelligence to react.'

Does that performance indicate that you're now at your best?

'No, it's not enough. This team has a huge potential, but we have lacked consistency until now. We found a good level today and we have to repeat that. Consistency gives you a chance to win something. Potential, nothing.'

Pleased with Dennis today?

'Yes, I'm pleased with his runs. It was maybe the first game when he had so many runs forward, behind the defenders. And he looked really sharp going forward. That's why I'm pleased. Because he looks like he has changed his game, and is playing really to go behind the defenders. The mixture he had today, between coming off the ball and running behind the defenders, was right.'

Bergkamp often plays too deep and does not vary his game enough, so I could not resist the obvious question: 'Have you asked him to do that?'

'Yes. He wants to do that as well. He's an intelligent player, and he adapts his game to his physical potential. So when he had some problems at the beginning of the season, and was not feeling as sharp as he is at the moment, he came deeper for the ball. When we don't play so well as a team he doesn't get as many balls behind the defenders, so he comes and tries to build up the game. And last year he was always in a situation where we wanted him to come to the ball, and Nicolas to go behind the defender. And this year we try to mix that with Kanu, and that takes some time as well.'

This was a very significant point. Wenger had just admitted that he had asked Bergkamp to make more runs behind the defence in Anelka's absence because he could do that better than Kanu. Basically, August through to November had been a period of transition in which Wenger had had to decide whether to play Suker or Kanu at centre-forward. He had looked at both and played both and decided on the younger Kanu.

It was suggested that the team had regrouped in the time off for international matches after the Spurs game. Wenger, in response, neither confirmed nor denied this. He simply said that the team was at a stage of the season where they had to react. He said that everybody at the club felt they had lost some games they should not have lost. 'But I think the team realised that they have to show more concentration. Look at our season. We lost at West Ham but we should have won. We won at Chelsea but we were 2–0 down.

And we were 2–0 down at Tottenham after twenty minutes. So we are missing something. I think that is down to concentration sometimes. Not the right concentration when you start the game – maybe you think it will be easier than it is. And I believe that the English Premier League is every year more difficult.'

The *Sun*'s Brian Woolnough asked about speculation that the Dutchmen might move, and noted that Overmars had not yet killed off the speculation himself.

'No, because both players have long-term contracts. Long-term contracts mean that I want the player to stay. When I sign a player for a long time it always means I have a lot of confidence in his quality and his commitment to the club. We have no special problems with Marc Overmars. It was just things coming out in the newspapers . . . that's down to you!'

Is Overmars now back to his best?

'Yes, he's back. Marc had a lack of preparation. He went into the season injured. He didn't play the first games. He's just back to his best now. Tonight you have seen the best Overmars because they've changed three times the player marking him. That's always a sign.'

Is he the quickest player in the Premiership?

'Over the first five yards, certainly. I believe as well that he has the intelligence. And the timing of his movement is intelligent. When you add that pace to the timing of his movement, he is always dangerous. Petit is an important player for him because he finds him, and because he covers him defensively.'

Bergkamp's best game of the season?

'Difficult to say. He had a very good game against Barcelona. But it's the game where he got what I want from him right. That means his runs, the way he balanced his game, was maybe the best, yes. That's what we miss a little bit. So it gets easier for the defenders to push in on every player if they know that you don't go in behind them. So it's easy for them to hold the line if you don't make the runs.'

Wenger almost always talks moderately, never over-reacting, never exaggerating, even when the adrenalin is flowing after matches. He is a natural teacher, always supportive, always encouraging, but always patiently demanding more from his players. Coaches always want more, and although Wenger wants more than most he knows that some Saturdays are a lot better than others. This was one of the best, so his face, voice and body language told the same story: he was very pleased. He had an almost tangible aura of satisfaction about him because, having seen Bergkamp outpace a defence as Anelka used to do, he seemed to be halfway towards solving the biggest problem in his team.

The five goals were proof that this was the best Wenger's Arsenal had ever played without Patrick Vieira. The key point was that Bergkamp and Overmars had pulled their fingers out because Vieira was not playing. They knew they had to do the business. Necessity had been the mother of Dutch invention.

The five goals were also excellent preparation for the start of a fresh European campaign, for the UEFA Cup now beckoned, if Arsenal were really up for it. Eight of the 32 Champions League clubs had now been eliminated from Europe, including AC Milan, and another eight third-placed clubs had parachuted into the 32-team third round of the UEFA Cup in an absurd new format. This gave Arsenal a chance to play at Highbury and redeem themselves with a few victories. There were five Italian clubs in the UEFA Cup – Juventus, Parma, Roma, Udinese and Bologna – and four Spanish clubs – Celta Vigo, Atlético Madrid, Deportivo La Coruña and Real Mallorca – so Arsenal were quite fortunate when they drew Nantes, who were second from bottom in the French league and had lost their last six games. The easy draw was a sign that Wenger's luck had changed because it virtually guaranteed him another four games in Europe.

Arsenal beat Nantes 3–0 at Highbury on 25 November, although the result was better than the performance. On the Sunday, for the Derby County match, Wenger made four changes, the most interesting change being Thierry Henry for Kanu. This meant that Bergkamp and Henry were partners again for the first time since the Liverpool game at Anfield in August, when Arsenal had lost 2–0.

It was obviously a big test for Henry, and when Dean Sturridge scored for Derby after two minutes he really was in the spotlight.

Wenger had left Kanu and Suker on the bench so that Henry could start, but now Arsenal were losing at home and the pressure had doubled. Any chance he missed now would trigger a groan twice as loud as those which had accompanied his misses in previous games. After eleven minutes Overmars made a speedy run from inside his own half and saw Henry making a run from right to left, so he passed forward and Henry hit a first-time shot across Mart Poom and just inside the post, a beautiful finish. So the score was 1–1 and we began to realise that Wenger's changes were not rotation, but an admission that the Bergkamp–Kanu partnership had not really worked against Nantes.

Henry's pace had already elongated the game, forcing Derby to sit back more than they would have done against Kanu, and that gave Petit room to dictate the play, which he did in magnificent style. Overmars spurted forward again and found Henry, who took one touch into the box and fired across Poom for 2–1. So Thierry Henry came good at last and won the fans over. But was it a flash in the pan? Could Henry replace Anelka as a striker who terrorised Premiership defences every Saturday?

What Wenger calls 'our game' is a very fast, precise passing game which is based on explosive choreography, a game which, for the sake of convenience, we might call 'Bergkamp football'. The Derby match was a return to Bergkamp football: direct, dynamic, penetrating attacks. The fact that Bergkamp had a stinker was ironic, but Overmars and Petit played Bergkamp football on a day when Dennis did not.

Only three weeks earlier Wenger had told us that Henry could not time his runs, so his best position 'at the moment' was on the wing. The $64,000 question now was: Can Henry score regularly? Arsenal's attack often failed because the movement was not varied enough and if the attack was to be consistently effective Henry would have to improve because his on-the-ball play was far better than his off-the-ball movement. The Derby game was only the second time Wenger had selected Thierry Henry as Bergkamp's strike partner and he had scored two goals. After four months of experimenting he had at last found his best pair of strikers. But, this being football, as soon as something goes right, something else goes wrong. Bergkamp had gone off with a calf injury and would miss the next eight Premiership games, so Kanu partnered Henry in five of those games. Bergkamp did not partner Henry again till February.

The return leg against Nantes on 9 December was really an appendix to the first leg rather than a real second leg, and the game turned into an entertaining battle which finished 3–3. Wenger was angry with his team for not taking it seriously enough. When the draw for the fourth round was made he found that his next game would be at home to Spanish league leaders Deportivo La Coruña, who were like a Spanish Dynamo Kiev: well organised and technically sound in midfield and defence, giving very little away.

Then, on Monday, 13 December, Arsenal met Blackpool in the third round of the FA Cup. The date was an innovation everyone hated, since the third round had always been played on the first Saturday of January. Blackpool were third from bottom in Nationwide Division Two, and after fifteen minutes it was a massacre, but still goalless. Blackpool struggled to cope with Arsenal's pace, skill and movement and Arsenal struggled to cope with ninety per cent possession. Then, after 23 minutes, Overmars squared the ball to Grimandi who hit a fine shot into the bottom corner, his third goal in three matches. Phil Clarkson equalised, but Adams and Overmars soon made it 3–1. Oleg Luzhny, at centre-back between Dixon and Adams, covered well, headed solidly, passed accurately and ran confidently with the ball when space opened up for him. It was a successful experiment.

Thierry Henry was improving with every game, and he scored in a 1–1 draw with Wimbledon on 18 December, although that was little consolation for the loss of two vital points. However, a quick scan of the Arsenal teamsheet – Manninger; Dixon, Grimandi, Luzhny, Winterburn; Overmars, Ljungberg, Petit, Silvinho; Kanu, Henry – suggested that failure had been almost inevitable. The enforced changes had broken up all the vital partnerships in the team. Any team needs partnerships which cement the side together, and there were five key partnerships in this Arsenal team: Seaman–Adams, Bergkamp–Overmars, Bergkamp–Parlour, Adams–Keown and Petit–Vieira. This match was the first time all five of those partnerships were missing from the team. It was the dodgiest team Wenger had ever fielded in the Premiership.

ROBBIE KEANE IS FLICKING FANTASTIC

Footballers are made by their mums and dads.
                    Mick McCarthy, Republic of Ireland manager

The game at Coventry on Boxing Day, a Sunday, must have made Wenger wonder why he had not signed Robbie Keane, the talented young Irish international. He must have thought, 'How many times have my scouts seen this boy play?' Aston Villa boss John Gregory had offered Wolves £5 million for Keane, but Gordon Strachan, who had just raised £10 million by selling Boateng and Huckerby, signed him for £6 million.

Arsenal started the match feebly, Petit misplacing passes and overhitting corners, Kanu sleepwalking, and Belgian loan striker Roussel winning balls in the air against Keown, who had just come back after seven weeks out. Then McAllister hit a thirty-yarder which deflected in off Keown's back for 1–0 after six minutes, and Coventry made it 2–0 when their Moroccan international Mustapha Hadji curled a right-foot shot just inside the post. Seaman thought the shot was going wide and embarrassed himself by not going for it straight away, then panicked and ran along his line. Kanu and Overmars had stinkers, but Ljungberg managed to get a goal back for Arsenal.

Then Robbie Keane scored an extraordinary goal to make it 3–1. There was a long free-kick, Carlton Palmer won the header against Petit, nodded the ball to Roussel, who headed down past the rusty Keown, and Keane was on the ball in a flash, flicking it sharply up and across Seaman so that it looped in by the far post. Very few players in Britain could have reached that ball as quickly as Keane did, and none could have flicked it so early, so hard and so accurately. He instinctively did the only thing he could have done to score from where he was. It was a goal made in the womb. As the Republic of Ireland manager Mick McCarthy says, 'Footballers are made by their mums and dads.' Then Suker, just onside, collected a long diagonal pass from Petit, left Telfer on his backside, swerved inside Breen and scored with a left-foot toe-poke across Hedman.

The Keane strike had been the highlight of Coventry's 3–2 win. We all knew that Wenger had wanted Robbie Fowler, who was not for sale, but Robbie Keane had been available – a cheeky dribbler with lightning feet and exceptional movement, an agile volleyer, an aggressive competitor and an electric poacher, very smart at gliding down the channels and bending his runs to stay onside. He can also head the ball and is a natural finisher. Strachan had effectively signed a £14 million player for only £6 million and left Leeds, Chelsea and Arsenal looking stupid. For Wenger, the most annoying thing of all was that Robbie Keane would have been dynamite alongside Overmars and Bergkamp because he is sparky and they are cool. The chemistry would have been perfect. He would have been exactly the right player to replace Anelka, but Arsenal blew it, big-time.

Wenger had now seen his team lose five Premiership games since August, so this latest defeat made Leeds on 28 December a must-win game. The shock team news was that Keown, Dixon and Winterburn were not playing. The back four was Luzhny, Grimandi, Adams and Silvinho. Clearly, Wenger feared the pace and energy of this bubbling Leeds side and wanted to reinvigorate his side with fresh, speedy full-backs. This game marked the moment when Nigel Winterburn stopped being Arsenal's first-choice left-back after thirteen years of astonishingly consistent service.

Tony Adams was soon thundering into tackles and making interceptions like the Adams of old, the fearless, ferociously competitive warrior-athlete, and we immediately knew we were watching an all-or-nothing performance by one of English football's supreme gladiators, a man who was reaching down deep inside himself to dominate this vital game. Many fans were gobsmacked. They did not know that Adams could still play like this. The way he played that day was a statement which said, 'I want another title before I pack up.' It said, 'Leeds will win this Premiership over my dead body.' Adams was also sending a message to Leeds manager David O'Leary, who played for Arsenal for twenty years and made 722 appearances, a club record. That message might have been, 'You know I was a boozer who pissed the bed, but I'm still playing and I'm still a winner.'

Leeds competed very energetically and aggressively. Vieira was being caught in possession more than usual, but as the game went on he began to improve, giving us glimpses of his steely power. This was a rough, tough game to come back into after such a long suspension. Alan Smith, a pitbull of a player, jumped into Petit, who screamed at referee Graham Poll.

The first goal was scored after 34 minutes when Kanu spun away from Radebe and shot left-footed. Nigel Martyn dived to his left and got both hands to the ball, but Ljungberg stabbed in the rebound. The game had been intense until the first goal, and when Smith kicked Grimandi in the chest, and was booked, one wondered whether it would finish with 22 players on the pitch.

Seaman had nothing to do except punch away a couple of crosses, and as the second half went on Leeds just never got going, while Thierry Henry looked full of running, full of improvisation, very positive. Arsenal made it 2–0 when Kanu gave Henry a great pass and he went inside Radebe and hit a fine left-foot shot – his most explosive goal so far at Highbury, his most Anelka-like goal.

So Wenger saw his new players come through with flying colours. Silvinho had been very quick and sharp, a model of energy and concentration; Ljungberg had had an excellent game – feisty, skilful, productive, riding tackles and recovering, sticking his foot in here, there and everywhere, a jack-in-the-box who ambushed defenders; and Kanu was back to his best form, playing a big role in both goals. Near the end, Thierry Henry had produced a brilliant bit of showboating when he flew on to the ball on the left touchline and juggled it as he sprinted, playing keepy-uppy, kicking the ball six to ten inches in the air as he ran along. An astonishing sight: Henry dribbling the ball in mid-air! It was an incredible and spontaneous demonstration of balance and coordination which made the nearby Junior Gunners laugh out loud. Hooray, Henry! Wenger had also, of course, watched Adams at his best. He had toyed with the Leeds strikers, dispossessing them and accepting their fouls philosophically, shrugging off the kicks and elbows of Bridges and Smith as the fleabites of novices. George Graham had said it many times since 1986, and Wenger had agreed with him: Adams is a colossus.

It was a handsome 2–0 victory over the league leaders, an immensely satisfying one for Wenger. Arsenal had ended 1999 in third place with a win which brought them to within five points of Leeds.

LIVERPOOL MAKE WENGER ANGRY AGAIN

Since I've been in football, when you don't win people always say, 'Do they want it enough?' It's the same old story.

Arsène Wenger

In the FA Cup fourth round on 9 January 2000 Arsenal played Leicester at Highbury, and afterwards Arsène Wenger and Martin O'Neill revealed that all the significant action had taken place before kick-off in this dull 0–0 draw. Wenger said he had originally picked his team without Kanu, and O'Neill said that Emile Heskey almost did not play. It was a reminder that backstage life at football clubs is a lot more improvised than the fans imagine.

All week Kanu had been at the centre of an acrimonious tug-of-war between club and country, and it had been reported that FIFA would kick Arsenal out of the FA Cup if they refused to release the Nigerian for the African Nations Cup. Wenger said, 'I planned to play without him yesterday. Last night I had a chat with the manager of the team who told me there's no way he plays for Arsenal. OK – now we change again because I got the clearance at one o'clock. He was in a Nigerian restaurant last night. He was not even with us because I was sure he couldn't play. So I let him come to join the team at one o'clock.' Martin O'Neill, charcoal-suited and bespectacled, quirky and funny as always, in turn revealed that Heskey had travelled down to London that morning separately from the rest of the squad. 'We went for a walk at twelve o'clock. He wasn't feeling very well at all. I asked him if he could give us 25 minutes in the game. Just as a boost for us all. I said, "Have a think about it. Give me a shout at half past one." I didn't speak to him at half one. I just asked him when we were in the dressing room at a quarter to three. He said: "I'll give it a go." For him to play the whole game, I'm delighted.'

The draw for the fifth round was made before the press conferences, so both managers knew that the winners of the replay would be away to Chelsea or Nottingham Forest. Wenger was asked what he thought of the draw. He smiled and said, 'It's very difficult to go to Nottingham Forest.' Everyone laughed. A grim day at Highbury had ended with a good joke.

At Leicester on 19 January the replay finished goalless again, and Arsenal lost the penalty shoot-out, just as they had at Middlesbrough in the Worthington Cup fourth round on 30 November. Then they beat Sunderland 4–1 in the Premiership, Suker and Henry each scoring twice, which put them in reasonable shape for their next game – at Old Trafford on 24 January.

Many pundits reckoned this game would be a walkover for the treble winners because United, having been allowed to drop out of the 1999/2000 FA Cup, would be refreshed after their working holiday at the Club World Championship in Brazil, while Arsenal had no strikers. But Wenger, a student of the fixture lists, knew that United would be rusty, lacking their usual rhythm. They were poor in Rio, especially against Vasco Da Gama, and they were bound to lack fluency and sharpness. English teams find form by playing matches, not by sunbathing.

Wenger selected two strikers who had not yet played together, Henry and Ljungberg. Sure enough, United were a rabble in front of 58,293 people, the biggest crowd in Premiership history, and the Swede's gutsy attitude paid off after eleven minutes when Henry headed the ball on and he put his head in where Stam's boot almost caught him in the face, kept going, and whacked the ball under Bosnich's body. Arsenal were the better side and should have won, but Seaman missed a punch and Yorke hooked the ball back to give Sheringham a tap-in.

Ljungberg and Henry had done well together, but Wenger did not pick the same pair at Bradford on 5 February. Instead, he brought back Suker. Henry scored but Arsenal lost 2–1 and Suker did not start another Premiership game until the last day of the season at Newcastle. Then there was a problem with the increasingly temperamental Emmanuel Petit, who did an interview in the *Express* talking about how he feared every game would be his last, that he was worried his knee would fold after the next bad tackle. He said Wenger had had a go at him after the Leicester game, questioning his commitment. Petit was a ball-winning midfielder. If he was scared to tackle, what use was he?

Despite talking on the phone to Liverpool manager Gerard Houllier several times a month, Wenger never seems to be at his best after contests against his friend. Arsenal 0 Liverpool 1 on 13 February was a defeat which effectively put the Gunners out of a title race which had, ironically, opened up slightly with Newcastle's 3–0 victory over Manchester United. It was a cruel disappointment for Wenger and he was very sour and bad-tempered after the game. Arsenal had now won only two of their last nine matches. Was Wenger angry with his own players, or was he disgusted that Liverpool had played so negatively? Surely, after their dismal 0–0 draw last season, he had expected Houllier's team to shut up shop if they scored first?

Was it a significant blow for you, Arsène?

'Because we lost the game, of course. I think it was a poor game. That's even more disappointing, on both sides. I personally thought the two sides were poor.' Wenger had never before lost a match, come in and said both sides were poor, so I asked him if Arsenal had done enough to deserve a point. 'I think we deserved a point. Just because we at least tried to play, and tried to break Liverpool down, even if I think we didn't do enough to force it and we were not enough of a threat to break their defence down. I think it can be explained by the fact that we lost Petit at half-time, and by the fact that some players come back after a long injury and are not sharp enough at the moment to be dangerous.'

How deep is any concern you might have about qualification for the Champions League next season?

'It's very deep, because Chelsea's one point behind. Liverpool is three points ahead. It will be very difficult for us.'

Why has it gone wrong?

'I think we had too many players out through the whole season. If you look at the number of games some players have played together it's not enough.'

Kenny Goldman of ClubCall then asked, 'Is it a striker problem?'

'No. It is a problem, of course. But when you lose Kanu in the middle of the season, and Bergkamp is injured, and Overmars is injured, it's an explanation. We've lost three strikers – nine weeks for Bergkamp, six weeks for Kanu and six weeks for Overmars. That just explains that up front we have a problem.'

Who do you think the championship race is between now?

'Manchester United and Leeds.'

Just those two?

'Yes.'

Nigel Clarke of the *Daily Mail* asked, 'Is getting back on track going to provide you with the most difficult task since you've been here?'

'No, I've had difficult periods every year.'

This sounded, at last, more like a typical Wenger reply to a leading question. Clarke continued: 'You've always finished third, first, second – and now you appear to be slipping out of it.'

'Yes, but it's not over. There are thirteen games to go and we will see in the end where we stand.'

Have you considered playing Suker and Henry up front with Bergkamp behind them?

Wenger was very annoyed by this question, which is the sort of thing armchair tacticians talk about. His reply was emphatic: 'No, never. Not for one second.'

Brian Woolnough then mentioned a comment by Ray Parlour after the Bradford game, when he said that Bradford wanted to win the game more than Arsenal.

'Listen, when you lose games you have to accept that negative things always come out. I've no doubt about the state of mind or the commitment of the team. You can always find thousands of reasons but you always have to see what is important. Since I've been in football, when you don't win people always say, "Do they want it enough?" It's the same old story. But I have no problem about that. It's not about commitment, it's about quality. We miss quality at the moment.'

Kenny Goldman: 'You've had more shots on goal than any other team –'

'And we are less efficient. That's down to quality. And the way many teams play against Arsenal. They know how we play, so they just drop back and wait and defend deep, and then if we don't score first we always have a problem. And I think as well we are a little bit impatient at the back because we know that we have a problem, we need to score. So we don't have the patience at the back to avoid making a mistake.'

Wenger never interrupts a question. It was obvious that he wanted this press conference to end very soon. But first he was asked about Tony Adams, who had a toe injury caused by a swinging dressing-room door pushed by Petit. Wenger described his centre-back as 'short physically'.

If he was picked by England on Thursday, for the Argentina game, that would be OK?

'No chance. We live in a crazy world, but not one where the players don't play for the club but play for the national team.'

Clarke: 'Are you saying that Adams is not fit to play for England?'

'No, it's not that he's not fit. It's just not acceptable that he plays for England without having played for Arsenal.'

Clarke: 'So you won't allow him to join up?'

'No chance. Especially for a friendly. It's not like the country has to see if he is good enough. If he's fit in June [for Euro 2000], that is important. But at the moment he cannot play for the national team if he isn't playing for us.'

Jack Steggles of the *Daily Star* asked, 'Was it his decision not to play or yours?'

'It was my decision because I make the decisions. But deeply inside he agreed with that, because he didn't feel ready.'

And that was it. Seven minutes of Mr Wenger reacting to one of his worst days at the office since Blackburn stuffed Arsenal 3–1 at Highbury in December 1997. The good ship Gooner had been torpedoed by Camara's early goal and it was surprising that he did not give Liverpool a bit more credit. Perhaps his most revealing line was 'We at least tried to play', which suggested he was mad at

Houllier rather than his own team. Sky's stats gave Arsenal 65% possession.

It was mid-February and Arsenal were fourth in the table. If Wenger took stock of his resources he might have had mixed feelings because he had already seen the best years of seven of the players who started the Liverpool game. Only Silvinho, Henry, Vieira and Ljungberg could possibly improve. Seaman, Dixon, Keown, Grimandi, Parlour, Petit and Bergkamp could not get any better. Keown would do well to stay at the same level for a year, while Parlour might sustain his efforts for another three years. Silvinho, however, was establishing himself as an adventurous, dynamic footballer who wanted the ball all the time, and Ljungberg had done well against Liverpool. A week later it still looked like a cardinal error not to play him as a striker at Bradford after he had played out of his skin at Old Trafford. Arsenal lacked bite in the box and the Swede was giving them that.

Thierry Henry had also adapted well and learned English quickly, and he was liked by the other players. He had scored eleven goals and was quite good against Liverpool. He startled Westerveld with a thumping shot, powered past right-back Heggem to force a good block-save, headed a Silvinho corner a foot over the bar and had a good shot stopped by Westerveld's foot. Grimandi, too, had been solid. Still a journeyman, still a bit green, still getting done when he should not be, but mobile, durable, brave and a decent passer. Arsenal would have been in mid-table without his efforts so far that season. He had proved after all to be a worthwhile signing.

All in all, though, in mid-February 2000 Arsène Wenger was having a rough time, and the strain was showing. He would probably have been fine without the Anelka saga, but that had been partly his fault. He had thought he could find a way to keep Anelka for another year.

On 26 February Arsenal beat Southampton 3–1 at Highbury. Wenger was calm and businesslike, as usual, but very detached, talking about the match as if it had happened three days ago rather than half an hour before. Intriguingly, he said that constant competition for places was more important than having a settled first eleven.

'That was much more like Arsenal,' said Wenger. 'We had the needed reaction today and the needed performance. Not only because we won, but concentration-wise, spirit-wise, I would say we had what I expected of the team. It was a great test today, not of the ability of the players, but of our desire still to be at the top in our job. And I think we reacted well. I played Ljungberg on the left because I needed him there today. Because Overmars was a little bit short. He's maybe the player who can play everywhere. And he may be the most improved player of the season, compared to last season, when he had some problems to adapt and everybody said maybe he's not an Arsenal player. Don't forget, he's only 22. He has shown since the beginning of the season that he's one of the most consistent players in our team.'

When everyone's back and you've got a full team, will you play your best team in every game?

'No. If you say I'll play the same team every time, no matter how they play, the competition inside the squad goes, and that's not right. I'll play the team that has the best chance of winning the game, and I'll try to create stability in our shape and in the players who play well together. For example, when you play at home, Kanu–Bergkamp works better than when you play away. Because you get more space away and so you need more players who will go in behind the defenders. You need more pace away.'

Arsenal then beat Deportivo La Coruña 5–1 and while the scoreline was a surprise it was not a mystery. It was just one of those nights where everything went right. Bulgarian referee Ouzounov allowed the game to flow and it turned into a thrilling spectacle. Dixon ! Henry ! Djalminha penalty for 2–1! Djalminha sent off! Henry scored again for 3–1! Kanu made it 4–1! A Bergkamp free-kick for 5–1! Ouzounov was conned by Flavio, who dived when Ljungberg made minimal contact, and Djalminha showed his class by floating the penalty down the middle while Seaman dived to one side. The referee was also conned by Grimandi, who over-reacted to a butt in the chest by Djalminha to get the little sorcerer sent off.

The next two games were both away from home in early March. Lee Dixon scored in the 1–1 draw at Aston Villa and after that Wenger had to play a bizarre back four at Middlesbrough: Luzhny, Grimandi, Petit and Silvinho. This was the first time Petit had played at centreback for Arsenal and it was also the last. It was little wonder they lost 2–1. In the UEFA Cup they lost 2–1 in La Coruna, and then they beat Werder Bremen 2–0 at Highbury and 4–2 in Bremen, courtesy of a Ray Parlour hat-trick.

MORE DUTCH RUMBLINGS

We missed two chances with Arsenal to win the Champions League. In your career you don't get too many chances to win such a big trophy. Who has the patience to wait for the next time with the same club?

Marc Overmars

Both Arsène Wenger and George Graham were smiling on Sunday, 19 March after Arsenal beat Spurs 2–1 with an own-goal and a Thierry Henry penalty. Wenger said, 'Thierry keeps doing it. He keeps improving, and he has just to keep fit and to work hard. He shows he has large potential because he has started to improve in the air. He's cool enough to take the penalties and I think he had a tremendous game again today. He is the penalty-taker at the moment.'

Do you feel Grimandi's sending-off was justified?

'It was a second yellow card. It was unfortunate. Gilles didn't want to make a bad tackle. But that happens sometimes when you're tired; you're a little bit late and you get a yellow card. He's a physical player. He's a defender. He has to win the ball for us and sometimes he gets a yellow card. But for me he had a tremendous game against Werder Bremen, and today again. I feel sorry for him that he got this second yellow card, because at the moment he's a very important player for us.'

For Wenger, there is always a big difference between a player who is sent off for a wild tackle or a serious misdemeanour and someone who picks up a second yellow card, which can be for something innocuous.

George Graham, the former king of the Gooners, appeared at the press conference in a navy suit, dark blue shirt and club tie. He had played a memorable role in the sporting life of Europe's biggest city, won six trophies for Arsenal and one for Spurs, but he now seemed to have become a cabaret turn. What is cabaret? Cabaret is when you sing the same old songs again and again and again. Cabaret is an act, but you try to hide your boredom, try to make it meaningful, try to make it convincing, try to make it real.

Was it a close game, George?

'Yeah, I think so. First half we started nice and brightly, a few corners, a few poor efforts on goal from Iversen and Ginola, should maybe have done a litle bit better. I agree with Arsène. I think they looked tired, too many games. They were there to be beaten today. We just couldn't capitalise on it second half. We had lots of possession but didn't really create enough.'

Why did you play Ginola on the right?

'I wanted to see how good a defender Silvinho was.'

How good is he?

'I don't know. I still don't know. David created the chance, great cross and a lovely little flick. If you consider Arsenal's two goals – one's an own goal and one's a penalty.'

Wenger had mentioned the special atmosphere at Highbury that day, but would it still have been special had Spurs not been managed by George Graham? Rivalry is the lifeblood of football, but in terms of the Premiership Leeds, Liverpool and United were Arsenal's rivals now, not Tottenham.

The following Sunday, Wenger must have been shocked by a Joe Melling story in the *Mail on Sunday*, its headline OVERMARS TEMPTED BY BARCELONA CHALLENGE. The winger had made some comments which summed up his point of view perfectly. 'We have missed two chances with Arsenal to win the Champions League. In your career you don't get too many chances to win such a big trophy. Who has the patience to wait for the next time with the same club? Has every player still got the same desire and willpower to win that trophy?' Overmars reckoned he had developed considerably and had become a match-winner. 'At Arsenal I have become a more complete player. I can play as a midfielder now. I can decide matches, I can score goals and I can give the team something extra. But there is room for another ten per cent of improvement. To get that extra I may have to go to another football country where I will experience different challenges.'

Arsenal played Coventry on the day the piece appeared, and a remarkable thing happened at Highbury: Petit started tackling again after months of not tackling, and it made a big difference. They beat Coventry 3–0, but they were still fourth in the league. Arsenal never really got going in a tedious first half, but then they raised their game, Henry scoring his eighteenth goal of the season. Vieira played him in with a superbly weighted through-pass, Henry accelerated, took one touch and swept it confidently past the advancing Ogrizovic. This was real Wenger football: dynamic, skilful, direct and unstoppable. Straight down the middle – Grimandi, Vieira, Henry, bang!

Petit had been pressing Coventry in the first half, even pressing them in their own penalty area, and was flying into tackles. He was involved in everything. In the second half he took a free-kick wide on the right, the ball bounced into a crowded penalty area, hit Shaw and broke to Grimandi, who buried his shot from seven yards. Kanu then waltzed through to collect a Petit chip over the top and delayed for an eternity of seconds before dummying Ogrizovic on to his backside and stroking the ball home sweetly from two yards. In the next game they played Wimbledon and Kanu got two and Henry came on as sub, took a penalty and scored.

After that came the UEFA Cup semi-final first leg at Highbury against Lens, Arsenal ideally needing a two- or three-goal cushion to take to France on 20 April. Lens were missing several key defenders, and when the game started the centre-backs were shaky. The goalkeeper, Warmuz, who was also the captain, was obviously expecting that. So when Petit launched a fifty-yard pass, Warmuz raced out of his penalty area to claim the ball but Bergkamp zoomed past him and scored beautifully. After that goal, Arsenal dominated for the next fifteen minutes, but then Lens improved and matched them for energy with five players in midfield closing down their angles, swarming like bees, pressing the pressers, forcing errors and breaking quite well at times. It was a brave effort in damage limitation to keep Arsenal to 1–0.

Lens coach François Brisson came into the post-match press conference first. A strongly built guy with short black hair and a serious, businesslike manner, he seemed relaxed and satisfied. The reporters talked to him in French, and there was no translation. Then Wenger came in.

Will that be enough, Arsène?

'I don't know. I just think that we were a little bit frustrated coming off. The performance was not maybe our best of the season. The result was not too bad because we kept a clean sheet and could score a goal. But it was very difficult to get our passing together because they played very well, closed us down, and when they dropped physically in the second half we couldn't improve our level any more. They were wobbling in the last 25 or 30 minutes but we had nothing more to give and we couldn't kill the game off.

'Our target is clear: we have to go out there and try to score a goal. But having seen them tonight you can see that it will be difficult. But they have two difficult games now. They play against Metz and against Paris Saint Germain. We have a difficult game at Leeds. We'll see. Psychologically, championship games can have an importance in the second leg.'

It was a quirk of fate that two Premiership clubs who were also UEFA Cup semi-finalists should have to play each other in a league game between the first and second legs of their respective ties, against Lens and Galatasaray. But if Wenger really believed that football is a game of sequences, he would have had no worries as his team bus arrived at Elland Road. Leeds had lost their last five games while Arsenal had won their last six.

The visitors handed the Leeds players bouquets before the game in memory of the two supporters who had been murdered in Istanbul the previous week. It was a scene reminiscent of Anfield in 1989 when the Arsenal players had given the Liverpool players flowers in memory of the Hillsborough disaster, before beating them 2–0 to take the title.

Arsenal produced a powerfully efficient team performance on the Sunday, thrashing Leeds 4–0 and completing seven wins in a row. Wenger had fielded his strongest side so that they would have no excuses for not winning, and they had demonstrated the high degree of ruthlessness needed to sustain unbeaten runs in professional football. Ljungberg had been preferred to Overmars, a landmark selection by Wenger. It was the first time the Swede had been chosen over the Dutchman when both were fit – the manager had obviously seen that Joe Melling interview. Ljungberg was voted Sky's Man of the Match, on his 23rd birthday.

Arsenal then went to Lens and won 2–1 to reach the UEFA Cup Final. Bergkamp and Silvinho were excellent, but Vieira was better than both of them against a fast, aggressive French side who made Arsenal work very hard for their victory. Overall, the UEFA Cup had suited them and they had scored 21 goals in eight games. Thierry Henry, who had not started a Champions League game, had now played seven UEFA Cup ties and scored seven goals. If only he had arrived on 4 June, not 4 August. Arsenal now faced Galatasaray in Copenhagen on 17 May, the Turks having drawn 2–2 at Elland Road.

TWELVE IN A ROW

The ball rebounded against his hand, yes. But that doesn't mean they had to concede the goal. It was 35 yards out on the right side.

Arsène Wenger

Three days after the victory over Lens, Arsenal won 3–2 at Watford. Henry scored twice, but then he missed the trip to Everton on the 29th, where Petit made Overmars the star by picking him out with a series of defence-splitting passes. Vieira, rested, sat on the bench with a face like thunder. The only goal of the game was a vintage 1998 one: Overmars sprinted into the Everton half, chested the ball forward, guided it brilliantly into his stride with his left foot and, with David Weir backing off in terror, hit the ball between Paul Gerrard and the near post. The shot was very relaxed, very fluent, with lots of disguise, the greatest Robbie Fowler goal of his career.

Arsenal had now won ten games in a row, and they only had to keep it going for five more games, against West Ham, Chelsea,

Sheffield Wednesday, Newcastle – and Galatasaray. Every match is a potential banana skin, of course, but ten wins was the best possible confidence-builder for these last five games.

The West Ham game at Highbury on 2 May turned out to be the most controversial of the season. Arsenal badly missed the pace of Henry, who was injured, and Kanu was feeble against Stimac. Five minutes before half-time di Canio put the Hammers a goal up, and it was still 1–0 after 56 minutes, when Wenger made one of his best ever substitutions: Petit for Dixon. Time was running out when Overmars got past Foe and rifled a low shot inside the post. Twenty-one minutes left to win the game. In the last ten Arsenal played fast, fluent, inventive football, and then, in stoppage time, Petit handled the ball on the right side and hit a tremendous shot which deflected off Stimac into the net. Incredibly, referee Paul Durkin allowed the goal, in the face of furious protests from the West Ham players.

There was only one question for Harry Redknapp after the match. Do you feel you've been robbed tonight, Harry?

'Oh, for sure. We were robbed tonight, yeah. It was handball. It was our throw-in in the first place. Luzhny's come right in front of him and kicked the ball out of play. And the linesman's just naturally put his flag that way because he's been doing it all night. And then the ball comes in to Petit and he handballs it.' Not surprisingly, Harry had the hump with Durkin because he had come with a team of 'odds and sods' and reckoned the Hammers deserved better than to lose to a handball in stoppage time.

I had the inevitable question ready for Wenger. Were you lucky tonight?

'I don't think so. Because I believe that overall we deserved to win. And it was an exciting game, a cracking game, with a high pace. West Ham played very well but I believe overall my team has shown a great spirit and great quality and never gave up tonight. In the end you can say it's a lucky three points because we scored in the last minute. But if there was to be a winner tonight it's Arsenal.'

Brian Woolnough asked about the Petit handball.

'The ball rebounded against his hand, yes. But that doesn't mean they had to concede the goal. It was 35 yards out on the right side.'

So that was it. A handball, a late goal, a fiery finish, an angry Harry, a plausible Arsène, another three points, second place, and a bigger, harder game to come against Chelsea and George Weah.

On a very warm 6 May Thierry Henry scored twice against Chelsea, whose minds were on their forthcoming FA Cup Final against Aston Villa. A through-ball from Vieira was misjudged by Leboeuf and Henry rounded de Goey to slot home his 24th goal of the season. Soon after that Bergkamp sent Henry racing through against Desailly. His shoulder-charge knocked Desailly over like a skittle and he scored from a narrow angle through de Goey's legs. Poyet volleyed inside the post with ten minutes left.

Manager Luca Vialli reckoned Chelsea had lost the midfield battle, and that Henry was virtually unstoppable. Wenger said that Arsenal had been expecting a difficult last 25 minutes but their spirit, determination and organisation saw them through. He also paid tribute to Henry, saying he had shown tremendous strength to beat Desailly for the second goal. Television replays explained the incident: Desailly was standing still and Henry was flying, so his speed did the damage, demonstrating a simple law of physics: force equals mass times acceleration. The collision provided an exciting and comical moment, although it was not funny for Desailly, who did not claim a foul, as some players might have done. His handsome face just registered disbelief and indignation.

In the last home game against struggling Sheffield Wednesday on 9 May, it was obvious that the players all wanted to avoid injury eight days before the UEFA Cup Final. Arsenal had already achieved second place in the league (of their twelve straight wins, eight had come in the Premiership), so they started without their three strategic brains: Adams, Petit and Bergkamp.

It was a still, sticky night, unsuited to a high-tempo game, so Arsenal took a long time to score, Henry crossing for Dixon to net the opener after 34 minutes. In the second half Sibon and de Bilde came on as subs for Wednesday, each got a goal to make it 2–1, then Alan Quinn beat the offside trap and went round Seaman far too easily for 3–1. Silvinho was sent on, and his 25-yard shot reduced the deficit, and then Henry made it 3–3. That was the final score, and Wednesday were relegated. Their manager, Peter

Shreeves, said the turning point was Silvinho's goal because its quality had lifted the crowd. With their minds firmly on Copenhagen, Wenger fielded a reserve team at Newcastle in the last league game and Arsenal lost 4–2.

In the build-up to the final, Leeds manager David O'Leary did his old club no favours by saying that Galatasaray were far inferior to them. 'There's only one winner,' he said. 'Arsenal as a team are so superior to Galatasaray. I still have many friends at Highbury and I'm certain Tony Adams will be lifting the cup on Wednesday night. I don't even see it as a close game. I can see them winning by two or three goals.'

UEFA CUP FINAL MEDIA DAY

It's been quite unbelievable the way the club's moved on from six years ago. Every single aspect of the club has changed, and I can't emphasise enough how much Arsène's had to do with that. I think he's been a massive influence on the club.

Lee Dixon

Before the Chelsea game Wenger and his players hosted a media day at their superb Shenley Training Centre. From the outside, the training complex is just a place where footballers practise and park their Porsches and BMWs, but from the inside, it is immediately apparent that Shenley is a serious place of work for serious footballers which cost serious money to build. The high-tech complex was designed to Wenger's specification and is luxurious, reflecting the status of his gifted, multinational squad of players. It is a 2,500-square-metre glazed building which houses a senior squad gymnasium, state-of-the-art medical equipment, and offices for the coaches, physio, doctor and youth officer. A hydrotherapy unit, with swimming pools, jacuzzi and sauna, plays an important part in the warm-down routines and is used a lot on the day after matches. There are ten immaculate pitches including two designed for high-intensity use, with polypropylene strips inserted into the top soil layer to aid drainage and prevent divoting, and two also have underground heating.

When you are there for a few hours everything else melts away and the world is simplified. The working life of the players and coaches is divided into match days and preparation days, each day existing in relation to the match that has just been played and the match that is about to be played. There are newspapers and TV sets tuned to news and sports channels, but they reflect an external reality which is a lot less relevant than the internal realities of who is fit, who is injured, who is playing well in training. A footballer's life revolves around the fixture list, the clock, meal times and travel schedules.

On this media day reporters were welcomed into what is normally the restaurant, a huge first-floor room with glass walls and French windows leading on to balconies down both sides. There were large circular tables, each seating eight people, sofas at both ends and help-yourself coffee, bottled water and Danish pastries. Wenger wore a dark blue suit and did a general press conference and another for the Sunday papers. He said that a cup final can always go either way, unless you are playing a team three divisions below you. 'Some people will say Galatasaray is favourite but I wouldn't say that. We have a fifty-fifty chance. And we just have to go for it. In a cup final you just try to win it.' He said that this season's UEFA Cup competition was full of strong teams. 'You had La Coruña, who can be champions in Spain, Monaco, who will be champions in France, Juventus, who can be champions in Italy, maybe. You had Roma, Parma, Udinese and Leeds. So it was a highly competitive UEFA Cup. You cannot consider it as a consolation trophy if you look at the teams who were in there, and you had all the cup winners as well. It's a great achievement to be there, and if it's taken sixteen years for an English club to be in there again, it's not easy.'

He also spoke again about how going out of the Champions League had been very, very disappointing for everyone. 'Today, when you are at a club like Arsenal, the players feel that if they are not in the Champions League they are not at the top. It's such a big thing now, created by the media, that if they are not there they feel, "I'm wasting my time, I'm not at the top." To achieve something at the end of the season will give the players the feeling that they did not fight for nothing.'

Wenger confirmed that he had not seen Galatasaray himself, but he had sent scouts and reviewed videos and he admitted that sometimes as a young manager he was too obsessed by his opponents. 'You watch them and watch them and re-watch, and you forget about your own team. It's good to concentrate on your own strengths.'

He then talked about the return of Tony Adams in a way that showed his tolerance and ability to analyse character. 'He came back with a lot of other big players and the team feels more secure when he is there. The team felt, with everybody being back, stronger again, psychologically. It was a huge boost to have everybody back. I think when you come out of such a huge problem as he had, you have to find a new balance in your life. That takes time. He has found a new balance in his life. When I arrived he was just trying to get out of the problem and stabilise his situation. It wasn't difficult for me because he's a very intelligent guy. He had a little bit of a rough image and I was surprised to discover somebody who is very intelligent and sensitive. But he had been hiding that behind different behaviour.'

Tony Adams himself – big and rangy with long, untidy hair, wearing a pair of jeans, a striped shirt and a short-sleeved grey sweater – clearly felt a strong sense of duty towards his beloved club. 'Physically, today, I feel well. I've been very frustrated and very impatient. I had a double hernia operation in September and played 25 straight games, and I don't think that was very wise. I should have taken it a bit slower perhaps. So basically over the last month or so I've done a lot of work in the gym and it's been a slower comeback this time. I wish we could play once on Saturday afternoon, three o'clock, once a week – that would be the ideal thing.'

Lee Dixon, in black jeans and navy shirt, talked about the changes in the skipper since he conquered alcoholism. 'I can't speak highly enough about that side of his life,' he said. 'If you knew him before and you know him now, as a person he's totally different and he's a nicer person to be around. A few years ago he wasn't a nice person to be around all of the time. Although he was still a mate, he had problems and we didn't really know how to help him. You can have a conversation with him now about all sorts of things. He's done it all himself with hard work and determination. It just shows the character of the man.'

Only Adams, Dixon and Seaman remained from the 1994 side that beat Parma in the same Parken Stadium in Copenhagen, where they were now due to face Galatasaray, the first Turkish club to reach a European final. Dixon was asked about his memories of the Parma final. 'I remember thinking when the final whistle went, "How the hell have we won that?" Because we got absolutely battered for ninety minutes. We were the underdogs and we played like underdogs, got absolutely hammered and won 1–0.' He reckoned the transformation the club had undergone in the intervening years was mostly due to the manager. 'It's been quite unbelievable the way the club's moved on from six years ago. Every single aspect of the club has changed, and I can't emphasise enough how much Arsène's had to do with that. I think he's been a massive influence on the club. Certainly the club would have moved forward, but whether it would have gone forward at this pace – I don't think it would have been possible under anybody else. The team, the facilities, the stadium, everything, just the professionalism in the way the club's run. Everything's spot-on. If there's any problem, he sorts it out. Simple as that. And he doesn't allow complacency to breed in any part of the club.'

Thierry Henry was as friendly and laid-back as usual, wearing trainers – as all the players did – faded jeans and a light navy jacket over a pale-green knitted cotton top. He was revealing when he talked about Arsenal's pressing style, and about his struggles to score in the first four months of the season. 'Manu and Patrick, when they are in great condition, they can win the ball high on the pitch, and I can make some good runs. We scored so many goals like that this year. Some teams think they can destroy us, but Manu and Patrick can take the ball high around the pitch and we can counter-attack with me or Marc or Dennis or Kanu. So I think we always play like that.'

He said that when he first started to play football he always felt like a striker. 'I lost my confidence when I played as a winger because you have to cross for the striker. At the beginning, when I first arrived at Monaco, I was sixteen years old and I was a striker with the youth team. After, they put me in the first squad and I played as a winger and I started to lose my confidence in front of goal. I played four years. I knew what to do in front of the goalkeeper, but I didn't have that feeling any more. I think this year I missed so many chances, I missed more chances than I scored goals. So it was a little bit difficult at the beginning because all the time Patrick used to tease me. It was funny, but it was true as well. I remember I missed so many chances. Some chances were difficult, but many of the chances I was missing were not difficult. I think playing striker is the most difficult position, along with the goalkeeper. When he makes a mistake it's a goal. With a striker, when you don't score for one game, or two or three or four, you lose your confidence and people talk about you. They say, "He's not fit any more, he's not like before." You have to score to stay confident.'

He was then asked if during this period he had ever gone to Wenger and said, 'Look, it's not working, I must go back on the wing.'

'One day I wanted to do it. I didn't do it because I have a lot of confidence in Arsène. But it was so hard. In my mind it was so hard because I was always in the French squad as a winger. And everybody in Europe used to know me as a winger. So one day I thought, "I have to speak with the boss." Then when I arrived at the training camp I said, "No, it's all right." You know, sometimes you have players who stop when they have a little problem, but I thought, "I'll just have to keep going, and maybe we'll see at the end of the season." The day it clicked was Derby at home. We were losing 1–0 and I scored two goals. I was like a proper striker, I made a run. I can remember, it was Marc Overmars sent me twice in the goal. He gave me the first goal and I scored with my left foot – it was an easy goal. And I made a good run with Marc again. And I started to have more confidence. Sometimes when you score two goals you feel like a striker. So the last time France picked me I played as a striker.'

Such sentiments are common among top strikers, whose jobs consist of goals and misses seen by millions of people every weekend. In a *Gazzetta Italia* interview, Christian Vieri of Inter Milan once said something very simple and very profound on this point: 'Only a striker knows what it's like to score – and not to score.' But it was good to know that before Arsenal's first European final for five years Thierry Henry was now feeling like a proper striker.

GALATASARAY

We improved in the second half, but really we could not find our true game today.

Arsène Wenger

In Copenhagen, Arsenal seemed to be intimidated by the pre-match hooliganism in the city centre and the Turkish-dominated atmosphere in the stadium. Adams and Keown were shaky from the start, and anxiety spread forward into the rest of the team. When Adams headed out early on and Arif volleyed, the ball hit Keown and deflected just wide of the post. Arsenal were on the back foot right from the kick-off and as the first half wore on they seemed to be too diagrammatic, too shape-conscious, broken up into three separate units of defence, midfield and attack, players staying in their boxes fifteen yards apart. Bergkamp was having to forage back among four Turks just to get a touch of the ball on the left side of midfield because Petit never made a tackle, never got into the game. Vieira and Okan were booked for fouls on each other, Overmars was giving a hundred per cent, scrapping with Capone and fouling him, but Petit was a jogging passenger. Overmars managed to recover a Bergkamp flick and drill in a low shot which Taffarel saved at the near post, but Galatasaray dominated possession, which is what happens when you are effectively playing with ten men.

At half-time in the BBC studio, Martin O'Neill reminded the viewers that world-class players can play badly. Ljungberg spoke to Garth Crooks and said, 'It's good. It's 0–0. Because I think Galatasaray are gonna get tired in the second half. Galatasaray have been running a lot in the first half and hopefully they're gonna get tired in the second half. They've been pressing a lot and I don't think they're gonna last for ninety minutes.' O'Neill reacted to that. 'It's a dangerous way to think. That that's how you're gonna win a game – the other side gets tired.'

In the second half a Bergkamp–Vieira move put Parlour into a good position, but his cross hit the near post. Then Hakan Sukur was through and Keown, with a last-ditch tackle, just managed to divert the ball on to the post. Later, Henry hit a fine cross to give Keown a golden chance, but he spooned over the bar from four yards. Arsenal were dominating the game at last, and then, on 74 minutes, Wenger took off Bergkamp and brought on Kanu. To little effect.

Who would score the golden goal in extra time? One shot, one header, one mistake and it would be all over. Arsenal got on top again and looked like winning. Henry had a run, but he shot from a silly angle. Then Hagi dribbled, Adams tackled well, and the ball went loose between them. Adams moved to impede the Romanian's recovery before playing the ball himself, as you do, so Hagi pulled his shorts and grabbed him round the waist. Adams flailed backwards with his arms, so Hagi slapped Adams on the back with his little fist. Spanish referee Antonio Lopez Nieto handed Adams a yellow card and Hagi a red card, and after that Galatasaray just sat back and played for penalties.

During half-time of extra time, Wenger could be seen prowling the touchline with his hands in his trouser pockets. Should he have taken a defender off and gone for broke? Grimandi, strong in the air, full of running, might have given them more presence in the box. Blocked and frustrated in the centre of the park, should he have tried to work the flank more using Silvinho's energetic overlaps? Had he backed himself into a corner by taking Bergkamp off? Did he not need to add to Bergkamp, rather than replace him? What a hellish experience it must be for a coach when the last match of the season, a UEFA Cup Final, becomes a journey to the outer limits of his faith, his ideas, his strength, his nerve-endings. Sometimes the hardest part of being a coach is to do nothing. Anybody can throw new bodies on, but if you keep faith, believe in your players, it often comes right.

Suddenly, the season almost worked out when Parlour hit a fantastic cross from the corner flag. Henry jumped well at the far post and headed down firmly, but Taffarel parried. Arsenal kept coming forward. Kanu swerved in from the right wing and smacked in a shot which Taffarel again parried, this time against Popescu's legs and back to Kanu, whose second shot was saved again by the keeper. A Galatasaray cross from the left byline then skimmed low across Seaman's goalmouth with no takers. Wenger put on Suker for Overmars for the last six minutes. Both teams were exhausted, though, and the last throw of the dice was a Petit free-kick from the right side. He swung the ball into the right area, Adams challenged, but the referee whistled for a push, as he did too often on set-piece plays.

The penalty shoot-out did not look promising as the kicks were to be taken at the Turkish end, facing a wall of noise. David Seaman had done his job well so far but he does not save penalties any more and Arsenal had already lost shoot-outs at Middlesbrough and Leicester.

Ergun took a perfect cool penalty, left-footed, just inside the post, beating Seaman's dive. Davor Suker checked his run and smacked his penalty against the inside of the post and it came out. When Hakan Sukur hit a slick shot high into the net for 2–0 there was bedlam behind the goal. Parlour was now under a lot of pressure from the crowd. But he fired his penalty perfectly into the bottom corner to Taffarel's right for 2–1.

Davala sent Seaman the wrong way for 3–1. Patrick Vieira seemed to rush his run-up, not taking time to compose himself. He hit his penalty hard and centrally and it came back off the underside of the bar. Then Popescu hit a classy shot into the bottom corner to clinch the first European trophy ever won by a Turkish club.

Man for man, Galatasaray had been more up for it than Arsenal. They had defended deep, broken up the rhythm by diving, worked the angles in midfield, played in little triangles and always seemed to have an extra player until Hagi was sent off. Coach Fatih Terim had really done his homework, and had got a swarm of players round Vieira and Bergkamp at key moments. Their pressing was backed up by craftsmanship, players who were resourceful and patient when it came to keeping possession. Terim's tactics nullified Henry's pace and isolated Bergkamp, who nevertheless played well in bursts and was furious when he was taken off.

Arsenal had looked too schematic, too German, with too little play round the ball and not enough support runs close to the ball, not enough improvisation. Ljungberg, with his energy and devilment, might have added a lot from the bench by getting into the box and matching Galatasaray's fiery commitment. Wenger had relied on pace to win it early, and on fitness to win it later on if pace was not decisive, and on supersub Kanu if pace and fitness failed to produce a goal. But none of those three factors was significant on the night. Petit had been abysmal, but Wenger was either too loyal or too conservative to substitute a World Cup winner.

The manager was furious that referee Nieto did not toss for ends to decide where the shoot-out would take place. UEFA officials, in response, claimed that the toss to decide ends for extra time also counted for where the penalties were taken. Wenger said, 'I can't agree with that. The referee may be saying that now but I don't believe it and I think it was unfair. Nobody has seen this toss of the coin which is supposed to have happened. The referee just told Tony Adams that it was what he had decided.'

On the game as a whole, he said, 'We had a not very good first half and in the end lost to a good Galatasaray side. We improved in the second half, but really we could not find our true game today. It is very disappointing because this is the third cup we have missed this season through penalty shoot-outs. We lost in the FA Cup and the Worthington Cup in that way too, and it is very difficult to take. If we had won the penalty shoot-out it would not have made any difference to the quality of our game.'

Wenger was probably the only manager in England who would have said that winning in a cup final on penalties would not have changed the fact that they had played badly. It showed how idealistic he was, how high his expectations were in terms of the exciting, entertaining football he expected his team to play. He really wanted to win that UEFA Cup Final, and he was devastated by the defeat. He later told Philippe Auclair of *France Football* that it took him a week to get over it.

8. 2000/01: THE SEASON OF ROTATION

In the summer of 2000 Wenger sold Marc Overmars and Emmanuel Petit to Barcelona for £28 million. Overmars had been a world-class player when he was scoring goals, Petit a world-class player when he was tackling, but Arsenal had been turning into Chelsea because those two players were just not performing in Premiership away games.

The manager again decided to invest in foreign players. On 11 July Edu, the £6 million replacement for Petit, arrived at Heathrow but was sent back to Brazil for having a fake passport. He had a Portuguese grandfather and was eligible for dual nationality, but only after his father had acquired the necessary documents from Lisbon, which might take six months, so he went back to São Paulo and continued to play for Corinthians. This was a severe blow to Wenger. Should he wait for Edu or buy someone else?

He then signed French winger Robert Pires for £6 million from Marseilles to replace Overmars, and Lauren, a versatile Cameroon player from Real Mallorca, for £7.2 million. He also acquired Latvian centre-back Igor Stepanovs for £1 million from FC Skonto Riga, and was looking at Lithuanian striker Tomas Danilevicius from Lausanne in Switzerland.

Tomas was Lithuania's under-21 centre-forward. He had been having secret trials with Arsenal for a week when the club took him to a pre-season tournament in Amsterdam to celebrate the centenary of Ajax. During the match against Barcelona, Silvinho rolled the ball to Tomas, who cleverly dummied Guardiola and rifled a shot past Richard Dutruel. Arsenal lost the game 2–1, but Tomas looked like he might be another Marian Pahars, the lively, brave little Latvian at Southampton. Big players from small countries might be just what was needed by Wenger, who said of Tomas, 'He's fast, he has good presence, he's good in the air and he's scored a great goal.' In fact, Tomas seemed almost too good to be true and Wenger made a bid for him.

The acquisition of Sylvain Wiltord proved problematic for many weeks. Wenger initially offered £8 million, but Bordeaux wanted £15 million. Four years earlier Wiltord had played for Rennes, who had sold him for £1.75 million to Deportivo La Coruña. Before Wiltord had even so much as played a game in Spain he was sold on to Bordeaux for £2 million, with a sell-on clause which gave the Spanish club 35% of any future transfer fee. That clause was due to expire in June 2001, so Bordeaux wanted Wiltord to stay and play another season so they could keep the full transfer fee.

For Wenger and other Champions League coaches the biggest date in the summer calendar was 31 August, the deadline for registration of squads with UEFA. As the deadline approached, Wenger said of the Wiltord negotiations, 'We will make the deadline or not the player.' In other words, he wanted Wiltord before 31 August or not at all. He eventually signed him for £12.5 million just before the Charlton game on 26 August.

Wenger now had a very odd quartet of strikers. The first was the best left-winger in the world, a player so gifted that there had been 26 moments in the season before when he had made scoring look easy, and made people think he was a striker. Alongside Henry was Wenger's second striker, an injury-prone Dutchman who had not been on an aircraft for six years and had only scored six Premiership goals in 1999/2000. The third was a Nigerian whose heart foundation was helping sick kids and who could not fully plug into the reality of Premiership football, where you had to believe that getting three points at Coventry is the most important thing in the world. Kanu also wanted Wenger to pay his huge salary while he vanished to Sydney for a month to play in another Olympic Games – a strange impertinence.

Now that gifted but often problematic trio had been joined by a new Frenchman who should have been a centre-forward who could head the ball. Instead, Wiltord was a five-foot-eight-inch buzzbomb who liked to get the ball in wide positions and come inside and have a shot. So Messrs Henry, Bergkamp, Kanu and Wiltord was an odd firm of strikers, a very unbalanced quartet indeed, and rotating them would prove a test for any manager. Finding one productive strike partnership would be hard, let alone two or three. It had taken many months for Bergkamp to help the great left-winger to score the goals that made Thierry Henry, in his own mind, a striker again.

PASSIONATE VIRTUOSITY

I want to make one thing clear: I will never leave Arsenal.

Patrick Vieira

In Rotterdam on 2 July Patrick Vieira played for France against Italy in the Euro 2000 final. France were within twenty seconds of losing the match when Sylvain Wiltord equalised. Then David Trezeguet scored the golden goal and Vieira added a European Championship medal to his World Cup medal from 1998.

Seven weeks later it was back to business with Arsenal, whose first Premiership game was at the Stadium of Light in Sunderland on 19 August. The team played very well but missed eight chances and conceded the only goal of the game when former Gunner Niall Quinn headed home a cross in the 53rd minute. Seaman bottled that cross, jumping outside the huge Irishman. Vieira had been targeted for special attention throughout, and in the closing seconds, when Darren Williams grabbed him round the waist, Vieira kept running, swung his arm and caught Williams with a back-handed slap on the neck. Williams went down pretending to be hurt and referee Steve Dunn sent Vieira off. Most neutrals thought Williams should have gone as well, especially when the camera caught Williams winking at the Sunderland bench. After the match, fourth official Paul Taylor claimed that he had been manhandled by Arsène Wenger during an argument in the tunnel between Henry and Williams. The *Sunday Telegraph*'s Colin Malam thought Arsenal's opening day a harsh one. 'Sunderland won a match yesterday that they could easily have lost 6–1,' he wrote. 'Just to compound their misery, Arsenal had Patrick Vieira sent off again right at the end of the match. The tall Frenchman, man of the match by a mile, was shown the red card for retaliation when fouled by Sunderland substitute Darren Williams, who escaped with just a yellow card.'

Far worse was in store. Three days later at Highbury, during the second half of the match with Liverpool, referee Graham Poll – who had had a reasonable first half, sending off Gary McAllister for a clumsy two-footed lunge which injured Vieira – completely lost the plot for half an hour. He gave Jamie Carragher a yellow card for elbowing Vieira, then booked Vieira for reacting. Then, three minutes later, Vieira slid in for a loose ball, won it, and was himself deliberately kicked by Dietmar Hamann. Amazingly, Poll gave Vieira his second red card in four days.

At least Arsenal won the game, 2–0 – the first time Wenger had beaten Liverpool since arriving at Arsenal, and the club's first win over the Merseysiders in seven seasons – and Lauren had a fine home debut in Parlour's wide position, scoring, like Ljungberg, in his first game. He won a corner which really should have been a goal kick, Silvinho took it, and the Cameroon new boy knocked the ball in off Adams. Thierry Henry had scored the second goal and was named Man of the Match, but he did not care about that because he was so upset about Patrick. In a live interview on Sky Sports Henry was almost in tears because his friend was being so cruelly abused by opponents and officials. Vieira had cleared his locker and left the stadium before the match finished. He said he was quitting English football.

The next day, a Wednesday, Wenger was charged by the Football Association with 'alleged threatening behaviour and physical intimidation' after the Sunderland game. Under the new guidelines, 'jostling or holding' a match official was punishable by a twelve-match ban and a fine of four weeks' wages. A statement from the club read, 'Arsène is certainly surprised by the charge. He is looking forward to providing the FA with a detailed explanation of events.'

That Saturday, against Charlton, the sympathetic Arsenal fans sang Vieira's name even before kick-off, and they continued to sing his name after the game started. After nineteen minutes, Vieira glided forward on to Kanu's sublime pass and scored by baffling keeper Dean Kiely with a right-foot stepover and a left-foot flick over his body, a Kanu-type goal. Then Charlton's Andy Hunt scored twice and the visitors led 2–1 at half-time, which dampened down the atmosphere considerably until Thierry Henry equalised within forty seconds of the restart. It seemed that Arsenal would surely win now, but a Graeme Stuart near-post volley made it 3–2 to Charlton. Two minutes later Vieira was set up by Kanu again and he fired a 25-yard shot into the bottom corner. Henry scored Arsenal's fourth, then Vieira fed Silvinho, who made it 5–3.

After two traumas in four days which had left him in the depths of despair, Patrick Vieira had come out and played like a super-gladiator. This comeback performance was majestic, a statement of intent, an expression of loyalty, an exhibition of skill and spirit that spoke louder than any words could have done. Wenger's teams for the last five years have always been a blend of warriors and technicians, but that day Vieira was a warrior-technician who played with passionate virtuosity. In football, as in jazz, you admire technique and you admire passion, but it is the combination of the two that is exciting – when they play brilliantly from the heart. There is nothing more thrilling than passionate virtuosity, and that was exactly what we saw that day. In that super-motivated mood, Patrick Vieira was colossal, phenomenal, fictional, a supremely strong anchorman who played deep in his own half but cruised forward like a twenty-first-century Becken-bauer to win the game. No other player in England, no other player in the world, could have started the week with two red cards and ended it with two goals of such quality.

Naturally, Arsène Wenger was delighted. 'I'm pleased that we could win this game after such a controversial week, and as well by the performance of Patrick Vieira today. Because he was outstanding and exceptional. Not only because he's a great player, but mentally his response was great. I think he had a little bit less aggression. One of the positive effects of this whole controversial situation was that today there were less fouls on him. Charlton tried to play football against him. Some people asked me if I thought of leaving him out. And I said, "Never for a minute did I think of not playing him." Because I know how strong this guy is mentally. And he has shown that today. I never thought he would walk out on Arsenal. He's committed to the club. He's committed to the fans. He knows how much people love him here. And how much he has improved since he has arrived here.'

Vieira said later, 'The day after the Liverpool game I spoke to the manager and to Mr Dein. What we talked about was enough for me to keep going and to want to stay at Arsenal. The sending-off was frustrating. I said things straight after the game and that is the time when you are emotional. You can't make an important decision when you are feeling like that. But I want to make one thing clear: I will never leave Arsenal.'

THE 2000 AGM

Concerning my future, I'm very happy at Arsenal at the moment. And I'm pleased as well that the directors want me to stay.

Arsène Wenger

The AGM on 7 September was notable for chairman Peter Hill-Wood's comment that the new stadium at nearby Ashburton Grove would cost £200 million. A few shareholders moaned and groaned, perhaps believing that there was, somewhere, a perfect football club with perfect directors, perfect players and a perfect manager. So when you give them a very good team, a superb manager and ambitious plans for a new stadium, and you hand them a press release as they walk in detailing a £47 million share deal with Granada Media, they will still complain.

So it was fitting when shareholder Martin Wengrow stood up and made some comments which caught the mood of the silent majority, simple words that were as well-timed as Silvinho's Exocet at Stamford Bridge the previous night. 'With all due respect to the earlier speakers, I would just like to say a very big thank you to Mr Wenger for the fantastic quality of footballers he's brought to this club.' Loud applause. 'Also for the fantastic quality of the football that's played. I've never looked forward more to coming to Highbury every week in fifty years than I do at the moment. I'd just like to say that whatever the outcome of the negotiations, thank you very much indeed for being here. I think we all hope that you do extend your contract. I think everybody here, every Arsenal fan, perceives you to be very much an Arsenal person. We sense that the club has got into you as it has us. We'd be immensely proud and absolutely delighted if the directors make every effort to keep you here. I think you can lead us right into this century with loads of success, and I hope it's your last job in football. We love you!'

The applause which followed lasted eighteen seconds. It was the applause of 800 people thanking someone for saying what the earlier speakers should have said.

Wenger then stood up and spoke in his lucid, modest way. 'What can I say after that?' he said. There was laughter. 'Good afternoon, everybody. It's quite impressive to face you. Because usually I can never see you during the whole season. You're behind me, or on the other side in the stand. Judging by your questions you're quite an offensive team.' Laughter. 'I like that! I'd like to thank the gentleman who was so nice to me, but I feel that we can do better. We have to do better and we want to do better. Concerning my future, I'm very happy at Arsenal at the moment. And I'm pleased as well that the directors want me to stay. And I don't see why we can't find an agreement!'

The shareholders were ecstatic. Everyone was dreading going into a new stadium without the guiding hand of Wenger because, at this moment in time, he seemed to be the only man on the planet who could ensure that Arsenal would have a team as good as their new stadium. Clearly, the club would pay whatever it took to keep him, matching whatever he was offered by Milan, Real Madrid or Barcelona. If it took £2 million a season to keep him, or £4 million, so be it.

As the autumn progressed, Wenger was pleased to see his Brazilian left-back begin to score vital goals. Silvinho, a steal at £4 million a year ago, had replaced Nigel Winterburn and was proving to be a special player who could do special things, even if he would never be able to defend as heroically as Winterburn had done for thirteen years. Silvinho's excellent distribution put him on a par with the muscular Roberto Carlos of Real Madrid. However, Carlos is a power player, an elemental force, a rumble of thunder, while the compact Silvinho is a zigzag streak of lightning who can deliver a better final ball.

Against Charlton on 26 August he had scored the fifth goal in the 89th minute, racing on to Vieira's pass, swerving into the box and firing across Kiely in fine style. Against Chelsea on 6 September he had enjoyed an eventful night. He got a yellow card for a foul on Panucci, collided with Luzhny to allow Hasselbaink to score a sensational twenty-yarder, lost Zola for the second Chelsea goal, played Henry in to make it 2–1 and then saved the game when a ball went loose on the edge of the Chelsea box. He pounced on it and smashed a banana shot just inside the post to earn a 2–2 draw. That 86th-minute equaliser meant that Arsenal were now unbeaten by Chelsea in five years.

In Arsenal's first Champions League game of the season, against Sparta in Prague a week after that Chelsea game, he scored in the 33rd minute. Kanu hit a long diagonal pass that Pires chased to the corner flag. Pires then found the Brazilian on the corner of the penalty area, where he was unsupported with nothing on, and Silvinho just skipped inside Mynar, quick as a hummingbird's wing, darted towards the goal, swerved left again and clipped the ball across the advancing keeper Postulka for the only goal of the game.

After that Silvinho did not score in the next fifteen games, but his next goal, when it came during the match in Moscow with Spartak at the end of November in stage two of the Champions League (for which Arsenal had at last qualified), was one of the finest ever seen in that competition, a classic demonstration of how to destroy a sweeper defence with a breathtakingly quick counter-attack. And it happened just 77 seconds into the game. Silvinho won the ball deep inside his own half, played it infield to Pires and then zoomed off on an 83-metre sprint across the snowy grass and icy mud. Pires passed to Henry, who accelerated towards the Russian sweeper and right-back. Henry, four yards outside the penalty area, facing Ananko and Tchuisse, nutmegged them, taking out both defenders with a sublime pass through Ananko's legs which played in Silvinho, who glided round the Spartak keeper, Filiminov, and gently rolled his shot into the net. The best thing about the goal was that the defenders did nothing wrong. It was just a shame that Moscow Spartak beat Arsenal 4-1 that night.

PIRES, LAUREN, WILTORD

Tonight is more about Arsenal than the Champions League.

Sir Alex Ferguson in Eindhoven

Wenger took Robert Pires to Sunderland on 19 August and gave him his first look at Premiership football from the bench, so that the culture shock would not be too great. His 66th-minute appearance as a sub for Ljungberg went unnoticed amid all the controversy of the game, but he went on, after the Liverpool game, to feature in the next four matches against Charlton, Chelsea, Bradford and Coventry.

A right-footed left-winger, the canny Pires was Arsenal's best player at Chelsea in the 2–2 draw. He carried the ball cleverly, passed carefully, held the side together during some rough patches and put two corners on Grimandi's head. Without him Arsenal would have been swamped and beaten. Lauren was also proving to be an energetic, resilient, solid craftsman who could pass the ball early and accurately. He started the game wide right, played well, and also looked good when he switched to right-back.

Pires was improving with every game, and against Coventry on 16 September he was the hub of the team in a 2–1 win. Artful, versatile and consistently constructive, he redefined Arsenal's attacking options, cruising forward, turning Carlton Palmer inside out and embarrassing Marc Edworthy. He hardly wasted a pass all afternoon and set up six shots on goal. Sylvain Wiltord also had some good moments. Ray Parlour looked three yards offside when Luzhny's seventy-yard pass bounced off him, but there was no flag and Wiltord buried a left-foot shot past Hedman. The new striker was chunky and combative, able to twist sharply away from opponents without losing his balance. On Wiltord, Wenger said after the match, 'Once he's in his stride he's very fast, and I believe he has shown the potential. He's quick on the turn, good movement. But he is still lacking fitness. He has no preparation at all at the moment, just two games. He's a goalscorer and he has shown that today – he created two or three chances.'

Are things different now you have four strikers?

'It's very good, especially when you have many games. It is very bad when you have not many games.'

Is Pires the player who can make you great again this season?

'What is interesting is that he has a good mixture between individual and team play. And he could play central as well.'

You've said he could be a possible successor to Zinedine Zidane for France.

'He's the closest I know to being a successor to Zidane. Unfortunately, he's too close age-wise to Zidane, so that will not leave him much time. But I think as well they can play together. That's why I want him to play on the flank. Because he has shown one-on-one he can pass anybody. He's very quick. He doesn't look it.'

What kind of man is he?

'A very nice guy. A happy boy, he's very nice with everybody. He has real team spirit. I wanted to buy him when he moved from Metz to Marseilles and I made a bid. I couldn't get him at that time. Fortunately, I could do it during the European Championship. If I had not done it just before the final it would have been over for us.'

The Arsenal–Lazio game at Highbury on 27 September featured Wenger's most radical team selection ever when he played Bergkamp wide on the right in a 4–3–3 formation. It took 43 minutes to work and everyone had a lot of doubts during that time because Lazio's defensive awareness in terms of covering all the angles around their box was excellent. It looked as if Arsenal would not score in a month of Wednesdays until Kanu crossed high and perfectly, Bergkamp appeared on the left to head the ball down, and Ljungberg swept it past the keeper. After 55 minutes Luzhny intercepted and played a first-time pass to Bergkamp, who powered infield and slipped the ball between Negro's legs, which allowed Ljungberg to go past Lombardo and side-foot the goal that ended the contest.

The other European news that night was that Sir Alex Ferguson had decided to rest six players, including Giggs and Beckham, in Eindhoven with an eye on the Premiership clash at Highbury that Sunday, and United had lost 3–1 to PSV. He said, 'Tonight is more about Arsenal than the Champions League.' Thus Fergie set himself up for looking like a fool if he did not beat Arsenal, and that was exactly what happened on the Sunday afternoon, Thierry Henry scoring a long-range goal with an outrageous flick-up and volley which looped over Barthez into the top corner.

Wenger said that Henry had been very worried about not scoring for six games. 'It was playing on his mind that he didn't score the goals he wanted to score. And sometimes you do something completely crazy; you don't think, you just do it. Maybe if he'd had a one-on-one with Barthez he'd have missed it. When you have a little doubt in your mind, doing something completely unexpected helps you. Just do it, don't think about it. That was important for him. He's never gone through a period where he didn't score. Because he's new in the position it played too big a role in his mind. It's the first time since he's been in this position that he didn't score for a while. It's part of the learning process in this position, for me. I talked to him about it. But you can say what you want – when a player is so desperate to score you can only show confidence in him. They need it to survive.'

The fans were already warming to Pires, whose style is unique because he shuffles and waits and dummies and changes his mind at the last moment. As he carries the ball he is always thinking and rethinking the best pass. He takes his time, reviews his options, and if he does not like them he reviews his options again. Then he makes his choice. So Pires does one thing better than Overmars ever did: he gives his team-mates the time to run into good positions. He demonstrated this on 14 October when he created the winning goal against Aston Villa after 61 minutes. As he cruised down the middle of the field, Bergkamp and Henry scissored, Bergkamp going left and Henry gliding right, the latter taking the ball and shooting early through Alpay's legs and past David James, who was standing tall, not crouching. The game was Pires's comeback after going off with a hamstring against Ukrainians Shakhtar Donetsk on 20 September, a game in which Arsenal had gone 2–0 down but won 3–2 thanks to a goal from Wiltord and two from Martin Keown.

On 17 October Arsenal travelled to Rome for the return against Lazio, who went ahead via Pavel Nedved's fluke-of-the-season deflected goal in the 24th minute. Then, in the 88th minute, sub Wiltord made a long pass down the left wing and Pires, another sub, knocked the ball forward for himself to the edge of the penalty area where, with sublime disguise, he almost ran past the ball. The advancing Peruzzi realised just too late what was coming and was helpless as Pires curved a shot over him and into the net for a handsome equaliser. Rome was a good moment for the Frenchman with the Spanish name to score his first goal for Arsenal, giving Monsieur Wenger yet another reason to be cheerful: his team now had three wins and a draw from four Champions League games. He must have asked himself, 'Why the hell did we play those two seasons at Wembley?'

November was always going to be a tricky month because in the first week two strange games were scheduled, matches which hovered somewhere outside normal sporting reality because they did not have to be won – Ipswich in the Worthington Cup and the dead Champions League game in Donetsk. The Arsenal mindset is all about playing hard, concentrating and winning, so matches you do not have to win are weirdly artificial and mysterious, a parallel universe, a disturbing place where you never go and never want to go. If the full first team does not play, or does not try, is it a real game? Does it count? Is it part of your sequence?

The main team problem at this time was the integration of Wiltord, which was still proving difficult. A striker needs games and needs goals, and, like Anelka in 1997/98, Wiltord could not improve unless he was in the team. Wenger tried to play him as often as he could and paid a price. Wiltord's do-it-yourself style, coming in from flank positions, made him more of a deputy for Thierry Henry than a suitable partner.

There was an unexpected trauma the day before the Worthington Cup tie when reserve manager Georgie Armstrong collapsed at the training ground and died of a brain haemorrhage. Despite this tragedy, the game went ahead. Five reserves made their debuts, Ipswich scored an early goal, Stepanovs equalised with a header from a Vivas corner, and Ipswich got a last-minute winner.

The Premiership game at Middlesbrough on 4 November took place exactly seventeen years after Tony Adams' debut for Arsenal.

Ljungberg was clattered in the box by keeper Mark Crossley, who was harshly sent off, so Marlon Beresford came on for Hamilton Ricard and got his first touch when he picked Henry's penalty out of the net. Nobody realised then that this would be Arsenal's only win in seven games during November.

Donetsk, in the deepest Ukraine, far beyond Kiev, was a city nobody wanted to visit for a sixth Champions League game that did not matter. Keown, scorer of two goals against Shakhtar at Highbury, made two expensive mistakes in a 3–0 defeat, and then learned to his dismay that England caretaker manager Peter Taylor had left the over-thirties out of his squad. Every Arsenal player was at Georgie's funeral in Cambridge the next day, which left Friday to prepare for the visit of Derby, the only team in the four divisions so far without a win. In the swirling wind and rain Rory Delap missed three good chances. Wenger played Bergkamp behind Wiltord and Henry, which did not work and Arsenal were lucky to get a 0–0 draw. Having too many strikers was proving as problematic as having too few, and when he tried Kanu with Bergkamp and Wiltord at Everton on 18 November, things seemed even worse. Weakened by the absence of Vieira, and with Luzhny having a nightmare at left centre-back, they lost 2–0.

Spartak Moscow was the first game of Group Stage Two of the Champions League and a major event in the Russian capital, an 82,000 sell-out where £4 tickets were being sold on the black market for £60. The partially frozen pitch was passed fit just two hours before kick-off, and Spartak responded to Silvinho's goal with a whirlwind of creative movement and slick passes into well-timed runs, earning themselves a handsome 4–1 win which could easily have been 8–1. When the draw was made Wenger had said that Spartak Moscow were 'a very, very good team'. He was right about that.

The game at Leeds on the 26th showed that Henry was uncomfortable with a short passing game. He had been playing in avenues for a year and now Wenger was asking him to play in triangles. Most of Arsenal's triangles were telegraphed, and Radebe and Woodgate saw them coming a mile off. Wiltord dribbled in his own half and lost the ball four times, once before the decisive goal when his short pass did not find Lauren and Dacourt broke forward, was fouled by Parlour, and took a free-kick which looped in off Lauren's shoulder. Overall, though, Arsenal were unlucky. They deserved a draw, but Wiltord and Henry were a long way off from being effective strike partners. Wiltord at least got better as the game went on. Henry got worse.

For the first time under Wenger Arsenal had lost three games in a row, so for the match against Southampton a week later he rested Henry and gave Wiltord a chance with Bergkamp, who can make anybody look good, especially when he is in gladiator mode, roaring all over the field like a Rolls-Royce in overdrive, giving a performance that seemed to say, 'Yes, we have had a shocking run of one win in seven games, but I did not play in five of those games and I'm going to turn this round, starting right now!' The improved passing rhythm suggested that Wenger had put the last five days to very good use. A whole week without having to visit Russia was a big help, and his team had recaptured ninety per cent of their dynamism and eighty per cent of their fluidity. Even so, the winning goal was a long time coming. Arsenal hit the post three times before Vieira's miscued header dribbled in off Lundekvam's shoulder in the 85th minute.

ARSENAL 2 BAYERN MUNICH 2

We should have won.

Arsène Wenger

Arsenal had never previously met Bayern Munich in European competition, so the game on 5 December was a massive opportunity for them, an open door which, should they drive through it, would put the club one giant step up the stairway to heaven. A team which beats Lazio is noticed, but a team which beats Bayern Munich is respected. Bayern, like Real Madrid, are the establishment.

Wenger knew that his rival, Ottmar Hitzfeld, would want a tight game, because in an open game Bayern might get slaughtered. The Germans had won only two of their last eight games in the Bundesliga and had been lucky to scramble a 1–0 win against

Lyon, so their results were better than their performances. Wenger brought Ashley Cole in for the injured Silvinho, showing that he trusted the youngster at left-back, while Luzhny kept his place at right-back. Henry had not scored for six games, and in seven Champions League games so far he had not scored either.

Bayern started by playing some solid keep-ball, but then Vieira won the ball cleverly from right-back Willie Sagnol, spun and passed to Pires, who moved forward on the left side and pushed a crossfield pass towards the penalty area. Henry dummied, Kanu played him in with a disguised pass and Henry swept his shot past Kahn. Arsenal had scored with their first attack. Usually a laid-back player, one of the coolest dudes in football boots, even when he scores, Thierry Henry now raced away to the corner flag like a demented man, screaming his head off, releasing the tension, so much tension, so much frustration. He had obviously been wound up as tight as a spring and now, after this perfectly executed goal, he let it all hang out. His eyes were bulging and he pummelled invisible enemies with both fists as he ran. He was more pumped up than we had ever seen him. Manic? Just a little bit!

Arsenal had taken 42 minutes to score against Lazio (Ljungberg) and seven minutes against Shakhtar Donetsk (Lauren), but now they had breached the defence of the big boys inside four minutes with a stylish goal that must have given immense technical satisfaction to Wenger. The geometry of the move was exquisite, the speed stunning.

Amazingly, after conceding that early goal, Bayern carried on playing negatively as if nothing had happened, refusing to respond by trying to get the goal back, as a British side would do. Their one promising moment came five minutes before half-time when Effenberg produced a moment of EffenVision, launching a stupendous seventy-yard pass from the left-back position. The ball sailed just beyond Keown's attempt to intercept, Adams could not reach it, Cole was sucked infield to cover Adams, and Elber prodded the ball back to Scholl, whose shot swerved a yard wide of Manninger's post. It was their first shot of the game.

At half-time Hitzfeld took off Sagnol, moved Salahamidzic to right-back and brought on Paulo Sergio against Ashley Cole, who had played confidently for 45 minutes. Bayern started the second half at a higher tempo, but on 55 minutes Henry zoomed down the left and set up an awkward half-chance on the edge of the box for Kanu, who guided his low shot towards the far bottom corner. Kahn dived and managed to touch the ball, but it went in. Another excellent goal, another big step towards the quarter-finals, another moment of sublime satisfaction for Wenger. This was how he wanted his team to play. This was the football he loved. Goals of such quality were a vindication of his ideas, his faith in pace, his confidence in slick, explosive moves between sprinting strikers. Kanu and Henry had been rested at Southampton three days before and now both had scored – and they had made each other's goals. Rotation had worked at last.

In his twentieth Champions League game as Arsenal manager, Wenger was now beating the big boys. He had just gone 2–0 up against Bayern Munich and his team looked capable of beating anybody, but just as he was starting to enjoy his most exhilarating European night so far, Salahamidzic raced down the touchline, collided with Pires and fell over. It was a debatable foul, but Effenberg quickly took the free-kick from the right touchline. Vieira, jogging back, turned to find himself slightly out of position, jumped knowing he could not reach the ball, obscuring the view of Luzhny, who was standing behind him. Elber laid the ball back to Tarnat and his shot rifled into the bottom corner for 2–1.

Arsenal had broken one of the most basic rules of professional football by conceding a goal just after scoring. Wenger now had to suffer the agony of watching his team fall apart. For the next ten minutes they were unable to string even two passes together. The whole season seemed to be trembling in the balance.

When Jeremies tanked down the left wing and crossed blind, Keown headed the ball out and Sforza volleyed it forward to Elber, then ran for a flick-on which he could not reach. As he went Sforza brushed Ljungberg and tumbled just outside the box, claiming a shirt-tug. It was one of the most blatant dives of the season so far. Italian referee Stefano Braschi should have waved play on – the replay showed only minimal contact between Ljungberg's hand and Sforza's elbow – but he gave a free-kick.

The wall lined up, Scholl dummied, Ljungberg encroached, Scholl appealed and Tarnat smacked his shot into the wall. Braschi booked Ljungberg and ordered a retake. Unfortunately, Manninger did not read Scholl's intent, for it was he, not Tarnat, who replaced the ball, and everyone knows that the player who places the ball is usually the one who takes the free-kick. Scholl whipped it over the wall and into the corner of the net for 2–2.

After that, Wenger must have been thinking, 'If we had scored the second goal before half-time, or if we had passed the ball around just for ten minutes at 2–0, we would have won.' Near the end Wenger lost his temper with the fourth official, who refused to allow him to shout a message to his players. So the big night turned out to be a roller-coaster ride of thrilling success and dramatic failure, a game which promised everything and delivered, in the end, a bitter lesson: Arsenal and referee Braschi had been mugged by crafty diving.

The events of that evening took a lot out of Wenger, who rolls with the punches better than most managers. When he came into the press conference he looked weary and sounded drained. His voice lacked its usual energy. 'It's very disappointing and very frustrating,' he said, 'because I felt we'd done the most important thing in getting a 2–0 lead. But at that level you know you can't lose concentration. I felt straight away after the second goal, we lost a little bit, subconsciously, concentration – and were punished straight away. I'm especially angry at the first goal because I think it's unbelievable, how we gave a goal away. You could see straight away, the way we cleared the ball, the way we were positioned, that we could concede a goal.'

This was an unusual thing to say, especially given his low-angle view of a free-kick taken on the opposite side of the field, so reporters asked him to elaborate.

It was collective bad defending?

'Yes.'

You could actually see from the touchline, before they took the free-kick, that you were in trouble?

'Yes,' he replied. But he would not name individuals. He merely went on to say, 'That of course gave mental strength to Bayern and we lost confidence. On the free-kick I think we were unlucky. They miss the first free-kick and he gives it again. Then Scholl took it well.'

Brian Woolnough asked, 'Do you think you can still go through?'

'I think we can still go through, yes, because Lyon beat Spartak Moscow tonight. That shows that everybody still has chances. It was, of course, important to win tonight, but crucial not to lose. And in the end we got a point. It looks as if everybody can beat everybody in this group. The most disappointing thing tonight is that we should have won. We got a goal early on, and if you look at how many saves Alex Manninger has made tonight, you will be surprised. I can't remember a real difficult save for him.'

Brian Glanville then asked Wenger if he thought his team had looked demoralised after conceding the first goal.

'It looks a little bit like that. The team has lost confidence straight away. We were still in the goal we scored, instead of being conscious that it was important in the next five minutes not to concede a goal.'

After Wenger was asked a question in German, which he answered in German, Woolnough wanted to know what he had been gesticulating about near the end of the game.

'We had two free-kicks with one minute and thirty seconds to go. We had everybody up in the box and we played a short ball. That is difficult to understand. I just wanted to tell the players to put the ball in the box because in the last minute they can panic and make a mistake and you have a chance, when you have twenty players in the box, to score a goal. And that's all. The fourth official didn't let me do it. It was a little bit ridiculous.'

'You were much better than them until the first goal you conceded,' Woolnough observed.

'Yes. That was the turning point.'

Another reporter said he could not remember the last time Wenger looked so angry and disappointed. Was it getting him down?

'No, I'm not down at all. I just feel that when you see your team giving everything you want them to be rewarded. And it's frustrating when you feel that your players gave everything and got only a point. If you can find a manager in the world who leads 2–0 at that level and is happy when he comes out with a 2–2, I would like to be introduced to him.'

That was his exit line, and in the circumstances it was a good one. Wenger must have known his team were still on a learning curve, and that with a few more tight Champions League games under their belts they might not have contrived to snatch this draw from the jaws of victory. He also knew that Arsenal had been the better side on the night. They had scored two excellent goals in open play, had hit the post and twice had viable penalty shouts in the same attack, for a push on Keown and a clear handball by Sforza, who admitted handling the following day. The best side does not always win, however, and Wenger, a coach for nearly twenty years, had been through many, many games where he had told himself, 'We should have won!' Every footballer and every fan has said those same words. Nevertheless, he was probably seething when he studied the video, which showed how clever and systematic Bayern's gamesmanship had been. They created nothing in open play. They had a few shots wide, but Manninger did not have to make a real save all night. Tony Adams conceded only one foul in the whole game and that was a bad call near the end by Braschi, after Elber had backed into Adams. Adams was furious, tried to pick Elber up, and almost ripped his shirt off. Quite simply, Bayern played for free-kicks throughout the game. But nobody said much about it, which proves that you can fool most of the people all of the time.

Overall, Arsenal's 2-2 draw with Bayern Munich was a night when the performances of each team reflected the personalities and priorities of their respective managers. Hitzfeld was 51 and a pragmatic tactician who was in the results business, not the entertainment business; Wenger, also 51 but nine months younger, was more idealistic, in love with the beautiful game, dreaming of the perfect attacking performance backed by defensive concentration. Hitzfeld must have left Highbury a content man; Wenger, having seen his team lose their shape, focus and nerve, the weaknesses in his side suddenly becoming obvious, was savagely disappointed. In those ultra-tense final seconds he was as furious as we had ever seen him.

In all their European games Arsenal had never really been outplayed, except by Kiev and Galatasaray, and they had chances to win those games. In most of those games there had been a very fine line between success and failure. Wenger knew that Bayern Munich could be beaten, he knew how they could be beaten, and a win at Highbury would have been deeply satisfying. But the year 2000 was about to end and that big victory, that night of satisfaction, was still proving elusive, still hovering just out of reach.

Arsenal were now bottom of Group C with one point from their first two games, but their Champions League fate was still in their own hands. They could still beat Lyon twice and they could also take three points from the Spartak Moscow match at Highbury. But the next match was not until February, so it was time to focus again on the Premiership. Arsenal got straight back into the groove by thrashing Newcastle 5–0 on 9 December.

The press conference after that game reminded us that the restaurateur's son from Alsace had a lot in common with the miner's son from Durham. Bobby Robson is one of the most compelling personalities in the game because he gives you something you do not get from other managers: a sense that Premier League football is still a sport. He really loves a football match, and thinks it is important, but he knows it is only a football match. He was a gracious loser whose enthusiasm lit up the early-evening darkness as much as Ray Parlour's hat-trick had done.

'We got smashed,' Robson admitted. 'It's as simple as that. Once the first goal went in, then the second one soon after that, it was a case of damage limitation. Because Arsenal were hungry. Apart from their quality, excellent quality on the pitch, all over – every single player was a top-class player, and their passing and movement was top class – I just thought they had a terrific desire. And yet all of their goals were not a result of great possession football, where they're making seven, eight passes, and you're chasing the ball and you can't get the ball and then they get through you. They were breaking up our attacks and playing very effective two-pass, three-pass, four-pass movements, with the move being finished on the fourth or the third pass.

'I mean, Adams gets the ball in midfield and hits the ball over the top, Henry gets in behind Aaron Hughes and finishes – two passes, goal. Second goal is a mistake by Griffin. We lost the ball down by the left corner flag, it gets played through, Parlour makes a straight run through between the two young centre-halves, it's a terrific finish. And Kanu did the same for the third goal after half-time. Ball over the top, no clever passing movements, just effective, simple, early football – got in behind our two young centre-halves. And that was the difference: we had two young players learning the game; Henry and Kanu are two gifted, intelligent, experienced international players. It's like you playing against me – you wouldn't win. Parlour's come in, fresh as a daisy, didn't play Tuesday night against Bayern, so he's able to make strong runs out of midfield. We couldn't cope with it. Three times he's done it, three times he's scored. So it's not a game for me to get angry with my players in public. I won't do that. We've lost 5–0, forget about it.'

ANFIELD AND OLD TRAFFORD

I have had worse experiences, but the size of the score makes this a very bad one.

Arsène Wenger in Manchester

The two biggest tests of the 2000/01 Premiership season were the away games against Liverpool in December and Manchester United in February. Arsenal failed both, and the most interesting thing about the failures was that Wenger picked the right team at Anfield and the wrong team at Old Trafford. The 4–0 thrashing in the first game was entirely the fault of the players, while the 6–1 humiliation in Manchester was mainly the fault of the manager. The latter was surprising, since Wenger had mostly been a model of consistency in his team selections, picking his strongest team without trying to do anything radical or clever. He obviously believes that tinkering baffles your own team as much as your opponents because it breaks up rhythms, partnerships, angles, understandings.

When Arsenal visited Anfield two days before Christmas, Liverpool had just won 1–0 at Old Trafford. If they beat Arsenal now they were back in the big time, but if Arsenal beat Liverpool then they themselves were still very much title contenders. Both managers knew it would be a battle so they picked their most aggressive players: Owen instead of Fowler, Murphy instead of Smicer, Ljungberg instead of Pires.

Arsenal started brightly, but then Babbel launched a long throw from the right, Vieira headed out, and Gerrard hit a phenomenal half-volley from twenty yards that flew into the bottom corner. Liverpool had scored with their first shot of the game. Parlour was denied a penalty when he took on Carragher, who fell and knocked the ball away craftily with his arm, and as the first half wore on it was Arsenal playing all the football in an intense game on a soggy, sandy, bumpy pitch. Again in the second half it was all Arsenal for fifteen minutes, Vieira playing twenty yards further forward, but then Heskey made a long run to the left corner, turned Keown, barged him away and hit a shot which Manninger fumbled to give Owen a tap-in. The build-up to the third goal began when Heskey, again using his strength, muscled Parlour off the ball near the centre circle. Biscan played a simple ball to substitute Smicer and he played a cute pass through for Barmby's run inside Silvinho, who stood like a statue and let him go. Barmby clipped the ball neatly past Manninger. Finally, when Parlour let a long ball bounce off his thighs it went to Heskey, who found Barmby, who played in substitute Robbie Fowler for the fourth.

Only time would tell whether this game signalled Liverpool's arrival as England's number two team. Gerard Houllier had won nothing yet, but his best players were all English, apart from centre-back Sami Hyypia, who has now become as important to Liverpool as Vieira is to Arsenal. Hyypia was a reminder that great players at big clubs are invariably spinal players – goalkeepers, centre-backs, midfield anchormen and centre-forwards. Houllier had bought two spinal players, Hyypia and Heskey, while Wenger, after almost five years, had signed only one.

In their must-win games Liverpool usually play very defensively, even at home, hitting long balls up to Owen and Heskey, and their formidable unit of six tall defenders invariably works against Arsenal, who play avenue football, looking to support each other by gliding quickly down central avenues near the man with the ball. So when Arsenal play Liverpool they are usually reduced to shooting from 25 yards, as they were here.

Their next game, on Boxing Day, was against Leicester at Highbury, where Latvian centre-back Stepanovs came in for his Premiership debut. Arsenal were average for half an hour, but then Henry scored from 25 yards and they stormed home 6–1 winners. A 4–0 defeat away had been followed by a 6–1 victory at home – all very up and down, which was very much the story in January 2001 too: a defeat at the hands of Charlton, uninspiring draws against Chelsea and Leicester, a 6–0 demolition of QPR in the FA Cup. At least they were not conceding goals, and that trend continued into February, Arsenal keeping six clean sheets in a row. They beat Coventry 1–0 on 3 February and Ipswich 1–0 a week later, then they went to Lyon and won with a second-half header by Henry. The clean sheets were ended by Chelsea on the 17th in the FA Cup fifth round tie at Highbury, but Arsenal won 3–1, Wiltord coming on as a sub to score two goals. But they could only draw 1–1 with Lyon at Highbury in a game where Edmilson, a Brazilian centre-back Wenger had tried to sign, had a seesaw night. He was nudged off the ball illegally by Bergkamp, who scored, and then he equalised in stoppage time with a booming header.

The team Wenger had selected to face Lyon was Seaman; Dixon, Grimandi, Luzhny, Cole; Ljungberg, Parlour, Vieira, Pires; Bergkamp and Henry. But when he went to Old Trafford four days later, he tinkered, making some changes he should not have made and picking only four outfield players in the positions they should have played in. The new selections were illogical, perhaps the most misguided in his five years as Arsenal manager, showing how easy it is for rotation to become confusion.

The team Wenger fielded against Manchester United on 25 February was Seaman; Luzhny, Grimandi, Stepanovs, Cole; Pires, Parlour, Vieira, Silvinho; Wiltord and Henry. Wenger knew that Arsenal had never won a game in which Wiltord and Henry had started together, but he still dropped Bergkamp. Pires should have stayed on the left to support young Cole, Luzhny should have been at right centre-back to partner the relatively inexperienced Stepanovs, since they had done very well together against Chelsea, and Grimandi should have played in central midfield, where he had battled bravely against Keane and Scholes in the past. The manager knew that Manchester United's off-the-ball movement in attack was the best in England, but he still picked two centre-backs who had never played together. Furthermore, the compromise of playing Silvinho in front of Cole, especially after Wenger had gone on record saying he was not convinced by Silvinho in midfield, was bizarre and self-defeating. And his best option at right-back, in the absence of the injured Dixon, was Vivas, who came on as a sub.

Arsenal might have lost at Old Trafford anyway, but Wenger's selections were unfathomable. The make-up of the team was criticised by many fans, but not by the press, none of whom mentioned his kamikaze line-up. United were always going to score goals against such a side, and the first one came after just two minutes and eight seconds. A Scholes dummy baffled the entire back four, and he returned the ball to the unmarked Dwight Yorke, who let the ball bounce in off his thigh from three yards. Henry equalised after a lovely move, but Yorke scored again when Grimandi played him onside, Beckham hit a magnificent long pass over Stepanovs' head for Yorke to make it 3–1, Yorke left Stepanovs floundering on the halfway line to set up Keane for 4–1, then Grimandi sold himself to Butt, who crossed for Solskjær. After only 38 minutes, the score was Manchester United 5 Arsenal 1. Sheringham made it six in the last minute of normal time.

It was a humiliating experience for Wenger, who had to sit there in a stadium packed with 67,000 people knowing that hundreds of millions were watching on television all over the world, many of them in France. The scoreline equalled Arsenal's worst-ever defeat at Old Trafford, in 1952. They were still in second place but they were now sixteen points behind United – and their hard-earned goal difference had been ruined.

'I have had worse experiences, but the size of the score makes this a very bad one,' Wenger said later. 'Defensively we were too poor. Nobody was communicating, we had no leaders, and there were times when we looked like a youth team. We are not into March yet and it hurts me that the title is already over. It's not good for the league, and I'm not proud of that.'

TYLER ON PREMIERSHIP MANAGERS

I don't hear much grumbling about Arsène, whereas there are Liverpool players who grumble about Houllier.

Martin Tyler

Sky Sports commentator Martin Tyler has a knowledge of Premier League football which is second to none, and he has known all the key personalities for many years. When we spoke in January he said that he had worked on the Sunderland–Arsenal and Arsenal–Liverpool games in August, and he believed Vieira was unlucky on both occasions. 'He's now played twenty matches without being booked. As an aside, it has taken a little bit off his game.

'What is Arsenal's form now? Three wins in the last eleven Premiership games? After the Charlton game on New Year's Day I said, "Are you worried about second place?" Because Manchester United were playing that night. And Wenger said, "Yes, it could be second, third, fourth, fifth or sixth the way we are at the moment."

'There's a feeling that if they hit it off they can wallop anybody. But it's a bit more off the cuff now. It's an obvious thing to say, but if Adams or Keown don't play they haven't got that thou-shalt-not-pass look about them. Silvinho was at fault for the Charlton goal at the far post – he allowed Jonatan Johansson to make up quite a lot of ground to get his head to that. I thought Stepanovs did all right on Saturday against Chelsea, and he has good, brave qualities, and he accepts responsibility on the ball as well, but he's only had five or six games. Stepanovs might not be here if Upson hadn't had that knee injury.

'Ashley Cole does look a prospect, but he was a year too young to replace Winterburn. I'm still not sure whether Silvinho's an Arsenal player, but he's a fine player. Freddie Ljungberg is fantastic, he has got English spirit. It's a dangerous thing to say it's a lack of Englishmen. Overmars and Petit were shoulder-shruggers.

Petit hasn't been replaced, Overmars has. Edu is very good on the ball, but I don't think he will be that sort of player. I'm going from glimpses of him, really.

'We're talking about Arsenal not playing well, and it has been like that for a period now. Arsène was manager of the month for October. In November they lost five games in league and League Cup and Europe. In December they did some silly things but they still put five past Newcastle and six past Leicester. I don't think they've scored the second goal enough. They did win at Middlesbrough with a penalty and they didn't need a second goal against a team who were struggling. Derby they didn't even get one, Everton they didn't even get one, Leeds they didn't get one, but they should have done. And then one was enough to beat Southampton, they blew Newcastle away, should have got more than one at Tottenham for their second-half showing but had to wait till right at the end. They were in it at Liverpool till 2–0. I thought they did all right for an hour and then they fell away – most un-Arsenal-like. We did that game. Two up against Sunderland is the one contrary argument to that. They should have got a second against Chelsea when Leboeuf was paddling about. I would say the second goal has been very elusive for a little while now. But when they get it they're likely to get five.'

We wondered why Lithuanian striker Tomas had not been involved against Chelsea the previous Saturday. Then Tyler mentioned that Jermaine Pennant had been summoned from the youth team in the morning. 'Bergkamp was genuinely sick. He tried to do some running and, being a foreigner, he decided that the most sensible thing to do was not to play. Instead of giving it a go and seeing how he felt. And maybe producing one bit of magic. He definitely was ill. There's no problem with his contract, other than Dutch tax laws. There's some deal about how he juggles figures around to make sure he gets the maximum. He's Sheringham with pace. But, unfortunately, he's not Sheringham with goals.

'That's another point that you should look at. The dependence on Thierry Henry, it's frightening. Bergkamp has two goals in his last 29, Kanu has scored one Premiership goal this season. You don't get many from Parlour, although he gets his occasional good days when he cashes in on the team winning 5–0. But he doesn't win many games 1–0 for you. The bonus has been Vieira, although the Premier League are trying to take a goal off him, the Southampton game. Henry needs a sidekick in there. If you wanted to do one thing to get the team right, you'd get someone in there. The rest would tend to fall into place.'

So we talked about what Sylvain Wiltord had offered so far.

'The football people I know in France say, "Give him time." They think he has got something. He's a personality player and you need that personality to be fostered generally. Not to be seen as a squad player. People have likened him to Ian Wright, but Ian Wright ran on adrenalin, and that adrenalin came from being the main man. Wiltord looks like he's got the ability to be the main man. But Ian Wright would have struggled to be the main man with Thierry Henry in the team, to be fair.'

Tyler went on to point out that Wenger, knowing the age of his goalkeeper and defenders, was open to criticism. 'Seaman will probably be replaced as well. On the goal, he was knocked by Keown, not a Chelsea player. He's not the greatest in those physical situations. I thought he kept goal well actually, apart from that. So the big criticism is that he has not replaced the key elements. Wenger's argument is, "I can't patch the team up, I've got to get the right people. They're not there."

'Petit was a pain in the backside for the manager, and the players. It was so stupid. I was in Amsterdam in August when he came back to play against Arsenal. And they gave him a shirt. All the players signed a shirt for him – and he burst into tears! It was, "I don't know why I'm going!" and all this. And they said, "Oh, you've been a pain in the backside to us, go and enjoy yourself at Barcelona. Thanks very much, but we've now had enough." Marc pretty much the same. He's a Dutchman and the noughts on the end of the pay cheque are important. But for all his jumping out of tackles, look at what Arsenal did when he was here. His ratio of goals to games was excellent for a wide player. And he scored in the important games. He scored a lot of goals and Pires ain't gonna get double figures. They scored 112 goals last season, which David Dein told me was in the top four of all-time for Arsenal. That's two seasons on from the Double. It didn't crumble overnight, but it's in danger. If Arsenal finish sixth this season it's a transitional season.'

Tyler said that back in 1996 and 1997 Wenger had a great edge on French footballers, and that was illustrated by his shrewd captures of Vieira and Anelka. 'But now it is Fulham who are getting the great young French players. Houllier's come in since Arsène came here. It's that much more difficult now. The foreign influence is so strong in our football now that everyone's looking in France.

'Arsène is the most cerebral manager that you could ever want to work alongside as a broadcaster. A most sophisticated and civilised human being, somebody who does nothing but enhance the role of football manager. As far as I'm aware he wants to stay, but this is the crunch, because he's never been under any pressure. Only the pressure to win when you're expected to win. He's never been really under pressure to sort out a losing team. Arsène is getting some criticism now and if you stay there long enough you will. There is a life-span for a football manager, at one club, and he is coming into that territory, isn't he? It's absolutely fascinating. They are a wonderful club, Arsenal, and they are a massive club.' However, Tyler also made the point that Sir Alex Ferguson had been at Old Trafford for fourteen years and there had been some lean periods during that time. 'I think Arsène should be entitled to a lean period. I don't think there's any pressure from within the club. What we're talking about is a media perception of what is interesting viewing at the moment, to see how a masterful manager deals with the ravages of time on the key elements of his team and the fallibility of certain foreign players within the demands of our football. Vieira, you couldn't ask for a better player. Freddie, we've just talked about. It may be that some of the others will come good. It's the blending of it, the chemistry.'

Tyler believes that the big wages players now earn make a fundamental difference to the way managers operate, compared to ten years ago. 'Alex Ferguson could not start his management now, as he is. He was tried and trusted, and he had this reputation, so he could be the Victorian father figure with them. But I don't think anybody could do that now. Not in the Premiership. You can do it lower down. Gary Hill is a bit like that at Dagenham & Redbridge. He's a very strong disciplinarian. Nowadays it's management by personality, by respect. You have to be either very, very good at it, like Venables – he walks into Middlesbrough and transforms it because people know straight away they're learning – or like Peter Reid, who is mentally stronger than anybody else at the club, so nobody else can challenge him.

'And there's management by intellect. I think Wenger's the best example of that. I don't hear much grumbling about Arsène, whereas there are Liverpool players who grumble about Houllier. He is a very imposing person, he's kept himself in fantastic shape. He's totally devoted to it. He is an absolute football nut and that's why he likes it here. Because he's in that culture. In France, that isn't the culture.'

NO MORE CABARET

I'm hoping they still want to employ me. I've done a lot of good things, maybe.

David Pleat

Sylvain Wiltord had played poorly in some league games, dribbling in his own half, losing the ball and shooting wildly from silly positions, but the FA Cup proved to be his salvation. He scored the only goal of the game at Carlisle in the third round, scored twice at QPR as Arsenal romped through, then scored twice again against Chelsea. On 3 March he grabbed his first hat-trick against a weak West Ham side, and then he got an early goal in the 3–1 victory in the FA Cup quarter-final against Blackburn.

Ashley Cole was improving too. On 28 March he made his debut for England in Albania after just nine Premiership starts for Arsenal. Sven-Goran Eriksson's new-look England won 3–1, and the twenty-year-old left-back was struck by a metal lipstick case thrown from the crowd as the players celebrated Andy Cole's long-awaited first goal for his country.

Wenger was in Paris that night to watch France play Japan, and *France Football*'s London correspondent Philippe Auclair did an interview, which he kindly translated for this book. Wenger made it clear that, like Steve Perryman, he had been captivated by the refreshing innocence of Japanese football and that he would return there one day.

'Nagoya got in touch with me,' he recalled. 'I had never been to Japan before. I had worked ten seasons in the French first division without ever taking the time to stop. I knew nothing about Japanese football and my knowledge of the culture of this country was far from perfect. Those years I spent in Japan have been a turning point in my life. Whether we like it or not, European culture is a little one-dimensional. When we go from one country to the other in Europe we don't really feel like we're changing culture. In Japan I was confronted by a completely different culture, by different values, and this at a time when I probably needed it. When one invests himself to that point in football, the only priority is win, win and win. You end up by pushing away the rest of your life. Even if there are cultural differences within Europe, we have lost the power to discern them.

'In Japan I was forced to open my eyes, and to take stock, and to think about the values I had been taught in my youth, and about the life that I had led until then. It was a determining experience for me on a personal plane, but also on a football plane, because I rediscovered the pleasure of coaching. It was as if I had been brought back to the France of the forties and fifties when professional football was only starting and when the players were discovering profes-sionalism. For the first time in my career I was obliged to hide the ball from the players so that they couldn't train. That was something extraordinary, that we are not used to any more at home. But the enriching process has been reciprocal. I built a training centre in Nagoya and it was my inspiration for the one we built at Arsenal.

'Will I come back to Japan some day? The answer is yes. That is absolutely certain. We all have places where we have lived something unique and Japan is that for me. I will go back because of curiosity, nostalgia. Maybe privately, maybe in football – that I cannot exclude.'

Wenger also spoke of the giant strides Japanese football had taken in recent years, but France thrashed them 5–0 and they looked decades away from being able to win a World Cup, even in their own backyard. Wenger knew that, however much he loved the country, he was much more likely to win a major trophy managing Arsenal – or France.

Back in the Premiership at the end of March, there were ructions at White Hart Lane. Tottenham chairman Alan Sugar had sold most of his shares to ENIC, an investment company whose board surprisingly sacked George Graham, days before the Premiership game at Highbury and the FA Cup semi-final with Arsenal at Old Trafford. Southampton manager Glenn Hoddle almost immediately invoked his £800,000 buy-out clause and rejoined his alma mater, ostensibly to restore Tottenham's DNA and bring back style and glory. The timing of Graham's departure was as bizarre as the timing of Hoddle's arrival, raising serious doubts about the competence of ENIC. Did they really think Hoddle could walk in, beat Arsenal, and then beat Liverpool in Cardiff?

David Pleat, Tottenham's director of football and commentating, took over for the league game on 31 March, and a young side packed with reserves competed well against the Gunners, losing only 2–0 as Hoddle watched from the stand. Henry and Wiltord were the strikers against Spurs Reserves, with Kanu on the bench, which suggested that Bergkamp would not recover from his Achilles injury in time for the forthcoming Champions League game against Valencia at Highbury. It looked as if Wenger did not want Kanu to be injured playing in a game Arsenal could win without him, although they never really looked like scoring early on.

In the second half, Wiltord, unmarked, shot two yards over the bar, but Pires scored, at last, after 69 minutes, neatly skipping inside Iversen and blasting his shot low across Sullivan. Kanu, on for Lauren, won the ball in the centre circle to release Henry, who flew down the middle of the field at phenomenal speed, backed Chris Perry into the box, went round him, stumbled and just managed to jab the ball past Sullivan. Despite this defeat, Pleat hoped he would still have a job with Hoddle in charge. 'I'm hoping they still want to employ me. I've done a lot of good things, maybe.'

Glenn Hoddle had just six days with the Tottenham team to prepare for the FA Cup semi-final at Old Trafford on 8 April, and on the day he gambled on the fitness of Sol Campbell, who had not trained after twisting his ankle on England duty in Albania. Gary Doherty put Spurs ahead with an early header, but the body language of Adams and Vieira clearly said, 'We are better than you, and we will win.' The equaliser was not far away. Campbell was off the field receiving treatment when Pires sent a fine free-kick into the box and Vieira got in front of Chris Perry to head past Sullivan. Vieira, fittingly, then launched the move for the winning goal when he broke powerfully forward and played a pass wide to Wiltord, whose low cross was converted by Pires at the far post. The match had been one-way traffic with Arsenal having eleven shots on target against Tottenham's four and nine corners against none. The Spurs Reserves had been better at Highbury than the first team were at Old Trafford.

VALENCIA'S AWAY GOAL

We are still in a situation where we can put everything right and have a great season. Tonight is a big occasion because Valencia have proved consistently to be one of the best sides in Europe. If we can win through this one, everything is possible.

Arsène Wenger

Another Henry goal had ensured a win for Arsenal over Spartak on 6 March, which was just as well because a week later they were inexplicably pitiful in Munich, losing 1–0. They finished stage two level on points with Lyon, but progressed to their first ever Champions League quarter-final on the back of their 1–0 win in Lyon.

Arsenal were up against last year's finalists, Valencia, with the first leg at Highbury. This was knockout football, not a mini-league. Away goals would count double if aggregate scores were level, so a clean sheet would be vital. In Europe, as in the Premiership, Wenger had proved to be an attacking coach but a conservative tactician, although at times he was, perhaps, not conservative enough.

Early on in the game, when Pires placed a corner to the far post, Vieira headed against the bar from two yards – a bad miss. After half an hour Arsenal seemed to have run out of ideas. Seaman had to save with his foot after the giant John Carew went round him, and then, on 40 minutes, Mendieta crossed into the box and the ball squirted out to centre-back Ayala, who volleyed expertly past Seaman. Valencia were 1–0 up at half-time. Would this be Arsenal's first Champions League defeat at Highbury? Dutch referee Dick Jol, one of Europe's very best, was sensibly letting quite a lot go and was guilty of no very bad decisions, but he was having one of those watch-me-I'm-no-homer nights, giving every fifty-fifty decision to Valencia.

For the second half Wenger switched to 4–3–3, bringing on Wiltord for Ljungberg, and Arsenal raised the tempo. Vieira powered past Aimar and Mendieta and fed Wiltord on the left; he cut the ball back to Kanu, whose touch failed. The ball went loose towards Pires, who backheeled neatly to Henry, who banged it in from ten yards for 1–1. Then Vieira, fouled in midfield by Angloma, took a quick, short free-kick to Kanu, Parlour burst on to the ball, skipped sharply beyond Kanu's marker, the huge Pellegrino, with a terrific change of pace and slammed a 27-yard thunderbolt high into the net. Highbury went wild with delight. Two goals in 107 seconds had the old East Stand rocking on its foundations, a slightly alarming new experience for this reporter, who had sat there in an apparently solid structure through dozens of jump-to-your-feet goals.

Five minutes after Parlour's cannonball, Vieira released Henry and a semi-final place looked certain if he could just slip the ball past Canizares's legs, but he swerved round the keeper, had to slow down, and Angloma just reached the ball first. Still, there was no reply from Valencia and this was undoubtedly Wenger's most exciting Champions League win, a quantum leap forward, although the score had left the tie very finely balanced indeed.

Arsenal had failed to support their strikers in the first half, as the manager had said they should, but in the second, when they played high-energy football, pressurising ferociously, it had worked because that is their most effective way of playing. They cannot play cagey cat-and-mouse football like Bayern Munich. Their game is based on speed and energy, skill and momentum, so they are the kings of coming-at-you football but the dunces of wait-and-see football.

Robert Pires was impressed by the support that night, as he told Alex Hayes of the *Independent*. 'What a racket! I've never heard anything like it. The Arsenal fans never cease to amaze me. It's wonderful to play for a club where every man, woman and child screams for you at the top of their lungs.' Last season Pires had been captain of Marseilles, a club with serious administrative problems and a disappointed, hostile crowd, so he was definitely enjoying happier times. 'It's an unbelievable sensation to be standing on the pitch when the whole crowd erupts,' he continued. 'When Ray scored the winner on Wednesday, I thought Highbury was going to collapse. As a Frenchman, I had never experienced that kind of support. That's why I sometimes stand back and just look around me. The intensity is such that I often think the fans are about to pour on to the pitch.'

That week Bayern Munich president Franz Beckenbauer was brave enough to come out and say that German players and coaches were resorting to 'dirty tricks' to fool referees and it was time to stop diving. 'We only have to look over the borders to England, Spain or Italy,' he said. 'There is no play-acting any more. After a foul, players bounce right back up and keep going.' Wenger would undoubtedly have agreed with that sentiment.

Kanu was called up to join the Nigeria squad for a World Cup qualifier against Sierra Leone, scheduled just four days after the Valencia second leg, so Wenger had to ask for him to be allowed to fly out to Africa from Spain. For Arsenal's midweek game at Maine Road on 11 April he played the Nigerian but rested six players. Midfielder Edu had arrived in January, and Wenger now gave him his first start in this side: Seaman; Keown, Luzhny, Stepanovs, Cole; Lauren, Parlour, Edu, Ljungberg; Kanu and Wiltord. Struggling Manchester City, five points adrift of fourth-from-bottom Middlesbrough, were still outclassed. Ljungberg scored after eight and sixteen minutes, Wiltord grabbed Arsenal's second goal in between, and Kanu added a fourth after 36 minutes. Arsenal now had sixty points, thirteen behind Manchester United but seven clear of Ipswich and Leeds. City manager Joe Royle said,

'We're not giving up, but they were awesome. They gave us a spanking. On that form they could win the Champions League. They were on a different planet to us.'

On the Friday Wenger said he had no plans to spend heavily on strengthening his squad in the summer. 'Knowing the difficulties players have adapting to the English game, I would like to keep the same team. The new players have adapted well now, although it took them some time. They have found their confidence and there is a balance about the team. I would like to see that carried through into next year. I will sign only one or two players. Not more. And I am happy with midfield and up front. We are quite solid there.' He was more preoccupied with retaining his current players. 'It would be frustrating if anybody wanted to leave now. I think everyone is happy and will want to stay here. I want to keep everyone. The key to it, of course, is making sure we are in the Champions League again next season. That is why our remaining league games are so important.'

Arsenal were second in the table, had reached the FA Cup Final and were in the quarter-final of the biggest tournament in Europe, if not the world, holding a 2–1 lead from the first leg, but some people were still complaining that it was a transitional season. 'I hope I have many transitional seasons like this one,' said Wenger. 'The Champions League is a huge ambition, personally and for the club, and once you are in the quarter-finals the competition is open to everybody. We were lucky to go through because our minds were not right in Munich, but the fact that Valencia scored an away goal against us at Highbury means we have to play and be positive in Spain. You have to show character. You have to stay calm. We cannot play for a nil-nil. That way, we would get punished. I will play with at least two up.' During this interview Wenger also revealed that Vicente, Valencia's nineteen-year-old left-winger, was a player he had tried to sign last summer. 'He came here with his agent and I was very hopeful we would get him, but in the end the fact that he comes from Valencia was probably decisive in signing for them. Either that or they made him a slightly better offer.'

The Maine Road walkover may have lulled Arsenal into a false sense of superiority for their next game against lowly

Middlesbrough on 14 April. Edu had a traumatic home debut, scoring an own-goal after 33 minutes. Silvinho scored a second own-goal, then Hamilton Ricard scored early in the second half. A team which had managed only two shots on target had won 3–0. It was Arsenal's first league defeat at home for fourteen months and their worst since the Premiership's opening day in August 1993, when Mick Quinn scored a hat-trick for Coventry. The defeat also allowed Manchester United to celebrate their third consecutive title. 'Everything seemed to go against us,' Wenger said afterwards, 'but that can happen when your concentration is not right. My worry is finishing second in the table, and now that looks much more difficult. We could have gone seven points clear of third place today, but now the gap is only four and Leeds, Liverpool and Ipswich can all still catch us.

'I congratulate United,' he added. 'What they've done is remarkable. We have to accept that they are a better team. Everybody wants to beat them but they already have a good team and a big financial potential to buy even more players this summer. It's going to be difficult to catch them. It's boring for you and frustrating for me, but it's a fact. Once United had the title in the bag they could relax and it became easier for them to win. The difference was in October and November when we slipped away. Just because United dominated doesn't mean everyone else is bad. But the table doesn't lie. We were too poor away from home.' Wenger then made an untypically defeatist comment, saying that Sir Alex Ferguson's retirement need not signal the end of United's domination. 'I don't think Ferguson leaving will stop United, as long as they can keep the players they have at the moment and buy right. That is the most important thing for them, although the other teams can improve, you never know.'

Wenger took his team to Spain a day earlier than usual to prepare for the match, the most vital of Arsenal's season so far. 'We know our defenders will have to be at their best,' he said. 'You know we will need a big game from David Seaman and something similar from Martin Keown and Tony Adams. Because without that you have no chance, and they know that. We have to show our potential and our quality. We are not a defensive team, though.

Our team is frustrated if it can't get out and play. We are still in a situation where we can put everything right and have a great season. Tonight is a big occasion because Valencia have proved consistently to be one of the best sides in Europe. If we can win through this one, everything is possible.'

It was a great motivating line, and it needed to be. In recent years the Mestalla Stadium had become the most impregnable football fortress in Europe, the home of a very proud and consistent team. Valencia's Champions League record was played fourteen, won ten, drawn four, lost none, 26 goals for and just seven against. It was going to be very tough, and unfortunately, on the night, Arsenal were not quite good enough. The game was close, though, and at the end of the first half Arsenal's steady performance had silenced the 48,000 crowd. Wenger had not started Kanu, who had missed three chances against Middlesbrough three days earlier. What did that tell us? Did it mean Kanu would not be at Arsenal next season, or that his mind was already in Sierra Leone? It was still there to be won early in the second half, but Wiltord and Henry did not click. Valencia had Ayala's away goal in the bag, so it was always likely to be Fiorentina revisited – a very tight one-goal game.

This second leg was 0–0 for 74 minutes and Arsenal did not show enough initiative in those 74 minutes. In the 75th, Angloma hit a hard cross, dipping towards the near post, and Carew sent a header bouncing down across Seaman, who reacted late, still got a full hand to it but only managed to push it into the net. It was 2–2 on aggregate, but Valencia were through to face Leeds, who had beaten Deportivo La Coruña 3–2 on aggregate.

Overall, the 90 minutes showed the limitations of Wenger's straight 4–4–2 selection. Most teams who play 4–4–2 depend a lot on crosses, but Arsenal did not hit crosses because Wiltord and Henry play avenue football, dribble-and-shoot football. If you do not cross the ball, you need a creative half-striker to link the play, giving time for midfielders to make supporting runs, and Arsenal did not do that enough. They defended intelligently, but attacked stupidly. As usual, far too much depended on Thierry Henry.

The bonus on the night was Ashley Cole, who got close enough to make Carew shoot wide from a promising position in the first half and, just before the goal, completed a seventy-yard dribble before being obstructed by Angloma. In the final minutes, when Adams was playing centre-forward and Valencia broke three against three, Cole took the ball off Zahovic with a tremendous covering tackle in the box when Keown was beaten, just as Winterburn would have done. He was now, clearly, a better defender than Silvinho. Arsenal had lost a quarter-final but found a left-back.

At the pre-Everton press conference that Friday, Wenger said that he would be signing new players in the summer, but not massive names. Five years on, Wenger was still the straight-shooting corporate gentleman he was in 1996, still willing to shoulder all the responsibility. 'We have a good game,' he said, 'but maybe not good enough. I accept that. There are lots of ingredients. It's up to me to make the right changes.' Valencia had been his 53rd match of the season, and there is nothing as instructive as 53 competitive games to help you clarify your strengths and weaknesses. Typically, though, he also cited the need for stability, pointing out that the Bayern Munich team which had just beaten Manchester United contained eight of the same players who had lost to United in the 1999 final in the Nou Camp.

THE CARDIFF COLLAPSE

As soon as Michael scored it was a different game. Their defence was superb, but when we scored they lost authority.

Gerard Houllier

During the season Wenger had gradually converted fiery Freddie Ljungberg into a right winger who could score with his left foot. He grabbed the first goal in a 4–1 win against Everton, and, after Arsenal had won 2–1 at Derby, Ljungberg again scored the first against Leeds, who were beaten 2–1 on the Saturday before their Champions League semi-final second leg in Valencia, where Leeds lost 3–0. After the Leeds game Sylvain Wiltord was seen leaving Highbury with four suitcases, heading for Paris, where he spent Saturday night, Sunday and Monday. A club statement later said he had permission to attend a charity event and reporters who noticed his absence from training on Tuesday were told that Wiltord was 'injured'.

Among the many previews of the FA Cup final the most perceptive remark came from Arsenal's Head Youth Coach Don Howe who said, 'Steven Gerrard is going to be a tremendous player. I liken him to a young Stefan Effenberg at Bayern Munich. He is big, strong and gets around the whole pitch. He also has a terrific shot and we must not allow him the space if he moves towards goal.'

Jean-Marc Butterlin of *L'Equipe*, the French sports newspaper, reckoned that Wenger's strength lies in his close relationship with his players. 'He has a true love for them, as if they were his children,' said Butterlin. 'He expects a lot of them but he loves watching them develop into what he wants. For him, it is very, very important that each player keeps developing. His players are as important as his team. Thierry Henry and Nicolas Anelka are prime examples of players he's pampered while he watched them grow up. He says he likes players for the childlike side of their personality, for the purity of play while they are cocooned in his team.'

Staging the FA Cup final in Cardiff made the match a unique event for both sets of fans. Londoners and Liverpudlians mingled happily in the sunshine and the new Millennium Stadium had a more invigorating atmosphere than Wembley, plus better sightlines and adequate knee-room. Wenger picked all five of his French players, so Grimandi, a journeyman, was preferred in central midfield to Lauren, who had been player of the tournament in the African Nations in 2000 and an Olympic champion with Cameroon in Sydney in the autumn. Lauren had also scored Arsenal's first Premiership goal of the season – against Liverpool. Wiltord started rather than Kanu, who had scored only four goals all season after seventeen the year before. A manager's selections are often self-justifying, of course. If you pay £12 million for Wiltord you want to play him to justify your outlay, and if you are keen to unload him, you put him in the shop window and hope he scores. Bergkamp had missed the last nine games with an

Achilles tendon injury, so he was on the bench alongside Kanu, Parlour, Lauren and Manninger.

As expected, Liverpool defended deep, and nothing much happened for seventeen minutes. Then Vieira made a tackle on Heskey, poking the ball to Ljungberg, whose pass allowed Henry to race behind Hyypia, cruise round keeper Westerveld and shoot from a narrow angle. The ball was going into the net when centre-back Henchoz blocked it with his left arm, but assistant referee Kevin Pike kept his flag down. At the other end Michael Owen threatened but Adams stood his ground cleverly, and then, when Heskey flicked on Babbel's long throw, and Owen shot, Keown made a magnificent block.

At the start of the second half Seaman saved a Heskey header and then Pires gave Henry a one-on-one with Westerveld, but he bottled it. Where Ian Wright or Michael Owen would have seen only the goal, Henry saw the keeper, and his outstretched boot missed the ball by three inches. Henry collided with Westerveld, fell on his back, and flicked the loose ball to Ashley Cole, whose shot was cleared off the line by Hyypia.

Then Henry beat Henchoz and side-footed a silly shot which hit Hyypia and rebounded to Ljungberg, whose chip over the advancing Westerveld was headed off the line by Hyypia. Arsenal had so far produced four shots on target: one saved, one handballed and two cleared off the line.

After 72 minutes Liverpool, still very negative, ran out of luck. Carragher backpassed, Westerveld kicked wide to Babbel, who backpassed again, and this time the keeper scuffed his clearance to Grimandi, who volleyed to Pires and his slide-rule pass picked out Ljungberg's diagonal run. The sparky Swede took the ball sweetly round the keeper, clipped it into the net from seven yards, and Wenger leapt off the bench with both fists clenched. He had just seen a gem, one of his team's finest 'narrow' goals, a perfect combination between two wide players who baffled the Liverpool defence by linking with each other, missing out the strikers, to create a goal worthy of the occasion.

The game opened up immediately, and when Ljungberg's long pass released Henry, he swerved round Henchoz, who fell and diverted the ball with his trailing arm, so that the shot became awkward for Henry, and his side-foot stab was parried by the keeper. Incredibly, Henry miskicked the rebound and Hyypia cleared off the line for the third time.

Wiltord slipped three or four times, as if he was wearing the wrong studs, and he showed once again that he cannot play with Henry. By now the game was crying out for Bergkamp but Wenger brought on Parlour for Wiltord in 75 minutes. This was utter folly. It was really two changes rather than one, since Ljungberg switched into a striking role. Good substitutes, like Sheringham, are invariably technicians, not warriors, because warriors take a while to warm up, a point proved by Houllier's subs – McAllister, Berger and Fowler – whose skill allowed them to get into the game immediately.

As soon as Parlour came on, Arsenal's attacks stopped and their problems started. Keown had to make another superb tackle on Owen in the box. Unfortunately, the demoralised Henry had switched off mentally and was caught offside four times in the remaining eighteen minutes; Bergkamp might have revived him during that crucial period. Parlour played a role in Liverpool's equaliser when he got on the wrong side of Carragher and made a challenge he did not have to make. McAllister's free-kick ricocheted vertically off Keown's head, Babbel just beat Adams in the air, and Owen half-volleyed home, a fine strike by a great reflex player. So it was 1–1 after 83 minutes.

Extra time looked likely when Keown went forward for an Arsenal free-kick after 87 minutes, leaving Dixon and Adams at the back. Pires hit the free-kick feebly and as it bounced Kanu, who had replaced Ljungberg, did not compete with Heskey. The Liverpool striker brushed the Nigerian aside and pushed the ball to Berger, who launched a long 'Petit pass', a 70-yard defence-stretcher. The acceleration of Owen was electrifying, just like Overmars and Anelka in the 1998 final. He held off Dixon, sped wide of Adams and shot low across Seaman for a memorable winner. From Pires' free-kick to the goal at the other end took only eleven seconds. Seaman did not check his angles or advance to give Owen a smaller target.

Bergkamp came on for Dixon with 90 minutes on the clock, so a season which had started in controversy at Sunderland now ended in farce. Liverpool had never beaten Arsenal in any cup final and they should not have won in Cardiff, but at least the Millennium collapse gave the manager a perfect X-ray of his team. Football is a game of partnerships and Patrick Vieira had no partner. Thierry Henry had no partner either, so he carried too big a burden. The back five were magnificent and then, on a hot day, they fell part in the last ten minutes. Michael Owen's first goal had triggered a familiar ailment: Bayernitis. It was the concede-and-crumble scenario all over again. When Arsenal let a goal in they just went to pieces and started giving the ball away. As Gerard Houllier noted, 'As soon as Michael scored it was a different game. Their defence was superb, but when we scored they lost authority.'

Arsène Wenger had picked the wrong team in an FA Cup final, but he had looked like winning the game anyway. Attack had been his best means of defence for 83 minutes and attacking had worked so well that Seaman had only needed to make one save, which was one less than Henchoz. Parlour for Wiltord when Arsenal were 1–0 up was an inexplicable and disruptive substitution which he will probably regret for the rest of his days. Afterwards Wenger said, 'This is a little bit the image of our season. We always looked like we should win the big games but we can't finish it and we lose the concentration. We need some players because we've lost two big games, Valencia and now today, in the last fifteen minutes – and that is not a coincidence.'

Significantly, Wiltord was not in the squad for the last two Premiership games. On the Tuesday night at Newcastle Bergkamp played for an hour in the 0–0 draw which clinched the runners-up spot and an automatic Champions League place. If Bergkamp was fit enough to start in Newcastle, why did he not come on earlier in Cardiff? On the final Premiership Saturday Arsenal met Southampton in an emotional final match at The Dell, the home of the Saints for 103 years. Arsenal led 1–0 through Cole, and then led 2–1 thanks to Ljungberg, but eventually lost 3–2. Matt Le Tissier, a supreme technician, came on and scored the winner in the 89th minute. The only good news was that Wiltord had said he never wanted to play for Arsenal again.

At Wembley in 1998, after the FA Cup final win over Newcastle, I had asked Wenger, 'Are you specifically looking for a striker who can head the ball?' He smiled and said, 'That's a good question.' Three years later I was still waiting for an answer. The point had been emphasised on Wednesday 16 May when Liverpool played Alavés in a thrilling UEFA Cup final in Dortmund, winning 5–4 in extra time against nine men with a golden own-goal. Three of the Alavés goals were headers.

9. 2001/02: THE SEASON OF THE SQUAD

On 25 May 2001, Patrick Vieira told *L'Equipe* that he was in talks with Arsenal about leaving. He was still moaning about the departure of Petit and Overmars. Meanwhile, Wiltord and Lauren had admitted being lonely and homesick. The Frenchman loved nightclubbing and been fined for turning up late for training, but promised to change his ways, as bad boys always do. Wenger had allowed Wiltord to go on holiday early and he now said, 'I am very happy at Arsenal, but I know there have been mistakes. There is much more to come from me.'

Lauren had lived in Spain since the age of four and was on holiday in Mallorca with his wife. 'My first year in England has been positive, apart from the time I was out injured,' he said. 'It is always a joy for me to return to Mallorca; I have a lot of friends here and I miss them. I feel a bit nostalgic, but I am sure that next year I will feel more comfortable and not miss things quite as much.'

Feyenoord goalkeeper Jerzy Dudek had visited Shenley and agreed personal terms, but the Rotterdam club wanted £8.6 million and Arsenal had offered £6 million. As Poland's keeper he naturally wanted to protect that position if he joined Arsenal. 'I don't want to go to be a reserve. I have told them of my concerns. It would be too much to risk my international career.' Wenger said he wanted new players, but had to be careful and think about many things. 'It can be dangerous to bring in too many players at once and upset the spirit at the club. We need to strengthen and I will buy players, but two, maybe three, and in the right areas. I know that. We have to look at the options tactically, and with our formation, like Robert Pires and whether he could play in the middle. There are many ways of changing the team. It is more important that we build on what we have and strengthen from there and that means we will never sell Patrick. He will stay and be successful with us. We have come very close in the biggest games this season. It shows we need something extra, but it also means we are not far away and I think sometimes disappointments can inspire success.'

On Sunday 10 June, Wenger was in Yokohama as a television commentator to see Vieira score the winner as France beat Japan in the Confederations Cup Final. In the absence of Zidane, Pires had partnered Vieira in central midfield, and he talked about taking his Arsenal form into the tournament, which was exactly what Petit had done in 1998.

'All the French players who came to Arsenal under Wenger have exploded,' said Pires. 'Certainly, he has instilled confidence into my game. The success I've had with France in Japan was just a continuation of a really enjoyable year I had at Arsenal. Arsène has worked so hard on my confidence. The simple thing is he puts enormous trust in you. He has spoken to me a lot and made me aware of my place in the whole environment of the game. But then he knows me well, since I was at Metz.

'It's interesting how he works on you. At the beginning, he speaks to you a lot. Then he leaves you, lets you relax in your mind and become calm about what you're doing. Then, once you are on the pitch, it's up to you to demonstrate your worth back to him. The way he talks, it makes the pleasure of playing come back. He does it progressively until something sparks inside you. He says simple things and they make you want to work for him. He takes only six minutes to announce the team line-up and talk before each game. Then, the rest of it is up to us, to think while we're in the dressing room about what we are going to do.'

Wenger was reconsidering his personnel, seeking to define the missing pieces of the jigsaw. Clearly, Vieira needed a left-footed partner with a good passing range, Keown needed a younger partner with pace, and Henry needed someone who was quick enough to play with him, brave enough to get in where it hurts, bright enough to run behind defences at the right moment and skilful enough to play one-touch football at high speed.

Very few British strikers fitted that description, perhaps only Robbie Keane and Francis Jeffers, the Everton kid Wenger now signed for £10 million on the same day that Chelsea paid £11 million for West Ham's Frank Lampard. He said, 'I have signed Francis because he is a good player and has the qualities I need in my team. We play football based on mobility and technique here and he is a good runner off the ball. Maybe people will be surprised that I have signed an Englishman but I looked at his quality and not his passport. You need an English base and the right mixture at a club.'

Jeffers was twenty and had been injury-prone. He was a goal-poacher who knew where to run, and Wenger explained his virtues in considerable detail. 'Francis has the qualities we have missed in the team. He is obsessed with scoring goals and we haven't had a player like that. I want to develop him as a team player. As soon as I knew Francis was available I wanted him here. English players are used to the hardness of the Premiership. Francis knows what it means to go to Southampton or Newcastle and fight. He scored seven goals in the first nine games last season before he was injured and five of them were away.'

On Tuesday 19 June, he signed Giovanni van Bronckhorst, 26, from Rangers. The Dutchman said he had spoken to Wenger on Friday and it felt right: 'The ambition, the way he trains, the way the team plays, his vision really suited me.'

The Vieira situation, however, remained a major drama. The star flew back to London and told Wenger and Dein that he wanted to leave. Then he went on holiday to Miami with Sheryl, his girlfriend. Two weeks later he launched a stunning attack on Arsenal in *The Sun*, saying, 'I need to leave because I want to win more trophies and I just cannot see that happening at Arsenal. Certainly not over the next few years, anyway. Comparing Arsenal to the big clubs in Europe this season is going to be quite ridiculous.'

On the signings of Jeffers and van Bronckhorst, he said, 'Arsène Wenger has signed two 'hopeful' players who haven't proved themselves in the Premiership yet. One of them is a boy of twenty. You can't compete with the best clubs in Europe by making these kind of signings.'

Gilles Grimandi was adamant that these quotes had been made up because his friend never talked like that. Grimandi told his website, 'He will never get the same level of love, respect and admiration that he enjoys at Highbury anywhere else. He's like a God at Arsenal, I can honestly say I've never known anything like it.'

Recognising an agent's handiwork, David Dein issued a statement. 'Patrick Vieira is an Arsenal player and is not for sale at any price.' Wenger was deeply depressed by this turn of events, since he had developed Vieira into the complete footballer: warrior, ball-winner, standard-bearer, and, now, playmaker. The season's OPTA stats showed that Vieira was Arsenal's best passer of the ball with 1,500 passes, 300 more than anyone else, and 82 per cent of his passes were successful. He won more tackles than any of his team-mates, and scored five goals with four assists. He was one of the giants of the modern game, the finest player in the Premiership.

But was Patrick Vieira bigger than the club? Did he think he was bigger than Arsenal? If he did, could they keep him? Should they keep him? What were their options in this ugly situation? If Vieira was on £30,000 a week and Wenger thought he was half the team, should he double his wages, demand a big season from him, and sell him in June 2002? Clearly, if Frank Lampard was worth £11 million, Anelka was worth £23 million and if Figo was worth £37 million, then Vieira, who was 25 and in his prime, must now be worth £40 million.

Vieira had grown up in poverty in Dakar, Senegal, and when he was seven he emigrated with his brother Nicoro to join his mother Rose in Trappes, a Paris suburb mainly populated by immigrant families. He had captained Cannes at eighteen and come to Arsenal via AC Milan, for whom he played only twice. He now seemed to be at a crossroads in his life.

On Tuesday 3 July, a controversial transfer coup was announced: Sol Campbell had left Tottenham on a free transfer and signed a four-year contract with Arsenal. He was reported to be on a salary of £45,000 plus a huge signing-on fee paid in instalments over his five-year contract, making him the highest-paid footballer in British history.

One on one, Campbell, 26, was a magnificent gladiator, although he sometimes struggled to read crosses. His other main quality, after his athleticism, was his calm temperament. 'I tried to attract him here because he is the best,' said Wenger. 'After chatting to him I felt he is a very ambitious guy who wants to improve and play at the top level. That convinced me he is the right player for us.' He hoped that the arrival of Campbell would help him to persuade Vieira to stay, and he admitted that Campbell had asked him whether he was confident of keeping Vieira.

On 6 July he signed Ipswich goalkeeper Richard Wright, 23, for a reported £6 million fee. Freddie Ljungberg agreed a new five-year deal on 11 July, and he also signed young Japanese midfielder Junichi Inamoto on loan with an option to buy him for £4 million after one year.

Amazingly, Sir Alex Ferguson now accused Arsenal of double standards because they had signed Sol Campbell but refused to release Vieira. 'We know he has asked to leave,' said Ferguson. 'Are Arsenal going to condemn the boy for wanting to come to United?' It was, of course, nonsensical to compare Vieira and Campbell, since Vieira was in the middle of a long contract till 2004. Did Fergie really entertain hopes that Arsenal would sell Vieira to him? Or was it just a exercise to destabilise his rivals? The United boss soon bought Juan Sebastian Veron from Lazio for a British record transfer fee of £28 million.

There was intense speculation about whether Vieira would turn up for training on Monday 16 July, but he arrived at 9.42a.m. in his black Cherokee Jeep and left an hour after the other players, driving over the grass to a side exit to escape reporters.

Insiders soon whispered that when Vieira reported for training Dein and Wenger had sat him down and told him that Arsenal would hold him to his contract for the next three years. If he didn't like it, he could play for the reserves. But he was not going anywhere. This information explained Vieira's silence and his refusal to apologise for the media manipulation of his agent Marc Roger. But would Vieira sulk? Would he care as much as he did before? Would he play as well as he had done for the last five years?

On a happier note, Philippe Auclair did an interview in *France Football*, where Wenger talked in glowing terms about the talents of Robert Pires. 'Personally, I look at the player and what do I see? He asks for the ball, and then he gives it to a team-mate. Already that's not bad. Then, he passes it to a player who is in front of him. That is even better. Lastly, he gives it at the right moment. Not many players can do that. He can also accelerate, he's a team player, passes a lot. When he went to Marseille, I already wanted to sign him. For me he is a fantastic football player and, on top of all that, he loves what he does.'

On 5 August, Alex Manninger joined Fiorentina on loan, and Wenger then picked up Stathis Tavlaridis, twenty, a promising Greek defender who had trained with Arsenal for ten days. After warm-up games in Austria, the squad came back for a friendly at Norwich, where, surprisingly, Vieira wore the skipper's armband, even though Keown was playing. On Wednesday 8 August, Vieira was appointed club vice-captain, so he would lead the team when Tony Adams was absent.

Pires reckoned that the club would have faced an exodus if Vieira had been allowed to quit, saying, 'If you let a player of Patrick's stature leave, then your whole credibility is shot to pieces.' When France met Denmark in Nantes on 15 August, Pires scored the only goal of the game and dedicated it to Wenger. 'If I play so well with France it is because of Arsenal,' he said. 'I got my confidence back thanks to them, they trust me. I found there the quality of game I had lost. Every time I leave Arsenal to go and play with Les Bleus, Wenger tells me, "Play as you know and take initiatives." I've had the chance to play under excellent coaches in my career but there is something extra with Wenger, he deeply loves football and his players.'

With the new season about to kick-off, Wenger was saying he was happy to have more options. Most of his players were now between 20 and 26 years of age, so it was his youngest squad and last year's new boys were now bedded in. 'I'm very happy with the signings we have made, but just as encouraging is that we have kept the players who were here last year. The ones who arrived a year ago like Sylvain Wiltord, Robert Pires and Lauren should show the benefit of having had a season to get used to English football.'

CAMPBELL RETURNS TO THE LANE

We look very solid, especially away from home.

Arsène Wenger

In the first game at Middlesbrough the team was Seaman, Lauren, Adams, Campbell, Cole, Parlour, Vieira, Pires, Ljungberg, Wiltord and Henry. They won 4–0 and Henry, who scored the first goal, said, 'I saw something today I never saw last season – we played as a team in attack and in defence. It's the most important thing in football.' Regrettably, Parlour earned a second yellow card for a mistimed tackle on Ehiogu.

On the following Tuesday night, they faced Leeds and referee Jeff Winter booked Bakke, Dacourt, Bowyer and Mills in the first seventeen minutes. When Mills was fouled by Pires outside the box, Winter allowed Ian Harte to take a free-kick quickly and Leeds went 1–0 up. Wiltord soon equalised with a diving header. When Alan Smith was injured, Batty came on and that gave Leeds three against three in the middle and pushed Bowyer onto Cole, who had been unmarked. That change shut the door and Kewell soon jinked round Lauren and passed to Viduka, who beat Adams and scored, giving Leeds their first league victory at Highbury for seven years, even though Bowyer and Mills had been sent off. Wenger said, 'It's a real blow for us to lose a game like this. If you're going to have a good season, you have to be strong at home. It's very frustrating.'

The conundrum facing every football coach is this: how do I make one part of my team stronger without making another part weaker? Interestingly, Wenger had re-configured his attack for these two games, using three players in midfield – Parlour, Vieira and Pires – with Ljungberg and Wiltord wide, plus Henry. The narrow midfielders had dominated against Leeds, but Arsenal had failed to score first. Henry and Wiltord rarely set up goals for each other and this system admitted their incompatability by playing them on opposite sides of the field.

After the Leeds defeat, Wenger gave van Bronckhorst his debut and started Bergkamp, not Henry, against Leicester. On a blazing hot day, Leicester struggled to keep the ball for more than a few seconds. Bergkamp played an advanced game at centre-forward, feeding Wiltord on the right, and Pires set up goals for Ljungberg, then Wiltord. When Henry came on, he made it 3–0. Then Vieira and Dennis Wise were sent off after going head-to-head in a one-sided game which had become calmer in the cruel heat. Kanu headed a fourth in stoppage time.

When Wenger came into the press conference, I asked him if it was the hottest day's football he had ever known at Highbury. He smiled and said, 'I felt we played in Yaounde or Angola. It was African heat. It looked like we were serious in the first half, tried to get a good pace in the game. And of course we dropped physically in the second half.'

Asked about Vieira's dismissal, he said, 'Patrick at that stage of the game was already physically a little bit tired. He had played his fourth game in nine days and maybe he was a little bit nervous. Because he has not, at the moment, really found his game.' The Sunday papers reported that it had been the hottest bank holiday in London since 1943.

The Champions' League deadline was approaching and Arsenal sold Silvinho, 27, to Celta Vigo, just in time for him to register to play in the UEFA Cup. In a remarkable twist, Liverpool signed Jerzy Dudek for £4.85 million and threw him in against Aston Villa the following day. Sander Westerveld had made a late error to lose a game at Bolton.

Arsenal were scheduled to play Real Mallorca, FC Schalke 04 and Panathinaikos in the Champions' League but France had arranged a friendly in far-flung Chile, a ridiculous journey. Wenger, angry before the trip, would be furious when he saw the impact on his team's next performance at Chelsea. Vieira and Parlour were suspended, but he rested Campbell, Ljungberg and Jeffers because he was thinking ahead to his 11 September date, saying, 'That gives me five fresh players for Mallorca.' At Stamford Bridge, Henry snapped up a rebound from a Pires shot, but Hasselbaink equalised with a penalty after Keown brought down Zola. Hasselbaink was then sent off after tangling with Keown.

On that Tuesday morning the Al-Qaida suicide hijackers crashed jets into the World Trade Centre and the Pentagon, a terrorist outrage which shocked the whole world and made UEFA wonder whether the eight games should go ahead that night. It was decided that Wednesday's games should be postponed, but Tuesday's should be played because thousands of fans had travelled.

Vieira led Arsenal for the first time in a competitive game and saw Ashley Cole make a crazy tackle on Albert Luque in the box and get sent off after only eleven minutes. Engonga cheekily floated the penalty down the middle, past Seaman, and that was the only goal of the game. Henry was clipped by Nadal in the box, but Danish referee Knud Fisker gave him a yellow card for diving.

Incredibly, none of Arsenal's five games so far had ended with 22 players and seven of the sixteen red cards so far shown in the Premiership had come in games involving Arsenal, so there was an avalanche of bad publicity. They went to newly-promoted Fulham and might have had six goals instead of one at half-time. Ljungberg scored the first goal and set up Henry for the second before Bergkamp made it 3–1 from Wiltord's pass. So Arsenal headed the table after five games and Wenger said, 'I think we can stay at the top. Why not? Other teams are dropping points. It could be a lot closer than last year. We look very solid, especially away from home. We look determined, mentally right.'

A frightening drama unfolded at Anfield during Liverpool's game against Leeds. Gerard Houllier spoke to the players in the dressing room, then complained to the club doctor of chest pains. He was taken to hospital immediately, had heart surgery that night, and a tragedy was narrowly averted.

Otherwise, Arsenal's autumn continued along familiar lines with a 1–0 defeat in Athens, where Henry berated the referee after the game, and a 2–1 win against Panathinakos at home. They qualified by beating Mallorca 3–1 at Highbury, which made Schalke in Gelsenkirchen a dead game. Vieira was rested, Parlour captained the team for the first time, and Luzhny was dismissed for an off-the-ball scuffle with Jörg Böhme as Schalke won 3–1.

They remained in the top two in the Premiership until their usual November slump began against Charlton with a 4–2 defeat in which Richard Wright was at fault for two goals. It was Wenger's biggest home defeat in the Premiership and he was very upset by the booing, but said nothing on the record. One could sympathise with his distress, since every team loses matches.

In the Worthington Cup, his second team beat Ferguson's third team 4–0 and after that it was White Hart Lane, which the tabloids hyped up with headlines like SOL TO FACE HATE MOB. On 17 November, sure enough, the Arsenal team bus was bombarded with bottles and beer cans. When Campbell had come on as a sub at Chelsea he had looked fat, and he was ponderous against Schalke. But now he was a well-conditioned athlete and Wenger said he was only a kilo above his optimum weight.

The fans held up abusive banners, released two thousand balloons with the word JUDAS printed on them, and jeered his every touch. But Sol Campbell announced himself as an Arsenal player with a thunderous tackle on Poyet, winning the ball. That tackle said: I am an Arsenal player now. He played superbly in a tight game and Pires eventually put Arsenal ahead with a 25-yard curler. In stoppage time, when Gus Poyet hit a volley from outside the box, Wright tried to catch the ball and fumbled it over the line.

Still, Campbell had earned the respect of his teammates on the traumatic day, and he now faced another challenge in Spain. Wenger warned that Deportivo were not the quickest side in the world, but could win matches just by passing the ball well. 'La Coruña are better than Barcelona at the moment,' he noted. 'They have tremendous intelligence.' He said that Richard Wright had a great game at Tottenham and then made a mistake in the last seconds. Wenger, more forgiving than Houllier when it came to goalkeeping blunders, added, 'Richard had a bad day against Charlton but 24 hours later he bounced back with a clean sheet against United in the Worthington Cup. That makes you think he has the calibre to play for Arsenal, because it takes a special strength of character to play here.'

Deportivo had just beaten Manchester United twice and they now had Diego Tristan, a powerful centre forward with guile. Wenger said, 'Sol was brilliant against Tottenham but, though this game will be mentally easier for him, it will be a lot more difficult technically. Against Spurs, it was all route one with lots of high balls and I know Sol and Martin Keown can always cope with that.

Against La Coruña, it will be a Brazilian type of game, with everything on the ground. They play on the break and Tristan always knows where to go. He is an intelligent player, brilliant at exploiting the spaces left by defenders. You cannot afford to let your concentration drop for one second.'

He admitted, 'Deportivo are one of the best teams, better than anything we faced in the first group. They are good enough to be European champions. We do seem to have a bit of a mental block when it comes to playing away in Europe and we have to get over that. My players have the character and determination to achieve something in Europe. This is the chance for them to show I'm right not to be worried by our recent record. We are not lacking quality, but there is a confidence problem at the back. We are being punished for every technical mistake we make. We just need to get through one game without losing concentration and we will be on the way.'

Early on, as Arsenal defended, Campbell made two good blocks but then blasted the loose ball against Tristan, only to see it ricochet to Makaay, whose shot bounced past Wright for 1–0. Soon after that, during a deceptively sleepy passage of play, Valeron launched a perfect diagonal pass to Tristan, who ambled inside Lauren and hit a shot which Wright should have saved at his near post. That mistake effectively ended the match after 25 minutes.

The game must have been among the longest of Wenger's career. Every tackle was too short, the passing was atrocious, and Henry, caught offside in the 5th, 24th, 32nd and 89th minutes, was cautioned when he petulantly lashed at the ball, kicking it away after conceding a throw.

Deportivo were organised, with good habits. They used the whole width of the pitch and were not scared to pass the ball backwards and sideways, while Arsenal played narrowly and impatiently, always trying to go forward. Mauro Silva anchored everything and Emerson, another tenacious Brazilian, was strong enough to dominate van Bronckhorst, and to mix it with Vieira. Wenger admitted it was wrong to start Richard Wright, even though the doctors had said his jarred knee was OK. Stuart Taylor had replaced him at half time.

The next game was against Manchester United at Highbury on Sunday 25 November, the seventeenth clash between the managers whose rivalry had defined English football for half a decade. Remarkably, United had only won two of their last nine games, while Arsenal had only won two of their last eight. Ferguson had lost authority because he was retiring at the end of the season, and Wenger seemed to have lost authority because he had not signed his contract yet.

'Alex has done marvellously well, but his club has such potential they will continue to be tough, no matter who comes in after him,' said Wenger. 'It will not be a relief when he retires. They have the money to buy a good manager, the money to buy good players. It will go on. United have twice our budget, but I don't envy that because, frankly, I enjoy our rivalry. I want to go as far as I can with my team.'

Santa Claus turned up a month early in the shape of a goalkeeper with a shaved head. United had scored with their first attack when Sylvestre picked out Scholes, who beat keeper Stuart Taylor on his Premiership debut, but that was their only shot on target. The equaliser came when Gary Neville passed to Pires, who played the ball across to Ljungberg, whose jabbed shot flew sharply over Fabien Barthez and into the net. Barthez had made good saves to keep the score at 1–1 but after 80 minutes he booted Beckham's back-pass straight to Henry, who made it 2–1. Then Barthez raced out to challenge Henry for Vieira's lofted through pass and fumbled the ball, another gift for Henry.

At Ipswich, defender Titus Bramble made an early error, passing to Henry, who set up Ljungberg for 1–0. When the Swede was brought down by Mark Venus, Henry converted the penalty for 2–0.

Then it was the big night at Highbury against Juventus, who started impressively. Stuart Taylor made important saves, especially one from Del Piero, and Cole was outstanding in a hectic first fifteen minutes, while Kanu and Henry were clueless. When Vieira powered through for a shot after 21 minutes, Gianlugi Buffon spilled it and Ljungberg popped up to net the rebound.

Then Arsenal won a free-kick 22 yards out and Henry took one step and hit the ball over the wall and down into the top corner. Buffon took half a step towards the shot and stopped, knowing he could not reach a strike that was stunning in its velocity and accuracy. It was also utterly unexpected. If Henry could do that, why had he waited three years?

Juve then got a goal back when Taylor saved Trezeguet's shot and Campbell's clearance off the line hit the keeper for an unlucky own-goal. After that it was a very intense, absorbing contest, balanced on a knife-edge at 2–1. The rugged Montero had been reading Kanu like an open book, so Kanu was replaced by Bergkamp, who soon turned Montero inside out before flicking Ljungberg through for 3–1. Having created two goals for Freddie against last year's Italians, Lazio, Bergkamp now took eleven touches to conjure the *coup de grace* against Juventus. Would Wiltord have read that situation? Would he have made that run to score from Bergkamp's sublime pass? Not in a thousand years.

Overall, this thrilling 3–1 victory was what Arsenal had promised against Bayern Munich but did not deliver. It was the same brand of speed-football that sliced Bayern to ribbons for fifty minutes, but this time they sustained it and gave the manager his first win against the big boys. A year on from the Munich meltdown, Arsenal had finished the job. They were learning.

WENGER SIGNS TILL 2005

We can win everything.

Arsène Wenger

Having now won four games in a row for the first time all season, the manager decided to sign his contract, so the media were summoned to the training ground on Friday 7 December.

David Dein, Danny Fiszman, Wenger and Peter Hill-Wood sat together at a long table backed by small posters that said LET ARSENAL SUPPORT ISLINGTON. The stadium decision was due at a council meeting on the following Monday night and Wenger's signature at this moment, after so much speculation and delay, suggested that approval of the club's plans would be granted at last.

'Good afternoon, ladies and gentlemen, and welcome,' said Peter Hill-Wood, who always relishes a role as the bringer of glad tidings. 'Arsène has agreed to sign a new contract with us which will keep him at the club till at least 2005. It's marvellous news. He's done an absolutely fantastic job since his arrival in 1996 and our future could not be in better hands.'

Wenger said that he hoped we would suffer him for a few more years. 'I've decided to stay because I believe I have a group of players that I respect and admire and have a lot of potential to bring this club to where I want them to be. That means at the top level in Europe and in the world. The directors have shared that kind of ambition with me. And that's why I decided to stay, giving me the freedom to work and to achieve our target. The club has a huge potential supporters-wise, and the fans have always been loyal to me since I'm here.'

He was asked whether this would encourage players to extend their contracts. 'Well, we have a strong bunch of players. All the young players have longer contracts and the experienced players have a big part to play as well in the future of the club. Overall, I think 99 per cent of the players will stay. When I'm committed, I'm committed. I don't accept get-out clauses for the players. You're in a project or out of it, and not in between. So if it goes well, you stay. I'm part of the future of the club and I will fight very hard to achieve our target. I'm not in or out. I'm in, and definitely.

'No matter where you work in the world, if you get up in the morning and you're not happy to go to your job, it's not worth doing it. The relationship I have with the directors of this club is predominant. You have a deep feeling when you make such a decision. I'm 52 years old, I know that I will not take five more contracts. In fairness, I had good possibilities, and when you face such a decision you have deep feelings in yourself that tell you the truth. Are you happy here, or not?'

Hill-Wood said that other clubs had asked to speak to Wenger, but he refused to admit that one of them had been Manchester United. Then the daily papers chatted to Dein, while, simultaneously, in the next room, the Sunday papers had an audience with Fiszman and Hill-Wood.

Dein emphasised that the manager was intimately involved in everything the club was doing. 'This development here at the training ground is Arsène's brainchild. He was concerned with every minor detail down to the teacups. And he's involved, obviously, in making sure that the new stadium's gonna be successful. We need a new stadium to compete with the biggest clubs in Europe because financially, without a new stadium, we cannot afford to pay the sort of salaries that we currently do.

'Personally, I always thought he was going to stay. To me, he's a miracle-worker. He revolutionised the club. We owe a lot to him. He has brought world class players to the club. He's developed players to world class stature. Together with Liam Brady, he's developed our youth policy to make sure we've got youngsters coming through, as you saw on Tuesday night. Our back five, when you consider, we had Stuart Taylor and Ashley Cole who came through our youth team. Without being unkind to Juventus, what did they pay for their back five? It's not just about money. It's that he believes in seeing that youth does develop through the ranks as well as combining with other talent, which he's been so successful in doing.'

He said he had known Arsène for fourteen years and had been privileged to see him operate at close quarters in France. 'I'd seen him work at Monaco, seen how he dealt with players, with the press, the public in general. His demeanour, his intelligence. He's a hybrid. He's highly intelligent, he speaks five or six languages. Cool, calm and collected. A great tactician. Knows a lot about medicine. It's very rare that you find that – he knows what an injury is all about. He knows when to bring players on and when to bring them off in a game. This is all part of a manager's ability. He has got an encyclopaedic knowledge of players. I don't think there's anybody I've ever met who could challenge him for his knowledge on players around the world. The ambition of the club is that one day when he gets to the point when he can't take it every day in a tracksuit, he'd be the ideal person to be technical director.'

Wenger said that the players each have ambitions and it is up to a coach to provide a framework in which they can express themselves. 'We can win everything, in my opinion, because we have a big squad and huge potential. I think we have shown that by beating Manchester United and Juventus in recent weeks. If we can beat teams like that quite comfortably, it tells you a lot about the potential of the players. You ask anybody at Juventus what they want to achieve and they will say they want to win the League and the European Cup. Ask anybody at Man United and they will say exactly the same. So, when we do what we have done to them, why should we not say that, too?

'My ambition is for Arsenal to become the best in Europe, starting this season. That means we've got to remove Man United and many other teams who have the same ambition. But I believe we can do it because we have young players, we have potential and we have stability. We have also gathered experience in the Champions' League over the past three years. That will help us a lot.'

He had no qualms about four more years in a very stressful job, saying, 'It's a choice between a passionate life and a really quiet life and for me that's no choice. I came into this job so I could stay in football and I thought it would lead me to extreme emotions and tell me a lot about myself. I was not wrong. Maybe I will die two or three years earlier. Maybe ten. But I could also have died with a boring life. It's the life I wanted.'

Philippe Auclair had introduced me to *France Football* editor Gerard Ernault and Arnaud Ramsay, another French reporter, and we chatted for a while and then went downstairs and asked the receptionist to call a taxi to St Albans station. Philippe explained that Gerard had come over to present the French Player of the Year trophy to Patrick Vieira today, before this press conference had been arranged.

As we were standing in the foyer, Vieira came down the stairs wearing a long navy blue mac, tight black trousers and snazzy silverblue trainers. He was carrying a large bag in one hand and a red mobile phone in the other and he asked Philippe if he needed a lift.

'There's four of us,' said Philippe.

'Oh, that's alright, come with me,' said Patrick.

So we asked the receptionist to cancel the cab and walked out to the car park where I stood by the passenger door of the black

Chrysler Jeep while the others piled in the back. Then Patrick appeared by my elbow and said, 'It's a left-hand drive.' I could not see the steering wheel through the dark windows.

We rolled out of Shenley and out of Hertfordshire and down past Totteridge and through Mill Hill and into Hendon and most of the chat was in French. Patrick, an easy-going, agreeable character, was just as relaxed as any other superstar on his way home from work.When Gerard asked where the players live Patrick said that Gilles was in Hampstead, Robert was near Baker Street, and, '*Thierry habite a cinq minutes de chez moi.*'

His radio was tuned to Choice FM, so I asked him if he ever listened to Jazz FM. He said he likes to listen to the station at night on long drives, but Choice during the day.

'Do you go to any concerts?'

'Sometimes, yes. The last one I went to was R. Kelly. It was good.'

'He produced Aaliyah's first album, didn't he?'

'Yes, he was married to her,' said Patrick.

I mentioned Tuesday night's success, saying that it must be a proud feeling to be captain of Arsenal when you beat Juventus 3–1.

'I didn't think we'd do that. It's a good feeling – but we lost to Charlton.'

'Arsène said that was complacency,' I said.

'Did he?' said Patrick, a little surprised.

We cruised down Finchley Road and turned left up Frognal and he dropped us at the bottom of Holly Hill, opposite Hampstead tube station and we said thanks and cheerio. Philippe has a close relationship with Arsène, so he was delighted by today's news and wanted to celebrate with a pint.

As we strolled down Hampstead High Street towards a pub he knows, George Graham came out of a shop two yards in front of us. He was wearing a black leather jacket and looked fit, fashionable, sporty, a bit macho, a working playboy. The poor boy from Glasgow became a footballer, then a Londoner, then a manager, then a millionaire and now he lives here with Sting, Boy George, Danny Fiszman and all the other Hampstead millionaires. George is a Sky Sports pundit now and has remained friendly with

Fiszman, so he knows what is going on at Arsenal. I had sparred with him at press conferences for eight years, developed a rapport, and enjoyed our one-on-one interviews.

He grinned, shook my hand, and said, 'Hi, how are you doing?'

George said he was impressed by how well Arsenal were playing these days and I introduced him to the French guys and told him that Patrick has just dropped us off.

'Will Vieira be here next season?' said George.

'I didn't ask him that,' I replied.

'Why not? It's your job!' he said, laughing.

Old habits die hard and George still likes to keep everybody on their toes. It was good to see him looking so well and it brought back many happy memories.

ARSENAL 1 NEWCASTLE 3

Some people round here don't know how to lose.

Bobby Robson

Arsenal needed to beat Aston Villa at Highbury to stay second but they went behind when Dion Dublin flicked on and Upson reacted late to a run by Merson, who lobbed the advancing Taylor. Steve Stone's low shot made it 2–0, so Wenger gambled with two changes at half-time: Keown for Upson, Wiltord for Ljungberg. Immediately, Wiltord made it 2–1. Then Vieira robbed Samuel in the right back position, saw Henry just onside, and hit a superlative cross, left-footed, to his pal, who killed the ball perfectly, dummied Enckelman on to his knee, and slotted the ball past him for 2–2.

After that the pressure built until a pass from Pires released Henry, who slipped the ball neatly past Enckelman for a 92nd minute winner. Arsenal had so far won twelve games and Henry had scored in all of those victories. At the end of the season he said that this goal, while not his most beautiful, was his favourite.

On the following Monday night, Islington Council gave the go-ahead for the new stadium. Wenger took kids and squad players to Blackburn for the Worthington Cup quarter-final and they were thrashed 4–0. When asked about Inamoto he said, 'Well, I took him off at half-time and he wasn't injured.'

At home to Newcastle, they scored first when Henry hooked the ball across for Cole to turn back for Pires. Then Kanu missed two sitters, which would prove expensive. Referee Graham Poll gave Parlour an early yellow card after his arm caught Dabizas, and then sent him off for a slightly late tackle on Shearer, who asked the ref to be lenient. At half-time Henry walked off alongside Poll, shaking his head.

After an hour, Arsenal were guilty of dopey defending when substitute Lua Lua took a quick corner to the near post. Stuart Taylor was still organising at the far side and Henry was strolling back, the nearest player to Andy O'Brien, who headed in from two yards. It was a very soft goal. Then Cole feigned injury to get Bellamy sent off. When Bellamy's arm caught Cole on the neck he went down as if he had been punched and Poll gave Bellamy a straight red card.

Five minutes from time, Lauren Robert was through on Taylor and Campbell made, from behind, a magnificent recovery tackle, toe-ending the ball out for a corner. It might have been the best tackle of the season, but Poll awarded a penalty. A good referee looks at where the ball goes. Such incidents are like an l.b.w. in cricket – you can't give a decision if you're not a hundred per cent sure. Shearer scored from the spot and Robert made it 3–1 at the death to give the Newcastle their first win in London for 30 matches.

Graham Poll had certainly ruined the contest but when the final whistle went, the game was over. Henry, furious, approached Poll accusingly, shouting, 'Why did you kill the game?' Keown tried to restrain Henry but he was pushed away, as was Gary Lewin. Such a tantrum was silly, self-defeating and, ultimately, pathetic. As Bobby Robson said, 'Some people round here don't know how to lose.' Quite. Bellamy's red card was later rescinded on appeal.

At that moment in December it looked as if Arsenal's appalling disciplinary record, 39 red cards since Wenger arrived, would derail their title challenge. Henry looked set for a long suspension. Vieira, booked seven times in all competitions and sent off against Chelsea, was suspended for Sunday's game at Liverpool, and

Lauren would miss the Middlesbrough game after accumulating five yellow cards. Parlour would sit out the New Year's Day game at Leicester and the FA Cup third round tie at Watford.

The press slaughtered Wenger, saying that he never saw fouls by his own players, never condemned them publicly, did not punish them privately or even, it seemed, speak to them about discipline. But it was all ancient news, really. Wenger was prepared to live with the red cards and the bad publicity. His attitude was: we play the game very fast, we go for ball, and sometimes we miss the ball, so we get cards which are deserved, and other cards that are undeserved – that's my kind of football and I will never apologise for it because we are not a dirty team.

Many acres of newsprint had been devoted to this controversy, but Wenger had once summed it up in nine words when he said, 'I'm never going to tell them not to tackle.'

The next game was at Anfield, where van Bronckhorst was muscled over in the box by Henchoz. He got up without claiming a penalty but referee Paul Durkin gave him a second yellow card for diving. That injustice really ignited the team and, with Parlour playing out of his skin, they roared into a 2–0 lead.

The first goal was a Henry penalty after Ljungberg ran on to Kanu's pass and Dudek could not avoid colliding with him. Early in the second half Gerrard made a sloppy pass to Pires, who left him for dead and teed up a low cross for ever-ready Freddie to stab home from four yards. Litmanen netted a late header. It was Arsenal's first Premiership victory at Anfield for nine years.

At Chelsea, they fell behind when a Melchiot throw, chested by Hasselbaink, rebounded off Vieira for Lampard to fire low into the bottom corner. Campbell headed in a corner for 1–1 and eventually van Bronckhorst took a free-kick, Melchiot headed out, and Wiltord smashed in the winner.

The Middlesbrough match at Highbury was tense and messy, with both keepers unemployed except for Mark Crossley once saving a Pires shot, knocking it onto the post. Then Campbell miskicked a back-pass and Noel Whelan scored and Arsenal were 1–0 down at half-time. Pires hauled them back into it with a looping thirty-yarder, helped by Henry's obstruction on Paul Ince, which the referee missed. Bergkamp, on as a sub, won the game with a curling cross over the defence for Cole to head in.

In the FA Cup Third Round, they outclassed Watford and then drew Liverpool in the Fourth Round at Highbury. They had three league games before that and the first, oddly enough, was at home to Liverpool. Arsenal were one player short down the left side because Upson, while playing well at left back, lacked the attacking brio of the injured Cole, but at the other end Campbell and Keown were so tight that Michael Owen had no goal attempts. Anelka, on loan from Paris St. Germain, had one shot blocked. Bergkamp replaced Kanu, became the third man on the left, and they scored immediately. Campbell hit a long ball into the corner, Bergkamp held off Carragher cleverly, played a cute ball to Pires, and his pass allowed Ljungberg to stab in from six yards. Then Riise zoomed down the flank and scored from Gerrard's long diagonal pass as keeper Stuart Taylor froze. Taylor had one decision to make in the match and he got it wrong, so the game finished 1–1.The team was looking good, but could they win a trophy without a goalkeeper?

It was now mid-January and the fans were still wondering about Vieira. Arsenal needed him, France needed him, and Real Madrid thought they needed him, but Vieira's mediocre performances seemed to indicate that he did not want to be at Arsenal. His mind was not on the job. He tackled less often, gave the ball away more, and got sillier bookings than ever before. Then Wenger gave the players two days off and Vieira was spotted at Barajas airport in Madrid. The world's greatest club had apparently offered him £3.5 million a year for five years. Who could turn down that kind of money?

Some fans were dismayed; others angry. When Vieira was suspended at Anfield, Parlour had inspired the team and they won 2–1 with ten men. But when Parlour was suspended at Highbury, Vieira was not concentrating. There was plenty of time to score again after Riise equalised: 21 minutes. But how could Vieira concentrate on winning that game if he knew he would be on a plane to Madrid in the morning?

Sunday's visit to Leeds fizzled out into a 1–1 draw. Wilcox beat Luzhny to create Fowler's early header past Wright, who was back in goal, and then Pires started and finished the move for the equaliser. But Wilcox fell against Ljungberg, twisting the Swede's ankle and putting him out for the next eight weeks. Those two 1–1 draws put pressure on the game at Leicester, where van Bronckhorst lifted the anxiety by heading his first goal in a 3–1 win.

ARSENAL 0 DEPORTIVO LA CORUÑA 2

What he does is close to genius.

Wenger on Bergkamp's goal at Newcastle

Arsenal v Liverpool was an FA Cup Fourth Round tie that had monsoon rain, gusting wind, a pulsating atmosphere, van Bronckhorst's best game so far, some dogged defending, a miss or two by Owen, and a sulky cameo by Anelka, who was withdrawn at half time.

We saw a collective sense of purpose, and a style of play, which had now evolved to the point where the team could prosper without Lauren and Ljungberg, and despite losing the injured Pires after twenty minutes, and despite the sending off of Keown and Bergkamp.

They only scored one goal, but they only needed one. When Wright kicked long, Henry controlled the ball beautifully on his body, played a one-two with van Bronckhorst, and crossed left-footed for Bergkamp to glance a header beyond Dudek from seven yards. It was champagne football: sharp early passes, lightning sprints, a sudden thrust into the box, an unstoppable goal.

In the second half there were three red cards. Keown impeded Owen on a breakaway and referee Mike Riley sent him off. Bergkamp, furious after a handball had not been given against Hyypia, made a malicious-looking tackle which just missed Carragher's ankle, so he walked as well. Then Carragher stupidly threw a coin back into the crowd.

A 3–2 win at Blackburn was a thriller in which Robert Pires started the move for the first goal, when Wiltord's cross reached Bergkamp at the far post, gave Henry a 60-yard pass for the second, and slipped Bergkamp in for the winner after Blackburn had levelled at 2–2. Playing like this, Pires made anything seem possible. Luzhny had been sent off for tripping Tugay.

At home to Southampton, Vieira went off injured, and then Cole got a knee injury which put him out for the next eleven games. Wiltord scored just before half-time but Richard Wright was a bag of nerves, blasting pass-backs here, there and everywhere. Southampton took over and Joe Tessem headed an equaliser. But Edu had looked the part, at last.

On 6 February, Manchester United PLC informed the Stock Exchange that they were in talks with Sir Alex about him staying on as manager. They had failed to tempt Eriksson, Hitzfeld and Capello.

Arsenal went to Everton on 10 February, a week before manager Walter Smith was sacked. Stepanovs was booked early on, as was Campbell, but after that Campbell held the defence together. He has a knack of playing athletically, and robustly, but not riskily, so he never gets a second yellow card. Everton were the better side in the first half but after an hour Vieira played a lovely chipped pass, Wiltord shinned it, the ball looped across the goal – and went in.

When the team was motoring, and enjoying this unbeaten run, new players coming in were jumping onto a moving vehicle and were carried along by the momentum. As February continued, Vieira was superb in a 4–1 win against Fulham and he blotted out Michael Ballack in a phenomenal 4–1 demolition of Bayer Leverskusen. At Newcastle he played with all his old flair, power and authority in a 2–0 victory. Why had he improved so much in those three games? Had he decided to stay?

Pires later described how Vieira kept the French boys together, on and off the field. 'Patrick is so important to the team. He gives us rhythm, his positional play is excellent and he always makes a good pass. He's intelligent and he's the soul of the team. When he's not playing well, the team are not playing well. Patrick, Thierry, Sylvain and me are close. I've known Patrick for eight years now. For us, he's also very important outside football. He knows London very well, and where to go out. But as far as his future is concerned it's his decision, not ours. Of course, it would be great if he stays.

But you know he's been here six years already, and so, whatever he decides, we will respect it.'

2 March saw a league game at Newcastle and Henry's delayed misconduct charge was to be heard by the FA on the following Wednesday. 'I cannot believe that Henry has not been in front of the FA yet,' said Bobby Robson. 'After all, it's coming up to three months since we played that game. Perhaps this shows what power Arsenal have in the game today.' The visitors made the break-through with an outrageous goal after eleven minutes. Vieira won the ball from Lauren Robert and played it up to Bergkamp, who passed wide and square to Pires and then cruised upfield, collected a crossfield pass from Pires, and flicked the ball, left-footed, past Dabizas, ducked in behind him, and side-footed past Shay Given into the corner from ten yards.

'Unbelievable,' said Wenger. 'You don't see that kind of thing too many times, but you're blessed when you come to a stadium and witness something like that. It wasn't only a magnificent goal, but an extremely important one. That's why I enjoyed it so much. What he does is close to genius. I'm always wary of using those kind of words, but I think in his case they're justified. He's a player who gets close to perfection.'

ITV pundit Ally McCoist made a complete fool of himself by doubting that dazzling Dennis had wholly intended this demon-stration of footballing magic, which was later voted Goal of the Season. McCoist was obliged to apologise in a later programme. Bergkamp, incidentally, had made the second goal that day, flighting a free-kick for Sol Campbell to score with a header.

After that 2–0 win, Wenger said he believed his team were good enough to claim a treble of Champions' League, Premiership and FA Cup, just as Manchester United had done in 1999. 'I just want to take the club as far as I can and like at every big club it is a construction,' he said. 'There is a scaffolding you build up and up and up. The club now has recognition in Europe but we want more. We want to become the biggest club in the world. I believe the club is in progression, it is on the move. If you look at the potential of Arsenal with the new stadium, you cannot say you want to be the second best in the world.

'I understand other clubs have the same target but I don't know why we should be behind anyone in our ambitions. The secret to becoming the biggest club in the world is having good players and making good decisions. Nothing more. And that is our goal. As long as our attitude and commitment is right, I expect us to win every game. But it is important to be vigilant because all our hopes can disappear very quickly if we get careless.'

With ten league games left, Arsenal were three points better off than at the same stage in 1998. In the next game, against Derby on 5 March, Bergkamp put Pires through for the winner, his eleventh goal of the season. Television captured their exquisite skill: Wiltord's diagonal pass went over a defender's head and Bergkamp, the king of two-touch, took one touch on the turn, then flicked into the stride of Pires, who guided the ball precisely four feet in front of himself and swept his shot past Andy Oakes, a young keeper who was having a good game.

It was their seventeenth match without defeat since losing to Newcastle at Highbury in December and Wenger said, 'The championship is now in our hands and as long as we win our games we don't have to worry about anyone else.' When the FA banned Henry for three games Wenger decided not to appeal as it would play on Henry's mind.

Meanwhile, Bergkamp had tipped Pires for the PFA Player of the Year Award, saying, 'He has been absolutely awesome all season and I've nothing but respect for the man. He has so much intelligence and skill it's terrifying. One of his main strengths is his ability to keep possession of the ball. I think he's possibly the best player I've ever seen at Arsenal in terms of holding on to the ball come what may. I'm a big fan of Robert and enjoy playing with him.'

For the FA Cup Sixth Round tie at Newcastle, the teamsheet contained four shocks. Pires, Bergkamp and Seaman were on the bench, while Ljungberg, who had missed twelve games, started after not playing for the reserves. They scored an early goal when Wiltord crossed low to the near post for Edu but then Lauren Robert accelerated on to Shearer's flick-on and fired past Wright, so it went to a replay.

In the Champions' League, Deportivo La Coruna and Arsenal both had seven points from four games and Wenger was again raising the stakes with upbeat comments. He said, 'If we beat La Coruna, we will qualify for the last eight – and I am convinced we will. The players are more confident now than at any other time since I took charge at Highbury six years ago.' To say this after being outplayed at the Riazor in November seemed reckless, but football is a game of sequences and Arsenal were really enjoying their 18-match unbeaten run.

The night promised a fascinating clash of styles, since Arsenal are spectacular sprinters who win games by overwhelming opponents, and Deportivo are canny passers who win by outsmarting them. Unfortunately, Arsenal had been playing an FA Cup tie while Depor were resting eight players at the weekend, and they looked tired. The match began promisingly but the crowd became quiet and apprehensive after twenty minutes as they saw their team run out of ideas. When Wiltord turned carelessly, Mauro Silva read the turn and backheeled smartly to Fran, who fed Romero's overlap run to the touchline. Romero cut the ball back to Valeron, Campbell went to ground for the block, and Valeron stroked home his shot with a matador's panache, an elegant, deadly thrust.

When Fran crossed, Tristan headed back, Valeron shot again from eight yards, and Seaman made a superb save. By then, after only 35 minutes, the game looked over. Then Vieira lost the ball to Victor upfield and did not chase back immediately as a captain should. Depor played six passes round and through the Arsenal defence as Grimandi missed a tackle, Vieira, back now, missed a tackle, Campbell missed a tackle, Luzhny missed a tackle, Lauren missed a tackle and then Naybet's shot was deflected in off Stepanovs. Deportivo destroyed Arsenal in that move, toying with them as no team has toyed with them.

After half-time, Arsenal cranked up the tempo for a while but it was a storm in a teacup. Hope flickered when Ljungberg came on and immediately raced behind the defence to touch Bergkamp's pass beyond Molina, who brought him down. But Henry's penalty was feeble and Molina saved it.

Deportivo won fair and square with sophisticated teamwork, sometimes reading Arsenal's passes before they had even decided to make the pass. They may not have the best players in Europe, but they might have the best shape, the sweetest rhythm, and the most fully-realised style of play. With two left-footed players, Fran and Romero, they had a good balance, and Mauro Silva was immense in a team that was well-equipped to defend a 2–0 lead. At the end, the Arsenal fans gave them a standing ovation.

This defeat, Wenger's first in seventeen European matches at Highbury, left qualification out of Arsenal's hands and facing a game in Turin against Juventus, who were bottom of the group and could not qualify. So Arsenal could win and still go out, but they could also lose and go through if Deportivo beat Leverkusen in La Coruna to win the group. Matchday 12 threatened to be a weird evening.

On Sunday afternoon, Edu scored at Aston Villa, Seaman made a sensational penalty save from Gareth Barry, Pires cleverly lobbed Schmeichel for a second goal, but a Dublin header made it 2–1 and gave Arsenal a tense last twenty minutes. Lee Dixon came on as a sub on his 38th birthday.

Juventus were one point behind joint-leaders Inter and Roma, so their minds were on the title race and they fielded a reserve side. When Wenger heard the Deportivo team, containing only Mauro Silva, Cesar and Naybet from the eleven who started at Highbury, he feared the worst. Ten minutes into the game, his assistant had a phone call from their man in La Coruna, saying that Depor were not up for it. Arsenal lost their game when Zalayeta scored with a header from a corner. The bottom line, on Matchday 12, was that Juve's reserves were motivated but Deportivo's reserves were not, losing 3–1 to allow Leverkusen to win the group. So Arsenal's European campaign was over for another year.

LJUNGBERG SCORES SEVEN IN SEVEN

This could be the first of many for me.

Sol Campbell

Wenger had said boldly on Sky Sports that he was one hundred per cent certain that Arsenal would win the title. Had any manager ever said that since the league started in 1888? That he was one hundred per cent certain his team would be champions? It had always been one of the rules of football, as fundamental as having eleven players on each side and four corner flags, that a manager always said, 'We'll take each game as it comes.'

One of Dennis Bergkamp's lifetime dreams was to play in an FA Cup Final, so he was on fire in the replay against Newcastle on 23 March. Magisterial, razor-sharp, always thinking one move ahead, always purposeful, never flashy, never guilty of showboating, Bergkamp made a goal for Pires in 62 seconds, chipped against the bar in five minutes, scored from a Pires pass in ten minutes, chipped against the post in 22 minutes, and created the third goal in 49 minutes.

At 2–0, Newcastle fought back with admirable spirit, but just after half-time Luzhny made a run, got fouled, and Bergkamp sent the free-kick dipping down into the area for Sol Campbell to head in from seven yards. Newcastle kept playing, rarely fouled, had some decent shots and headers, and Kieron Dyer did well on his long-awaited comeback. But they were outclasssed, as Bobby Robson admitted. 'Arsenal were far better than us,' he said. 'They had a genius in Bergkamp. We didn't have a genius.'

Unfortunately, Pires, jumping to avoid a lunge by Dabizas, had landed awkwardly and damaged the medial ligament of his right knee. He had been the best player in the Premiership, but he would now miss the World Cup. Pires had scored thirteen goals and had assists in fifteen other goals. Only David Beckham, twice, and Nol Solano had ever accumulated fifteen Premiership assists in a season, and they played more games.

Arsenal celebrated Easter with two 3–0 victories and the ferocity of those performances seemed to contain an element of, 'Let's win it for Robert.' On the Saturday, they had some luck against Sunderland, but on Monday they played devastating football at Charlton. Henry raced on to Campbell's clearance to fire past Dean Kiely, sprinted to the corner flag, and kicked it out of the ground, a violent celebration we had never seen before. Then Henry turned Richard Rufus inside out to release Bergkamp, who glided round Kiely and crossed to give Ljungberg his first goal since his return.

Another sparkling move allowed Henry to make it 3–0 after 25 minutes. Manchester United went to Spain and outplayed Deportivo for a 2–0 victory which kept Ferguson on course for a European Cup Final in his home town of Glasgow on 15 May.

Talking about Bergkamp's form, and his finest goals, Wenger said, 'With Dennis in the team you expect him to create chance after chance for everybody. And with Robert Pires unavailable we rely more and more on that. Dennis is really confident at the moment and as creative as ever, but what is different this season is that he looks more physically fresh. Maybe that's because he has played less games this season, so he now looks very sharp. Personally, I like the goals he scores with his head – like the ones against Real Mallorca and Dynamo Kiev. When you see how good he is technically at heading the ball it's a shame that he does not score more like that. Also, I don't get to see my team score many headed goals, so when they happen I always enjoy them!'

The home game against Tottenham was level at 1–1 after 86 minutes. Ljungberg had scored from Bergkamp's pass and Sheringham equalised from a dubious penalty when Poyet ran into Seaman. Then Dean Richards wrestled Henry to the ground. Referee Mark Halsey gave another penalty. The immaculate Lauren waited for Kasey Keller to move and then rolled the ball gently down the middle.

The FA Cup semi-final was at Old Trafford, where Middlesbrough's substitute centreback, Gianluca Festa, scored an own-goal to send Arsenal to Cardiff again, while Chelsea beat Fulham at Villa Park with a goal by John Terry.

Against Ipswich, after an hour of tension, frustration and doubt, Ljungberg grabbed both goals from crosses, not passes. Bergkamp was energetic and productive, but Henry seemed to have lost his bottle. Would he score again this season? On that showing it looked unlikely. Was he carrying an injury we did not know about?

Arsenal were jittery against West Ham at Highbury and Kanoute was unlucky not to score when Ashley Cole kicked his shot away after it had crossed the line. Eventually, a majestic pass from Bergkamp released Ljungberg and he beat David James comfortably. Then Ljungberg crossed from the left for Kanu to make it 2–0.

By now, Ferguson could see that an unprecedented fourth consecutive Premiership trophy was likely to elude him, but he claimed that Arsenal might pay for an apparent 'over-confidence'. On 29 April, Arsenal went to Bolton, who were now safe from relegation. It was a massive match, bigger than the FA Cup Final, since they could blow the title if they lost, but Bergkamp laid on two passes in seven minutes to give Ljungberg and Wiltord the goals. They now had a lead of five points over Manchester United with two games remaining.

On a sunny Saturday, 4 May, Arsenal returned to the magnificent Millennium Stadium as favourites to win the FA Cup Final. Wenger dropped Edu, started Parlour, and preferred Seaman to Wright, who had played in the previous rounds. It was a harsh decision but the correct one.

Claudio Ranieri had figured out that Wiltord and Henry can rarely time their runs off the ball, so Chelsea defended with a very high line. Where Liverpool had defended the box the year before, and allowed Arsenal the space to create sweet passing moves, the blues defended the halfway line as much as possible, squeezing Bergkamp out of the spaces he uses to create his killer passes. Lampard did remarkably well against Vieira, whose passing was shabby.

In that tight first half, Bergkamp released Ljungberg twice with passes down the middle but the flag went up because Henry had strayed offside on both occasions. Wiltord crossed for Lauren, whose header deflected over the bar off Le Saux's head. Vieira then picked out Bergkamp's run with a diagonal pass from the halfway line but his header floated just wide. Hasselbaink was carrying a calf injury and when he and Gudjohnsen managed a one-two just before half time, Gudjohnsen was wrongly flagged offside. Then Gudjohnsen hit a dipping shot which forced Seaman to make the best save of the game.

Chelsea dominated after half-time and the first goal came from a counter-attack: Cole to Vieira to Parlour to Adams to Wiltord, who evaded Desailly and jabbed the ball to Parlour, who fired a 22-yard shot into the far corner of the net. It was a glorious moment for Romford Ray after a mixed campaign with three red cards and only one previous goal – against Gillingham. Then Edu found Ljungberg just inside Arsenal's half. Three red shirts faced six blues but the little man suddenly spurted forward with immense drive and optimism, beyond the blue defence, like a scrum-half going for the line. Amazingly, he held off substitute John Terry, stumbled, recovered and curled his shot round Cudicini for 2–0.

Fiery Freddie had conjured up a real do-it-yourself goal, his seventh in his last seven games. Charity workers in Cardiff had been soliciting donations in return for dye-jobs, so thousands of fans had red hair in tribute to the man of the moment and now, to the tune of the Andy Williams hit 'Can't Take My Eyes Off You', they were singing, 'We love you Freddie, because you've got red hair, we love you Freddie, because you're everywhere.'

At the final whistle, Tony Adams hugged Sol Campbell, who later said, 'I must admit it was really nice with Tony at the end. He's got a few winner's medals under his belt and hopefully I can join him this could be the first of many for me. It's a start. I'm going to enjoy this. I've won the Worthington Cup with Spurs, but this is great. It's been a fantastic season, the way everyone in the squad has chipped in. It's nice that everyone has played a part in some unbelievable performances.'

UEFA chief Lennart Johansson, a lifelong Arsenal fan, handed out the medals one by one, with Tony Adams last in line. Adams and Vieira held up the trophy together. Would either of them be playing for Arsenal next season? The retirement of Adams looked likely and Vieira's flaccid performance suggested he might be at Real Madrid. Maybe he was just tired. A year ago against Liverpool he had been the best player on the pitch and lost. Now, against Chelsea, Vieira had been average and won. A funny old game, football. Arsenal were now one point away from the first League and FA Cup double ever to be won Cup-first.

CHAMPIONS AT OLD TRAFFORD

He's given people patience. And a lot of love.

Tony Adams

In the Champions' League semi-final, Manchester United had lost to Bayer Leverkusen on away goals, so Ferguson's fairytale was over. When the press said Veron was a luxury player who had disrupted their shape, Ferguson erupted at Carrington, the training ground, swearing at reporters. Defending Veron, his parting words were, 'He's a f****** great player.' He added 'Youse are all f****** idiots.' Skipper Roy Keane also spoke out, questioning the commitment of some United players.

When reporters next saw Wenger, he mischievously asked, 'What are all these asterisks in the newspaper?' He said that he never thought that Arsenal might not win the title. 'It does not cross my mind. I don't know if Alex Ferguson is rattled or if he will congratulate us if we do it, but the table doesn't lie. It's always right. We have coped with the pressure and we will show it again in what is a big pressure game. You do not take your foot off the pedal when you are so close.'

He highlighted the turning point: the 2–1 win at Liverpool with ten men. He said that victory was the day the players really believed they could win the Premiership. 'This season is the season of the squad, a mental strength that has kept us together. What relaxes me is knowing the effort the team is putting in. I have never had to ask myself this question this season. I can go home knowing this team will give their last drop of blood for me.'

After the Cardiff consummation, Wenger said the players felt relief after such a long wait for another trophy. They had dinner together, but it was a low-key affair because everyone knew that the job was not yet done. He said, 'We expect United to be at their best, don't worry about that. They won't want to lose the title on their own ground, but we don't want to lose it, either. Winning the title at Old Trafford will have no special significance.'

Gooners who read that comment must have giggled. Winning the title at Old Trafford will have no special significance? Who did Arsène think he was kidding? It would be wonderful to win the title in Sir Alex F*******'s own back yard, but it would also be fantastic to win it with a win, rather than a draw. The league is about points, of course, but psychological ascendancy over your main rivals is very important.

Wenger made three changes: Keown for Adams, who had a knee injury, Edu for Henry, and Kanu for Bergkamp. Henry had 'a small knee injury'. Outside the stadium the United fans were not really buzzing, since they did not give Everton a prayer at Highbury on the final day. Wenger looked relaxed on the bench, because it was a win-win-win situation. He already had silverware in the bank and if he did not win tonight a draw would be enough for the title, and even if he lost Arsenal would still be champions on Saturday.

It was extraordinary how the match reflected the temperaments of the rival managers: United were spiky and energetic, while Arsenal were also combative, but in a more cerebral manner, more detached and in control of their game. The Red Devils started aggressively to show Keane they still had fire in their bellies, and they had a few near-misses before the real mayhem began. Referee Paul Durkin issued three yellow cards in six minutes after Scholes clattered into Edu, Phil Neville scythed down Wiltord, and Keane came in late as Vieira controlled a high-bouncing ball. Keane's boot just missed Vieira's thigh, but his arm smacked Vieira's face. That was the end of Keane and the end of the contest, really.

Edu was busy, competitive and positionally solid, the revelation of the night. When Silvestre moved up the left he lost possession to Parlour, who passed short to Wiltord, who found the diagonal run of Ljungberg, who beat Blanc and hit a low shot. Barthez saved and the ball rebounded to Wiltord on his weaker left foot . . . and he scored the goal that won the Double.

When the final whistle came, the beaming Wenger was hugged by physio Gary Lewin, Edu lifted Ljungberg off his feet, Wiltord and Lauren danced a jig of delight, and Wenger walked over to embrace Vieira. He had seen his men produce a truly heroic team performance, a classic of containment and counter-attack, with the defensive and offensive elements executed confidently. It was exactly the kind of away performance they needed in the Champions' League.

Winning the title again was even more satisfying than it had been in 1998, said Wenger, who regarded this Double as his greatest achievement in England. 'I feel very happy because this team got what they deserved and we did it in style. I personally believe that what this team has achieved is tremendous and will remain in history. We have 84 points, we have played 19 games away in the League without losing one and we have scored in every game. The character of this team is extraordinary. This is not only a team of good players. It is a team of togetherness. We wanted there to be a shift of power. Winning it in my first full season almost felt natural, but I have lost a few times since then and realised how hard it is.'

The papers gave high praise to the new champions the next day, when the best headline was on a Tim Rich piece in *The Independent*: WENGER'S INVINCIBLES CLAIM GRAND PRIZE IN BARE-KNUCKLE TITLE FIGHT.

There was a festival atmosphere at Highbury as Lee Dixon led out the side against Everton in his last game before retirement. After imbecilic defending by Alan Stubbs and Stepanovs, among others, they won 4–3. Henry, playing with his right knee strapped, scored twice and crossed for sub Francis Jeffers to head Arsenal into a 4–2 lead. Bergkamp had netted the first and generously set up the second for Henry, whose 24 league goals won him the Golden Boot.

Then came the presentations. The 22 players who had played ten games or more collected their medals as did Pat Rice, Gary Lewin and first team coach Bora Primorac. Then, at last, came Robert Pires and, as he held up the trophy, the other players bowed down to him in a we-are-not-worthy salute. The pantomime was amusing but also a sincere statement of thanks, for without the consistent creativity of Pires they would not have been collecting these medals as champions. He had been voted Footballer of the Year by the English journalists.

Liverpool had finished second, with Dudek and Riise proving to be phenomenal signings. Manchester United, now demoralised, were third after a 0–0 draw with Charlton, their first scoreless game in the Premiership for three years. Arsenal had 87 points, Liverpool 84 and United 77.

Tony Adams gave an interview to Sky, saying that the manager had won the League this time, not the players. He explained how much he enjoyed the day-to-day life at the training ground and praised Wenger's cool leadership and his shrewd deployment of the squad.

'It takes a man at the helm. Maybe '98 was the players winning it, but I do believe it's the manager that's won this one. Throughout the season he's been extremely confident, unflappable. I dunno how best to describe him. But he's been self-assured, he's been dignified, he's been calm, he's been trusting, he's been faithful. He's given people patience. And a lot of love. I think the man deserves all the credit he can get.'

Wenger managed his players with tolerance, accepting their mistakes without being punitive or judgemental. He was also patient because he knew that you succeed after you fail, not before, so he kept faith with the new players and gave them time to settle in. He said, 'I am convinced that the biggest problem in modern football is impatience with new players. There are many big examples of this impatience, like when Patrick was at Milan and Thierry at Juventus. All coaches are under a lot of pressure that if a player does not perform in the first six months everybody starts to question our buying policy. Arsenal fans were always very patient with our players and it has worked out. Take Pires this year and Pires last year.'

While 2000–01 had been the season when rotation did not quite work, 2001–02 was the season where enforced rotation, due to a succession of injuries, worked remarkably well. Bergkamp had needed a year to adjust to not starting every match. Arguably, Wenger's first choice team was Seaman, Lauren, Campbell, Adams, Cole, Ljungberg, Parlour, Vieira, Pires, Bergkamp and Henry, but that eleven never played once in the sixty games. He had ten in the first two games, missing Bergkamp, and ten in the FA Cup Final, when he was missing Pires. So it was, truly, the season of the squad, and it looked as if, from now on, all seasons would be like this. The concept of the 'first team' had become obsolete.

Back in May 2001, Wenger had talked about needing 'a depth of stability in defence', but five players had turned out at left back, including Juan, the young Brazilian who played against Gillingham, and there had been a bewildering succession of centre-back partnerships. Three goalkeepers collected medals, which was unprecedented.

Despite all that disruption, the improvement in their defensive record during February, March, April and May was staggering: they had not been behind in a Premiership game since Fowler scored at Elland Road on 20 January. Team spirit had played a big part, confidence had grown while the vehicle was motoring, but the consistency, the twelve clean sheets, still seemed somewhat hard to explain. Perhaps the return of Adams and Dixon, who were training with the team again, had made everything more solid. Lauren admitted that Dixon had given him tips about positioning, and he was now covering runs instead of ball-watching. The clean sheets really started when Seaman came back to the side in February, and Campbell's recovery pace meant that mistakes could usually be rectified.

The professor, a master of man-management and mind-management, had guided his team to a 29-game unbeaten run in domestic football. It was revealed that Wenger held a team meeting on 23 December where he asked the players to stop getting red cards. Bergkamp was sent off after that, against Liverpool, and Luzhny went at Blackburn, but maybe there was no mystery about their improved disciplinary record. Success generally improves a team's behaviour. Players get red cards when they are struggling and frustrated and losing, not when they are cruising and winning. Patrick Vieira had played more than anyone else, but produced only half a dozen great games in all competitions. He was pacing himself, like most of the French World Cup winners, planning to peak in Japan in June. Often he was sloppy in the first half, much better in the second, perhaps after Wenger had a word.

Freddie Ljungberg had been playing exceptionally well when he was injured in January. He came back in March and was red hot in April and May. He scored the vital first goal so often. Of his seventeen goals, eleven were first goals. Two of the other six goals were in matches where he had scored the first goal. He was the first player to score in consecutive FA Cup Finals for forty years.

Remarkably, Wenger had sorted out their away form in the Premiership. Their record had improved from five wins, seven draws and seven defeats to fourteen wins and five draws, so his next task was obvious: to improve Arsenal's away form in Europe.

How would he do that? By signing players who would slightly change Arsenal's style, allowing more flexibility and greater possession? Did he now accept that the high-tempo attacking which worked so well at Highbury, and which destroyed Juventus and Bayer Leverkusen, does not work away from home in the Champions' League?

They needed to keep the ball for longer, consolidate at the back, and score some goals from crosses. Their definitive away performance was in Lyon, when they kept possession well and Henry headed home a cross by Ashley Cole and they won 1–0. That match always looked like a template to follow for the future, but they never played well enough to repeat that victory, although they were close in Leverkusen.

On 13 May, Wenger was quoted in L'Equipe saying, 'I can't imagine finishing my life without winning the European Cup.' Two days later he flew to Glasgow to see the European Cup Final in which Real Madrid met Leverkusen. The German underdogs, without Ze Roberto and skipper Nowoty, outplayed Madrid, but they were beaten by a stunning volley from Zidane.

Wenger's contract was due to end in 2005, by which time he would have been managing Arsenal for nine years, but Ashburton Grove looked unlikely to open before 2005–6. In the meantime, he was still enjoying his daily work at Shenley and he loved the competition, the matches. As he said, 'It's the life I wanted.'

When George Graham was sacked in 1995, the directors had resolved that no future manager would ever have that much power again, but Wenger now oversaw a vastly expanded operation with many coaches, physios, masseurs and other full time staff. In 1996 Ashley Cole had been a 14-year-old boy looked after by a part-time schoolteacher who earned £45 a week, but now he was a 21-year-old playing for England in the World Cup.

Film director Orson Welles, a maverick genius, once called RKO Studios 'the biggest electric train set a boy ever had,' but Arsène Wenger would probably say that managing Arsenal was the biggest train set a French boy ever had. A man motivated by an ideal of how the game could be, he was now close to creating his perfect football machine: a stylish, athletic, attacking team which could keep clean sheets.

Since London is the biggest city in Europe, it was logical for Arsenal to try to become the biggest club in the world. A new stadium alone cannot do that, of course, but it could provide the money to make winning the European Cup more likely.

Or maybe Arsenal could reach the final next year. Could Arsène Wenger win the European Cup at Old Trafford in May 2003?

10. 2002/03: THE SEASON OF 15 DRAWS

Ronaldinho's free-kick is one of those unforgettable moments in English football history.

World Cup 2002 Quarter-finals, Shizuoka, Japan: the score is 1–1 and Brazil get a free-kick on the right side, 35 yards from England's goal. Roberto Carlos and Rivaldo let the youngster take it and he scores by floating the ball over David Seaman and into the far corner. The goal is no fluke. It is an outrageous free-kick by a Brazilian genius. His body shape proves it was deliberate, and he looks only at the goal, not at the players hoping for a header 12 yards out from the far post. Ronaldinho did not miskick that ball by 12 yards.

Such a moment had been coming for a long time. When a baseball player gets too old the Americans say he has 'lost a step' and Seaman, 38, had lost a step years before. Between 1989 and 1996 he had been well protected by the best defence in England, and when Vieira, Petit and Parlour were in midfield, he had even less to do. Seaman was the hero of Euro 96 and as the years rolled on he could still make great saves, but he did not command his penalty area after his ribs were broken by Ole Gunnar Solskjaer on 16 November 1996. He did not come out so much or so confidently, so his defenders were gradually pushed back into the goalmouth when defending crosses and free-kicks.

However, his decline had been a taboo subject. To criticise David Seaman MBE was unpatriotic and he had remained as Arsenal's No.1, while Richard Wright, who had never recovered from his trauma in La Coruña, was sold to Everton for £3.5 million. Alex Manninger went to Espanyol for £1 million and Wenger signed a Swedish keeper, Rami Shaaban, 27, from Djurgaarden IF for £600,000, plus the Lille center-back Pascal Cygan for £2.1 million, and Kolo Toure from the Ivory Coast for £500,000. He phoned PSV Eindhoven about Mark van Bommel, but PSV would not budge from their price of £15 million, so he bought Gilberto Silva from Atletico Mineiro for £4.5 million.

Retirements had created a leadership vacuum and left Dennis Bergkamp wondering, 'Who will do the shouting, organising and motivating without Tony Adams and Lee Dixon? That was always a major, major strength of both those players.'

In the Community Shield, Arsenal met Liverpool, and Gilberto scored the only goal, charging onto Bergkamp's pass to blast a left-foot shot through the legs of Jerzy Dudek. The following weekend the Premiership kicked off with 132 foreign players and just 88 Englishmen, and Arsenal's Rolls-Royce teamwork made it a short match against promoted Birmingham, as they raced to a 2–0 lead in 23 minutes. They went to Upton Park seeking their 15th straight league win, but Joe Cole and Frederic Kanoute gave West Ham a two-goal lead after 65 minutes. Then Henry scored a wonder goal, Kanoute missed a penalty, and Wiltord made it 2–2. If the Hammers had held on, their season might have been completely different.

Against West Brom, Arsenal cruised to a 3–0 lead in 24 minutes. It was far too easy and they came out for the second half with a different head on and Scott Dobie scored. After that goal, amazingly, Arsenal got the jitters. If Adams and Dixon had been playing, they would not have been so shaky when leading 3–1 at home. But they went on to win 5–2.

The Chelsea-Arsenal match was the tamest for ten years and Arsenal were dominating until Zola's 40-yard free-kick bounced three yards from goal and went into the net. Patrick Vieira was harshly sent off by referee Andy D'Urso after a tackle which Zola skipped over and another where Gronkjaer hurt himself by kicking Vieira's boot. A Kolo Toure header earned a draw.

After that, Arsenal won the next nine games by playing the most stylish, entertaining football they had played in their entire history. Fluent, powerful and confident, as champions should be, they could now spurt, score, slow it down, spurt again, score another, and stroll to the final whistle. Skipper Vieira was back to his regal best – concentrating well, striding forward and passing beautifully – the hub of a football machine that now had more gears. With Sol

Campbell developing into a better player than he had ever been at Spurs, Gilberto adding extra power, Henry demonstrating sublime skills at breathtaking pace, and Bergkamp pulling out all the stops for what might be his swansong season, Arsenal were playing keep-ball better than they had done at any time in the last six years.

So hopes were high for the Champions League campaign, which would begin at home to Borussia Dortmund on 17 September, followed by away games against PSV Eindhoven and Auxerre. But, after they had beaten Charlton 3–0 and Dortmund 2–0 and Bolton 2–1, Wenger made a comment for which he would be castigated. He said, 'It looks easy from the outside when we dominate some games – but it is a consequence of a big effort and a lot of hard work by the players. If we have the right attitude, we can go through the season unbeaten. I'm not tempting fate by saying what I believe.'

Arsenal kicked off in Eindhoven and lost the ball, but Ljungberg won it back, released Henry on the left, and he crossed for Gilberto to grab the fastest goal in Champions League history in 20.07 seconds. Ljungberg made it 2–0, Henry doubled the tally to 4–0, and Vieira said, 'We know we can beat anybody. We feel really strong.'

Toure made the first goal and scored the second in a spectacular 4–1 win at Leeds, and, in Auxerre, new boy Gilberto grabbed another priceless goal. 'They're capable of scoring within five seconds of getting the ball back,' said coach Guy Roux. 'Their forwards have devilish skill like I haven't seen in a long time.'

In *France Football*, Vieira said he would far rather win the Champions League with Arsenal than with Real Madrid and he noted that Arsenal played with more freedom than France, so Thierry Henry can score at any time. 'He can make the difference at any given moment, and to stretch the point, you could say that we all play for him, in a way.' A revealing line: 'We all play for him, in a way.'

Vieira was exceptional in a 3–1 win over Sunderland, whose player-coach Niall Quinn said, 'They're playing football like they're the kings of Europe, not just the kings of the Premiership.' And it was that victory which overtook Manchester United's previous benchmark of 29 Premiership games unbeaten.

ROONEY SHATTERS THE EUPHORIA

Arsenal are the strongest team in Europe at the moment

Roma coach Fabio Capello

After that came an international break which worried Wenger. England drew 2–2 with Macedonia, and Seaman took more flak when Artim Sakiri scored directly from a corner. France thrashed Slovenia 5–0, flew to Malta and went 3–0 up in an hour, but Jacques Santini left Henry, Vieira and Wiltord on for 90 minutes.

The Arsenal team had not played together for 14 days, so they lacked their normal fluency at Everton, who were a rejuvenated side. Ljungberg got the first goal, Radzinski equalised, and a tight battle developed. But then Everton's chunky substitute Wayne Rooney controlled a high ball from Gravesen and smashed a dipping 25-yard shot in off the underside of the bar. Rooney became the Premiership's youngest-ever goalscorer five days short of his 17th birthday.

In that moment a bubble was burst, a state of euphoria destroyed. Footballers who had forgotten what it was like to lose came back to earth with a painful bump, as the magic carpet was yanked from under them. Arsenal's aura of invincibility was suddenly shattered.

Cleverly, Wenger hailed Rooney as the greatest prospect in English football, declaring, 'He is the biggest talent I've seen since I arrived in England. There has certainly not been an under-20 player as good as him since I became a manager here. We were beaten by a special goal from a very special talent.'

On his 53rd birthday, Wenger welcomed Auxerre to Highbury, who started at a high tempo and went 2–0 up in 27 minutes and then sat deep and blotted out Henry, whose one good run set up a goal for Kanu. After that, Arsenal were denied further chances, being forced to hit long balls. It was like Senegal beating France. At Blackburn, Edu volleyed an own-goal and then equalised from a free-kick, but Tugay slid a ball between Campbell and Lauren for Ostenstad, whose square pass gave Yorke the winner. Arsenal had 27 shots and Brad Friedel made 14 saves, some of them world class. The champions had now lost three games in a row.

In Dortmund, the home team hit the post twice in 14 minutes before Arsenal got out of first gear. Henry scored with a free-kick, but had a poor game, giving up too easily, which annoyed the fans. Seaman had no chance with a Gilberto own-goal, but bottled a 50-50 with Jan Koller, who touched the ball, jumped over him and fell. The replays showed no contact and Wenger said, 'Like on many occasions, the referee made a difference. All credit to him, he scored a good second goal for them. I was happy for him. He deserves a good mention.' Four consecutive defeats was Arsenal's worst run since 1983 and Wenger had responded with sarcasm.

Liverpool stormed seven points clear by beating West Ham at Anfield, but Arsenal scraped home at Fulham, courtesy of a surreal own-goal by Steve Marlet. A relieved Wenger said, 'I would have preferred to win this match with a different goal, but I'll take that one. If you lose four, it has to be a concern because confidence is a fragile thing. We're not used to losing runs.'

In the Worthington Cup Arsenal's Second XI went 2–0 up against Sunderland at Highbury and then conceded three headers to lose 3–2. At home to Newcastle, Wiltord scored, and that 1–0 win cut the gap at the top of the Premiership, with Liverpool losing at Middlesbrough. Rami Shaaban made his debut against PSV Eindhoven in the Champions League, Seaman having strained a groin muscle, but Arsenal had already qualified and it was a 0–0 draw. Toure was sent off, but Cygan played solidly, as did Shaaban. For the second group stage they were drawn against Valencia, Roma and Ajax.

When Spurs came to Highbury on 16 November, Henry, deep in his own half, controlled Vieira's header on his body, exploded away from Etherington, swerved past Steve Carr and Ledley King, and aimed a left-foot shot just inside the post – an electrifying solo goal. The 3–0 win put the champions back on top.

Gilberto had flown to South Korea to play for Brazil, so Edu started at Southampton, where Bergkamp scored the first goal. James Beattie replied from a free-kick awarded for a fair challenge by Cygan on Delgado. When Campbell brought Delgado down, referee Paul Durkin gave him a red card and Beattie's penalty put the Saints ahead. Then Toure headed into his own net off Delgado for 3–1. There were more chances at both ends before Pires, replacing Bergkamp, made it 3–2.

Rome loomed as a huge test for Shaaban. He had kept clean sheets against PSV and Spurs but he now saw Cassano's miscued shot dribble in off the post after only four minutes. Amazingly, Henry equalised within two minutes and after that both sides kept it tight until the last fifteen, when Henry scored two more goals. Roma coach Fabio Capello accepted defeat graciously, saying 'Arsenal are the strongest team in Europe at the moment. They punish you at the first mistake and are always united. They run for each other the whole time. They never stop.' Back home, Henry starred in a 3–1 win against Aston Villa at Highbury, but Cygan and Campbell looked dodgy against Vassell and Dublin.

As December started, Manchester United were motoring after wins against Newcastle, Basle and Liverpool and their next game was Arsenal at Old Trafford. In a Sky interview, Tony Adams urged his team to stop treating the Premiership as their No.2 priority. Adams tipped United, suggesting that Arsenal's defending in domestic games was not as professional as it was in Europe. It was a good call: United were fiery and won 2–0. Arsenal were still top but their sequence of scoring in 55 Premiership games had ended.

Adams criticised the midfield balance, saying, 'I can now say publicly what I used to say to Arsène Wenger privately on occasion, that the most crucial area of any game is getting the numbers and balance right in midfield. Freddie Ljungberg and Robert Pires are wonderful players going forward, but I don't think you can play them both away from home. I believe Arsenal are missing Ray Parlour.'

The second group stage of the Champions League continued at Highbury against Valencia, whose left winger, Vicente, reckoned that Henry often 'lacks character at key moments'. He added, 'I've seen him play lots of times and he tries to be so elegant that he might as well go on to the pitch wearing his dinner jacket. He's too laid back. If you keep him tightly marked he hardly makes a contribution.' On the night both teams seemed to respect each other too much and a keenly anticipated clash fizzled out in a 0–0 draw.

Only Cole, Parlour, Campbell and Keown were really up for the following derby at White Hart Lane, a 1–1 draw in which Seaman embarrassed himself by trying to dribble round Robbie Keane. It looked as if Adams was right: the foreigners were concentrating on the Champions League. So the key question became: How long can a team keep fluctuating from bad to good without losing the ability to be good when it wants to be good?

In the run-up to Christmas, a 2–0 home win over Middlesbrough put Arsenal two points above Chelsea, but at West Brom they struggled to create openings, and Dichio headed home a Koumas corner. Then Jeffers clipped in a neat equaliser. Vieira, superb throughout, blocked Adam Chambers' clearance and the ball rebounded for Henry to score the winner. Unfortunately, during training on Christmas Eve, Rami Shaaban broke his leg.

Liverpool at Highbury was a tale of two penalties. Gerrard's long pass found Baros looking for Campbell's outstretched foot to trip over. He went down and Danny Murphy converted. Baros could not have scored from such a narrow angle and sometimes a defender has to say: 'OK, you've beaten me, now beat my keeper!' Jeffers came on for Wiltord and spun onto Bergkamp's jabbed pass into the box, Riise put an arm across him, Jeffers dived, and Henry smashed the penalty down the middle.

December had been a disappointing month with only two wins in six games, but January began well as Chelsea arrived to find Vieira in super-gladiator mode. Arsenal led 3–0 after 83 minutes before a loss of concentration let Chelsea pull back to 3–2. The players looked tired after four games in 11 days, especially Gilberto, who was now running on World Cup legs, but they had maintained their five-point advantage at the top. Never before had Arsenal earned so many points by New Year's Day. Centre-back Matthew Upson, disillusioned by his lack of first-team action, wanted a move, so he was sold to Birmingham for an initial £1 million during the January transfer window.

They now had easy games against Oxford, Birmingham, West Ham and Farnborough, and four wins took them to Anfield for a thriller which again showed how Arsenal failed to kill off opponents. Henry scored early and almost created another goal five minutes before the interval, then Heskey set up Riise for a scorching shot into the far corner. Seaman had no chance and neither did Dudek when Bergkamp's shot deflected off the heel of Henchoz for 2–1.When Baros came on, Wenger took Bergkamp off and brought on Luzhny as a third centre-back. By removing Bergkamp, Wenger was saying to Liverpool, 'You have the ball for the next six minutes'. Baros and Luzhny chased a ball which looked over the line before either touched it, a dubious corner was cleared, but Diao crossed and Heskey headed in for 2–2.

The Fulham game was poised at 1–1 for an hour until substitute Jeffers changed the game, creating the winner for Pires. Despite the team's dodgy moments, Bergkamp said he felt part of something really special. 'I don't want to get too philosophical, but I honestly think that this Arsenal side have rewritten the rules of football.'

At Newcastle a fast and furious battle developed. Henry made it 1–0, but early in the second half, Cole gave the ball to Laurent Robert, who beat Vieira and Lauren to rifle in the equaliser. There was more than half an hour left and only a late save by Seaman denied Newcastle victory. Another draw meant that after 27 games Arsenal had 57 points and Manchester United had 54.

The FA Cup took Arsenal to Old Trafford. Henry and Bergkamp were rested, and also Gilberto, who was recovering from Brazil's friendly in China. Scholes kicked Vieira twice to start a fracas, and van Nistelrooy kicked Keown and slammed his arm into Lauren's forehead. Vieira, furious at these assaults, was booked for dissent.

Then Beckham flighted a 40-yard pass for Giggs, who went round Seaman and Campbell, but fired over an open goal. That was the turning point. When Edu took a free-kick, the wall jumped. The ball hit Beckham's shoulder, wrong-footing Barthez for 1–0, and then a swift move set up Wiltord, who swerved past Wes Brown and thumped in the second. Remarkably, Seaman did not have one shot to save.

Media frenzy erupted when the front page of Monday's *Sun* carried a photograph showing Beckham arriving for training with a cut over his left eyebrow. The injury occurred in the dressing room when an angry Ferguson kicked a loose boot, which hit Beckham's face.

Ajax coach Ronald Koeman knew how penetrating Arsenal had been against PSV, but he could also see that they were predictable. His side, with seven players of 21 or under, started shakily at Highbury and conceded an early goal to Wiltord. Then De Jong made it 1–1 and Ajax settled down and contained Arsenal by defending deep, attacking wide and improving as the game went on, with the little South African, Pienaar, typifying their effervescent spirit. It is at such moments that Wenger seems to be a very conservative selector, too rigid in his thinking. He has a master plan, a way of playing, and a first eleven which is set in stone, Edu had done enough in Manchester to keep his place.

When Arsenal won 5–1 at Maine Road, Manchester City manager Kevin Keegan said, 'Arsenal, in my opinion, will win the Champions League. They're on a different planet.' Amsterdam was next and Wenger admitted that 'other teams adapt to your style of play'. But, positive as ever, he added, 'We've taken a big step forward in Europe over the last three years and now believe we can win anywhere against anyone.'

This time there was less fire and trickery about Ajax, who played in a more functional, programmed style, which worked until Vieira made a magnificent tackle, got up, found Henry, who found Pires, who put Bergkamp in on the right. But he scuffed his shot beyond the far post. The Ajax kids prevented similar counter-thrusts by skirmishing energetically just inside Arsenal's half, the zone from which their killer passes are so often launched, and defending the box in depth against a side which does not score from crosses. Meanwhile, Roma had become the first team to win a Champions League game in Valencia.

March kicked off with a 2–0 home win against Charlton which put Arsenal eight points clear, so the season now depended on the next four games – Chelsea, Roma, Blackburn and Valencia. Two games at home, then two away. The treble was still possible, but Ashley Cole, their only left-back, was out for a month after a hernia operation.

The Chelsea cup tie was a superb contest for an hour. John Terry scored with an early header, Cudicini saved Henry's penalty, Jeffers levelled, and Henry bamboozled the advancing Cudicini with a spin to put Arsenal 2–1 up at half-time. The game turned on the double substitution of Pires and Wiltord for Jeffers and Ljungberg in 64 minutes. After that, Arsenal lost shape and fluency, and when Toure came on for Henry there was no goal threat. Chelsea, already chasing the game, were further galvanised. Zenden's corner was flicked into the danger area by Melchiot, where Campbell kicked the ball against Lampard and the rebound dribbled over the line to set up a replay.

The Roma game was yet another draw. Vieira played out of his skin, but nobody else did, and Arsenal could not defeat ten men after Totti was sent off for jumping into Keown arm-first and slapping him on the ear. Montella missed a late header and it finished 1–1.

In another *Observer* piece, Tony Adams said that Wenger goes on long walks round the training ground, mulling over the selection most suited to the next match, and asks physio Gary Lewin which players are feeling stiff or tired. 'Then he will look at the statistics he has from the games. He will see which players are in the best shape. For example, he may look at the chart of, say, Robert Pires. He may have run 14 kilometres during the last game and compare it to another midfielder – Ray Parlour, for instance. If he is deciding between the two for a spot in the team, he will look at those figures. If Robert has run more than Ray, then he will deduce he is in better shape and he will get the nod. He is what I call a physiological manager. He goes a lot on physical shape.'

At Blackburn, Arsenal were without Vieira, Campbell and Cole, so it was a cruel blow when Keown pulled a hamstring. He went off when the score was 0–0, and the defence collapsed, with van Bronckhorst exposed by Keith Gillespie. Duff and Tugay scored.

Wenger's fiftieth Champions League match in charge of Arsenal would be a moment of truth. They would qualify for the quarter-finals, if they won or drew in Valencia, but they had just drawn with Chelsea, drawn with Roma, and lost at Blackburn, so form was not on their side and neither was history: Arsenal had never won in Spain.

Surprisingly, Pires was given the Bergkamp role, with Ljungberg on the left and Wiltord on the right, and they faced canny veterans who were especially good at containing quick-passing thrusts through the middle, which was more than could be said for the defenders at the other end. When Cygan followed Juan Sanchez into midfield, Aimar released Carew to rifle a shot inside Taylor's near post. Then Pires slipped Henry through to side-foot his trademark shot round Canizares. Nobody scores a one-on-one from 19 yards so sweetly. But Wiltord idiotically lost the ball to Vicente, who crossed for Carew to head the winner. Ajax drew 1–1 in Rome, so Valencia won the group with nine points, followed by Ajax on eight, Arsenal on seven and Roma on five.

A European campaign, which had started so marvellously in Eindhoven, had ended with yet another crushing disappointment, but Patrick Vieira now showed his colossal competitive spirit by putting the team on his back and carrying them to two wins in three days against Everton and Chelsea. With Vieira playing like this, a double Double was still possible and the title race promised to be the most exciting finish in the eleven-year history of the Premiership.

COLLAPSING INTO CARDIFF

I hope that, for the next 20 years, we will have seasons as disappointing as this one.

Arsène Wenger

Arsenal's regained momentum was now interrupted for England's crucial Euro 2004 qualifier against Turkey, with Wayne Rooney making a fine debut in a 2–0 victory.

Unfortunately, when the team re-assembled at Villa Park it looked a feeble imitation of the outfit that had hammered Chelsea 3–1. Ljungberg gave them the lead, but deputy left-back Toure miskicked an Alback shot into his own net and the last half hour was pitiful. Arsenal's eight-point lead had vanished in 29 days and they now led United only on goal difference.

The following weekend United won 6–2 at Newcastle while the FA Cup semi-finals brought predictable wins for Southampton against Watford, and Arsenal against Sheffield United. Ljungberg scored again, Vieira went off with a serious knee injury, and Seaman clawed a Peschisolido header off the line at the death.

At Highbury, Vieira led the team out against Manchester United with his knee bandaged. Van Nistelrooy raced away from Campbell to score, and Vieira had to limp off. Arsenal then got lucky, as Cole's shot was deflected in off Henry's calf, and when Henry, clearly offside, took a Gilberto pass and netted with no flag raised. But Giggs replied immediately with a header and 1t finished 2–2. Late on, Sol Campbell threw an arm that caught Solskjaer and referee Mark Halsey gave him his second red card of the season. Campbell was now banned for the last three games, plus the FA Cup Final.

To keep the contest going until the last day, Arsenal now needed to win at Middlesbrough and Bolton. Skipper Ray Parlour was the catalyst at the Riverside, making more tackles in the first 20 minutes than Gilberto had made since Christmas, and setting the tone. Cygan also played well in a 2–0 win. But United beat Blackburn 3–1 and they now topped the table on 74 points with three games to play. Arsenal had 71 points with four to play, so if both teams kept winning, they would finish level on 83 points and the title would be decided on goal difference, goals scored, or, possibly, a play-off,

At the Reebok, Bolton, who were fighting relegation, dominated a goalless first half. Henry created a tap-in for Wiltord, Pires side-footed a second, but then Okocha crunched Ljungberg's ankle. It looked as if Bergkamp would replace the crippled Swede, but Luzhny came on. Then, suddenly, Cygan pulled a calf muscle, and a Gardner tackle put Lauren out of the game with a twisted ankle.

Incredibly, three players had gone off injured in the 15 minutes since Pires had put them 2–0 up. Luzhny scuffed a clearance and Frandsen's shot rebounded to Djorkaeff, who made it 2–1 and then produced a dipping free-kick which went in off Keown's head. Champions should defend better than that. It was another lead lost, another draw, another bitterly disappointing day. Wenger made a comment he had never made before, admitting that his players 'wanted to do the minimum to win'.

The team that could not hold a lead never got in front when Leeds came to Highbury on 4 May. Wilcox hit a very long pass and Kewell deftly handled the ball towards his left foot and hit a sensational cross-shot past Seaman. Keown did not appeal, none of the officials saw the handball, and, astonishingly, the Sky commentators and studio pundits missed it as well.

Henry headed the equaliser after Parlour's 30-yarder was tipped onto the post by Robinson, and Harte hit a free-kick which went off Cole's head to make it 2–1 to Leeds. Still, Arsenal were playing well and Henry found Pires, who set up Bergkamp for 2–2, and they looked like winning when Henry stepped inside Mills to hit a swerving shot against the far post. There was still time and it looked as if Henry might score, but substitute Jermaine Pennant ignored a pass to Bergkamp, preferring to turn the other way into three Leeds players. Matteo took the ball off him and released Viduka, who was coming back in an offside position. The flag stayed down and Viduka scored the goal that gave Sir Alex Ferguson another title.

In the final analysis, Arsenal lacked experienced defensive cover and lost 14 points in away games when they were leading. The team could lift you up to the skies but could not nail down a result. They were the most attractive attacking team in England, but you don't get points for artistic impression. Professional football is about results and their results were not quite good enough. They drew 15 of their 59 games in all competitions. Manchester United were champions because they won 13 of their last 16 league games and drew three.

Back in the Sixties, the legendary Matt Busby had told Best, Law and Charlton to just go out and play. Busby's philosophy was 'We are the stars, let them mark us'. Forty years later, Ferguson's rivalry with Wenger tended to obscure what their teams had in common: Arsenal always come to play, and Manchester United always come to play. Maybe Arsène Wenger was really just Sir Matt Busby with a BSc.

Ten days before the FA Cup Final, Southampton suffered a 6–1 humiliation at Highbury, so boss Gordon Strachan chose damage limitation tactics, dropping right-winger Fernandes, pushing Telfer forward and introducing Baird, a young right-back, to tighten up that flank.

It was a one-sided final in which Henry missed early chances and Pires scored his 16th goal of the season. Vieira and Campbell, two spinal players, were badly missed, so Arsenal were too inhibited to kill the game off. Brett Ormerod eventually hit a terrific volley which skipper Seaman palmed away and after that scare it was keep-ball and time-wasting. That led to drama in stoppage time when Matt Oakley swung over a perfect corner and James Beattie powered in a header, which Cole blocked on the line. Bergkamp was the classiest player on the pitch and Gilberto had his best game for three months.

Thierry Henry, who had racked up 24 Premiership goals and an unprecedented 20 assists, won PFA Player of the Year and FWA Footballer of the Year, plus Goal of the Season for his slalom against Spurs, but he had still not scored in a final.

Seven years on from his ambassadorial arrival on that sunny autumn Sunday, Arsène Wenger had stayed true to his mission statement. Arsenal were playing stylish, power football, scoring dozens of thrilling goals, breaking many records, and had collected five trophies. No manager in Arsenal's history had kept them in the top two for six years in a row and one of his comments after Cardiff reminded us that the Arsène Wenger we love most is the droll Professor who says things like, 'I hope that, for the next 20 years, we will have seasons as disappointing as this one'.

In the Champions League semi-final Real Madrid were beaten by Juventus, who met AC Milan in the final and lost a penalty shoot-out after a 0–0 draw.

Madrid were again linked with Arsène Wenger, who was alleged to be frustrated by the delay in building Ashburton Grove, and to have had a meeting with them in Paris. But while Wenger would probably love to manage Raul, Ronaldo, Figo and Zidane, would he enjoy managing Jorge Valdano, the sporting director, and Florentino Perez, the president who bought their superstars? One recalled the words of Tibource Darrou, the fitness coach Wenger uses in Antibes, in a new book, *The French Revolution*. He said, 'The day Arsène stops managing Arsenal, he stops managing for good.

What he lives here is a dream. He did not need to invest one penny, but he manages the money of the club, he is the boss. What else could he dream of?'

Index

Doris Lessing

was born of British parents in Persia (now Iran) in 1919 and was taken to Southern Rhodesia (now Zimbabwe) when she was five. She spent her childhood on a large farm there and first came to England in 1949. She brought with her the manuscript of her first novel, *The Grass is Singing*, which was published in 1950 with outstanding success in Britain, in America, and in ten European countries. Since then her international reputation not only as a novelist but as a non-fiction and short story writer has flourished. For her collection of short novels, *Five*, she was honoured with the 1954 Somerset Maugham Award. She was awarded the Austrian State Prize for European Literature in 1981, and the German Federal Republic Shakespeare Prize of 1982. Among her other celebrated novels are *The Golden Notebook*, *The Summer Before the Dark*, *The Memoirs of a Survivor* and the five volume *Children of Violence* series. Her short stories have been collected in a number of volumes, including *To Room Nineteen* and *The Temptation of Jack Orkney*; while her African stories appear in *This Was the Old Chief's Country* and *The Sun Between Their Feet*. *Shikasta*, the first in a series of five novels with the overall title of *Canopus in Argos: Archives*, was published in 1979. Her novel *The Good Terrorist* won the W. H. Smith Literary Award for 1985, and the Mondello Prize in Italy that year. *The Fifth Child* won the Grinzane Cavour Prize in Italy, an award voted on by students in their final year at school. *The Making of the Representative for Planet 8* was made into an opera with Philip Glass, libretto by the author, and premièred in Houston. Her most recent works include *London Observed*, *African Laughter* and the first volume of her autobiography, *Under My Skin*.

By the same author

NOVELS

The Grass is Singing
The Golden Notebook
Briefing for a Descent into Hell
The Summer Before the Dark
The Memoirs of a Survivor
Diary of a Good Neighbour
If the Old Could . . .
The Good Terrorist
The Fifth Child

'Canopus in Argos: Archives'
  series

Re: Colonised Planet 5, Shikasta
The Marriages Between Zones
  Three, Four, and Five
The Sirian Experiments
The Making of the Representative
  for Planet 8
Documents Relating to the
  Sentimental Agents in the
  Volyen Empire

'Children of Violence'
  novel-sequence

Martha Quest
A Proper Marriage
A Ripple from the Storm
Landlocked
The Four-Gated City

DRAMA

Play with a Tiger
Each His Own
The Singing Door

SHORT STORIES

Five
The Habit of Loving
A Man and Two Women
The Story of a Non-Marrying
  Man and Other Stories
Winter in July
The Black Madonna
This Was the Old Chief's Country
  (Collected African Stories,
  Vol. 1)
The Sun Between Their Feet
  (Collected African Stories,
  Vol. 2)
To Room Nineteen (Collected
  Stories, Vol. 1)
The Temptation of Jack Orkney
  (Collected Stories, Vol. 2)
London Observed

POETRY

Fourteen Poems

NON-FICTION

In Pursuit of the English
Particularly Cats
Rufus the Survivor
Going Home
A Small Personal Voice
Prisons We Choose to Live Inside
The Wind Blows Away Our Words
African Laughter
Under My Skin

DORIS LESSING

The Memoirs of a Survivor

Flamingo

An Imprint of HarperCollinsPublishers

Flamingo
An Imprint of HarperCollins*Publishers*
77–85 Fulham Palace Road,
Hammersmith, London W6 8JB

Published by Flamingo 1995
9 8 7 6 5 4 3 2 1

First published in Great Britain by
The Octagon Press 1974

Previously published by
Picador 1976

Copyright © 1974 The Octagon Press

Author photograph by Caroline Forbes © 1994

ISBN 0 00 649325 4

Set in Baskerville

Printed in Great Britain by
HarperCollinsManufacturing Glasgow

This book is for my son Peter.

The Memoirs of a Survivor

We all remember that time. It was no different for me than for others. Yet we do tell each other over and over again the particularities of the events we shared, and the repetition, the listening, is as if we are saying : 'It was like that for you, too? Then that confirms it, yes, it was so, it must have been, I wasn't imagining things.' We match or dispute like people who have seen remarkable creatures on a journey : 'Did you see that big blue fish? Oh, the one you saw was yellow!' But the sea we travelled over was the same, the protracted period of unease and tension before the end was the same for everybody, everywhere; in the smaller units of our cities – streets, a cluster of tall blocks of flats, a hotel, as in cities, nations, a continent ... yes, I agree that this is pretty highflown imagery considering the nature of the events in question : bizarre fish, oceans, and so forth. But perhaps it wouldn't be out of place here to comment on the way we – everyone – will look back over a period in life, over a sequence of events, and find much more there than they did at the time. This is true even of events as dispiriting as the litter left on a common after a public holiday. People will compare notes, as if wishing or hoping for confirmation of something the events themselves had not licensed – far from it, something they had seemed to exclude altogether. Happiness? That's a word I have taken up from time to time in my life, looked at – but I never did find that it held its shape. A meaning, then; a purpose? At any rate, the past, looked back on in this frame of mind, seems steeped in a substance that had seemed foreign to it, was extraneous to the experiencing of it. Is it possible that

7

this is the stuff of real memory? Nostalgia, no; I'm not talking of that, the craving, the regret – not that poisoned itch. Nor is it a question of the importance each one of us tries to add to our not very significant pasts: '*I* was there, you know. *I* saw that.'

But it is because of this propensity of ours that perhaps I may be permitted the fancy metaphors. I *did* see fish in that sea, as if whales and dolphins had chosen to show themselves coloured scarlet and green, but did not understand at the time what it was I was seeing, and certainly did not know how much my own personal experience was common, was shared: this is what, looking back, we acknowledge first – our similarities, not our differences.

One of the things we now know was true for everybody, but which each of us privately thought was evidence of a stubbornly-preserved originality of mind, was that we apprehended what was going on in ways that were not official. Not respectable. Newscasts and newspapers and pronouncements were what we were used to, what we by no means despised: without them we would have become despondent, anxious, for of course one must have the stamp of the official, particularly in a time when nothing is going according to expectation. But the truth was that every one of us became aware at some point that it was not from official sources we were getting the facts which were building up into a very different picture from the publicised one. Sequences of words were crystallising events into a picture, almost a story: *And then this happened, and so-and-so said* ... but more and more often these were words dropped during a casual conversation, and perhaps even by oneself. 'Yes, of course!' one would think. 'That's it. I've known that for some time. It's just that I haven't actually heard it put like that, I hadn't grasped it ...'

Attitudes towards authority, towards Them and They, were increasingly contradictory, and we all believed that we were living in a peculiarly anarchistic community. Of course not. Everywhere was the same. But perhaps it would be better to develop this later, stopping only to remark that the use of the word 'it' is always a sign of crisis, of public anxiety. There is a gulf between: 'Why the hell do they have to be so incompetent!' and 'God, things are awful!' just as 'Things are awful' is a different matter again from 'It is starting here too,' or 'Have you heard any more about it?'

I shall begin this account at a time before we were talking about 'it'. We were still in the stage of generalised unease. Things weren't too good, they were even pretty bad. A great many things were bad, breaking down, giving up, or 'giving cause for alarm', as the newscasts might put it. But 'it', in the sense of something felt as an immediate threat which could not be averted, no.

I was living in a block of flats, which was one of several such blocks. I was on the ground floor, at earth-level; not as it were in some aerial village with invisible paths beaten from window to window by the inquisitive or the speculative eye among birds following their roads, while traffic and human affairs were far below. No, I was one of those who looked up, imagining how things might be up there in higher regions where windows admitted a finer air, and where front doors led to the public lifts and so down, down, to the sound of traffic, the smells of chemicals and of plant life ... the street. These were not flats built by a town council, the walls scribbled with graffiti, the lifts stained with urine, the walls of lobbies smeared with excrement: these were not the vertical streets of the poor, but were built by private money, and were heavy, were settled widely over the valuable soil – the formerly valuable soil. The walls were thick, for families who could afford to pay for privacy. At the entrance was a largeish hall, carpeted; and there were even stands of flowers, artificial but handsome enough. There was a caretaker. These blocks were models of what such buildings should be for solidity and decency.

But by that time, with so many people gone from the city, the families who lived in these blocks were not all the class for whom the buildings had been put up. Just as, for years, all through the eroding streets of the poor, empty houses had been taken over by squatters settling in families or groups of families, so that for a long time it had been impossible to say: This is a working class area, this is homogeneous – so, too, in these great buildings once tenanted only by the well-to-do, by the professional and business people, were now families or clans of poor people. What it amounted to was that a flat, a house, belonged to the people who had the enterprise to move into it. So, in the corridors and halls of the building I lived in you could meet, as in a street or a market, every sort of person.

A Professor and his wife and his daughter lived in the twin set of rooms to mine down the corridor; immediately above me was a family of Indians with many relatives and dependants. I mention these two sets of people, because they were closest to me, and because I want to make the point that it is not as if an awareness of what went on behind walls and ceilings had been lacking before the start of – what? Here I do find difficulty, because there is nothing I can pinpoint, make definite ... now I am talking not about the public pressures and events we encapsulate in words like 'They' 'Them' 'It' and so on, but my own private discoveries which became so urgent and which were making such a claim on me at that time. I can't say: 'On such and such a day I knew that behind the wall a certain quality of life was being lived.' Not even: 'It was in the spring of that year that...', No, the consciousness of that other life, developing there so close to me, hidden from me, was a slow thing, coming precisely into the category of understanding we describe in the word *realise*, with its connotation of a gradual opening into comprehension. Such an opening, a growing, may be an affair of weeks, months, years. And of course one can 'know' something, and not 'know' it. (One can also know something and then forget it!) Looking back I can say definitely that the growth of that other life or form of being behind that wall had been at the back of my mind for a long time before I *realised* what it was I had been listening to, listening for. But I can't set down a date or a time. Certainly this inner preoccupation predated the other, public, concern to which I've given, I hope it is not thought frivolously, the word 'it'.

Even at my dimmest and thickest I did know that what I was becoming conscious of, what I was on the edge of *realising*, was different in quality from what in fact went on around me: above my head, the lively, busy, warming family life of the

Indians, who came, I believe, from Kenya; and different again from what I heard from the rooms inhabited by Professor White and his family – the wall of whose kitchen was also the wall of mine, through which, although it was a thick wall, we had news of each other.

Not realising, or allowing myself to take in, the full implications of the fact that something was going on behind the wall of my living-room was because beyond it was a corridor. To be precise about it, what I was hearing was impossible. The sounds that come from a corridor, even a much-used one, are limited. It is for getting from one place to another: people walk along corridors singly, in pairs, in groups, talking or not talking. This corridor led from the front hall of the building, past the door into my flat, then on to the White's front door, and so around to the flats on the east side of the ground floor of the building. Along that corridor went the Professor and the members of his family and their visitors, myself and my visitors, the two families from the east side and their visitors. So it was used a good deal. Often one had to be aware of feet and voices, distanced by the solidity of that wall, but I would say to myself: 'That must be the Professor, surely he is early today?' Or: 'That sounds like Janet back from school.'

Yet there did come that moment when I had to admit that there was a room behind that wall, perhaps more than one, even a set of rooms, occupying the same space as, or rather, overlapping with, the corridor. The realisation of what I was hearing, the knowledge that I had been aware of something of the kind for a long time, became strong in me, at the time that I knew I would almost certainly have to leave this city. Of course by now everyone had a sense of this: knowing that we would have to leave was not confined to me. This is an example of something I have already mentioned: an idea coming into everyone's mind at the same time and without intervention from the authorities. That is to say, it was not announced through the loudspeakers, or on public platforms, in the newspapers, on the radio, the television. God knows that announcements of all kinds were continually being made: yet these were not absorbed by the populace as was this other information. On the whole people tended to disregard what the authorities said – no, that is not quite true. The public information was discussed and argued and complained about, but it had a different impact. Suppose I said it was regarded almost as an entertainment? – no, that is not right either. People did not act on what they heard, that is the point : not unless they were forced to. But this other information, coming from no one knew where, the news that was 'in the air', put everyone into action. For instance, weeks before the official announcement that a certain basic foodstuff was to be rationed, I ran into Mr Mehta and his wife in the hall – the old couple, the grandparents. They were dragging between them a sack of potatoes; I, too, had a supply. We nodded and smiled, mutually commending our foresight. Similarly I remember Mrs White and myself exchanging good mornings on the paved area in front of the main entrance. She said, quite casually : 'We shouldn't leave things too long.' And I replied : 'We've got some months yet, but we ought to be making preparations, I agree.' We were talking about what everyone was, the need to leave this city. There had been no public intimation that people should leave. Nor, for that matter, was there ever any recognition on the part of the authorities that the city was emptying. It might be mentioned in passing, as a symptom of something else, as a temporary phenomenon, but not as the big fact in our lives.

There was no single reason for people leaving. We knew that all public services had stopped to the south and to the east, and that this state of affairs was spreading our way. We knew that everyone had left that part of the country, except for bands of people, mostly youngsters, who lived on what they could find : crops left ungathered in the fields, animals that had escaped slaughter before everything had broken down. These bands, or gangs, had not, to begin with, been particularly violent or harmful to the few people who had refused to leave. They even 'co-operated with the forces of law and order', as the newscasts put it. Then, as food became more scarce, and whatever the danger was that had first set populations on the move away from it came closer, the gangs became dangerous, and when they passed through the suburbs of our city, people ran inside and stayed out of their way.

This had been going on for months. Warnings, first by rumour, then through the news-sources, that gangs were moving through such and such an area where the inhabitants had gone behind their locked doors until the danger had passed; that new gangs were approaching this or that area, where people would be well-advised to look after their lives, and their property; that another district, formerly dangerous, was now safe again – such alarms were part of our lives.

Where I lived, on the north side of the city, the streets were not roadways for the migrating gangs until a long time after the southern suburbs had become accustomed to them. Even when parts of our own town took anarchy for granted, we in the north talked and thought of ourselves as immune. The trouble would vanish, dissolve, take itself off ... Such is the strength of what we are used to, the first two or three appearances of gangs in our northern suburbs seemed to us isolated incidents, not likely to be repeated. Slowly, we came to understand that it was our periods of peace, of normality, and not the days of looting and fighting, which were going to be unusual now.

And so – we would have to move. Yes, we would go. Not quite yet. But it would soon be necessary, and we knew it ... and all this time my ordinary life was the foreground, the lit area – if I can put it like that – of a mystery that was taking place, had been going on for a long time, 'somewhere else'. I was feeling more and more that my ordinary daytime life was irrelevant. Unimportant. That wall had become to me – but how can I put it? – I was going to say, an obsession. That word implies that I am ready to betray the wall, what it stood for, am prepared to resign it to the regions of the pathological? Or that I felt uneasy then or now about my interest in it? No, I was feeling as if the centre of gravity of my life had moved, balances had shifted somewhere, and I was beginning to believe – uncomfortably, still – that what went on behind the wall might be every bit as important as my ordinary life in that neat and comfortable, if shabby, flat. I would stand in my living-room – the colours were predominantly cream, yellow, white, or at least enough of these to make it seem that walking into the room was walking into sunlight – I would wait there, and look quietly at the wall. Solid. Ordinary. A wall without a door or a window in it : the door from the lobby of the flat was in the room's side wall. There was a fireplace, not in the middle of it but rather to one side, so that there was a large expanse of this wall quite empty : I had not put up pictures or hangings. The 'white' of the walls had darkened and did not give off much light unless the sunlight lay on it. Once there had been wallpaper. It had been painted over, but under the paint outlines of flowers, leaves, birds were still visible. When in the mornings the sun did fall on part of that wall, the half-obliterated pattern showed so clearly that the mind followed suggestions of trees and a garden into a belief that the wash of light was making colour – greens, yellow, a certain shade of clear shell pink. It was not a high wall : the ceilings of the room were a comfortable height.

As you can see, there is nothing I can think of to say about this wall that could lift it out of the commonplace. Yet, standing there and looking at it, or thinking about it while I did other things about the flat, the sense and feel of it always in my mind, was like holding an egg to one's ear that is due to hatch. The warm smooth shape on one's palm is throbbing. Behind the fragile lime which, although it can be crushed between two fingers, is inviolable because of the necessities of the chick's time, the precise and accurate time it needs to get itself out of the dark prison, it is as if a weight redistributes itself, as when a child shifts position in the womb. There is the faintest jar. Another. The chick, head under its wing, is pecking its way out, and already the minutest fragments of lime are collecting on the shell where in a moment the first black starry hole will appear. I even found I was putting my ear to the wall, as one would to a fertile egg, listening, waiting. Not for the sounds of Mrs White's, or the Professor's, movements. They might have just gone out or just come in; the ordinary sounds of the corridor might in fact be there. No, what I was hearing was from somewhere else. Yet they were ordinary sounds in themselves : furniture being shifted : voices, but from very far off; a child crying. Nothing clear. But they were familiar, I had been hearing them all my life.

One morning I stood with my after-breakfast cigarette – I allowed myself this one real cigarette a day – and through clouds of blue coiling smoke looked at how the yellowness of the sun stretched in a foreshortened oblong, making the wall itself seem higher in the middle than at its ends. I looked at the glow and the pulse of the yellow, looked as if I were listening, thinking how, as the seasons changed, so did the shape and extent and position of this patch of morning light – and then I was through the wall and I knew what was there. I did not at that first time achieve much more than that there were a set of rooms. The rooms were disused, had been for some time. Years, perhaps. There was no furniture. Paint had flaked off the wall in places, and lay in tiny shards on the floorboards with scraps of paper and dead flies and dust. I did not go in, but stood there on the margin between the two worlds, my familiar flat and these rooms which had been quietly waiting there all this time. I stood and looked, feeding with my eyes. I felt the most vivid expectancy, a longing : this place held what I needed, knew was there, had been waiting for – oh yes, all my life, all my life. I knew this place, recognised it, and before I had actually absorbed the information through my eyes that the walls were much higher than mine, there were many windows and doors, and that it was a large, light, airy, delightful flat, or house. In a further room I glimpsed a painter's ladder; and then, just as the sunlight faded out on my wall when a cloud absorbed the sun, I saw someone in white painter's overalls lifting a roller to lay white paint over the faded and stained surface.

I forgot this occurrence. I went on with the little routines of my life, conscious of the life behind the wall, but not remembering my visit there. It was not until a few days later that I again stood, cigarette in hand, in the mid-morning hour, looking through drifting smoke at the sunlight laid there on the wall, and I thought : Hello! I've been through there, of course I have. How did I manage to forget? And again the wall dissolved and I was through. There were more rooms than I had suspected the first time. I had a strong sense of that, though I did not see them all. Nor did I, on that occasion, see the man or the woman in overalls. The rooms were empty. To make them habitable, what work needed to be done! Yes, I could see that it would take weeks, months ... I stood there marking fallen plaster, the corner of a ceiling stained with damp, dirty or damaged walls. Yet it was on that morning when I was beginning to understand how much work needed to be done that I saw, just for the ghost of a second – well, what? But I can hardly say. Perhaps it was more of a feeling than some-thing seen. There was a sweetness, certainly – a welcome, a reassurance. Perhaps I did see a face, or the shadow of one. The face I saw clearly later was familiar to me, but it is possible that that face, seen as everything ended, appears in my memory in this place, this early second visit : it had reflected itself back, needing no more to use as a host or as a mirror than the emotion of sweet longing, which hunger was its proper air. This was the rightful inhabitant of the rooms behind the wall. I had no doubt of it then or later. The *exiled* inhabitant; for surely she could not live, never could have lived, in that chill empty shell full of dirty and stale air?

When I again knew myself to be standing in my living-room, the cigarette half-burned down, I was left with the conviction of a promise, which did not leave me no matter how difficult things became later, both in my own life, and in these hidden rooms.

———————◆———————

The child was left with me in this way. I was in the kitchen, and, hearing a sound, went into the living room, and saw a man and a half-grown girl standing there. I did not know either of them, and advanced with the intention of clearing up a mistake. The thought in my mind was that I must have left my front door open. They turned to face me. I remember how I was even then, and at once, struck by the bright hard nervous smile on the girl's face. The man – middleaged, ordinarily dressed, quite unremarkable in every way – said : 'This is the child.' He was already on the way out. He had laid his hand on her shoulder, had smiled and nodded to her, was turning away.

I said : 'But surely. . . .'

'No, there's no mistake. She's your responsibility.'

He was at the door.

'But wait a minute. . . .'

'She is Emily Cartright. Look after her.' And he had gone.

We stood there, the child and I, looking at each other. I remember the room had a wash of sun : it was still morning. I was wondering how the two had got in, but this already seemed irrelevant, since the man had gone. I now ran to the window : a street with a few trees along the pavement, a bus-stop with its familiar queue of people waiting, waiting; and on the wide pavement opposite, underneath the trees there, some children from the Mehta's flat upstairs playing with a ball – dark-skinned boys and girls, all dazzling white shirts, crisp pink and blue dresses, white teeth, gleaming hair. But the man I was looking for – not a sign.

I turned back to the child; but now I took my time over it, and was wondering what to say, how to present myself, how to handle her – all the pathetic little techniques and tricks of our self-definition. She was watching me, carefully, closely : the thought came into my mind that this was the expert assessment of possibilities by a prisoner observing a new jailer. Already my heart was heavy : anxiety! My intelligence was not yet making much of what was happening.

'Emily?' I said tentatively, hoping that she would choose to answer the questions in my mind.

'Emily Mary Cartright,' she said, in a manner that matched her bright impervious voice and smile. Pert? At any rate a hard, an enamelled presence. I was trying to get past, or around it; I was conscious that I was desperately making signals – my smile, gestures – that might perhaps reach something softer and warmer which must be there behind that cold defence of hers.

'Well, will you sit down? Or can I make you something to eat? Some tea? I do have some real tea, but of course . . .'

'I'd like to see my room please,' she said. And now her eyes were, quite without her knowing it, an appeal, She needed, she needed very much, to know what walls, what shelter, she was going to be able to pull around her, like a blanket, for comfort.

'Well,' I said, 'I haven't thought yet, I don't quite . . . I must . . .' Her face seemed to shrivel. But she preserved her bright desperation. 'You see,' I went on, 'I wasn't expecting . . . let's see now.' She waited. Stubbornly, she waited. She knew that she was to live with me. She knew that her shelter, her four walls, her den, the little space that was hers and which she could creep into was here somewhere. 'There's the spare room,' I said. 'I call it that. But it isn't very . . .' But I went, and I remember how helplessly and unhappily I did, into the little front lobby, and through it to the spare room.

The flat was on the front of the building, the south side. The living-room took up most of the space : its size was why I had taken the flat. At the end away from the entrance lobby, so that you had to walk through the living-room to get to it, was the kitchen, on the corner of the building. This was quite large, with cupboards and storage space, and was used for eating as well. From the entrance lobby went two doors, one to the living-room, one to the room I called a spare room. This room was connected with the bathroom. My bedroom was on the front of the building, reached from the living-room. The bathroom, lobby, spare room, took up the same space as my bedroom, which was not large. It will be seen that the spare room was very small. It had a small high window. It was stuffy. There was no way of making it attractive. I never used it except for keeping things in or, with apologies, for a friend staying the night.

'I'm sorry that it is so small and dark . . . perhaps we should . . .'

'No, no, I don't mind,' she said, in the cool jaunty way which was so much hers; but she was looking at the bed with longing, and I knew she had found her refuge, hers, here it was at last. 'It's lovely,' she said. 'Oh yes, you don't believe me, you don't know what . . .' But she left the possibility of an explanation of what she had been experiencing, and waited, her whole body expressing how she wanted me to leave.

'And we'll have to share the bathroom,' I said.

'Oh, I'll be ever so tidy,' she assured me. 'I'm really very good, you know, I won't make a mess, I never do.'

I knew that if I were not in this flat, if she did not feel she must behave well, she would be between the blankets, she would already be far away from the world.

'I won't be a tick,' she assured me. 'I must get tidy. I'll be as quick as I can.'

I left her and waited for her in the living-room, first standing by the window looking out, wondering perhaps if fresh surprises were on the way. Then I sat down, rather, I imagine, in the attitude of The Thinker, or some such concentrated pose.

Yes, it was extraordinary. Yes, it was all impossible. But after all, I had accepted the 'impossible'. I lived with it. I had abandoned all expectations of the ordinary for my inner world, my real life in that place. And as for the public, the outer world, it had been a long time since that offered the normal. Could one perhaps describe that period as 'the ordinariness of the extraordinary?' Well, the reader should have no difficulty here: these words are a description of the times we have lived through. (A description of all life? – probably, but it is not much help to think so.)

But these words convey perfectly the atmosphere of what was happening when Emily was brought to me. While everything, all forms of social organisation, broke up, we lived on, adjusting our lives, as if nothing fundamental was happening. It was amazing how determined, how stubborn, how self-renewing, were the attempts to lead an ordinary life. When nothing, or very little, was left of what we had been used to, had taken for granted even ten years before, we went on talking and behaving as if those old forms were still ours. And indeed, order of the old kind – food, amenities, even luxuries, *did* exist at higher levels, we all knew that; though of course those who enjoyed these things did not draw attention to themselves. Order could also exist in pockets, of space, of time – through periods of weeks and months or in a particular district. Inside them, people would live and talk and even think as if nothing had changed.

When something really bad happened, as when an area got devastated, people might move out for days, or weeks, to stay with relatives or friends, and then move back, perhaps to a looted house, to take up their jobs, their housekeeping – their order. We can get used to anything at all; this is a commonplace, of course, but perhaps you have to live through such a time to see how horribly true it is. There is nothing that people won't try to accommodate into 'ordinary life'. It was precisely this which gave that time its peculiar flavour; the combination of the bizarre, the hectic, the frightening, the threatening, an atmosphere of siege or war – with what was customary, ordinary, even decent.

For instance, on the newscasts and in the papers they would pursue for days the story of a single kidnapped child, taken from its pram perhaps by some poor unhappy woman. The police would be combing suburbs and the countryside in hundreds, looking for the child, and for the woman, to punish her. But the next news flash would be about the mass deaths of hundreds, thousands, or even millions of people. We still believed, wanted to believe, that the first, the concern about the single child, the need to punish the individual criminal, even if it took days and weeks and hundreds of our hard-worked police force to do it, was what really represented us; the second, the catastrophe, was, as such items of news had always been for people not actually in the threatened area, an unfortunate and minor – or at least not crucial – accident, which interrupted the even flow, the development, of civilisation.

This is the sort of thing we accepted as normal. Yet for all of us there were moments when *the game we were all agreeing to play* simply could not stand up to events : we would be gripped by feelings of unreality, like nausea. Perhaps this feeling, that the ground was dissolving under our feet, was the real enemy . . . or we believed it to be so. Perhaps our tacit agreement that nothing *much*, or at least, nothing irrecoverable, was happening, was because for us the enemy was Reality, was to allow ourselves to know what was happening. Perhaps our pretences, everyone's pretences, which in the moments when we felt naked, defenceless, seemed like playacting and absurd, should be regarded as admirable? Or perhaps they were necessary, like the games of children who can make playacting a way of keeping reality a long way from their weaknesses? But increasingly, all the time, one had to defeat the need, simply, to laugh: oh, not a good laughter, far from it. Rather bellows and yells of derision.

For instance again: in the same week as a horde of two hundred or so hooligans had surged through our neighbourhood, leaving a corpse on the pavement across from the street from my windows, leaving smashed windows, looted shops, the remains of bonfires, a group of middleaged women, self-appointed vigilantes were making formal protests to the police about an amateur theatricals group some youngsters had set up. This group had written and put on a play describing the tensions inside an ordinary family living in a block of flats like ours, a family which had taken in half a dozen refugees from the eastern counties. (As long as travellers were with the migrating gangs they were 'hooligans', but when they hived off to find shelter with some family or household they were 'refugees'). A household that had held five people suddenly held twelve, and the resulting frictions led to adultery and an incident where 'a young girl seduced a man old enough to be her grandfather' as the good women indignantly described it. They managed to organise a not-very-well-attended meeting about the 'decay of family life', about 'immorality', about 'sexual indulgence'. This was comic, of course. Unless it was sad. Unless – as I've suggested – it was admirable; a sign of the vitality of the said 'ordinary life' which would in the end defeat chaos, disorder, the malevolence of events.

Or what can one say about the innumerable citizens' groups that came into existence right up to the end, for any ethical or social purpose you could think of: to improve old age pensions, at a time when money was giving way to barter; to supply vitamin tablets to school children; to provide a visiting service for housebound invalids; to arrange formal legal adoption for abandoned children; to forbid the news of any violent or 'unpleasant' event, so as not to 'put ideas into young people's heads'; to reason with the gangs of hooligans as they came through the streets, or alternatively, to birch them; to go around and about the streets, exhorting people 'to restore a sense of decency to their sexual practices'; to agree not to eat the meat of cats and dogs; and so on, and on, and on – there was really no end to it. Farce. Splitting into a hurricane; standing in front of a mirror to touch up one's face or straighten a tie as the house crashes around one; extending the relaxed accommodating hand of the Royal handshake to a barbarian who will certainly bend and take a good bite out of it . . . these similes come to mind. Analogies were being made then, of course, in the conversations that were our meat and drink, and by the professional comedians.

In such an atmosphere, in a time of such happenings, that an unknown man should arrive in my home with a child, saying she was my responsibility, and then leave without further remark, was not as strange as all that.

When Emily at last came out of her bedroom, having changed her dress and washed from her face what looked like an assault of miserable tears, she said: 'The room will be a bit small for Hugo and me, but it doesn't matter a bit.'

I saw that she had beside her a dog, no a cat. What was it? An animal, at any rate. It was the size of a bulldog, and shaped more like a dog than a cat, but its face was that of a cat.

It was yellow. Its hide was harsh and rough. It had cat's eyes and whiskers. It had a long whip-like tail. An ugly beast. Hugo. She sat herself down carefully in my deep old sofa opposite the fireplace, and the beast got up beside her, and sat there, as close as he could get, and she put her arm about him. She looked at me, from beside the animal's cat face. They both looked at me, Hugo with his green eyes, and Emily with her defensive shrewd hazel eyes.

She was a large child, of about twelve. Not a child, really; but in that half-way place where soon she would be a girl. She would be pretty, at least goodlooking. Well-made: she had small hands and feet, and good limbs that were brown with health and sun. Her hair was dark and straight, parted on one side, held with a clip.

We talked. Or rather, we offered each other little remarks, both waiting for that switch to be turned somewhere which would make our being together easier. While she sat there silent her brooding dark gaze, her mouth with its definite possibilities of humour, her air of patient thoughtful attention made her seem someone I could like very much. But then, just as I was sure she was about to respond in kind to my attempts, my feeling of pleasure in her potentialities, there would come to life in her the vivacious self-presenting little *madam* – the old-fashioned world was right for her : there was something old-fashioned in her image of herself. Or perhaps it was someone else's idea of her?

She chattered : 'I'm awfully hungry, and so is Hugo. Poor Hugo. He hasn't eaten today. And neither have I, if the truth must be told.'

I made my apologies and hastened out to the shops to buy whatever cat or dog foods I could find for Hugo. It took some time to find a shop which still stocked such things. I was an object of interest to the shop assistant, an animal-lover, who applauded my intention to stand up for my right to keep 'pets' in these days. I also interested one or two of the other customers, and I was careful not to say where I lived, when one asked me, and went home by a misleading route, and made sure I was not being followed. On the way I visited several shops looking for things I usually did not bother with, they were so hard to track down, so expensive. But at last I did find some biscuits and sweets of a quite decent quality – whatever I thought might appeal to a child. I had plenty of dried apples and pears, and stocks of basic foodstuffs. When at last I got back home she was asleep on the sofa, and Hugo was asleep beside her. His yellow face was on her shoulder, her arm was around his neck. On the floor beside her was her little suitcase, as flimsy as a small child's week-end case. It had in it some neatly-folded dresses and a jersey and a pair of jeans. These seemed to be all she owned in the way of clothes. I would not have been sur-prised to see a teddy or a doll. Instead there was a Bible, a book of photographs of animals, some science fiction paperbacks.

I made as welcoming a meal as I could for both her and Hugo. I woke them with difficulty : they were in the exhausted state that follows relief after long tension. When they had eaten they wanted to go off to bed, though it was still mid-afternoon.

And that was how Emily was left with me.

In those first few days she slept and she slept. Because of this, and because of her invincible obedience, I was unconsciously thinking of her as younger than she was. I sat waiting quietly in my living-room, knowing that she was asleep, exactly as one does with a small child. I did a little mending for her, washed and ironed her clothes. But mostly, I sat and looked at that wall and waited. I could not help thinking that to have a child with me, just as the wall was beginning to open itself up, would be a nuisance, and in fact she and her animal were very much in the way. This made me feel guilty. All kinds of emotions I had not felt for a long time came to life in me again, and I longed simply to walk through the wall and never come back. But this would be irresponsible; it would mean turning my back on my responsibilities.

It was a day or two after Emily came: I was beyond the wall, and I kept opening doors, or turning the corners of long passages to find another room or suite of rooms. Empty. That is, I did not see any one, although the feeling of someone's presence was so strong I even kept turning my head quickly, as if this person could be expected to step out from behind a wall in the few seconds my back had been turned. Empty but inhabited. Empty but furnished ... wandering there, between tall white walls, from room to room, I saw that the place was filled with furniture. I knew these sofas, these chairs. But why? From what time in my life did they date? They were not my taste. Yet it seemed that they had been mine, or an intimate friend's.

The drawing-room had pale pink silk curtains, a grey carpet with delicate pink and green flowers laid on it, many small tables and cabinets. The sofas and chairs were covered in tapestry, had pastel cushions placed exactly here and there. It was a room too formal and too self-sufficient ever to have been mine. Yet I knew everything in it. I walked there, slowly filling with irritated despair. Everything I looked at would have to be replaced or mended or cleaned, for nothing was whole, or fresh. Each chair would have to be re-covered, for the material was frayed. The sofas were grimy. The curtains had little rents and the roughened patches moths leave, each with its miniscule holes. The carpet showed its threads. And so with all the many rooms of this place, which was giving a feeling of things slipping away from me through clumsy and stiff fingers. The whole place should be cleared out, I kept saying to myself. It should be emptied, and what was in it now should be burned or thrown away. Bare rooms would be better than this infinitely genteel shabbiness, the gimcrackery. Room after room after room – there was no end to them, or to the work I had to do. Now I kept looking for the empty room that had in it a painter's ladder and a half-glimpsed figure in overalls: if I could see this, it would mean a start had been made. But there were no empty rooms, every one was crammed with objects, all needing attention.

It must not be thought that all my energy was going into this hidden place. For days at a time I did not think of it. The knowledge of it, being there, in whatever shape it was using for the moment, came to me in flashes during my ordinary life, more and more often. But I would forget it, too, for days. When I was actually through that wall, nothing else seemed real; and even the new and serious preoccupations of my life – Emily and her attendant animal – slid away, were far off, were part of another distant life which did not much concern me. And this is my difficulty in describing that time : looking back now it is as if two ways of life, two lives, two worlds, lay side by side and closely connected. But then, one life excluded the other, and I did not expect the two worlds ever to link up. I had not thought at all of their being able to do so, and I would have said this was not possible. Particularly now, when Emily was there; particularly when I had so many problems that centred on her being with me.

The main problem was, and remained for some time, that she was so infinitely obliging and obedient. When I got up in the morning she was already up, dressed in one of her neat little dresses, the clothes of a good child whose mother needs her children to be well dressed, even remarkably so. Her hair was brushed. Her teeth were cleaned. She was waiting for me in the living-room, with her Hugo, and instantly she began chattering, offering this or that to me, how she had slept marvellously, or how she had dreamed, or how she had had this amusing or foolish or valuable thought – and all in a rushing almost frantic way of forestalling some demand or criticism from me. And then she began about breakfast, how she would 'adore' to cook it – 'oh, she would simply love to, please', for really she was ever so handy and capable. And so she and I would go into the kitchen, the beast padding behind us, and I and Hugo sat watching her preparations. And she was, indeed, competent and nifty. And then we ate whatever it was, Hugo's head at her waist-level, his eyes calmly watching her, me, our hands, our faces, and when he was offered a bit of food he took it delicately, like a cat. Then she would offer to wash up. 'No, no, I love washing-up, incredible as it might seem, but I really do!' And she washed up and made the kitchen neat. Her bedroom had been tidied already, but not her bed, which was always a nest or womb of coiled blankets and pillows. I never reproved her for this; on the contrary, I was delighted that there was one place she felt was her own, that she could make her refuge, where she could hide away from this really awful need always to be so bright and good. Sometimes, unpredictably, during the day, she went to her room – abruptly, as if *something* had been too much. She shut the door and, I knew, crawled into the heap of disorder and there she lay and recovered . . . but from what? In the living-room she sat on my old sofa, her legs curled up, in a pose which was as much an offering to what might be expected of her as was her manner, her obedience. She watched me, as if anticipating commands or needs, or she might read. Her taste in reading was adult: seeing her there, with what she had chosen, made her bright child's manner even more impossible, almost as if she were deliberately insulting me. Or she would sit with her arm round the yellow beast, and he licked her hand, and put his cat's face on her arm and purred, a sound which rumbled through the rooms of my flat.

Had she been some kind of a prisoner?

I did not ask. I never, not once, asked her a question. And

she did not volunteer information. Meanwhile my heart ached for her, recognising her manner for what it was; and, at the same time, while I was really quite soft and ridiculous with pity for her, I was in a frenzy of irritation, because of my inability ever, even for a moment, to get behind the guard she had set up. There she was, the solemn, serious little girl, in her good little girl's dress, showing every mark of the solitary child, all self-consciousness and observation, and then off she'd go, chattering and rattling, being 'amusing', offering me little skills and capacities as a return for – but what? I did not feel myself to be so formidable. I almost felt myself not to exist, in my own right. I was a continuation, for her, of parents, or a parent, a guardian, foster-parents. And when we left here, presumably I would hand her over to someone else? The man who had given her into my care would come to take her back? Her parents would arrive? Otherwise, what was I going to do with her? When I started my travels north or west, joining the general movement of the population away from the southern and eastern parts of the country, what would I be moving into? What sort of life? I did not know. But I had not envisaged a child, never a responsibility of such a total sort ... and besides, even in the few days she had been here she had changed. Her breasts were shaping, pushing out the child's bodice. Her round face with its attractive dark eyes needed very little to shape it into a young girl's face. A 'little' girl was one thing, and bad enough – 'child with her pet' ... but the 'young girl' would be quite another, and particularly in these times.

It will sound contradictory when I say that another thing that bothered me was her indolence. Of course there wasn't very much to do in my flat. She sat for hours at my window and watched, absorbed, everything that went on. She entertained me with comment: this was a deliberate and measured offering; she had been known, it was clear, for her 'amusing' comments. Here again I did not know quite what it was I had to reckon with, for these were certainly not a little girl's perceptions. Or perhaps I was out of date, and this was what one had to expect in this time, for what strains and stresses did children now not have to accept and make part of themselves?

Professor White would come out of the lobby and down the steps, and then stop, looking up and down the street, almost in a military way: *Who goes there!* Then, reassured, he stood for a moment: almost he could be imagined pulling on a pair of gloves, adjusting a hat. He was a slight man, young for a professor, still in his thirties; a precise, an ashy, man with everything in his life in its proper place. On to Emily's face would come a smile as she watched him, a sour little smile, as if she was thinking: I've got *you,* you can't escape me! And over her attendant animal's pricked yellow ears she would say: 'He looks as if he was pulling on a pair of gloves!' (Yes, this was her observation.) And then: 'He must have a terrible temper!' 'But why? Why do you think so?' 'Why? Well, of course, all that control, everything so neat and clean, he must burst out somewhere.' And, once, 'If he has a mistress...' – the use of the old-fashioned word was deliberate, part of the act – 'then she would have to be someone with a bad reputation, someone rather awful, or *he* would have to think she was, or other people would have to think so even if he didn't. Because he would have to feel wicked, don't you see?' Well, of course she was right.

I found myself making excuses to sit there, to hear what she would come out with. But I was reluctant too, watching the knife being slipped in so neatly, so precisely, and again and again.

Of Janet White, a girl of about her age: 'She'll spend her life looking for someone like Daddy, but where will she find him. I mean *now*, he won't exist.' She meant, of course, the general break-up of things, times which were not conducive to the production of professors with very clean white shirts and a secret passion for the unrespectable – since respectability itself was sentenced to death, and with it the distinctions his secret needs must feed on. The professor she called The White Rabbit. His daughter she called Daddy's Girl, making the point that in doing so she was of course describing herself: 'What else, after all?' When I suggested that she might enjoy making a friend of Janet, she said: 'What, me and her?'

There she sat, most of the day, lolling in a large chair that she pulled up for the purpose : a child, presenting herself as one. One could almost see the white socks on her plump well-turned legs, the bow in her hair. But what one really did see was different. She wore jeans and a shirt she had ironed that morning whose top two buttons were undone. Her hair was now parted in the middle, and at a stroke she was turned into a young beauty : yes, already, there she was.

And, as if in acknowledgement of this step forward into vulnerability, now her worst, or best, comments were for the boys who went past : this one's way of walking which she knew represented an uncertainty about himself; that one's flashy way of dressing : the other one's bad skin, or unkempt hair. These unattractive grubs represented a force, an imperative which there was no way of evading, and like a girl on a too high swing she was shrieking in thrilled terror.

She was dreadful in her accuracy. She depressed me – oh, for many reasons; my own past being one of them. Yet she did not suspect this, she really did believe – so the bright manner, her confident glances at me said – that she was, as usual, 'paying her way'; and this time by her perspicacity. She simply could not let anyone pass without swallowing them, and regurgitating them covered in her slime : the clever child, the one who could not be deceived, who could not have anything put over on her : who had been applauded for being like this, had been taught it.

And yet I came into the room once and saw her talking through the window with Janet White : she was earnest, warm, apparently sincere. If she did not like Janet White, she intended Janet White to like her. Infinite promises were made by both girls on the lines of joint forays into the markets, visits, a walk. And when Janet went off, smiling because of the warmth she had absorbed from Emily, Emily said : 'She's heard her parents talking about me, and now she'll report back.' True enough, of course.

The point was that there wasn't anybody who came near her, into her line of sight, who was not experienced by her as a threat. This *was* how her experience, whatever that had been, had 'set' her. I found I was trying to put myself in her place, tried to be her, to understand how it was that people must pass and repass sharply outlined by her need to criticise – to defend; and found I was thinking that this was only what everyone did, what I did, but there was something in her which enlarged the tendency, had set it forth, exaggerated. For of course, when someone new approaches us, we are all caution; we take that person's measure; a thousand incredibly rapid measurements and assessments go on, putting him, her, in an exact place, to end in the silent judgement : yes, this one's for me; no, we have nothing in common; no, he, she, is a threat . . . watch out! Danger! And so on. But it was not until Emily heightened it all for me that I realised what a prison we were all in, how impossible it was for any one of us to let a man or a woman or a child come near without the defensive inspection, the rapid, sharp, cold analysis. But the reaction was so fast, such a habit – probably the first ever taught us by our parents – that we did not realise how much we were in its grip.

'Look how she walks,' Emily would say, 'look at that fat old woman.' (The woman, of course, was about forty-five or fifty; she might even be thirty!) 'When she was young, people said she had a sexy walk – "Oh what a sexy little wriggle you have there, ooh you sexy thing you!" ' And her parody was horrible because of its accuracy : the woman, the wife of a former stockbroker who had become a junk-dealer, and who lived on the floor above, was given to a hundred little winsome tricks of mouth and eyes and hips. This is what Emily saw of her : it was what everybody must see first of her; and on these tricks she was likely to be judged, by most people. It was impossible not to hear Emily without feeling one's whole being, one's sense of oneself, lowered, drained. It was an assault on one's vitality : listening to her was to acknowledge the limits we all live inside.

I suggested she might like to go to school – 'for something to do', I added hastily, as I saw her quizzical look. This look was not measured : it was her genuine reaction. So I was catching a glimpse of what I had needed for some time : to know what she thought of me, made of me – it was tolerance.

She said, 'But what's the point?'

What was the point? Most schools had given up the attempt

of teaching; they had become, for the poorer people at least, extensions of the army, of the apparatus for keeping the population under control. There were still schools for the children of the privileged class, the administrators and overseers. Janet White went to one of them. But I thought too much of Emily to offer to send her to one, even if I was able to get a place for her. It was not that the education there was bad. It was irrelevant. It merited – a quizzical look.

'Not much point, I agree. And I suppose we won't be here long, anyway.'

'Where do you think you'll go then?'

This broke my heart: her forlorn isolation had never shown itself so sharply; she had spoken tentatively, even delicately, as if she had no right to ask, as if she had no right to my care, my protection – no share in my future.

Because of my emotion, I was more definite about my plans than I felt. I had, in fact, often wondered if a certain family I had known in north Wales would shelter me. They were good farming folk – yes, that is exactly the measure of my fantasies about them. 'Good farming folk' was how safety, refuge, peace, – utopia – shaped itself in very many people's minds in those days. But I did know Mary and George Dolgelly, had been familiar with their farm, had visited their guesthouse, open through the summers. If I made my way there, I might perhaps live there for a while? I was handy, liked to live simply, was as much at home out of cities as in them .. of course, these qualifications belonged these days to large numbers of people, particularly the young, who could increasingly turn their hands to any job that needed doing. I did not imagine the Dolgellys would find me a prize. But at least they would not, I believed, find me a burden. And a child? Or rather a young girl? An attractive, challenging girl? Well, they had children of their own ... you can see that my thoughts had been pretty conventional, not very inventive. I talked to Emily, on these lines, while she listened, her sour little smile slowly giving way to amusement. But amusement concealed from politeness: I could not yet bring myself to believe that it was affection. She knew this fantasy for what it was; yet she enjoyed it, as I did. She asked me to describe the farm : I had once spent a week there, camping on a moor, with silvery water in little channels on a purple hillside. I took a can to Mary and George every morning for new milk, buying at the same time a loaf of their homemade bread. An idyll. I developed it, let it gather detail. We would take rooms in the guesthouse, and Emily would 'help with the chickens' – a storybook touch, that. We would eat at the guesthouse table, a long wooden table. There was an old-fashioned stove in a recess. Stews and soups would simmer there, real food, and we would eat as much as we liked . . . no, that was not realistic, but as much as we needed, of real bread, real cheese, fresh vegetables, perhaps even, sometimes, a little good meat. There would be the smell of herbs from the bunches hanging to dry. The girl listened to all this, and I could not keep my eyes off her face, where the knowing sharp little smile alternated with her need to shield *me* from my inexperience, my sheltered condition! Stronger than anything else, was something she was quite unconscious of, would certainly destroy all evidence of if she knew she was betraying weakness. Stronger than the tricks, the need to please and to buy, the painful obedience, was this : a hunger, a need, a pure thing, which made her face lose its hard brightness, her eyes their defensiveness. She was a passion of longing. For what? Well, that is not so easy, it never is! But I recognised it, knew it, and talk of the farm in the Welsh hills did as well as anything to bring it out, to make it shine there : good bread, uncontaminated water from a deep well, fresh vegetables; love, kindness, the deep shelter of a family. And so we talked about the farm, our future, hers and mine, like a fable where we would walk hand in hand, together. And then 'life' would begin, life as it ought to be, as it had been promised – by whom? When? Where? – to everybody on this earth.

This idyllic time – of not more than a few days, in fact – came abruptly to an end. One warm afternoon I looked out and saw under the plane trees of the opposite pavement about sixty young people, and recognised them as a pack of travellers on their way through the city. This recognition was not always easy, unless there were as many as this, for if you saw two or three or four of such a troop separated from the others, you might think they were students who still – though there weren't many of them – were to be seen in our city. Or they could be the sons and daughters of ordinary people. Seen together, they were instantly unmistakable. Why? No, not only that a mass of young people in these days could mean nothing else. They had relinquished individuality, that was the point, individual judgement and responsibility, and this showed in a hundred ways, not least by one's instinctive reaction in an encounter with them, which was always a sharp apprehension, for one knew that in a confrontation – if it came to that – there would be a pack judgement. They could not stand being alone for long; the mass was their home, their place of self-recognition. They were like dogs coming together in a park or a waste place. The sweet doggie belonging to the matron (her smart voluminous coiffure a defence against the fear visible in her pet, whose coat is an old lady's thin curls showing the aged pink scalp but sheltered by a home-knitted scarlet wool coat); the great Afghan, made to range forty miles a day without feeling it, shut it into his little house, his little garden; the mongrel, bred from survivors; the spaniel, by nature a hunting dog – all these dear family companions, Togo and Bonzo and Fluff and Wolf, having sniffed each other's bums and established precedence, off they go, a pack, a unit ... this description is true of course of any group of people of any age anywhere, if their roles are not already defined for them in an institution. The gangs of 'kids' were only showing the way to their elders, who soon copied them; a 'pack of youngsters' nearly always, and increasingly, included older people, even families, but the label remained. That is how people spoke of the moving hordes – this last word at least was accurate before the end, when it seemed as if a whole population was on the move.

On this afternoon, with the trees above them heavy and full, the sun making a festival – it was September, and still warm –

the pack settled down on the pavement, building a big fire and arranging their possessions in a heap with a guard stationed by it : two young boys armed with heavy sticks. The whole area had emptied, as always happened. The police were not to be seen; the authorities could not cope with this problem and did not want to : they were happy to be rid of these gangs who were in the process of taking elsewhere the problems they raised. Every ground-floor window for miles around was closed and the curtains drawn, but faces could be seen packing all the higher windows of the blocks around us. The young people stood around the fire in groups, and some couples had their arms around each other. A girl played a guitar. The smell of roasting meat was strong, and no one liked to think too much about it. I wondered if Hugo was safe. I had not become fond of this animal, but I was worried for Emily's sake. Then I realised she was not in the living-room or the kitchen. I knocked on her bedroom door, and opened it : the piled stuffy nest of bedclothes she crept into for shelter against the world was there, but she was not, and Hugo was not. I remembered that in the mass of young people was a young girl in tight jeans and a pink shirt who was like Emily. But it had been Emily, and now, from the window, I watched her. She stood near the fire, a bottle in her hand, laughing, one of the gang, the crowd, the team, the pack. Standing close against her legs, fearful for himself, was the yellow animal : he had been hidden by the press of the crowd. I saw she was shouting, arguing. She retreated, her hand on Hugo's head. Slowly she backed away, and then turned and ran, the animal bounding beside her : to see him thus even momentarily was a painful reminder of his power, his capacity, his range, now feebled by the little rooms that held his life and his movements. A great shout of raucous laughter went up from the young people; and from this it was evident they had been teasing her about Hugo. They had not really intended to kill him; they had been pretending that they would; she had believed them. All this meant they had not considered her as one of themselves, even potentially. Yet there were children as young as she among them. She had not challenged them as a child, no; but as a young girl, an equal –

34

that must have been it, and they had not accepted her. All this came into my mind, had been reasoned out by me, by the time she came into the living-room, white, trembling, terrified. She sat down on the floor and put her arms around her Hugo, and hugged him close, swaying a little, back and forth, saying, or singing, or sobbing: 'Oh no, no, no, dear Hugo, I wouldn't, I couldn't, I wouldn't let them, don't be so frightened.' For he trembled as much as she did. He had his head on her shoulder, in their usual way of mutual comfort at such times.

But, in a moment, seeing I was there and that I had understood her rejection by the adult group she had challenged, she went red, she became angry. She pushed Hugo away and stood up, her face struggling for control. She became smiling and hard, and she laughed and said: 'They are quite fun really, I don't see why people say such nasty things about them.' She went to the window to watch them out there lifting the bottles to their mouths, passing around hunks of food as they shared their meal. Emily was subdued: perhaps she was even afraid, wondering how she could have gone out to them at all. Yet every one of us, the hundreds of people at our windows, knew that, watching them, we were examining our own possibilities, our future.

Soon, without looking at me, Emily pushed Hugo into her bedroom and shut the door, and she was off out of the flat and across the road again. Now the light of the fire made a tight bright space under the singeing trees. All the lower windows were dark but reflected the blaze or a cold gleam of light from a half-moon that stood between two towers of flats. The upper windows were full of heads outlined against varying kinds and degrees of light. But some of the ordinary citizens had already joined the young people, curious to find out where they had come from, where they were going; Emily was not the only one. I must confess that I had more than once visited an encampment for an evening. Not in this part of the town: no, I was fearful of my neighbours, of their condemnation, but I had seen faces I knew from my own neighbourhood: we were all doing the same, from the same calculation.

I was not fearful for what might happen to Emily if she

behaved sensibly. If she did not then I planned to cross the street and rescue her. I watched all night. Sometimes I was able to see her, sometimes not. Most of the time she was with a group of boys younger than the rest. She was the only girl, and she did behave foolishly, challenging them, asserting herself. But they were all drunk, and she was only one of the many ingredients of their intoxication.

There were people lying asleep on the pavement, their heads on a bundled sweater or on their forearms. They slept uncaring while the others milled about. This careless sleep, confident that the others would not tread on them, that they would be protected, said more than anything could about the kind of toughness these youngsters had acquired, the trust they had for each other. But general sleep was not what had been planned. The fire had died down. It would soon be morning. I saw that they were all gathering to move on. I had a bad half hour, wondering if Emily would leave with them. But after some embraces, loud and ribald, like the embraces and the jesting of tarts and soldiers when a regiment is moving off, and after she had run along beside them on the pavement for a few yards, she came slowly back – no, not to me, I knew better than to think that, but to Hugo. As she came in her face was visible for a moment in the light from the corridor, a lonely sorrowful face, and not at all the face of a child. But by the time she had reached the living-room the mask was on. 'That was a nice evening, say what you like,' she remarked. I had not said anything, and I said nothing now. 'Apart from eating people, they are very nice, I think,' she said, with an exaggerated yawn. 'And do they eat people?' 'Well, I didn't ask, but I'd expect so, wouldn't you?' She opened the door to her little room, and Hugo came out, his green eyes watchful on her face, and she said to him : 'It's all right, I haven't done anything you wouldn't have done, I promise you.' And with this unhappy remark, and a hard little laugh, she went off, saying over her shoulder : 'I could do worse than go off with them one of these days, that's what I think. They enjoy themselves, at least.'

Well, I preferred that good night to many others we had

exchanged when at ten o'clock she would cry, 'Oh, it's my bedtime, off I go' – and a dutiful good night kiss hung between us, a ghost, like the invisible white gloves of Professor White.

It happened that during that early autumn, day after day, fresh gangs came through. And, day after day, Emily was with them. She did not ask if she could. And I wasn't going to forbid her, for I knew she would not obey me. I had no authority. She was not my child. We avoided a confrontation. She was there whenever the pavements opposite were crowded and the fire blazing. On two occasions she was very drunk, and once she had a torn shirt and bite marks on her neck. She said : 'I suppose you think I've lost my virginity? Well, I haven't, though it was a close thing, I grant you.' And then the cold little addition, her signature, 'If it matters, which I doubt.'

'I think it matters,' I said.

'Oh, do you? Well, you are an optimist, I suppose. Something of that kind. What do you think, Hugo?'

That sequence of travelling gangs came to an end. The pavements up and down the street were blackened and cracked with the fires that had been blazing there for so many nights, the leaves of the plane trees hung limp and blasted, bones and bits of fur and broken glass lay everywhere, the waste lot behind was trampled and filthy. Now the police materialised, were busy taking notes and interviewing people. The cleaners came around. The pavements went back to normal. Everything went back to normal for a time, and the ground floor windows had lights in them at night.

It was about then I understood that the events on the pavements and what went on between me and Emily might have a connection with what I saw on my visits behind the wall.

Moving through the tall quiet white walls, as impermanent as theatre sets, knowing that the real inhabitant was there, always there just behind the next wall, to be glimpsed on the opening of the next door or the one beyond that, I came on a room, long, deep-ceilinged, once a beautiful room, which I recognised, which I knew (from where, though?) and it was in such disorder I felt sick and I was afraid. The place looked as if savages had been in it; as if soldiers had bivouacked there. The chairs and sofas had been deliberately slashed and jabbed with bayonets or knives, stuffing was spewing out everywhere, brocade curtains had been ripped off the brass rods and left in heaps. The room might have been used as a butcher's shop : there were feathers, blood, bits of offal. I began cleaning it. I laboured, used many buckets of hot water, scrubbed, mended. I opened tall windows to an eighteenth century garden where plants grew in patterns of squares among low hedges. Sun and wind were invited into that room and cleaned it. I was by myself all the time; yet did not feel myself to be. Then it was done. The old sofas and chairs stood there repaired and clean. The curtains were stacked for the cleaners. I walked around in it for a long time, for it was a room large enough for pacing; and I stood at the windows, seeing hollyhocks and damask roses, smelling lavender, roses, rosemary, verbena, conscious of memories assaulting me, claiming, insinuating. One was from my 'real' life, for it was nagging and tugging at me that the pavements where the fires had burned and the trees had scorched were part of the stuff and the substance of this room. But there was the tug of nostalgia for the room itself, the life that had been lived there, would continue the moment I had left. And for the garden, whose every little turn or corner I knew in my bones. Above all, for the inhabitant who was somewhere near, probably watching me; who, when I had left, would walk in and nod approval at the work of cleaning I had done and then perhaps go out to walk in the garden.

What I found next was in a very different setting : above all, in a different atmosphere. It was the first of the 'personal' experiences. This was the word I used for them from the start. And the atmosphere was unmistakable always, as soon as I entered whatever scene it was. That is, between the feeling or texture or mood of the scenes which were not 'personal', like, for instance, the long quiet room that had been so devastated, or any of the events, no matter how wearying or difficult or discouraging, that I saw in this or that setting – between these and the 'personal' scenes a world lay; the two kinds 'personal' (though not necessarily, to me) and the other, existed in spheres quite different and separated. One, the 'personal' was instantly to be recognised by the air that was its prison, by the emotions that were its creatures. The impersonal scenes might bring discouragement or problems that had to be solved, like the rehabilitation of walls or furniture, cleaning, putting order into chaos – but in that realm there was a lightness, a freedom, a feeling of possibility. Yes, that was it, the space and the knowledge of the possibility of alternative action. One could refuse to clean that room, clear that patch of earth; one could walk into another room altogether, choose another scene. But to enter the 'personal' was to enter a prison, where nothing could happen but what one saw happening, where the air was tight and limited, and above all where time was a strict unalterable law and long, oh my God, it went on, and on and on, minute by decreed minute, with no escape but the slow wearing away of one after another.

It was again a tall room, but this time square and without grace, and there were tall but heavy windows, with dark red velvet curtains. A fire burned, and in front of it was a strong fireguard, like a wire meat cover. On this were airing a great many thick or flimsy napkins, baby's napkins of the old-fashioned sort, and many white vests and binders, long and short dresses, robes, jackets, little socks. An Edwardian layette, emitting that odour which is not quite scorch, but near to it : heated airless materials. There was a rocking horse. Alphabet books. A cradle with muslin flounces, minute blue and green flowers on white . . . I realised what a relief the colour was, for everything was white, white clothing, white cot and cradle and covers and blankets and sheets and baskets. A white-painted room. A little white clock that would have been described in a catalogue as a Nursery Clock. White. The clock's tick was soft and little and incessant.

A small girl of about four sat on a hearthrug, with the clothing that was set to air between her and the flames. She wore a dark blue velvet dress. She had dark hair parted on one side and held by a large white ribbon. She had intensely serious, already defensive hazel eyes.

On the bed was a baby, being bundled for the night. The

baby was chuckling. A nurse or attendant hung over the baby; but only a broad white back was visible. The little girl's look as she watched the loving nurse bending over the brother was enough, it said everything. But there was more : another figure, immensely tall, large and powerful came into the room; it was a personage all ruthless energy, and she too, bent over the baby, and the two females joined in a ceremony of loving while the baby wriggled and responded and cooed. And the little girl watched. Everything around her was enormous : the room so large, warm and high, the two women so tall and strong and disliking, the furniture daunting and difficult, the clock with its soft hurrying which told everyone what to do, was obeyed by everyone, consulted, constantly watched.

Being invited into this scene was to be absorbed into child-space; I saw it as a small child might – that is, enormous and implacable; but at the same time I kept with me my knowledge that it was tiny and implacable – because petty, unimportant. This was a tyranny of the unimportant, of the mindless. Claustrophobia, airlessness, a suffocation of the mind, of aspiration. And all endless, for this was child-time, where one day's end could hardly be glimpsed from its beginning, ordered by the hard white clock. Each day was like something to be climbed, like the great obdurate chairs, a bed higher than one's head, obstacles and challenges overcome by the aid of large hands that gripped and pulled and pushed – hands which, seen at work on that baby, seemed to be tender and considerate. The baby was high in the air, held up in the nurse's arms. The baby was laughing. The mother wanted to take the baby from the nurse, but the nurse held tight and said : 'Oh no, this one, this is *my* baby, he's my baby.' 'Oh no, Nurse,' said the strong tower of a mother, taller than anything in the room, taller than the big nurse, almost as high as the ceiling : 'Oh no,' she said, smiling but with her lips tight, 'he's *my* baby.' 'No, this is my baby,' said the nurse now rocking and crooning the infant, 'he's my darling baby, but the other one, she's your baby, Emily is yours, madam.' And she turned her back on the mother in a show of emotional independence, while she loved and rocked the baby. At which the mother smiled, a smile different from the other, and not understood by the little girl, except that it led to her being pulled up roughly on the mother's hand, and told : 'Why aren't you undressed? I told you to get undressed.' And there began a rapid uncomfortable scrambling and pushing; she was trying to remain steady on her feet, while layers of clothes were pulled off her. First the blue velvet dress of which she was proud, because it suited her – she had been told so by voices of all kinds insisting against each other high over her head, but it had many little buttons up the inside of her arm and down her back, each one taking so long to undo while the big fingers hurt and bruised. Then off came the petticoat, quite fast but scratching at her chin, then long white tights too big for her which released a warm likeable smell into the air : the mother noticed it and made a grimace. 'And now into bed with you,' she said as she hastily pulled down a white nightdress over the child's head.

Emily crept into her bed near the window, hauling herself up by the head-rail, for to her it was a big bed; and she lifted a corner of the heavy red velvet to look out at the stars. At the same time she watched the two large people, the mother and the nurse, tending the baby. Her face was old and weary. She seemed to understand it all, to have foreseen it, to be living through it because she had to, feeling it as a thick heaviness all around her – time, through which she must push herself, till she could be free of it. For none of them could help themselves, not the mother, that feared and powerful woman, not the nurse, bad-tempered because of her life, not the baby, for whom she, the little girl, already felt a passion of love that melted her, made her helpless. And she, the child, could not help herself either, not at all; and when the mother said in her impatient rough way, which came out as a sort of gaiety, a courage that even then the child recognised as a demand on her compassion : 'Emily, you should lie down. Off to sleep with you,' she lay down; and watched the two women taking the baby into another room from where could be heard a man's voice, the father's. A ceremony of good night, and she was excluded : they had forgotten she had not been taken to say good night to her father. She turned herself over, back to the hot white room, where the red flames pulsed out heat, filled the heavy white clothes on the bars with hot smells, made red shadows in the caves behind the edges of the red curtains, made a prickling heat start up all over her under the heavy bedclothes. She took hold of the dangling red tassels on the curtains, brought them close to her, and lay pulling them, pulling them. . . .

This small child was of course the Emily who had been given into my care, but I did not understand for some days that I had been watching a scene from her childhood, (but that was impossible, of course, since no such childhood existed these days, it was obsolete), a scene, then, from her memory, or her history, which had formed her. . . . I was sitting with her one morning, and some movement she made told me what should have been obvious. Then I kept glancing at that young face, such a troubling mixture of the child and the young girl, and could see in it her solitary four-year-old self. Emily. I wondered if she remembered anything of her memories, or experiences, that were being 'run' like a film behind my living-room wall, which at the moment – the sun lighting a slant of air and the white paint where the flowery pattern of the paper maintained its frail but stubborn being – was a transparent screen : this was one of the moments when the two worlds were close together, when it was easy to remember that it was possible simply to walk through. I sat and looked at the wall, and fancied I heard sounds that certainly were not part of 'my' world at all : a poker being energetically used in a grate, small feet running, a child's voice.

I wondered if I should say something to Emily, ask her questions? But I did not dare, that was the truth. I was afraid of her. It was my helplessness with her I feared.

She was wearing her old jeans that were much too tight for her, a bulging little pink shirt.

'You ought to have some new clothes,' I said.

'Why? Don't you think I look nice, then?' The awful 'brightness' of it; but there was dismay as well . . . she had gathered herself together, ready to withstand criticism.

'You look very nice. But you've grown out of those clothes.'

'Oh dear, I didn't realise it was as bad as that.'

And she took herself away from me and lay on the long brown sofa with Hugo beside her. She was not actually sucking her thumb, but she might just as well have been.

I ought to describe her attitude to me? But it is difficult. I don't think she often saw me. When brought to me first by that man, whoever he was, she saw an elderly person, saw me very clearly, sharp, minutely, in detail. But since then I don't think she had for one moment, not in all the weeks she had been with me, seen more than an elderly person, with the characteristics to be expected of one. She had no idea of course of the terror I felt on her account, the anxiety, the need to protect. She did not know that the care of her had filled my life, water soaking a sponge . . . but did I have the right to complain? Had I not, like all the other adults, talked of 'the youth', 'the youngsters', 'the kids' and so on. Did I not still, unless I made an effort not to? Besides, there is little excuse for the elderly to push the young away from them into compartments of their minds labelled : 'This I do not understand,' or 'This I will not understand' – for every one of them has been young . . . should I be ashamed of writing this commonplace when so few middleaged and elderly people are able to vivify it by practice? When so few are able to acknowledge their memories? The old have been young; the young have never been old . . . these remarks or some like them have been in a thousand diaries, books of moral precepts, commonplace books, proverbs and so on, and what difference have they made? Well, I would say not very much . . . Emily saw some dry, controlled, distant old person. I frightened her, representing to her that unimaginable thing, old age. But for my part, she, her condition, was as close to me as my own memories.

When she went to lie on the sofa, her back to me, she was sulking. She was making use of me to check her impulse to step forward away from childhood into being a girl, a young girl with clothes and mannerisms and words regulated precisely to that condition.

Her conflict was great, and so her use of me was inordinate and tiresome, and it all went on for some weeks, while she complained that I criticised her appearance, and it was my fault she was going to have to spend money on clothes, and that she did or did not like how she looked – that she did not want to wear nothing but trousers and shirts and sweaters for the whole of her life, and wanted 'something decent to wear at last'; but that since my generation had made such a mess of everything, hers had nothing interesting to wear, people her age were left with ancient fashion magazines and dreams of the delicious and dead past . . . and so it went on, and on.

And now it wasn't only that she was older and her body showing it: she was putting on weight. She would lie all day on the sofa with her yellow dog-like cat, or cat-like dog, she would lie hugging him and petting him and stroking him, she would suck sweets and eat bread and jam and fondle the animal and daydream. Or she sat at the window making her sharp little comments, eating. Or she would supply herself with stacks of bread and jam, cake, apples, and arrange a scene in the middle of the floor with old books and magazines, lying face down with Hugo sprawled across the back of her thighs: there she would read and dream and eat her way through a whole morning, a whole day, days at a time.

It drove me quite wild with irritation: yet I could remember doing it myself.

Suddenly she would leap up and go to the mirror and cry out: 'Oh, dear, I'll be getting so fat you'll think I'm even more ugly than you do now!' Or: 'I won't be able to get into any clothes even when you do let me buy some new ones, I know you don't really want me to have new ones, you just say so, you think I'm being frivolous and heartless, when so many people can't even eat.'

I could only reiterate that I would be delighted if she bought herself some clothes. She could go to the secondhand markets and shops, as most people did. Or, if she liked, she could go to the real shops – just this once. For buying clothes or materials in the shops was by that time a status symbol; the shops were really used only by the administrating class, by – as most people called them, The Talkers. I knew she was attracted by the idea of actually going to a real shop. But she ignored the money I had left in a drawer for her, and went on eating and dreaming.

I was out a good deal, busy on that common occupation, gathering news. For while I had, like everyone else, a radio, while I was a member of a newspaper circle – shortage of newsprint made it necessary for groups of people to buy newspapers and journals in common and circulate them – I, like everyone else, looked for news, real news, where people congregated in the streets, in bars and pubs and teahouses. All over the city were these groups of people, moving from one place to another, pub to teahouse to bar to outside the shops that still sold television. These groups were like an additional organ burgeoning on the official organs of news : all the time new groups, or couples, or individuals added themselves to a scene, stood listening, mingling, offering what they themselves had heard – news having become a sort of currency – giving in exchange for rumour and gossip, gossip and rumour. Then we moved on, and stopped; moved on and stopped again, as if movement itself could allay the permanent unease we all felt. News gathered in this way was often common talk days or even weeks before it was given official life in the newscasts. Of course it was often inaccurate. But then all news is inaccurate. What people were trying to do, in their continual moving about and around, nosing out news, taking in information, was to isolate residues of truth in rumour, for there was nearly always that. We felt we had to have this precious residue : it was our due, our right. Having it made us feel safer and gave us identity. Not getting it, or enough of it, deprived us, made us anxious.

This is how we saw it then. Now I think something different : that what we were doing was talking. We talked. Just like those people above us who spent their lives in their eternal and interminable conferences, talking about what was happening, what should happen, what they fondly hoped they could make happen – but of course never did – we talked. We called them The Talkers . . . and ourselves spent hours of every day talking and listening to talk.

Mostly, of course, we wanted to know what was happening in the territories to the east and to the south – referred to as 'out there' or 'down there' – because we knew that what happened there would sooner or later affect us. We had to know

45

what gangs were approaching, or rumoured to be approaching – gangs which, as I've said, were not all 'kids' and 'youngsters' now, were made up of every kind and age of person, were more and more tribes, were the new social unit; we had to know what shortages were expected or might be abating; if another suburb had decided entirely to turn its back on gas, electricity and oil and revert to candle power and ingenuity; if a new rubbish dump had been found, and if so, could ordinary people get access to its riches; where there were shops that might have hides or old blankets or rose hips for vitamin syrups, or recycled plastic objects, or metal things like sieves and sauce-pans, or whatever it was, whatever might be cast up from the dead time of plenty.

Of course, such contriving and patching and making do began to parallel our ordinary living, our affluence and waste and overeating, at a very early stage, long before the time of which I am writing now. We were all experts at making a great deal out of very little, even while we all still had a lot, and were still being incited by advertisements to spend and use and discard.

Sometimes I left Emily – fearful, of course, for what might happen in my absence, but thinking the risk worth it – to make trips a good way out from the city, to villages, farms, other towns. These might take two or three days, since the trains and buses were so infrequent and unreliable, and the cars, nearly all of them used by officialdom, so reluctant to offer lifts be-cause of the fear of ordinary people felt by the official class. I walked, having rediscovered the uses of my feet, like most people.

One day I returned to the flat and to Emily with half a dozen sheepskins. Other things as well, which I put away in cupboards and hiding places with supplies of all kinds for future and still only partly imagined contingencies, but it was the skins that were important, since they started her off on a new phase of her development. At first she pretended to ignore them. Then I saw her standing in front of a long mirror I had in the hall, or lobby, and she was pinning them on her. She seemed to be aiming at a savage-princess effect, but as soon as she knew I had noticed and was interested, she returned to her place on the sofa with Hugo, returned to her daydream which excluded the time we were in fact living through. Yet I believe she was intrigued by the business of survival, its resources and tricks and little contrivances. I remember that it was at that time she took pleasure in creating a dish of dumplings and gravy, using nothing but some old onions, withering potatoes and herbs, presenting it with a flourish like a chef's. She liked the markets where she tracked down things I would never have bothered myself with. She enjoyed – what I always found irritating and could not help contrasting with the simplicities and efficiencies of the past – building up the fire to heat water for washing and cooking. She scolded me for being prepared to use stocks of wood I had, and insisted on running out to some deserted building to bring back old skirting boards and suchlike, which she proceeded to split, using an axe skilfully then and there on the carpet, shielding this with old rags from even worse wear than it had suffered already. Yes, she was very handy, and this said everything about her experiences before she had come to me. And she knew I was watching and drawing my conclusions; and this sent her back to the sofa, for her need to be secret, her need not to be understood and found out was stronger, even now, than anything. Yet I was comforted, seeing her skills and her resources, and the heavy load of foreboding I carried about with me because of her future was lightened : how could this heavy, dreaming, erratic child, so absorbed in herself, in fantasy, in the past, survive what we would all have to survive? And I began to realise just how dark a foreboding it was, how I had come to watch and grieve over her, how sharp was my anxiety when she was out in empty buildings and waste lots. 'Why do you think I can't look after myself?' she cried, in a rage of irritation, though of course, being Emily and so instructed in the need to please, to placate, she smiled and tried to hide it : the real irritation, her real emotions, she must hide and dim, while her pretend angers and sulks, the adolescent's necessary play-acting, were on display all the time.

Now I was thankful Hugo was there. He was not a difficult animal (I nearly said person!) to share a home with. He did not seem to sleep much : he kept watch. I believe this was how he saw his function : he was to look after her. He preferred Emily to feed him, but would eat if I put his food down. He wished to be her only friend and love; yet was courteous with me – I am afraid that is the only word for it. He looked forward to his trip out of doors on his heavy chain in the evenings, was disappointed if Emily could not take him, went obligingly with me. He ate the nasty substances that were being sold as dog food, but preferred the remains from our plates and showed that he did.

Not that there was ever much left : Emily ate and ate, and she had taken to wearing her little shirts outside her bursting trousers. She stood glooming at herself in front of the mirror, her jaws moving over sweets or bread. I said nothing; I made a point of saying nothing, even when she challenged me : 'It suits me to be fat, don't you think?' Or : 'I'll make better eating when cooked for the feast.' But whatever she said, however she joked, she ate. She lay on the floor, her hand automatically conveying bread, more bread, cake, potato mixtures, fruit dumplings, to her mouth, while her eyes followed the lines of print in some old book she had picked up but would soon let drop while she stared in front of her, her eyes glazed. Hour after hour. Day after day. Sometimes she would jump up to make herself some beverage or other, and offer me a cup, then she forgot me. Her mouth was always in movement, chewing, tasting, absorbed in itself, so that she seemed all mouth, and everything else in her was subordinated to that; it seemed as if even the intake of words through her eyes was another form of eating, and her day-dreaming a consumption of material, which was bloating her as much as her food.

And, then, suddenly, it all went into reverse. Of course it did not seem sudden at the time. It is now, looking back, that it is all so obvious : even, I am afraid, banal and mechanical, as the inevitable does seem – in retrospect.

Some youths from our blocks of flats took to hanging about on the opposite pavement and the waste lot, under the scorched trees. These youths were sharing in lost glory and adventure : memories of the time when migrating tribes had lit fires and feasted there. They pointed out to each other the blackened parts of the pavement, told and re-told episodes from the epic. At first there were two or three, then half a dozen, then . . . Emily had forsaken her dreaming to watch them. Not that you could make out from her face anything but scorn of them. I remember I felt pity for the raucous adolescent boys, so desperately wanting to be noticed and looked at, who were so forlorn and unappetising in their lumpish bodies; pity for her, the fat girl looking out of her window, the princess in disguise. I marvelled that such a short time, a few years, would transform these grubs into beauties. But I was wrong : time had so speeded up that years were not needed any longer . . . one evening Emily sauntered out and stood in front of the building with a look like a jeer, while her body pleaded and demanded. The boys ignored her. Then they made some comments about her figure. She came indoors, sat thoughtfully in her sofa corner for some hours – and stopped eating.

She lost weight fast. She was living on herb teas and yeast extracts. And now I watched the reverse process, a shape emerging whole and clear while increments of lard melted away around it.

I began to remonstrate : you must eat something, you should set yourself a proper diet. But she did not hear me. I was distant from her need to make herself worthy of the heroes of the pavement . . . quite a few of them now that the days were lengthening and spring healed the scarred trees.

We were watching, though I still did not recognise this, the birth of a gang, a pack, a tribe. It would be pleasant to be able to say now that I was aware of the processes going on in front of me. Now I judge myself to have been blind. How else do things work always unless by imitation bred of the passion to be like? All the processes of society are based on it, all individual development. For some reason it was something that we seemed to have a conspiracy to ignore or not to mention, even while most singlemindedly engaged in it. There was some sort of conspiracy of belief that people – children, adults, everyone – grew by an acquisition of unconnected habits, of isolated bits of knowledge, like choosing things off a counter : 'Yes, I'll have that one,' or 'No, I don't want that one!' But in fact people develop for good or for bad by swallowing whole other people, atmospheres, events, places – develop by admiration. Often enough unconsciously, of course. We are the company we keep.

In front of my eyes, on that pavement, for weeks, for months, I could have watched as in a textbook or a laboratory, the genesis, growth and flowering of society's new unit. But I did no such thing, for I was absorbed in Emily, my concern for her. Those processes went on, and I observed them; details did stand out for me; I watched for the effects of this or that event on Emily. It is only now, looking back, I see what an opportunity I missed.

Emily was not the only young girl preparing herself to take her place as a woman among other women. Janet White, for instance: before her parents stopped her, Janet passed a dozen times a day outside our windows in front of the jeering boys. There was a period when boys and girls, on opposite sides of the road, stood in hostile battalions exchanging taunts and abuse.

Then it was noticeable that they jeered less, stood more often in silence, or quietly talked among themselves, though always watching the other groups while pretending not to.

Inside the flat Emily remembered the sheepskins. Again she arranged them around her, belted them tight, swaggered about in them with her hair loose.

She came to me: 'I found that sewing machine. Can I use it?'

'Of course. But don't you want to buy clothes? That thing is so old. It must be thirty-five years old.'

'It works.'

The money I had given her was still in the drawer. This she now took out and quickly, almost secretively, walked the five or six miles to the centre of the city where the big shops were with the goods for the official class, or for anyone who could afford them. Nearly always the same thing. She came back with some good cloth from the pre-crisis time. She came back with sewing cottons and a tape measure and scissors. She also visited the secondhand shops and the market stalls, and the

floor of her room was heaped with loot, with booty. She invited
Janet White in from the pavement, having of course first
politely asked my permission, and the two nymphs squeezed
themselves into the tiny room, and chattered and competed,
and arranged their images this way and that way before the
long mirror – a ritual which was repeated when Janet White
in her turn went off on her foray to capture materials and old
clothes . . . repeated in Janet's room along the corridor. And
this led to her being forbidden the street and the pleasures of
the tribe and warned not to take Emily for a friend. For Janet
was destined differently. To tell the truth I did not realise how
high the Whites were placed in the administrative circles; but
then, they were not the only official family to half-hide themselves in this way, living quietly, in an ordinary flat, apparently
like everyone else but with access to sources of food, goods,
clothes, transport, denied to most.

Emily did not seem to mind Janet discarding her. There
followed a period of weeks when she was every bit as self-
absorbed as when she had been eating, dreaming, indolent, but
now she was full of energy and self-denial, at least for food,
and I watched. I watched endlessly, for I had never seen anything like this for concentration.

For if she, Emily, had gone inwards, as much now in this
new activity as she had when lazy and dreaming, at least now
what she felt herself to be was all visible, presented to me in
the shape of her fantastic costumes.

Her first self-portrait . . . she had found an old dress, white
with sprigs of pink flowers. Parts were stained and worn. These
she cut away. Bits of lace and tulle, beads, scarves, were added
and removed to a kaleidoscope garment that changed with
her needs. Most often it was a bride's dress. Then it was a young
girl's dress – that ambiguous declaration of naiveté more usually
made by a maturer vision than that of the wearer, an eye that
sees the fragility of certain types of young girls' clothes as the
expression of the evanescence of that flesh. It was nightdress
when she wore its transparency over her naked body. It was
evening dress, and sometimes when she did not intend this, for
a hardness in her, the watchfulness of her defences, took away

innocence from anything she wore, so that she might have flowers in her hands and in her hair, in an attempt at her version of Primavera, yet she had about her the look of a woman who has calculated the exact amount of flesh she will show at a dinner party. This dress was for me an emotional experience. I was frightened by it. Again, this was a question of my helplessness with her. I believed her capable of going out on the pavement wearing it. Now I judge myself to have been stupid : the elderly tend not to see – they have forgotten! – that hidden person in the young creature, the strongest and most powerful member among the cast of characters inhabiting an adolescent body, the self which instructs, chooses experience – and protects.

And then, to see this creation now, at such a time of savagery and anarchy, this archetype of a girl's dress – or rather, this composite of archetypes; the way this child, this little girl, had found the materials for her dreams in the rubbish heaps of our old civilisation, had found them, worked on them, and in spite of everything had made her images of herself come to life ... but such old images, so indestructible, and so *irrelevant* – all this was too much for me, and I retired from the scene, determined to say nothing, show nothing, betray nothing. And it was lucky I did. She wore the thing about the flat, a naked girl only just veiled; she wore it flauntingly, bashfully, daringly, fearfully; she was 'trying on' not a dress, but self-portraits, and I might as well not have been there, she took no notice of me. Well, of course, the pressures on everyone's privacy had taught us how to absent ourselves into inner solitudes, we were all adept at being with others and not being with them.

But I really did not know whether to laugh or to cry; I did a little of both, of course when she could not see me. For she was so ludicrous, as well as so brave and resourceful, with her straight, honest, hazel eyes – her English good-comrade's eyes, unsubtle, judging, wary; with her attempts at make-up on a fresh little face, languishing away there behind harem veils, her body stiff in 'seductive' poses. This dress possessed her for weeks. Then one day she took scissors and cut off the bottom in a gesture of derisive impatience : something had not worked, or had worked for her and it was all over, not needed. She threw the jaded bundle into a drawer and began on a new invention of herself.

There was a late, and prolonged, cold spell. There was even a little snow. In my flat warmth was a much-coaxed visitor, and like everyone else we were wearing almost as many clothes indoors as we did out. Emily took the sheepskins and made a long dramatic tunic. This she belted with some scarlet chiffon, and she wore it over an old shirt she had taken from my cupboard. Without asking. I cannot say how delighted I was when she did this. It showed she felt she had some rights with me, at last. The child's right to be naughty, for one; but it was more than that: an elderly or a mature person finds some young one simply taking something, a personal thing, particularly if it is a strong expression or statement of a phase of life (as a pink-sprigged white dress is for a young girl) and what a release it is, a shock, cold water on shrinking flesh if you like, but a liberation. *This is more mine than yours* – says the act of the theft; *more mine because I need it more, it fits my stage of life better than it does yours, you have outgrown it . . .* and perhaps the exhilaration it releases is even a hint of an event still in the future, that moment when the person sees in the eyes of people the statement– still unconscious, perhaps: You can hand over your life now, you don't need it any longer, we will live it for you, please go.

The shirt had been among my clothes for thirty years, had once been a sophisticated thing, was of fine green silk. Now it went under Emily's sheepskin swagger, and just as I was wrestling with the need to say: 'For heaven's sake, you can't wear that brigand's outfit out of doors, it is an invitation to assault! – she allowed the contraption to fall apart, for it was only tacked and pinned together, no more permanent than a daydream.

And so we went on. She did not go out of the flat, not in any of her fantasies; and I observed that these were becoming more utilitarian.

Chrysalis after chrysalis was outgrown, and then, because of her shame at having wasted so much, she asked abruptly and gracelessly but in her over-polite and *awful* way for some more money, and went off by herself to the markets. She came back with some secondhand clothes that in one giant's step took her from being a child with fantastic visions of herself into a girl – a woman, rather. She was thirteen then, not yet fourteen; but she might as well have been seventeen or eighteen, and it had happened in an explosion of days. Now I thought that probably the heroes of the pavement would be beneath her; that she, a young woman, would demand what nature would in fact have chosen for her, a young man of seventeen, eighteen, even more.

But the crowd, the pack, the gang – not yet a tribe, but on its way to being one, had suffered forced growth, as she had. A few weeks had done it. While snow had bleached the pavements and heightened the black of tree branches frilled and dangling with new green – had shrunk away and returned again, while Emily had mated herself in imagination with romantic heroes and chief executives and harem tyrants, a dozen or so young men had emerged from their disguises as louts and yokels, and at evening stood around under the trees swaggering in colourful clothes, and the girls of the neighbourhood had come out to join them. Now sometimes as many as thirty or more young people were being watched in the lengthening afternoons of early spring from hundreds of windows. By now it had dawned on the neighbourhood that a phenomenon we had believed could belong only to the regions 'out there' was being born before our eyes, in our own streets, where until now it had seemed that at worst nothing could happen but the passage of some alien migrations.

We heard that the same thing was to be observed in other parts of our city. It was not only on our pavements that the young people were gathering in admiration and then emulation of the migrating tribes; and, while emulating, became. We all knew, we understood, and it was spoken of in the teashops and pubs and at all the usual gathering places : it was discussed, making news, making things happen. We knew that soon our young people would leave; we made the ritual noises of wonder and alarm; but now it was happening everyone knew it had been bound to happen, and we marvelled at our lack of foresight ... and at the shortsightedness of others, whose neighbourhoods were still without this phenomenon and who believed they were immune.

Emily began showing herself off. First from our window; making sure she had been seen, and then on the pavement outside, strolling there as if unaware of the young people across the road. This period took longer than I expected, or than she needed to be accepted. I think, now it came to the point, she was afraid of taking this big step away from shelter, from childhood, from the freedom of fantasy: for now she looked like the other girls and must behave and think like them. And how did they look? Well, the key to the clothes of the migrating ones was of course practicality, it had to be: utility stylised. Trousers, jackets, sweaters and scarves, everything thick and strong and warm. But from the markets, the rubbish dumps, the old warehouses, came what seemed an endless supply of old 'fashionable' clothes that could be adapted or at any rate transformed into bits and pieces of all kinds. So what they looked like was gipsies, of the old sort, and for the same reason. They had to be warm and free to move; their feet would have to carry them long distances. But an exuberancy of fancy kept them colourful, and warm weather brought them out like butterflies.

There came a day when Emily walked across the street and added herself to the crowd there, as if it were quite easy for her to do this. Almost at once she accepted a cigarette from the boy who seemed to be the strongest personality there, allowed it to be lit for her, and smoked with ease. I had never seen her smoke. She was there while the light faded out of the sky around the tall buildings with their little glimmering windows. She was there long afterwards. The young people were a half-visible mass under the branches. They stood talking softly, smoking, drinking from bottles they kept lodged in their jacket pockets; or they sat on the little parapet that surrounded the paving of the nearest blocks of flats. That space of pavements and waste lot, with the trees and the weeds, bounded on one side by the little parapet, on the other by an old wall, had become defined, like an arena or a theatre. The crowds there had claimed it, shaped it: we would not again be able to see that space as anything but where the tribe was forming.

But Hugo was not there. She had hugged him, kissed him, talked to him, whispered into his ugly yellow ears. But she had left him.

He sat on a chair at the window and watched her, making sure that the curtains concealed him.

Coming suddenly into the room a stranger would have to say: 'That's a very yellow dog!' Then: 'Is it a dog, though?' What I saw of him, though Emily never did, for he was turned to face her entrance from the moment she crossed the street to come home, was a straw-yellow dog sitting with its back to the room, absolutely still, hour after hour, its whip-tail sticking out through the bars of the chair, all of him expressing a sad and watchful patience. A dog. A dog's emotions – fidelity, humility, endurance. Seen thus from the back, Hugo aroused the emotions most dogs do: compassion, discomfort, as if for a kind of prisoner or slave. But then he would turn his head and, expecting to see the warm abject lovingness of a dog's eyes, fellow-feeling vanished away: this was no dog, half-humanised. His strong green eyes blazed. Inhuman. Cat's eyes, a genus foreign to man, not sorry and abject and pleading. Cat's eyes in a dog's body – cat's eyes and face. This beast, whose ugliness drew one's eyes as good looks do, so that I was always finding myself staring at him, trying to come to terms with him and understand the right he assumed to be there in my life – this aberration, this freak, kept watch over Emily, and with as much devotion as I did. And it was Hugo who was hugged, caressed, loved when she returned at night smelling of smoke, of drink, and full of the dangerous vitality she had absorbed from the wild company she had been part of for so many hours.

She was with them now every day from early afternoon until midnight and after; and I and the animal would be sitting behind the curtains, peering out at the dark, for there was only the one street lamp, and nothing much could be seen of the crowd milling about out there, except the pallor of faces, little gleams and flashes as cigarettes were lit, nothing heard of their talking together until they laughed, or sang for a while, or when voices rose wildly in a quarrel – and at such times I could feel Hugo trembling and shrinking. But quarrels were soon quelled by general consent, a communal veto.

And when we knew Emily was coming back, both of us, Hugo and myself, would quickly leave our post and go to where we could be believed to be asleep, or at least not spying on her.

———◆———

Throughout this period, whenever I was drawn in through the flowers and leaves submerged under half-transparent white paint, I found rooms disordered or damaged. I never saw who or what did it, or even caught a glimpse of the agent. It was seeming to me more and more that in inheriting this extension of my ordinary life, I had been handed, again, a task. Which I was not able to carry through. For no matter how I swept, picked up and replaced overturned chairs, tables, objects; scrubbed floors and rubbed down walls, whenever I re-entered the rooms after a spell away in my real life all had to be done again. It was like what one reads of a poltergeist's tricks. Already my entrance into that place was with a lowered vitality, a sense of foreboding, instead of the lively and loving anticipation I had felt on first being able to move there . . . I really do have to make it clear here that this feeling of discouragement was not at all like the misery that accompanied the 'personal' scenes; no, even at the worst, the disorder and anarchy of the rooms were nothing like as bad as the shut-in stuffiness of the family, the 'personal'; it was always a liberation to step away from my 'real' life into this other place, so full of possibilities, of alternatives. When I talk of 'lowering' here, I mean only in terms of the generally freer air of this region; I could not compare it with the constrictions and confinements of the place, or the time, where that family lived out its little puppet play.

But what laws, or needs, did the unknown destroyer obey? I would find myself in the long but irregular passage, like a wide hallway that extended itself indefinitely full of doors and little enclaves where a table might stand with flowers or a statue, pictures, objects of all kinds, each with an exact place – and open a door on a room next to it and there everything would be awry. A violent wind would be blowing the curtains straight out into the room, knocking over small tables, sweeping books off the arms of chairs, littering the carpet with ash and cigarette stubs from an ashtray which was wheeling there, ready to topple. Opening another door, everything stood as it ought : there was order, a room not only ready for its occupants, as neat as a hotel bedroom, but one which he, she, they, had just left, for I could feel a personality or presences in a room seen through a half-open door. Which, entering, perhaps only a moment later, I might find in chaos, as if it were a room in a doll's house, and the hand of the little girl had been inserted through the ceiling and knocked everything over on a freak of impulse or bad temper.

I decided that what I had to do was to repaint the rooms ... I talk as if they were a permanent, recognisable, stable set of rooms, as in a house or a flat, instead of a place which changed each time I saw it. First, paint : what was the use of tidying, or cleaning furniture that would have to stand between such forlorn and shabby walls? I found paints. Tins of different sizes and colours stood waiting on spread newspapers on the floor in one of the rooms that was temporarily empty – I had seen it furnished only a few minutes before. There were brushes and bottles of turpentine and the painter's ladder I had seen during one of my early visits here. I started on a room I knew well : it was the drawing-room that had brocade curtains and pink and green silks and old wood. I stacked what was usable in the middle of the room under dust-sheets. I scrubbed down the ceiling and walls with sugar soap, with hot water, with detergents. Layer after layer of white paint went on, first dull and flat, then increasingly fine, until the last one covered everything with a clear softly shining enamel, white as new snow or fine china. It was like standing inside a cleaned-out eggshell; I felt that accretions of grime had been taken off which had been preventing a living thing from breathing. I left the furniture there in the centre of the room under its shrouds, for it seemed too shabby now for such a fine room, and I felt that there seemed little point in setting it out: when I returned the poltergeist would have flung everything about or thrown muck at the walls. But no, it was not so, this did not happen; or I think it did not – for I never saw that room again. And it was not that I looked for it and failed to find it ... would it be accurate to say that I forgot it? That would be to talk of that place in terms of our ordinary living. While I was in that room, the task made sense; there was continuity to what I did, a future, and I was in a continuing relation to the invisible destructive creature, or force, just as I was with the other beneficent presence. But this feeling of relatedness, of connection, of context, belonged to that particular visit to the room, and on the next visit it was not the same room, and my preoccupation with it was altered – and so with the other rooms, other scenes, whose flavours and scents held total authenticity for the time they lasted and not a moment longer.

I have been writing, with no particular reluctance or lack of enjoyment, descriptions of the realm of anarchy, of change, of impermanence; now I must return to the 'personal' and it is with dismay, a not-wanting. . . .

I had approached a door, apprehensive, but also curious to see if I would open it on the poltergeist's work, but instead it was a scene of clean tidiness, a room that oppressed and discouraged because of its statement that here everything had its place and its time, that nothing could change or move out of its order.

The walls were ruthless; the furniture heavy, polished, shining; sofas and chairs were like large people making conversation; the legs of a great table bruised the carpet.

There were people. Real people, not forces, or presences. Dominant among them was a woman, one I had seen before, knew well. She was tall, large, with a clean-china healthiness, all blue eyes, pink cheeks, and the jolly no-nonsense mouth of a schoolgirl. Her hair was brown and there was a great deal of it piled on the top of her head and firmly held there. She was dressed for company; she wore good clothes, expensive, fashionable, and inside them her body seemed to be trying to assert itself – timidly, but with a certain courage, even gallantry. Her arms and legs looked uncomfortable; she had not wanted to put on these clothes, but had felt she must : she would discard them with a small laugh, a sigh, and 'Thank the Lord for that, what a relief !'

She was talking to a woman, the visitor, whose back was to me. I could watch her face, her eyes. Those eyes, unclouded by self-criticism, like skies that have been blue for too many weeks, and will continue blue and regular for weeks yet, for it is nowhere near the time for the season to change – her eyes were blank, did not see the woman she was talking to, nor the small child in her lap, whom she bumped up and down energetically, using her heel as a spring. Nor did she see the little girl who stood a short way from her mother, watching, listening, all her senses stretched, as if every pore took in information in the form of warnings, threats, messages of dislike. From this child emanated strong waves of painful emotion. It was guilt. She was condemned. And, as I recognised this emotion and the group of people there in the heavy comfortable room, the scene formalised itself like a Victorian problem picture or a photograph from an old fashioned play. Over it was written in emphatic script : GUILT.

In the background was a man, looking uncomfortable. He was a soldier, or had been one. He was tall, and built well, but held himself as if it were hard to maintain purpose and self-respect. His conventionally handsome face was sensitive and easily pained, and was half-hidden by a large moustache.

The woman, the wife and mother, was talking; she talked, she talked, she went on and on as if no one but herself existed in that room or beyond it, as if she were alone and her husband and her children – the little girl particularly, who knew she was the chief culprit, the one being complained of – couldn't hear her.

'But I simply did not expect it, no one ever warns one how it is going to be, it is too much. By the time the end of the day has come I'm not fit for anything at all but sleep, my mind is just a fog, it's a scramble . . . as for reading or any serious sort of thing, that is out of the question. Emily will wake at six, I've trained her to stay quiet until seven, but from then on, I'm on the go, the go, the go, all day, it is one thing after another, and when you think that at one time I was quite known for my intelligence, well that is just a joke, I'm afraid.'

The man, very still, sat back in his chair, smoking. The ash on his cigarette lengthened itself and dropped. He frowned, gave his wife an irritated look, hastily pulled an ashtray towards him in a way that said at the same time he should have remembered the ashtray before, but that if he felt like dropping ash he was entitled to. He went on smoking. The little girl, who was about five or six, had her thumb in her mouth. Her face was shadowed and bleak because of the pressure of criticism on her, her existence.

She was a dark-haired child, with dark eyes like her father's, full of pain – guilt.

'No one has any idea, do they, until they have children, what it means. It's all I can do just to keep up with the rush of things, the meals one after another, the food, let alone giving the children the attention they should have. I know that Emily is ready for more than I have time to give her, but she is such a demanding child, so difficult, she always has taken a lot out of me, she wants to be read to and played with all the time, but I'm cooking, I'm ordering food, I'm at it all day, well you know how it is, there isn't time for what there has to be done, I simply don't have time for the child. I did manage to get a girl for a time last year, but that was really more trouble than it was worth, really, all their problems and their crises and you have to deal with them, she took up as much of my time as Emily does, but I did get an hour to myself after lunch and I put my feet up for a bit, but I did not find I had the energy to read, let alone study, no one knows how it is, what it means, no, children do for you, they do you in, I'm not what I was, I know that only too well I am afraid.'

The child on her knee, two or three years old, a heavy passive child dressed in white wool that smelled damp, was being jogged faster now; his eyes were glazing as the world bounced up and down around him, his adenoidal mouth was open and slack, the full cheeks quivering.

The husband, passive but really tense with irritation – with guilt – smoked on, listening, frowning.

'But what can you give out when you get nothing in? I am empty, drained; I am exhausted by lunchtime and all I want is to sleep by then. And when you think of what I used to be, what I was capable of! I never thought of being tired, I never imagined I could become the sort of woman who would never have time to open a book. But there it is.'

She sighed, quite unselfconsciously. She was like a child, that tall, solid, confident woman; she needed understanding as a child does. She sat looking inward into the demands of her days and her nights. No one else was there for her, because she felt she was talking to herself : they could not hear, or would not. She was trapped, but did not know why she felt this, for her marriage and her children were what she personally had wanted and had aimed for – what society had chosen for her. Nothing in her education or experience had prepared her for what she did in fact feel, and she was isolated in her distress and her bafflement, sometimes even believing that she might perhaps be ill in some way.

The little girl, Emily, had left the chair where she had been standing and holding tight to the arm, sheltering from the storm of abuse and criticism. She now went to her father, and stood by his knee, watching that great powerful woman her mother, whose hands were so hurtful. She was shrinking closer and closer to her father who, it seemed, was unaware of her. He made a clumsy movement, knocking off his ashtray, and his instinctive retrieval of it caused his elbow to jog Emily. She fell back, dropped away, like something left behind as a rush of water goes past, or a stream of air. She drifted to the floor and lay there, face downwards, thumb in her mouth.

The hard accusing voice went on and on, would always go on, had always gone on, nothing could stop it, could stop these emotions, this pain, this guilt at ever having been born at all, born to cause such pain and annoyance and difficulty. The voice would nag on there for ever, could never be turned off, and even when the sound was turned low in memory, there must be a permanent pressure of dislike, resentment. Often in my ordinary life I would hear the sound of a voice, a bitter and low complaint just the other side of sense : there it was, in one of rooms behind the wall, still there, always there ... standing at the window I watched Emily, the bright attractive girl who always had people around her listening to her chatter, her laugh, her little clevernesses. She was always aware of everything that went on, nothing could escape her in the movements and happenings of that crowd; while talking with one group, it seemed as if even her back and shoulders were taking in information from another. And yet she was isolated, alone; the 'attractiveness' was like a shell of bright paint, and from inside it she watched and listened. It was the intensity of her self-awareness that made her alone; this did not leave her, even at her most feverish, when she was tipsy or drunk, or singing with the others. It was as if she had an invisible deformity, a hump on her back, perhaps, visible only to herself ... and to me, as I stood watching her in a way I never could when she was close to me at home.

Emily might not see me at all. So much aware of what went on among her companions, she had eyes for every little outside. But she did notice me once or twice, and then it was odd to see how she would look at me, just as if I could not see her looking. It was as if the act of her gazing out from the protection of that crowd gave her immunity, was a different thing from looking at someone inside it, demanding a different code. A long, level thoughtful stare, not unfriendly, merely detached, her real self visible, and then would come the bright hard smile, the wave of the hand – friendliness, as far as it was licensed by her companions. As soon as she lost sight of me, my existence vanished for her; she was back again, enclosed by them, the prisoner of her situation.

While I stood there at my window, Hugo watchful beside me, observing her, I saw how the numbers on the pavement had grown : fifty or more of them now, and, looking up at the innumerable windows full of faces, that overhung the scene, knew that we all had one thing in common : we were wondering how soon this throng, or part of it, would move on and away, how soon 'the youngsters' would be off ... it would not be long now. And Emily? She would go with them? I stood by the watching yellow beast who would never let me fondle him, but who seemed to like my being there, close, the friend of his mistress, his love – I stood there and thought that any day I could approach that window and find the opposite pavement empty, the street cleaners swilling water and disinfectant, clearing away all memories of the tribe. And Hugo and I would be alone, and I would have betrayed my trust.

She did sit with her yellow animal in the mornings, she fed him his meat substitutes and his vegetables, she fondled him and talked to him, she took him at night into her little room where he lay by her bed as she slept. She loved him, there was no doubt of that, as much as ever she had done. But she was not able to include him into her real life on the pavement.

One early evening, she came in at the time when the life outside was at its most lively, its noisiest – that is, just as the lights were beginning to appear at their different heights in the darkening air. She came in, and with a look of trepidation which she was trying to hide from me, she said to Hugo: 'Come on, come with me and be introduced.'

She had forgotten her earlier experiment? No, of course not; but it seemed to her that things could have changed. She was now well-known out there – more, she must feel herself to be a founder-member of this particular tribe: she had helped to form it.

He did not want to go. Oh, no, he very much did not want to go with her. He was laying the responsibility for what might happen on her in the way he stood up, signifying his willingness, or at least his agreement, to go with her.

She led the way out, and he followed. She had not put him on his heavy chain. She was, in leaving her animal unprotected, making her pack responsible for their behaviour.

I watched the young girl, slender and vulnerable even in her thick trousers, her boots, her jacket, her scarves, cross the road, with her beast following soberly after her. She was afraid, that was obvious, as she stood on the edge of one of the bright chattering noisy groups which always seemed lit with an inner violence of excitement or of readiness for excitement. She kept her hand down on the beast's head, for reassurance. People turned and saw her, saw Hugo. Both the girl and the animal had their backs to me; I was able to see the throng of faces as Emily and Hugo saw them. I did not like what I saw ... if I had been out there I would have wanted to run, to get away ... But she stuck it out for a time. Her hand always kept down, close to Hugo's head, fondling his ears, patting him, soothing, she moved quietly among the clans, determined to make her test, to sound out her position with them. She stayed out with him as dusk came down and the lively crowds were absorbed into a mingle of light and dark, where sound – a laugh, a raised voice, the clink of a bottle – was heightened, and went travelling out in every direction to the now invisible watchers at their windows, carrying messages of excitement or alarm.

When she brought him in she seemed tired. She was saddened. She was much closer to the commonplace level where I, as one of the elderly, lived. Her eyes saw me, as she sat eating her bean salad, her little hunk of bread, seemed really to see the room we sat in. As for me, I was full of apprehension : I believed her sadness was because she had decided her Hugo could not safely travel with the tribe – I thought her mad even to have considered it – and that she had decided to leave with them, to jettison him.

After the meal she sat for a long time at the window. She gazed at the scene she was usually a part of. The animal sat, not beside her, but quietly in a corner. You could believe he was weeping, or would, if he knew how. He sorrowed inwardly. His lids lowered themselves as crises of pain gripped him, and he would give a great shiver.

When Emily went to bed she had to call him several times, and he went at last, slowly, with a quiet dignified padding. But he was in inner isolation from her : he was protecting himself.

Next morning she offered to go out and forage for supplies. She had not done this for some time, and again I felt this was sort of token apology because she meant to leave.

We two sat on quietly in the long room, where the sunlight had left because it was already midday. I was at one side of it, and Hugo lay stretched, head on paws, along the outer wall of the room where he could not be seen from the windows above him.

We heard footsteps outside which stopped, then became stealthy. We heard voices that had been loud, suddenly soft.

A young girl's voice? – no, a boy's; but it was hard to tell. Two heads appeared at the window, trying to see in the comparative dusk of the room : the light was brilliant outside.

'It's here,' said one of the Mehta boys from upstairs.

'I've seen him at the window,' said a black youth. I had observed him often with the others on the pavement, a slim, lithe, likeable boy. A third head appeared between the other two : a white girl, from one of the blocks of flats.

'Stewed dog,' she said daintily, 'well *I'm* not going to eat it.'

'Oh go on,' said the black boy, 'I've seen what you eat.'

I heard a rattling sound; it was Hugo. He was trembling, and his claws were rattling on the floorboards.

Then the girl saw me sitting there, recognised me, and put on the bright uncaring grin the pack allowed outsiders.

'Oh,' she said, 'We thought . . .'

'No,' I said. 'I am living here. I haven't left.'

The three faces briefly turned towards each other, brown, white, black, as they put on for each other's benefit *we've made a mess of it* grimaces. They faded outwards, leaving the window empty.

There was a soft moaning from Hugo.

'It's all right,' I said. 'They've gone.'

The rattling sound increased. Then the animal heaved himself up and crept away, with an attempt at dignity, towards the door into the open kitchen, which was the farthest he could go from the dangerous window. He did not want me to observe his loss of self-possession. He was ashamed of having lost it. The moaning I had heard was as much shame as because he was afraid.

When Emily came in, a good girl, daughter-of-the-house, it was evening. She was tired, had had to visit many places to find supplies. But she was pleased with herself. The rations at that time were minimal, because of the winter, just finished : swedes, potatoes, cabbage, onions. That was about it. But she had managed to find a few eggs, a little fish, and even – a prize – a strongly scented, unshrivelled lemon. I told her, when she had finished showing off her booty, what had happened. At once her good spirits went. She sat quiet, head lowered, eyes concealed from me by the thick, white, heavily-lashed lids. Then, without looking at me, turning herself from me, she went to find her Hugo, to comfort him.

And then a little later, out she went to the pavement and stayed there until very late.

I remember how I sat on and on in the dark. I was putting off the moment of lighting the candles, thinking that the soft square of light which was how my window looked from across the street, would remind the cannibals out there of Hugo. Who was back in the place along the wall, where he could not easily be seen. He was as still as if asleep, but his eyes were open. When I did light the candles he did not move or even blink.

Looking back I see myself sitting in the long room with its comfortable old furniture, with Emily's things in the little space she allotted for them, and the yellow beast lying quietly, suffering. And there for backdrop was the ambiguous wall, which could so easily dissolve, dissolving, too, all this extraneous life, and the anxieties and pressures of the time – creating, of course, its own. Shadowily present, there it stood, its pattern of fruits and leaves and flowers obliterated by the dim light. That is how I see it, see us, that time : the long room, dimly lit, with me and Hugo there, thinking of Emily away across the street among crowds that shifted and ebbed and thinned and left – and behind us that other indefinite region, shifting and melting and changing, where walls and doors and rooms and gardens and people continually recreated themselves, like clouds.

That night there was a moon. There seemed more light outside my room than in it. The pavements were crammed. There was a lot of noise.

It was clear that the crowd had split into two parts : one part was about to take to the roads.

I looked for Emily with these people, but could not see her.

Then I did see her: she was with the people who were staying behind. We all – I, Hugo, the part of the crowd not yet ready to make the journey, and the hundreds of people at the windows all around and above – watched as the departing ones formed up into a regiment, four or five abreast. They did not seem to be taking much with them, but summer lay ahead, and the country they were heading for was still, or so we believed, not yet much pillaged. They were mostly very young, people not yet twenty, but included a family of mother and father with three small children. A baby was carried in the arms of a friend, the mother took an infant on her back in a sling, the father had the biggest child on his shoulders. There were leaders, three men: not the middleaged or older men, but the older ones among the young people. Of these two went at the front with their women, and one came at the end with his: he had two girls attached to him. There were about forty people altogether in this band.

They had a cart or trolley, similar to the ones that had been used at airports and railway stations. This had some parcels of root vegetables and grain on it, and the little bundles of the travellers. Also, at the last moment, a couple of youths, laughing but still shamefaced or at least self-conscious, pushed on to this trolley a great limp parcel which exuded blood.

There were slim bundles of reeds on the cart – these were hawked from door to door by then; and three girls carried them as flaring torches, one at the front, one at the back, one in the middle, torches much brighter than the inadequate, when it was not altogether absent, street lighting. And off they went, along the road north-west, lit by the torches that dripped dangerous fire close above their heads. They were singing. They sang Show Me the Way to Go Home – without, or so it seemed, any consciousness of its ludicrous pathos. They sang We Shall Not be Moved, and Down by the Riverside.

They had gone, and left on the pavements were still a good many people. They seemed subdued, and soon dispersed. Emily came in, silent. She looked for Hugo – he had returned to his place along the wall, and she sat near him, and pulled his front half over her lap. She sat there hugging him, bent over him. I could see the big yellow head lying on her arm, could hear him, at last, purr and croon.

Now I knew that while she wanted more than anything to be off into that savage gamblers' future with the migrating ones, she was not prepared to sacrifice her Hugo. Or at least, was in conflict. And I dared to hope. Yet, even while I did, I wondered why I thought it mattered that she should stay. Stay with what? Me? Did I believe it mattered that she should stay where she had been left by that man? Well, my faith in that was beginning to dim: but her survival mattered, presumably, and who could say where she was likely to be safest? Did I believe that she should stay with her animal? Yes, I did; absurdly, of course, for he was only a beast. But he was hers, she loved him, she must care for him; she could not leave him without harm to herself. So I told myself, argued with myself, comforted myself – argued, too, with that invisible mentor, the man who had dropped Emily with me and gone off: how was I to know what to do? Or how to think? If I was making mistakes, then whose fault was it? He had not told me anything, or left instructions; there was no way at all of my knowing how I was expected to be living, how Emily should be living.

Behind the wall I found a room that was tall, not very large, and I think six-sided. There was no furniture in it, only a rough trestle around two of the sides. On the floor was spread a carpet, but it was a carpet without its life: it had a design, an intricate one, but the colours had an imminent existence, a potential, no more. There had been a fair or a market here, and this had left a quantity of rags, dress materials, scraps of Eastern embroideries of the kind that have tiny mirrors buttonhole-stitched into them, old clothes – everything in that line you can think of. Some people were standing about the room. At first it seemed that they were doing nothing at all; they looked idle and undecided. Then one of them detached a piece of material from the jumble on the trestles, and bent to match it with the carpet – behold, the pattern answered that part of the carpet. This piece was laid exactly on the design, and brought it to life.

It was like a child's game, giant-sized; only it was not a game, it was serious, important not only to the people actually engaged in this work, but to everyone. Then another person bent with a piece chosen from the multi-coloured heap on the trestles, bent, matched and straightened again to gaze down. There they stood, about a dozen people, quite silent, turning their eyes from the patterns of the carpet to the tangle of stuffs and back again. A recognition, the quick move, a smile of pleasure or of relief, a congratulatory glance from one of the others . . . there was no competition here, only the soberest and most loving co-operation. I entered the room, I stood on the carpet looking down as they did at its incompleteness, pattern without colour, except where the pieces had already been laid in a match, so that parts of the carpet had a bleak gleam, like one that has been bleached, and other parts glowed up, fulfilled, perfect. I, too, sought for fragments of materials that could bring life to the carpet, and did in fact find one, and bent down to match and fit, before some pressure moved me on again. I realised that everywhere around, in all the other rooms, were people who would in their turn drift in here, see this central activity, find their matching piece – would lay it down, and drift off again to other tasks. I left that tall room whose ceiling vanished upwards into dark where I thought I saw the shine of a star, a room whose lower part was in a bright light that enclosed the silent concentrated figures like stage-lighting. I left them and moved on. The room disappeared. I could not find it when I turned my head to see it again, so as to mark where it was. But I knew it was there waiting, I knew it had not disappeared, and the work in it continued, must continue, would go on always.

———◆———

This time seems now to have gone on and on, yet in fact it was quite short, a matter of months. So much was happening, and every hour seemed crammed with new experience. Yet in appearance all I did was to live quietly there, in that room, with Hugo, with Emily. Inside it was all chaos . . . the feeling one is taken over by, at the times in one's life when everything is in change, movement, destruction – or reconstruction, but that is not always evident at the time – a feeling of helplessness, as if one were being whirled about in a dust-devil or a centrifuge.

Yet I had no alternative but to go on doing exactly what I was. Watching and waiting. Watching, for the most part, Emily . . . who had been a stranger, so it seemed, for years. But of course this was not so, it was anxiety for her that stretched the hours. The yellow beast, melancholy, his sorrow swallowed – I swear this was so, though he was no more than animal – in the determination to be stoic, not to show his wounds, sat quietly either at the window in a place behind the curtains where he could easily dodge back and down, or stretched along the wall, in a mourner's position, his head on his forepaws, his green eyes steady and open. He lay there hour after hour, contemplating his – thoughts. Why not? He thought, he judged, as animals can be seen to do, if observed without prejudice. I must say here, since it has to be said somewhere about Hugo, that I think the series of comments automatically evoked by this kind of statement, the ticker-tape remarks to do with 'anthropomorphism' are beside the point. Our emotional life is shared with the animals; we flatter ourselves that human emotions are so much more complicated than theirs. Perhaps the only emotion not known to a cat or a dog is – romantic love. And even then, we have to wonder. What is the emotional devotion of a dog for his master or mistress but something like that sort of love, all pining and yearning and 'give me, give me'. What was Hugo's love for Emily but that? As for our thoughts, our intellectual apparatus, our rationalisms and our logics and our deductions and so on, it can be said with absolute certainty that dogs and cats and monkeys cannot make a rocket to fly to the moon or weave artificial dress materials out of the by-products of petroleum, but as we sit in the ruins of this variety of intelligence, it is hard to give it much value : I suppose we are under-valuing it now as we over-valued it then. It will have to find its place : I believe a pretty low place, at that.

I think that all this time, human beings have been watched by creatures whose perceptions and understanding have been so far in advance of anything we have been able to accept, because of our vanity, that we would be appalled if we were able to know, would be humiliated. We have been living with them as blundering, blind, callous, cruel murderers and torturers, and they have watched and known us. And this is the reason we refused to acknowledge the intelligence of the creatures that surround us : the shock to our *amour propre* would be too much, the judgement we would have to make on ourselves too horrible : it is exactly the same process that can make someone go on and on committing a crime, or a cruelty, knowing it : the stopping and having to see what has been done would be too painful, one cannot face it.

But people need slaves and victims and appendages, and of course many of our 'pets' are that because they have been made into what we think they should be, just as human beings can become what they are expected to be. But not all, not by any means; all the time, through our lives, we are accompanied, everywhere we go, by creatures who judge us, and who behave at times with a nobility which is ... we call it human.

Hugo, this botch of a creature, was in his relations with Emily as delicate as a faithful lover who is content with very little provided he is not banished from the beloved presence. This is what he had imposed on himself : he would not make demands, not ask, not be a nuisance. He was waiting. As I was. He watched, as I did.

I was spending long hours with him. Or I sat at the times when the sunlight was on the wall, waiting for it to open, to unfold. Or I went about the streets, taking in news and rumours and information with the rest, wondering what to do for the best, and deciding to do nothing for the time being; wondering how long this city would stand, eroded as it was in every way, its services going and gone, its people fleeing, its food supplies worsening, its law and order consisting more and more of what the citizens imposed on themselves, an instinctive self-restraint, even a caring for others who were in the same straits.

There seemed to be a new sharpness in the tension of waiting.

For one thing, the weather – the summer had come hot and dry, the sun had a dusty look. The pavement opposite my window had filled up again. But there was less interest now in what went on out there : the windows held fewer heads, people had become used to it all. Everyone knew that again and again the street's edge would half-empty as another tribe took off, and we acknowledged with mixed feelings the chance that had chosen our street as a gathering place for the migrations from our part of the city : parents at least knew what their children were doing, even if they did not like it. We became accustomed to watching a mixed lot of people collect along the pavement with their pathetic bits of baggage, and then depart, singing their old wartime songs, or revolutionary songs that seemed as inappropriate as sex songs are to old age. And Emily did not leave. She would run after them a little way with some of the other girls, and then come home, subdued, to put her arms around her Hugo, her dark head down on his yellow coat. It was as if they both wept. They huddled together, creatures in sorrow, comforting each other.

The next thing was that Emily fell in love . . . I am conscious that this seems a term inappropriate to the times I am describing. It was with a young man who seemed likely to lead the next contingent out and away from the city. He was, despite his swash-buckling clothes, a thoughtful young man, or at least one slow to judgement; an observer by temperament, perhaps, but pushed into action by the time? He was, at any rate, the natural guardian of the younger ones, the distressed, the forlorn. He was known for this, teased for it, sometimes criticised : softness of this sort was superfluous to the demands of survival. Perhaps this was why he appealed to Emily.

I believe her trust in him was such that she even thought of taking Hugo out to the mob for another trial, but this must have gone from her to Hugo, for he felt it : he shivered and shrank, and she had to put her arms around him, and say : 'No, I won't Hugo, I promise I won't. Did you hear? – I promised, didn't I?'

Well, then, so there it was, she was infatuated. It was 'the first love' of tradition. Which is to say that half a dozen puppy loves, each one as agonising and every bit as intense and serious as later 'adult' loves had passed; this love was 'first' and 'serious' because it was returned, or at least acknowledged.

I remember I used to wonder if these young people, living as they had to from hand to mouth, who would never shut themselves off in couples behind walls unless it was for a few days or hours in a deserted house somewhere, or a shed in a field, would ever say to each other: *I love you. Do you love me? Will our love last?* – and so on. All of which phrases seemed more and more like the keys or documents of possession to states and conditions now obsolete.

But Emily was suffering, she was in pain, as one is at that age, as fresh as a new loaf and loving a hero of twenty-two. Who had inexplicably, even eerily, chosen her. She was his girl, chosen from many, and known as such. She was beside him on the pavement, went with him on expeditions, and people felt pleasure and even importance when they called to her: 'Gerald says . . .' 'Gerald wants you to. . . .'

From pain she would soar at once to exaltation, and stood there beside him, flushed and beautiful, her eyes soft. Or fling herself down in the sofa-corner, to be by herself for a bit, or at least away from him, for it was all too much, too powerful, she needed a respite. She was radiant with amazement, not seeing me or her surroundings, and I knew she was saying to herself: But he's chosen *me, me* . . . and this did not mean *And I'm only thirteen!* That was a thought for people my age. A girl was ready for mating when her body was.

But these young people's lives were communal, and mating was far from being the focus or pivot of a relationship when they chose each other. No, any individual consummations were nothing beside this act of mingling constantly with others, as if some giant rite of eating were taking place, everyone tasting and licking and regurgitating everyone else, making themselves known to others and others known to them in this tasting and sampling – eyeing each other, rubbing shoulders and bodies, talking, exchanging emanations.

But while Emily was part of this communal act, the communal feast, she was at the same time feeling as girls traditionally did. She wanted, I knew, to be alone with Gerald : she would have liked that experience, the old one.

But she never was alone with him.

What she wanted was inappropriate. She felt in the wrong, even criminal, at least very much to be blamed. She was an anachronism.

I did not say anything, for our relations were not such that I could ask, or she likely to volunteer.

All I knew was what I could see for myself : that she was being filled over and over again with a violence of need that exploded in her, dazzling her eyes and shaking her body so that she was astonished – needs which could never be slaked by an embrace on the floorboards of an empty room or in the corner of a field. All around her the business of living went on, but Gerald was always at the heart of it : wherever she turned herself in some task or duty, there he was, so efficient and practical and busy with important things, but she, Emily, was possessed by a savage enemy, was raging with joy and grief. And if she betrayed what she felt by a wrong look or a word, what then? She would lose her home here, among these people, *her* tribe . . . And this was why she had so often to slip away indoors, to creep near her familiar Hugo, and put her arms around him. At which he might give a muffled groan, since he knew very well the use she was making of him.

There was this juxtaposition : Emily lay with her cheek on rough yellow fur, one still-childish hand enclosing a ragged ear, her tense body expressing emptiness and longing. The wall beside me opened, reminding me again how easily and unexpectedly it could, and I was walking towards a door from which voices came. And frenetic laughter, squeals, protests. I opened the door on that world whose air was irritation, confinement, littleness. A brightly-coloured world : the colours were flat and loud as in old calendars. A hot close place, everything very large, over-lifesize, difficult : this was again the child's view that I was imprisoned in. Largeness and smallness; violence of emotion and its insignificance – contradictions, impossibilities, were built into and formed part of the substance of whatever one saw when that particular climate was entered. It was a bedroom. Again, a fire burned in the wall behind a tall metal guard. Again it was a thick, heavy, absorbing room, with time as its air, the tick of a clock felt as a condition of one's every moment and thought. The room was full of a hot light: a reddish light barred and crossed with shadow lay over the walls, across the ceiling, and on the immensely long soft white curtains that filled a wall opposite the two beds: father's and mother's beds, husband's bed and wife's bed.

The curtains for some reason filled me with anguish, the soft weight of them. They were of white lawn or muslin that had a raised spot woven in, and were lined and lined again. A white that was made for lightness and transparency to let in sun and night-air had been taken hold of and thickened and made heavy and hung up in shrouds to shut out air and light, to reflect hot flame-light from the metal-barred fireplace.

On one side of the room the mother sat with her boy-infant, always in his damp wool. Her arms were about him, she was absorbed in him. In a large chair set against the curtains the soldier-like man sat with his knees apart, gripping between them the small girl who stood shrieking. On his face, under the moustache, was a small tight smile. He was 'tickling' the child. This was a 'game', the bedtime 'game', a ritual. The elder child was being played with, was being made tired, was being given her allowance of attention, before being put to bed, and it was a service by the father to the mother, who could not cope with the demands of her day, the demands of Emily. The child wore a long nightie, with frills at wrists and at the neck. Her hair had been brushed and was held by ribbon. A few minutes ago she had been a clean neat pretty little girl in a white nightdress, with a white ribbon in her hair, but now she was hot and sweating, and her body was contorting and twisting to escape the man's great hands that squeezed and dug into her ribs, to escape the great cruel face that bent so close over her with its look of private satisfaction. The room seemed filled with a hot anguish, the fear of being held tight there, the need for being held and tortured, since this was how she pleased her captors. She shrieked: 'No, no, no, no . . . helpless, being explored and laid bare by this man.

76

The mother was indifferent. She did not know what was going on, or what the little girl suffered. For it was a 'game' and the squeals and protests were from her own childhood and therefore in order, healthy, licensed. From her came a blankness, the indifference of ignorance. She cooed and talked to her stolid open-mouthed infant while the father went on with his task, from time to time looking at his wife with a wonderfully complex expression – guilt, but he was unaware of that; appeal, because he felt this was wrong and ought to be stopped; astonishment that it was allowable and by her, who not only did not protest, but actively encouraged him in the 'game'; and, mingled with all these, a look that was never far from his face at any time, of sheer incredulity at the impossibility of everything. He let his knees go slack, and pretended to release the child, who nearly fell, reached for a knee to steady herself, but before she could run away, was caught again as the knees clapped together on either side of her. The exquisite torture began again. 'There, there, there, Emily,' muttered the great man, flooding her in an odour of tobacco and unwashed clothes. 'Now then, that's it, there you are you see,' he went on, as the fingers thicker than any of her ribs dug into her sides and she screamed and pleaded.

This scene faded like a spark or like a nightmare, and the same man was sitting in the same room but in a chair near the bed. He wore a heavy brown dressing gown of some very thick rough wool, a soldier's garment, and he smoked and sat watching his wife. The large healthy woman was discarding her clothes in a rapid efficient way on her side of the bed near the fire : only now it was summer, and the fireplace had red flowers standing in it. The curtains hung limp and still, very white, but drawn back to show areas of black glass which reflected the man, the room, the movements of the woman. She was unaware of her husband, who sat there watching her nakedness emerge. She was talking, she was creating her day for him, for herself : 'And by four o'clock I was quite exhausted, the girl had her half day, and Baby was awake all morning, he did not have his sleep, and Emily was very trying and demanding today . . . and . . . and . . . .' The plaint went on, while she stood naked, looking about her for pyjamas. She was a fine solid woman with clear white flesh, her breasts small and round. The nipples were virginal for a woman who had had two children : small and with narrow pink aureoles. Her plentiful brown hair fell down her back, and she scratched first her scalp, then under one arm, lifting it to expose wisps of long brown hair. On to her face came a look of intense satisfaction which would have appalled her if she could have seen it. She scratched the other armpit, then allowed herself to scratch, voluptuously, with both hands, her ribs, her hips, her stomach. Her hands did not stray lower. She stood there scratching vigorously for a long time, a couple of minutes, while red marks appeared on the solid white flesh behind the energetic fingers, and from time to time she gave a great shudder of pleasure, masked as cold. Her husband sat quiet and watched. On his face was a small smile. He lifted his cigarette to his mouth and took a deep lungful, and slowly let it out, allowing it to trickle from half-open mouth and nostrils.

His wife had finished with her scratching, and was bundling herself into pink-spotted cotton pyjamas, in which she looked like a jolly schoolgirl. Her face was unconsciously greedy – for sleep. She was already in imagination drifting to oblivion. She got efficiently into bed, as if her husband did not exist, and in one movement lay down and turned her back to him. She yawned. Then she remembered him : there was something she ought to do before allowing herself this supreme pleasure. She turned over and said 'Good night old thing,' and was at once sucked down and lay asleep, facing him. He sat on, smoking, now openly examining her at his leisure. The amusement was there, incredulity, and, at the same time, an austerity that had begun, from the look of it, as a variety of moral exhaustion, even a lack of vitality, and had long ago become a judgement on himself and on others.

He now put his cigarette out, and got up from the chair, gently, as if afraid of waking a child. He went into the next room, which was the nursery with its red velvet curtains, its white, white, white everywhere. Two cots, one small one, one large. He walked delicately, a large man among a thousand tiny items of nursery use, past the small cot, to the large one. He stood at the foot of it and looked at the little girl, now asleep. Her cheeks flamed scarlet. Beads of sweat stood on her forehead. She was only lightly asleep. She kicked off the bed-clothes as he watched, turned herself and lay, her nightgown around her waist, showing small buttocks and the backs of pretty legs. The man bent lower and gazed, and gazed ... a noise from the bedroom, his wife turning over and perhaps saying something in her sleep, made him stand straight and look – guilty, but defiant, and above all, angry. Angry at what? At everything, that is the answer. There was silence again. Lower down in this tall house a clocked chimed: it was only eleven. The little girl tossed herself over again and lay on her back, naked, stomach thrust up, vulva prominent. The man's face added another emotion to those already written there. Suddenly, but in spite of everything not roughly, he pulled a cover over the child and tucked it in tight. At once she began to squirm and whimper. The room was much too hot. The windows were closed. He was about to open one, but remembered a prohibition. He turned himself about and walked out of the nursery without looking again at the two cots, where the little boy lay silent, his mouth open, but where the girl was toss-ing and struggling to get out, to get out, to get out.

In a room that had windows open to a formal garden, a room that had a 'feel' to it of another country somewhere, different from the rooms in this house, was a small bed in which the girl lay. She was older, and she was sick and fretful. Paler, thinner than at any time I had seen her, her dark hair was damp and sticky, and there was the smell of stale sweat. All around her lay books, toys, comics. She was moving rest-lessly and continuously, rubbing her limbs together, tossing about, turning over, crooning to herself, muttering complaints and commands to someone. She was an earthquake of fevers, energies, desires, angers, need. In came the tall large woman, preoccupied with a glass she was carrying. At the sight of the glass the girl brightened: here at least was a diversion, and she half sat up. But already her mother had set down the glass and was turning away to another duty.

'Stay with me,' pleaded the girl.

'I can't, I have to see to Baby.'

'Why do you always call him Baby?'

'I don't know, really, of course it is time . . . he's quite old enough to . . . but I keep forgetting.'

'Please, please.'

'Oh very well, for a minute.'

The woman sat on the extreme edge of the bed, looked harried, looked as she always did, burdened and irritated. But she was also pleased.

'Drink your lemonade.'

'I don't want to. Mummy, cuddle me, cuddle me . . .'

'Oh, Emily!'

With a flattered laugh, the woman bent forward, offering herself. The little girl put her arms up around the woman's neck, and hung there. But she got no encouragement. 'Cuddle me, cuddle me,' she was crooning, as if to herself, and it might just as well have been to herself, since the woman was so puzzled by it all. She suffered the small hot arms for a little, but then she could not help herself – her dislike of flesh raised her own hands, to put the child's arms away from her. 'There, that's enough,' she said. But she stayed, a little. Duty made her stay. Duty to what? Sickness, very likely. 'A sick child needs its mother.' Something of that sort. Between the little girl's hot needful yearning body, which wanted to be quieted with a caress, with warmth, wanted to lie near a large strong wall of a body, a safe body which would not tickle and torment and squeeze; wanted safely and assurance – between her and the mother's regularly breathing, calm body, all self-sufficiency and duty, was a blankness, an unawareness; there was no contact, no mutual comfort.

The little girl lay back and then reached for the glass and drank eagerly. The moment the glass was empty the mother got up and said : 'I'll make you another one.'

'Oh stay with me, stay with me.'

'I can't Emily. You are being difficult again.'

'Can Daddy come?'

'But he's busy.'

'Can't he read to me?'

'You can read to yourself now, you're a big girl.'

The woman went out with the empty glass. The girl took a half-eaten biscuit from under the pillow and picked up a book and read and ate, ate and read, her limbs always on the move, tossing and rearranging themselves, her unoccupied hand touching her cheek, her hair, her shoulders, feeling her flesh everywhere, lower and lower down, near to her cunt, her 'private parts' – but from there the hand was quickly withdrawn, as if that area had barbed wire around it. Then she stroked her thighs, crossed and uncrossed them, moved and twisted and read and ate and ate and read.

There lay Emily now on my living-room floor.

'Dear Hugo ... dear, dear Hugo – you are *my* Hugo, you are my love, Hugo ...'

And I was filled with that ridiculous impatience, the helplessness, of the adult who watches a young thing growing. There she was enclosed in her age, but in a continuum with those scenes behind the wall, a hinterland which had formed her – yet she could not see them or know about them, and it would be of no use my telling her: if I did she would hear words, no more. From that shadowy region behind her came the dictate: *You are this, and this and this – this is what you have to be, and not that;* and the biological demands of her age took a precise and predictable and clocklike stake on her life, making her exactly like this and that. And so it would go on, it had to go on, and I must watch; and in due time she would fill like a container with substances and experiences; she would be delivered by these midwives, some recognisable, understood, and common to everyone, some to be deduced only from their methods of operation – she would become mature, that ideal condition envisaged as the justification of all previous experience, an apex of achievement, inevitable and peculiar to her. This apex is how we see things, it is a biological summit we see: growth, the achievement on the top of the curve of her existence as an animal, then a falling away towards death. Nonsense of course, absurd; but it was hard to subdue in myself this view of her, shut off impatience as I watched her rolling and snuggling beside her purring yellow beast, to make myself acknowledge that this stage of her life was every bit as valid as the one ahead of her – perhaps to be summed up or encapsulated in the image of a capable but serene smile – and that what I was really waiting for (just as, somewhere inside herself *she* must be) was the moment she would step off this merry-go-round, this escalator carrying her from the dark into the dark. Step off in entirely . . . And then?

———◆———

There was a new development in the life on the pavement. It was bound up with Gerald; with, precisely, his need to protect the weak, his identification with them, that quality which could not be included in the little balance sheets of survival. There were suddenly children out there, nine, ten, eleven years old, not attached to families, but by themselves. Some had parents they had run away from, or whom they did see, but only occasionally. Some had no parents at all. What had happened to them? It was hard to say. Officially of course children still had parents and homes and that kind of thing, and if not, they had to be in care or custody; officially children even went to school regularly. But nothing like this was the practice. Sometimes children attached themselves to other families, their own parents being unable to cope with the pressures, not knowing where to find food and supplies, or simply losing interest and throwing them out to fend for themselves as people had once done with dogs and cats that no longer gave pleasure. Some parents were dead, because of violence, or epidemics. Others had gone away out of the city and left their children behind. These waifs tended to be ignored by the authorities unless attention was specifically drawn to them, but people might feed them or take them into their own homes. They were still part of society, wished to be part, and hung around where people lived. They were quite unlike those children whom I will have to describe quite soon, who had put themselves outside society altogether, were our enemies.

Gerald noticed that a dozen or so children were literally living on the pavement, and began to look after them in an organised way. Emily of course adored him for this, and defended him against the inevitable criticism. It was mostly of old people that it was said they should be allowed to die – I can tell you that this added a new dimension of terror to the lives of the elderly, already tenuous – that the weaker had to go to the wall : this was already happening, and was not a process that should be checked by sickly sentiment. But Gerald took his stand. He began by defending them when people tried to chase them away. They were sleeping on the waste lot behind the pavement, and complaints started about the smell and the litter. Soon would happen what we all feared more than anything at all : the authorities would have to intervene.

There were empty houses and flats all around; about half a mile off was a large empty house, in good condition. There Gerald took the children. It had long ago lost its electricity supply, but by then hardly anyone paid for electricity. The water was still connected. The windows had been broken, but shutters were made for the ground floor and they used old bits of polythene for the upper floor windows.

Gerald had become a father or elder brother to the children. He got food for them. Partly, he begged from shops. People were so generous. That was an odd thing : mutual aid and self-sacrifice went side by side with the callousness. And he took expeditions off to the country to get what supplies could still be bought or purloined. And, best of all, there was a large garden at the back of the house, and he taught them how to cultivate it. This was guarded day and night by the older children armed with guns or sticks, or bows and arrows or catapults.

There it was : warmth, caring, a family.

Emily believed herself to have acquired a ready-made family.

Now began a new, queer time. She was living with me, 'in my care' – a joke, that, but it was still the reason for our being together. She was certainly living with her Hugo, whom she could not bear to leave. But every evening, after an early supper (and I even arranged for this meal to be at a time which would more easily accommodate her new life) she would say : 'I think I'll be off now, if you don't mind.' And without waiting for an answer, but giving me a small guilty, even amused smile, she went, having kissed Hugo in a little private ceremony that was like a pact or promise. She came back, usually, at mid-morning.

I was worried, of course, about pregnancy; but the conventions of our association made it impossible to ask questions, and in any case I suspected that what I regarded as an impossible burden that could drag her down, destroy her, would be greeted by her with : 'Well, what of it? Other people have had babies and managed, haven't they?' I was worried, too, that her attachment to this new family would become so strong that she would simply wander off, away from us, from Hugo and me. There *we* were, the two of us, waiting. Waiting was our occupation. We kept each other company. But he was not mine, not my animal, most definitely he was not that. He waited, listening, for Emily : his green eyes steady and watchful. He was always ready to get up and meet her at the door – I knew she was coming minutes before she appeared, for he smelled or heard or intuited her presence when she was still streets away. At the door the two pairs of eyes, the green, the brown, engaged in a dazzling beam of emotion. Then she embraced him, fed him, and bathed. There were no baths or showers in Gerald's community yet. She dressed herself and at once went out to the pavement.

This period, too, seemed to go on interminably. That summer was a long one, the weather the same day after day. It was hot, stuffy, noisy, dusty. Emily, like the other girls, had reverted with the hot weather to earlier styles of dress, shedding the thick garments that had to be worn for utility. She pulled out the old sewing machine again and made herself some bright fanciful dresses out of old clothes from the stalls, or she wore the old dresses themselves. Very strange those pavements looked, to someone my age, with decades of different fashions on display there all at the same time, obliterating that sequence of memory, which goes : 'That was the year when we wore. . . .'

Every day, from early afternoon onwards, Gerald, with the children from the community house, would be on the pavement, so Emily was separated from her 'family' only for a couple of hours each day when she paid her visit home to dress and bath, and for an hour or so each evening, when she took a meal with me. Or rather, with Hugo. I think, too, that coming home for this brief time was a necessity to her emotionally: she needed a respite from her emotions, her happiness. In that other house it was all a great crescendo of joy, of success, of fulfilment, of doing, of making, of being needed. She would return from it like someone running in laughing from a heavy storm, or from too-loud band music. She would alight on my sofa smiling, poised ready for flight, basking, friendly to the whole world. She could not prevent herself smiling all the time, wherever she was, so that people kept looking at her, then came to talk to her, touch her, share in the vitality that flowed off her, making a pool or reservoir of life. And in that radiant face we could still see the incredulous: But why *me*? This happening to *me!*

Well, and of course such intensity could not last. At its peak it was already threatened: she kept collapsing into little depressions and fatigues and irritations when the elation of only an hour or so before seemed impossible. Then up she would swoop again into joy.

Soon I saw that Emily was not the only girl Gerald favoured, she was by no means the only one helping him with that household. I saw she was not sure of her position with him. Sometimes she did not go to his house, but stayed with me; and I believed this was because she was trying to 'show' him, or even confirm for herself that she still had some independence of will.

From the rumour markets I heard that the young man Gerald was 'seducing all those young girls, it is shocking.' Funny, to hear all those old words, seduce, immoral, shocking and so on; and that they had no force in them was proved by the fact that nothing was done. When citizens are moved one way or another they show it, but no one really cared much that young women of thirteen, fourteen, had sexual relations. We had returned to an earlier time of man's condition.

And what was Emily feeling now? Again, her emotions had not accommodated change. Only a few weeks, even days, after it was passed, she saw herself as the widow of a dead bliss, a paradise: she would have liked that time to have gone on for ever when she felt herself to be a sun drawing everybody in towards her, when she shed light and warmth on them, a joy which she manufactured with her lover Gerald. But not finding herself first, or alone, with him, finding herself uncertain and unsupported there, where she felt her centre to be, she lost her bloom, her lustre; she became peaked, she sat about listlessly, and had to force herself up into activity. I was pleased that this had happened: I could not help it. I still felt she should be with me, because that man – guardian, protector or whatever he was – had asked me to care for her. And if she was being let down by Gerald – which was how she felt it – then this was painful but at least she would not go off with him when he took his turn to lead off a tribe. If he now would leave at all, having made this new community.

I waited, watched ... walking through a light screen of leaves, flowers, birds, blossom, the essence of woodland brought to life in the effaced patterns of the wallpaper, I moved through rooms that seemed to have aged since I saw them last. The walls had thinned, had lost substance to the air, to time; everywhere on the forest floor stood slight tall walls, all upright still and in their proper pattern of angles, but ghosts of walls, like the flats in a theatre. They soared into boughs, lost themselves in leaves; and the sunlight lay shallow and clear on them where the leafy shadow patterns did not. Earth had blown in, and fresh grass and flowers grew everywhere.

I walked from room to room through the unsubstantial walls, looking for their occupant, their inhabitant, the one whose presence I could feel strongly even now, when the forest had almost taken the place over.

Someone ... yes, indeed, there was somebody. Close .. I walked soft over the grass along the slant of an eggshell wall making not a sound, knowing that at the end, where the intersecting wall had fallen and decayed long ago, I would easily and at last turn my head and see – whoever it was ... a strong soft presence, an intimate, whose face would be known to me, had always been known to me. But, when I came to the end of the wall, a small stream lay bubbling there through grass, so clear that the fishes on their ground of bright pebbles looked up with their round eyes at me as if there was no water between me and them, as if they hung in air at my feet.

Straying through room after room all open to the leaves and the sky, floored with the unpoisoned grasses and flowers of the old world, I saw how extensive was this place, with no boundaries or end that I could find, much larger than I had ever understood. Long ago, when it had stood up thick and strong, a protection from the forest and from the weather, how very many must have lived here, multitudes, yet all had been subdued to the one Presence who was the air they breathed – though they did not know it, was the Whole they were minuscule parts of, their living and their dying as little their personal choice or wanting as the fates and fortunes of molecules in a leaf are theirs.

I walked back again, towards the border region on whose other side was my 'real' life, and found that here was a set of rooms still solid, still unthinned, with floors and ceilings intact, but as I looked I saw how the floorboards were beginning to give, had collapsed in some places; then that there were ragged holes in them, then that in fact these were not really floorboards, only a few rotting planks lying about on earth that was putting out shoots of green. I pulled the planks away, exposing clean earth and insects that were vigorously at their work of re-creation. I pulled back heavy lined curtains to let the sunlight in. The smell of growth came up strong from the stuffy old room, and I ran from there, and pushed my way back through fine leafy screens, leaving that place, or realm, to clean growth and working insects because – I had to. After all, it was never myself who ordained that now I must interrupt my ordinary life, since it was time to step from one life into another; not I who thinned the sunlight wall; not I who set the stage behind it. I had never had a choice. Very strong was the feeling that I did as I was bid and as I must; that I was being taken, was being led, was being shown, was held always in the hollow of a great hand which enclosed my life, and used me for purposes I was too much beetle or earthworm to understand.

Because of this feeling, born of the experiences behind that wall, I was changing. A restlessness, a hunger that had been with me all my life, that had always been accompanied by a rage of protest, (but against what?) was being assuaged. I found that I was more often, simply, waiting. I watched to see what would happen next. I observed. I looked at every new event quietly, to see if I could understand it.

———◆———

What happened next was June.

One afternoon, when Emily had been home with me and Hugo a full day and a night, had not gone at all to the communal household, a little girl came to the door asking for her. I say 'a little girl' conscious of the absurdity of the phrase with its associations of freshness and promise. But after all, she was one: a very thin child, with strong prominent bones. Her eyes were pale blue. She had pale hair that looked dirty hanging to her shoulders and half-hiding an appealing little face. She was small for her age, could have been eight or nine, but was in fact eleven. In other words she was two years younger than Emily, who was a young woman and loved – precariously – by the king, Gerald. But her breasts were stubby little points, and her body altogether in the chrysalis stage.

'Where is Emily?' she demanded. Her voice – but I shall only say that it was at the extreme away from 'good English', the norm once used for announcements, news, or by officialdom. I could hardly understand her, her accent was so degraded. I am not talking about the words she used, which were always sharp enough when one had uncoded them, were stubborn and strong attempts to lay hold of meanings and ideas every bit as clear and good as those expressed in tutored speech. The peremptoriness of the 'Where is Emily?' was not from rudeness; but because of the effort she had to put into it, the determination to be understood and to be led to Emily, or that

88

Emily should be brought out to her. It was, too, because she was a person who had not been brought up to believe she had rights. Yet she set herself towards goals, she wanted things and achieved them : she would reach her Emily without the help of words, skills, manners – without rights.

'She's here,' I said. 'And please come in.'

She followed me, stiff with the determination that had got her here. Her eyes were everywhere, and the thought came into my mind that she was pricing what she saw. Or, rather, valuing, since 'pricing' was somewhat out-of-date.

When she saw Emily, today a languid suffering young woman on a chair by the window, her two bare feet set side by side side on her attendant yellow beast, the child's face lit with a heartbreakingly sweet smile all confidence and love, and she ran forward, forgetting herself. And Emily, seeing her, smiled and forgot her troubles – love-troubles and goodness knows what else, and the two girls went into the tiny room that was Emily's. Two girls in a young girls' friendship, despite one being already a woman, and one still a child, with a child's face and body. But not, as I discovered, with a child's imaginings, for she was in love with Gerald. And, after having suffered jealousy because of the favourite Emily, by turns hating and denigrating her or feverishly and slavishly admiring her, now she was her sister in sorrow when Gerald was being loved, served, by another girl, or girls.

It was morning when she came; and at lunchtime the two emerged from the bedroom and Emily asked with her unfailing visitor's manners : 'If you don't mind, I would like to ask June to have a sandwich or something.'

Later in the day the two tired of the stuffy room, and came into the living-room, and sat on the floor on either side of Hugo and talked while they patted and petted him. June was wanting advice and information on all kinds of practical matters, and particularly about the garden, which was Emily's responsibility, since Emily understood about all that kind of thing.

She did? *I* knew nothing of this in Emily, who with me had not showed the slightest interest in such matters, not even in the potted plants.

I sat listening to their talk, reconstructing from it the life of their community . . . how very odd it was that all over our cities, side by side with citizens who still used electric light, drew water for which they had paid from taps, expected their rubbish to be collected, were these houses which were as if the technological revolution had never occurred at all. The big house fifteen minutes' walk away had been an old people's home. It had large grounds. Shrubs and flowerbeds had been cleared and now there were only vegetables. There was even a little shed in which a few fowls were kept – another illegality that went on everywhere, and to which the authorities turned a blind eye. The household bought – or acquired in some way – flour, dried legumes, honey. But they were about to get a hive of bees. They also bought the substitutes 'chicken' and 'beef' and 'lamb' and concocted the usual unappetising meals with them. Unappetising only to some : there were plenty of young people who had eaten nothing else in their lives, and who now preferred the substitute to the real thing. As I've said, we learn to like what we get.

The place was a conglomeration of little workshops : they made soap and candles and wove materials and dyed them; they cured leather; they dried and preserved food; they reconstructed and made furniture.

And so they all lived, Gerald's gang, thirty of them now, with pressure always on them to expand, since so many people wanted to join them and had to be refused : there was no space.

It was not that I was surprised to learn of all this. I had heard it all before in various forms. For instance, there had been a community of young adults and small children not far away where even the water system and sewage had broken down. They had made a privy in the garden, a pit with a packing-case over it, and a can of ashes for the smell and the flies. They bought water from the door, or tapped the mains as they could, and cadged baths from friends : there was a time when my bathroom was being used by them. But that group drifted off somewhere. All over our city were these pockets of life reverting to the primitive, the hand-to-mouth. Part of a house . . . then the whole house . . . a group of houses . . . a street

. . . an area of streets. People looking down from a high building saw how these nucleii of barbarism took hold and spread. At first the observers were all sharp hostility and fear. They made the sounds of disapproval, of rectitude, but they were in fact learning as they, the still fortunate, watched these savages from whose every finger sprouted new skills and talents. In some parts of the city whole suburbs had reverted. Miles of people, all growing their potatoes and onions and carrots and cabbages and setting guard on them day and night, raising chickens and ducks, making their sewage into compost, buying or selling water, using empty rooms or an empty house to breed rabbits or even a pig – people no longer in neat little families, but huddled together in groups and clans whose structure evolved under the pressures of necessity. At night such an area withdrew itself into a dangerous obscurity where no one dared go, with its spare or absent street lighting, its potholed pavements and rutted streets, the windows showing the minuscule flickering of candles or the shallow glow of some improvised light on a wall or a ceiling. Even in the daytime, to walk there seeing wary faces half-visible behind shutters, knowing that bows and arrows, catapults, or even guns were held trained for use on you if you transgressed – such an expedition was like a foray into enemy territory, or into the past of the human race.

Yet even at that late stage, there was a level of our society which managed to live as if nothing much was happening – nothing irreparable. The ruling class – but that was a dead phrase, so they said; very well then, the kind of person who ran things, administered, sat on councils and committees, made decisions. *Talked.* The bureaucracy. An international bureaucracy. But when has it not been true? – that the section of a society which gets the most out of it maintains in itself, and for as long as it can in others, an illusion of security, permanence, order.

It seems to me that this has something to do, at bottom, with conscience, a vestigial organ in humanity which still demands that there should be some sort of justice or equity; feels that it is intolerable (this *is* felt by most people, somewhere, or at least occasionally) that some people do well while others starve and fail. This is the most powerful of mechanisms for, to begin with, the maintaining of a society, and then its undermining, its rotting, its collapse . . . yes of course this is not new, has been going on throughout history, very likely and as far as we know. Has there been a time in our country when the ruling class was not living inside its glass bell of respectability or of wealth, shutting its eyes to what went on outside? Could there be any real difference when this 'ruling class' used words like justice, fair play, equity, order, or even socialism? – used them, might even have believed in them, or believed in them for a time; but meanwhile everything fell to pieces while still, as always, the administrators lived cushioned against the worst, trying to talk away, wish away, legislate away, the worst – for to admit that it was happening was to admit themselves useless, admit the extra security they enjoyed was theft and not payment for services rendered . . .

And yet in a way everybody played a part in this conspiracy that nothing much was happening – or that it was happening, but one day things would go into reverse and hey presto! back we would be in the good old days. Which, though? That was a matter of temperament: if you have nothing, you are free to choose among dreams and fantasies. I fancied a rather elegant sort of feudalism – without wars of course, or injustice. Emily, having never experienced or suffered it, would have liked the Age of Affluence back again.

I played the game of complicity like everyone else. I renewed my lease during this period and it was for seven years: of course I knew that we didn't have anything like that time left. I remember a discussion with Emily and June about replacing our curtains. Emily wanted some muslin curtains in yellow that she had seen in some exchange-shop. I argued in favour of a thicker material, to keep out noise. June agreed with Emily: muslin, if properly lined – and there was a stall that sold nothing but old lining materials only two miles away – hung well, and was warm. After all, thicker material, supposedly warmer, hung so stiffly that draughts could get in around the edges . . . yes, but once this thick material had been washed, it would lose its stiffness: . . . this was the sort of conversation we were all capable of having; we might spend days or weeks on a decision. Real decisions, necessary ones, such as that electricity would have to be given up altogether, were likely to be made with a minimum of discussion; they were forced on us – it was that summer that I arranged for my electricity to be disconnected. Just before June's visit, in fact. Her first visit: soon she was coming every day, and usually found us in discussions about lighting and heating. She told us that there was a man in a small town about twelve miles away selling devices of the sort once used for camping. No, they were not the same devices, but he had evolved all kinds of new ones: she had seen some, we should get them too. She and Emily discussed it, decided not to make the expedition by themselves, and asked Gerald to go with them. Off they went and came back late one afternoon loaded with every kind of gadget and trick for light and heat. And here was Gerald, in my living-room. From near by this young chieftain was not so formidable; he seemed harassed, he was even forlorn – his continual glances towards Emily had anxiety in them, and he spent all the time he was there asking her for advice about this or about that . . . she gave it, she was really extraordinarily practical and sensible. I was seeing something of their relationship – I mean, the one beneath that other perhaps less powerful bond which was evident and on the surface, and to which Emily was responding: beyond this almost conventional business of girl in love with boss of the gang, one saw a very young man, overburdened and over-responsible and unsure, asking for support, even tenderness. He had gone off with Emily and June to 'help carry supplies in for Emily and her friend for the winter', but this was not only kindheartedness – he had plenty of that – but a way of saying to Emily that he needed her back in his household. A payment, perhaps; a bribe, if you want to be cynical. She was dallying with going back. Robustly tired after the long walk carrying such a load, looking flushed and sunburned and pretty, she coquetted with him, made herself scarce and difficult. As for June, not yet able to play this game, she was quiet, watching, very much excluded. Emily, feeling power over Gerald, was using it; she stretched, and luxuriated in her body, and played with Hugo's head and ears and smiled at Gerald . . . yes, she would go back with him to his house, since he so much wanted it, wanted *her*. And after an hour or so of it, off they went, the three of them, Emily and Gerald first, June tagging on behind. Parents and a child was what it looked like – what it felt like, I guessed, at least to June.

And now I suppose it must be asked and answered why Emily did not choose to be a chieftainess, a leader on her own account? Well, why not? Yes, I did ask myself this, of course. The attitudes of women towards themselves and to men, the standards women had set up for themselves, the gallantry of their fight for equality, the decades-long and very painful questioning of their roles, their functions – all this makes it difficult for me now to say, simply, that Emily was in love. Why did she not have her own band, her own houseful of brave foragers and pilferers, of makers and bakers and growers of their own food? Why was it not she of whom it was said: 'There was that house, it was standing empty, Emily has got a gang together and they've moved in. Yes, it's very good there, let's see if she will let us come too.'

There was nothing to stop her. No law, written or unwritten, said she should not, and her capacities and talents were every bit as varied as Gerald's or anybody else's. But she did not. I don't think it occurred to her.

The trouble was, she did love Gerald; and this longing for him, for his attention and his notice, the need to be the one who sustained and comforted him, who connected him with the earth, who held him steady in her common sense and her warmth – this need drained her of the initiative she would need to be a leader of a commune. She wanted no more than to be the leader of the commune's woman. His only woman, of course.

This is a history, after all, and I hope a truthful one.

———◆———

One afternoon I returned from a news-gathering excursion,

and found my rooms had been disturbed, and in exactly the same way as the place behind the wall might be disturbed by the 'poltergeist', or anarchic principle. This was my thought as I stood there looking at a chair overturned, books spilled on the floor. There was a general disorder, an emptiness, and above all, an alien feel to the place. Then, one by one, specific lacks and absences became evident. Supplies of food had gone, stocks of valuable cereals, tinned goods, dried fruits: candles, skins, polythene sheeting – the obvious things. Very well, then – thieves had broken in, and I was lucky it had not happened before. But then I saw that possessions only retrospectively valuable were missing: a television set unused for months, a tape recorder, electric lamps, a food mixer. The city had warehouses full of electric contrivances no longer useful for anything, and I began to think that these thieves were freakish or silly. I saw that Hugo lay stretched in his place along the outer wall; he had not been disturbed by the intruders. This was strange, and no sooner had I become convinced of the inexplicable nature of this robbery, than the sound of voices I knew well took me to the window. There I stood to watch a little procession of the goods being brought back again. On a dozen heads, children's heads, were balanced the television, sacks of fuel and food, all sorts of bags and boxes. The faces became visible, brown and white and black, when they tilted up in response to Emily's voice: 'There now, we're too late!' – meaning that I was back and stood at the window watching. I saw Emily coming behind the others. She was in charge: supervising, looking responsible, annoyed – officious. I had not seen her in this role before, this was a new Emily to me. June was there too, beside Emily. I knew all these faces – the children were from Gerald's household.

In a moment, boxes, bundles and cases were filing into my living-room, the children beneath them. When the floor was covered with what had been taken, the children began to edge out again, looking at Emily but never at me: I might as well have been invisible.

'And now say you're sorry,' she ordered.

They smiled, the feeble awkward smile that goes with: *Oh*

how she does go on! They were obeying Emily, but she was found overbearing: those embarrassed, affectionate smiles were not the first she had wrung out of them, I could see. I became even more curious about her role in that other house.

'No, come on,' said Emily. 'It's the least you can do.'

June's thin shoulders shrugged, and she said: 'We are sorry. But we have brought them back, haven't we?' My attempt to transcribe this is: 'Aow, w'srry, 't wiv brung'm beck, ivnt wee?'

In this effort of speech was the energy of frustration: this child, like others formed by our old time which above all had been verbal, to do with words, the exchange of them, the use of them, had been excluded from all that richness. We (meaning the educated) had never found a way of sharing that plenty with the lower reaches of our society. Even in two women standing on a street's edge bartering their few sentences of gossip had been the explosive effort of frustration: the deprived, thinned speech of the poor had always had somewhere in it the energy of a resentment (unconscious perhaps, but there) fed by the knowledge of skills and ease just beyond them, and whose place in their talk was taken by the constant repetition of the phrases – like crutches – 'you know?' and 'you know what I mean?' and 'isn't it?' and all the rest, phrases which made up a good part of everything they said. Words in their mouths – now in June's – had a labouring effortful quality – dreadful, because of the fluencies so easily available, but to others.

The children went off at last, June lingering behind. From her look around the room I could see she did not want to go. She was regretting, not the act, but the consequences of it, which might sever her from her beloved Emily.

'What was that about?' I asked.

Emily's bossiness dropped from her, and she slumped, a worried and tired child, near Hugo. He licked her cheek.

'Well, they fancied some of your things, that's all.'

'Yes, but...' My feeling was, *But I'm a friend and they shouldn't have picked on me!* Emily caught this, and with her dry little smile she said: 'June had been here, she knew the lay-out, so when the kids were wondering what place to do next, she suggested yours.'

'Makes sense, I suppose.'

'Yes,' she insisted, raising serious eyes to me, so that I shouldn't make light of her emphasis. 'Yes, it does make sense.'

'You mean, I shouldn't think there was anything personal in it?'

Again the smile, pathetic because of its knowingness, its precocity – but what an old-fashioned word that was, depending for its force on certain standards.

'Oh no, it was personal . . . a compliment if you like!'

She put her face into Hugo's yellow fur and laughed. I knew she needed to hide her face from the effort of presenting it all bright and eager, good and clever. Her two worlds, Gerald's place, my place, had overlapped in a threatening way. I could feel that in her, understand it. But there was an exhaustion in her, a strain that I did not understand – though I believed I had caught a glimpse of the reason in her relations with the children. Her problem was not so much that she was only one of the contenders for Gerald's favour, but that the burdens on her were much too heavy for someone her age?

I asked: 'Why did they bother with the electrical goods?'

'Because they were there,' she replied, over-short; and I knew she was disappointed in me. I had not understood the differences between *them* – a category in which she sometimes did and sometimes did not include herself – and me.

Now she was looking at me. Not without affection, I'm glad to say, but it was quizzical. She was wondering whether to attempt something with me – if it would be resented? would be understood?

She said: 'Have you been upstairs recently?'

'No, I suppose not. Should I have?'

'Well then – yes, yes, I think you should!' And as she made up her mind to go ahead with whatever it was she became whimsical, gay, a little girl charming or disarming a parent or adult; she cried out: 'But we must find something to put things on – yes, this will do. And of course if the lift isn't working – and most of the time it isn't these days, oh dear!'

In a moment she was flying about the rooms, gathering together every electrical object I had, except for the radio, without which we were still convinced we could not live – the news from other countries might just as well be from other planets, so far away did they seem now; and in any case, things went on there just the same as they did with us. Mixers, the television, lamps – these I have already mentioned. To these were added a hair dryer, a massager, a grill, a toaster, a roaster, a coffee pot, a kettle, a vacuum cleaner. They were all piled together on a double-layered trolley.

'Come, come, come, come,' she cried gaily, gently, her serious eyes ever on me, for fear I might be taking offence, and out we went, pushing the over-loaded trolley. The hall was full of people : they streamed up and down the stairs, or waited for the lift – which was working; they laughed and talked and shouted. It was a crowd alight and a-glitter, restless, animated, fervent; everyone looked as if he or she had a fever. Now I realised that of course I had become used to seeing the hall and the pavement immediately outside the building full of this crowd, but I had not understood. This was because along the corridors of the lower floors of the building, all was as it had been : quietness, sobriety, and doors marked 1, 2, 3, behind which lived Mr and Mrs Jones and family, Miss Foster and Miss Baxter, Mr and Mrs Smith and Miss Alicia Smith – little self-contained units, the old world.

We waited for our turn for the lift, pushed the loaded trolley into it, and went up with a crush of people who glanced at our goods and did not think much of them. On the top floor we pushed the trolley into the passage, and Emily stood for a moment, undecided : I could see it was not because she did not know her way, but because she was working out what would be best for me : precisely, what would be *good* for me !

Up here it was the same as on the ground floor : rooms all round the building with a corridor behind them; single rooms off that, a court in the middle – but here the court was of course a well, or gulf. There was a great bustle and movement up here, too. Doors stood open everywhere. It was like the approach to a street market, people with bundles of goods in their arms, or an old pram loaded with this or that, a man carefully holding a wrapped precious thing above his head so that no one could bump into it. It was hard to remember that in the lower parts of the building was quiet and the sense of people giving each other space. A room opposite the lift had a great mound of stuff, right up to the ceiling, and around it crouched children sorting things out into their categories. A child smiled up at Emily and explained: 'I'm just helping with this load, its just come in,' and Emily said: 'That's good, I'm glad,' reassuring the child. Again, there was in this exchange something which made me wonder: the little girl had been overready to explain herself. But we were in the entrance to another room, where an irregular gap in the wall, like bomb damage, communicated with the room we had left – the heap of things had hidden the gap. Through it were being taken by hand, or trundled on various kinds of little cart, certain categories of goods: this room was for containers – jars, bottles, cans and so on, and they were in every sort of material, from glass to cardboard. About a dozen children were at the work of carrying the containers from the heap next door through the gap, into this room: the one thing these markets were not short of, the one commodity no one had been short of for a long time, was labour, was hands to work at whatever was needed. In the corner stood two youths, on guard, with weapons: guns, knives, knuckle dusters. It was not until we stood outside the door of yet another room, where the atmosphere was altogether lower, and more listless, and where there was no guard, that I understood the contents of the rooms with the two armed boys were valuable, but that this room held stuff not valued at all: electrical goods like these we were pushing on our trolley.

We stood there for a while, watching the bustle and movement, watching the children at work.

'They get money, you see,' said Emily. 'Or get something in exchange – even the kids at school come here for an hour or so.'

And I saw that indeed, among these children, some of whose faces were familiar enough, from the pavement, were some better-dressed, cleaner, but above all with that wary self-contained I'm-only-here-on-my-own-terms-look that distinguishes the youngsters of a privileged class when engaged in work that is beneath their conception of themselves. They were here, in short, doing the equivalent of the holiday tasks of middleclass children in the old days – packing goods for firms, cleaning in restaurants, selling behind the counter. Yes, I could have noticed this without Emily, in time; but her shrewd eyes were on me hastening the process; she really was finding me slow to take in, to adapt, and when I did not seem to have understood as quickly as she thought I should, set herself to explain. It seemed that as people left these upper floors empty, to flee from the city, dealers had moved in. It was a large building, much heavier and better-built than most, with good thick floors that could take weight. Mr Mehta had bought rights in a rubbish dump before the government had commandeered all rubbish dumps, and was in business with various people – one was Gerald's father, a man who had once run a business making cosmetics. Usable stuff from the dump was brought here, and sorted out, mostly by children. People came up here to trade. A lot of the goods were taken down again to the street markets and shops.

Goods that were broken and could be mended were put right here : we passed rooms where skilled people, mostly older ones, sat and mended – gadgets, broken saucepans, clothes, furniture. There was in these rooms a great liveliness and interest : people stood around watching. An old man, a watch-mender, sat in a corner, under a light specially rigged up for him, and around him, fascinated, hardly drawing breath, pressed in a thick crowd – so thick that a guard kept asking them to stand back, and when they did not held them with a cudgel. They hardly noticed this, so intent were they, old and young, men and women, watching this precious skill – an old man's hands at work in the tiny machinery.

There was a woman fitting lenses to spectacle frames. She had an oculist's chart on the wall, and according to its findings was handing out second-hand spectacles to people who stood in a line and who, one after another, took from her a pair that she considered suitable. An oculist from the old days; and she, too, had a crowd of admirers. A chair-mender, a basket-mender surrounded with his twisted rushes and reeds, a knife-grinder – here they all were, the old skills, each with a guard, each watched by marvelling barbarians.

What wasn't to be seen in the rooms we passed through, one after another? String and bottles, piles of plastic and polythene pieces – the most valuable, perhaps, of all commodities; bits of metal, wire flex, plastic tape; books and hats and clothes. There was a room full of things that seemed quite new and good and had reached the rubbish dumps shielded from dirt and spoiling : a jersey in a plastic bag, umbrellas, artificial flowers, a carton full of corks.

And everywhere the pressing lively people, here as much for the show as for the goods. There was even a little café in one room, selling herbal teas, bread, spirits. A lot of people seemed tipsy, but they often do at markets, without alcohol. It was hard to tell the sellers from the buyers, the owners from the visitors; it was a polyglot crowd, a good-natured crowd, who respected the orders and instructions of the many guards; an orderly crowd, and one able in the new manner to settle among themselves disputes and differences quickly and without bad feeling being allowed to fester. People joked, showed each other their purchases, and even bought and sold from each other, without going to the formality of engaging the services of the official traders – a process which was quite in order and approved of. What the traders wanted was a crowd, was plenty of people, was the flow of goods, in and out.

We made a tour of the entire floor, and, having been greeted by innumerable people – many of the people from the pavement were up here, again entered the room for electrical goods and pushed forward our trolley. For this merchandise we were given a few vouchers, and I said to Emily that since it was her enterprise that had brought us there, she should have the spending of the results of it. She looked quizzical – I had come to expect this, and understood it was because I might be expecting too much in the way of a return. And what would be done, I wanted to know, with our toasters and roasters? Well, they would be dismantled for their parts, and these parts would be incorporated into other objects – obviously they were of no use as they were? Surely I didn't mind seeing them go? Well, if I didn't mind, she would very much like to take to Gerald's house – was I sure I didn't mind? – some stuff for the kitchen, because they were short. We found an old saucepan, an enamel jug, a plastic bowl, a scrubbing brush : this was what we got in exchange for the electrical equipment of what had been, after all, a lavishly equipped flat.

Back in our flat, Emily put off her little girl charm, without which she could never have brought herself to take me up on an expedition she clearly felt was into her territory and a long way from mine; and sat observing me. She was wondering, I suppose, unflattering though that was, if I had really understood that goods, 'things,' were different commodities for her and for children like June; in some ways more precious, because irreplaceable, but also without value . . . no, that is not right, without personal value : things did not belong to people as they did once. Of course, this had been true among some people long before the time of getting and having had passed : all sorts of experiments in communalism had been worked through, apart from the fact that people like 'the Ryans' had dispensed with ideas of mine and thine, and this without any theories or ideas about it. June was June Ryan; her family had been the despair of the authorities long before the collapse of the old society, when things had still been assumed to be normal. And, as a Ryan . . . But more of this later, when I describe 'the Ryans' in their proper place . . .

Why am I postponing it? This place will do as well as another. In my wanting to postpone what has to be said for the sake of the narrative about the Ryans, no more than an extension and a reflection of the attitudes and emotions of the said authorities towards 'the Ryans'? The point being that 'the Ryans', meaning a way of life, were unassimilatable, both in theory – theories about society and how it worked – and in practice?

To describe them, their circumstances – nothing here that the reader won't have heard a hundred times : it was a textbook case, as the social workers kept exclaiming. An Irish labourer had married a Polish refugee. Both were Catholics. In due time there were eleven children. He drank, was brutal, was intermittently affectionate. She drank, was hysterical, incompetent, unpredictably loving. The children would not stay in school. Welfare authorities, housing authorities, the police, the psychologists, all knew the Ryans. Then the two older boys were in court for stealing, and went to Borstal for a time. The second – not the oldest – girl, got pregnant. She was fifteen. No, there is nothing unfamiliar about any of it, but the Ryans' case seemed to be bigger and more hopeless because there were so many of them, and because both parents were large and colourful characters whose sayings were likely to be quoted at conferences and at meetings : it often happens that a single case takes wing out of its anonymity and represents others : in our city alone there were thousands of 'Ryans' of all kinds, colours, nations, unknown except to their neighbours and to the authorities, and these people in due time found themselves in prison, Borstal, remand homes, and so on. But some charity interested itself in the Ryan family, they were installed in a house : efforts were made to keep them together.

This was how the picture looked to officialdom, doing as well as it could; how it looked in reports; how a newspaper, choosing the Ryans out of so many because of this quality they had of being more visible than others, presented them. *Below the Poverty Line and Lower* this was called. A book recording a dozen cases, the Ryans among them, was : *Rejects of the Affluent Society*. A young man just out of university whose aunt was a welfare worker on the case, had collected notes for a book, *The Barbarians We Make,* comparing the Ryans to those who pulled down Rome from its heights.

The Ryans . . .

How about the Ryan house, for a start? Well, it was filthy, and what furniture it had fit for a rubbish dump. Nothing on the bare floors but dirt, a bone, a plate of rancid cat's food : dogs and cats, like children, were fed impulsively. There was never much heat, so the thirteen Ryans and their friends – the Ryans attracted others and kept them in orbit – were always in one room, huddling. The parents were usually drunk and sometimes the children were, too. The friends were of all colours, and often remarkable, with lives out of the ordinary, and they all sat about, eating biscuits or chips and talking, talking; but sometimes the mother or an older girl cooked up some potatoes with a bit of meat, or opened some tins of something, and it became a festival. Chips and sweet drinks and tea with six or eight spoons of white sugar to each cup – such was the diet of the Ryans, so they were always listless, or on some unnatural peak of vitality while the sugar jigged in their arteries. They sat and talked and talked; the room was lively with that perpetually renewed chronicle, *The Ryans Against the World.* How the three middle children had been set on in the playground by a rival gang or family, but had won; or how the welfare woman had left a piece of paper saying that the fifth child, Mary, had to go to the clinic on Wednesday, and really must try to remember this time, for her rash ought to be attended to; how Paul had found a car unlocked and had taken – whatever was there, because it was there. Two of the girls had visited a chain store and had come back with twenty small plastic purses, two pounds of coffee, gardening shears, some spices from the Indian shelf, and six plastic cullenders. These articles would lie about unused, or might be bartered for other objects : the thieving was for the sake of the act, not of possession. The black girl Tessa, Ruth's friend, and Tessa's brother, and Ruth's other friend Irene and her sister had watched the television all the afternoon in one of the friendly television shops on the main street which did not chase away children who sidled in for an afternoon's free viewing – the Ryans' set was always broken. Stephen had met a dog on the street, and had gone to the canal and thrown sticks for the dog and the dog was ever so clever, it brought back three, no five, even six sticks at once . . . they talked, they talked; they drank and made their day, their lives, through vivid shrewd comment; and when they went to bed, it was three, four, six in the morning – but they did not undress, no one in that house undressed to go to bed, for it was never bedtime. A child would drop off where he sat, on his sister's lap, and stay there asleep, or be set down on the floor on a coat. By morning the four beds of the house each had three or four bodies in them, with the dogs and cats, all close together, warm, warming, protecting. No one got up till ten, eleven, mid-afternoon : if a Ryan found a job, he or she lost it in a week, because it was impossible to get up on time.

They lived on welfare, unless Mr Ryan aroused himself, became sober, and found a job: he was a carpenter. Then money flowed in, and they got clothes and shoes. These garments were worn communally, for no one owned this jersey or that dress. Children wore what fitted and what lay nearest. New clothes might easily be in rags the day after they arrived in the house, for some reason or another.

The children went on a 'job' when the mood took them – which was often. June, the thin sweet-faced little girl, was leader from the age of about seven. Four or five children would slide their way into a flat or a shop and emerge with – money? No, not so, that was not the point; or if it was money, then their pockets would be stacked for days with wads of notes which would fall out or be given away or 'lifted' by someone else. No, they were more likely to return with a marble table lamp, a stack of coffee tables which they had seen on a television advertisement and fancied the look of, a mirror with a pink plastic frame, and cigarettes – which last were valued and instantly shared out.

The point was, the goal of the saints and philosophers was theirs by birthright: *The Way of the Ryans,* it might be called. Each day, each experience, was sufficient unto itself, each act divorced from its consequences. 'If you steal that you will have to go to prison.' 'If you don't eat properly you will suffer from vitamin deficiencies.' 'If you spend that money now there won't be any to pay the rent on Friday.' These truths, always being presented to them by the officials in and out of the house, could never stay in a Ryan head.

And surely the priests and spiritual preceptors were abashed? To be attached to property is bad? What property? A Ryan had none, not even a shirt or a comb. To be the slave to habit is a chain? What habits – unless to have none is a habit of a kind. Regard they neighbour as thyself? – This grace of the very poor was theirs: within the clan which was the Ryans and their friends, white black and brown, who came and went day and night in and out of the house, was infinite giving and tolerance, was a generosity of judgement, a delicacy of understanding not given to many more fortunate people, or at least not without hard jostling with event and circumstance.

One ought not to care for appearances? – It was a long time since the Ryans had been able to afford this luxury.

One ought not to be puffed up, should not stand upon one's rights, should be humble and non-demanding? – Five minutes in the Ryan household would have any middleclass person indignantly on the telephone to his lawyer.

Feckless and irresponsible, hopeless, futureless, uneducated and ineducable – if they could read and write their names they did well; debased and depressed and depraved – but what could you expect when four or five people of any sex or age slept together in one bed? – dirty, unhealthy, louse-ridden and limp with bad feeding when they weren't on a momentary 'high' . . . in short and to be done with it, everything that our old society regarded as bad the Ryans were. Everything that our old society aimed at the Ryans did not even attempt, they had opted out, it was all too much for them.

The poor Ryans, doomed and damned; the dangerous Ryans, such a threat to us all, to our ways of thinking; the lucky Ryans, whose minute-by-hour life, communal and hugger-mugger, seemed all enjoyment and sensation : they liked being together. They liked each other.

When the bad times started, or rather, were *seen* to be starting, a very different thing, the Ryans and all the others like them were suddenly in a different light. First of all – but of course, this is a sociological cliché, some of the boys found places in the police or one of the many military or semi-military organisations that sprang up. And then, it was these people who took most easily to the hand-to-mouth life in the wandering tribes : nothing very much had changed for them, for when had they not been on the move, from room to broken-down house to council flat to hostel in a squatters' street? They ate badly? They were eating better and more healthily now than when civilisation had fed them. They were ignorant and illiterate? They were surviving capably and with enjoyment, which was more than could be said of so many of the middle-class people, who either lived on pretending nothing was *really* happening, only a reorganisation of society; or who faded away in a variety of ways, not able to bear an existence where respectability and gain could no longer measure the worth of a person.

'The Ryans', no longer an extreme, disappeared into society, were absorbed by it. As for our Ryans, the actual family described here, there was still a nucleus somewhere near, the mother and three of the smaller children : the father had died in an accident to do with drink. All the older children had left the city, except for two in the police. June had attached herself to Gerald's household, and one of her younger brothers was there part of the time. 'The Ryans' had turned out to be nothing special, after all. In their humble, non-demanding way they had been part of our society, even when they had seemed not to be : they had been formed by it, were obedient to it. They were as far from what was to come afterwards, and quite soon – when 'the gang of kids from the Underground' appeared in our lives and wrecked Gerald's household – as we were, or had been, from 'the Ryans'.

I use that phrase *Gerald's house* as people had once said *the Ryans,* meaning a way of life. Temporary ways of life, both : all of our ways of living, our compromises, our little adaptations – transitory, all of them, none could last.

But while they lasted, so much clung to and worked at, like Emily with her duties in Gerald's house. Which I now visited, for Emily and I had not been back down in our rooms for more than a few minutes when the doorbell went and it was June, all bright anxious smiles. At first she did not mention the robbery, but sat on the floor with her arms around Hugo. Her eyes were on the move around the room, to see where the things she had taken away and been forced to return, now were. Most were out of sight, back in cupboards and storeplaces, but there was a bundle of fur pieces on a chair, and at last she said, in a spurt of desperate restitution : 'That's all right, is it? I mean, it's all right?' – and even got up to pat the fur, as if it were an animal she might have hurt. I would have liked to laugh, or to smile, but Emily was frowning at me, very fierce indeed, and she said gently to June : 'Yes, everything is fine, thank you.' At which the child brightened up at once, and she said, turning her attention to me with difficulty : 'Will you visit us? I mean

Gerald says it is all right. I asked him, you see? I said to him, can she come, do you see what I mean?'

'I'd like to very much,' I said, having consulted Emily with my eyes. She was smiling: it was the smile of a mother or a guardian.

But first Emily had to prepare herself: she emerged in due time from the bathroom, her hair newly-washed and combed down, her clothes neat, her breasts outlined in blue cotton, cheeks soft and fresh and smelling of soap – a tidy package of a girl, all ready to present herself to her responsibilities, to Gerald. But her eyes were sombre, defensive, worried, and there beside her was June the child, and her face was laid open and absolutely undefended in a trustful smile at Emily the woman – her friend.

We walked, the three of us, through streets dusty and as usual littered with paper, cans, every kind of debris. It would be necessary to pass a tall hotel built in tourism's last fling, and I was watching to see the route Emily would choose: every individual picked out a careful way between hazards in these streets, and one could tell a good deal about a person's nature by whether she chose to go past a dubious building, taking a chance she might be seen from it as prey or a target, or move into another street altogether; by whether she boldly called greetings into defended gardens or walked past quickly with an averted face. Emily went direct, walking carelessly through all the rubbish. Not for the first time I marvelled at the different standards for in and out of doors: inside her home, Emily was as pernickety as a little cat, but outside she seeme dnot to see what she walked through.

The hotel had been taken over by squatters long ago: another obsolete word. But all kinds of people lived there, although as a machine the place was useless, like all the complicated buildings which had depended on technicalities.

Looking up the tall shaft, today outlined against an over-hot and dusty sky, it showed ragged and patched, like lace: windows had been smashed or blown in. Yet the upper parts of it bristled everywhere with devices. Outside one window would be a whirr of light – someone had rigged up a little windmill for catching wind and turning it into power for hot water or lighting. Outside others were slanting discs held out on what looked from down in the street like spider webs: these were solar snares of various kinds. And among these up-to-the-minute contraptions danced and dangled coloured washing held out into the air on timeless string and wood.

Up there it looked gay and even frivolous, with the blue sky as backdrop; down here rubbish was banked up all around the building, with pathways cleared through it to the doors. The smell – but I'll ignore that, as Emily and June seemed able to do so easily.

Recently I had gone into the building, had gone up to the very top: there I stood, looking down over the city which – I suppose not surprisingly – did not *look* so very different than it did in the years before the machines stopped working. I had gazed down and fancied myself back in time: all of us did this a great deal, matching and comparing, balancing facts in our minds to make them fit, to orient ourselves against them. The present was so remarkable and dreamlike that to accommodate it meant this process had to be used: *It was like that, was it? Yes, it was like that, but now....* As I stood up there, thinking that there was one thing missing, an aeroplane, a jet rising up or descending to the airport and dominating the sky, I heard a soft droning, a bee's sound, no louder, and there it was – a plane. A little one, like a grasshopper, painted bright red, all alone in the empty sky where once so many great machines had filled our lives with noise. There it was, a survivor, holding perhaps the police or the army or high officials off to some conference somewhere to talk, talk, talk and pass resolutions about our situation, the sad plight of people everywhere in the world – it was pretty to look at, it lifted the spirits, to see that little thing glittering up there in emptiness, off to some place which no one looking up at it could get near these days except in imagination.

I had walked slowly down through the erstwhile hotel, exploring, examining. I had been reminded of a new township built for African labourers outside a large mine in Africa that I saw in the after all not-so-long-ago days when the continents were close together, were a day's journey away. The township covered acres, had been built all at one time, and was made of thousands of identical little 'houses', each consisting of a room and a small kitchen, a lavatory with a wash-basin. But in one house you would see the pattern of tribal village life brought to the town almost unchanged: a fire burned in the centre of the brick floor, a roll of blankets stood in a corner, and two saucepans and a mug in another. In the next 'house' a scene of Victorian respectability: a sideboard, dining table, a bed, all in hideous varnish, with a dozen crocheted articles for ornament, and a picture of Royalty on the wall opposite the entrance so that the Queen, in full military regalia and the observer could exchange glances of approval over this interior. In between these extremes was every variation and compromise: well, that was what this hotel had become, it was a set of vertical streets in which you could find everything, from a respectably clean family making jokes about conditions in England before the advent of proper sewage disposal and carrying chamber pots and pails down flight after flight of stairs to the one lavatory that still worked, to people living, eating, sleeping on the floor, who burned fuel on a sheet of asbestos and pissed out of the window – a faint spray descending from the heavens these days need not mean imminent rain or condensing steam.

From the possibility of which event I wanted to hurry on and away, instead of standing there, among rubbish, gazing up; particularly as I could see through the windows of the ground floor a couple of young men with guns: they guarded the building, or part of it, or just their own room, or rooms – who knew? But June, seeing them, exclaimed and called out and looked pleased – in the way she had of being pleased, as if every little event offered her undeserved riches of pleasure. With an apology to Emily for keeping her waiting (*my* presence she had the greatest difficulty in remembering at all), in she went, while we two, Emily and I, stood there in a cloud of flies, watching a scene through a window of June being embraced and embracing – one of the two young men had visited in the Ryan house, which meant he had been almost part of the family. Now he gave her a dozen pigeons: the guns were airguns; the pigeons would come back – they had flown off as we arrived – and settle again over the rubbish where they had been feeding. We left, carrying the dead birds which would do for the household's next meal, hearing the silken whirring of many wings, and the pop, pop, pop of the airguns.

We crossed some old railway lines, flourishing now with plants, some of which Emily pulled up, as she passed, for medicine and flavourings. Soon we were at the side of the house. Yes, I had walked past it, out of curiosity, in my walks, but had never wanted to go in, fearing as always to encroach on Emily. Again June waved at a youth standing behind ground floor shutters that were half-open because of the heat, and again some weapon or other was put aside. We entered into a room which was very bare and clean – this struck me first of all, for I had not shed old associations with 'the Ryans'. No furniture at all, but there were curtains, and the shutters were scrubbed and whole, and mats and mattresses were rolled and stood along the walls. I was being taken from room to room on a rapid tour, while I looked for the communal rooms – dining-room, sitting-room, and so on. There was a long room for eating, with trestles and benches, everything scrubbed bare; but otherwise each room was self-sufficient as a workroom or as a home. We opened door after door on groups of children sitting on mattresses which were also beds; they were talking, or engaged on some task, and on the walls were hanging clothes and belongings. It could be seen that natural affinities and alliances had made, were making, of this community a series of smaller groups.

There was a kitchen, a large room where half of the floor had been covered with asbestos sheets and then corrugated iron sheets, where fires of whatever fuel was available could burn. There was a fire burning now, and a meal being prepared by two youngsters who, when they saw it was Emily, stood aside to let her taste and examine : it was a stew, made of meat substitute with potatoes. She said it was good, but what about a few herbs, and offered them the handfuls she had gathered off the railway lines. And here were some pigeons : they could pluck them if they liked, or otherwise find somebody who would like an extra task – no, she, Emily would find someone and send them to do it.

I understood now what I had half-noticed before: the way the children reacted when they saw Emily: this was how people respond to Authority. And now, because she had criticised the stew, a boy knelt and chopped the greenstuff on a board with a piece of sharpened steel: he had been given an order, or so he felt, and was obeying her.

Emily's eyes were on me: she wanted to know what I had seen, what I made of it, what I was thinking. She looked so worried that June instinctively put her hand into Emily's and smiled at her – all this was such a sharp little presentation of a situation that I did not avoid it by pretending I had noticed nothing.

Only a few days before Emily had come in late from this household, and had said to me: 'It is impossible not to have a pecking order. No matter how you try not to.' And she had been not far off tears, and a little girl's tears at that.

And I said: 'You aren't the first person to have that difficulty!'

'Yes, but it isn't what we meant, what we planned. Gerald and I talked it over, right at the start, it was all discussed, there wasn't going to be any of that old nonsense, people in charge telling people what to do, all that *horrible* stuff.'

I had said to her: 'Everybody has been taught to find a place in a structure – that as a first lesson. To obey. Isn't that so? And so that is what everybody does.'

'But most of these children have never had any education at all.'

She was all indignation and incredulity. A grown-up – a very grown-up and responsible – question she was asking: after all, it is one that most adults never ask. But what had confronted me there had been a young girl in whose eyes kept appearing – only to be driven down, fought down – the needs of a child for reassurance, the sullen reproach against circumstances of a very young person, not an adult at all.

'It starts when you are born,' I said. 'She's a good girl. She's

a bad girl. Have you been a good girl today? I hear you've
been a bad girl. Oh she's so *good*, such a good child...
don't you remember?' She had stared at me; she had not really
heard. 'Its all false, it's got to do with nothing real, but we are
all in it all our lives – you're a good little girl, you're a bad
little girl. 'Do as I tell you and I'll tell you you are good.' It's
a trap and we are all in it.'

'We *decided* it wasn't going to happen,' she said.

'Well,' I had said, 'you don't get a democracy by passing
resolutions or thinking democracy is an attractive idea. And
that's what we have always done. On the one hand 'you're a
good little girl, a bad little girl', and institutions and hierarchies
and a place in the pecking order, and on the other passing
resolutions about democracy, or saying how democratic we are.
So there is no reason for you to feel so bad about it. All that
has happened is what always happens.'

She had got to her feet : she was angry, confused, impatient
with me.

'Look,' she said. 'We had everything so that we could make
a new start. There was no need for it to get like it's got. That's
the point, I'm afraid.' and she had gone off to the kitchen, to
get away from the subject.

And now she was standing in the kitchen of her, or Gerald's,
household, angry, confused, resentful.

That child hurrying over his task, not looking up because
the overseer still stood there and might criticise – this humiliated
her, 'But *why*,' she whispered, staring at me, really – I could
see – wanting an answer, an explanation. And June stood smiling there beside her, not understanding, but gazing in pity at
her poor friend who was so upset.

'Oh all right, never mind!' said Emily at last, turning away
from me, June, the scene and going out, but asking as she
went : 'Where's Gerald? He said he would be here.'

'He went with Maureen to the market,' said one of the
children.

'He didn't leave a message?'

'He said we must tell you that we must have our heads done
today.'

'Oh he did did he!' But then, already relieved of her distress, she said: 'Right, tell everyone to get to the hall.' And she led the way to the garden.

It was a fine garden in every way, planned, prepared, organised, full of good things all for use – potatoes, leeks, onions, cabbages, the lot – and not a weed or a flower in sight. Some children were at work there, and as they saw Emily they quickened their pace of work.

Suddenly she exclaimed: 'Oh, no, no, I said the spinach should be left until next week, it's being overpicked.' A child of about seven quite openly grimaced at June – it was that face which is made to say: Who does she think she is, bossing us? – that absolutely routine reaction, to be observed in one form or another anywhere there are groups, hierarchies, institutions. In short, everywhere. But Emily saw it, suffered, and softened her voice: 'But I did say leave it, didn't I? Can't you see for yourself? The leaves are still tiny.'

'I'll show Pat,' said June, quickly.

'It doesn't matter really,' said Emily.

Before we left the garden Emily had again to exclaim and explain: wood ash from the fires to control fly on the cabbages had been laid too close around the stems. 'Can't you *see*?' said Emily to the child, a black child this time, who stood rigid in front of her, his face agonised with the effort of taking this criticism, when he felt he was doing so well. 'It shouldn't be close to the stem, you should make a circle, like this . . .' And she knelt down on the damp soil and trickled ash out of a plastic bag around the cabbage stem. She did it neatly and quickly, she was so expert; and the child sighed and looked at June, who put her arm around him. When Emily looked up from her task with the ash, she saw the two children, one in the protective embrace of the other, allied against her, the boss. She went scarlet, and said: 'I'm sorry if I spoke sharply, I didn't mean to.' At which both children, disengaging themselves from each other, fell in on either side of her and went, distressed by her distress, through the paths of that exemplary garden, towards the house. I followed, forgotten. The black child had put his hand on Emily's forearm; June had hold of her other hand;

Emily was walking blind between them, and I knew this was because her eyes were full of tears.

At the back door she went ahead by herself, the black child following. June fell back to be with me. She smiled at me, really seeing me for this one time : her shy, open, defenceless smile offered me her inadequacy, her deprivation – her history. At the same time her eyes asked that I should not criticise Emily, for she could not bear Emily to be disliked.

In the hall, or dining-room, the trestles had bowls of water set all along them that smelled of a strong herb; there were fine combs and bits of old cloth. Beside the trestles stood the children, and the older ones, with Emily, began to comb through the scalps presented to them.

Emily had forgotten me. Then she saw me and called : 'Would you like to stay and eat with us?'

But I could see she did not want me to.

I had scarcely turned to take myself off, when I heard her anxiety ring out : 'Did Gerald say when he would be back? Did Maureen say anything? Surely he said something about how long they would be?'

Back in my home, I saw, through the window, Gerald arriving on the pavement with a girl, presumably Maureen, and he stood surrounded as usual with the younger children, some from his household, some not. He probably saw his loitering there for hours at a time as a function. I suppose it was. Collecting information, as we all had to; attracting new recruits for his household – but he had more applicants than he could take in; simply showing himself, displaying his qualities among the four or five other young men who were the natural leaders – was this the equivalent of a male going out to hunt while the women kept themselves busy at home? I entertained these thoughts as I stood with Hugo beside me, watching the young man in his brigand's outfit prominent among the people there, with so many young girls hanging about, catching his eye, waiting to talk to him . . . old thoughts, about stale social patterns. Yet one had them, they did not die. Just as the old patterns kept repeating themselves, re-forming themselves even when events seemed to license any experiment or deviation or mutation, so did the old thoughts, which matched the patterns. I kept hearing Emily's shrill, over-pressured voice: 'Where's Gerald, where is he?' as she stood in her woman's place, combing nits and lice out of the younger children's heads, while Gerald was probably planning some expedition to capture supplies from somewhere, for no one could say of him that he was unresourceful or lazy.

Later he was gone from the pavement, and Maureen, too. Soon after that Emily came home. She was very tired and did not try to conceal it. She sank down at once beside the animal, and rested, while I made the supper. I served it, and washed up while she rested again. It seemed to me that my visiting that other house and seeing how much she had to do there, enabled her at last to relax with me, to sit and allow herself to be served by me. When I finished the washing up, I made us both a cup of tea, and sat with her on into the dusk of that summer evening, while she sat limp beside her Hugo.

Outside, the noise and clamour of the pavement under a colourful sunset. In here, was quiet, a soft light, the purring of the animal as he licked Emily's forearm. In here, the sound of a girl crying, like a child, with small fastidious sniffs and gulps. She did not want me to know she was crying but did not care enough to move away.

The wall opened. Behind it was an intensely blue sky, a blue sharply clear and cold, blue that never was in nature. From horizon to horizon the sky stood uniformly filled with colour, and with nowhere in it that depth which leads the eye inwards to speculation or relief, the blue that changes with the light. No, this was a sky all self-sufficiency, which could not change or reflect. The tall sharp broken walls reached up into it, and to look at them was to experience their tough hardness, like flakes of old paint magnified. Glittering white were these shards of wall, as the sky was blue, a menacing hardened world.

Emily came into view, her frowning face bent over a task. She wore a soft blue smocklike garment, like an old-fashioned child from a nursery, and she held a broom made of twigs, the kind used in gardens, and she was massing fallen leaves into heaps that were everywhere on the grass that floored this broken house. But as she swept, as she made her piles, the leaves gathered again around her feet. She swept faster, faster, her face scarlet, desperate. Her broom whirled in a cloud of yellow and orange leaves. She was trying to empty the house of leaves so that the wind could not spread them out again. One room was clear, then another; but outside the leaves lay as high as her knees, the whole world was thickly covered with the leaves that descended as fast as snowflakes everywhere from the horrible sky. The world was being submerged in dead leaves, smothered in them. She turned herself about in an impulsive movement of panic to see what was happening inside the rooms she had cleared: already the piles she had made were being submerged. She ran desperately through the unroofed rooms, to see if here, or here, or here, would be a place that was still covered over and sheltered, still safe from the smothering fall of dead vegetable matter. She did not see me. Her stare, fixed, wide, horrified, passed over me. She saw only the fragments of the walls that could not shelter her, nor keep out the sibilant drift. She stood back against the wall and leaned on her futile little broom, and looked and listened as the leaves rustled and fell over and about her and over the whole world in a storm of decay. She vanished, a staring little figure, a small bright-coloured girl, like a painted china ornament for a cabinet or a shelf, a vivid clot of colour on painted whiteness, the horrible whiteness of the nursery world that opened out of the parents' bedroom where the summer or a storm or a snow-world lay on the other side of thick curtains.

White. White shawls and blankets and bedding and pillows. In an interminable plain of white an infant lay buried and unable to free its arms. It stared at a white ceiling. Turning its head it saw a white wall one way and the edge of a white cupboard the other. White enamel. White walls. White wood.

The infant was not alone; something was moving about, a heavy tramping creature, each footstep making the cot shake. Thud, thud, went the heavy feet, and there was a clash of metal on stone. The infant lifted its head and could not see, it strained to hold its head up from the damp heat of the pillow, but had to let go and fall back, into the soft heat. Never, not until she would come to lie helpless on her deathbed, all strength gone from her limbs, nothing left to her but the consciousness behind her eyes, would she again be as helpless as she was now. The enormous tramping creature came thudding to the cot, whose iron bars shook and rattled, and as the great face bent over her, she was excavated from the hot white and whisked up, losing her breath, and was gripped in hands that pressed on her ribs. She was dirty. Already. Dirty. The sound of the word was disapproval, disgust, dislike. It meant being bundled about, turned this way and that, between hard knocking hands, like a piece of filleted fish on a slab, or a chicken being stuffed.

Dirty, dirty... the harsh cold sound of the word, to me watching this scene, was the air of the 'personal', the unalterability of the laws of this world. Whiteness, dislike sounding in a word, a frigidity, a smothering, as the air fell and fell, dragged down by a storm of white in which the puppets jerked on their strings... *Suppose, then, that the dams were to fill up with ice and the snows came down for ever, an eternal descent of white; suppose the rooms filled up with cold powder, all water gone and crystallised, all warmth held latent in dry chill air that shocked and starved the lungs*... a scene of the parents' bedroom, where the white curtains are drawn back, drifts of white dotted muslin. Beyond these the snow is white on white again, for the sky is blotted out. The two great beds lifted high, high, half-way to the smothering white ceiling, are filled. Mother in one, father in the other. There is a new thing in the room, a cot, all white again, a gelid glittering white. A tall thing, this cot, not as high as the towering beds that have the great people in them, but still beyond one's reach. A white figure bustles in, the one whose bosom is a full slope, which is hard. A bundle is lifted from the cot. While the two people in the beds smile encouragingly, this bundle is held out and presented to her face. The bundle smells, it smells: sharp, and dangerous are these odours, like scissors, or hard tormenting hands. Such a desolation and an aloneness as no one in the world (except everyone in the world) has felt, she feels now, and the violence of her pain is such that she can do nothing but stand there, stiff, staring first at the bundle, then at the great white-clothed nurse, then at the mother and the father smiling in their beds.

She could have sunk down and away from the sight of them, the smiling ones, the great people held up high there against the ceiling in their warm stifling room, red and white, white and red, red carpet, the red flames crowding there in the fireplace. It is all too much, too high, too large, too powerful; she does not want anything but to creep away and hide somewhere, to let it all slide away from her. But she is being presented again and again with the smelling bundle.

'Now, then, Emily, this is your baby,' comes the smiling but peremptory voice from the large woman's bed. 'It is your baby, Emily.'

This lie confuses her. Is it a game, a joke, at which she must laugh and protest, as when her father 'tickles' her, a torture which will recur in nightmares for years afterwards? Should she now laugh and protest and wriggle? She stares around at the faces, the mother, the father, the nurse, for all have betrayed her. This is not her baby, and they know it, so why . . . But again and again they say: 'This is your baby, Emily, and you must love him.'

The bundle was being pushed against her, and she was supposed to put her arms out and hold it. Another deception, for she was not holding it, the nurse did. But now they were smiling and commending her for holding the thing in her arms. And so it was all too much, the lies were too much, the love was too much. They were too strong for her. And she did hold the baby: it was always being lifted down to her, against her, towards her. She held it and she loved it with a passionate violent protective love that had at its heart a trick and a betrayal, heat with a core of ice. . . .

Now the room is the one with the red velvet curtains, and a little girl of about four, dressed in a flowered smock, is standing over a pudgy open-mouthed infant who sits slackly on a piece of linoleum stretched across the carpet.

'No, not like that, like this,' she commands, as the little boy, gazing in admiration at this strong and clever mentor of his, attempts to put a block on another block. It topples off. 'Like *this*,' she shrills, and feverishly kneels and puts blocks one on top of another, very fast and skilfully. She is quite absorbed, every atom of her, in her need to do this, to do it well, to show she can do it, to prove to herself she can do it. The amiable infant sits there, is watching, is impressed, but to do it is the thing, yes, to do it, to place the blocks one above the other, perfectly, corner to corner, edge to edge: 'No, not like that, like *this!*' The words ring through the room, the room next door, the rooms downstairs, the garden. 'Like *this*, Baby, don't you see? Like *this*.'

Things continued to be easier between Emily and me, because of my visit to her other home. I was able, for instance, to comment on her smeared face and swollen eyes one morning. She had not been to Gerald's place the day before, and showed no signs of going now. It was already midday and she had not dressed. She wore what she had slept in, a cotton shift-like garment that had once been a summer evening dress. She was on the floor, her arms around Hugo.

'I don't really see what I am doing there at all,' she said, and meant it as a question.

'I should have said you were doing everything there.'

She held her look steadily on me; she smiled – bitter, and not self-consciously so. 'Yes, but if I didn't, someone would.'

Now, this I did not expect: it was, if you like, too adult a thought. Even while I was privately commending her on it, I was also reacting with alarm, for the other side of this thought, its shadow, is dark indeed, and leads to every sort of listlessness and despair: it is often the first step, to be precise about it, towards suicide . . . at the very least, it is the most deadly of the energy-drainers.

But I sidestepped with: 'Very true. True for everyone of us. But that doesn't mean to say we can all stay in bed! But the thought in *my* mind is, why do you feel like this now? This moment. What triggered it off?'

She smiled – oh yes, she was very quick, very shrewd: 'Well I'm not going to cut my throat!' And then, in a complete switch of level, a plunge, she cried out: 'But if I did, what of it?'

'Is it Maureen?' I asked. I could think of nothing else to offer.

My stupidity enabled her to check herself; she was back again, on her own level. She looked at me; she looked – oh, those looks, which I took one after another, light mocking blows. This one meant: *Oh, a melodrama! He does not love me, he loves another!*

'Maureen . . .' she let slip out of her, like a shrug, and did in fact shrug. But then, condescending, she allowed: 'It is not Maureen, actually, at this very minute it is June.'

And she waited and watched, with her little sour smile, for my '*What*, nonsense, it can't be!'

'It's not right, is it?' she mimicked.

'But she's – how old?'

'Actually, she is eleven, but she says she is twelve.'

She was smiling now, and out of her own, her real philosophy: my energetic disapproval was feeding energy into her, and she even sat up and laughed. My tongue was rejecting, one after another, an assortment of verbalisations, not one of which, I knew, could earn anything less than mockery. Finally, she did mock me again with: 'Well, she can't get pregnant, that's something at least.'

I wasn't going to capitulate. 'All the same,' I said, 'it can't possibly be good for her.'

Her smile changed: it was a little sad, envious perhaps; it meant: You forget we are not in a position to afford your standards. *We* are not so fortunate remember?

Because of this smile, I stayed quiet, and then she said: '*You're* thinking, Oh she's just a child, how wrong! – that sort of thing, but *I'm* thinking, June was my friend and now she isn't.'

And now I really was silenced. For what nonsense was this? If June was not a friend now, she would be in a week, when Gerald went on to one of the others. In one moment – and it seemed that this happened a dozen times a day – Emily had switched from a realm of sophistication far beyond me (making that word mean an acceptance, an understanding, of how things work) to being a child, really a child, and even as they used to be . . . I shrugged, leaving her to it. I could not help it, this switchbacking conversation had been too much for me.

Emily felt the shrug as a condemnation of her, and she cried out : 'I've never had anyone before, not anyone really close, like June.' And her face was turned away to hide a child's tears.

And that is how blind one can be about a thing. For I had been seeing the child June adoring the 'older woman', as was natural, and is a stage in every person's growth. I had never understood how much Emily depended on that thin sharp-faced waif, who not only *looked* three years younger, but was in a different realm altogether, as different as childhood is from young womanhood.

I could only offer : 'You know he will get tired of her and you will be friends again.'

She almost shrieked in her exasperation at my old-fashioned ways and thoughts : 'It is not a question of getting *tired*.'

'What then. Tell me.'

She looked at me, in her turn shrugged and said : 'Well, things are quite different, aren't they . . . he just has to – make the rounds, I suppose. Like a cat marking his territory.' And she laughed, a little, at the thought.

'Well, whatever your original and brilliant new customs are, the point is, June will be free quite soon, surely ?'

'But I miss her *now*,' she wept, a little girl again, thumbs sweeping tears from her eyes; but up she jumped, and said, as an adult : 'Anyway, I have to go there, whether I like it or not.' and off she did go, red-eyed, miserable, full of a suppressed anger that showed in every movement. She went because her sense of duty would not let her do otherwise.

Behind my flowery wall was a straight-upstanding, a tall, fine, white-shining house. I looked at it from some way off, then came closer, noting that this was the first time I had approached a house from outside, instead of finding myself inside another building from the moment I crossed the mysterious frontier. It was a solid and well-kept house, in style rather like the Cape Dutch, whose every sober curve speaks of the burgher, the bourgeois. The house shone, with a peculiar soft glisten. It was made of a substance which was familiar in itself, but not when shaped into a house. I broke a piece off it and ate : sweet, dissolving on the tongue. A sugar house, like the one in fairy tales; or if not sugar, then the edible substance they once used to wrap bars of nougat. I kept breaking off bits and eating and tasting . . . it was compulsively edible, because it was unsatisfying, cloying : one could eat and eat and never be filled with this white insipidity. There was Emily, breaking off whole pieces of the roof and cramming them into her healthy mouth; there, too, was June, languidly picking and choosing. A fragment of wall, a piece of windowpane . . . we ate and ate our way into the house like termites, our stomachs laden but unsatisfied, unable to stop ourselves, but nauseated. Eating my way around a corner I saw a room in that region I knew was the 'personal'. I knew the room. A small room, with strong sunlight coming through the window. A stone floor, and a cot in the middle of it, and in the cot, a child, a small girl. Emily, absorbed, oblivious. She was eating – chocolate. No, excrement. She had opened her bowels into the freshness of the white bed and had taken handfuls of the stuff and smeared it everywhere with quick shrieks of triumph and joy. She had smeared it on sheets and blankets, over the wood of the cot, over herself, over her face and into her hair, and there she sat, a little monkey, thoughtfully tasting and digesting.

This scene – child, cot, sunlit room – diminished sharply, dwindled in the beam of my vision, and was whisked away to be replaced by the same scene made smaller, reduced by the necessity to diminish and so to contain pain; for suddenly there were heavy clanging steps on the stone, a loud angry voice, slaps, heavy breathing – there were low mutters and then exclamations of disgust, and the child yelling and screaming, first in anger, and then after an interval when she was half-drowned by the vigour with which she was scrubbed and swished about in a deep and over-hot bath, in despair. She wept in innocent despair, as the big woman snuffed and sniffed at her, to see if the stink of shit had been washed away but found (still, in spite of the too-hot water that had scalded and burned, in spite of the scrubbing which had left the fragile skin painful and red) a faint tainted odour, so that she had to keep on exclaiming in disgust and in fright. The mother was exclaiming over and over again in dislike of her; the child was sobbing with exhaustion. She was dumped down in a playpen, and her cot was taken out for a scrubbing and a disinfecting. Alone in her disgrace, she sobbed on and on.

A child crying. The miserable lost sound of incomprehension.

'You are a naughty girl, Emily, naughty, naughty, naughty disgusting, filthy, dirty, dirty, dirty dirty dirty dirty, a dirty girl Emily, you are a dirty *naughty,* oh *disgusting,* you are a filthy dirty dirty girl, Emily.'

I wandered looking for her in adjacent rooms, but never finding the right one, though I could hear Emily's misery sometimes very close. Often I knew her to be through a single wall: I could have touched her if there had not been a wall there. But, following that wall to its end, it led beyond the 'personal' and I was out on a bright green lawn or small field with summer trees standing about its edges. On the lawn was an egg. It was the size of a small house, but poised so lightly it moved in a breeze. Around this brilliant white egg, under a bright sky, moved Emily, her mother, and her father, and – this was as improbable an association of people as one could conceive – June too, close to Emily. There they strayed, contented in the sunlight, with the light breeze moving their clothes. They touched the egg. They stood back and looked at it. They smiled; they were altogether full of delight and pleasure. They laid their faces to the smooth healthy slope of the egg's surface, so that their cheeks could experience it; they smelled it; they gently rocked it with their fingertips. All this scene was large and light and pleasurable, was freedom – and from it I turned a corner sharp back to a narrow and dark passageway and the sound of a child's crying . . . of course I had been mistaken, she had not been behind *that* wall at all, there was another one, and I knew exactly where it was. I began to run, I ran, I had to reach her. I was conscious that I was also reluctant, for I was not looking forward to the moment when I, too, would smell that faint contaminating smell in her hair, her skin. I was setting myself a task as I ran: I was not to show my repugnance, as her mother had done with her sharply indrawn breath, a controlled retching, the muscles of her stomach convulsing again and again, her quivering dislike of the child communicating itself down through the arms which lifted Emily up and away from the scene of her pleasure, and dropped her sharp and punishing into the bath where the water, from the need for haste, was still cold, but where very hot water was flooding and the two streams of very hot and very cold water swirled all around her, scalding and freezing her legs and stomach. But I could not find her, I never did find her, and the crying went on and on and on, and I could hear it in the day, in my 'real' life.

I've said, I think, that when I was in one world – the region behind the flowery wall of my living-room, the ordinary logical time-dominated world of everyday did not exist; that when in my 'ordinary' life I forgot, and sometimes for days at a time, that the wall could open, had opened, would open again, and then I would simply move through into that other space. But now began a period when something of the flavour of the place behind the wall did continuously invade my real life. It was manifested at first in the sobbing of a child. Very faint, very distant. Sometimes inaudible, or nearly so, and my ears would strain after it and then lose it. It would begin again, and get quite loud, and even when I was perhaps talking to Emily herself, or standing at the window watching events outside. I heard the sobbing of a child, a child alone, disliked, repudiated; and at the same time, beside it, I could hear the complaint of the mother, the woman's plaint, and the two sounds went on side by side, theme and descant.

I sat listening. I sat by myself and listened. It was warm, over-warm; it was that hot final summer. There was often thunder, sudden dry storms; there was restlessness in the streets, the need to move . . . I would make little tasks for myself, because I had to move. I sat, or kept myself busy, and I listened. One morning Emily came in, all brisk and lively, and, seeing me at work setting plums on trays to dry, she joined me. She was wearing that morning a striped cotton shirt, and jeans. The shirt lacked a button at breast-level, and gaped, showing her already strong breasts. She looked tired, as well as full of energy; she had not yet bathed, and a smell of sex came from her. She was fulfilled and easy, a bit sad, but humorously so. She was, in short, a woman, and she sat smiling and wiping plums with slow easy movements, all the hungers, the drives and the needs pounded and hunted out of her, exorcised in the recent lovemaking. And all the time, that child was crying. I was looking at her; I was thinking as the elderly do, wrestling with time, the sheer cussedness of the thing – futilely (but they cannot help it), using the thought over and over again as a kind of measure or guideline: *That was fourteen years ago, less, when you wept so painfully and for so long because of your incomprehension and because of your scalded buttocks and thighs and legs. Fourteen years for me is so short a time, it weighs so light in my scale: in yours, in your scale, it is everything, your whole life.*

She, thinking of time, speaking of it as a girl was once expected to while she marked the slow overtaking of the milestones one by one into womanhood and freedom, said 'I'm coming up to fifteen,' because she had just passed her fourteenth birthday. She had said that only yesterday; she was capable of talking like that, even pertly and with a fling of her hair, like a 'young girl'. Meanwhile she had just come from lovemaking, and no girl's lovemaking at that.

All that morning I listened to the sobbing while I sat working with her. But Emily heard nothing, though I couldn't believe it.

'Can't you hear someone crying?' I asked, as casual as could be, while I was twisting and turning inwardly not to hear that miserable sound.

'No, can you?' And off she went to stand at the window, Hugo beside her. She was looking to see if Gerald had arrived yet. He had not. She went to bath, to dress; at the window she stood waiting – yes, he was just arriving. And now she would stand there a little longer, careful not to see him, so as to assert her independence, to emphasise this other life of hers with me. She would linger half an hour, an hour. She would even sit down again with her ugly yellow animal, fondling and teasing him. Her silence would grow tense, her stares out of the window more stylised: *Girl at Window Oblivious of her Lover.* Then her hand on the animal's head, stroking and patting, would forget him, would fall away. Gerald had seen her. He had noticed her *not* noticing him. He had turned away: unlike her, he genuinely did not care very much, or rather, he did care, but not at all in the same way. At any rate, now, this afternoon, June was there, and Maureen, a dozen other girls. And Emily could not bear it. She went, with a kiss for her Hugo. As for me I got the ritual: 'I'll just go out for a little if that is all right with you.'

And in a moment she was with them, her family, her tribe, her life. A striking-looking girl, with her dark hair flat on either side of a pale, too-earnest face, she was where Gerald was, who swaggered there with the knives in his belt, his whiskers, his strong brown arms. Good Lord, how many centuries had we overturned, how many long slow steps of man's upclimbing did Emily undo when she crossed from my flat to the life on the pavement! And what promise, what possibilities, what experiments, what variations on the human theme had been cancelled out! Watching, I fell into despair at the precariousness of every human attempt and effort, and I left the window. It was that afternoon I tried deliberately to reach behind the wall: I stood there a long time looking and waiting. The wall did not have light lying there now, was uniform, dull, blank. I went up and pressed my palms against it, and moved my hands all over it, feeling and sensing, trying everything to make the heavy solidity of the thing go down under the pressure of my will. It was nonsense, I knew that; it was never because of my, or anybody's, wanting when that wall went down and made a bridge or a door. But the interminable low sobbing, the miserable child, was driving me frantic, was depriving me of ordinary sense ... yet by turning my head I could see her, a lusty young girl on the pavement, unsmiling perhaps, because of her innate seriousness, but very far indeed from weeping. It was the child I wanted to pick up and kiss and soothe. And the child was so close, it was a question only of finding the right place on the wall to press, as in the old stories. A particular flower in the pattern, or a point found by counting just so many inches from here to there and then gently pushed . . . but of course, I knew there could be nothing in a deliberate attempt of the will. Yet I stood there all afternoon, and into the evening, as it darkened outside and the flares were lit on the pavement, showing the crowding masses eating, drinking, milling about in their clans and alliances. I let my palms move over the wall, slowly, inch by inch, but I did not find a way in that day, nor the next, I never did find that weeping child who remained there, sobbing hopelessly alone and disowned, and with long years in front of her to live through before time could put strength into her and set her free.

I never found Emily. But I did find . . . the thing is, what I did find was inevitable. I could have foreseen it. The finding had about it, had in it as its quintessence, the banality, the tedium, the smallness, the restriction, of that 'personal' dimension. What else could I find – unexpectedly, it goes without saying – when behind that wall I ran and ran along passages, along corridors, into rooms where I *knew* she must be but where she was not, until at last I found her: a blonde blue-eyed child, but the blue eyes were reddened and sullen with weeping. Who else could it possibly be but Emily's mother, the large carthorse woman, her tormentor, the world's image? It was not Emily I took up in my arms, and whose weeping I tried to shush. Up went the little arms, desperate for comfort, but they would be one day those great arms that had never been taught tenderness; the face, scarlet with need, was solaced at last into a pain-drained exhaustion as the fair little child collapsed, head on my shoulder, and the soft wisps of gold baby-hair came up dry and pretty as I rubbed the dank strands gently through my fingers, to absorb the sweat. A pretty, fair little girl, at last finding comfort in my arms . . . and who was it I saw at an earlier stage than the scene where a little girl joyously smeared the chocolate-brown faeces into her hair, her face, her bedding? For once, following a low sobbing, I walked into a room that was all white and clean and sterile, the nightmare colour of Emily's deprivation. A nursery. Whose? This was before a brother or sister had been born, for she was tiny, a baby, and alone. The mother was elsewhere, it was not time to feed. The baby was desperate with hunger. Need clawed in her belly, she was being eaten alive by the need for food. She yelled inside the thick smothering warmth; sweat scattered off her scarlet little face; she twisted her head to find a breast, a bottle, anything: she wanted liquid, warmth, food, comfort. She twisted and fought and screamed. And screamed – for time must pass before she was fed, the strict order of the regime said it must be so: nothing could move that obdurate woman there, who had set her own needs and her relation with her baby according to some timetable alien to them both, and who would obey it to the end. I knew I was seeing an incident that was repeated again and again in Emily's? her mother's? – early life. It was a continuing thing; had gone on, day after day, month after month. There had been a screaming and hungry, then a whimpering and sullen, baby, wanting the next meal which did not come, or if it did come, was not enough. There was something in that strong impervious woman which made this so, dictated it. Necessity. The strict laws of this small personal world. Heat. Hunger. A fighting of emotion. The hot red running of flames from a barred fireplace on white walls, white wool, white wood, white, white. The smell of sick rising from the wet that grated under the chin, the smell of wet heavy wool. And smallness, extreme smallness, weakness, a helplessness reaching out and crying for the little crumbs of food, freedom, variation of choice which were all that could reach this little hot place where the puppets jerk to their invisible strings.

———◆———

I think this is the right place to say something more about 'it'. Though of course there is no 'right' place or time, since there was no particular moment marking – then or now – 'its' beginning. And yet there did come a period when everyone was talking about 'it'; and we knew we had not been doing this until recently : there was a different ingredient in our lives.

Perhaps I would have done better to have begun this chronicle with an attempt at a full description of 'it'. But is it possible to write an account of anything at all without 'it' – in some shape or another – being the main theme? Perhaps, indeed, 'it' is the secret theme of all literature and history, like writing in invisible ink between the lines, which springs up, sharply black, dimming the old print we knew so well, as life, personal or public, unfolds unexpectedly and we see something where we never thought we could – we see 'it' as the ground-swell of events, experience . . . Very well then, but what *was* 'it'? . . . I am sure that ever since there were men on earth 'it' has been talked of precisely in this way in times of crisis, since it is in crisis 'it' becomes visible, and our conceit sinks before its force. For 'it' is a force, a power, taking the form of earthquake, a visiting comet whose balefulness hangs closer night by night distorting all thought by fear – 'it' can be, has been, pestilence, a war, the alteration of climate, a tyranny that twists men's minds, the savagery of a religion.

'It', in short, is the word for helpless ignorance, or of helpless awareness. It is a word for man's inadequacy?

'Have you heard anything new about it?'

'So and so said last that it . . .'

Worse still when the stage is reached of 'Have you heard anything new', when 'it' has absorbed everything into itself, and nothing else can be meant when people ask what is moving in our world, what moves our world. It. Only it, a much worse word than 'they'; for 'they' at least are humanity too, can be moved, are helpless, like ourselves.

'It', perhaps – on this occasion in history – was above all a consciousness of something ending.

How would Emily put what she felt into words? She would describe this, perhaps, in terms of that image of her sweeping, sweeping, the sorcerer's apprentice put to work in a spiteful garden against floods of dying leaves that she could never clean away no matter how hard she tried. Her sense of duty but expressed in images – she could not say of herself that yes, she was a good little girl and not a bad dirty little girl; a good little girl who must love cherish and protect her brother, her baby, the defenceless, the powerless, the amiably indifferently smiling, who sat there all loose and slack in their damp strong-smelling white wool. 'It was so hard,' she might say. 'Everything was so difficult, such an effort, such a burden, all those children in the house, not one of them would do a thing to help unless I got at them all the time, they turned me into a tyrant and laughed at me, but there was no need for that, they could have had something equal and easy if they had done their parts but no, I always had to overlook everything, comb their dirty hair and see if they had washed and then all those sores that they got when they wouldn't eat sensibly, and the horrible smell of disinfectants all the time that the government supplied and the way June got sick, it drove me crazy with worry, she kept getting ill for no particular reason – that was it, there was never any good reason for things, and I worked and I worked and it was always the same, something happened and then it all came to nothing.'

Yes, that is probably how Emily's version of that time would sound.

June, returning with Emily to my flat one day, about a fortnight after her induction into womanhood – I put it like that because this was how she obviously felt it – had changed physically, and in every way. Her experience had marked her face, which was even more defenceless, in her sad-waif style, than before. And she was looking older than Emily. Her body still had the flat thickness through the waist of a child, and her breasts had fattened without shaping. Anxiety, or love, had made her eat enough to put on weight. We saw her, that eleven-year-old, as she would look as a middleaged woman: the thick working body, the face that accommodated, that always seemed able to accommodate, two opposing qualities: the victim's patient helplessness, the sharp inquisitiveness of the user.

June was not well. Our questions brought out of her that this was nothing new, she hadn't been too good 'for quite a time'. Symptoms? 'I dunno, jst feel bad, you know what I mean.'

She had stomach pains and frequent headaches. She lacked energy – but energy cannot be expected of a Ryan. She 'jst didn't feel good anywhere at all, it comes and goes, reely'.

This affliction was not only June's; it was known to a good many of us.

Vague aches and pains; indispositions that came and went, but not according to the terms and times prescribed by the physicians; infections that seemed to be from a common source, since they would go through the community like an epidemic, but not with an epidemic's uniformity – they demonstrated their presence in different symptoms with every victim; rashes that did not seem to have any cause; nervous diseases that could end in bouts of insanity or produce tics or paralyses; tumours and skin diseases; aches and pains that 'wandered' about the body; new diseases altogether that for a time were categorised with the old ones for lack of information until it became clear that these *were* new diseases; mysterious deaths; exhaustions and listlessness that kept people lying about or in bed for weeks and caused relatives and even themselves to use the words *malinger* and *neurotic* and so on but then, suddenly vanishing, released the poor sufferers from criticism and self-doubt. In short there had been for a long time a general increase in illness, both traditional and newly-evolved, and if June complained of 'just not feeling good anywhere, do you see what I mean?' – then we did, for it was common enough to be classed as a recognisable illness in itself. June decided to move in with us, 'for a few days,' she said, but what she needed was to evade the pressures, psychological or otherwise, of Gerald's household, and Emily and I knew, if June did not, that she would have liked to leave there altogether.

I offered the big sofa in the living-room to June, but she preferred a mattress on Emily's floor, and even, I think, slept on it, though of course I wondered. Silently wondered. Too often had I experienced a sharp shocked reaction to questions asked innocently. I really did not know if Emily and June would consider lesbianism as the most normal thing in the world, or as improper. Styles in morals had changed so sharply and so often in my lifetime, and were so different in various sections of the community, that I had learned long ago to accept whatever was the norm for that particular time and place. I rather believe that the two girls slept in each other's arms for comfort. Of course I could have no doubt, after what Emily had told me, about how she must feel now she had the child, her 'real friend', alone with her there. Almost alone – there was me and there was Hugo. But at least there weren't so many others around all the time.

Emily tried to 'nurse' June. That is to say, she fussed and offered food. But a Ryan doesn't eat like an ordinary citizen : June nibbled, all fancies and antipathies. Probably she was, as Emily said, suffering from vitamin deficiencies, but she said : 'That doesn't make sense to my mind : I never eat any different, do I? But I feel bad inside and everywhere now, don't I, and I didn't before.'

So if June were asked to say what 'it' was like for her, she would very likely answer : 'Well, I dunno reely, I feel bad inside and everywhere.'

Perhaps, after all, one has to end by characterising 'it' as a sort of cloud or emanation, but invisible, like the water vapour you know is present in the air of the room you sit in, makes part of the air you know is there when you look out of a window – your eye is traversing air, so your intellect tells you when you look at a sparrow pecking insects off a twig; and you know that the air is part water vapour which at any moment – as a slap of cold air comes in from somewhere else – will condense as mist or fall as rain. 'It' was everywhere, in everything, moved in our blood, our minds. 'It' was nothing that could be described once and for all, or pinned down, or kept stationary; 'it' was an illness, a tiredness, boils; 'it' was the pain of watching Emily, a fourteen-year-old girl, locked inside her necessity to – sweep away dead leaves; 'it' was the price or unreliability of the electricity supply; the way telephones didn't work; the migrating tribes of cannibals; was 'them' and their antics; 'it' was, finally, what you experienced . . . and was in the space behind the wall, moved the players behind the wall, just as much there as in our ordinary world where one hour followed another and life obeyed the unities, like a certain kind of play.

As that summer ended there was as bad a state of affairs in the space behind the wall as on this side, with us. Or perhaps it was only that I was seeing what went on there more clearly. Instead of entering into a room, or a passageway, where there was a door which opened into other rooms and passages, so that I was within a sense of opportunities and possibilities, but limited always to the next turn of the corridor, the opening of the next door – the sense of plenty, of space always opening out and away kept within a framework of order within which I was placed, as part of it – now it seemed as if a perspective had shifted and I was seeing the sets of rooms from above, or as if I were able to move through them so fast I could visit them all at once and exhaust them. At any rate, the feeling of surprise, of expectancy, had gone, and I could even say that these sets and suites of rooms, until so recently full of alternatives and possibilities, had absorbed into them something of the claustrophobic air of the realm of the 'personal' with its rigid necessities. And yet the disorder there had never been so great. Sometimes it seemed to me as if all those rooms had been set up, carefully, correct to the last detail, simply in order to be knocked flat again; as if a vast house had been taken over and decorated to display a hundred different manners, modes, epochs – but quite arbitrarily, not consecutively and in order to give a sense of the growth of one style into another. Set up, perfected – and then knocked flat.

I cannot begin to give an idea of the mess in those rooms. Perhaps I could not go into a room at all, it was so heaped with cracking and splintering furniture. Other rooms had been used, or so they looked, as refuse dumps: stinking piles of rubbish filled them. Some had their furniture neatly set out in them, but the roofs had gone, or the walls gaped. Once I saw in the centre of a formal and rich room – French, Second Empire, as lifeless as if it had been arranged for a museum – the remains of a fire built on a piece of old iron, some sleeping bags left anyhow, a big pot full of cold boiled potatoes near the wall in line with a dozen pairs of boots. I knew the soldiers would come back suddenly, and if I wanted to keep my life I should leave. Already there was a corpse, with dried blood staining the carpet around it.

And yet, with all these evidences of destructiveness, even now I could not move behind the wall without feeling something of the old expectation, hope, even longing. And rightly, for when the anarchy was at its height, and I had almost lost the habit of expecting anything but smashed and dirtied rooms, there was a visit when I found this – I was in a garden between four walls, old brick walls, and there was a fresh delightful sky above me that I knew was the sky of another world, not ours. This garden did have a few flowers in it, but mostly it had vegetables. There were beds neatly filled with greenery – carrot tops, lettuces, radishes, and there were tomatoes, and gooseberry bushes and ripening melons. Some beds were raked and ready for planting, others had been turned and left open to the sun and the air. It was a place filled with industry, usefulness, hope. I walked there under a fruitful sky, and thought of how people would be fed from this garden. But this wasn't all, for I became aware that under this garden was another. I was able easily to make my way down into it along a sloping ramp of earth, and there were even steps of, I think, stone. I was down in the lower garden which was immediately under the first, and occupied the same area : the feeling of comfort and security this gave me is really not describable. Nor was this lower garden any less supplied with sun, wind, rain, than the upper one. Here, too, were the tall warm walls of weathered brick, and the beds in various stages of preparedness and use. There was an ex- quisite old rose growing on one wall. It was a soft yellow, and its scent was in all the air of the garden. Some pinks and mignonette grew near a sunny old stone : these were the old flowers, rather small, but subtle and individual : all the old cottage flowers were here, among the leeks and the garlics and the mints. There was a gardener. I saw him at the moment I realised I was listening with pleasure to the sound of water running near my feet where there was a channel of earth, with tiny herbs and grasses growing along its edges. Near the wall the channel was of stone, and wider : the gardener was bending over the stone runnel where it came into the garden from outside through a low opening that was green and soft with moss. Around every bed was a stream of clear water, the garden was a network of water channels. And, looking up and beyond the wall, I saw that the water came from the mountains four or five miles away. There was snow on them, although it was midsummer, and this was melted snow-water, very cold, and tasting of the air that blew across the mountains. The gardener turned when I ran towards him to ask if he had news of the person whose presence was so strong in this place, as pervasive as the rose-scent, but he only nodded and turned back to his duties of controlling the flow of water, of seeing that it ran equably among the beds. I looked across at the mountains and at the plain between, where there were villages and large stone houses in gardens, and I thought that what I was looking at was the under-world – and one just as extensive and productive – of the level to which I now had to return. I walked up to the first level again, and saw the old walls warm with evening sunlight, heard water running everywhere though I had not heard it when I stood here before; I took small cautious steps from one solid but moist spot to the next, with the smell of apple-mint coming up from my knees and the sound of bees in my ears. I looked at the food the earth was making, which would keep the next winter safe for us, for the world's people. Gardens beneath gardens, gardens above gardens : the food-giving surfaces of the earth doubled, trebled, endless – the plenty of it, the richness, the generosity . . .

And back in my ordinary life I watched June listless in a deep chair, shaking her head with a patient smile at a plate of food being held towards her by Emily.

'But she has to eat, hasn't she?' said Emily to me, sharp with worry, and when the child continued to smile and refuse, Emily whirled about and set the plate down in front of Hugo who, knowing he was being used to demonstrate rejection, as if she were tipping food into a rubbish bin, turned his face away. I saw Emily then, all loving remorse, sit by her neglected slave, and put her face down into his fur, as once she had so often been used to do. I saw how he turned his head a little towards her, despite his intention not to show response, let alone pleasure. Despite himself, he licked her hand a little, with a look on him that a person has when doing something he doesn't want to do, but can't stop . . . and she sat and wept, she wept. There they were, the three of them, June with her malady, whatever it was, the ugly yellow beast in his humility, suffering his heartache, and the fierce young woman. I sat quiet among the three of them, and thought of the gardens that lay one above another so close to us, behind a wall which at this time of the day – it was evening – lay quite blank and with no depth in it, no promise. I thought of what riches there were in store for these creatures and all the others like them; and though it was hard to maintain a knowledge of that other world with its scent and running waters and its many plants while I sat here in this dull shabby daytime room, the pavement outside seething as usual with its tribal life – I did hold it. I kept it in my mind. I was able to do this. Yes, towards the end it was so; intimations of that life, or lives, became more powerful and frequent in 'ordinary' life, as if that place were feeding and sustaining us, and wished us to know it. A wind blew from one place to the other; the air of one place was the air of the other; as I came to the window after an escape into the space behind the wall there would be a moment of doubt, my mind would sway and have to steady itself as I reassured myself that no, what I was looking at was reality, was real life; I was standing foursquare in what everybody would concur was normality.

———◆———

By the end of that summer there were hundreds of people of all ages on the pavement. Gerald was now only one of a dozen or so leaders. Among them was a middle-aged man – a new development, this. There was also a woman, who led a small band of girls. They were self-consciously and loudly critical of male authority, male organisation, as if they had set themselves a duty always to be there commenting on everything the men did. They were a chorus of condemnation. Yet the leader seemed to find it necessary to spend a great deal of energy preventing individuals of her flock from straying off and attaching themselves to the men. This caused a good deal of not always good-natured comment from the men, sometimes from the other women. But the problems and difficulties everyone had to face made this kind of disagreement seem minor. And it was an efficient group, showing great tenderness to each other and to children, always ready with information – still the most important of the commodities – and generous with what food and goods they had.

It was to the women's group that we lost June.

It happened like this. Emily had again taken to spending most of her days and nights at the other house: duty had taken her back, for messages had come that she was needed. She wanted June to move with her, and June did listen Emily's persuasions, agreed with her – but did not go. I began to think that I was to lose Emily, my real charge, for June, and I did not feel any particular responsibility for her. I liked the child, though her listless presence lowered the atmosphere of my home, making me listless, too, and keeping Hugo in a permanent sorrow of jealousy. I was pleased enough when she roused herself to talk to me: for the most part she lay in a corner of the sofa, doing nothing at all. But the truth was, I would have liked her to leave. She asked after Gerald when Emily came flying home to cook a meal of her favourite chips, to make pots of precious tea, to serve her cups half-filled with precious sugar: she listened, and asked after this and that person; she liked to gossip. She said to me, to Emily, and doubtless to herself, that she was going, yes, she would go tomorrow. She confronted Emily's frenzies and anxieties with: 'I'll come over tomorrow, yes I will, Emily,' – but she stayed where she was.

On the pavement Emily was being very energetic. Gerald's troop was about fifty strong, with the people actually living in his household and the others who had gravitated towards him from the crowds who kept coming in, and in, during the long hot afternoons.

Emily was always to be seen near Gerald, prominent in her role of adviser, source of information. I now did what I had once been careful to avoid, for fear of upsetting Emily, of disturbing some balance. I crossed the street myself 'to see what was going on' – as if I had not been watching what went on for so many months! But this was how all the older citizens described their first, or indeed their subsequent trips to the pavement – described them often, right up to the moment when they put together a blanket, some warm clothes and a little food to leave the city with a tribe passing through, or one taking off from our pavement. I even wondered if perhaps this visit of mine away from my flat to across the street was a sign of an inner intention to leave which I knew nothing about yet. This was so attractive an idea that as soon as it had entered my head, it took possession and I had to fight it down. My first trip to the pavement – to stand there, to mill around with the others for an hour or so, was really to hear what it was that Emily so ably and for so many hours every day, dispensed out there. Well, I was astounded . . . how often had this girl taken me by surprise! Now I drifted around among this restless, lively, ruthless crowd and saw how everyone, not only those who seemed ready to owe allegiance to Gerald, turned to her for news, information, advice. And she was ready with it. Yes, there were dried apples in such and such a shop in that suburb. No, the bus for a village twenty miles west was not cancelled altogether, it still ran once a week until December, and there was a trip next Monday at ten a.m., but you would have to be there in the queue the night before and must be prepared to fight for your place : it would be worth it, for it was said there were plentiful supplies of apples and plums. A farmer was coming in by cart every Friday with mutton fat and hides, and could be found at . . . Big strong horses were for sale, or barter. And yes, there was a house four streets away quite suitable for stabling. As for fodder, that could be procured, but better still, grow it, and for one horse you would need . . . A variety of chemical devices for cooking and lighting were being constructed tomorrow afternoon at the second floor of the old Plaza Hotel; assistance was needed and would be paid for in the form of the said devices. Wood ash, horse manure, compost, would be for sale under the old motorway at Smith Street at 3 p.m. on Sunday. Lessons in making your own wind-generators, to be paid for in food and fuel . . . air cleansers and purifiers, water cleansers, earth sterilisers . . . laying fowls and coops for them . . . knife sharpeners . . a man who knew the plan of the underground sewers and the rivers that ran into them was piping water to the surface at . . . The street between X Road and Y Crescent was growing superb crops of yarrow and colts-foot, and on the corner of Piltdown Way was a patch of potatoes people had planted and then forgotten: they had probably left the city. Emily knew all these things and many more and was much sought-after, by virtue of her energy and her equipment, in that scene like a fair where hundreds of egos clashed and competed and fed each other – Emily, Gerald's girl. So she was referred to, so spoken of. This surprised me, knowing the state of affairs in that house I had visited. This was yet another emotional, or at least verbal, hangover from the past? A man had a woman, an official woman, like a first wife, even when he virtually ran a harem? . . . if one could use one old-fashioned term, then why not another? I did try the word out on June: 'Gerald's harem,' I said; and her little face puzzled up at me. She had heard the word, but had not associated it with anything that could come close to her. But yes, she had seen a film, and yes Gerald had a harem. She, June, was part of it. She even giggled, looking at me with those pale blue eyes that seemed always to be swallowing astonish-ment. There she lay, seeing herself as a harem girl, a little ageing woman with her childish flat waist, her child's eyes, her pale hair dragged to one side.

Emily of course had marked my appearance on the pave-ment, and was assuming I was ready to migrate. And how attractive it was there with those masses of vigorous people, all so resourceful in the ways of this hand-to-mouth world, so easy and inventive in everything they did. What a relief it would be to throw off, in one movement like a shrug of the shoulders, all the old ways, the old problems – these, once one took a step across the street to join the tribes would dissolve, lose importance. Housekeeping now could be just as accurately described as cavekeeping, and was such a piddling, fiddly business. The shell of one's life was a setting for 'every modern convenience'; but inside the shell one bartered and captured and even stole, one burned candles and huddled over fires made of wood split with an axe. And these people, these tribes, were going to turn their backs on it all, and simply take to the roads. Yes, of course they would have to stop somewhere, find an empty village, and take it over; or settle where the farmers that survived would let them, in return for their labour or for acting as private armies. They would have to make for themselves some sort of order again, even if it was no more than that appropriate to outlaws living in and off a forest in the north. Responsibilities and duties there would have to be, and they would harden and stultify, probably very soon. But in the meantime, for weeks, months, perhaps with luck even a year or so, an earlier life of mankind would rule : disciplined, but democratic – when these people were at their best even a child's voice was listened to with respect; all property worries gone; all sexual taboos gone – except for the new ones, but new ones are always more bearable than the old; all problems shared and carried in common. Free. Free, at least from what was left of 'civilisation' and its burdens. Infinitely enviable, infinitely desirable, and how I longed simply to close my home up and go. But how could I? There was Emily. As long as she stayed, I would. I began again to talk tentatively of the Dolgellys, of how we would ask for a shed there and build it up and make it into a home . . . June as well, of course. For from the frantic anxiety Emily showed, I could see it would not be possible for Emily to be separated from June.

And Hugo? The truth is she did not have time for him, and I was thinking that if he had been what kept her here before, this was not true now.

I believe that he gave up hope altogether during that time when Emily was hardly ever with us, and only flew in to see June. One day I saw him sitting openly at the window, all of his ugly stubbornly yellow self visible to anyone who chose to look. It was a challenge, or indifference. He was seen, of course.

Some youngsters crossed the street to look at the yellow animal sitting there, gazing steadily back at them with his cat's eyes. It occurred to me that some of the youngest there, the real children of five or six years old, might never have seen a cat or a dog as a 'pet' to love and make part of a family.

'Oh, he is ugly,' I heard, and saw the children make faces and drift off. No, there would be nothing to help Hugo when the time came for him; no one could say: 'Oh don't kill him, he's such a handsome beast.'

Well . . . Emily came in one evening and saw the blaze of yellow at the window. Hugo was vividly there, illuminated by a flare from the late sunset, and by the candles. She was shocked, knowing at once why he should have chosen to disobey the instincts of self-protection.

'Hugo,' she said, 'oh my dear Hugo . . .' He kept his back to her, even when she put her hands on either side of his neck and brought her face down into his fur. He would not soften, and she knew he was saying that she had given him up, and did not care for him.

She coaxed him off the high seat and sat with him on the floor. She began to cry, an irritable, irritating, sniffing sort of weeping that was from exhaustion. I could see that. So could June, who watched without moving. And so could Hugo. He licked her hand at last and lay himself patiently down, saying to her by the way he did this: *It is to please you. I don't care to live if you don't care for me.*

Now Emily was all conflict, all anxiety. She kept rushing back and forth from my flat to that house, between there and the pavement. June, she had to see June, to bring her the bits of food she liked, to make the gesture of getting her into bed at a decent hour, for, left to herself, June would be in that sofa-corner until four or six in the morning, doing nothing, except perhaps to mark the interior movements of her illness, whatever that might be. And Hugo, she had to make a point of fussing over Hugo, of loving him. It was as if she had set herself the duty of paying attention to Hugo, measured, like a medicine or a food. And there was myself, the dry old guardian, the mentor – a pull of some sort, I suppose. There were the children, always sending after her if she stayed away from that house for too long. She was worn out; she was cross and sharp and harried and it was a misery to see her at it.

And then, suddenly, it was all over.

It was solved : June left.

She got herself out of the sofa one day and was on the pavement again. Why? I don't know. I never knew what moved June. At any rate, in the afternoons she was again with the crowds out there. She did not seem to be more part of one group than another : her flat, pale, effaced little person was to be seen as much in the other clans as in the one that Gerald held together. She was seen, but only once or twice, in the women's group. And then the women's group had gone and June had gone with them.

And yes, we did not believe it, did not even, at first, know what had happened. June was not in my flat. She was not on the pavement. She was not in Gerald's house. Emily ran frantically about, asking questions. At that point she was stunned. June had left, just like that, without even leaving a message? Yes, that's what it looked like : she had been heard to say, so someone reported, that she felt like moving on.

It was this business of June's not having said goodbye, of not leaving a message, that Emily could not swallow. June had not given any indication at all? – we talked it over, the crumbs we had between us, and at last we were able to offer to the situation the fact that June had said on the day she left : 'Well, ta, I'll be seeing you around, I expect.' But she had not directed this particularly, to Emily or to me. How could we have understood this was her farewell before going away for good?

It was the inconsequence of the act that shocked. June did not believe we were worth the effort of saying goodbye? She had not said a real goodbye because she thought we would stop her? No, we could not believe that was it : she would have stayed as readily as she had left. The shocking truth was that June did not feel *she* was worth the effort : her leaving us, she must have felt, was of no importance. In spite of the fact that Emily was so devoted, and anxious and loving? Yes, in spite of that. June did not value herself. Love, devotion, effort, could only pour into her, a jug without a bottom, and then pour out, leaving no trace. She deserved nothing, was owed nothing, could not really be loved and therefore could not be missed. So she had gone. Probably one of the women had been kind to her, and to this little glow of affection June had responded, as she had to Emily's. She had gone because she could leave one day as well as another. It did not matter, she did not matter. At last we agreed that the energetic and virile woman who led that band had captured the listless June with her energy, at a time when Emily did not have enough to go around.

Emily could not take it in.

And then, she began to cry. At first the violent shocked tears, the working face and blank staring eyes of a child, which express only: What, is this happening to *me*! It's impossible! It isn't *fair*! – Floods of tears, noisy sobs, exclamations of anger and disgust, but all the time the as it were painted eyes, untouched: *Me*, it is *me* sitting here, to whom this frightful injustice has occurred . . . a great fuss and a noise and a crying out, this kind of tears, but hardly intolerable, not painful, not a woman's tears . . .

Which came next.

Emily, eyes shut, her hands on her thighs, rocked herself back and forth and from side to side, and she was weeping as a woman weeps, which is to say as if the earth were bleeding. I nearly said *as if the earth had decided to have a good cry* – but it would be dishonest to take the edge off it. Listening, I certainly would not have been able to do less than pay homage to the rock-bottom quality of the act of crying as a grown woman cries.

Who else can cry like that? Not an old woman. The tears of old age can be miserable, can be abject, as bad as anything you like. But they are tears that know better than to demand justice, they have learned too much, they do not have that abysmal quality as of blood ebbing away. A small child can cry as if all the lonely misery of the universe is his alone – it is not the pain in a woman's crying that is the point, no, it is finality of the acceptance of a wrong. So it was, is now and must ever be, say those closed oozing eyes, the rocking body, the grief. Grief – yes, an act of mourning, that's it. Some enemy has been faced, has been tackled, but a battle has been lost, all the chips are down, everything is spent, nothing is left, nothing can be expected ... yes, in spite of myself, every word I put down is on the edge of farce, somewhere there is a yell of laughter – just as there is when a woman cries in precisely that way. For, in life, there is often a yell of laughter, which is every bit as intolerable as the tears. I sat there, I went on sitting, watching Emily the eternal woman at her task of weeping. I wished I could go away, knowing it would make no difference to her whether I was there or not. I would have liked to give her something, comfort, friendly arms – a nice cup of tea? (Which in due time I would offer.) No, I had to listen. To grief, to the expression of the intolerable. What on earth, the observer has to ask – husband, lover, mother, friend, even someone who has at some point wept those tears herself, but particularly, of course, husband or lover, 'What in the name of God can you possibly have expected of me, of life, that you can now cry like that? Can't you see that it is impossible, *you* are impossible, *no one* could ever have been promised enough to make such tears even feasible ... can't you see that?' But it is no use. The blinded eyes stare through you, they are seeing some ancient enemy which is, thank heavens, not yourself. No, it is Life or Fate or Destiny, some such force which has struck that woman to the heart, and for ever will she sit, rocking in her archaic and dreadful grief, and the sobs which are being torn out of her are one of the pillars on which everything has to rest. Nothing less could justify them.

In due course, Emily keeled over, lay in a huddle on the floor and, the ritual subsiding into another key altogether, she snuffled and hiccupped like a child and finally went to sleep.

But when she woke up she did not go back to the other house, she did not go out to the pavement. There she sat, coming to terms. And there she would have stayed for good, very likely, if she had not been challenged.

Gerald came over to see her. Yes, he had been in before, and often, for advice. Because his coming was nothing new, we did not know that his problem, our problem, was anything new. And he didn't, at this stage.

He wanted to talk about 'a gang of new kids' for whom he felt a responsibility. They were living in the Underground, coming up in forays for food and supplies. Nothing new about that, either. A lot of people had taken to a subterranean existence, though they were felt to be a bit odd, with so many empty homes and hotels. But they could be actively wanted by the police, or criminal in some way, feeling the Underground to be safer.

These 'kids', then, were living like moles or rats in the earth, and Gerald felt he should do something about it, and he wanted Emily's support and help. He was desperate for her to rouse herself, and to energise him with her belief and her competence.

He was all appeal; Emily all listlessness and distance. The situation was comic enough. Emily, a woman, was sitting there expressing with every bit of her the dry: You want me back, you need me – look at you, a suitor, practically on your knees, but when you have me you don't value me, you take me for granted. *And what about the others?* Irony inspired her pose and gestures, set a gleam of intelligence that was wholly critical on her eyelids. On his side he knew he was being reproached, and that he certainly must be guilty of something or other, but he had had no idea until this moment of how deeply she felt it, how great his crime must be. He was searching his memory for behaviour which at the time he had committed it he had felt as delinquent, and which he could see now – if he really tried and he *was* prepared to try – as faulty ... is this, perhaps, the primal comic situation?

He stuck it out. So did she. He was like a boy in his torn jersey and worn jeans. A very young man indeed was this brigand, the young chieftain. He looked tired, he looked anxious; he looked as if he needed to put his head on someone's shoulder and be told, There, there! He looked as if he needed a good feed and to have his sleep out for once. Is there any need to describe what happened? Emily smiled at last, drily, and for herself – for *he* could not see why she smiled, and she would not be disloyal to him in sharing it with me; she roused herself in response to the appeal which he had no idea he was making, the real one, for he went on logically explaining and exhorting. In a short time they were discussing the problems of their household like two young parents. Then off she went with him, and for some days I did not see her, and only by fits and starts did I come to understand the nature of this new problem, and what was so difficult about these particular 'kids'. Not only from Emily, did I learn : when I joined the people on the pavement everybody was talking about them; they were everyone's problem.

A new one. In understanding why this was, we householders had to come to terms with how far we had travelled from that state when we swapped tales and rumours about 'those people out there', about the migrating tribes and gangs. Once, and only a short time ago, to watch – and fearfully – a mob go past our windows was the limit of our descent into anarchy. Once, a few months ago, we had seen these gangs as altogether outside any kind of order. Now we wondered if and when we should join them. But above all the point was that when studied, when understood, their packs and tribes had structure, like those of primitive man or of animals, where in fact a strict order prevails. A short time with people living this sort of life, and one grasped the rules – all unwritten, of course, but one knew what to expect.

And this was precisely where these new children were different. No one knew what to expect. Before, the numerous children without parents attached themselves willingly to families or to other clans or tribes. They were wild and difficult, problematical, heartbreaking; they were not like the children of a stable society : but they could be handled inside the terms of what was known and understood.

Not so this new gang of 'kids'. Gangs, rather : soon we learned that there were others; it was not only in our district that such packs of very young children defied all attempts at assimilation. For they were very young. The oldest were nine, ten. They seemed never to have had parents, never to have known the softening of the family. Some had been born in the underground and abandoned. How had they survived? No one knew. But this was what these children knew how to do. They stole what they needed to live on, which was very little indeed. They wore clothes – just enough. They were . . . no, they were *not* like animals who have been licked and purred over, and, like people, have found their way to good behaviour by watching exemplars. They were not a pack either, but an assortment of individuals together only for the sake of the protection in numbers. They had no loyalty to each other, or, if so, a fitful and unpredictable loyalty. They would be hunting in a group one hour, and murdering one of their number the next. They ganged up on each other according to the impulse of the moment. There were no friendships among them, only minute-by-minute alliances, and they seemed to have no memory of what had happened even minutes before. There were thirty or forty in the pack in our neighbourhood, and for the first time I saw people showing the uncontrolled reactions of real panic. They were going to call the police, the army; they would have the children smoked out of the Underground . . .

A woman from the building I lived in had gone out with some food to see 'if anything could be done for them', and had met a couple on a foray. She had offered them food, which they had eaten then and there, tearing it and snapping and snarling at each other. She had waited, wanting to talk, to offer help, more food, even perhaps homes. They finished the food and went off, without looking at her. She had sat down : it was in an old warehouse near the Underground entrance, where grass and shrubs were growing up through the floor, a place both sheltered and open, so that she could run for it if she had to. And she did have to . . . as she sat there, she saw that all around her were the children, creeping closer. They had bows and arrows. She, unable to believe, as she put it, 'that they really were past hope' had talked quietly to them, of what she could offer, of what they risked living as they did. She understood, and with real terror, that they *did not understand her.* No, it was not that they did not understand speech, for they were communicating with each other in words that were recognisable, if only just – they *were* words, and not grunts and barks and screams. She sat on, knowing that an impulse would be enough to lift a bow up and send an arrow her way. She talked for as long as she could make herself. It was like, she said, talking into a vacuum – it was the most uncanny experience of her life. 'When I looked at them, they were only kids, that was what I couldn't get into my thick head, they were just children . . . but they are wicked. In the end I got up and left. And the thing that was worst of all was when one of them came running after me and tugged at my skirt. I couldn't believe it. I knew he would have stuck a knife into me as easily. He had his finger in his mouth, and he was pulling at my skirt. He was grinning. It was just an impulse, do you see? He didn't know what he was doing. The next minute there was a yell and they were all after me. I ran, I can tell you, and I only escaped by nipping into that old Park Hotel at the corner and I shook them off by barricading myself into a room on the fourth floor until dark.'

These were the children Gerald had decided must be rescued by his household. Where would they all fit in? Well, somewhere, and if they didn't, there was that other big house just across the road, and perhaps Emily and he could run the two houses between them?

There was much resistance to the idea. From everybody. Emily too. But Gerald wore them down: he always did, because after all it was he who maintained them, got food and supplies – he who took responsibility. If he said it could be done, then perhaps . . . and they were just 'little kids', he was right about that. 'Just little kids, how can we let them rot out there?'

I believe that the others in the house comforted themselves with 'they won't come anyway'. They were wrong. Gerald could make people believe in him. He went down the Underground, heavily armed and showing it. Yes, he was terrified . . . they crept from holes and corners and tunnels, they seemed able to see without much light whereas he was half-blinded by the flare of the torch. He was alone down there, and he was an enemy, since everybody was, offering them something they did not even know the words for. But he was able to make them follow him. He walked back from the Underground like a Pied

Piper, and the twenty or so children who followed him ran and shouted all over the house, flinging open doors and slamming them, putting their fists through the precious polythene in the windows. Smelling food being cooked, they stood crowded together waiting for it to come their way. They saw people sitting down, children their own ages with the adults, a sight that was astonishing to them. They were subdued, it seemed; or at least their reflexes were temporarily put out. Or perhaps they were curious? They would not sit down at table – they never had, they would not sit down on the floor in an orderly way to be served, but they did stand snatching at food which was passed to them on trays, and bolted it down, their bright hard eyes watching everything, trying to understand. When there was not enough food to fill their aroused expectations, they ran shrieking and jeering through the house, destroying everything.

At once that household broke up. Gerald would not listen to reason, to the appeals of the existing inhabitants. There was something about the situation of those children which Gerald could not tolerate; he had to have them in there, he had to try, and now he would not throw them out. By then it was too late. The others left. It took a few hours for Gerald and Emily to find their 'family' all gone, while they were house-parents of children who were savages. Gerald had apparently actually believed that they could be taught rules which had been made for everyone's sake. Rules? They could hardly understand what was said: they had no idea of a house as a machine. They wrecked everything, tore up the vegetables in the garden, sat at windows throwing filth at passers-by like monkeys. They were drunk; they had taught themselves drunkenness.

From my window I saw that Emily had her arm in bandages, and went over to ask what was wrong.

'Oh, nothing much,' said she, with her dry little humour, and then told how she and Gerald, descending that morning to the lower regions of the house, had found the children squatting and scratching all together, like monkeys in a too-small cage. There were bits of half-cooked meat about. They had been roasting rats : near the house was an entrance to some sewers.

Nothing *under* the earth could be alien to these children, and they had crept down there with their catapults and bows and arrows.

Upstairs, Emily and Gerald had had a talk about tactics. Their situation was bleak. They had not been able to find any of their own children – not one. These had all left for other communes or households, or had decided that this was the moment to join a caravan going out of the city for good. The two were completely alone with these new children. They at last decided that a sharp business-like descent into the lower part of the house, and a reasonable but stern talk, must be attempted. What they envisaged was, in fact, the immemorial 'sensible' talk of adults appealing to children's better sense before retribution had to fall. The trouble was, no retribution was possible, everything had already happened to these outcasts. Emily and Gerald realised they had nothing to threaten them with, and nothing to offer but the old arguments that life is more comfortable for a community if the members keep the place clean, share work, respect each other's individuality. And the children had survived without such thoughts ever having come near them.

But, not being able to think of anything else, the two young parents did go down, and one of the brats had suddenly run at Emily and hit her with a cudgel. Had hit her again and shouted – in a moment another little child had jumped in to attack. Gerald, going to rescue Emily, had found himself, too, being hit, bitten, scratched, and by a dozen or so of them. It had taken all their strength to fight off these children, not one of whom was over ten, and yet the inhibition against hitting or hurting a child was so strong that it 'paralysed our arms', as Emily explained. 'How can you hit a child?' Gerald had demanded, even though Emily's arm was badly bruised. Standing there, embattled, blood all over the place, the two young people had fended off children, and, screaming above their screams, had tried to reason and persuade. The response to these exhortations was that the children had got themselves into a tight knot in a corner of the room, facing out, teeth bared, holding their cudgels ready to repel an attack, as if the words had been missiles. At last Emily and Gerald removed themselves, had another discussion, decided more must be attempted, but did not know what. That night, lying in their bed at the top of the house, they smelled smoke : the children had set fire to the ground floor, just as if the house were not their shelter. The fire was put out, and again the little savages cowered behind their weapons while Gerald, beside himself with emotion – for he simply could not endure that these children were not to be saved (for what, of course, was a question not one of us would ask) – Gerald pleaded and reasoned and persuaded. A stone from a catapult just missed his eye, and cut open his cheekbone.

What was to be done?

The children could not be thrown out. Who was to throw them out? No, with his own hands, Gerald had opened the gates to the invaders, who would now stay. Why not! They had piles of bedding, clothing, a fireplace to burn fuel in – they had never been warm before. Yes, almost certainly the house would soon burn down. It had been tidy and clean; now there was food everywhere, on floor, walls, ceilings. It stank of shit : the children used landings, even the rooms they slept in. They did not even have the cleanliness of animals, their instincts for responsibility. In every way they were worse than animals, and worse than men.

They menaced everyone in the neighbourhood, and there was to be a big meeting about it tomorrow on the pavement. People were coming from the flats and from the houses round about. I was invited. That the barriers were completely down between the citizens and the life on the pavement showed how serious a threat were these children.

Next afternoon I went out, careful to leave Hugo in my bedroom, the door locked, the curtains drawn.

It was an autumn afternoon, the sun low and cold. Leaves were flying everywhere. We stood in a great mass, five hundred or more, and people kept coming in to join us. On a little improvised platform of bricks were the half a dozen leaders. Emily was up there with Gerald.

Before the talking began, the children who were to be discussed arrived and stood a little apart, listening. There were now about forty of them. I remember that we were all encouraged they were with us, had come at all – community feeling of a kind, perhaps? At least they had understood there was to be a meeting that concerned them; they had taken in words, and understood them in the same way we did ... then they began stamping around and chanting: *I am the king of the castle, you are a dirty rascal.* It was terrifying. This ancient children's song was a war-song, they had made it one, they were living it. But more than that, we could all see how familiar words could slip out of key – how quickly things could change, we could change ... *Had* changed: those children were ourselves. We knew it. We stood there, sullen and uncomfortable, listening. It was in accompaniment to this shrill jeering chant that Gerald began to describe the situation. Meanwhile there was apprehension, a restlessness in the crowd, which was due to more than the presence of the children, or our knowledge of ourselves. For this was like a 'mass meeting' of the ordinary world, and we had every reason to fear such meetings. Above all what we feared more than anything was the attention of Authority – that 'they' should be alerted. Gerald, reasonable as he always was, explained how essential it was, for the sake of us all to rescue the child, and we, standing shoulder to shoulder, again listening to a person talking down at us from a platform, were thinking that this was one street in one of many suburbs, that our comfortable habit of seeing only ourselves, our pavements and their energetic life, was a way of being able to cope with the fear. A useful way: we were not important, and the city was large. We were able to continue our precarious little lives because of our good sense, which enabled *Them* to take no notice of us. What they chose to overlook was all the time more; but they still would not stand for the burning down of a house or a street, or for a gang of children who were under no one's control terrorising everyone. They had their spies among us. They knew what went on.

Perhaps, in describing as I have done only what went on among ourselves, in our neighbourhood, I have not been able to give a clear enough picture of how our by now very remarkable society worked ... for after all, it *was* working. All this time, while ordinary life simply dissolved away, or found new shapes, the structure of government continued, though heavy and cumbersome and becoming all the time more ramified. Nearly everyone who had a job at all was in administration – yes, of course we ordinary people joked that the machinery of government was maintained so that privileged folk could have jobs and salaries. And there was some truth in it. What government really did was to adjust itself to events, while pretending, probably even to itself, that it initiated them. And the law courts worked on, plenty of them; the processes of law were infinitely tricky and prolonged, or sudden and Draconian, as if the impatience of the practitioners of law with their own processes and precedents got itself impressed by the way law could suddenly be dispensed with altogether, be overridden and re-written – and then what had been substituted went grinding along as heavily as before. The prisons were as full as ever, though expedients were always being found to empty them : so many crimes were being committed, and there seemed to be new and unforeseen categories of crime every day. Reform schools, Borstals, welfare homes, old age homes – all these proliferated, and they were savage and dreadful places.

Everything worked. Worked somehow. Worked on an edge, on one side of which was what authority tolerated, on the other, what it could not : this meeting was well over the edge. And very soon the police would arrive in a fleet of cars and drag off these children and put them behind bars in a 'home' where they wouldn't survive a week. Nobody, knowing their history, could feel anything but compassion for them; not one of us wished for them an end in a 'home' – but neither did we want, we could not tolerate, a visit of the police which would bring to official notice a hundred living arrangements that were not legal. Houses being lived in by people who didn't own them, gardens growing food for people who had no right to eat it, the ground floors of deserted houses accommodating horses and donkeys which were transport for the innumerable little businesses that illegally flourished, the little businesses themselves where all the riches of our old technology were being so ingeniously adapted and transformed, minuscule turkey farms, chicken runs, rabbit sheds – all this new life, like growth pushing up under old trees, was illegal. None of it should exist. None of it, officially, existed; and when 'they' were forced into seeing these things, they sent in troops or the police to sweep it all away. Such a visit would be referred to in a headline, a broadsheet, a newscast as 'Such and such a Street was cleaned out today'. And everyone knew exactly what had happened and thanked fortune it was someone else's street.

Such a 'cleanout' was what everybody feared more than anything, and yet we were tempting 'Them' by gathering together. Gerald talked on, in an emotional desperate way, as if the act of talking itself could produce some solution. He said at one point that the only way to cope with the 'kids' was to separate them and put them into households in ones and twos. I remember the jeering that went up from the children, and their white angry faces. They stopped their pathetic war-dance and stood huddled, facing outwards, weapons at the ready.

A young man appeared over the heads of the crowd: he had his arm around the trunk of a tree and was holding himself there. 'What are we doing this for?' he shouted. 'If they came now that would be the end of us, never mind about those kids. And if you want to know what I think, we should inform the police and be done with it. We can't cope with it. Gerald has tried – haven't you Gerald?'

And he disappeared, sliding down the trunk.

Emily now spoke. It looked as if someone had asked her to. She stood on the pile of bricks, serious, worried, and said: 'What can you expect? These kids defend themselves. That's what they have learned. Perhaps we should persevere with them? I'll volunteer if others will.'

'No, no, no,' came from everywhere in the crowd. Someone shouted out: 'You've got a broken arm from them by the look of it.'

'Rumour broke the arm, not the kids,' said Emily smiling, and a few people laughed.

And there we stood. It is not often a crowd so large can remain silent, in indecision. To call the police would be a real descent away from what we could tolerate in ourselves, and we could not bring ourselves to do it.

A man shouted: 'I'll call the police myself, and you can have it out with me afterwards. We've got to do it, or the whole neighbourhood will go up in flames one of these nights.'

And now the children themselves began edging away, still in their tight little band, clutching their sticks, their stones, their catapults.

Someone shouted: 'They're off'. They were. The crowd jostled and swayed, trying to see how the children ran across the road and disappeared into the dusk.

'Shame,' called a woman from the crowd. 'They're scared, poor little mites.'

At that moment there was a shout: 'The Police!' – and everyone was running. From the windows of my flat, Gerald, Emily and I and some others watched the great cars come roaring up, their lights flashing, their sirens shrieking. There was no one on the pavement. The cars drove by in a pack, around a block, and then back and around again. The shrieking, whining, clanging posse of monsters drove around and about our silent streets for half an hour or so, 'showing their teeth,' as we said, and then they went away.

What 'they' could not tolerate, could not tolerate even now, was the semblance of a public meeting, which might threaten them. Extraordinary and pathetic, for the last thing that interested anyone by this time was changing the form of government: we wanted only to forget it.

When the streets were quiet, Emily and Gerald went off to the other house, to see if the children had gone back there. But they had been and gone, taking with them all their little belongings – sticks and stones and weapons, bits of roast rat, uncooked potatoes.

The two had the house to themselves. There was nothing to prevent a new community being made there. The old one might be restored? No, of course it could not: something organic, which had grown naturally, had been destroyed.

———◆———

It was cold. There was very little fuel. In the long dark afternoons and evenings I sat with a single candle glimmering in my room. Or I would put it out, and let the fire light the room.

Sitting there one day, staring at the fire-flicker, I was through it and beyond – into the most incongruous scene you could imagine. How can I say 'ill-timed' of a world where time did not exist? All the same, even there, where one took what came, did not criticise the order of things, I was thinking: What a strange scene to show itself now!

I was with Hugo. Hugo was not just my accompaniment, an aide, as a dog is. He was a being, a person, in his own right, and necessary to the events I was seeing.

It was a girl's room, a schoolgirl's. Rather small, with conventional flowered curtains, a white spread for the bed, a desk with school books laid tidily, a school timetable pinned on a white cupboard. In the room, in front of a mirror that ordinarily was not part of the room at all (it had a little looking glass tacked to the wall above a washbasin), a long, capacious mirror all scrolled and gilded and curlicued and fluted, the sort of mirror one associated with a film set or a smart dress shop or the theatre – in front of this mirror, here only because the atmosphere and emotional necessities of the scene needed more than the sober small square looking glass, was a young woman. Was Emily, a girl presented or parcelled up as a young woman.

Hugo and I stood side by side, looking at her. My hand was on the beast's neck, and I could feel the tremors of his disquiet coming up into my hand from his misgiving heart. Emily was fourteen or so, but 'wellgrown' as once they had been used to put it. She was in evening dress. The dress was scarlet. It is hard to describe what my feelings were on seeing it, seeing her. They were certainly violent. I was shocked by the dress, or rather, that such dresses had ever been tolerated, ever been worn by any woman, because of what they made of the woman. But they had been taken for granted, had been seen as just another fashion, no worse or better than any.

The dress was tight around waist and bust : the word bust is accurate, those weren't breasts, that breathed and lifted or drooped and could change with emotion, or the month's changes : they made a single, inflated, bulging mound. Shoulders and back were naked. The dress was tight to the knees over hips and bottom – again the accurate word, for Emily's buttocks were rounded out into a single protuberance. Below, it twirled and flared around her ankles. It was a dress of blatant vulgarity. It was also, in a perverted way, non-sexual, for all its advertisement of the body, and embodied the fantasies of a certain kind of man who, dressing a woman thus, made her a doll, ridiculous, both provocative and helpless; disarmed her, made her something to hate, to pity, to fear – a grotesque. In this monstrosity of a dress, which was a conventional garment worn by hundreds of thousands of women within my lifetime, coveted by women, admired by women in innumerable mirrors, used by women to clothe their masochistic fantasies – inside this scarlet horror stood Emily, turning her head this way and that before the glass. Her hair was 'up', leaving her nape bare. She had scarlet nails. In Emily's lifetime the fashion had never been thus – there had been no fashion at all, at least, for ordinary people, but here she was, a few paces from us, and, sensing us there, her faithful animal and her anxious guardian, she turned her head, slow, slow, and looked at us with long lowered lashes, her lips held apart for fantasy kisses. Into the room came the large tall woman, Emily's mother, and her appearance at once diminished Emily, made her smaller, so that she began to dwindle from the moment the mother stood there. Emily faced her and, as she shrank in size acted out her provocative sex, writhing and letting her tongue protrude from her mouth. The mother gazed, horrified full of dislike, while her daughter got smaller and smaller, was a tiny scarlet doll, with its pouting bosom, its bottom outlined from waist to knees. The little doll twisted and postured, and then vanished in a flash of red smoke, like a morality tale of the flesh and the devil.

Hugo moved forward into the space before the mirror and sniffed and smelled at it, and then at the floor where Emily had stood. The mother's face was twisted with dislike, but now it was this beast that was affecting her so. 'Go away,' she said, in a low breathless voice – that voice squeezed out of us by an extremity of dislike or fear. 'Go away you dirty filthy animal.' And Hugo retreated to me, we backed away together before the advancing woman who had her fist raised to hit me, hit Hugo. We backed away, fast, then faster, while the woman advanced, grew large, became enormous, absorbing into herself Emily's girlhood room with its simpering conventionality, the incongruous mirror and – snap! – we were back in the living-room, in the dark place where the single candle bloomed in its hollow of light, where the small fire warmed a little space of air around it. I was sitting in my usual place. Hugo was upright near the wall, looking at me. We looked at each other. He was whimpering . . . no, the right word is crying. He was crying, in desolation, as a human does. He turned and crept away into my bedroom.

And that was the last time I saw Emily there in what I have called the 'personal'. I mean that I did not again enter scenes that showed her development as a girl, or baby, or child. That horrible mirror-scene, with its implications of perversity, was the end. Nor, entering that other world through – and this was new, too – the flames, or the husbanded glow of the fire as I sat beside it through these long autumn nights, did I find the rooms which opened and opened out from each other: or I did not think I had. Returning from a trip into that place I could not keep a clear memory of what I had experienced, where I had been. I would know that I *had* been there, from the emotions that sustained, or were draining, me : I had been fed there, from some capacious murmuring source all comfort and sweetness; I had been frightened and threatened. Or perhaps in, or under, the thick light of this room seemed now to shimmer another light which came from *there* – I had brought it with me and it stayed for a while, making me long for what it represented.

And when it faded, how slow and dim and heavy was the air . . . Hugo had developed a dry cough, and as we sat together, he might suddenly jump up and go to the window, nosing at it, his sides labouring, and I would open it, realising that I, too, was in a stupor from the fug and the heaviness of the room. We would stand there side by side, breathing the air that flowed in from outside, trying to flush our lungs clean with it.

———————◆———————

After some days when I had not seen Emily at all, I went to Gerald's house through streets which were disordered, as always, but seemed much cleaner. It was as if an excess of dirtiness and mess had erupted everywhere, but then winds, or at least movements of air, had taken some of it away. I saw no one during this walk.

I half expected to find that efforts had been made towards restoring the vegetable garden. No. It was wrecked and trampled, and some chickens were at work in it. A dog was creeping towards them under the bushes. This was so rare a sight that I had to stop and look. Not one dog, but a pack of dogs, and they were creeping on all sides towards the pecking chickens. I cannot tell you how uneasy this made me : there was something enormous waiting to burst in on me, some real movement and change in our situation : dogs! a pack of dogs, eleven or twelve of them, what could it possibly mean? And, watching them, my prickling skin and the cold sweat on my forehead told me I was afraid, and had good reason to be : the dogs could choose me instead of the chickens. I went as fast as I could inside the house. Which was clean and empty. Ascending through the house I was listening for life in the rooms off the landings – nothing. At the top of the house a closed door. I knocked and Emily opened it a crack – saw it was me, and let me in, shutting it fast again and bolting it. She was dressed in furs, trousers of rabbit or cat, a fur jacket, a grey fur cap pulled low over her face. She looked like a pantomime cat. But pale, and sorrowful. Where was Gerald?

She returned to a nest she had made for herself on the floor, of fur rugs and fur cushions. The room smelled like a den from the furs, but sniffing, trying it out, I realised that otherwise the air was fresh and sharp, and that I was breathing it in great gasps. Emily made a place for me in the rugs, and I sat and covered myself. It was very cold: no heating here. We sat quietly together – breathing.

She said: 'Now that the air outside has become impossible to breathe, I spend as much time as I can here.'

And I understood it was true: this was a moment when someone said something which crystallised into fact intimations only partly grasped that had been pointing towards on obvious conclusion... in this case, it was that the air we breathed had indeed become hard on our lungs, had been getting fouler and thicker for a long time. We had become used to it, were adapting: I, like everyone else, had been taking short reluctant breaths, as if rationing what we took into our lungs, our systems, could also ration the poisons – what poisons? But who could know, or say! This was 'it', again, in a new form – 'it', perhaps, in its original form?

Sitting in that room, whose floor was all covered with furs for lying and reclining, a room in which there was nothing to do but to lie, or to sit, I realised that I was – happy simply to be there, and breathe. Which I did, for a long time, while my head cleared and my spirits lightened. I looked out through clean polythene at a thick sky turbulent with clouds that held snow; I watched the light changing on the wall. From time to time Emily and I smiled at each other. It was very quiet everywhere. There came at one point a violent cackling and snarling from the garden, but we did not move. It ceased. Silence again. We sat on, without moving, just breathing.

There were machines in the room: one hanging from the ceiling, another on the floor, one nailed to a wall. These were for purifying the air, and they worked by sending out streams of electrons, negative ions – people had used them for some time; just as no one would dream of using water from the taps unless it had passed through one of the many types of water purifier. Air and water, water and air, the basics of our substance, the elements we swim in, move in, of which we are formed and reformed, continuously, perpetually recreated and renewed . . . for how long had we had to distrust them, evade them, treat them as possible enemies?

'You should take some machines home with you,' she said. 'There's a room full of them.'

'Gerald?'

'Yes, he went to a warehouse. There's a room of them under this one. But I'll help you carry them. How can you live in that filthy air?' and she said this in the way one does bring something out one has wanted to say, but has kept back.

She was smiling – and reproachful.

'Are you coming back . . .' – I hesitated to say 'home', but she said : 'Yes, I'll come home with you.'

'Hugo will be pleased,' I said, not meaning any reproach, but her eyes filled and she reddened.

'Why are you able to come now?' I asked, risking it; but she simply shook her head, meaning : I'll answer in a moment . . . And she did, when she had taken herself into control.

'There's no point in my staying here now.'

'Gerald has gone?'

'I don't know where he is. Not since he brought the machines.'

'He is making a new gang for himself?'

'Trying to.'

When she was on her feet, rolling up furs into big bundles to take with us, laying out others in which to wrap machines, there was a knock, and Emily went to see who it was. No, not Gerald, but a couple of children. At the sight of children, I was afraid. And I realised 'in a flash' – another one! that I, that everybody, had come to see all children as, simply, terrifying. Even before the arrival of the 'poor little kids' this had been true.

These two, dirty, bright-faced, sharp, wary, sat on the fur-floor, apart from us, and apart from each other. Each held a heavy stick, with a nail-studded knob, ready for use against us, and against each other.

'Thought I'd get a breath of fresh air,' said one, a red-headed boy, all milky skin and charming freckles. The other, a fair, angelic little girl, said, for herself : 'Yes, I wanted some fresh air.'

They sat and breathed and watched while we, keeping an eye on them, went on with the rolling and packing.

'Where are you going?' asked the girl.

'Tell Gerald he knows where to find me.'

This gave me too much food for thought for me to absorb at once.

These children were part of Gerald's new gang? Were they not members of the gang of children from the Underground? If this was true, then . . . perhaps that gang was only lethal as a unit, but the individuals were savable, and Gerald had been right? When our packs were ready, we left, the children coming with us; but they left us on seeing the butcher's yard that was the garden : feathers everywhere, bits of flesh, a dead dog. The children were cutting up the dog as we left, squatting on either side of the carcass, at work with sharp bits of steel.

We returned through streets which I pointed out to Emily as being, surely? less filthy – and noted her small checked reaction. Streets which had no one in them, not a soul apart from ourselves – I commented on this too, and heard her sigh. She was being patient with me.

In the lobby of the building we lived in, a great vase that had held flowers was lying in fragments outside the lift. There was a dead rat among the rubbish. As Emily took the animal by the tail to throw it out into the street, Professor White, Mrs White, and Janet, came along the corridor we jointly used. They had so far retained old ways that it was possible to say at once they were dressed for travelling – coats, scarves, suitcases. Seeing them thus, all three together, was a reminder of that other world or stratum of society, above ours, where people still presented themselves through clothes or belongings, for occasions. The Whites, as if nothing had happened to our world, were off on a journey, and Janet was saying : 'Oh quick, do let's go, let's go Mummy, Daddy, it's so horrid being here when there's no one left.' *Click* – there it was again, the few words flung out, emitted as if by the atmosphere itself, by 'it', summing up a new state of affairs that had not yet got itself summed up – or at least, not by me. I saw Emily's shrewd little glance at me, and she even instinctively moved a step closer, in a maternal gesture of protection for what might be a moment of weakness. I stood silent, watching the Whites fuss and arrange, seeing my past, our pasts: it looked comic. It *was* comic. We always had been ridiculous, little, self-important animals, acting our roles, playing our parts ... it was not pretty, watching the Whites, and seeing oneself. And then we all said goodbye, quite in the old style: it was nice to know you, I hope we'll meet again, all that kind of thing, as if nothing much was happening. They had discovered that a coach was going out of the city that afternoon, ten miles to the north, on some kind of official business. Not for the use of ordinary citizens, but they had bribed and urged their way into being on this coach, which would set them down a mile from the airport, with their luggage. An official flight was scheduled for the extreme north this afternoon: again, while no ordinary person could ever get on such a flight, the head of a department and his family might just manage it, if they had the money – astronomical, of course, not for fares, but again, for bribes. What bartering and promises and threats and appeals must have gone into this journey, what a fearful effort – and all of it entirely in the new style, our new mode, that of survival, of surviving at all costs – but not a trace of this showed in their manner: Goodbye, goodbye, it was nice to have you both as neighbours, see you soon perhaps, yes I do hope so, goodbye, pleasant journey.

We went into my flat, and from the windows watched them walk down the street carrying their heavy cases.

The rooms next to mine would be empty now. Empty ... it occurred to me that I had been seeing very few people around in the lobby, the corridors. What had happened to the market? I asked Emily and she shrugged, clearly feeling that I ought to know. I left my flat again, and went to the janitor's room down the passage. 'In case of emergency, apply to Flat 7, 5th Floor.' The way the notice hung there crooked, the silence from behind the door, told me that he and his family had gone off, had left : that notice might have been there for weeks. But I went to the lift, which did sometimes work, and pressed the bell. The machine shifted somewhere above, and I waited on, pressing and peering, but the lift did not come, so I used the stairs, up and up, floor after floor empty, with no liveliness of trading and bartering anywhere. The traders, the buyers, the goods, all were gone, and there was nobody in Flat 7, on the 5th floor, but at the top of the building, near the roof, I saw some youngsters feeding horses with pitchforks of hay, and I retreated, not wanting to be seen, since some of those at work there were young children. I crept down that passage, passing more rooms that held animals : a goat's head peered around a door, a pair of kingly lambs stood at the end of a corridor, and there was a shovelling and scraping from somewhere close and the smell of pigs. I tried the roof itself : up here was a flourishing market garden, with vegetables and herbs of all kinds, a polythene greenhouse, rabbits in cages, and a family, mother, father and three children, hard at work. They gave me the look of that time : *Who are you? Friend? Enemy?* – and waited, their implements held ready to use as weapons. Down I went again to the floor beneath and a child froze into a dark corner – he had been following me. His teeth were bared in a vindictive but calculated grin. I mean that the animosity was calculated, measured, so as to scare me. I could imagine him with a looking glass he had picked up in some corner, practising a variety of horrible expressions. I was indeed frightened : his hand, (like Emily's these days!) was held close to his chest, where the handle of a knife showed. I thought I knew his face, believed – he was red-haired and the right size – he was one of the urchins who had visited Emily that same day. But of course I made no appeal on such sentimental grounds as acquaintance, but glared back, and moved my right hand threateningly to where my – non-existent – knife was. He held his ground, and I walked on past him down the passage, looking into rooms, feeling him creep behind me, but at a good distance. I saw Gerald. He was sitting on heaps of furs surrounded by children – they were the 'Underground gang' and they were living in 'my' building. This gave me a real shock, and I went down-stairs, boldly passing the little boy, who was keeping up his business of scowling and threatening. Down, down, and into my flat, which after all I had seen seemed a strange little place of order, of old-fashioned amenities, of warmth. Emily had made up a fire, and was sitting next to it, opposite Hugo. They were looking at each other, not touching, looking long and quiet at each other. The girl entirely wrapped in furs, so it was hard to tell where her own glossy hair began and ended, and the poor beast, with his rough and yellow hide – Beauty and her Beast, in this guise, but Beauty was so close to her Beast now, wrapped in beast's clothing, as sharp and wary as a beast, surviving as one. Yes, Beauty had been brought down, brought very low ... I had a bad moment, watching the two there, thinking how very near we were to running and scurrying like rats along tunnels – but saw that the fire was solid and glowing, the air-machines we had brought were all at work, and the curtains had been drawn, with old blankets pinned over them. The air here was good, and clean, and I could feel my real self coming alive in it, but first I again left the flat and went out on the pavement. Dusk was coming down. Only a few people were on the gathering-place. They loitered there with a lost uncertain look : so many tribes had left, and these were the laggards. How dark everything was! Usually, as dusk came down, hundreds of candle flames seemed to float up and down and along the great buildings : people at their windows, looking down, and the rooms behind them shadowy in candlelight. But now, this evening, there were a few little glimmers high up in the darkness. From my windows nothing at all, yet my rooms were still alive : it was not possible now to tell from lights at windows who was in the building. No lights in the streets, only a thick heavy dark, the glow of a cigarette on the pavement, otherwise nothing. I found that I was standing there visualising the dark face of the building and a single candle flame – mine – alive in it. So things had been recently. Any-one passing would have known that here, alone, undefended, was a single person, or a single family. I had been crazy. Emily's little checked reactions of impatience or concern were understandable, understood. And, often enough, in the glow of that single flame must have been visible the patient watching outline of Hugo: yes, it was just as well she had come home – this time, or so it seemed, to look after me, not the other way around.

I went back into the flat. Emily had gone to bed. Hugo had not gone with her. Pride: and of course she would have understood it. He lay in front of the fire like any domestic beast, nose to the warmth, his green eyes watchful and open. I put my hand out to him and he allowed me a little tremor of his tail. I sat on for a long time, as the fire burned down, and listened to the absolute silence of the building. Yet above me was a farmyard, were animals, were the lethal children, was an old friend, Gerald: I went to bed, wrapping my head as peasants and simple people may do, against thoughts of danger, leaving just my face free – and woke next morning to find no water in the taps.

The building, as a machine, was dead.

That morning Gerald came down with two of the children, Redhair and a little black girl. He brought offerings of wine – for he had found an old wine merchant half-looted; and some blankets. Also, some food. Emily made the five of us some food, a porridge of some kind, with meat in it: it was good, and comforting.

Gerald wanted us to move to the top floor, where it would be easy for him to fix up a wind machine, one of the little windmills: we would have enough power to heat water, when we could get it. I said nothing, let Emily do the talking, make choices. She said no, it would be better to stay down here: she did not look at me as she said this, and it slowly came into me the reason was that up at the top of the building we would be more vulnerable to attack: we could not run away easily up there, whereas here it would be a question of jumping out of a window. This was why she said 'no' to his offer of a 'a large flat, really Emily, very big, and full of all sorts of food and stuff. And I could fix it up with power in a day – couldn't we . . . ?' he appealed to the children, who nodded and grinned. They sat on either side of him, those little things, about seven or eight years old: they were his, his creatures; he had made himself theirs; he had his gang, his tribe . . . but at the cost of doing what they wanted, serving them.

What he wanted was to have her back. He wanted her to go up with him, to live with him, as queen, or chief lady, or brigand's woman, among the children, his gang. And she did not want this; she most definitely did not. Not that she said it, but it was clear. And the children, sharp-eyed and alert, knew what the issue was. It was hard to know what they felt – there were none of the familiar signals to tell us. Their eyes turned from Emily to Gerald, from Gerald to Emily: they were wondering if Emily, like Gerald, could become one of them, kill with them, fight with them? Or they were thinking that she was pretty and nice and it would be pleasant to have her around with them? They saw her, or felt her, as filling the place of their mothers – if they remembered mothers, a family, at all? They were thinking that they should kill her, because of Gerald's, their possession's, love of her? Who could say?

Their eating habits were disgusting. Gerald said Use a spoon, look, like this . . . no, don't throw it on the floor! – in a way that showed that in his own rooms, his own cave, he no longer bothered with such niceties. His glance at Emily said that if she would be there with them, she could influence and civilise . . . but it was all no use, and the three, the man and the two little children, went off at midday, They would bring us fresh meat tomorrow: a sheep was going to be killed. He would come and see Emily soon: he spoke to her, it was Emily's place now. My flat was Emily's, and I was her elderly attendant. Well, why not?

She was silent when he had gone, and then Hugo came and sat with his face on her knee: he was saying: I can see that you have really chosen me at last, me against him, me instead of all the others!

It was funny and pathetic; but she flashed me glances that I was not to laugh: it was she who suppressed smiles, bit her lips, breathed deep to hold down laughter. She fussed and caressed: 'Dear Hugo, dear, dear Hugo . . .' I noted, and watched. I was seeing a mature woman, a woman who has had her fill of everything, but is still being asked from, demanded of, persuaded into giving: such a woman is generous indeed, her coffers and wells are always full and being given out. She loves – oh yes, but somewhere in her is a deadly weariness. She has known it all, and doesn't want any more – but what can she do? She knows herself – the eyes of men and boys say so – as a source – if she is not this, then she is nothing. So she still thinks; she has not yet shed that delusion. She gives. She gives. But with this weariness held in check and concealed . . . so she stroked her Hugo's head, made love to his ears, whispered affectionate nonsense to him. Over his head her eyes met mine: they were the eyes of a mature woman of about thirty-five, or forty . . . she would never willingly suffer any of it again. Like the jaded woman of our dead civilisation, she knew love like a fever, to be suffered, to be lived through: 'falling in love' was an illness to be endured, a trap which might lead her to betray her own nature, her good sense, and her real purposes. It was not a door to anything but itself: not a key to living. It was a state, a condition, sufficient unto itself, almost independent of its object . . . 'being in love'. If she *had* spoken of it, she would have spoken of it so, as I've written. But she did not want to talk. She exuded her weariness, her willingness to give out if absolutely necessary, to give without belief. Gerald, whom she had adored, the 'first love' of tradition; for whom she had waited, suffered, lain awake at nights – Gerald, her lover, now needed and wanted her, having worked through the cycle of *his* needs, but she no longer had the energy to rise and meet him.

When, later that day, Gerald came down again, alone, in an attempt to persuade her to return with him, she did talk to him. She talked and he listened. She told him what had happened to him, for he did not know.

After the community he had built up in his house had been broken up by the gang of 'kids' from the Underground, and when he had seen that none of his own household would return, he had put all his effort into getting Emily to stay with him, to make a new household. He had returned to the pavement, to attract the nucleus of a new tribe. But this did not happen, it had not happened. Why? Perhaps it was believed that he was in contact with the dangerous children, or that any new community he formed must attract them; perhaps the fact he had shown openly that he was prepared to settle for one woman, for Emily, instead of being free in his choices, bestowing favours on whoever he found in his bed, put off the girls – whatever law it was that operated, the result was that Gerald, formerly a young prince, perhaps the most regarded of all the young men on the pavement, found himself unfollowed, merely one of the youngsters who had to attach himself to a leader in order to survive . . . Gerald listened to all this, thoughtful, attentive, disagreeing with nothing Emily was saying.

'And then you decided it was better to have the children than to have nothing, or to be patient and wait. You simply had to have a gang at all costs. And you went back to them and took them over. But they have taken *you* over – can't you see? I bet you have to do exactly what they want, don't you? I am sure you never can stop them doing anything they want? And you have to go along with whatever it is?'

But now he had retreated, was not prepared to take this, could not listen.

'But they are just little kids,' he said. 'Isn't it better for them that they have me? I get them food and things. I look after them.'

'They had food and things before,' Emily said drily.

Too dry . . . he saw her as critical of him – that, and nothing more. There was no affection for him – so he felt it. Off he went, and did not come again for some days.

We were organising our life, our rooms.

We were supplied with clean air at the cost of sitting and turning a handle to recharge batteries from time to time. It was warm: Emily went out with an axe and returned with great bundles of wood. And, just as I was thinking that the shortage of water would drive us to the roads, there was a clop-clopping outside, and a donkey cart made its appearance, loaded with plastic buckets of water, wooden buckets, metal buckets.

'Wa-a-a-ter! Wa-a-a-ter!' – the old cry sounded through our

damp northern streets. Two girls of about eleven were selling the stuff, or rather, bartering. I went out with containers, and saw other people coming from the various blocks of flats around us. Not many, not more than fifty or so in all. I bought water dearly: the little girls had learned to be hard, to shake their heads and shrug at the prospect that people would do without water. For two buckets of good water – we were at least allowed to taste it before buying, I paid a sheepskin.

And then Gerald appeared, with about twenty of his gang – came with containers of every sort. Of course, there were all those animals up there, they needed water: but in a moment the gang had taken the water, simply grabbed it: they did not pay. I found myself shouting at Gerald that it was their livelihood, the little girls' – but he took no notice. I think he did not hear me. He stood on the alert, all vigilance, his eyes coldly assessing, while his children lifted down the buckets and ran off into the building with them, while the sellers complained, and the people who had come to buy water and had not yet been served, stood shouting and screaming. Then Gerald and the children had gone and it was my turn to be robbed. I stood with two filled buckets, and one of the men from the block of flats opposite held out his hand, lowering his head to glare into my eyes, baring his teeth. I handed over one bucket and ran indoors with the other. Emily had been watching through the window. She seemed sad. Also irritated: I could see the words she would use to scold Gerald forming in her mind.

A dish of clean water was put down for Hugo and he drank and drank. He stood beside the empty dish, head lowered: we filled it again, and he drank . . . a third of the bucket went in this way, and in our minds was the same thought – Hugo's, as well as ours. Emily sat by him and put her arms around him in the old way: he was not to worry or grieve, she would protect him, no one would attack him; he would have water if she had to go without or if I did . . .

When the water sellers came a couple of days later, they had men guarding the water with guns, and we bought in orderly queues. Gerald and his gang were not there. A woman in the queue said that 'that rotten lot' had opened up the Fleet River, and had started selling water on their own account. It was true, and for us, Hugo, Emily and me, a good turn of events, for Gerald brought us down a bucket of water every day and sometimes more.

'Well, we had to do it, we have to keep our animals watered, don't we?'

From the defensiveness of this, we knew that some hard battle had been fought. With the authorities? With other people using that source? – for of course old wells and springs had been opened everywhere over the city. If with the authorities, then how was it that Gerald and the children had won? – they must have done, to be able to reach and tap the supply.

'Well,' said Gerald, 'they haven't got enough troops to keep an eye on everything, have they? Most of them have gone, haven't they? I mean, there are more of us than there are of them, now . . .

◆————

And if everyone had gone, what were we – Emily and Hugo and I – doing here?

But we no longer thought about leaving, not seriously. We might talk a little about the Dolgellys, or say: Well, one of these days we really ought to be thinking . . .

Air, water, food, warmth – we had them all. Things were easier now than for a long time. There was less stress, less danger. And even the few people who were still lodged in the cracks and crevices of this great city kept leaving, leaving . . .

I watched a tribe go off as the autumn ended and winter came down. The last tribe, at least from our pavements. It was like all the others I had seen go, but better equipped, and typical of the caravans from our particular area: now, comparing notes, it seems that each neighbourhood had its peculiarities of travel, even styles! Yes, I can use that word . . . how quickly customs and habits do grow up! I remember hearing someone say, and this was quite in the early days of the departing tribes:

'Where is the shoe leather? We *always* have a supply of shoe leather.'

Perhaps it would be of interest if I described this late departure in more detail.

It was cold that morning. A low sky moved fast from west to east, a dark, pouring sea. The air was thick, and hard to breathe although there was a wind stirring and rolling drifts of the snow crumbs that lightly surfaced road and pavements. The ground seemed fluid. The tall buildings all around showed sharp and dark, or disappeared in snow flurries and cloud.

About fifty people had gathered, all rolled tightly into their furs. At the front were two young men with the two guns they owned prominently in evidence. Behind them came four more, with bows and arrows, sticks, knives. Then came a cart converted from a motor car: everything taken off down to wheel level, and boards laid over these to make a surface. The cart was being drawn by a horse, and on it was piled bundles of clothes and equipment, three small children, and hay for the horse. The older children were expected to walk.

Behind this cart walked the women and children, and behind them came another cart, and in the yokes were two youths. On this cart was a large version of the old hay box: a wooden container, insulated and padded, into which could be fitted pots which, taken off the boil just before the start of a journey, would go on simmering inside their nests and be ready to provide a meal at its end. After this second cart came a third, an old milk cart carrying food supplies: grains, dried vegetables, concentrates and so on. And a fourth cart, drawn by a donkey. It was arranged in cages. There were some laying hens. There were rabbits, not for eating, but for breeding: a dozen or so impregnated does. This last cart had a special guard of four armed boys.

It was the horse and the donkey that distinguished this caravan: our part of the city was known for its draft animals. Why we developed this speciality I don't know. Perhaps it was because there were riding stables in the old days, and these developed into breeding establishments when there was a need.

Even our little common had horses on it – under heavy guard night and day, of course.

Usually, when a column of people left for the journey north or west, people came out of the buildings to say goodbye, to wish them well, to send messages to friends and relatives who had gone on ahead. That morning only four people came. I and Hugo sat quietly in our window watching, as the tribe arranged itself and left, without fuss or farewells. Very different this departure from earlier ones, which had been so boisterous and gay. These people were subdued, seemed apprehensive, made themselves small and inconspicuous inside their furs : this caravan of theirs would make rich booty.

Emily did not even watch.

At the very last moment Gerald came out with half a dozen of the children, and they stood on the pavement until the last cart with its cackling load had gone out of sight beyond the church at the corner. Gerald turned then, and led his flock back inside the building. He saw me and nodded, but without smiling. He looked strained – as well he might. Even to see that band of infant savages was enough to make one's stomach muscles tighten in anxiety. And he lived among them, day and night : I believe he had run out with them to stop them attacking the loaded carts.

That night there was a knock on the door, and four of the children stood there : they were wild-eyed and excited. Emily simply shut the door on them and locked it. Then she put heavy chairs against it. A scuffling and whispering – the foot-steps retreated.

Emily looked at me, and mouthed over Hugo's head – it took me a few moments to work it out : *Roast Hugo.*

'Or roast Emily,' I said.

A few minutes later we heard screams coming from along the street, then the sound of many rushing feet, and children's shrill voices in triumph – all the sounds of a raid, a crime. We pushed aside our heavy curtains and were in time to see, through a glimmer from the snow that was being lit by a small moon, Gerald's gang, but without Gerald, dragging something up the front steps. It looked like a body. It need not have been anything of the kind, could have been a sack or a bundle. But the suspicion was there, and strong enough to make us believe it.

We sat on through the night quietly by our fire, waiting, listening.

There was nothing to prevent one or all of us becoming victims at any moment.

Nothing. Not the fact that Gerald, by himself or with a selection of the children, or even some of the children by themselves, might come down to visit us in the most normal way in the world. They brought us gifts. They brought flour and dried milk and eggs; sheets of polythene, cellotape, nails, tools of all kinds. They gave us fur rugs, coal, seeds, candles. They brought . . . the city around was almost empty, and all one had to do was to walk into unguarded buildings and warehouses and take what one fancied. But most of what was there were things no one would ever use again or want to : things that, in a few years time, if some survivor found them, he would have to ask : What on earth could this have been for?

As these children did already. You would see them squatting down over a pile of greeting cards, a pink nylon fluted lampshade, a polystyrene garden dwarf, a book or a record, turning them over and over : *What was this for? What did they do with it?*

But these visits, these gifts, did not mean that in another mood, on another occasion, they would not kill. And because of a whim, a fancy, an impulse.

Inconsequence . . .

Inconsequence again, as with the departure of little June. We sat there and brooded about it, talked about it, listening – far above our heads there was the neigh of a horse, and sheep baa-ing; birds whirled up past our windows on their way to the top of the building where there were the pickings of a farmyard for the effort of hopping through a broken window, was a vegetable garden, and even some trees. Inconsequence, a new thing in human psychology. New? Well, if it had always been there, it had been well channelled, disciplined, socialised.

Or we had become so used to the ways we saw it shown that we did not recognise it.

Once, not long ago, if a man or woman shook you by the hand, offered you gifts, you would have reason to expect that he, she, would not kill you at the next meeting because the idea had just that moment come into his head . . . this sounds, as usual, on the edge of farce. But farce depends on the normal, the usual, the standard. Without the *norm,* which is the source of farce, that particular form of laughter dries up.

I remembered June, when she first robbed my flat and I asked Emily : 'But why me?' The reply was : Because you are here, she knows you. Even : Because you are a friend.

We could believe that the children from upstairs might come down one night and kill us because we were their friends. They knew us.

One night, very late, sitting around the fire as it burned low, we heard voices outside the door and outside the window. We did not move or look for weapons. The three of us exchanged looks – it cannot be said that they were amused, no : we did not have so much philosophy, but I do claim these glances were of the order of humour. That morning we had given food to some of those brats who were outside now. We had sat eating with them. *Are you warm enough? Have another piece of bread. Would you like some more soup?*

We could not protect ourselves against so many : thirty or more in all, whispering beyond the door, below the window. And Gerald? No, that we could not believe. He was asleep, or away on some expedition.

Hugo turned himself, placing himself between Emily, whom he would defend, and the door. He looked at me, suggesting I should put myself between her and the window : of course it was Emily who must be defended.

The scuffling and whispering went on. There were some blows on the door. More scuffles. Then a burst of sound – shouts, and feet rushing away. What had happened? We did not know. Perhaps Gerald had heard of what they were doing, and had come to stop them. Perhaps they had simply changed their minds.

And next day some of the children, with Gerald, came down to us and we spent a pleasant time together ... I can say it, I can write it. But I cannot convey the normality of it, the ordinariness of sitting there, chatting, sharing food, of looking into a childish face and thinking : Well, well, it might have been you who planned to stick a knife into me last night !

And so it all went on.

We did not leave. If someone had asked : Do you mean to say that you two people are staying here, in danger, instead of leaving the city for the country where things are safe or safer, because of that animal, that ugly, bristly old beast there – you are prepared to die yourselves of hunger or cold or of being murdered, simply because of that beast ! – then we would have said : Of course not, we are not so absurd, we put human beings where they belong, higher than beasts, to be saved at all costs. Animals must be sacrificed for humans, that is right and proper and we will do it too, just like everybody else.

But it was not a question of Hugo any longer.

The question was, where would we be going? To what? There was silence from out there, the places so many people had set off to reach. Silence and cold ... no word ever came back, no one turned up again on our pavements and reported : 'I've come back from the north, from the west, and I ran into so and so and he said ...'

No, all we could see when we looked up and out were the low packed clouds of that winter hurrying towards us : dark cloud, dark cold cloud. For it snowed. The snow came down, the snow was up to our windowsills. And of all those people who had left, the multitudes, what had happened to them? They might as well have walked off the edge of a flat world ... On the radios, or occasionally from the loudspeaker of an official car – which, seen from our windows seemed like the relic of a dead epoch, came news from the east : yes, it seemed that there was life of a sort down there still. A few people even farmed, grew crops, made lives. 'Down there' – 'out there' – we did hear of these places, they were alive for us. And where we were was alive; the old city, near-empty as it was, held people, animals, and plants which grew and grew, taking over streets, pavements, the ground floors of buildings, forcing cracks in tarmac, racing up walls . . . life. When the spring came, what a burst of green life there would be, and the animals breeding and eating and flourishing.

But north and west, no. Nothing but cold and silence. We did not want to leave. And with whom? Emily, myself, and our beast – should we go by ourselves? There were no tribes leaving, no tribes even forming, and when we looked from our windows there was no one out there on the pavements. We were left in the cold dark of that interminable winter. Oh, it was so dark, it was such a low thick dark. All around us, the black tall towers stood up out of the snow that heaped around their bases, higher every day. No lights in those buildings now, nothing; and if a windowpane glinted in the long black nights, then it was from the moon, exposed momentarily between one hurrying cloud and another.

One afternoon, about an hour before the light went, Emily was by the window looking out, and she exclaimed: 'Oh no, no, *no!*' I joined her, and saw Gerald out there on the deep clean snow, high under stark branches. He wore his brave coat, but it was open, as if he did not care about the dreadful cold; he had nothing on his head, and he was moving about as if he were quite alone in the city and no one could see him. He was revisiting the scenes – so very recent, after all – of his triumphs, when he was lord of the pavement, chieftain of the gathering tribes? He looked about him at the exquisite crisp snow, up at the sky where low clouds were bringing dark inwards from the west, at the black trees touched up with white; he stood for minutes at a time, quite passive, staring, in thought or in abstraction. And Emily watched, and I could feel the fever of her anxiety rising. By now the three of us were there, watching Gerald; and of course other people were at their windows watching too. He had no weapons. His ungloved hands were in his pockets, or hung at his sides. He looked quite indifferent, had disarmed himself and did not care.

Then a small object hurtled past him, like a speeding bird.

He gave a rapid indifferent glance at the building and stayed where he was. There followed a small shower of stones : from the windows above us catapults were being trained on him, perhaps worse than catapults. A stone hit his shoulder : it might have hit his face, or even an eye. Now he deliberately turned and faced the building, and we saw he was presenting himself as a target. He let his hands fall loose at his sides, and he stood quietly there, not smiling, but unworried, unalarmed, waiting, his eyes steadily on something or somebody in windows probably a story up from us.

'Oh *no*,' said Emily again; and in a moment she had pulled around her shoulders a shawl, like a peasant woman, and she was out of the flat and I saw her running across the street. Hugo's breath was coming in anxious little whines, and his nose was misting the windowpane. I put my hand on his neck and he quieted a little. Emily had slid her arm under Gerald's, and was talking to him, coaxing him off that pavement and across the road towards us. There was a fusillade of stones, bits of metal, offal, rubbish. Blood appeared on Gerald's temple, and a stone, landing in Emily's middle, caused her to stagger back. Gerald, brought to life by the danger to her, now sheltered her with his arm, and he was bringing her in to the building. Above I could hear the children shouting and calling out, and their chant : 'I am the king of the castle...' The stamping and chanting went on above us, as Gerald and Emily arrived in the room where Hugo and I waited for them. Gerald was white and there was a deep gash on his forehead, which Emily bathed and fussed over. And he made her look to see if the stone had hurt her much : there was a bruise, no worse.

Emily made him sit by the fire, and sat by him, and rubbed his hands between hers.

He was very low, depressed. 'But they are just little kids,' he said again, looking at Emily, at me, at Hugo. 'That's all they are.' His face was all incredulity and pain : I don't know what it was in Gerald that could not – could not even now – bear what those children had become. I do know that it was deep in him, fundamental; and to give them up was to abandon – so he felt – the best part of himself.

'Do you know something, Em? – the little one, Denis, he's four years old, yes, he is. Do you know him, do you know the one I mean? He was down here with a me a few days back – the little one, with the cheeky face.'

'Yes, I do remember, but Gerald, you do have to accept . . .'

'Four,' he persisted, 'four. That's all. I worked it out from something he said. He was born the year the first lot of travellers came through this area. Yet he goes out with the others, he is as tough as the others. Did you know he was on that job – you know, the one that night?'

'A murder?' I asked, since Emily did not say anything, but went on rubbing his cold hands.

'Yes, well – but it was murder, I suppose. He was there. When I came back that night, I lost my temper, I was as sick as I could be. I said to them . . . and then one of them said that Denis had done it, he was the first to let go with what he'd got – a stone, I think. He was the first, and then after him, the others – four years old. And when I came back into the flat, do you know, the dead man was there, and they were all . . . and Denis was there, as large as life among them, taking his part – it's not their fault, how can it be their fault? How can you blame a kid of four?'

'No one is blaming them,' said Emily softly. Her eyes were bright, and her face was pale, and she was sitting by Gerald as if standing guard, protecting him, as if she had rescued him and now would not let go.

'No, but if no one saves them either, then that's the same as blaming them, isn't it? Isn't it?' he appealed to me;

We sat on through the long night, waiting. Of course we were expecting an attack, a visit, an embassy – something. Above us, in the great empty building there was no sound. And all that following day it snowed, and was dark and cold. We sat and waited, and nothing happened.

I knew that Emily was expecting Gerald to visit the top part of the building, to find out what went on. She was meaning to dissuade him. But he did not go; and all he said was, after some days: 'Well, perhaps they've moved somewhere else.'

'And the animals?' said Emily, fierce, thinking of those poor beasts up there.

He raised his head and looked at her and gave that short laugh which means someone has made an end to something in thought: a decision, but it is a decision beset with irony, or with conflict. 'If I go up there, well, I might be pulled back in again – and that's no good. And as for the animals, they have to take their chance like everyone else – there are other people up there still.'

And so we went on quietly, the four of us.

It all came to an end, but I can't say when it was after Gerald joined us. We had been there, waiting for winter to end, and we knew it was a long time, but not as long as our weary senses told us: an interminable time, but still not longer than a winter. Then, one morning, a weak yellow stain lay on the wall, and there, brought to life, was the hidden pattern. My feeling that this was what we had been waiting for was so strong that I called to the others, who were still asleep: 'Emily – Emily! Gerald and Emily, come quickly. Hugo, where are you?'

From her room padded that obdurate beast, Hugo, and behind him came Gerald and Emily, bundled in their furs, yawning, disheveled, not surprised, but looking their enquiry. Hugo was not surprised, not he: he stood, all alert and vivified beside the wall, looking into it as if at last what he wanted and needed and knew would happen was here, and he was ready for it.

Emily took Gerald by the hand, and with Hugo walked through the screen of the forest into ... and now it is hard to say exactly what happened. We were in that place which might present us with anything – rooms furnished this way or that and spanning the tastes and customs of millenia; walls broken, falling, growing again; a house roof like a forest floor sprouting grasses and birds' nests; rooms smashed, littered, robbed; a bright green lawn under thunderous and glaring clouds and on the lawn a giant black egg of pockmarked iron, but polished and glassy around which, and reflected in the black shine, stood Emily, Hugo, Gerald, her officer father, her large laughing gallant mother, and little Denis, the four-year-old criminal clinging to Gerald's hand, clutching it and looking up into his face, smiling – there they stood, looking at this iron egg until, broken by the force of their being there, it fell apart, and out of it came . . . a scene, perhaps, of people in a quiet room bending to lay matching pieces of patterned materials on a carpet that had no life in it until that moment when vitality was fed into it by these exactly-answering patches : but no, I did not see that, or if I did, not clearly . . . that world, presenting itself in a thousand little flashes, a jumble of little scenes, facets of another picture, all impermanent, was folding up as we stepped into it, was parcelling itself up, was vanishing, dwindling and going – all of it, trees and streams, grasses and rooms and people. But the one person I had been looking for all this time was there : there she was.

No, I am not able to say clearly what she was like. She was beautiful : it is a word that will do. I only saw her for a moment, in a time like the fading of a spark on dark air – a glimpse : she turned her face just once to me, and all I can say is . . . nothing at all.

Beside her, then, as she turned to walk on and away and ahead while the world folded itself up around her, was Emily, and beside Emily was Hugo, and lingering after them, Gerald. Emily, yes, but quite beyond herself, transmuted, and in another key, and the yellow beast Hugo fitted her new self : a splendid animal, handsome, all kindly dignity and command, he walked beside her and her hand was on his neck. Both walked quickly behind that One who went ahead showing them the way out of this collapsed little world into another order of world altogether. Both, just for an instant, turned their faces as they passed that other threshold. They smiled . . . seeing those faces Gerald was drawn after them, but still he hesitated in a fearful conflict, looking back and around, while the brilliant fragments whirled around him. And then, at the very last moment, they came, his children came running, clinging to his hands and his clothes, and they all followed quickly on after the others as the last walls dissolved.

Doris Lessing

Shikasta

Shikasta is the first volume in Doris Lessing's celebrated space fiction series, 'Canopus in Argos: Archives'.

In *Shikasta* the story of the final days of our planet is told through the reports of Johor, an emissary sent from Canopus. Twentieth-century Earth, named 'Shikasta, the stricken' by the kindly, paternalistic Canopeans who colonised it many centuries ago, is under the influence of the evil empire, Puttiora. War, famine, disease and environmental disasters ravage the planet. To Johor, mankind is a 'totally crazed species', racing towards annihilation: his orders to save humanity set him what seems to be an impossible task.

'Magnificent . . . an astounding book that sets out to chronicle the whole world of humanity, spirit, earth, stars, soul, virtue, evil, pre-Eden forever.'   Myrna Blumberg, *The Times*

'Profound, relevant and daring.'
                                    Rachel Billington, *Financial Times*

'*Shikasta* is a piercing diagnosis of the unease spreading through our civilisation. A powerful fable.'   W. L. Webb, *Guardian*

'*Shikasta* is at once a brief history of the world, a tract against human destructiveness, an ode to the natural beauties of this earth and a hymn to the music of the spheres.'   *Time*

🔺 *flamingo*

MODERN CLASSIC

Doris Lessing

This Was the Old Chief's Country

Collected African Stories
Volume One

Includes a new, previously uncollected story.

In this superb volume of African stories, Doris Lessing paints a magnificent portrait of the country in which she grew up. The cruelties of the white man towards the native, 'the amorphous black mass, like tadpoles, faceless, who existed merely to serve', the English settlers, ill at ease, the gamblers and moneymakers searching for diamonds and gold, and the presence, 'latent always in the blood', of Africa itself, its majestic beauty and timeless landscape: Doris Lessing draws them all together into a powerful, memorable vision.

'In story after story, Doris Lessing portrays the helpless collisions and alienations of the races. In "The Second Hut", a Rhodesian farmer is torn with anxiety and guilt about employing a poor Boer assistant with nine children because of the hostility between Boer and native workers. One brings away a sense of the sheer human impossibility of South Africa, as a place fit only for habitation by the imagination of exiles and of children. All else seems lost, betrayed and spoiled, except the glare of the sun, the dust, the boulders. An impressive collection.'

Gabriel Pearson, *Daily Telegraph*

'Doris Lessing's sense of setting is so immediate, the touch and taste of her continent is so strong, that Africa seems to become the universe.'

Newsweek

ISBN 0 586 09113 0

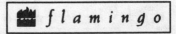

Doris Lessing

The Sun Between Their Feet

Collected African Stories
Volume Two

This much-acclaimed collection of stories vividly evokes both the grandeur of Africa, the glare of its sun and the wide open space, as well as the great, irresolvable tensions between whites and blacks. Tales of poor white farmers and their lonely wives, of storm air thick with locusts, of ants and pomegranate trees, black servants and the year of hunger in a native village – all combine to present a powerful image of a continent which seems incorruptible in spite of the people who plough, mine and plunder it to make their living. In Doris Lessing's own words, 'Africa gives you the knowledge that man is a small creature, among other creatures, in a large landscape.'

'Some stories are set in the Twenties, others in the war, others thereafter, but all draw with unhampered directness upon childhood sensation undiminished by distance and memory. With a boundless fecundity and flow, these stories are timeless, as though heat and wilderness took the place of time. Unblinkingly aware of how tortuous and intricate the whole question of identity is in Southern Africa, Doris Lessing has an extraordinarily generous and uncontemptuous feeling for the values of settler life without ever condoning its fundamental injustices.'

Gabriel Pearson, *Daily Telegraph*

'Doris Lessing can take what appears to be commonplace, mere passing anecdote and turn it deftly until its inner light is released: one feels that she has gazed upon the stories in her mind until that peculiar angle of vision, the angle that pierces obliquely but clean to the heart of a thing, has finally been found.'

Jacky Gillott, *The Times*

ISBN 0 00 654543 2

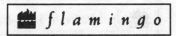

MODERN CLASSIC

Doris Lessing

To Room Nineteen

Collected Stories
Volume One

Includes a previously uncollected story and a new preface by the author.

For more than four decades, Doris Lessing's work has wittily and wryly observed the muddle and passion of human relations, unflinchingly dissected its truths and shown us the unique quality of her understanding.

From the magnificent 'To Room Nineteen', a study of a dry, controlled middle class marriage 'grounded in intelligence', to the shocking and sharp 'A Woman on a Roof', where a workman becomes obsessed with a pretty sunbather, this superb collection of stories from the 1950s through to the 1990s bears witness to Doris Lessing's extraordinary perspective on the human condition.

'The stories in *To Room Nineteen* are part of the intellectual apparatus of anybody alive in England in the Fifties. I can't begin to evaluate some of them objectively; "The Habit of Loving" and the dazzlingly cynical "One Off the Shortlist" shaped the way I, for one, perceived the world.'
Angela Carter, *Guardian*

'A major collection – rich, perceptive and cruelly honest. For Doris Lessing private lives, private sins and private blisses are aspects of history, so that even in short stories, she is a chronicler of her time and its conscience too.'
Lorna Sage, *Observer*

'On sex, Doris Lessing has few equals in understanding not only desire, but the rest – boredom, disappointment, erotic fury. On every subject there is a selfless, composed quality about her writing, a special combination of indignation and compassion.'
Diane Johnson, *New York Times*

ISBN 0 00 654806 7

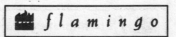

Doris Lessing

The Temptation of Jack Orkney

Collected Stories
Volume Two

Includes two previously uncollected stories and a new preface by the author.

Two marriages, both middle class, liberal and 'rather literary', share a shocking flaw, a 'secret cancer'. A young, beautiful woman from a working class family is courted by a very eligible, very upmarket man. An ageing actress falls in love for the first time but can only express her feelings through her stage performances because her happily married lover is sadly unobtainable. A dedicated, lifelong rationalist is tempted, after the death of his father, by the comforts of religious belief.

In this magnificent collection of stories spanning the last four decades, Doris Lessing's unique gift for observation, her wit, compassion and remarkable ability to illuminate the complexities of human life are all powerfully displayed.

'What do you say about Doris Lessing? She has shaped the attitudes of a whole generation of women; she has defined and punctured masculine pretensions and has torn strips off liberal double-think. This collection is, it goes without saying, a classic.'
                                                            Mary Hope, *Spectator*

'Intense and tender, valuable and drily humorous stories with streaks of gold. Dazzling.'
                                                    Myrna Blumberg, *The Times*

ISBN 0 00 654807 5

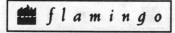

Doris Lessing

Martha Quest

'*Martha Quest* is a deeply felt and powerfully written account of a modern woman's progress.'
Sunday Times

The 'Children of Violence' series, a quintet of novels tracing the life of Martha Quest from her childhood in Africa to a post-nuclear Britain of AD 2000, first established Doris Lessing as a major radical writer. In this first volume, Martha, the young, rebellious daughter of a traditional Afrikaans family, finds her coming of age to be a great struggle for freedom and recognition. Intelligent and deeply compassionate, she sees the unpalatable political and social realities of the world in which she has grown up with an extraordinary clarity. Martha's vision of a just society takes her beyond the impoverished and rigid farming community to the city – an ill-matched marriage her means of escape.

'Stubborn, resilient, wry towards herself, Martha is Doris Lessing's most satisfying and complex characterization. She is a child of her times, of violence, who "could no more dissociate herself from the violence done by her than a tadpole can live out of water".'
The Times

flamingo

Doris Lessing

The Golden Notebook

'*The Golden Notebook* is euphoric, exhilarating, full of promise and provocation.'
Vogue

Anna Wulf is a young novelist with writer's block. Divorced, with a young child, and disillusioned by unsatisfactory relationships, she feels her life is falling apart. In fear of madness, she records her experiences in four coloured notebooks. The black notebook addresses her problems as a writer; the red her political life; the yellow her relationships and emotions; and the blue becomes a diary of everyday events. But it is a fifth notebook – the Golden Notebook – which is the key to her recovery and renaissance.

Bold and illuminating, fusing sex, politics, madness and motherhood, *The Golden Notebook* is at once a bold and perceptive portrait of the intellectual and moral climate of the 1950s – a society on the brink of feminism – and a powerful and revealing account of a woman searching for her own personal and political identity.

'Doris Lessing is a pioneer of feminist self-consciousness in its raw state . . . The truths contained in *The Golden Notebook* are indeed harsh. It can also be said that these particular truths have not been examined in so rigorous and exemplary a fashion since the first appearance of this extraordinary book. A seminal work.'
Anita Brookner, *London Review of Books*

'*The Golden Notebook* is the diary of a writer in shock, a young woman determined to forge a life as a 'free woman', as an 'intellectual'. Doris Lessing is a writer of considerable power, someone who can close her eyes and 'give' a situation by the sheer force of her emotional energy.'
Joan Didion, *New York Times*

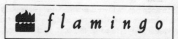

flamingo

Doris Lessing

Many Doris Lessing titles are available in Flamingo. Below is a selection.

Fiction
☐ London Observed £5.99
☐ The Fifth Child £4.99
☐ The Good Terrorist £6.99
☐ The Golden Notebook £6.99
☐ Winter in July £5.99
☐ Martha Quest £5.99
☐ A Proper Marriage £6.99
☐ Landlocked £5.99

Non-fiction
☐ Under My Skin, Volume One of My Autobiography to 1949
£20.00 (hardback)
☐ Particularly Cats and Rufus the Survivor £4.99
☐ In Pursuit of the English £5.99
☐ Going Home £5.99

You can buy Flamingo paperbacks at your local bookshop or newsagent. Or you can order them from HarperCollins Mail Order, Dept. 8, HarperCollins*Publishers*, Westerhill Road, Bishopbriggs, Glasgow G64 2QT. Please enclose a cheque or postal order, to the order of the cover price plus add £1.00 for the first and 25p for additional books ordered within the UK.

NAME (Block letters)_____

ADDRESS_____

_____

_____

While every effort is made to keep prices low, it is sometimes necessary to increase them at short notice. HarperCollins Publishers reserve the right to show new retail prices on covers which may differ from those previously advertised in the text or elsewhere.